UR III TABLETS FROM THE COLUMBIA UNIVERSITY LIBRARIES

Cornell University Studies in Assyriology and Sumerology
Volume 16
was made possible thanks to generous subventions by

An Anonymous Donor,

The Joseph Rosen Foundation,

Columbia University Libraries

and

The Occasional Publication Fund
Department of Near Eastern Studies
Cornell University

Cornell University Studies in
Assyriology and Sumerology
(CUSAS)

Volume 16

Ur III Tablets from The Columbia University Libraries

by

S. Garfinkle
H. Sauren
M. Van De Mieroop

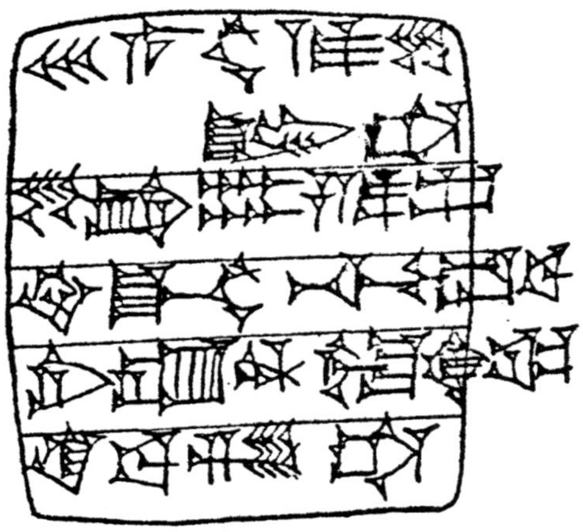

CDL Press
Bethesda, Maryland
2010

Library of Congress Cataloging-in-Publication

Garfinkle, Steven J.
Ur III tablets from the Columbia University Libraries / by S. Garfinkle, H. Sauren, M. Van De Mieroop.
p. cm. — (Cornell University studies in Assyriology and Sumerology ; v. 16)
ISBN 978-1-934309-28-5 (alk. paper)
1. Sumerian language—Texts. 2. Cuneiform tablets. 3. Babylonia—Economic conditions—Sources. 4. Ur (Extinct city) I. Sauren, Herbert, 1934– II. Van de Mieroop, Marc. III. Columbia University. Libraries. IV. Title. V. Series.

PJ4075.G26 2010
499'.95--dc22 2010013575

ISBN 9781934309285

Series Editor's Preface

The publication of the Columbia University Libraries cuneiform collection (now housed in the Rare Books and Manuscripts Collection, Butler Library) in the CUSAS series came about accidentally. During a casual conversation with Marc Van De Mieroop at Columbia University following the dissertation defense of Steven Garfinkle, I inquired about the status of the Columbia University Libraries tablets. He told me that Herbert Sauren had, in fact, copied all the tablets during the summer of 1975 but had subsequently retired to Portugal and no longer was interested in publishing his copies jointly with Van De Mieroop. I obtained Sauren's e-mail address and wrote to him asking if he still had his original copies. After a short correspondence, Sauren graciously sent me not only his original copies of the Columbia University tablets but many hundreds of copies of other still unpublished collections along with permission to arrange for their respective publications. Thus was set in motion the publication of the Columbia University collection. Garfinkle and Van De Mieroop collated the texts and the latter made preliminary transliterations and notes while Garfinkle prepared the texts and indices for this publication. The series editor made additional changes. The large number of texts precluded any significant commentary by the authors, as indicated in their introduction, but should, nevertheless, provide excellent opportunities for scholars to expand upon these new data. Their commitment to making these interesting texts available to the scholarly community coupled with the similar goals of the CUSAS series combined to make this publication possible. Although this volume incurred unexpected delays, it brings to a welcome conclusion the long-overdue publication of this significant collection.

Unlike the earlier volumes in this series, the Columbia University Libraries tablets represent texts from the earliest clandestine finds in Iraq, going back at least to 1895 (see detailed history of the collection below in the introduction). They augment or otherwise fill gaps in the well-known Ur III archives of Lagaš/Ĝirsu, Puzriš-Dagan, Umma, Gu'abba, Ur, and Nippur and provide substantial new data to enhance our understanding of these archives. We can only be grateful to the extensive efforts by Sauren, who copied the tablets, and to Van De Mieroop and Garfinkle, who brought this final publication to completion Thanks are due also to Jonathan and Jeannette Rosen and the Joseph Rosen Foundation, the Columbia University Libraries, the Anonymous Donor, and the Occasional Publication Fund of the Department of Near Eastern Studies, Cornell University for providing the generous subsidies that made the publication of this CUSAS volume possible.

David I. Owen
Curator of Tablet Collection
The Jonathan and Jeannette Rosen
Ancient Near Eastern Studies Seminar
Department of Near Eastern Studies
Cornell University, Ithaca
May, 2010

Preface

The cuneiform tablet collection of the Columbia University Libraries in New York is one of the oldest in North America, the bulk of it having been donated in 1896. From that early date, it has been partially published, and has been repeatedly cataloged, but no full publication of the collection has ever appeared. The intent of this book is to make available all the texts from the Ur III period (twenty-first century BCE) in a complete form, including hand copies, transliterations, and indices.

The largest part of the collection, 256 tablets and two envelopes, was donated by friends of Columbia University, who had acquired them in 1895 from the New York antiquities dealer, David Z. Noorian. Those tablets probably all derive from the site of Telloh, which was then being excavated by Ernest de Sarzec. They were certainly looted as part of the thousands of tablets reported by L. Heuzey to have been dug up illicitly after the French excavations of 1894.[1] Almost immediately upon their arrival at Columbia University twenty of them were published by William R. Arnold in his 1896 doctoral dissertation, *Ancient-Babylonian Temple Records in the Columbia University Library*. He first copied the texts imitating the signs as they appeared on the tablets, and then gave a "transliteration," reproducing the texts with Neo-Assyrian sign forms. In 1897, Robert Julius Lau published accurate copies of two, nearly identical, texts from the collection (CU 01.154 and 01.155, nos. 19–20 here).[2] Remarkably, he did not acknowledge this publication in his later book (see below), although the tablets are cataloged there as numbers 248 and 249.

In 1896, another thirty-two tablets were donated to Columbia University by L. A. Bernheimer, but their provenance and date are unclear, and their current location is uncertain. Similarly, the whereabouts of a gift of eighteen tablets by John Deneley Prince in 1902 is unknown. Three Ur III tablets from the latter gift were published in 1913 by Frederick A. Vanderburgh, as "Three Babylonian Tablets, Prince Collection, Columbia University."[3] The three are messenger texts very similar in content to a large part of the earliest donation, but they seemingly are not included in any of the later catalogs and publications, and cannot be found. Prince, who taught Slavic languages at Columbia University, was also an instructor of Sumerian and may have purchased the tablets as a teaching tool.

In 1906 Robert Julius Lau made a full catalogue of the original 1896 Ur III collection as his doctoral dissertation, which was published by Columbia University Press.[4] He also provided copies of sixty-one of them, five of which had

1. L. Heuzey and E. de Sarzec, *Découvertes en Chaldée* (Paris, 1884–1912), pp. 438–39.
2. "Two Old Babylonian Tablets," *Journal of the American Oriental Society* 18 (1897): 363–65.
3. *Journal of the American Oriental Society* 33 (1913): 24–32.
4. R. J. Lau, *Old Babylonian Temple Records*, (New York, 1906). A concordance is provided in this volume for the tablets previously published by Lau.

already been published by Arnold. Three of the 256 tablets included in his catalog are now unreadable (Lau's numbers 45, 140, and 198).

In 1934, David Eugene Smith, a professor of geography at Teachers College, Columbia University, donated sixteen tablets, which he had acquired from Edgar Banks. Eight of those were of Ur III date. In 1936, George Arthur Plimpton gave his collection to Columbia, including thirty-four cuneiform tablets, the famous mathematical tablet, Plimpton 322 among them.[5] At least ten of those were of Ur III date. The entire collection of tablets accumulated up to then was cataloged in 1943 by Isaac Mendelsohn, Professor of Semitic Languages, as *Catalogue of the Babylonian Tablets in the Libraries of Columbia University. A List of cuneiform documents from the Sumerian, Old-Babylonian, Kassite, and Neo-Babylonian periods, with photographic reproductions of selected seals, and clay objects.* Of the 380 items from all periods of Babylonian history, he listed 278 of Ur III date. Unfortunately, three have become illegible (Mendelsohn's numbers 58, 92, and 259) and three are actually Old Babylonian exercise texts (Mendelsohn's numbers 266–68); therefore, 272 of the Ur III texts identified by Mendelsohn are still in the collection.

In 1959, the collection of seventy-five tablets belonging to Paul Monroe, Professor at Teachers College, was donated by his children twelve years after his death. Thirty-five of these were of Ur III date. Subsequently, three small donations were made: four tablets in 1965 by Harry G. Friedman, two legated by Professor Lynn Thorndike in 1966, and two by Professor Frances Henne in 1973. Several of these probably had been originally acquired from Banks. When Robert David Freedman made a catalog of the Ur III texts in 1971 as a Master's Thesis at Columbia University, he reorganized the collection, mixing the various donations and numbering the tablets according to their provenance. He used the following system:

01 = Lagaš/Ĝirsu
02 = Puzriš-Dagan
03 = Umma
04 = Gu'abba
05 = Ur
06 = Nippur
07 = Borsippa
08 = dated texts without clear provenance
09 = undated texts without clear provenance

Freedman registered 315 tablets, which must have included some not accounted for in the above list of gifts. Unfortunately, in reorganizing the tablets he confused the question of provenance more than he clarified it. He broke up the large group of Ĝirsu tablets that made up the oldest part of the collection. We can assume that probably all of the 256 tablets cataloged by Lau in 1906 derived from Ĝirsu. Freedman lists only 185 tablets with that provenance. Moreover, his arguments to establish the Ur provenance are not very convincing. He clearly made a mistake by claiming that 07.01 (no. 77 here) was from Borsippa, whereas the toponym Kinunir shows it is from Ĝirsu, and he included a large number of Ĝirsu tablets in his categories without clear provenance. So the organization of the collection currently used at the library is not based on provenance, but on a spurious system of classification.

The tablets are now housed in the Rare Books and Manuscripts Library at Columbia's Butler Library, organized in boxes following Freedman's catalog. Some of the tablets still bear signs of the cotton wool in which they had previously been wrapped. While they have always been readily available to scholars, they were very rarely consulted as is the fate of many collections of this type. In the summer of 1975, Herbert Sauren, then Professor at the Université Catholique de Louvain, Belgium, copied the Ur III collection except for those tablets published by Lau in his 1906 book. Combining his copies with those by Lau, he made

5. O. Neugebauer and A. Sachs, *Mathematical Cuneiform Texts* (New Haven, 1945), Text A.

up plates of 319 items.[6] The intended publication on the model of his *Les tablettes cunéiformes de l'époque d'Ur des collections de la New York Public Library*[7] did not materialize, and in 1987 he asked Marc Van De Mieroop, who had been appointed at Columbia University, to collaborate on the project by providing transliterations. The latter made provisional transliterations on the basis of the hand copies, but did not pursue the project further due to other obligations. In the year 2000, when Steven J. Garfinkle finished his doctorate at Columbia University with a dissertation on the Ur III period, and when David Owen announced the creation of a new series of Ur III text publications, it was decided to finalize the project. Sauren provided the originals of his hand copies and notes. Garfinkle and Van De Mieroop made full transliterations based on the latter's provisional ones and by reading the tablets themselves in a series of visits to the collection in the spring of 2001. These are provided here along with Sauren's copies as a parallel record. They collated every tablet; whenever this lead to a different reading from the hand copy, this is indicated in the transliterations published here. Garfinkle made the indices and did all of the technical work preparing the publication. A total of 318 tablets is published here, a much delayed full publication of the Ur III texts from the Columbia University Libraries.

As is usual in a tablet collection of this nature, it contains texts that fit within Ur III archives already known and studied. For example, nos. 19 and 20 are part of the AS 9 dated records of the Saĝdana millhouse,[8] and nos. 37 to 41 to the Kennelman archive.[9] We have not attempted to indicate these archival provenances, although we understand the importance of such information. Our aim is to make these records available as soon as possible to all scholars working with Ur III data.

Marc Van De Mieroop
New York, April 2010

6. One of his copies does not correspond to a tablet at this time at Columbia University. Since Sauren copied numerous Ur III tablets around the time he visited Columbia, he may have mistakenly included this one in the Columbia collection. The tablet has been omitted from the publication here.

7. Publications de l'Institut Orientaliste de Louvain 19, 1978.

8. A. Uchitel, "Daily Word at the Sagdana Millhouse," *Acta Sumerologica* 6 (1984): 75–98.

9. P. Mander, *An Archive of Kennelmen and Other Workers in Ur III Lagash* (Naples, 1994).

Table of Contents

Series Editor's Preface .... *v*

Preface .... *vi*

Catalogue of Texts .... *xi*

Concordance .... *xx*

Lines Read according to Collation .... *xxiv*

The Texts 1

Indexes 293

- Glossary of Selected Terms 293
- Personal Names 317
- Divine Names 337
- Toponyms 338
- Temples, Households, and Institutions 339
- Fields, Storehouses, and Gardens 340

Seal Inscriptions 341

Catalogue of Texts

Text	Museum #	Provenance	Date	Description
1	08.38	Ĝirsu	-/-/Š 44	account of fields and hired labor, nì-ka$_9$-ak
2	09.06	Ĝirsu	[...]	list of land and oxen
3	09.35	Ĝirsu	[...]	account of land and officials
4	01.183	Ĝirsu	n.d.	land allotted to individuals
5	02.33	Ĝirsu	n.d	receipt of fields
6	01.83	Ĝirsu	IX/-/Š 47	receipt of barley for seeding
7	01.152	Ĝirsu	V/-/AS 8	ĝuruš for field work
8	01.156	Ĝirsu	VI/12/IS 1	receipt of barley for orchard workers
9	01.157	Ĝirsu	I/-/-	workers stacking sheaves
10	01.159	Ĝirsu	I/-/-	ĝuruš for field work
11	01.138	Ĝirsu	V/4/-	oxen, érin, and hired men for field work
12	01.142	Ĝirsu	VI/21/-	oxen for sowing and hired men for field work
13	01.163	Ĝirsu	VIII/-/-	oxen for sowing and hired men for field work
14	01.173	Ĝirsu	n.d.	account of érin performing bala, and hired workers 'sitting out' the bala, for fieldwork, nì-ka$_9$-ak
15	08.02	Ĝirsu	-/-/Š 39	barley to be winnowed
16	08.39	Ĝirsu	-/-/Š 47	barley to be winnowed
17	02.26	Ĝirsu	n.d.	barley to be winnowed
18	09.12	Ĝirsu	n.d.	barley to be winnowed
19	01.154	Ĝirsu	VI/10/AS 9	list of workers for the Saĝdana millhouse
20	01.155	Ĝirsu	VI/12/AS 9	list of workers for the Saĝdana millhouse
21	02.01	Ĝirsu	-/-/Š 25	list of workers of the household of Ninĝirsu
22	01.76	Ĝirsu	diri/-/Š 44	receipt of barley rations for érin
23	09.02	Ĝirsu	-/-/Š 45	barley rations for ĝuruš
24	01.119	Ĝirsu	VIII/-/Š 45	receipt of flour rations for érin performing bala
25	01.150	Ĝirsu	VIII/-/Š 46	receipt of barley rations for érin performing bala
26	01.80	Ĝirsu	X/-/Š 46	receipt of barley rations for érin performing bala
27	01.81	Ĝirsu	VIII/-/Š 47	receipt of barley rations for érin performing bala
28	01.82	Ĝirsu	VIII/-/Š 47	receipt of barley rations

TEXT	MUSEUM #	PROVENANCE	DATE	DESCRIPTION
29	01.151	Ĝirsu	I/-/AS 5	rations for géme Martu
30	01.95	Ĝirsu	VIII/-/IS 1	receipt of flour for female weavers; tablet and case
31	08.27	Ĝirsu	VII/-/-	barley rations for érin 'sitting out' the bala
32	01.99	Ĝirsu	VIII/-/-	receipt of barley rations for female weavers
33	01.149	Ĝirsu	[...]	barley rations for mounted messengers and géme
34	08.28	Ĝirsu	[...]	barley rations for female weavers and children
35	09.01	Ĝirsu	[...]	[disbursement] of rations
36	09.10	Ĝirsu	[...]	disbursement of rations
37	01.98	Ĝirsu	VIII/11/-	disbursement of bread
38	01.112	Ĝirsu	IX/23/-	disbursement of bread
39	01.108	Ĝirsu	XII/13/-	disbursement of bread and beer
40	01.115	Ĝirsu	XII/16/-	disbursement of bread and beer
41	01.116	Ĝirsu	XII/27/-	disbursement of bread
42	01.86	Ĝirsu	X/-/AS 1	receipt of barley as fodder
43	08.04	Ĝirsu	III/-/AS 3	barley as fodder for sheep
44	01.160	Ĝirsu	II/-/-	flour and barley as fodder
45	01.162	Ĝirsu	VIII/-/-	cereals as fodder for oxen
46	08.11	Ĝirsu	-/-/ŠS 9	barley for oxen
47	01.137	Ĝirsu	IV/27/-	barley for animals
48	01.139	Ĝirsu	V/10/-	barley for animals
49	01.140	Ĝirsu	V/24/-	barley for animals
50	01.141	Ĝirsu	VI/11/-	barley for animals
51	01.143	Ĝirsu	VI/18/-	barley for animals
52	01.144	Ĝirsu	VI/20/-	barley for animals
53	01.145	Ĝirsu	X/10/-	barley for animals
54	01.146	Ĝirsu	XII/5/-	barley for animals
55	01.147	Ĝirsu	XII?/6+/-	barley for animals
56	03.01	Ĝirsu	IV/-/Š 40	account of barley, nì-ka$_9$-ak
57	02.15	Ĝirsu	-/-/Š 40	account of barley, nì-ka$_9$-ak
58	08.37	Ĝirsu	-/-/Š 40	account of flour, nì-ka$_9$-ak
59	01.167	Ĝirsu	-/-/Š 45	account of bitumen, nì-ka$_9$-ak
60	02.16	Ĝirsu	-/-/Š 46	account of barley, nì-ka$_9$-ak
61	01.168	Ĝirsu	X/-/Š 47	account of barley, nì-ka$_9$-ak
62	01.169	Ĝirsu	XI/-/Š 47	account of barley and beer, nì-ka$_9$-ak
63	01.170	Ĝirsu	XII/-/AS 1	account of wool, nì-ka$_9$-ak
64	02.17	Ĝirsu	-/-/AS 1	account of flour, nì-ka$_9$-ak
65	02.18	Ĝirsu	IV/-/AS 2	account of cereals, nì-ka$_9$-ak
66	01.171	Ĝirsu	-/-/AS 2	account of barley loaded onto boats, nì-ka$_9$-ak

Text	Museum #	Provenance	Date	Description
67	01.172	Ĝirsu	XII/-/AS 4	account of animals disbursed for offerings, nì-ka$_9$-ak
68	01.166	Ĝirsu	IV/-/-	account of cereals, nì-ka$_9$-ak
69	09.28	Ĝirsu	[...]	account of barley, nì-ka$_9$
70	08.29	Ĝirsu	-/-/Š 36	account of animals and wool
71	08.22	Ĝirsu	-/-/Š 39	account of [ ]
72	04.01	Ĝirsu	-/-/Š 47	account of sheep and goats
73	04.02	Ĝirsu	-/4/Š 48	account of wool
74	08.41	Ĝirsu	-/4/AS 1	account of orchards and dates
75	04.03	Ĝirsu	-/5/AS 2	account of wool measured in gurdub
76	08.42	Ĝirsu	-/8/AS 2	account of wool and textiles
77	07.01	Ĝirsu	-/10/AS 2	account of wool measured in gurdub
78	08.03	Ĝirsu	[ ]/AS 2 or 3	account of sheep and goats
79	01.153	Ĝirsu	XI/-/AS 8	account of female workers
80	04.04	Ĝirsu	-/-/ŠS 8	account of workers
81	09.31	Ĝirsu	[ ]/ŠS 9	account of silver for a purchase
82	01.131	Ĝirsu	XII/-/IS 1	account of textiles
83	09.20	Ĝirsu	I/[ ]	account of [ ]
84	01.136	Ĝirsu	II/[ ]	account of animals
85	02.28	Ĝirsu	[...]	account of sheep and goats
86	09.11	Ĝirsu	[...]	account of cereals
87	09.15	Ĝirsu	[...]	account of cereals
88	09.16	Ĝirsu	[...]	account of barley
89	09.17	Ĝirsu	[...]	account of flour
90	09.18	Ĝirsu	[...]	account of ghee
91	09.21	Ĝirsu	[...]	account of cattle
92	09.23	Ĝirsu	[...]	account of animals
93	09.27	Ĝirsu	[...]	account of cereals
94	02.06	Ĝirsu	n.d.	account of cereals
95	09.13	Ĝirsu	n.d.	account of barley
96	09.24	Ĝirsu	n.d.	account of sheep
97	09.32	Ĝirsu	n.d.	account of dates
98	09.36	Ĝirsu	n.d.	account of personnel?
99	08.36	Ĝirsu	I/-/Š 34	delivery of textiles
100	01.118	Ĝirsu	n.d.	delivery of ghee
101	09.30	Ĝirsu	n.d.	delivery of silver from fishermen
102	08.40	Ĝirsu	XI/-/Š 27	vessels for the palace
103	01.101	Ĝirsu	V/-/Š 44	disbursement of beer
104	08.32	Ĝirsu	-/-/ŠS 1	disbursement of barley for shepherds

Text	Museum #	Provenance	Date	Description
105	01.102	Ĝirsu	I/-/ŠS 2	disbursement of flour to be put onto a boat
106	01.110	Ĝirsu	V/-/[ŠS 8]	disbursement of bran
107	01.105	Ĝirsu	X/-/ŠS 8	disbursement of bran
108	01.104	Ĝirsu	XII/-/ŠS 8	disbursement of bran
109	04.05	Ĝirsu	I/-/-	disbursement of emmer
110	01.161	Ĝirsu	IV/-/-	disbursement of beer
111	01.181	Ĝirsu	VII/-/-	disbursement of flour and bread
112	08.26	Ĝirsu	VII/-/-	disbursement of oil
113	01.69	Ĝirsu	XII/-/-	disbursement of beer and flour
114	01.72	Ĝirsu	XII/-/-	disbursement of flour
115	01.114	Ĝirsu	XII/-/-	disbursement of beer and flour for offerings
116	01.117	Ĝirsu	XII/-/-	disbursement of flour
117	01.134	Ĝirsu	XII/-/[ ]	regular offerings of beer and flour
118	08.16	Ĝirsu	[...]	disbursement of textiles
119	09.39	Ĝirsu	[...]	[disbursement] of dates and barley
120	08.01	Ĝirsu	-/-/Š 25	receipt of containers
121	08.09	Ĝirsu	IV/-/Š 42	receipt of barley
122	08.14	Ĝirsu	-/-/Š 43	receipt of ghee and wool
123	01.75	Ĝirsu	V/-/Š 44	receipt of [ ] and silver
124	01.77	Ĝirsu	I/-/Š 45	receipt of barley
125	01.121	Ĝirsu	V/-/Š 45?	receipt of copper rim
126	01.120	Ĝirsu	VIII/-/Š 45	receipt of cattle
127	01.78	Ĝirsu	X/-/Š 45	receipt of milled barley
128	01.79	Ĝirsu	IV/-/Š 46	receipt of emmer
129	03.02	Ĝirsu	-/-/Š 46	receipt of silver under the seal of the ensí
130	01.122	Ĝirsu	VI/-/Š 47	receipt of barley to purchase silver
131	08.05	Ĝirsu	III/-/Š 48	receipt of flour
132	08.15	Ĝirsu	-/-/Š 48	receipt of flour
133	01.123	Ĝirsu	II/-/AS 1	receipt of oxen for bala
134	01.84	Ĝirsu	III/10/AS 1	receipt of flour
135	01.85	Ĝirsu	V/-/AS 1	receipt of copper implement
136	01.174	Ĝirsu	X/-/AS 1	receipt of barley, še ur_5-ra
137	01.175	Ĝirsu	-/-/AS 1	receipt of barley, še ur_5-ra
138	01.176	Ĝirsu	-/-/AS 1	receipt of barley, še ur_5-ra
139	08.06	Ĝirsu	IV/-/AS 2	[receipt] of bread and beer
140	05.01	Ĝirsu	VI/-/AS 2	receipt of silver from sesame oil for the palace at Ur
141	01.125	Ĝirsu	X/-/AS 2	receipt of honey
142	08.30	Ĝirsu	-/-/AS 2	receipt of cattle

TEXT	MUSEUM #	PROVENANCE	DATE	DESCRIPTION
143	08.07	Ĝirsu	-/-/AS 2	receipt of silver for the palace
144	01.127	Ĝirsu	II/-/AS 3	receipt of fish
145	08.31	Ĝirsu	IV/-/AS 3	receipt of cattle
146	01.87	Ĝirsu	V/-/AS 3	receipt of aromatics
147	01.128	Ĝirsu	V/-/AS 3	receipt of silver for the palace
148	01.88	Ĝirsu	X/-/AS 3	receipt of barley loaded onto a boat
149	01.89	Ĝirsu	X/-/AS 3	receipt of wool
150	01.177	Ĝirsu	diri/-/AS 3	receipt of barley, še ur$_5$-ra
151	01.129	Ĝirsu	-/-/AS 3	receipt of aromatics
152	01.178	Ĝirsu	-/-/AS 3	receipt of barley, še ur$_5$-ra
153	02.11	Ĝirsu	-/-/AS 3	receipt of carcasses
154	02.12	Ĝirsu	-/-/AS 3	receipt of carcasses
155	08.17	Ĝirsu	-/-/AS 3	receipt of wool
156	08.18	Ĝirsu	-/-/AS 3	receipt of oil for the gods
157	01.90	Ĝirsu	II/-/AS 4	receipt of barley
158	08.19	Ĝirsu	-/-/AS 4	receipt of barley for a zabar-dab$_5$
159	08.08	Ĝirsu	-/-/AS 4	receipt of beer from the shipyard
160	01.91	Ĝirsu	II/-/AS 5	receipt of sesame for seeding
161	01.130	Ĝirsu	XI/-/AS 5	receipt of goat hair
162	08.20	Ĝirsu	-/-/AS 5	receipt of peas
163	01.124	Ĝirsu	III/-/AS 6	receipt of wax
164	01.92	Ĝirsu	VI/-/AS 6	receipt of carcasses; tablet and case
165	01.93	Ĝirsu	IX/-/AS 7	receipt of wooden parts for boats
166	01.94	Ĝirsu	IX/-/AS 7	receipt of vessels
167	08.24	Ĝirsu	-/-/AS 7	receipt of flour
168	01.179	Ĝirsu	X/-/ŠS 5	receipt of barley, še ur$_5$-ra
169	02.04	Ĝirsu	-/-/ŠS 5	receipt of silver
170	02.05	Ĝirsu	-/-/ŠS 5	receipt of silver and grain
171	08.10	Ĝirsu	VIII/3/ŠS 6	receipt of sheep
172	08.12	Ĝirsu	IV/-/IS 1?	receipt of oil
173	01.180	Ĝirsu	XII/-/IS 1	receipt of barley, še ur$_5$-ra
174	08.21	Ĝirsu	-/-/IS 1	receipt of barley; tablet and case
175	01.96	Ĝirsu	IV/-/-	receipt of barley
176	01.97	Ĝirsu	V/-/-	receipt of dates
177	01.132	Ĝirsu	VIII/7/-	receipt of flour
178	01.100	Ĝirsu	IX/-/-	receipt of beer
179	01.133	Ĝirsu	X/-/-	receipt of malt
180	08.34	Ĝirsu	-/-/Š 38	tablet basket tag
181	08.35	Ĝirsu	-/-/Š 41	tablet basket tag

Text	Museum #	Provenance	Date	Description
182	02.30	Ĝirsu	-/-/Š 46	tablet basket tag
183	02.31	Ĝirsu	-/-/Š 48	tablet basket tag
184	01.184	Ĝirsu	-/-/AS 2	tablet basket tag
185	01.01	Ĝirsu	I/4/-	messenger text
186	01.02	Ĝirsu	I/8/-	messenger text
187	01.03	Ĝirsu	I/17/-	messenger text
188	01.106	Ĝirsu	I/29/-	messenger text
189	01.04	Ĝirsu	I/-/-	messenger text
190	01.05	Ĝirsu	I/-/-	messenger text
191	01.06	Ĝirsu	I/-/-	messenger text
192	01.07	Ĝirsu	I/-/-	messenger text
193	01.158	Ĝirsu	I/-/-	messenger text
194	01.08	Ĝirsu	II/13/-	messenger text
195	01.09	Ĝirsu	II/-/-	messenger text
196	01.10	Ĝirsu	II/-/-	messenger text
197	01.107	Ĝirsu	II/-/-	messenger text
198	01.11	Ĝirsu	III/14/-	messenger text
199	01.12	Ĝirsu	III/-/-	messenger text
200	01.13	Ĝirsu	III/-/-	messenger text
201	08.25	Ĝirsu	III/-/AS 8	messenger text
202	01.14	Ĝirsu	IV/18/-	messenger text
203	01.15	Ĝirsu	IV/27/-	messenger text
204	01.16	Ĝirsu	IV/29/-	messenger text
205	01.17	Ĝirsu	IV/-/-	messenger text
206	01.18	Ĝirsu	IV/-/-	messenger text
207	01.19	Ĝirsu	IV/-/-	messenger text
208	01.20	Ĝirsu	IV/-/-	messenger text
209	01.21	Ĝirsu	IV/-/-	messenger text
210	01.22	Ĝirsu	V/2/-	messenger text
211	01.23	Ĝirsu	V/22/-	messenger text
212	01.109	Ĝirsu	V/24/-	messenger text
213	01.24	Ĝirsu	V/-/-	messenger text
214	01.25	Ĝirsu	V/-/-	messenger text
215	01.26	Ĝirsu	V/-/-	messenger text
216	01.27	Ĝirsu	V/-/-	messenger text
217	01.28	Ĝirsu	V/-/-	messenger text
218	01.29	Ĝirsu	V/-/-	messenger text
219	01.30	Ĝirsu	V/-/-	messenger text
220	01.31	Ĝirsu	V/-/-	messenger text

TEXT	MUSEUM #	PROVENANCE	DATE	DESCRIPTION
221	01.32	Ĝirsu	VI/5/-	messenger text
222	01.35	Ĝirsu	VI/16/-	messenger text
223	01.33	Ĝirsu	VI/-/-	messenger text
224	01.34	Ĝirsu	VI/-/-	messenger text
225	01.182	Ĝirsu	VI/-/AS 8	messenger text
226	01.111	Ĝirsu	VII/8/-	messenger text
227	01.36	Ĝirsu	VII/-/-	messenger text
228	01.37	Ĝirsu	VII/-/-	messenger text
229	01.38	Ĝirsu	VII/-/-	messenger text
230	01.39	Ĝirsu	VII/-/-	messenger text
231	01.40	Ĝirsu	VII/-/-	messenger text
232	01.41	Ĝirsu	VIII/2/-	messenger text
233	01.42	Ĝirsu	VIII/2/-	messenger text
234	01.43	Ĝirsu	VIII/30/-	messenger text
235	01.44	Ĝirsu	VIII/30/-	messenger text
236	01.45	Ĝirsu	VIII/-/-	messenger text
237	01.46	Ĝirsu	IX/5/-	messenger text
238	01.47	Ĝirsu	IX/13/-	messenger text
239	01.48	Ĝirsu	IX/21/-	messenger text
240	01.49	Ĝirsu	IX/24/-	messenger text
241	01.50	Ĝirsu	IX/-/-	messenger text
242	01.164	Ĝirsu	IX/-/-	messenger text
243	01.51	Ĝirsu	X/7/-	messenger text
244	01.52	Ĝirsu	X/8/-	messenger text
245	01.53	Ĝirsu	X/18/-	messenger text
246	01.54	Ĝirsu	X/20/-	messenger text
247	01.55	Ĝirsu	X/-/-	messenger text
248	01.56	Ĝirsu	X/-/-	messenger text
249	01.57	Ĝirsu	X/-/-	messenger text
250	01.58	Ĝirsu	XI/19/-	messenger text
251	01.59	Ĝirsu	XI/-/-	messenger text
252	01.60	Ĝirsu	XI/-/-	messenger text
253	01.61	Ĝirsu	XI/-/-	messenger text
254	01.62	Ĝirsu	XI/-/-	messenger text
255	01.63	Ĝirsu	XII/9/-	messenger text
256	01.64	Ĝirsu	XII/10/-	messenger text
257	01.66	Ĝirsu	XII/24/-	messenger text
258	01.65	Ĝirsu	XII/29/-	messenger text
259	01.67	Ĝirsu	XII/-/-	messenger text

TEXT	MUSEUM #	PROVENANCE	DATE	DESCRIPTION
260	01.68	Ĝirsu	XII/-/-	messenger text
261	01.70	Ĝirsu	XII/-/-	messenger text
262	01.71	Ĝirsu	XII/-/-	messenger text
263	01.73	Ĝirsu	XII/-/-	messenger text
264	01.113	Ĝirsu	XII/-/-	messenger text
265	01.165	Ĝirsu	XII/-/-	messenger text
266	01.74	Ĝirsu	[...]	messenger text
267	09.34	Ĝirsu	[...]	list of animals and assorted goods
268	09.41	Ĝirsu	n.d.	bulla with seal impression
269	09.33	Ĝirsu	[...]	unclear
270	01.185	Ĝirsu	I/-/AS 1	fragment
271	09.19	Ĝirsu	XI/-/[ ]	fragment
272	08.43	Umma	-/-/AS 8	account of onions
273	09.04	Umma	-/30/-	account of various commodities
274	03.08	Umma?	[...]	account of beer
275	03.05	Umma	III/-/ŠS 8	disbursement of apples
276	03.07	Umma	XII/-/-	disbursement of barley
277	09.05	Umma	n.d.	disbursement of fullers and hides
278	03.03	Umma	-/-/Š 48	receipt of animals
279	08.44	Umma	X/-/AS 5	receipt of leather
280	Henne 137	Umma	XI/-/AS 7	receipt of wooden parts for boats
281	03.06	Umma	X/-/-	receipt of date palm frond?
282	46.02	Ur	IX/-/IS 1	receipt of silver
283	46.01	Ur	I/30/IS 7	account of regular offerings of bread
284	09.26	Drehem	-/xii/ŠS 1	account of cattle and dairy products
285	08.33	Drehem	[-/-]/ŠS 9	account of goats
286	09.25	Drehem	[...]	account of cattle and sheep
287	01.135	Drehem	[ ]/12/-	deliveries of animals
288	02.14	Drehem	XII/-/Š 33	disbursement of dead cattle
289	02.08	Drehem	IV/-/Š 39	regular offerings of animals
290	02.27	Drehem	VIII/-/Š 42	regular offerings of sheep and goats
291	02.19	Drehem	II/-/Š 48	disbursement of cattle
292	02.20	Drehem	XI/16/AS 5	disbursement of lambs from Uruk
293	02.03	Drehem	VIII/-/ŠS 5	gift of textiles
294	06.01	Drehem	XI/-/-	[disbursement] of a commodity
295	02.29	Drehem	[...]	[disbursement] of lambs and goats
296	02.22	Drehem	XI/11/AS 2	withdrawal of a goat
297	02.21	Drehem	V/-/ŠS 4	withdrawal of a sheep
298	02.23	Drehem	I/29/ŠS 7	withdrawal of a gazelle

TEXT	MUSEUM #	PROVENANCE	DATE	DESCRIPTION
299	02.13	Drehem	VI/-/Š 39	receipt of [ ]
300	02.09	Drehem	VII/-/Š 45	receipt of dead cattle
301	02.10	Drehem	II/-/AS 2	receipt of dead animals
302	02.02	Drehem	XI/-/AS 2	receipt of animals
303	08.23	Drehem	II/9/AS 4	receipt of animals
304	Henne 136	Drehem	II/-/AS 4	receipt of dead animals
305	02.07	Drehem	XI/-/ŠS 4	receipt of hides
306	02.32	Drehem	VIII/21/ AS 8	list of various commodities
307	08.13	Adab?	-/-/Š 40	receipt of flour
308	02.24	unknown	[...]	account of oil
309	09.14	unknown	[...]	account of silver
310	09.22	unknown	n.d.	account of cereals
311	09.37	unknown	n.d.	account of workmen
312	02.25	unknown	[...]	pledge involving silver
313	09.09	unknown	[...]	barley for seeding furrows
314	09.07	unknown	[...]	list of ĝuruš and géme
315	09.03	unknown	[...]	fragment dealing with ghee
316	09.08	unknown	[...]	fragment
317	09.38	unknown	[...]	fragment
318	09.42	unknown	[...]	fragment
	01.103	-	-	fragment, not copied
	01.126	-	-	fragment, not copied
	03.04	-	[...]	fragment, not copied
	09.40	-	-	fragment, not copied

Concordance

MUS. #	TEXT #
01.01	185
01.02	186
01.03	187
01.04	189
01.05	190
01.06	191
01.07	192
01.08	194
01.09	195
01.100	178
01.10	196
01.101	103
01.102	105
01.104	108
01.105	107
01.106	188
01.107	197
01.108	39
01.109	212
01.110	106
01.11	198
01.111	226
01.112	38
01.113	264
01.114	115
01.115	40
01.116	41
01.117	116
01.118	100
01.119	24
01.120	126
01.12	199

MUS. #	TEXT #
01.121	125
01.122	130
01.123	133
01.124	163
01.125	141
01.127	144
01.128	147
01.129	151
01.130	161
01.13	200
01.131	82
01.132	177
01.133	179
01.134	117
01.135	287
01.136	84
01.137	47
01.138	11
01.139	48
01.140	49
01.14	202
01.141	50
01.142	12
01.143	51
01.144	52
01.145	53
01.146	54
01.147	55
01.149	33
01.150	25
01.15	203
01.151	29

MUS. #	TEXT #
01.152	7
01.153	79
01.154	19
01.155	20
01.156	8
01.157	9
01.158	193
01.159	10
01.160	44
01.16	204
01.161	110
01.162	45
01.163	13
01.164	242
01.165	265
01.166	68
01.167	59
01.168	61
01.169	62
01.170	63
01.17	205
01.171	66
01.172	67
01.173	14
01.174	136
01.175	137
01.176	138
01.177	150
01.178	152
01.179	168
01.180	173
01.18	206

MUS. #	TEXT #	MUS. #	TEXT #	MUS. #	TEXT #
01.181	111	01.53	245	01.92	164
01.182	225	01.54	246	01.93	165
01.183	4	01.55	247	01.94	166
01.184	184	01.56	248	01.95	30
01.185	270	01.57	249	01.96	175
01.19	207	01.58	250	01.97	176
01.20	208	01.59	251	01.98	37
01.21	209	01.60	252	01.99	32
01.22	210	01.61	253	02.01	21
01.23	211	01.62	254	02.02	302
01.24	213	01.63	255	02.03	293
01.25	214	01.64	256	02.04	169
01.26	215	01.65	258	02.05	170
01.27	216	01.66	257	02.06	94
01.28	217	01.67	259	02.07	305
01.29	218	01.68	260	02.08	289
01.30	219	01.69	113	02.09	300
01.31	220	01.70	261	02.10	301
01.32	221	01.71	262	02.11	153
01.33	223	01.72	114	02.12	154
01.34	224	01.73	263	02.13	299
01.35	222	01.74	266	02.14	288
01.36	227	01.75	123	02.15	57
01.37	228	01.76	22	02.16	60
01.38	229	01.77	124	02.17	64
01.39	230	01.78	127	02.18	65
01.40	231	01.79	128	02.19	291
01.41	232	01.80	26	02.20	292
01.42	233	01.81	27	02.21	297
01.43	234	01.82	28	02.22	296
01.44	235	01.83	6	02.23	298
01.45	236	01.84	134	02.24	308
01.46	237	01.85	135	02.25	312
01.47	238	01.86	42	02.26	17
01.48	239	01.87	146	02.27	290
01.49	240	01.88	148	02.28	85
01.50	241	01.89	149	02.29	295
01.51	243	01.90	157	02.30	182
01.52	244	01.91	160	02.31	183

MUS. #	TEXT #	MUS. #	TEXT #	MUS. #	TEXT #
02.32	306	08.20	162	09.12	18
02.33	5	08.21	174	09.13	95
03.01	56	08.22	71	09.14	309
03.02	129	08.23	303	09.15	87
03.03	278	08.24	167	09.16	88
03.05	275	08.25	201	09.17	89
03.06	281	08.26	112	09.18	90
03.07	276	08.27	31	09.19	271
03.08	274	08.28	34	09.20	83
04.01	72	08.29	70	09.21	91
04.02	73	08.30	142	09.22	310
04.03	75	08.31	145	09.23	92
04.04	80	08.32	104	09.24	96
04.05	109	08.33	285	09.25	286
05.01	140	08.34	180	09.26	284
06.01	294	08.35	181	09.27	93
07.01	77	08.36	99	09.28	69
08.01	120	08.37	58	09.30	101
08.02	15	08.38	1	09.31	81
08.03	78	08.39	16	09.32	97
08.04	43	08.40	102	09.33	269
08.05	131	08.41	74	09.34	267
08.06	139	08.42	76	09.35	3
08.07	143	08.43	272	09.36	98
08.08	159	08.44	279	09.37	311
08.09	121	09.01	35	09.38	317
08.10	171	09.02	23	09.39	119
08.11	46	09.03	315	09.41	268
08.12	172	09.04	273	09.42	318
08.13	307	09.05	277	46.01	283
08.14	122	09.06	2	46.02	282
08.15	132	09.07	314	Henne 136	304
08.16	118	09.08	316	Henne 137	280
08.17	155	09.09	313		
08.18	156	09.10	36		
08.19	158	09.11	86		

LAU #	TEXT #
1	53
4	22
5	180
9	26
16	153
17	27
22	232
25	24
27	113
44	137
46	30
73	189
79	156
82	146
84	133
85	136
87	114
88	116
91	31
92	111
95	34
96	75
98	165
99	183
100	182
102	160
105	122
106	6
110	186
114	192
126	40
127	213
141	120
148	140
157	102
159	77
160	73
161	70
162	184
171	72
172	11
173	80
177	59
178	92
179	96
183	5
185	181
194	65
208	130
211	173
212	141
236	147
238	66
240	60
242	57
244	267
251	67
252	56
253	64
254	14
256	1

Lines Read According to Collation

(Lines are preceded with an asterisk in the transliteration)*

TEXT	COLLATED LINE
1	5, 30, 47, 64, 79, 97, 98, 170, 211, 216, 298, 325, 327
2	11
3	81
5	1, 2, 3, 10, 12
6	2
8	1, 2
10	6, seal
14	24, 34, 74, 106, 116, 122, 123, 160, 178, 179
15	5, 10
16	3
18	6
21	1
22	4
23	17
24	1
25	1, 10
27	6, 9
29	3
33	12, 18
34	1–6, 11, 12
35	7
40	5, 7, 15, 18, 19
41	8
42	2, 4
50	19
53	14, 15, 20
56	2, 5, 24, 37, 39, 40, 50, 66, 69, 71
57	2, 4, 10, 13, 14, 20, 27, 33–41, 48, 49
59	4, 7, 12, 30
60	10, 16, 19, 22, 23, 25–30, 33, 36, 37
61	34, 36
62	29
63	8, 79, 105, 165
64	46, 49, 54, 63, 68–91, 94–109, 112, 114
65	6, 9, 17, 18, 19, 25
66	2, 4, 8, 21, 24
67	2, 8, 10, 12, 17, 20, 40, 46, 56, 57, 58, 63, 64, 66, 67, 69, 73, 79, 84, 95, 96, 107, 117, 118
68	3, 5, 13
70	3, 5, 8, 10, 11, 12, 18, 21
72	3, 5, 6, 8, 11, 12, 23
73	7, 18, 31, 34, 36, 37, 40, 52, 56
74	18
75	11
76	26, 38, 51
77	4, 8
80	2, 7, 14, 20
82	2, 4, 6, 9, 11, 14, 16–20, 22
86	15
89	6
90	10
91	1, 14, 15
92	8, 15, 17, 21
96	4, 11, 12, 19, 22, 23, 27

TEXT	COLLATED LINE
100	1
102	4, 7
109	1
111	2, 3
114	1, 3, 4
117	18
120	6, 8
124	1
125	4
131	6
133	4
136	5
141	3
146	2
151	3
164	seal l. 3
173	seal l. 2
182	3
183	6
184	19
186	8, 11
188	12
189	8, 19
192	12, 21
193	3
194	13, 15
197	16
200	1
206	19, 23, 26–28
213	3, 12, 20

TEXT	COLLATED LINE
219	11
222	11, 15
229	13
230	3
234	7, 16
236	22
240	3, 10
241	1, 6, 17
243	11, 13, 14, 17, 18, 21
246	9
249	4
253	13
259	3, 9, 15
263	9
267	4
269	7
273	41
277	3, 8, 11, 12, 14
283	20, 21
288	57, 86
289	10, 11
291	82
296	2
299	1, 6, seal
307	4, seal l. 3
308	6
312	3
313	9
315	6, 13
316	6, 9

I

(-/-/Š 44)

xi. 1. [ ] še gur lugal
2. [a-šà A]r-ša-ti-a [^{d}N]in-dár-a-ta
3. [ ] 3.0.0 gur
4. [a]-šà Sirara$_{4}$^{ki}-ḫé-ĝál-ta
★5. [L]ú-ku$_{5}$-da-mu dumu saĝa URU×gána*tenû*^{ki}
6. [ ] gur
7. [a-rá] 1-kam
8. [ ] gur
9. [a-rá] 2-kam
10. [ ] TUR
11. [a-r]á 1-kam
12. [a-r]á 2-kam
13. [k]alag-ga
14. [ ] NE [ ]-ta
15. [ ] LA
16. [ ] KAL
17. [ ] (BLANK)
18. [ ] (BLANK)
19. [x]
20. [ ] 5
21. [gu]r
22. [ ]-ta

(bottom of column i broken)

ii. 23. a-šà ^{ĝeš}tir-gaba-gíd-da
24. 225 iku 1.2.3-ta
25. 15.0.0 á-ḫun-ĝá
26. á-šà ^{ĝeš}tir-ma-nu
27. 234 iku 1.2.3-ta
28. 5.0.0 á-ḫun-ĝá
29. a-šà-gíd gána-gu-la
★30. 1332 iku 1.2.3-ta
31. 324 iku 1.4.0-ta
32. 144 iku 1.1.0-ta
33. a-šà im-bi-a-ba
34. 72 iku 1.1.0-ta
35. a-šà ^{d}Nin-ĝír-su
36. 270 iku 1.1.0-ta
37. a-šà ^{d}En-líl-lá
38. 7 amar 0.1.3-ta
39. še-bi 2.0.3 gur
40. (BLANK)
41. šu+níĝin 2469 iku 1.2.3-ta
42. šu+níĝin 324 iku 1.4.0-ta
43. šu+níĝin 510 iku 1.1.0-ta
44. še-bi 270.4.3 5 sìla gur
45. gána-apin-a
46. [ ] 9.0.0 gur
★47. [x] gána
48. [ama]r 0.1.3-ta
49. [x] gur
50. [x] 5
51. [gu]r

(bottom of column ii broken)

iii. 52. 18.3.0 gur
53. a-šà Sirara$_{4}$^{ki}-ḫé-ĝál-ta
54. 77.0.0 gur
55. a-šà Ar-ša-ti-a ù é-duru$_{5}$-Ur-^{ĝeš}gigir-ta
56. 64.0.0 gur
57. a-rá 1-kam
58. 2.0.4 a-rá 2-kam
59. ĝìr Ur-tur
60. 48.0.0 gur
61. a-rá 1-kam
62. 1.3.2 a-rá 2-kam
63. ĝìr Ur-ša$_{6}$-ga
★64. a-šà ĝeš-bi-ĝeš-e-ĝar-ra-ta
65. 10.0.0 gur ki Ur-^{d}Nanše dumu Na-ba-ša$_{6}$-ta
66. 89.2.1 gur
67. ki Lugal-síg-gíd-ta
68. (BLANK)
69. šu+níĝin 310.4.1 gur
70. šà-bi-ta
71. 666 iku 1.2.3-ta
72. 30.0.5 á-ḫun-ĝá
73. a-šà ^{ĝeš}tir-gaba-gíd-da
74. 234 iku 1.2.3-ta
75. 13.0.0 á-ḫun-ĝá
76. a-šà ^{ĝeš}tir-ma-nu
77. 234 iku 1.2.3-ta
78. 3.0.0 á-ḫun-ĝá
★79. a-šà ^{kuš}e-sír-dúb-ba
80. 234 iku 1.2.3-ta
81. 6.0.0 á-ḫun-ĝá
82. a-šà-gíd gána-gu-la
83. 90 iku 1.2.3-ta

iv. 84. 324 iku 1.4.0-ta
85. 216 iku 1.1.0-ta
86. a-šà im-bi-a-ba
87. 90 iku 1.1.0-ta

88. a-šà ^{d}Nin-ĝír-su
89. 216 iku 1.1.0-ta
90. a-šà ^{d}En-líl-lá
91. 5 amar 0.1.3-ta
92. še-bi 1.2.3 gur
93. 1.0.0 gur mur-gu$_4$ ḪU.KU.BU
94. (BLANK)
95. šu+níĝin 2268 iku 1.2.3-ta
96. šu+níĝin 324 iku 1.4.0-ta
★97. šu+níĝin 5[2]2 iku 1.1.0-ta
★98. še-bi 256.1.0 gur
99. gána-apin-a
100. šu+níĝin 52.0.5 gur
101. á-ḫun-ĝá
102. šu+níĝin 5 amar 0.1.3-ta
103. še-bi 1.2.3-ta
104. šu+níĝin 1.0.0 gur mur-gu$_4$ ḪU.KU.BU
105. (BLANK)
106. šu+níĝin 310.4.1 gur
107. zi-ga
108. diri 0.0.1 še
109. é šu-ga-lam-ma
110. é ^{d}Šul-gi-me
111. 49.0.0 gur
112. ì-dub a-šà Ar-ša-ti-a-ta
113. 14.3.0 gur
114. a-šà Sirara$_4^{ki}$-ḫé-ĝál-ta
115. 7.0.0 še-ba Ad-da-uru
116. ki Ma-ni-ta
117. 18.0.0 gur
118. Ur-saĝ-pa-è-ta
v. 119. 6.0.0 Ĝír-nun-ta
120. 50.0.4 5 sìla gur
121. ki Lugal-síg-gíd-ta
122. 5.2.3 gur
123. še-numun-ta gur-ra
124. 0.1.3 še amar ba-ug$_7$
125. 2.0.1 5 sìla gur
126. ki A-kal-la-ta
127. (BLANK)
128. šu+níĝin 152.3.0 gur
129. šà-bi-ta
130. 252 iku 1.2.3-ta
131. 4.0.0 á-ḫun-ĝá
132. a-šà NI-zi-na
133. 612 iku 1.2.3-ta
134. 6.0.0 á-ḫun-ĝá
135. a-šà-gíd gána-gu-la
136. 144 iku 1.2.3-ta
137. a-šà a-saĝ-dù-du
138. 36 iku 1.4.0-ta
139. 54 iku 1.1.0-ta
140. a-šà ĝír-ĝír
141. 306 iku 1.4.0-ta
142. 270 iku 1.1.0-ta
143. a-šà ^{d}En-líl-lá
144. 1.3.0 mur-gu$_4$ ḪU.KU.BU
145. 4 amar 0.1.3-ta
146. še-bi 1.1.0 gur
147. (BLANK)
148. šu+níĝin 1008 iku 1.2.3-ta
149. šu+níĝin 342 iku 1.4.0-ta
150. šu+níĝin 324 iku 1.1.0-ta
151. še-bi 139.4.0 gur
152. gána-apin-a
153. šu+níĝin 10.0.0 gur á-ḫun-ĝá
154. šu+níĝin 1.3.0 mur-gu$_4$ ḪU.K[U.BU]
vi. 155. šu+níĝin 4 amar 0.1.3 gur
156. še-bi 1.1.0 gur
157. (BLANK)
158. šu+níĝin 152.3.0 gur
159. zi-ga
160. Ma-an-sum
161. 49.0.0 gur
162. ì-dub a-šà Ar-ša-ti-a-^{d}Nin-dár-a-ta
163. 4.0.0 a-šà Ar-ša-ti-a-^{d}Nanše-ta
164. 36.0.0 gur
165. ì-dub Sirara$_4^{ki}$-ḫé-ĝál-ta
166. 18.0.0 gur
167. Ur-saĝ-pa-è-ta
168. 7.0.0 še-ba Ad-da-uru
169. ki Ma-ni-ta
★170. 6.0.0 Ĝír-nun-ta
171. 51.0.0 gur
172. ki Lugal-síg-g[íd-ta]
173. (BLANK)
174. šu+níĝin 17[1.0.0 gur]
175. šà-bi-[ta]
176. 594 [iku]
177. 6.0.0 á-[ḫun-ĝá]
178. a-šà ĝír-[ĝír]
179. 198 iku 1.[x.x-ta]
180. 6.0.0 á-[ḫun-ĝá]
181. a-šà a-s[ag-dù-du]
182. 146.5 ik[u]
183. 2.0.0 á-ḫ[un-ĝá]
184. a-šà NI-zi-[na]

185. 123 [iku]
186. 3.0.0 á-[ḫun-ĝá]
187. a-šà x [ ]
188. 90 iku 1.[x.x-ta]
189. a-[šà]
190. [ ]
(top of column vii broken)
vii. 191. [ ]
192. a-š[à]
193. 4 amar [0.1.3-ta]
194. še-bi [1.1.0 gur]
195. 1.0.0 mur-gu$_4$ Ḫ[U.KU.BU]
196. 2.0.1 5 sìl[a gur]
197. (BLANK)
198. šu+níĝin 972 [iku]
199. šu+níĝin 414 [iku]
200. šu+níĝin 360 iku [ ]
201. še-bi 120+[.x.x gur]
202. gána-apin-[a]
203. šu+níĝin 17.[x.x gur]
204. á-ḫun-[ĝá]
205. šu+níĝin 4 amar [0.1.3-ta]
206. še-bi 1.[1.0 gur]
207. šu+níĝin 1.0.0 mur-g[u$_4$ ḪU.KU.BU]
208. šu+níĝin 2.0.1 [5 sìla gur]
209. Ma-an-[sum]
210. (BLANK)
*211. šu+níĝin 160.[0.0] 5 [sìla gur]
212. zi-[ga]
213. lá-u$_x$ 1.0.4 [gur]
214. A-kal-[la]
215. é Nam-ḫ[a-ni]
*216. 57.4.0 [gur]
217. ì-dub a-šà [Sira]rà^{ki}-ḫé-[ĝál-ta]
218. 34.0.0 gur
219. ì-dub a-šà Ar-ša-ti-a-^{d}Nin-dar-a-ta
220. 8.0.0 gur
221. ì-dub a-šà Ar-š[a]-ti-a-^{d}Nanše-ta
222. 2.0.0 ki Ur-^{d}Nanše [dumu] Lú-du$_{10}$-ga-ta
viii. 223. 5.0.0 gur
224. Ĝír-nun-t[a]
225. 82.3.4 5 sìla gur
226. ki Lugal-síg-gíd-ta
227. 4.0.0 gur
228. ki Ma-ni-ta
229. 5.0.0 lá-u$_x$ su-ga
230. ki Ur-diĝir-ra-ta
231. (BLANK)
232. šu+níĝin 198.2.5 5 sìla gur
233. šà-bi-ta
234. 639 iku 1.2.3-ta
235. 12.0.0 á-ḫun-ĝá
236. a-šà-gíd gána
237. 258 iku 1.2.3-ta
238. 6.0.0 á-ḫun-ĝá
239. a-šà En-nu-lum-ma
240. 216 iku 1.2.3-ta
241. 4.0.0 á-ḫun-ĝá SA-kam
242. 10.0.0 gur á-ḫun-ĝá
243. a-šà uru-ni
244. 198 iku 1.2.3-ta
245. 180 iku 1.4.0-ta
246. 5.0.0 á-ḫun-ĝá
247. a-šà ^{d}Nin-mar-ki
248. 126 iku 1.2.3-ta
249. a-šà ĝír-ĝír
250. 324 iku 1.1.0-ta
251. a-šà ^{d}En-líl-lá
252. 4 amar 0.1.3-ta
253. še-bi 1.1.0 gur
254. 1.0.0 mur-gu$_4$ ḪU.KU.BU
255. (BLANK)
256. šu+níĝin 1437 iku 1.2.3-ta
257. šu+níĝin 180 iku 1.4.0-ta
ix. 258. šu+níĝin 324 1.1.0-ta
259. še-bi 159.1.4 5 sìla gur
260. gána-apin-a
261. šu+níĝin 37.0.0 gur
262. á-ḫun-ĝá
263. šu+níĝin 4 amar 0.1.3-ta
264. še-bi 1.1.0 gur
265. 1.0.0 mur-gu$_4$ ḪU.KU.BU
266. (BLANK)
267. šu+níĝin 198.2.4 5 sìla gur
268. zi-ga
269. Ur-^{d}Nin-mar-ki
270. 77.0.0 gur
271. ì-dub a-šà Ar-ša-ti-a-ta
272. 12.3.0 gur
273. ì-dub Sirara$_4^{ki}$-ḫé-ĝál-ta
274. 5.0.0 Ĝír-nun-ta
275. 103.3.1 5 sìla gur
276. ki Lugal-síg-gíd-ta
277. 8.0.0 gur
278. ki Ma-ni-ta
279. 2.0.0 lá-u$_x$ su-ga
280. ki Ur-diĝir-ra-ta

281. (BLANK)
282. šu+níĝin 208.1.1 5 síla gur
283. šà-bi-ta
284. 648 iku 1.2.3-ta
285. 15.0.0 á-ḫun-ĝá
286. a-šà En-nu-lum-ma
287. 261 iku 1.2.3-ta
288. 1.0.0 á-ḫun-ĝá
289. a-šà-gíd gána

x. 290. [26]4 iku 1.2.3-ta
291. [x].1.0 á-ḫun-ĝá
292. [a-šà] uru-ni
293. 18 iku 1.2.3-ta
294. 198 iku 1.4.0-ta
295. 6 á-ḫun-ĝá
296. a-šà ^{d}Nin-mar-ki
297. 126 iku 1.2.3-ta
★298. a-šà ĝír-ĝír
299. 324 iku 1.1.0-ta
300. a-šà ^{d}En-líl-lá
301. 7 amar 0.1.3-ta
302. še-bi 2.0.3 gur
303. 1.0.0 mur-gu$_{4}$ ḪU.KU.BU
304. (BLANK)
305. šu+níĝin 1461 iku 1.2.3-ta
306. šu+níĝin 198 iku 1.4.0-ta
307. šu+níĝin 324 iku 1.1.0-ta
308. še-bi 163.4 5 sìla gur
309. gána-apin-a
310. šu+níĝin 42.0.0 gur
311. á-ḫun-ĝá
312. šu+níĝin 7 amar 0.1.3-ta
313. še-bi 2.0.3-ta
314. šu+níĝin 1.0.0 mur-gu$_{4}$ ḪU.KU.BU
315. (BLANK)
316. šu+níĝin 208.1.1 5 sìla gur
317. zi-ga
318. Ur-^{d}Ig-alima
319. é ^{d}Nin-ĝeš-zi-da
320. 2250 iku 1.1.0-ta
321. še-bi 150 gur
322. 60.0.0 gur á-ḫun-ĝá
323. a-šà ^{d}En-líl-lá
324. (BLANK)
★325. šu+níĝin 8817 iku 1.2.3-ta

xi. *(top of column XI broken)*
326. [ ] x [ ] a
★327. [ ] 7.0.5 gur
328. [ ] á lú-ḫun-ĝá
329. šu+níĝin 31 amar 0.1.3-ta
330. še-bi 9.1.3 gur
331. šu+níĝin 5.3.0 gur
332. mur-gu$_{4}$ ḪU.KU.BU
333. zi-ga
334. šu+níĝin 1.0.3 5 sìla gur
335. lá-u$_{x}$-àm
336. šu+níĝin 0.0.1 gur
337. diri-àm
338. (BLANK)

xii. 339. (BLANK)
340. [nì-k]a$_{9}$-ak gána-gána-a
341. é ^{d}Šul-gi
342. é ^{d}Ig-alima
343. ù é ^{d}Nin-ĝeš-zi-da
344. (BLANK)
345. mu Si-mu-ur$_{4}$-ru-um^{ki}
346. Lu-lu-bu^{ki} a-rá 10 lá 1-kam-aš ba-ḫul

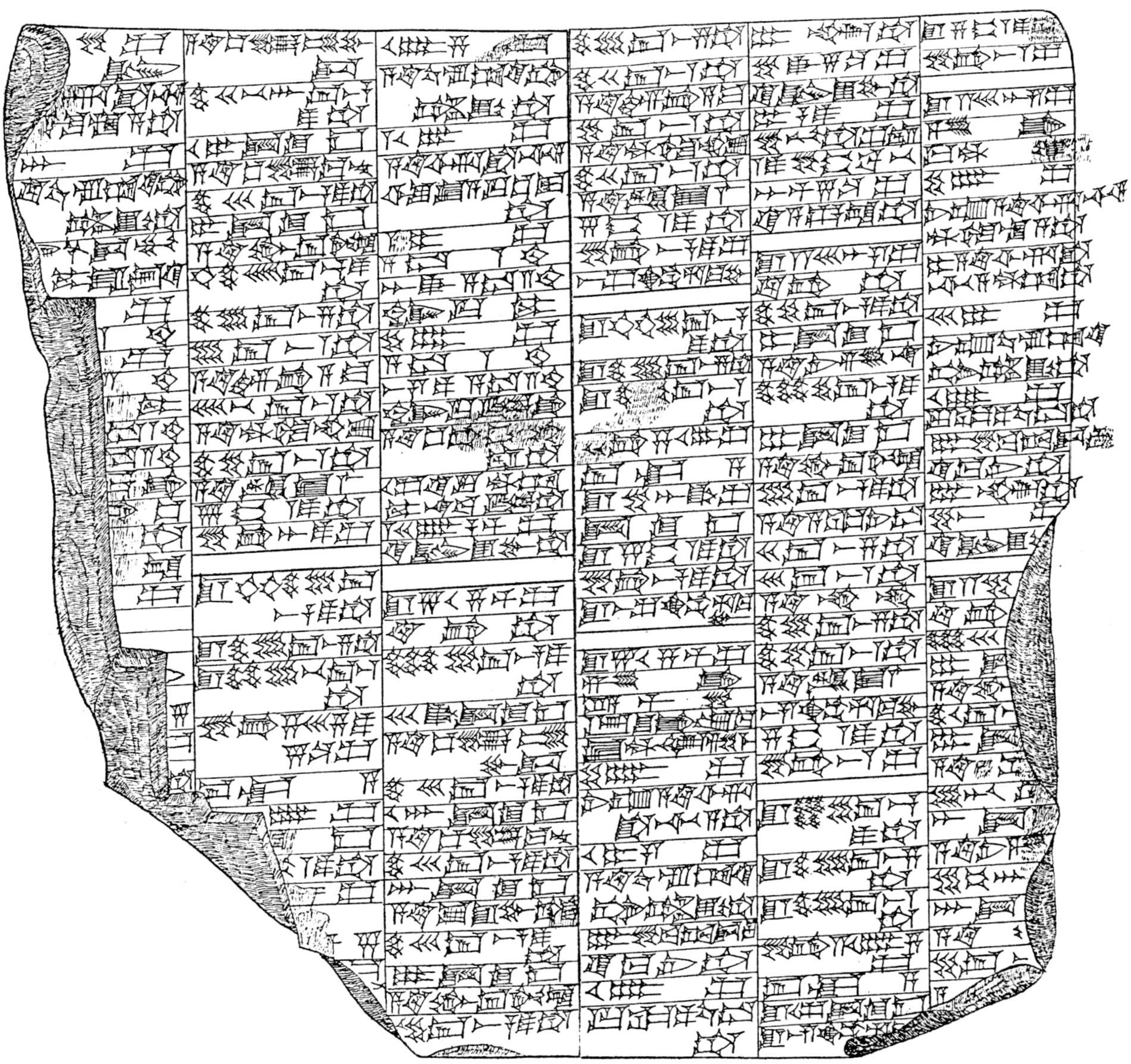

1 obverse

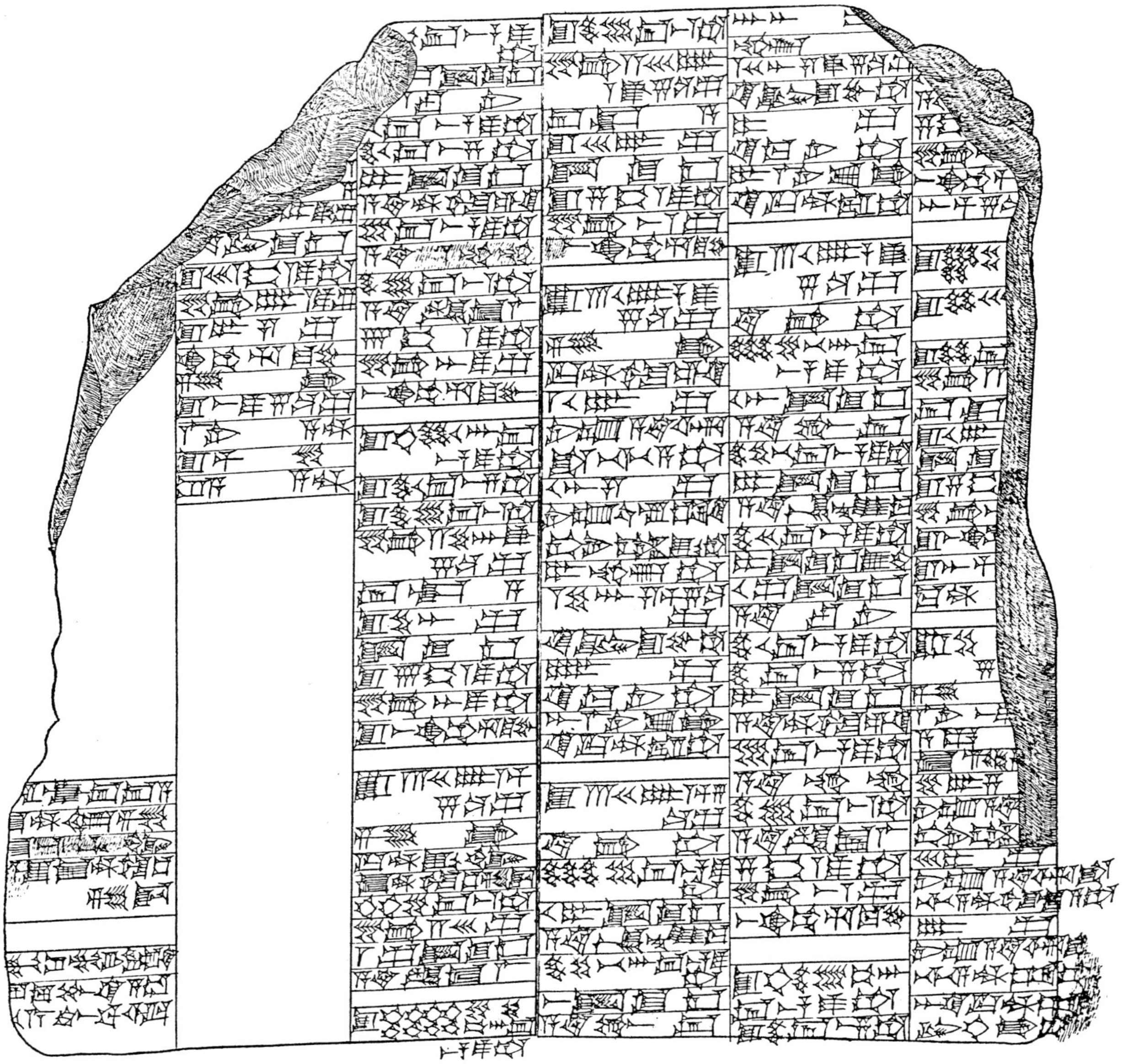

1 reverse

2 (date not preserved)

OBV.

(*top of obverse broken*)

1. [ ] ⸢Ur-^{d}Ba⸣-[ú]
2. kìšib Nam-zi-tar-[ra]
3. 1 (eše) Ùr-re-ba-d[u_7]
4. 1 (eše) 3 (iku) Ur-é-[ ]
5. 1 (bur) A-gu-[ ]
6. 1 (bur'u) 1 (bur) 2 (eše) 3+ (iku) [ ]
7. (*several lines broken*)
8. ⸢x x⸣ [ ]
9. 1 (bur'u) 3 (bur) 2 (eše) [ ]
10. šà Nina[^{ki}]

*11. 1 (bur) Lugal-[x]

12. šà Lag[aš^{ki}]

REV.

13. 20 gu_4 [ ]
14. 1 (bur) 1 (eše) [ ]
15. 1 (eše) 3 (iku) [ ]
16. 10 [gu_4]
17. 2+ (bur) 3+ (iku) [ ]

(*most of reverse broken*)

L.E.

18. mu-ús-s[a]

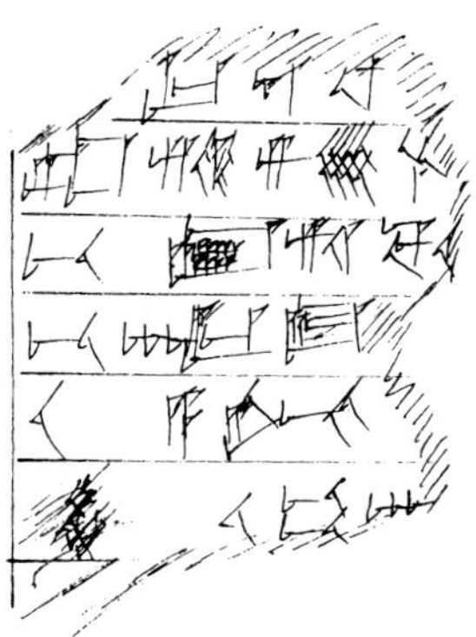

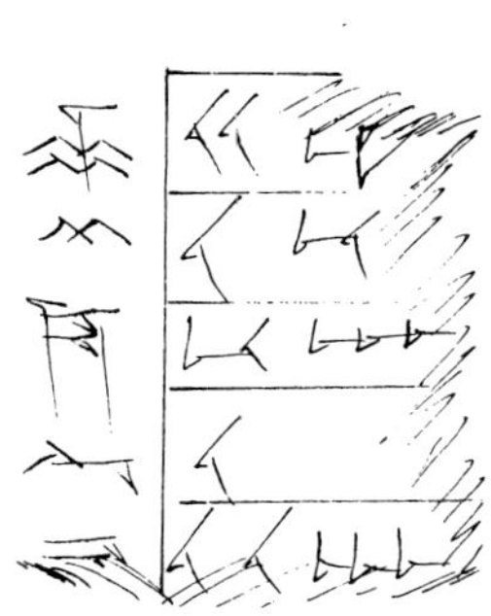

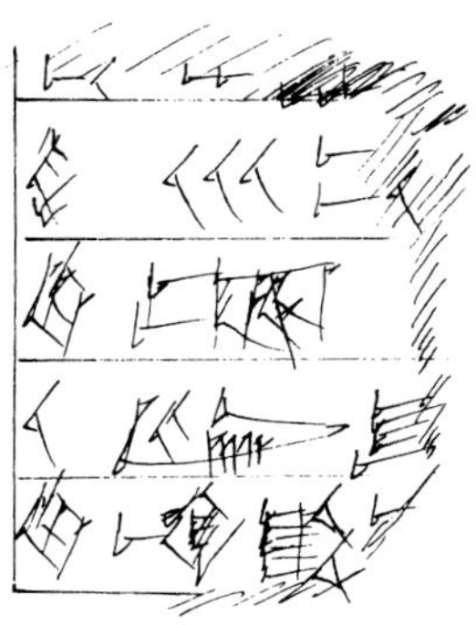

3 (date not preserved)

(at least one column missing)

i'. *(top of column i broken)*

1. [ ]x ta
2. [ ] 2.0.0 gur
3. [ ] šim
4. [ ] 6.0.0 gur
5. [ ] DÙ
6. [ ] ús saĝa
7. [i]ku 2.0.0 gur
8. [ ] 6.0.0 gur
9. [ ] lú šim
10. [ ] ĝeš-ì
11. [ ] é-a-me
12. [ ] (BLANK)
13. [ ] GIŠ
14. [ ]

(bottom of column i broken)

ii'. *(top of column ii broken)*

15. [ ] KA [ ]
16. 1 (eše) iku 1.0.0 gur
17. A-kal-la
18. 1 (eše) iku 1.0.0 gur
19. Mu-mu
20. nu-bànda-gu$_{4}$-me
21. lú-šuku-ra é-a-me
22. (BLANK)
23. a-šà ambar-a-šeš
24. 2 (eše) 3 iku 2.0.0 gur
25. ka-gur$_{7}$
26. 2 (eše) iku 2.0.0 gur
27. Al-mu nu-bànda-gu$_{4}$
28. lú-šuku-ra é-a-me
29. (BLANK)
30. a-šà [x]-bi-sur-ra
31. 4 iku 2.0.0 gur
32. Lú-sar
33. (BLANK)
34. [ ] KA.TUL

iii'. *(top of column iii broken)*

35. 1 (bur) iku [ ]
36. Ab-ba-[ ]
37. 1 (eše) 3 iku [ ]
38. SAĜ [ ]
39. 1 (eše) iku k[i]
40. En-nu-d[a]
41. 3 ugula x[ ] 1 (eše) iku-t[a]
42. 1 (eše) iku [ ]
43. sagi [ ]
44. 1 (bur) iku 3[.0.0 gur]
45. Al-[ ]
46. 1 (bur) iku 3.0.0 [gur]
47. A-kal-[la]
48. 2 (bur) 1 (eše) 3 iku [ ]

iv'.

49. šu+níĝin še ĝeš è-bi 150.0.0 gur lugal
50. saĝa
51. šu+níĝin 1 (bur) 1 (eše) iku 6.0.0 gur
52. ša$_{13}$-dub-ba
53. šu+níĝin 1 (bur) 1 (eše) iku 6.0.0 gur
54. ka-x
55. šu+níĝin 1 (bur) 1 (eše) iku 3.0.0 gur
56. ka-gur$_{7}$
57. šu+níĝin 1 (bur) iku 6.0.0 gur
58. šár-ra-ab-du
59. šu+níĝin 1 (bur'u) 1 iku 10.0.0 gur
60. [dub]-sar gu$_{4}$-apin
61. šu+níĝin 1 dub-sar
62. [ ] 2 (bur) iku [ ]

(bottom of column iv broken)

v'.

63. [ù]ĝ-ĝa$_{6}$
64. [šu+níĝin x] un-ĝa$_{6}$ 1 (bur) iku 4.0.0 gur
65. šu+níĝin 4 un-ĝa$_{6}$ 2 (eše) iku 4.0.0 gur
66. šu+níĝin 2 (eše) iku 1.0.0 gur
67. ugula ḫé-dab$_{5}$
68. šu+níĝin 1 (eše) en-nu-da-ambar-a
69. šu+níĝin 1 (bur) iku 1.0.0 gur
70. dub-sar érin-na
71. šu+níĝin 1 (bur) iku 3.0.0 gur
72. dub-sar a-šà érin-na
73. šu+níĝin 7 engar ĝeš-ì 4½ iku-ta
74. šu+níĝin 10 lá 1 aga-ús saĝa 4½ iku 1.0.0 gur-ta
75. šu+níĝin 1 aga-ús saĝa 1 (bur) iku [ ] gur

(bottom of column v broken)

vi'. *(top of column vi broken)*

76. [ ] gur
77. [ ] šim [x]-ta
78. [ ] 2.0.0 gur
79. [A]b-ba-uru
80. [ ] 2.0.0 gur

*81. [ ] ŠEŠ inim-ma
82. [x] mu lugal
83. [ ] sagi lugal
84. [x] 1.0.0 gur lú x-[ ] Ur-é

85. (BLANK)
86. [ ] x [ ]
(bottom of column vi broken)

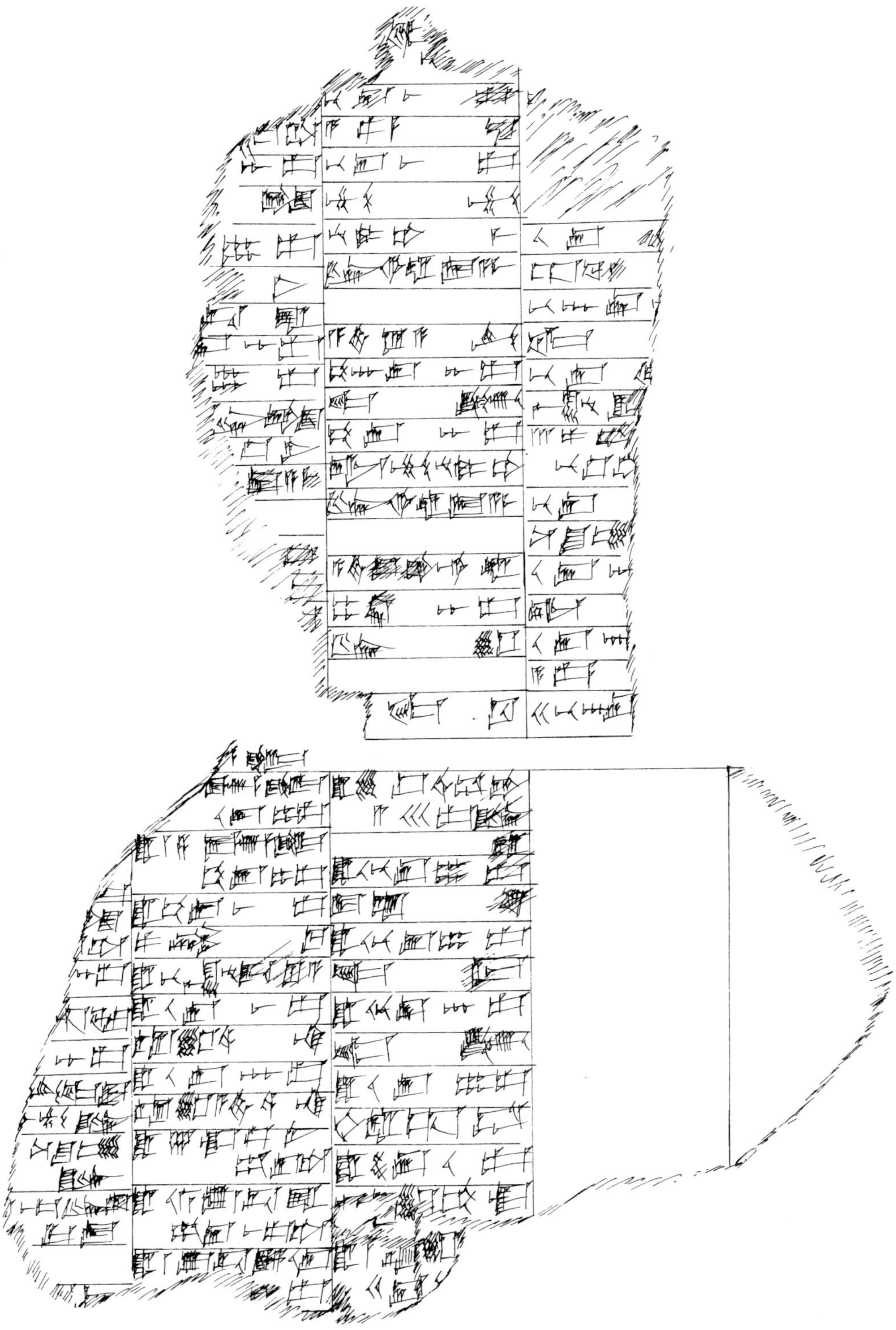

4

(not dated)

OBV.

1. [ ] iku
2. *A-ḫu-a*
3. Ur-^{ĝeš}gigir dumu Gi$_4$-ni-mu
4. Si-dù
5. Ka$_5$-a-mu
6. 4 (bur) Ur-^{d}Dumu-zi dub-nagar
7. 2[+] (bur) um-mi-a é-kišib-ba-ka

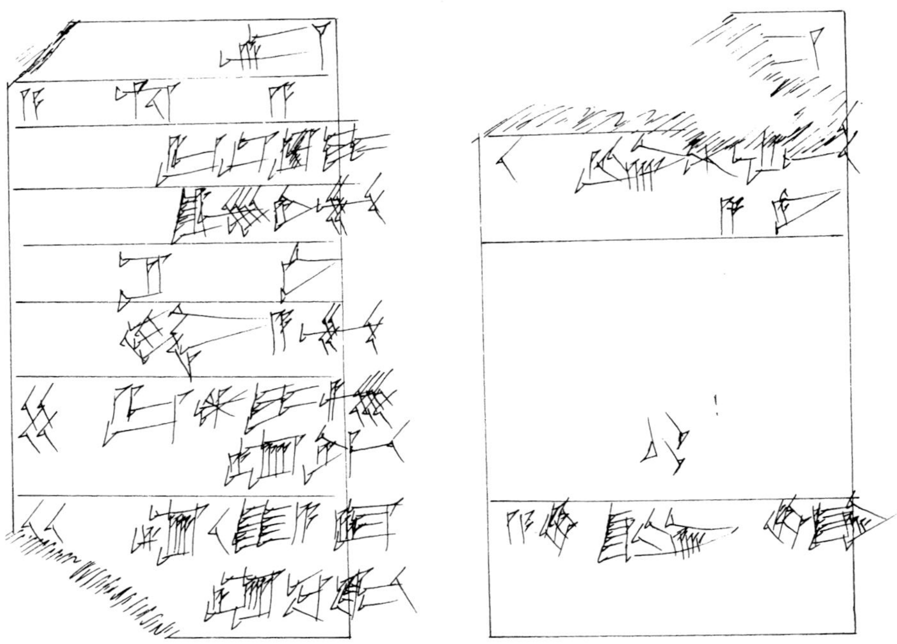

5

(not dated)

OBV.

*1. 1 (eše) 1 (sar) ^{d}Utu-[b]a-a-zi u$_4$ 10 ba-zal

*2. [ ] En-šà-kù-ge

*3. 1 (eše) 1 (sar) Ur-^{d}Ba-ú

4. 1 (eše) 1 (sar) Ur-^{d}Nin-ĝeš-zi-da

5. u$_4$ 23 ba-zal

6. 1 (eše) 5 (iku) Ab-ba-gi-na u$_4$ 28

7. [ ]

REV.

8. [x]

9. 1 (bur) Lú-diĝir-ra ⌜šeš⌝-a-ni

10. (BLANK)

11. a-šà Lugal-šà-ga

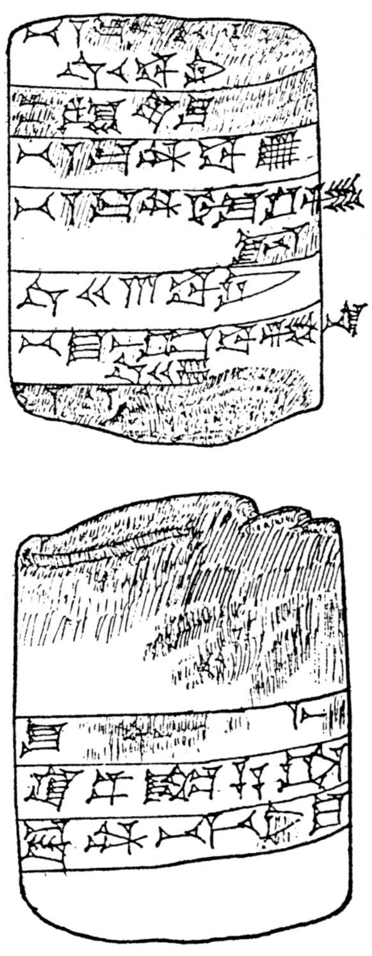

6

(IX/-/Š 47)

OBV.

1. 10.0.0 še gur lugal
*2. še-numun a-šà Bur-su-šè
3. ki Ur-^{d}Ba-ú-ta
4. é-nun saĝa-ta
5. Ur-^{d}Ig-alima

REV.

8. [ ]
9. (B L A N K)
*10. šu-gíd-me
11. ki Pa-ne-ZA-ta
*12. Za-an-ti ì-dab$_5$

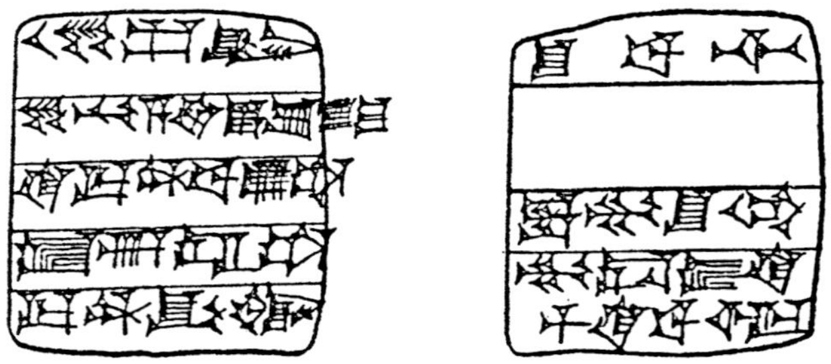

7

(V/-/AS 8)

OBV.

1. 71 ĝuruš u$_4$-1-šè
2. al ak
3. 750 ĝuruš u$_4$-1-šè
4. nì-gul ak
5. ki-sar
6. iti šu-numun
7. 630 ĝuruš u$_4$-1-šè

REV.

6. šu ba-ti
7. (B L A N K)
8. iti mu-šu-du$_7$
9. mu-ús-sa Ki-maš^{ki} ba-ḫul

8 (VI/12/IS 1)

OBV.

*1. sig$_7$-a 0.1.0 še Ur-^{d}IM dumu Amar-ka$_5$-a ⸢x-má⸣

*2. ^{ĝeš}kiri$_6$-Gar-šum^{ki}-šè

3. Ur-^{d}Inanna ì-dab$_5$

4. 0.1.0 En-šà-saĝ dumu Eren-da

5. 0.1.0 Na-ba-ša$_6$ dumu Lugal-ezen

REV.

6. Al-lí-ga ì-dab$_5$

7. im-e tak$_4$-a-me

8. (BLANK)

9. ^{ĝeš}tukul-e dab$_5$-ba-me

10. ĝìr Un-ĝa$_6$

11. iti ezen ^{d}Dumu-zi u$_4$ 12 ba-zal

12. mu ^{d}*I-bí*-^{d}Suen lugal

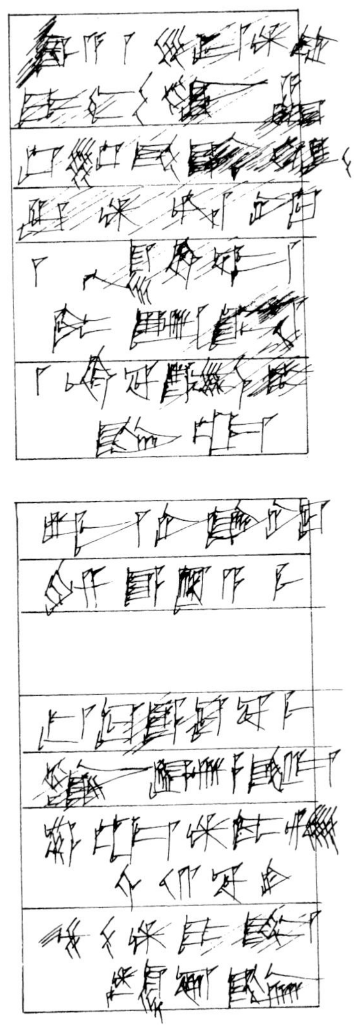

9

(I/-/-)

OBV.

1. 5 ĝuruš ḫé-dab$_5$
2. 144 karadin 0.0.3-ta
3. ugula Lú-da-gi-na
4. 5 ĝuruš 40 karadin 0.0.3-ta
5. ugula Lú-du-du
6. 11 ĝuruš 100 lá 2 karadin 0.0.3-ta
7. ugula Lú-diĝir-ra
8. 282 karadin 0.0.3-ta
9. ḫé-dab$_5$-me
10. 10 ĜIŠ.BI.AK
11. 10 Lú-tùr-[x]

REV.

12. Ur Lú-[ ]
13. [L]ú-^{d}Ĝeš-bar-⸢è⸣
14. [ ] ĝuruš [ ]
15. [ ] Lú-^{d}⸢Nanna⸣$^{?}$ engar
16. (BLANK)
17. [ ] x KI me
18. [Lú]-^{d}Utu-bar-ra engar
19. (BLANK)
20. [U]r-^{d}Ig-alima
21. 6 engar 50 karadin 0.0.3-ta
22. ⸢šà-gal⸣ Šeš-kal-la
23. gána ba-ga
24. iti buru$_x$(GÁN)-maš u$_4$ 4 ba-zal
25. šà uru-da NI.AB×MAŠ

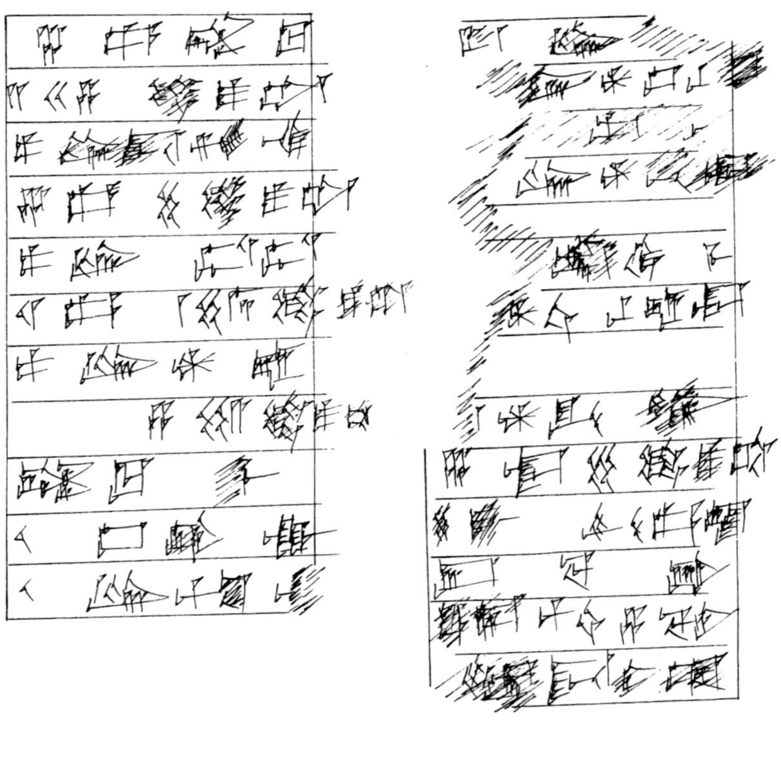

10

(I/-/-)

OBV.

1. 6 ĝuruš 3 ĝuruš ½
2. u$_4$ 4-šè
3. á še-kin-ku$_5$
4. 2 ĝuruš ½
5. u$_4$ 5-šè

REV.

*6. á še-kéš-rá
7. a-šà Ù-ma-ni-ka gub-ba
8. SEAL
9. é udu-me
10. ki Šà-kù-ge-ta
11. kìšib Ku-li
12. iti buru$_x$(GÁN)-maš

*Seal: Ku-li
dub-sar
dumu Lú-kiri$_4$-zal

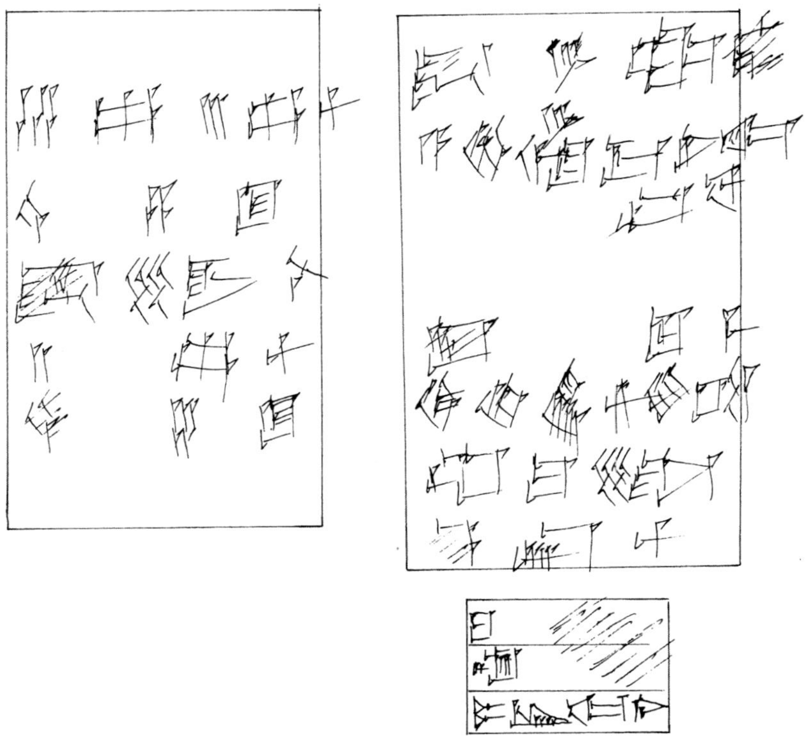

11 (V/4/-)

OBV.

1. 4 gu_4-ĝeš-ùr
2. 12 érin šà-gu_4
3. 5 lú-ḫun-ĝá
4. (BLANK)
5. é-[d]En-ki
6. 2 gu_4-ĝeš-ùr

REV.

7. 10 lá 1 érin šà-gu_4
8. (BLANK)
9. é-[x x]
10. (BLANK)
11. iti $munu_4$-kú
12. u_4 4-kam
13. a-šà da-ad

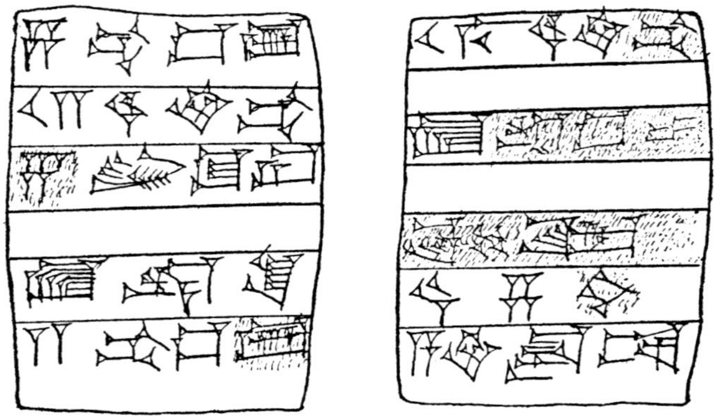

12 (VI/21/-)

OBV.

1. 1 gu$_4$-numun gána-ba
2. 20 ĝuruš lú-ḫun-ĝá
3. gána Ur-ša$_6$
4. 1 gu$_4$-numun 10 ĝuruš lú-ḫun-ĝá
5. gána Ìr
6. 1 gu$_4$-numun 3 ĝuruš lú-ḫun-ĝá
7. gána Ur-^{i_7}Nina^{ki}-šè-ĝen
8. 1 gu$_4$-numun 2 ĝuruš ḫun-ĝá
9. gána Ur-ki-gu-la
10. (B L A N K)
11. a-šà úkuš-x-zi
12. 1 gu$_4$-numun gána-ba
13. 1 gu$_4$-numun Lú-kal-la
14. 13 ĝuruš ḫun-ĝá

REV.

15. gána Ur-mes
16. [1 g]u$_4$-⸢numun gána⸣-ba
17. 5+.0.0 gur [ ] ta ĝuruš-šè
18. gána Ur-^{d}En-ki
19. 1 gu$_4$-num[un] gána-ba
20. 1 gu$_4$-numun Ur-^{d}[N]in-[ĝeš-z]i-da
21. 1 gu$_4$-numun Ur-^{d}[N]in-zu
22. 22 ĝuruš ḫun-ĝá 6 érin 6 [g]u$_4$
23. gána Ur-^{d}Suen
24. (B L A N K)
25. a-šà ^{ú}KI.NUMUN
26. iti ezen ^{d}Dumu-zi
27. u$_4$ 21-kam

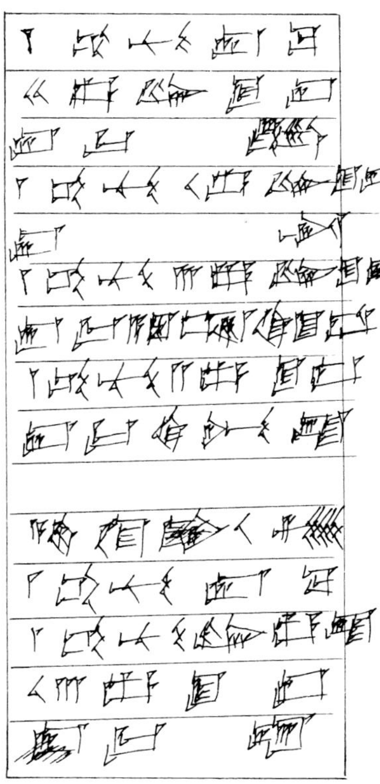

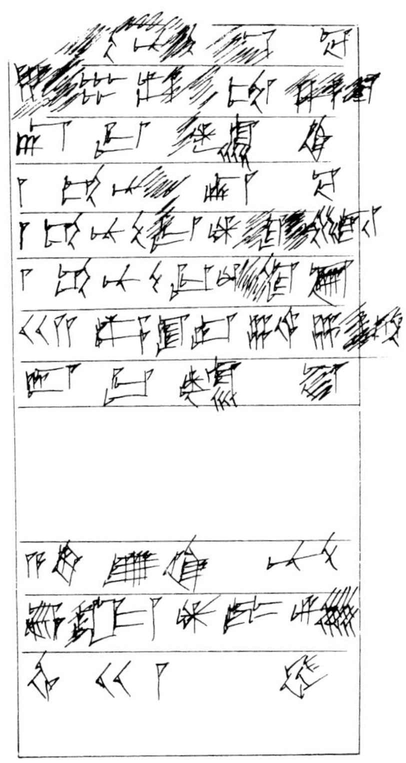

13

(VIII/-/-)

OBV.

1. [x x]
2. 246 ĝuruš ⸢x x x⸣
3. 1 gu$_4$-numun Ur-^{d}Ba-⸢ú⸣
4. 1 gu$_4$-numun Šeš-kal-la
5. 21 lú-ḫun-ĝá é-gal-la ĝen
6. 20 lú-ḫun-ĝá a x
7. 8 ĝuruš érin ḫun-ĝá
8. ⸢GÁ⸣ gi-na
9. [g]u$_4$-numun Ur-mes
10. [gu]$_4$-numun A-kal-la
11. [gu]$_4$-numun En-⸢ĝá-a⸣

REV.

12. [ ] x x x
13. [ ]
14. [ ] ⸢x⸣ a
15. [ ] ⸢x⸣ la
16. [ ]
17. [ ] ⸢x⸣
18. [ ]
19. ⸢x⸣ [ ] ḫi
20. u$_4$ [ ]
21. iti ezen [^{d}Ba]-ú

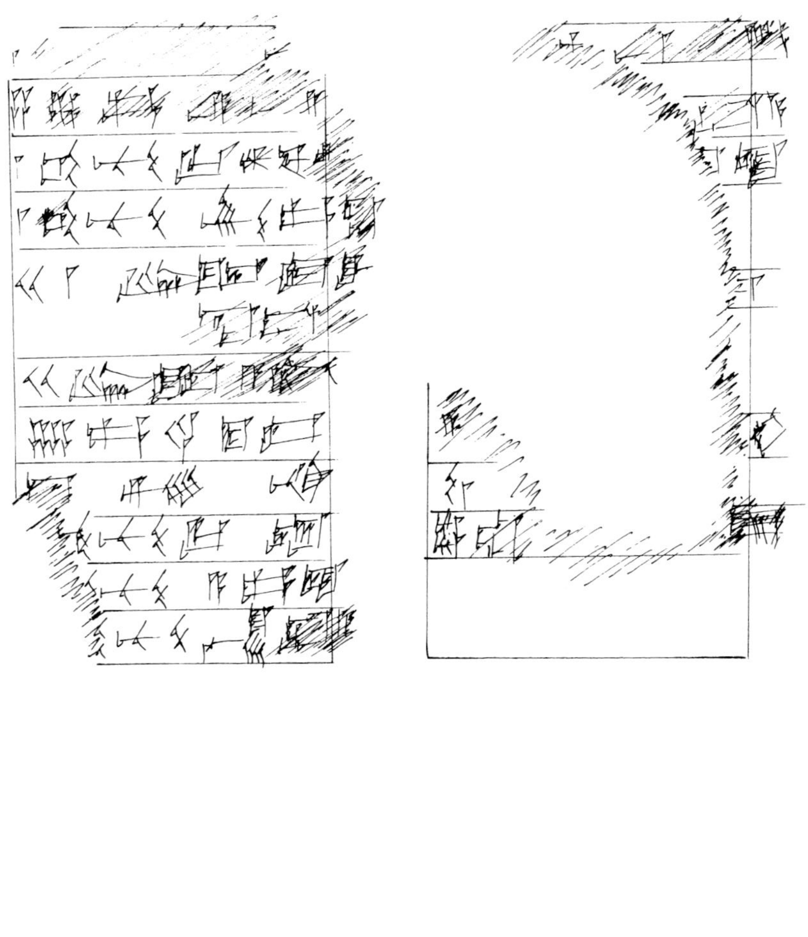

14 (not dated)

i. 1. 12 ĝuruš u$_4$ 30-šè
2. nu-bànda Ur-ša$_6$-ga dumu Lugal-igi
3. bala gub-ba
4. iti ezen ^{d}Dumu-zi
5. 10 engar u$_4$ 30-šè
6. 7 dumu-da-ba u$_4$ 30-šè
7. 3 un-ĝa$_6$ ⅓ u$_4$ 30-šè
8. 87 érin u$_4$ 30-šè
9. nu-bànda Ur-^{d}Ĝeš-bar-è
10. 33 érin u$_4$ 30-šè
11. nu-bànda *A-ḫu-a*
12. bala gub-ba
13. 12 érin 0.1.0-ta u$_4$ 20-šè
14. še-<bi> 2.2.0 gur lugal
15. ki Ur-é-ninnu-ta
16. nu-bànda Ur-ša$_6$-ga dumu Lugal-igi
17. 64 érin u$_4$ 1-šè
18. ki Ur-kisal-ta
19. 70 lá 1 érin u$_4$ 1-šè
20. ki Ur-^{d}Lama dumu Ur-ĝar-ta
21. iti ezen ^{d}Šul-gi
22. 64 érin 0.1.2-ta u$_4$ 20-šè
23. érin-ḫun-ĝá bala-tuš-a
*24. še-bi 17.0.2 gur
25. nu-bànda Ur-^{d}Ĝeš-bar-è
26. 5 érin u$_4$ 30-šè
27. bala gub-ba
28. 24 érin 0.1.0-ta u$_4$ 20-šè
29. érin-ḫun-ĝá bala-tuš-a
30. še-bi 4.4.0 gur
31. [n]u-bànda Lú-^{d}Nin-ĝír-su

ii. 32. 15 dumu ba-ug$_7$ u$_4$ 30-šè
33. é ^{d}Nin-mar-ki-me
*34. 33 érin 0.1.2-ta u$_4$ 30-šè
35. 5 érin 0.1.0-ta u$_4$ 20-šè
36. 6 érin 0.0.3-ta u$_4$ 20-šè
37. 4 érin 0.0.2-ta u$_4$ 20-šè
38. še-bi 10.3.2 gur
39. érin-ḫun-ĝá bala-tuš-a
40. nu-bànda *A-ḫu-a*
41. še-bi ki Ur-é-ninnu-ta
42. 16 érin u$_4$ 20-šè
43. bala-tuš-a še šu nu-ti-a
44. ugula Ur-^{d}Ba-ú dumu Lú-nimgir
45. 10 engar u$_4$ 30-šè
46. ní énsi-ta
47. 15 érin u$_4$-30-šè
48. ki Ur-^{d}Nanše-ta
49. 11 érin u$_4$ 30-šè
50. ki Lú-kiri$_4$-zal-ta
51. 3 érin u$_4$ 30-šè
52. ki Ur-kisal-ta
53. 2 érin u$_4$ 30-šè
54. ki Ur-^{d}Lama dumu Ur-ĝar-ta
55. nu-bànda Lú-^{d}Nin-ĝír-su
56. bala gub-ba
57. iti ezen ^{d}Ba-ú
58. 15 érin 0.0.2-ta u$_4$ 20-šè
59. še-bi 1.0.0 gur
60. ki Ur-é-ninnu-ta
61. érin ki Ur-^{d}Nanše-ta
62. 3 érin u$_4$ 20-šè
63. bala-tuš-a še šu nu-ti-a
64. ki Lú-kiri$_4$-zal-ta
65. 3 ĝuruš u$_4$ 20-šè
66. bala-tuš-a še šu nu-ti-a
67. ki Ur-kisal-ta
68. 2 érin u$_4$ 20-šè
69. bala-tuš-a še šu nu-ti-a

iii. 70. ki [ ]
71. 21 [ ]
72. bala-[ ]
73. 13 érin u$_4$ ⌜20⌝-[šè]
*74. bala-tuš-a še šu nu-ti
75. nu-bànda Lú-^{d}Nin-ĝír-su
76. 14 érin u$_4$ 30-šè
77. bala gub-ba
78. 10 engar u$_4$ 30-šè
79. nu-bànda Ur-^{d}Ĝeš-bar-è
80. 15 dumu ba-ug$_7$ u$_4$ 30-šè
81. é ^{d}Nin-mar-ki
82. 48 érin u$_4$ 30-šè
83. nu-bànda *A-ḫu-a*
84. 16 érin u$_4$ 30-šè
85. ugula Ur-^{d}Ba-ú dumu Lú-nimgir
86. bala gub-ba
87. iti mu-šu-du$_8$
88. 36 érin u$_4$ 30-šè
89. bala gub-ba
90. 16 érin 0.0.2 1 sìla-ta u$_4$ 20-šè
91. nu-bànda Lú-^{d}Nin-ĝír-su
92. 25 érin 0.0.1 5 (sìla)-ta u$_4$ 20-šè

93. še-bi 2.1.4 gur
94. ki Ur-é-ninnu-ta
95. bala-tuš-a še šu nu-ti-a
96. 40 lá 1 érin u$_4$ 30-šè
97. bala-tuš-a še šu nu-ti-a
98. nu-bànda Ur-^{d}Ĝeš-bar-è
99. 20 engar-búr u$_4$ 30-šè
100. 8 un-ĝa$_6$ igi-4-ĝál u$_4$ 30-šè
101. é ^{d}Dumu-zi-me
102. ní énsi-ta
103. 253 érin u$_4$ 1-šè
104. nu-bànda Ur-^{d}Utu
105. 221⅔ érin u$_4$ 1-šè
★106. nu-bànda Na-ba-š[a$_6$]
107. 80 érin u$_4$ 1-[šè]
108. nu-bànda Ur-tu[r dumu x-^{d}Nin]-ĝír-su

iv. *(top of column iv broken)*

109. é ^{d}[ ]
110. ki Ur-^{d}[ ]
111. iti amar-a-[a-si]
112. 2 (bur) 1 (eše) 3 i[ku]
113. gala [ ]
114. 20 iku [ ]
115. dam-gàr [ ]
★116. 1 (bur) 1 (eše) 3 i[ku]
117. ĝìr [ ]
118. á-bi [ ]
119. ki šabra [ ]
120. (B L A N K)
121. šu+níĝin 10 engar u$_4$ [ ]
★122. šu+níĝin 7 dumu-d[a-ba]
★123. šu+níĝin 3 un-[íl]
124. šu+níĝin 15 dum[u ba-ug$_7$]
125. šu+níĝin 380 é[rin]
126. bala gub-[ba]
127. šu+níĝin 204+[ ]
128. še-bi 30+[.0.0 gur]
129. ki Ur-é-[ninnu-ta]
130. érin-ḫun-ĝá [ ]
131. šu+níĝin 34 [ ]
132. šu+níĝin 20 [ ]
133. érin še šu nu-[ti-a]
134. šu+níĝin 60 [x]
135. á [ ]
136. ki [x]
137. šu-n[íĝin]
138. ér[in]

(bottom of column iv broken)

v. *(top of column v broken)*

139. iti [ ]
140. 370 [ ]
141. bala g[ub]
142. uru-ta [nu-è]
143. 500 [ ]
144. iti-ta [ ]
145. bala g[ub]
146. 180 érin [ ]
147. iti-ta [ ]
148. bala-tuš [ ]
149. iti amar-a-[a-si]
150. nu-bànda Lú-[ ]
151. 20 engar-bú[r]
152. 8 un-[íl igi-x]-ĝál [ ]
153. uru-ta nu-⸢è⸣
154. é ^{d}Dumu-z[i]
155. 1 nu-bànda gu$_4$ [ ]
156. uru-ta nu-⸢è⸣
157. é ^{d}[x]
158. (B L A N K)

(bottom of column v broken)

vi. 159. ĝuruš-e 0.0.1 [ ]

★160. á-bi 441 ⅓ u$_4$-1-šè
161. a-šà Nin-gána-gi-ambar-sur-ra
162. šu+níĝin 164 iku apin-a
163. ĝuruš-e 18 sar-ta
164. á-bi 911 u$_4$ 1-šè
165. a-šà Nam-šid apin-a
166. šu+níĝin 213 nindan-gíd gi-tab-ba
167. ĝuruš-1-e ½ nindan-ta
168. á-bi 426 u$_4$ 1-šè
169. šu+níĝin 2 ĝuruš u$_4$ 1-šè
170. im-du$_8$-a
171. a-šà Nin-e-gù-ba-dé
172. ki Ur-ša$_6$-ga dumu Ur-gu-la
173. šu+níĝin 605 dumu ba-ug$_7$ u$_4$ 1-šè
174. šu+níĝin 210 dumu-da-ba u$_4$ 1-šè
175. šu+níĝin 90 un-ĝa$_6$ ⅓ u$_4$ 1-šè
176. šu+níĝin 4 un-ĝa$_6$ igi-4-ĝál u$_4$ 1-šè
177. šu+níĝin 108 ĝuruš u$_4$ 1-šè
★178. [ ] še-íl-la
★179. šu+níĝin 60 lá 2 u$_4$ 1-šè tu-ra
180. (B L A N K)
181. zi-ga
182. šu+níĝin 53 ĝuruš u$_4$ 30-šè
183. uru-ta nu-è
184. šu+níĝin 1718 ĝuru[š]
185. iti-t[a zal-la]

vii. 186. šu+níĝin ĝuruš u$_4$ 1-šè
187. á-gul-la
188. bala gub-ba
189. šu+níĝin 8 ĝuruš u$_4$ 20-šè
190. uru-ta nu-è
191. šu+níĝin 1714 ĝuruš u$_4$ 1-šè
192. iti-ta zal-la
193. šu+níĝin ĝuruš u$_4$ 1-šè
194. á-gul-la
195. še-bi 37.1.3 gur
196. šu+níĝin 44 ĝuruš u$_4$ 30-šè
197. šu+níĝin 16 ĝuruš u$_4$ 20-šè
198. uru-ta nu-è-a
199. šu+níĝin 520 ĝuruš u$_4$ 1-šè
200. iti-ta zal-la
201. še šu nu-ti-a
202. (BLANK)
viii. 203. (BLANK)
204. nì-ka$_9$-ak
205. ki Ur-ĝar
206. (BLANK)

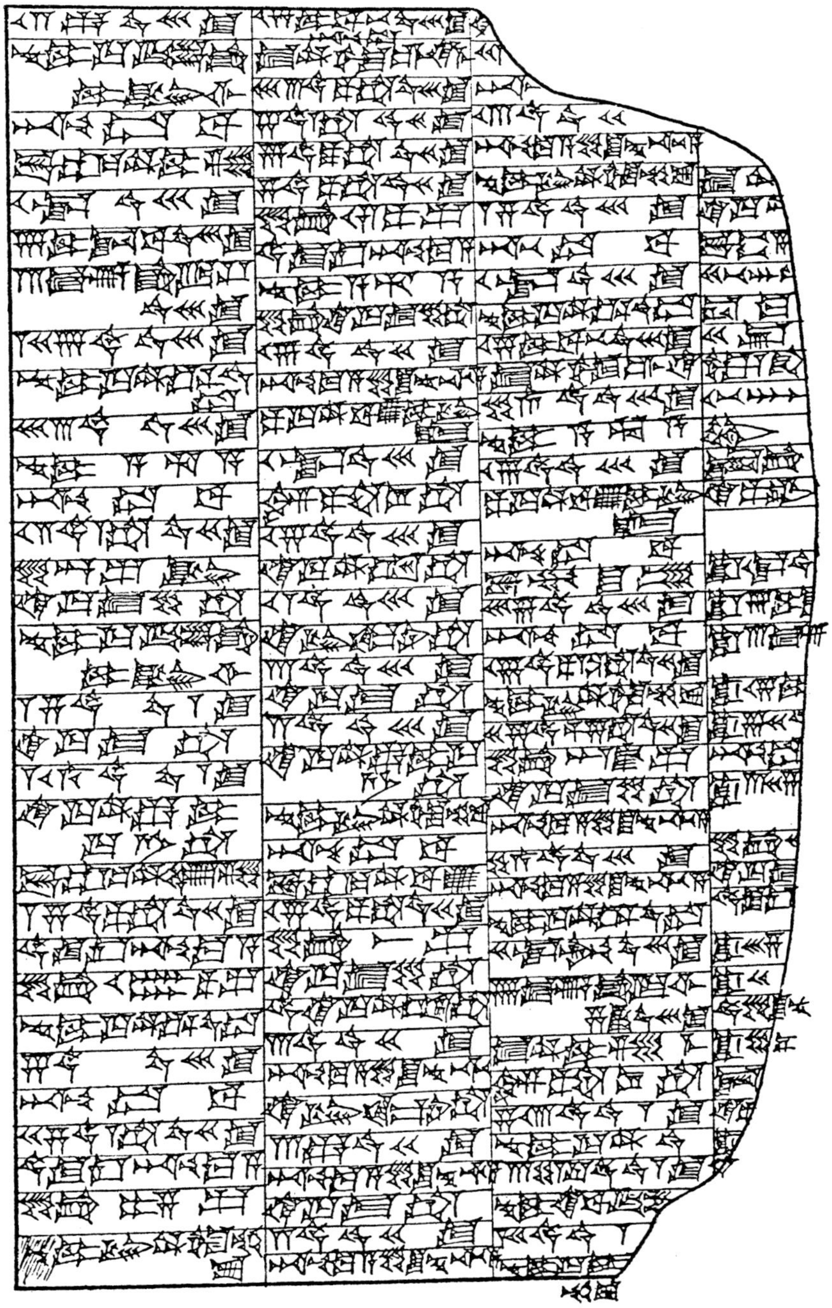

14 obverse

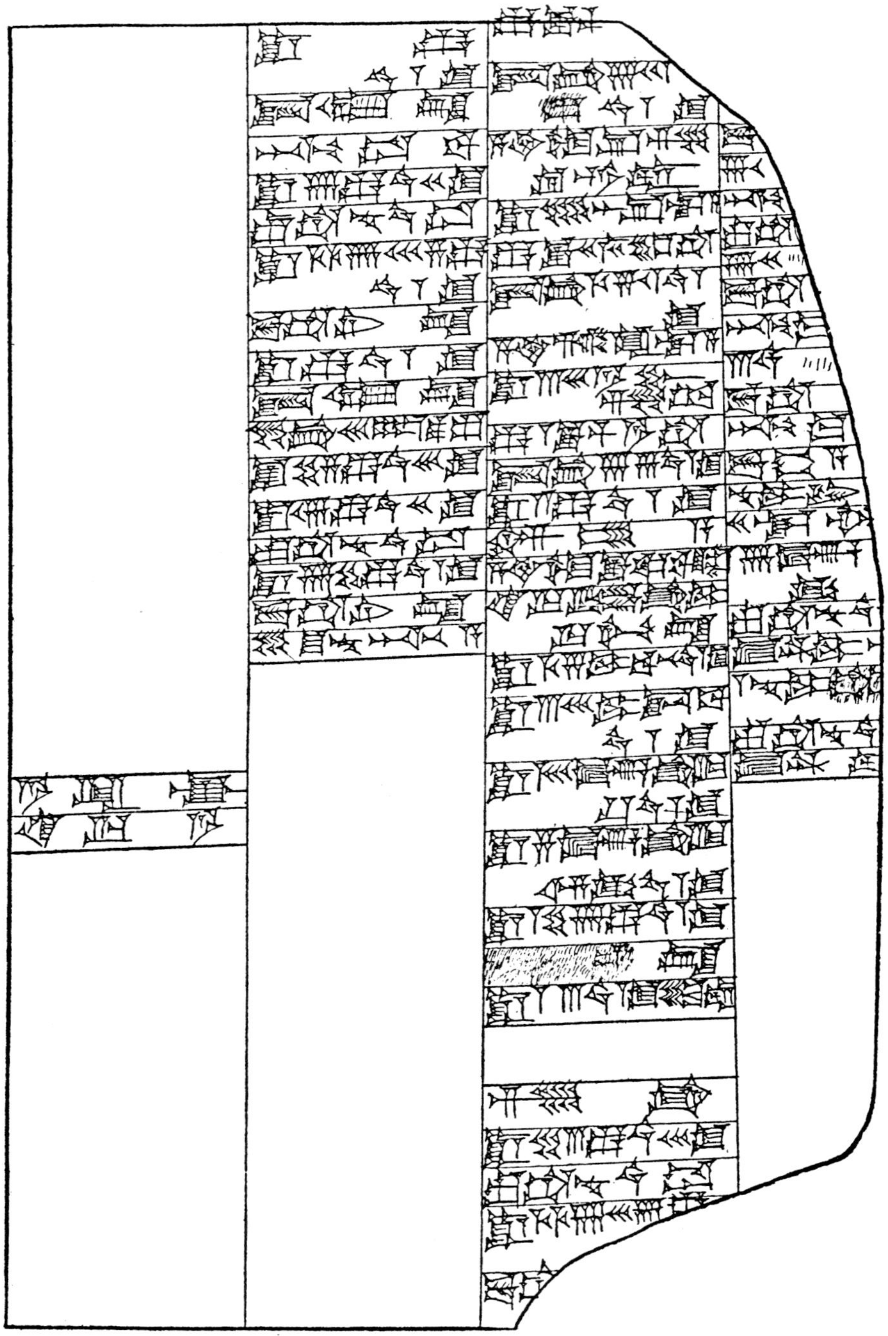

14 reverse

15

(-/-/Š 39)

OBV.

1. [x.x].2 še gur-saĝ-[ĝál]
2. [ ] LUL engar
3. [ ] gur
4. [ ] x engar
*5. [ ] nu-bànda gu$_4$
6. [ ] gur
7. [ka]l-la engar
8. [ ] gur
9. [D]U engar
*10. [ ]-ì-š[a$_6$] nu-bànda gu$_4$
11. [ ]
12. [ ]
13. Ur-^{d}[ ] engar
14. 0.4.0 gur

REV.

15. [x]-*ì-lí* ⌜nu-bànda-gu$_4$⌝
16. (B L A N K)
17. šu+níĝin 930.1.0 še gur-saĝ-ĝál-la
18. ĝìr Ur-^{d}Lama šeš Ì-kal-la
19. 8.2.0 gur
20. Ab-ba engar Ur-^{d}Ša-u$_x$-ša
21. ù Ur-Namma-ma engar
22. 14.2.0 gur
23. ^{d}Utu-du$_{10}$ engar ù Lugal-síg-gíd engar
24. ĝìr Ur-ša$_6$-ga dumu Ur-ki-gu-[la]
25. še ĝeš è-a
26. a-šà a-gú-na
27. mu-ús-sa bàd ma-da ba-dù-a <mu>-ús-sa-bi

16

(-/-/Š 47)

OBV.

1. 206.0.3 še gur lugal
2. Inim-ma-ni-zi engar
⋆3. gána-gu$_4$ Lú-igi-ša$_6$-ša$_6$ nu-bànda gu$_4$
4. a-šà NI-zi-na
5. 54.3.0 gur
6. Ḫé-na-a-a engar

REV.

7. gána-gu$_4$ Lugal-inim-gi-na nu-bànda gu$_4$
8. a-šà nam-niĝin$_5$-a-ni-du$_{10}$
9. še ĝeš è-a
10. ugula A-ab-ba
11. (BLANK)
12. mu-ús-sa Ki-maš^{ki} ba-ḫul

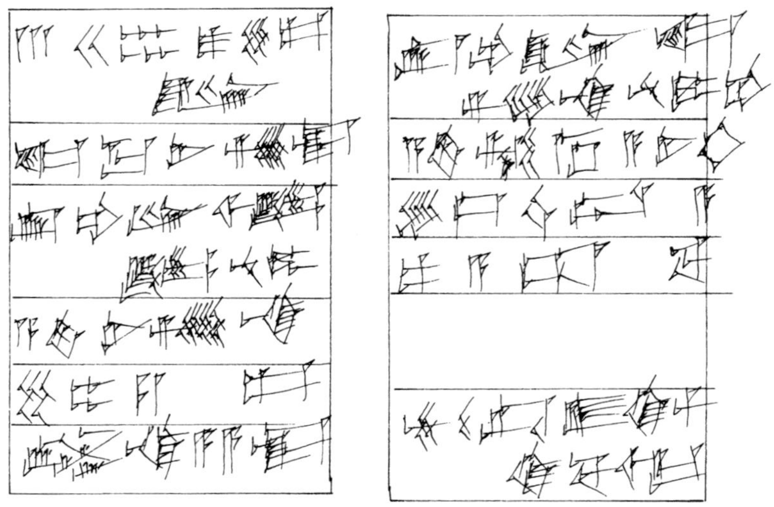

17 (not dated)

OBV.

1. 421.1.[x še gur] lugal
2. Šà-ge engar
3. gána-gu$_4$ Ur-gar nu-bànda gu$_4$
4. še in-bi nu-dé
5. a-šà ^{d}Nanše-gar-ra

REV.

6. (BLANK)
7. še ĝeš è-a
8. ugula Lugal-zà-ge-si
9. gu$_4$ ^{d}Nin-ĝeš-zi-da

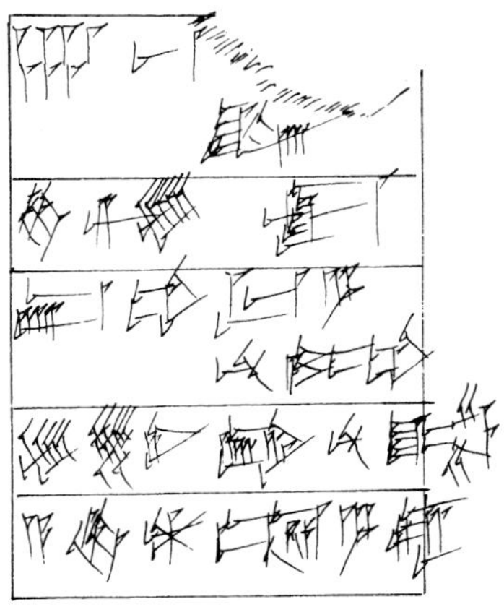

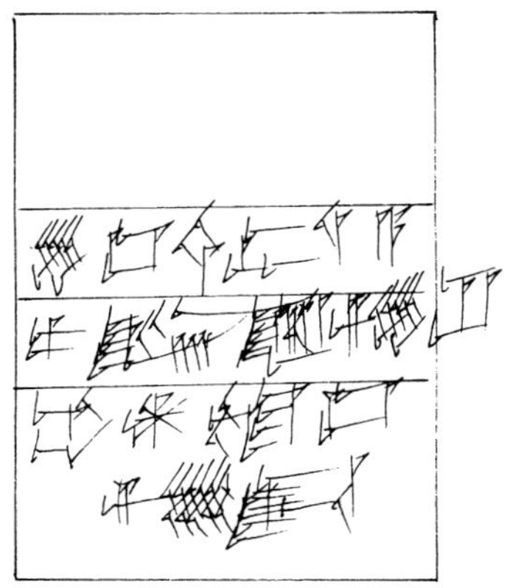

18 (not dated)

OBV.

1. 4.1.0 še gur lugal
2. Lú-^{d}Ab-Ú engar
3. 4.0.0 Ur-^{d}IM engar
4. 4.1.0 Ur-Namma-ma engar
5. 4.0.0 Ab-ba-gi-na

*6. 4.0.0 Un-ĝa$_6$ engar

REV.

7. (BLANK)
8. šu+níĝin 20.2 še gur
9. a-šà Igi-zi-mu-pàd
10. še ì-dé-a
11. (BLANK)
12. še ĝeš è-a ĝá-ĝá-dam

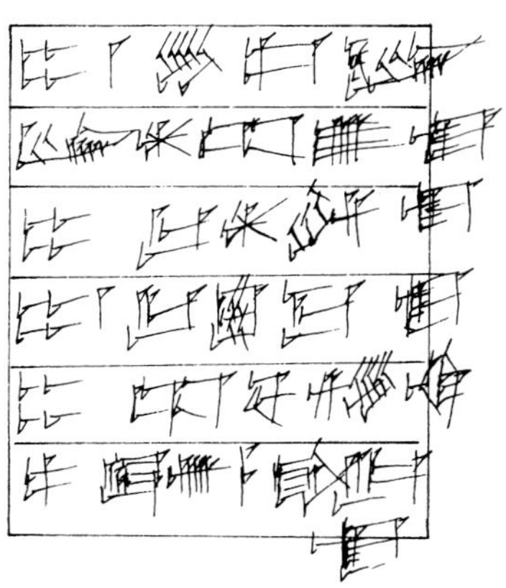

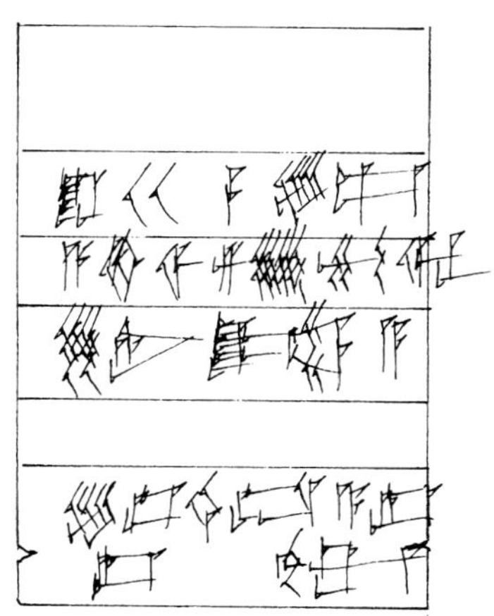

19 (VI/10/AS 9)

i. 1. Lú-^{d}Na-rú-a dumu Géme-^{d}Lama géme kar-kid
2. Ur-ki-gu-la šu-ḫa
3. Šul-lu$_{5}$ nu-^{ĝeš}kiri$_{6}$
4. Ur-^{d}Ḫendur-s[aĝ na]r
5. Ĝí[r]-su^{ki}-[ta]
6. ĝìr *A-b[u]-ni*
7. Ur-^{d}[Nin-ĝeš-zi-da] dumu [Géme-ba uš-bar]
8. Ur-^{d}⌜Ba⌝-[ú] gala
9. Lugal-unug^{ki}-šè
10. mu Lú-^{d}[En-ki]-šè
11. ki Lugal-pa-è
12. Ab-ba-kal-la aga-ús šabra-ta
13. mu ^{d}Utu-kalam-e-šè
14. Ba-ša$_{6}$-ga dumu ^{d}Nin-mar-ki-ka aslag

ii. 15. Ur-^{d}Nin-mar-ki tur
16. Ur-^{d}Nin-šar
17. Ur-^{d}Ba-ú šeš-a-ni
18. Lú-^{d}Na-rú-a túg-íl
19. (BLANK)
20. libir-àm
21. Ur-^{d}Nin-ĝeš-zi-da aslag
22. Nì-^{d}Ba-ú dumu-šeš-a-ni
23. mu Ĝìri-ni-ì-ša$_{6}$-šè
24. ki Ùr-re-ba-du$_{7}$
25. Nam-tar-íb-gu-ul dumu A-tu
26. Lú-^{d}Nin-šubur baḫar dumu Ba-ša$_{6}$-ga
27. ugula Ur-ki-gu-la
28. Ur-^{d}<Ḫendur>-saĝ dumu Lú-^{d}Ba-ú

iii. 29. ki Lugal-ezen
30. Ur-^{d}Da-mu ad-gub$_{5}$
31. ugula Lú-^{d}Nin-ĝír-su dumu Ba-zi
32. Ur-^{d}Igi-zi-bar-ra
33. nu-bànda Ur-^{d}Nanše
34. ^{d}Na-rú-a-palil muḫaldim
35. Ĝìri-ni-ì-dab$_{5}$ ìr Ur-ab-ba
36. Ur-^{d}Ba-ú ad-gub$_{5}$
37. ugula Da-da-a-ni
38. Ur-^{d}Ig-alima dam-gàr
39. Kù-^{d}Nanna dumu Uri$_{5}^{ki}$
40. Ur-^{d}Ba-ú dumu Ur-mes
41. (BLANK)
42. ^{ĝeš}tukul-e dab$_{5}$-ba-me
43. ĝìr Lú-^{d}Na-rú-a
44. ù Ur-^{d}Ba-ú
45. Ur-^{d}Ba-ú dam-gàr

iv. 46. Lú-^{d}Inanna ad-gub$_{5}$
47. ugula Lú-diĝir-ra
48. Nin-ki-ḫar-ša$_{6}$
49. Šà-ga-na géme
50. Géme-^{d}Ba-ú
51. (BLANK)
52. ḫé-dab$_{5}$-me
53. ugula Lú-me-lám
54. 26 ĝuruš 2 á ½ 3 géme
55. ḫé-dab$_{5}$-me
56. u$_{4}$-KU-a
57. é-kíkken-a gub-ba
58. šà Sag-da-na^{ki}
59. u$_{4}$ 10-kam
60. (BLANK)
61. iti ezen ^{d}Dumu-zi
62. mu en ^{d}Nanna Kar-zi-da ba-ḫun

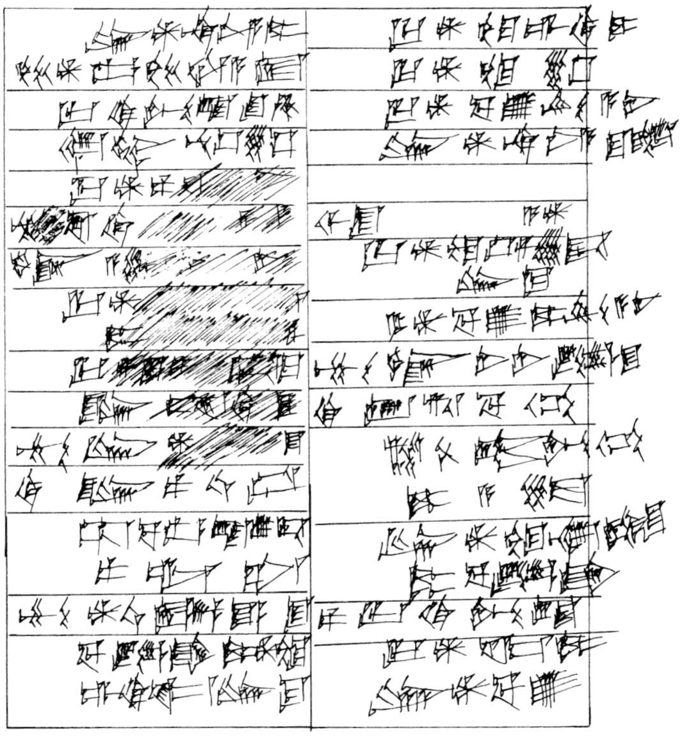

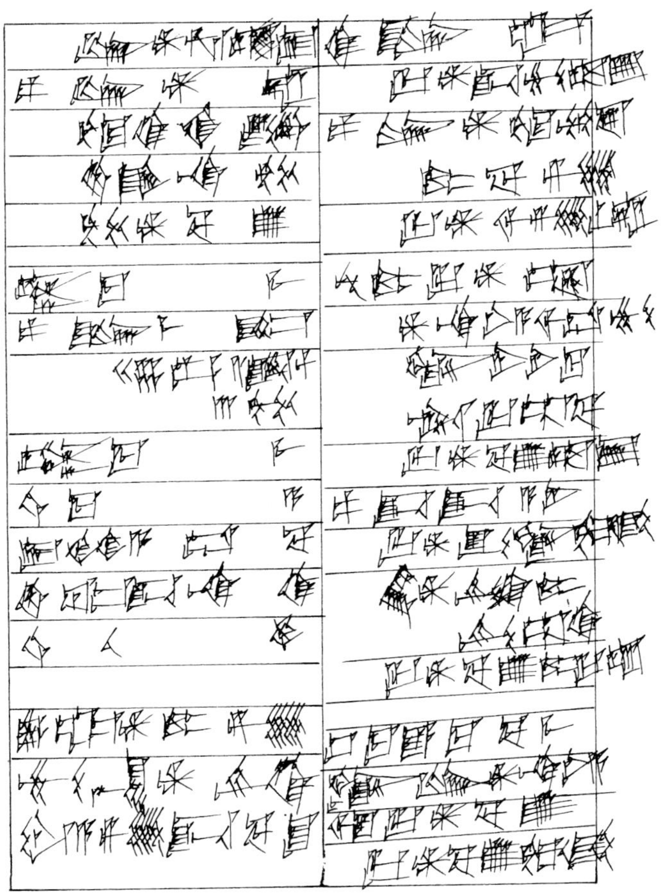

19 obverse (top), reverse (bottom)

20 (VI/12/AS)

i.

1. 1 Lú-^{d}Na-rú-a dumu Géme-^{d}Lama géme kar-kid
2. 1 Ur-ki-gu-la šu-ḫa
3. 1 Šul-lu$_{5}$ nu-^{ĝeš}kiri$_{6}$
4. 1 Ur-^{d}Ḫendur-saĝ nar
5. Ĝír-su^{ki}-ta
6. ĝìr *A-bu-ni*
7. 1 Ur-^{d}Nin-ĝeš-zi-da dumu Géme-ba uš-bar
8. 1 Ur-^{d}Ba-ú gala
9. 1 Lugal-unug^{ki}-šè
10. [m]u Lú-^{d}En-ki-šè
11. [ki L]ugal-pa-è
12. [Ab-b]a-kal-la aga-ús
13. [šabr]a-ta

(*several lines broken*)

ii.

14. ½ Ur-^{d}Nin-mar-ki tur
15. 1 Ur-^{d}Nin-šar
16. ½ Ur-^{d}Ba-ú šeš-a-ni
17. 1 Lú-^{d}Na-rú-a túg-íl
18. (BLANK)
19. libir-àm
20. 1 Ur-^{d}Nin-ĝeš-zi-da aslag
21. 1 Nì-^{d}Ba-ú dumu dumu-ni
22. mu Ĝìri-ni-ì-ša$_{6}$-šè
23. ki Ùr-re-ba-du$_{7}$
24. 1 Nam-tar-íb-gu-ul dumu A-tu
25. 1 Lú-^{d}Nin-šubur baḫar dumu Ba-ša$_{6}$-ga
26. [ugula Ur-ki-gu-la]

(*several lines broken*)

iii.

(*several lines broken*)

27. [Ur-^{d}Da-mu ad-gub$_{5}$]
28. [ugula Lú-^{d}Nin-ĝír-su dumu Ba-zi]
29. 1 Ur-^{d}Igi-zi-bar-r[a]
30. nu-bànda Ur-^{d}Nanše
31. 1 ^{d}Na-rú-a-palil muḫaldim
32. 1 Ĝìri-ni-ì-dab$_{5}$ ìr Ur-ab-ba
33. 1 Ur-^{d}Ba-ú ad-gub$_{5}$
34. ugula Da-da-a-ni
35. 1 Ur-^{d}Ig-alima dam-gàr
36. 1 Kù-^{d}Nanna dumu Uri$_{5}^{ki}$
37. 1 Ur-^{d}Ba-ú dumu Ur-mes
38. ĝìr Lú-^{d}Na-rú-a
39. ù Ur-^{d}Ba-ú
40. 1 Ur-^{d}Ba-ú dam-gàr
41. 1 Lú-^{d}Inanna ad-gub$_{5}$
42. ugula Lú-diĝir-ra

iv.

(*several lines broken*)

43. [x ĝuruš 2 á] ½ [x gé]me
44. [ḫ]é-dab$_{5}$-me
45. [ugu]la Lú-me-lám
46. ⸢é⸣-kíkken-a gub-ba
47. [š]à Sag-da-na^{ki}
48. (BLANK)
49. u$_{4}$ 12-kam
50. iti ezen ^{d}Dumu-zi
51. mu en ^{d}Nanna Kar-zi-da ba-ḫun

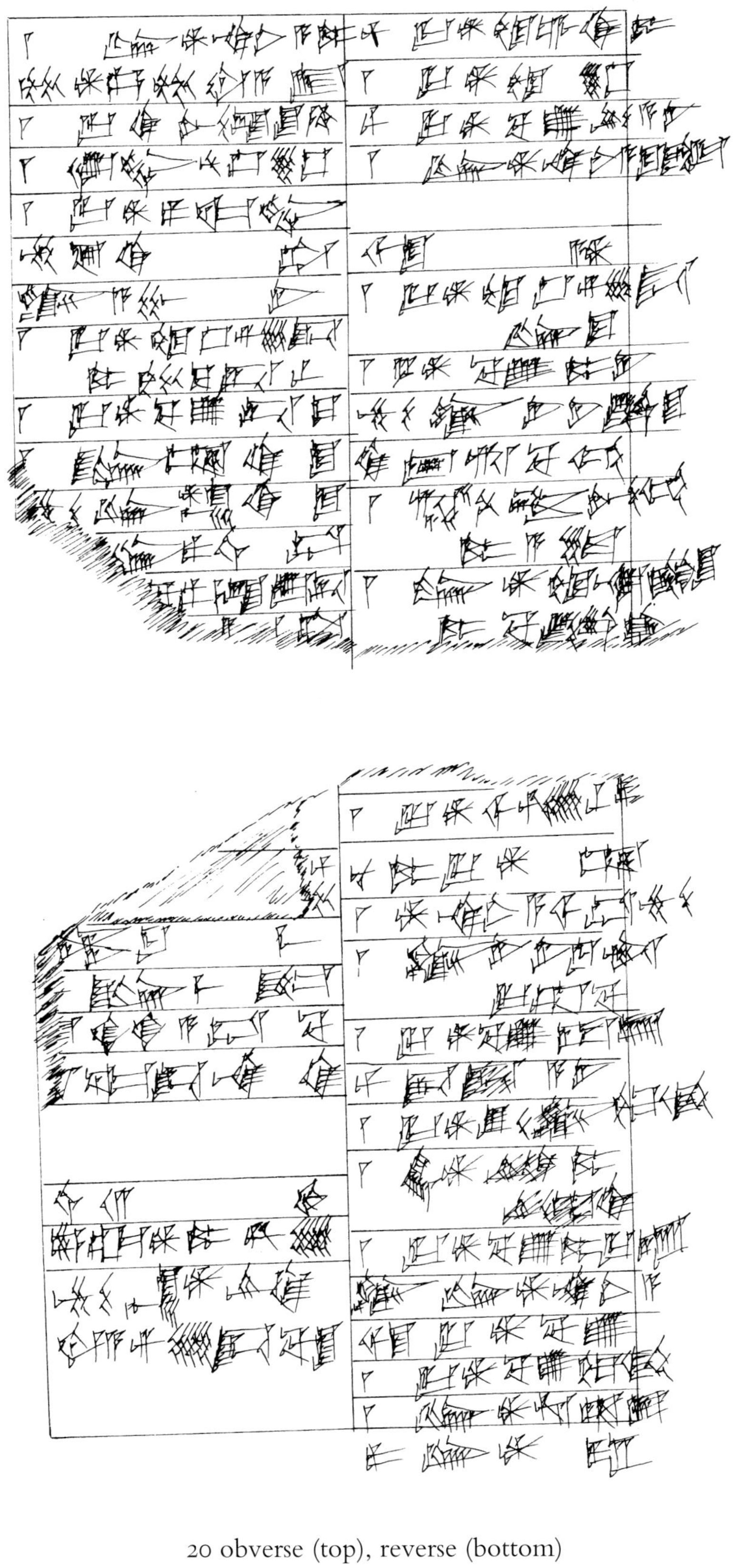

20 obverse (top), reverse (bottom)

21

(-/-/Š 25)

OBV.

*1. 1 ĜEŠ.DU$_8$.UN.ĜÁ
2. 1 Lugal-ezen
3. 1 Diĝir-ĝá-ì-ša$_6$
4. 1 A-kal-la
5. 1 ^{d}Nin-mar-ki-ka-ì-ša$_6$

REV.

6. 1 É-^{d}IM
7. UN.NE
8. dam-ni-me
9. šu ḫar-re-me
10. SEAL
11. é ^{d}Nin-ĝír-su
12. mu Si-mu-ru-um^{ki} ba-ḫul

Seal: Nam-zi-tar-ra
dub-sar
dumu Al-la-mu
šabra

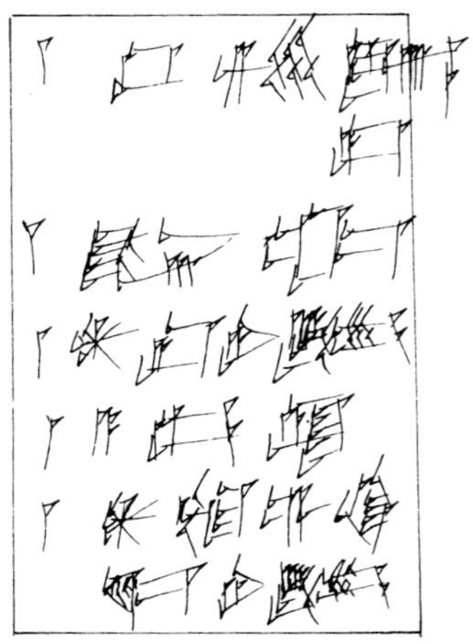

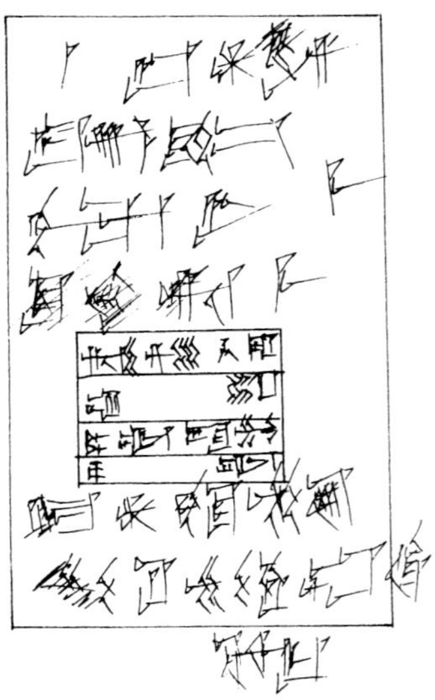

22

(diri/-/Š 44)

OBV.

1. 60 lá 1 ĝuruš 0.1.0 še lugal-ta
2. še-bi 11.4.0 gur
3. šà-gal érin-na-šè

*4. ì-dub a-šà ambar ⸢sur-ra⸣

5. ki Ur-^{d}Nin-gal-ta

REV.

6. Ur-gu-la ugula
7. šu ba-ti
8. [n]u-bànda ku$_5$-da
9. iti diri še-kin-ku$_5$
10. mu Si-mu-ur$_4$-um^{ki} Lu-lu-bu^{ki} a-rá 10 lá 1-kam ba-ḫul

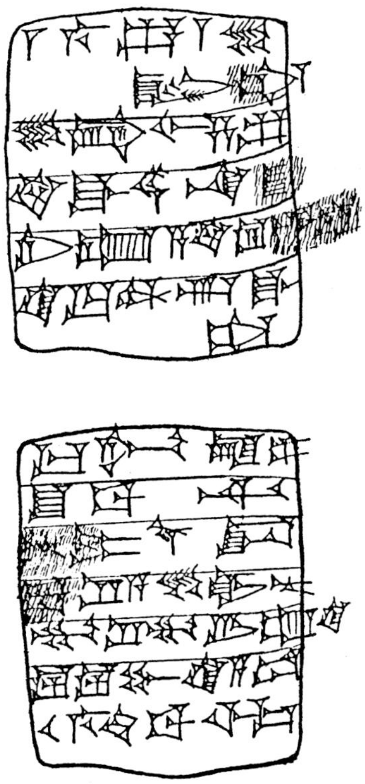

23

(-/-/Š 25)

OBV.

1. [0.1.0] še Ma-[an]-sum
2. 0.1.0 Gu$_4$-[x]
3. 0.1.0 Lugal-ú-šim [ ]
4. 0.0.2 zì Lugal-inim-silim-ma dumu [ ]
5. sig$_7$-a Lú-diĝir-ra dumu Ur-^{ĝeš}[gigir]
6. 0.1.0 Lú-^{d}Ba-ú
7. 0.0.3 Uru-ki-bi dumu géme-kíkken
8. 0.1.0 Ur-ša$_6$-ga
9. 0.1.0 Lú-aga
10. 0.0.4 Lugal-ba-ša$_6$
11. 0.0.2 Lugal-ḫé-ĝál
12. dumu Nin-inim-gi-na
13. 0.0.3 Ur-^{d}En-gal-du-du
14. dumu Lú-^{d}Nin-ĝír-su
15. 0.1.0 Lú-diĝir-ra dumu A-lum-m[a]
16. 0.0.4 Inim-^{d}Ba-ú-ì-gi
17. ★ 0.0.2 Ur-^{d}Ba-ú
18. 0.0.1 5 <sìla> ^{d}Inanna-k[a]
19. dumu Ur-dun ba-x-[ ]

REV.

20. (BLANK)
21. šu+níĝin 7 ĝuruš [0.1.0]
22. šu+níĝin 1 ĝuruš [sig$_7$-a]
23. šu+níĝin 2 ĝuruš [0.0.4]
24. šu+níĝin 3 ĝuruš [0.0.2]
25. šu+níĝin 2 tur [0.0.3]
26. šu+níĝin 1 [tur 0.0.1 5 sìla]
27. še-bi [ ] gur
28. (BLANK)
29. mu [x N]in-ĝír-s[u]
30. šà [ ]^{ki}
31. mu Ur-[bi-lum^{ki}] Si-mu-ur$_4$-[ru-um]^{ki} [ ]

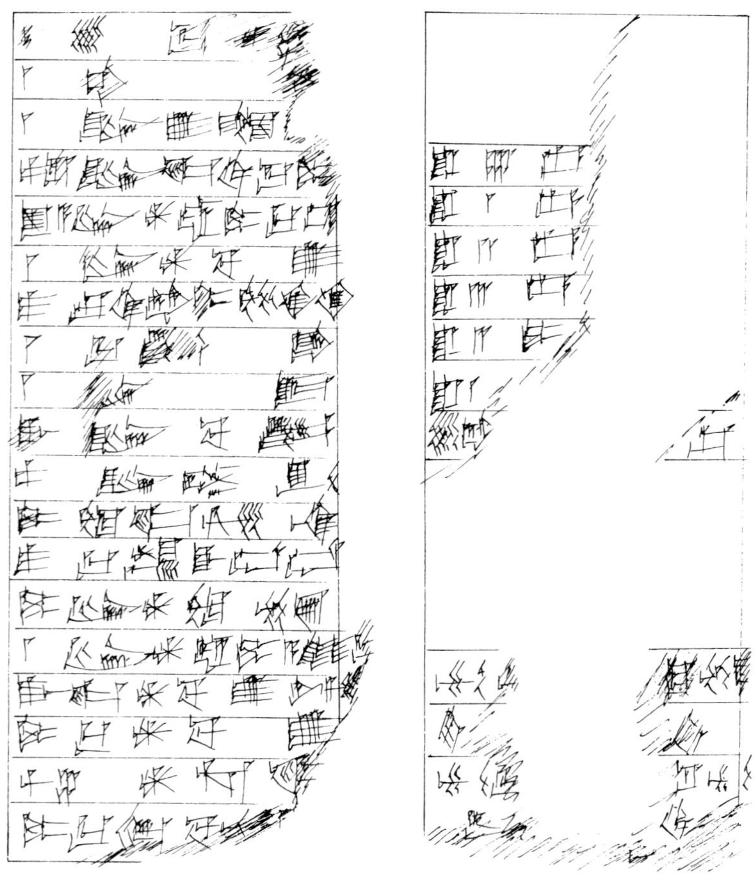

24

(VIII/-/Š 45)

OBV.

*1. 5.2.0 dabin gur lugal
2. šà-gal érin bala gub-ba
3. érin é-^{d}Ig-alima-ka
4. ki Ur-^{d}Nun-gal-ta

REV.

5. ì-dub a-šà ambar-sur-ra-ta
6. nu-bànda Ur-^{d}Nin-ĝeš-zi-da
7. iti ezen ^{d}Ba-ú
8. mu-ús-sa Si-mu-ru^{ki} Lu-lu-bu^{ki} a-rá 10 lá 1 ba-ḫul

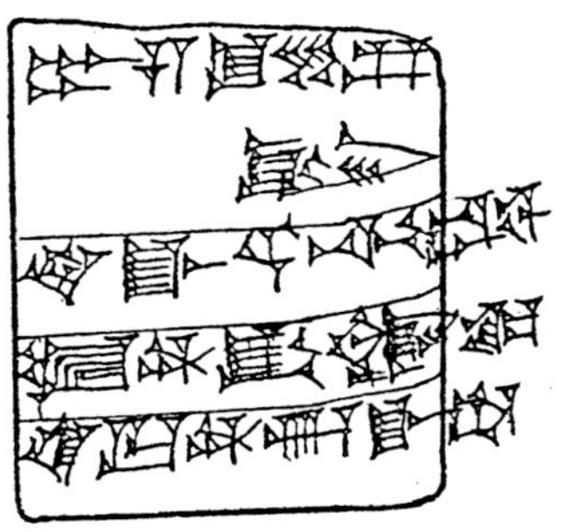

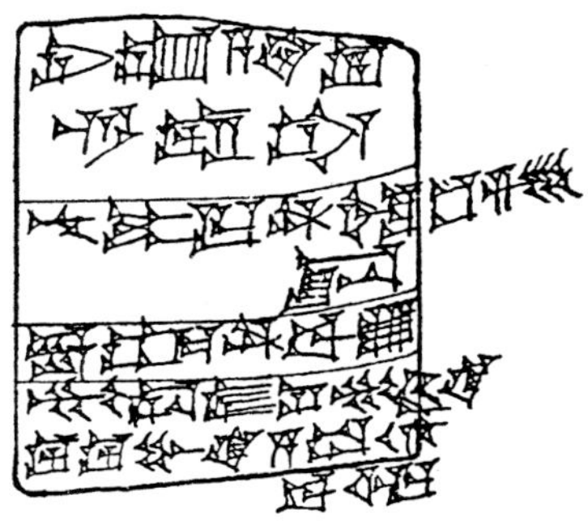

25

(VIII/-/Š 46)

OBV.

*1. 40 lá 1 ĝuruš 0.1.0 še lugal-ta
2. 7 ĝuruš 0.0.5-ta
3. ugula Ba-ša$_{6}$-ga
4. 33 ĝuruš 0.1.0-ta
5. 3 ĝuruš 0.0.5-ta
6. ugula Lú-^{d}Ba-ú
7. nu-bànda Nam-maḫ

REV.

8. še-bi [16.0.2] gur
9. šà-gal érin bala-gub-ba
*10. ì-dub Inim-ma-an-né
11. ki Ba-zi-ta
12. iti ezen ^{d}Ba-ú
13. mu Ki-maš^{ki} ba-ḫul

26

(X/-/Š 46)

OBV.

1. 30 lá 1 érin 0.1.3 še lugal-ta
2. še-bi 8.3.3 gur
3. šà-gal érin bala gub-ba
4. ì-dub ^{d}Nin-ḫur-saĝ
5. ki Ba-zi-ta

REV.

6. Ur-é-ninnu nu-bànda
7. šu ba-ti
8. é ^{d}Nin-ĝeš-zi-da-me
9. iti amar-a-a-si
10. mu Ki-maš^{ki} ba-ḫul

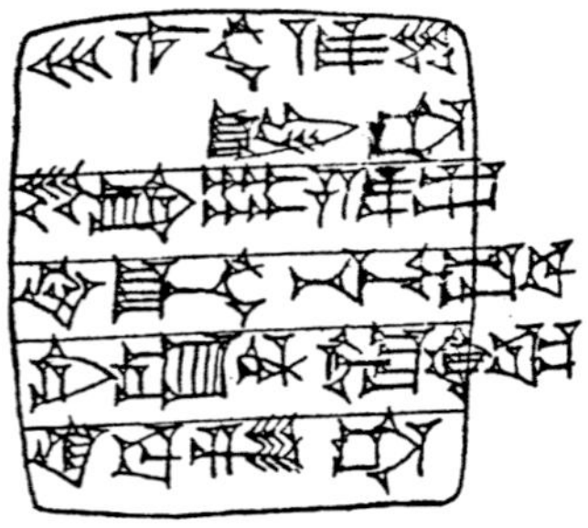

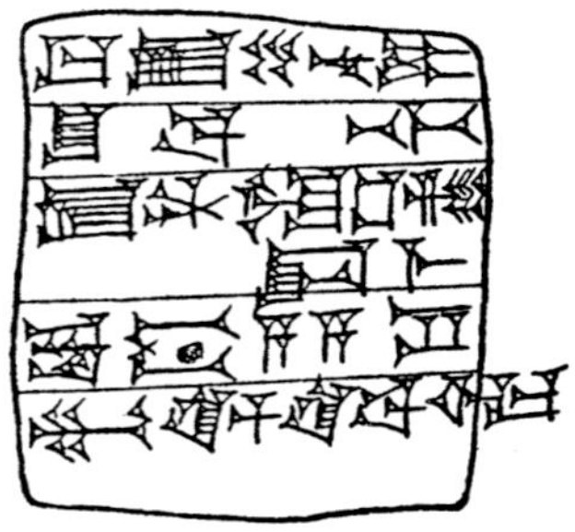

27

(VIII/-/Š 47)

OBV.

1. 26 ĝuruš 0.0.2 še lugal-ta
2. še-bi 1.3.4 gur
3. šà-gal érin bala gub-ba é gu-za-lá
4. ki Ur-^{d}Ba-ú-ta

REV.

5. ĝá-nun saĝa-ta

*6. nu-bànda Ur-⸢ša$_6$-ga⸣ gu-za-lá

7. Ur-^{d}Lama šu ba-ti
8. iti ezen ^{d}Ba-ú

*9. mu-ús-sa Ki-maš^{ki}

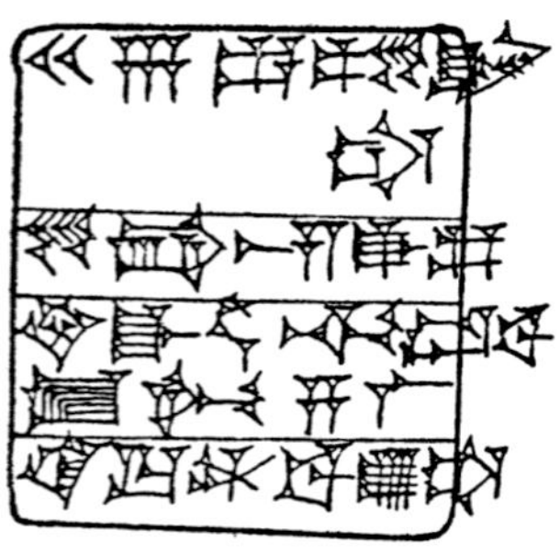

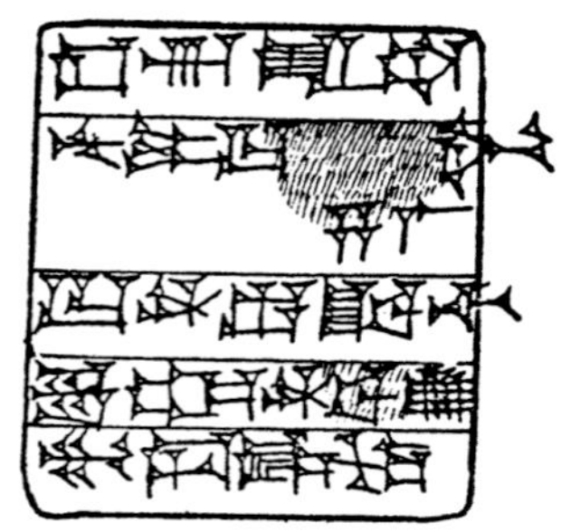

28

(VIII/-/Š 47)

OBV.

1. 17 [ ] še-gur lug[al]
2. še-ba é-[ ]
3. [x x] ^{d}Dumu-zi
4. ì-dub ambar-sug
5. ki [ ]-tu

REV.

6. Kù-^{d}Nin-ĝír-su
7. šu ba-ti
8. (BLANK)
9. iti ezen ^{d}Ba-ú
10. mu-ús-sa Ki-maš$^{[ki]}$ ba-hul

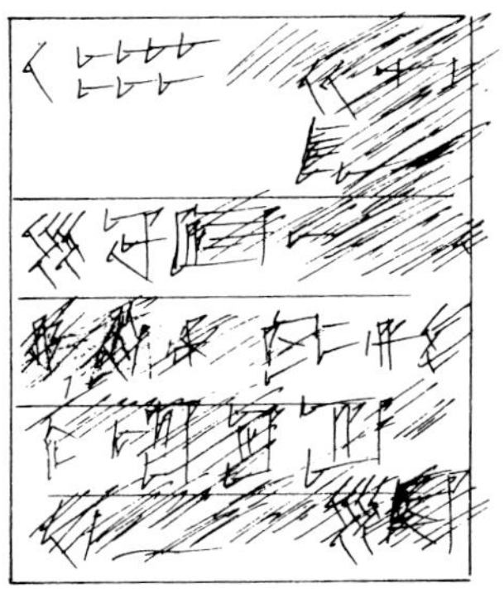

29

(I/-/AS 5)

OBV.

1. 0.0.4 Ad-du-EN
2. 0.0.4 Gu-na-ri
*3. géme Mar-tu gab-ús udu-gukkal-me
4. Nam-ḫa-ni na-gada
5. iti buru$_{x}$(GÁN)-maš-ta

REV.

6. šà Nina^{ki}
7. (BLANK)
8. mu en-unu$_{6}$-gal ^{d}Inanna ba-ḫun

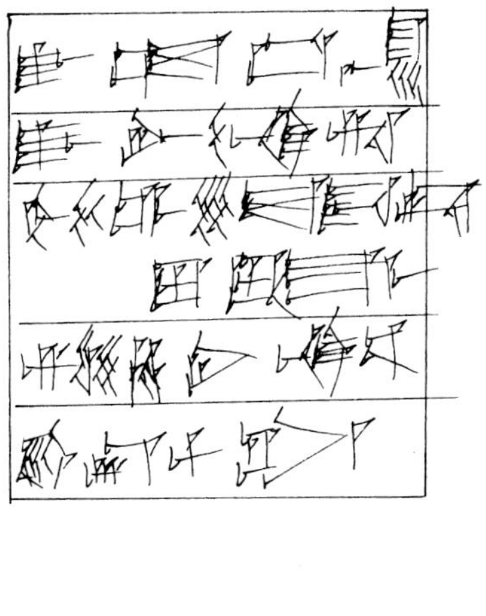

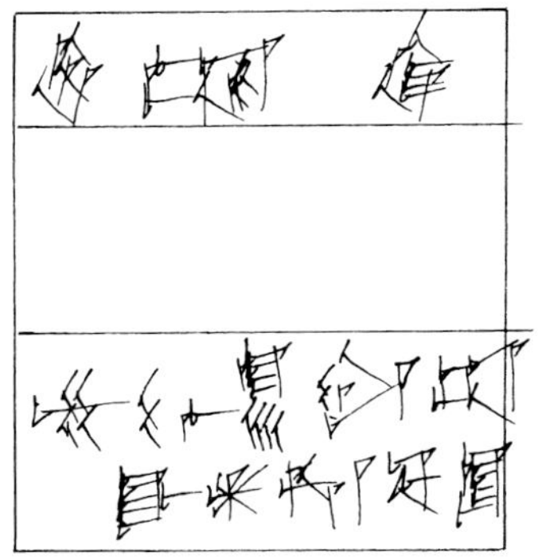

30

(VIII/-/IS 1)

TABLET

OBV.

1. 27.4.4 dabin gur
2. á géme-uš-bar Nina^{ki}-ka
3. má Lú-má-gur$_{8}$-ra

REV.

4. kišib Ur-^{d}Ba-ú dumu Ma-an-sì-na
5. Ur-^{d}Nanše-ke$_{4}$
6. šu ba-ti
7. iti ezen ^{d}Ba-ú
8. mu ^{d}*I-bí*-^{d}Suen lugal

CASE

OBV.

1. 27.4.4 dabin gur
2. á géme-uš-bar Nina^{ki}
3. SEAL
4. má Lú-má-gur$_{8}$-ra
5. kišib Ur-^{d}Nanše dumu Ku-li

REV.

6. SEAL
7. iti ezen ^{d}Ba-ú
8. mu ^{d}*I-bí*-^{d}Suen lugal

Seal: Ur-[ ]
dub-[sar]
dumu [ ]

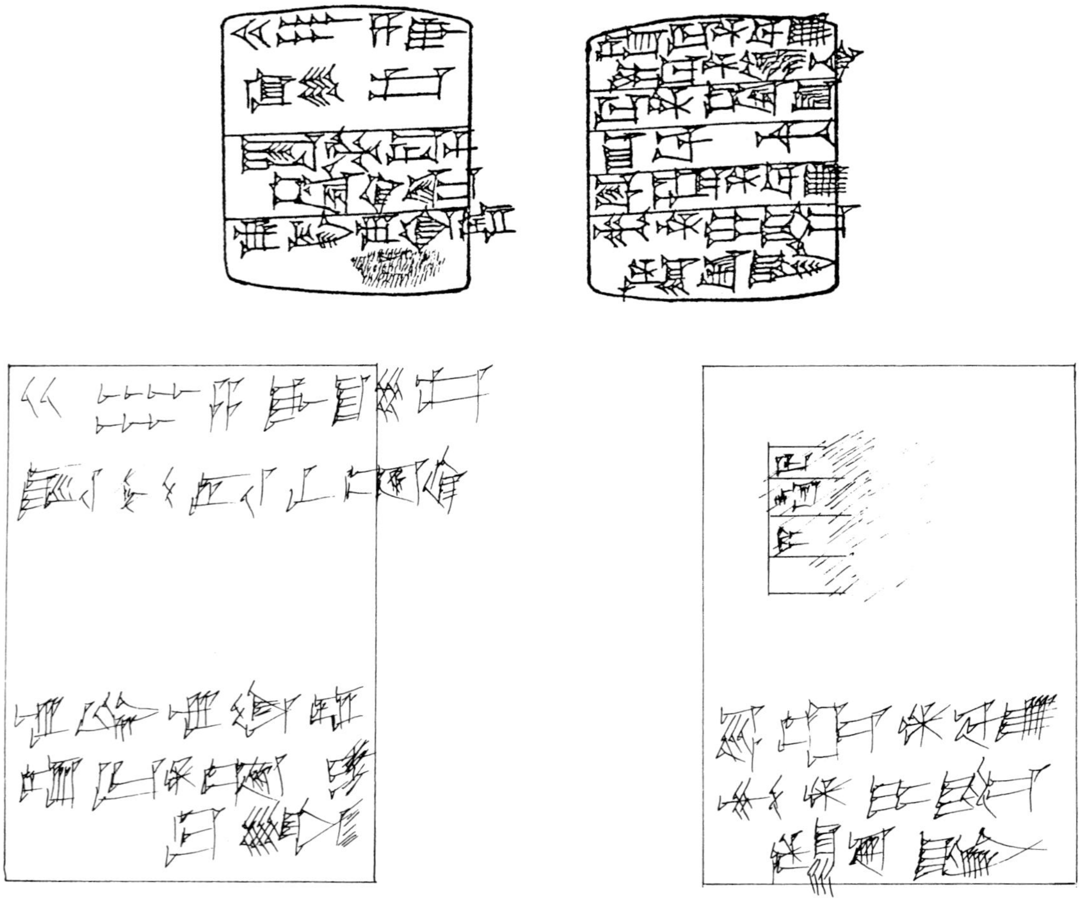

30 tablet (top), case (bottom)

31 (VII/-/-)

OBV.

1. 54 érin 0.1.3 še lugal-ta
2. še-ba 16.1.0 gur
3. érin bala-tuš-a

REV.

4. nu-bànda Su-šim-a
5. iti ezen ^{d}Šul-gi
6. ugula saĝa ^{d}Ĝá-tùm-du$_{10}$

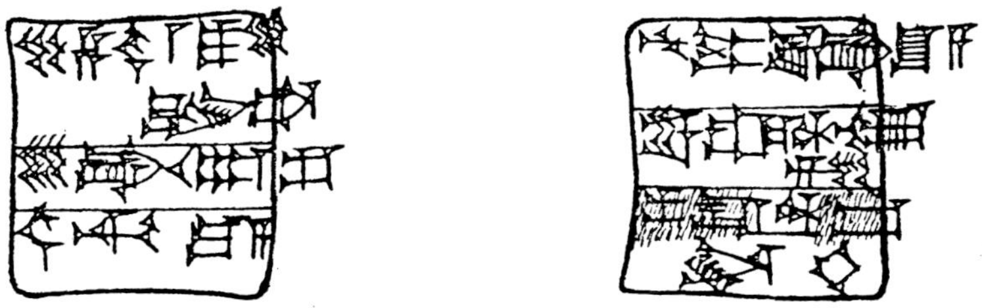

32 (VIII/-/-)

OBV.

1. 8.0.0 še gur lugal
2. še-ba géme uš-bar
3. ki Ur-zi-mu-ta
4. Ur-^{d}Da-mu
5. šu ba-ti
6. ĝìr Ur-^{d}Ba-ú

REV.

7. šà Nina^{ki}
8. iti ezen ^{d}Ba-ú
9. *(seal illegible)*

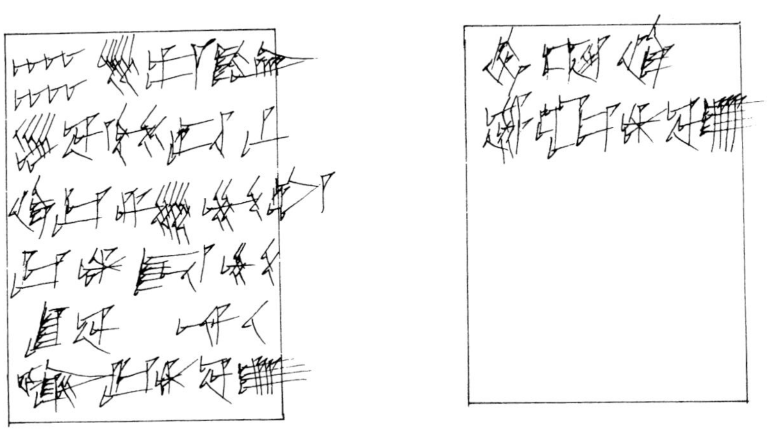

33

(date not preserved)

OBV.

1. 0.2.0 še ^{d}Šul-gi-ḫa-ma-ti
2. 0.1.0 *Li-bur-*^{d}Šul-gi
3. 0.0.3 *Šu-la-núm*
4. 2 géme 0.0.3-ta
5. 5 géme 0.0.2-ta
6. 0.1.0 Du-ú-du
7. [0.1.0] Na-bù-gu

REV.

8. 0.2.0 *A-ḫu-a*
9. 0.0.3 *A-bu-a*
10. 0.0.5 Ḫu-la-al
11. 0.0.5 *Puzur$_4$-ì-lí*

*12. 10 lá 1 rá-gaba sipa ur-⌜gi$_7$⌝-a

13. 0.2.0 ^{d}Šul-gi-*dan*
14. 1 géme 0.0.1 5 sìla
15. 0.1.0 *Ù-ṣe-mu-pe-li*
16. ki *Ṣe-lu-uš-Da-gan*
17. [ĝ]ìr ^{d}Šul-gi-ḫa-ma-ti

*18. [ ]-ḫul

19. *(seal illegible)*

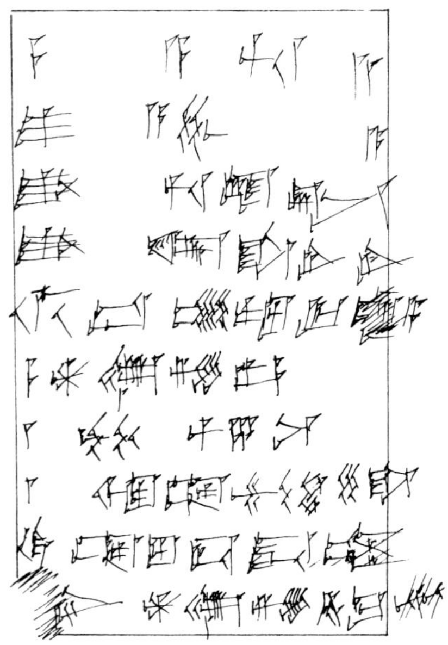

34

(date not preserved)

OBV.

★1. 16 géme 0.1.0-ta
★2. 2 géme 0.0.5-ta
★3. 93 géme 0.0.4-ta
★4. 44 géme 0.0.3-ta
★5. 8 géme á ½ 0.0.3-ta
★6. 6 géme šu-gi_4 0.0.2-ta
7. 33 dumu 0.0.2-ta
8. 28 dumu 0.0.1 5 sìla-ta

REV.

9. 30 lá 1 dumu 0.0.1-ta
10. še-ba-bi 25.4.0 gur lugal
★11. še-ba géme uš-bar-me
★12. ugula Ur-^{d}Da-mu
13. še-ba A-tu ì-du_8 é-la-la
14. Lú-[ ]-ki [ ]
15. [ ]

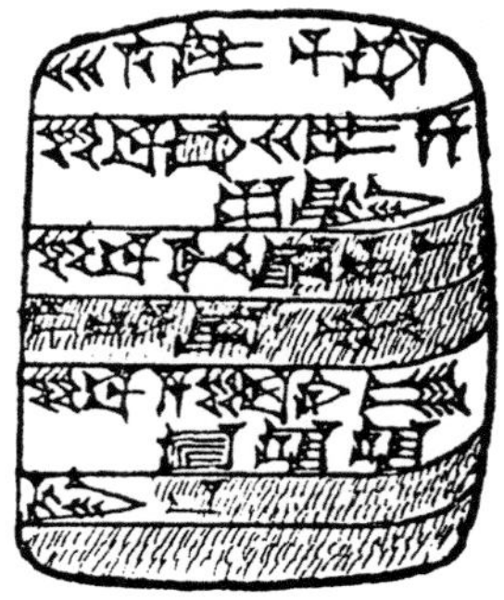

35

(date not preserved)

OBV.

(*top of obverse broken*)

1\. [Š]eš-k[al] géme [ ]

2\. 0.0.5 Lugal-má-gu[r$_8$-re] Gú-ab-ba^{ki} dumu Gém[e]

3\. 0.1.0 Šeš-a-ni dumu [ ] uš-bar Gú-a[b-ba^{ki}]

4\. 0.1.0 Ur-saĝ-ku$_5$ [x] dumu Ur-^{ĝeš}gigir nu-bànda [ ]

5\. 0.1.0 *Da-an-ni-núm* [ ]

6\. im-e tak$_4$-a

★7. 0.1.0 É-ḫi-li [x] dumu ^{d}En-lil-í[l]

REV.

8\. nu síg-ba á-n[a]

9\. 0.1.0 Šeš-kal-la x [ ] dumu E-⸢x⸣-[ ]

10\. 0.1.0 Lú-^{d}Dumu-z[i] Gù-dé-a [ ]

11\. ḫé-dab$_5$ al-[ ]

12\. (BLANK)

(*bottom of reverse broken*)

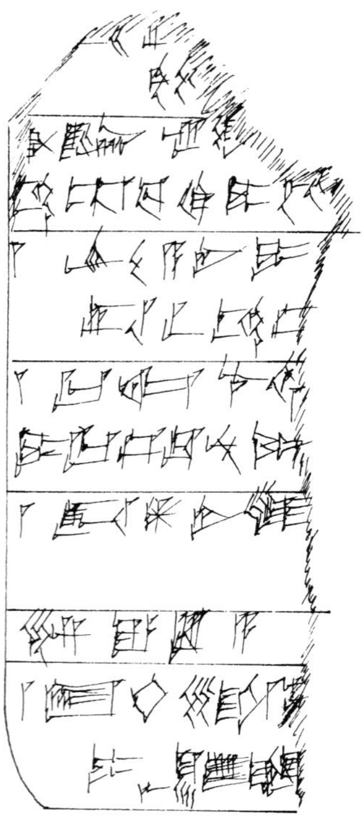

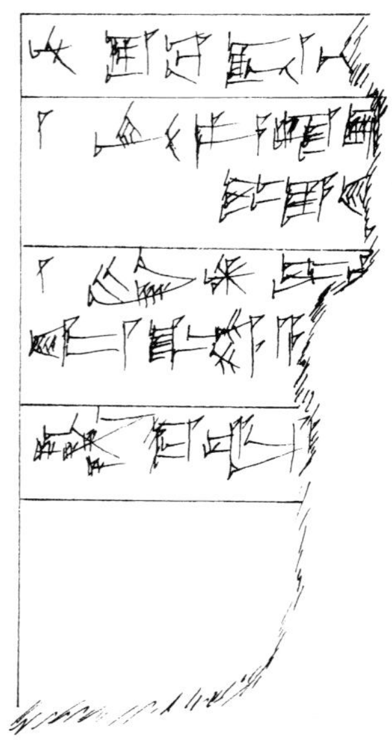

36 (date not preserved)

OBV.

(top of obverse broken)

1. ⸢dumu Ur-^{d}⸣[ ] ugula ur[ ]
2. 0.1.0 ^{d}Utu-ba-è šeš-[a-ni]
3. 0.0.5 Da-da-a Ir$_{11}$-da-ni
4. dumu Ur-^{d}Ḫendur-saĝ-me
5. 0.1.0 Šeš-kal-la dumu Géme-GU géme kar-^{kid}kid
6. 0.1.0 Ur-^{d}En-ki dumu Nin-a-ì-ša$_{6}$ géme kar-^{kid}kid

(bottom of obverse broken)

REV.

(top of reverse broken)

7. ⸢0.1.0 x⸣ [ ]
8. 0.1.4 Ur-^{d}En-ki nar ^{d}Ba-ú dumu Ur-^{d}SAR-da
9. ḫé-dab$_{5}$ Du$_{11}$-ga ⸢ba⸣-zi
10. (BLANK)
11. ^{ĝeš}tukul-e dab$_{5}$-ba-me
12. ĝìr Ab-ba-kal-la lú-^{ĝeš}tukul
13. ù Ur-^{d}Nin-⸢x-x-x⸣

(bottom of reverse broken)

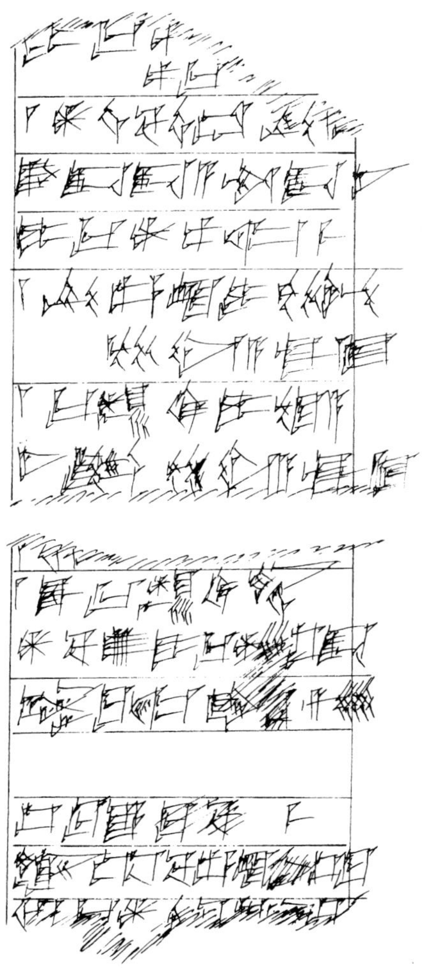

37

(VIII/11/-)

OBV.

1. 2 sìla ninda
2. Ur-^{d}Da-mu
3. 2 sìla ninda
4. Ùr-re-ba-du$_{7}$
5. 2 sìla Lú-^{d}Nin-tu é-udu
6. 2 sìla Du-šu-sig$_{7}$-a
7. 5 sìla Mar-tu-mí

REV.

8. 5 sìla lú-dab$_{5}$-ba en-nu
9. 6 sìla lú-dab$_{5}$-ba ĝá-nun-ĝeš-ka gub-ba
10. 5 sìla lú-mušen-dab$_{5}$ šu ba-ti
11. ĝìr Lú-ša$_{6}$-ga dumu Lú-gu-la
12. zi-ga u$_{4}$ 11-kam
13. iti ezen ^{d}Ba-ú

38

(IX/23/-)

OBV.

1. 0.0.1 ninda ur-gi$_7$-gal-gal
2. 2 sìla Ad-da
3. 2 sìla Ku$_5$-da
4. 0.0.2 4 sìla dub-sar-tur-tur
5. 5 sìla Mar-tu-mí
6. 6 sìla Ur-é-dar-a má-gín

REV.

7. 0.1.3 ninda Ér-è-a zabar-dab$_5$-ba-šè
8. ĝìr *I-šar-pá-dan*
9. 0.0.1 5 sìla ninda 1 sìla ninda ì-ra-ra
10. 1 ad$_x$ udu
11. BUR.LU-ma-al-gi$_4$ ù *I-šar-pá-dan* sízkur-šè ĝen-na
12. zi-ga u$_4$ 23-kam
13. iti mu-šu-du$_7$

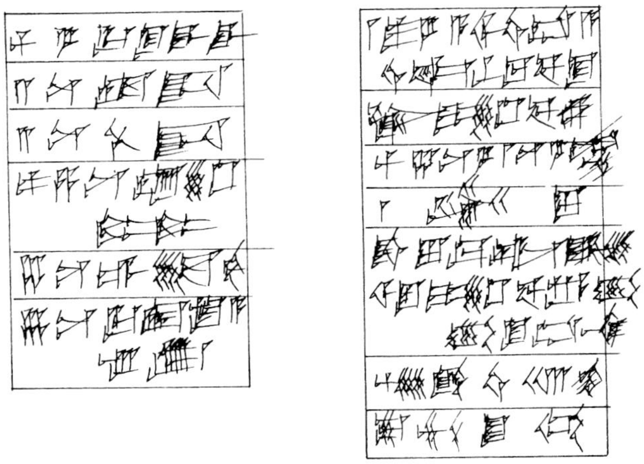

39

(XII/13/-)

OBV.

1. 2 sìla kaš 2 sìla ninda
2. *Šu*-[d]IM
3. 1 sìla Nì-ú-rum
4. lú-kisal-me
5. 2 sìla [d]Šul-gi-ḫa-ma-ti
6. 3 sìla Šar-ru-ru
7. 2 sìla Pi-mi-rí
8. 4 ur-gi$_7$ 2 sìla ninda-ta
9. 5 ur-gi$_7$ 1 sìla ninda-ta

REV.

10. ninda-bi 0.0.1 3 sìla
11. 2 sìla Pi-mu
12. 2 sìla Ad-da-uru
13. 2 sìla *Ši-ba-la-nim*
14. 1⅔ sìla *Puzur$_4$-Eš$_4$-tár*
15. sipa ur-me
16. 2 sìla kaš A-mu nagar
17. ĝìr ĝá-dub-ba
18. 2 sìla Lú-ba-ni-da
19. 1 sìla Ur-mes-bànda
20. ĝìr Ur-ĝar
21. zi-ga u$_4$ 13-kam
22. šà énsi
23. iti še-íl-la

40 (XII/16/-)

OBV.

1. 2 sìla kaš 2 sìla ninda
2. *Šu*-^{d}IM
3. 1 sìla Nì-ú-rum
4. lú-kisal-me

*5. 2 sìla ^{d}Šul-gi-ḫa-ma-ti
6. 3 sìla Šar-ru-ru
*7. 2 sìla Pi-mi-rí
8. ĝìr Ur-é-maḫ
9. 4 ur-gi$_7$ 2 sìla ninda-ta
10. 5 ur-gi$_7$ 1 sìla ninda-ta

REV.

11. ninda-bi 0.0.1 3 sìla
12. 2 sìla Pi-mu
13. 2 sìla Ad-da-uru
14. 2 sìla *Ši-ba-la-nim*
*15. 1⅓ sìla *Puzur*$_4$*-Eš*$_4$*-tár*
16. sipa ur-me
17. 2 sìla kaš A-mu nagar
*18. ĝìr ša$_{13}$-dub-ba
*19. 2 sìla Lú-ba-ni-da
20. 1 sìla Ur-mes-bànda
21. ĝìr Ur-ĝar
22. zi-ga u$_4$ 16-kam
23. šà énsi

L.E.

24. iti še-íl-la

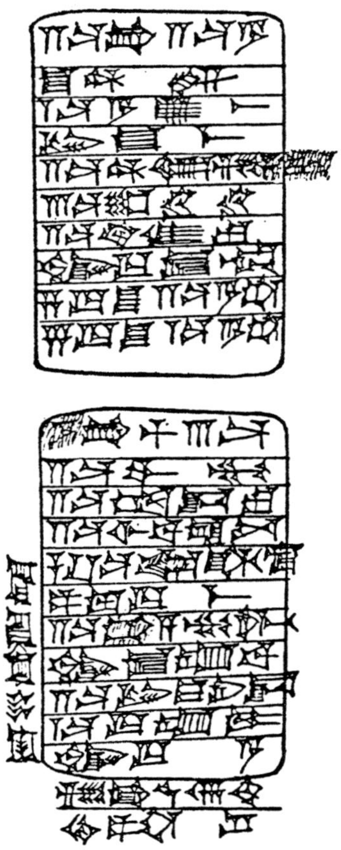

41 (XII/27/-)

OBV.

1. 2 sìla ninda Ur-^{d}Da-mu
2. 2 sìla Ùr-re-ba-du$_7$
3. 1 sìla Lú-^{d}En-líl-lá
4. ĝá-nun-da-tuš-a-me
5. 2 sìla Á-na-⌜mu⌝ sukkal
6. 1 sìla Ur-^{d}Ba-ú
7. 1 sìla Nimgir-di-ne

*8. érin é-tukul-me

9. 1 sìla Ur-^{ĝeš}gigir
10. 1 sìla Lú-diĝir-ra
11. dumu sipa ^{anše}kúnga-me
12. 2 udu ur-gi$_7$-re [ ]

REV.

13. ½ udu é-kaš$_4$
14. 1⅓ sìla *Ša-il-tum*
15. 1⅓ sìla Ad-mu-a
16. 1⅓ sìla Da-rí-ša
17. 1⅓ sìla *Ša-lim-mi*
18. 1⅓ sìla *Eš$_4$-tár-um-ni*
19. 1⅓ sìla A-li-šà-ge
20. Mar-tu-mí-me
21. 0.0.1 ninda ½ udu ĝìr *Ì-lí*-ša$_6$ ĝeš-šè ĝen-na
22. ĝìr Ur-^{d}Ig-alima rá-gaba
23. 5 sìla dumu lú-didli-me
24. ĝìr Lú-^{d}Nin-ĝír-su
25. zi-ga u$_4$ 27-kam
26. iti še-íl-la

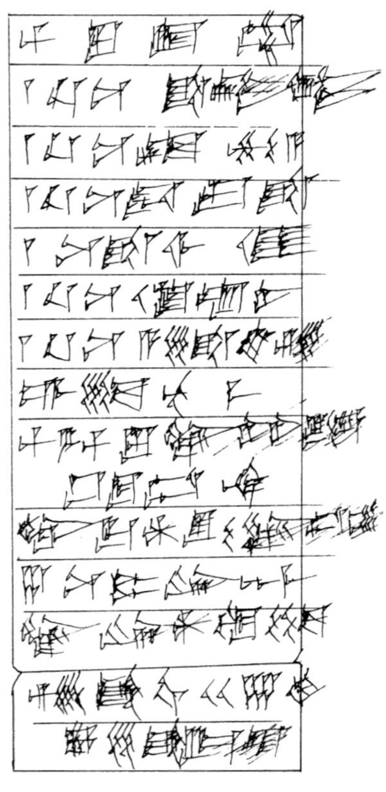

42

(X/-/AS 1)

OBV.

1. 6 sìla še lugal
*2. šà-gal èš-g[àr]
3. ki Ur-^{d}Hendur-saĝ
*4. ĝìr ^{d}Lama-ì-dab$_{5}$

REV.

5. šu ba-ti
6. (*seal illegible*)
7. iti amar-a-a-si
8. mu ^{d}Amar-^{d}Suen lugal

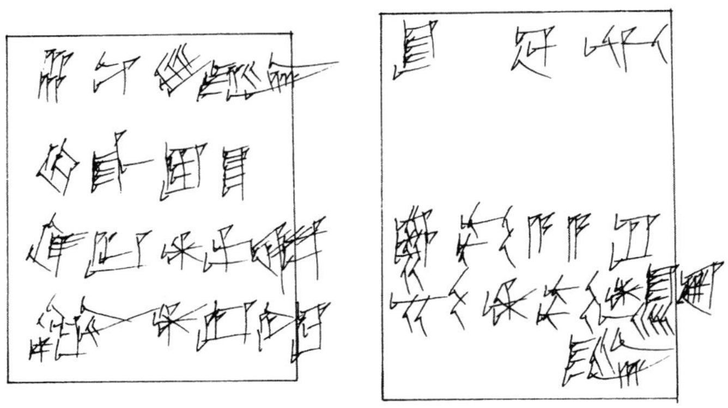

43

(III/-/AS 3)

OBV.

1. 3.0.0 še gur lugal
2. lá-u$_{x}$ su-ga
3. ki Ur-^{ĝeš}gigir-ta
4. šà-gal udu-šè

REV.

5. kišib Lugal-gú-gal
6. SEAL
7. iti ezen ^{d}Li$_{9}$-si$_{4}$
8. mu-ús-sa Ur-bí-lum^{ki} ba-ḫul

Seal: Lugal-gú-gal
dub-sar
dumu Lú-^{d}Ba-ú

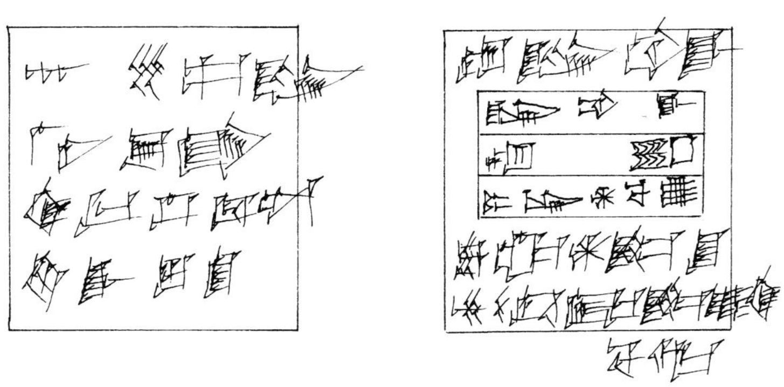

44

(II/-/-)

OBV.

1. 0.1.0 dabin lugal
2. Diĝir-*á-lí-ik* Mar-tu
3. 6 sìla zì-dub-dub
4. 4 sìla imĝaĝa$_3$
5. ^{d}Šul-pa-è
6. 0.0.1 zì-gu
7. Gù-dé-a
8. 0.1.0 dabin Pu-ga mušen-dù

REV.

9. mu mušen-šè dab$_5$-ba
10. 1.0.0 še gur
11. ki Gú-ab-ba^{ki}
12. 1.0.0 še gur
13. šà Á-sún
14. 1.0.0 še gur
15. šà Ḫu-rìm^{ki}
16. šà-gal anše zi-gúm-ma
17. iti gu$_4$-rá-bí-mú-mú

45

(VIII/-/-)

OBV.

1. 0.1.1 lá 1 sìla ninda-àr-ra
2. 0.2.0 duḫ-babbar
3. bisaĝ má-gur$_8$-ra
4. 0.0.5 še
5. ĝá-nun-ĝeš
6. šà-gal alim
7. 0.0.3 ninda-àr-ra
8. 0.0.5 duḫ

REV.

9. 0.1.1 duḫ-ĝi$_6$
10. šà-gal gu$_4$
11. á-u$_4$-te-na-bi
12. u$_4$ 28-kam
13. (BLANK)
14. iti ezen [d]Ba-ú

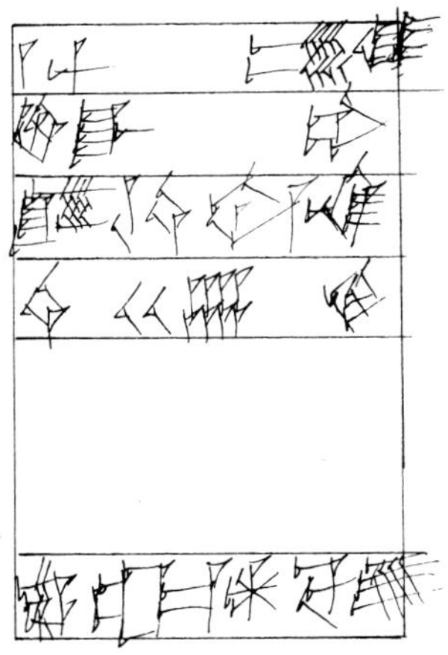

46

(-/-/ŠS 9)

OBV.

1. 210 gu$_4$ 0.4.3 še-ta
2. še-bi 189.0.0 gur
3. še-amar-e kú-a
4. kìšib Na-ba-ša$_6$

REV.

5. Lú-nita-gi-na
6. tum$_4$-dam
7. SEAL
8. mu é ^{d}Šára Umma^{ki} ba-dù

Seal: Lú-nita-gi-na
dub-sar

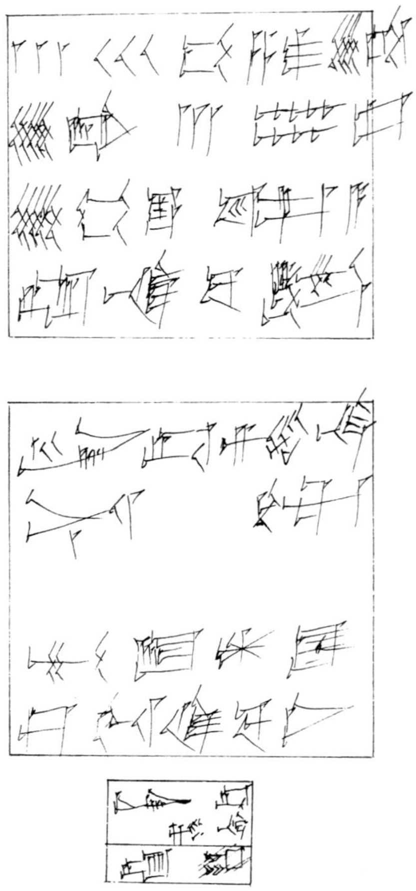

47

(IV/27/-)

OBV.

1. 91 udu 1½ sìla
2. 88 udu 1 sìla
3. še-bi 0.3.5 5 sìla
4. Nì-kal-la
5. 85 udu 1½ sìla
6. 104 udu 1 sìla
7. še-bi 0.3.5 5 sìla
8. Lú-kal-la
9. 85 udu 1½ sìla
10. 101 udu 1 sìla
11. še-bi 0.3.5
12. An-né
13. 88 udu 1½ sìla
14. 98 udu 1 sìla
15. še-bi 0.3.5

REV.

16. Lú-nì-šul
17. 120 udu 1 sìla
18. še-bi 0.2.0 Á-mu
19. 66 udu 1 sìla
20. še-bi 0.1.0 6 sìla
21. 42 sila$_4$ diri ½ sìla
22. še-bi 0.0.2 1 sìla
23. 10 gu$_4$ 8 sìla
24. 15 gu$_4$ 6 sìla
25. še-bi 0.2.5
26. 5 sìla šeg$_9$-bar
27. (BLANK)
28. iti šu-numun
29. u$_4$ 27-kam

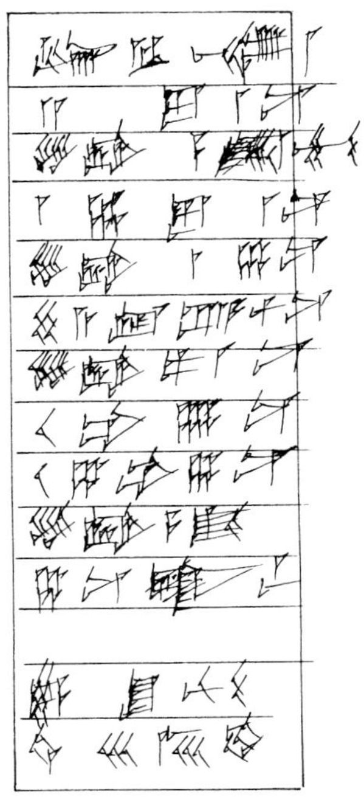

48

(V/10/-)

OBV.

1. 80 udu 1½ sìla
2. 65 udu 1 sìla
3. še-bi 0.3.0 ⸢5 sìla]
4. 80 udu 1½ sìla
5. 64 udu 1 sìla
6. [še]-bi 0.3.0 4 sìla
7. ⸢Lú⸣-kal-la
8. [x] udu 1[½] sìla
9. [ ] udu [ ]

(*bottom of obverse broken*)

REV.

(*top of reverse broken*)

10. [ ] gu$_{4}$ [8 sìla]
11. [5+] gu$_{4}$ 6 [sìla]
12. še-bi 0.2.0+ sìla
13. 5 sìla šeg$_{9}$-bar
14. (BLANK)
15. iti munu$_{4}$-kú
16. u$_{4}$ 10-kam

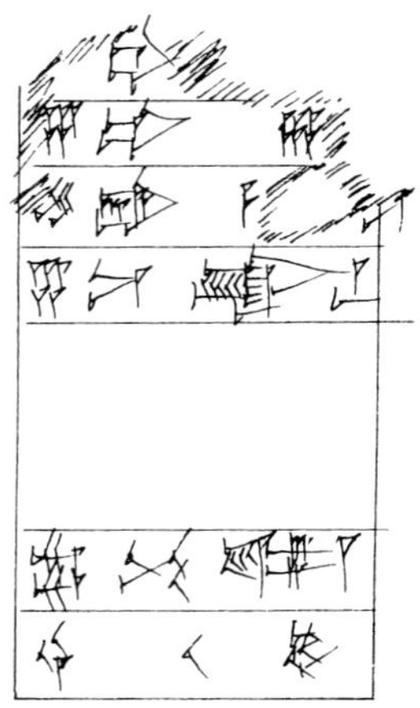

49

(V/24/-)

OBV.

1. 80 udu 1½ sìla
2. 68 udu 1 sìla
3. še-bi 0.3.0 8 sìla
4. Nì-kal-la
5. 80 udu 1½ sìla
6. 62 udu 1 sìla
7. še-bi 0.3.0 Lú-kal-la
8. 80 udu 1½ sìla
9. 67 udu 1 sìla
10. še-bi 0.3.0 7 sìla
11. An-né
12. 80 udu 1½ sìla
13. 62 udu 1 sìla

REV.

14. še-bi 0.3.0 Lú-^{d}Nin-šubur
15. 96 udu 1 sìla
16. še-bi 0.1.3 6 sìla
17. Á-na-mu
18. 90 lá 1 udu 1 sìla
19. še-bi 0.1.2 sá-du$_{11}$
20. 10 gu$_4$ 8 sìla
21. 7 gu$_4$ 6 sìla
22. 5 šeg$_9$-bar 1 sìla
23. še-bi 0.2.0 7 sìla
24. iti munu$_4$-kú
25. u$_4$ 24-kam

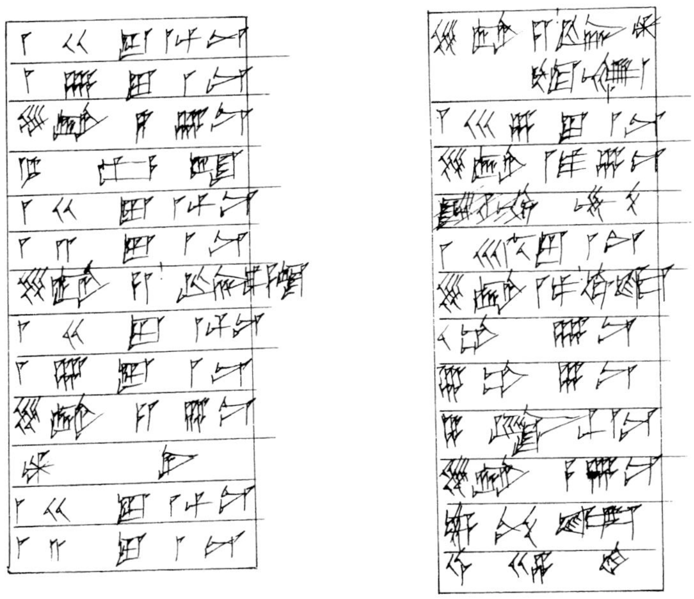

50 (VI/11/-)

OBV.

1. 80 udu 1½ sìla
2. 63 udu 1 sìla
3. še-bi 0.3.0 (*erasure*) Nì-kal-la
4. 80 udu 1½ sìla
5. 60 udu 1 sìla
6. še-bi 0.3.0 Lú-kal-la
7. 80 udu 1½ sìla
8. 64 udu 1 sìla
9. še-bi 0.3.0 An-né
10. 80 udu 1½ sìla
11. 60 udu 1 sìla
12. še-bi 0.3.0 Lú-^{d}Nin-šubur
13. 83 udu 1 sìla
14. še-bi 0.1.2 2 sìla

REV.

15. 76 udu 1 sìla
16. še-bi 0.1.1 6 sìla
17. 10 gu$_4$ 8 sìla
18. 10 lá 1 gu$_4$ 6 sìla
*19. še-bi 0.2.1 6 sìla
20. 5 sìla šeg$_9$-bar
21. (BLANK)
22. iti ezen ^{d}Dumu-zi
23. u$_4$ 11-kam

51

(VI/18/-)

OBV.

1. 140 udu 1½ sìla
2. 71 udu 1 sìla
3. še-bi 0.4.4 Nì-kal-la
4. 140 udu 1½ sìla
5. 71 udu 1 sìla
6. še-bi 0.4.4 Lú-kal-la
7. 140 udu 1½ sìla
8. 71 udu 1 sìla
9. še-bi 0.4.4 An-né
10. 140 udu 1½ sìla
11. 71 udu 1 sìla
12. še-bi 0.4.4
13. Lú-^{d}Nin-šubur

REV.

14. 153 udu 1 sìla
15. še-bi 0.2.3 3 sìla
16. Á-na-mu
17. 82 udu 1 sìla
18. še-bi 0.1.2 2 sìla
19. 10 gu$_4$ 8 sìla
20. 10 lá 1 gu$_4$ 6 sìla
21. 6 šeg$_9$-bar 1 sìla
22. še-bi 0.2.2
23. (BLANK)
24. iti ezen ^{d}Dumu-zi
25. u$_4$ 18-kam

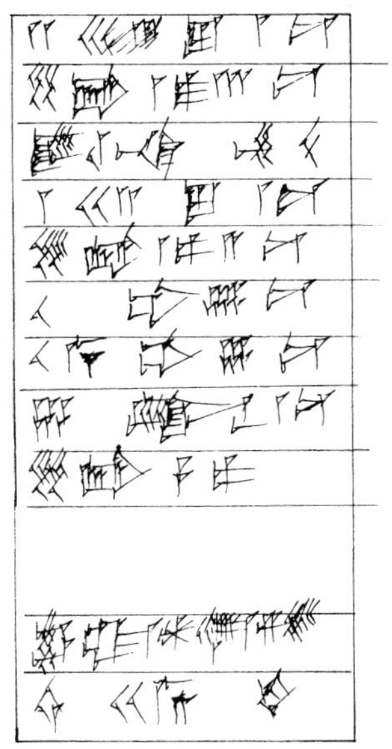

52

(VI/20/-)

OBV.

1. 140 udu 1½ sìla
2. 71 udu 1 sìla
3. še-bi 0.4.4 Nì-kal-la
4. 140 udu 1½ sìla
5. 71 udu 1 sìla
6. še-bi 0.4.4 Lú-kal-la
7. 140 udu 1½ sìla
8. 71 udu 1 sìla
9. še-bi 0.4.4 An-né
10. 140 udu 1½ sìla
11. 71 udu 1 sìla
12. še-bi 0.4.4
13. Lú-^{d}Nin-šubur
14. 153 udu 1 sìla

REV.

15. še-bi 0.2.3 3 sìla
16. Á-na-mu
17. 140 lá 1 udu 1 sìla
18. še-bi 0.2.2 sá-du$_{11}$
19. 10 gu$_{4}$ 8 sìla
20. 10 lá 1 gu$_{4}$ 6 sìla
21. 7 šeg$_{9}$-bar 2 sìla
22. 5 amar 3 sìla
23. še-bi 0.2.4 3 sìla
24. (BLANK)
25. u$_{4}$ 20-kam
26. iti ezen ^{d}Dumu-zi

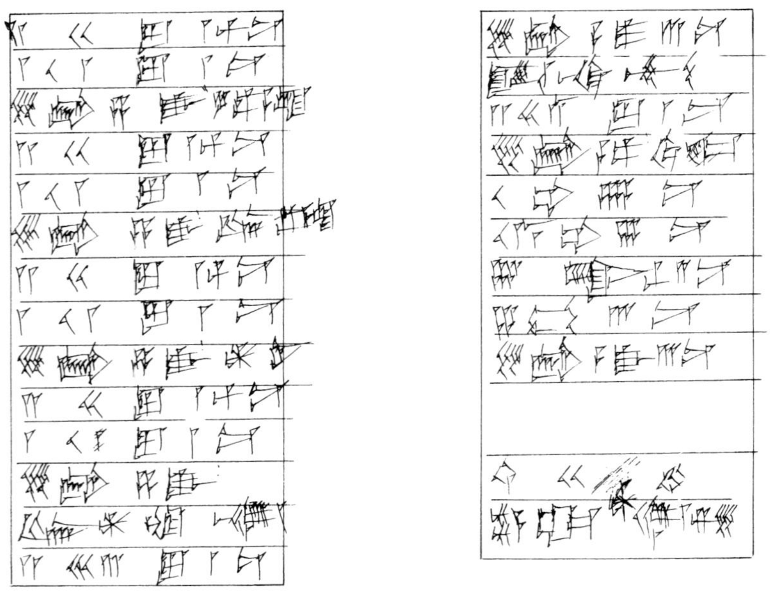

53

(X/10/-)

OBV.

1. 145 udu 1½ sìla
2. še-bi 0.3.3 7 sìla
3. Nì-kal-la
4. 140 udu 1½ sìla
5. še-bi 0.3.3 Lú-kal-la
6. 130 udu 1½ sìla
7. še-bi 0.3.1 5 sìla
8. An-né
9. 143 udu 1½ sìla
10. še-bi 0.3.3 4 sìla
11. Lú-^{d}Nin-šubur
12. 200 udu 1 sìla

REV.

13. še-bi 0.3.2
*14. Á-na-mu
*15. 322 udu 1 sìla
16. še-bi 1.0.2 2 sìla
17. 8 gu_4 8 sìla
18. 12 gu_4 6 sìla
19. 5 amar 3 sìla
*20. 7 $šeg_9$-bar 2 sìla
21. še-bi 0.2.4 5 sìla
22. (BLANK)
23. u_4 10-kam
24. iti amar-a-a-si

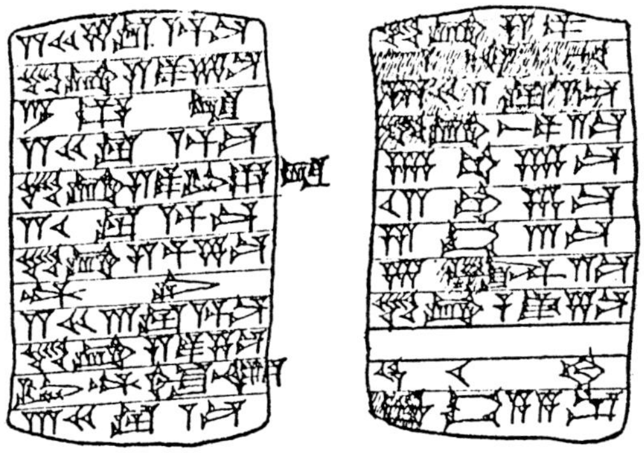

54

(XII/5/-)

OBV.

1. 200 udu 1½ sìla
2. še-bi 1 gur
3. Nì-kal-la
4. 160 udu 1½ sìla
5. še-bi 0.4.0 Lú-kal-la
6. 160 udu 1½ sìla
7. še-bi 0.4.0 An-né
8. 200 udu 1½ sìla
9. še-bi 1 gur
10. ^{d}Nanna-si-sá

REV.

11. 10 gu$_4$ 8 sìla
12. 10 lá 1 gu$_4$ 6 sìla
13. 7 šeg$_9$-bar 2 sìla
14. še-bi 0.2.2 8 sìla
15. Ur-ki-gu-la
16. (BLANK)
17. iti še-íl-la
18. u$_4$ 5-kam

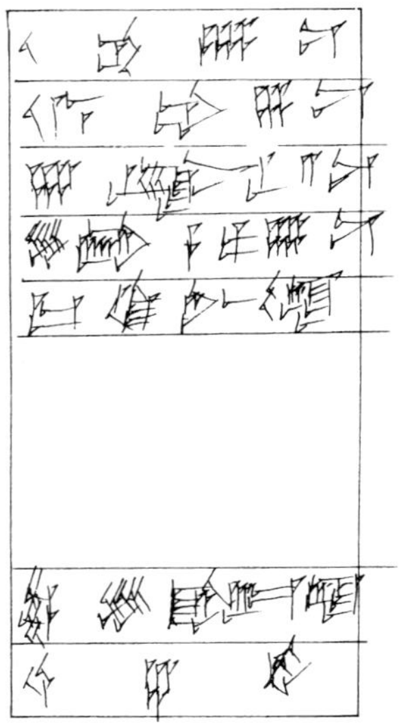

55

(XII?/6+/-)

OBV.

1. 30 lá 1 udu ì 1½ sìla
2. 95 udu 1½ sìla
3. še-bi 0.3.0 Nì-kal-la
4. 95 udu 1½ sìla
5. še-bi 0.2.2
6. Lú-kal-la
7. 95 udu [1½ sìla]
8. še-bi [0.2.2 An-né]
9. 95 udu [1½ sìla]
10. še-bi [0.2.2]

REV.

11. Lú-[d]Nin-šubur
12. 120 udu 1 sìla
13. še-bi 0.2.0
14. Á-na-mu
15. 27 máš ⅔ sìla
16. še-bi 0.0.1 8 sìla
17. sá-du$_{11}$-diĝir-ra
18. 42 sila$_4$ diri 1 sìla
19. (BLANK)
20. [u$_4$ 6+]-kam
21. [iti še-íl]-la

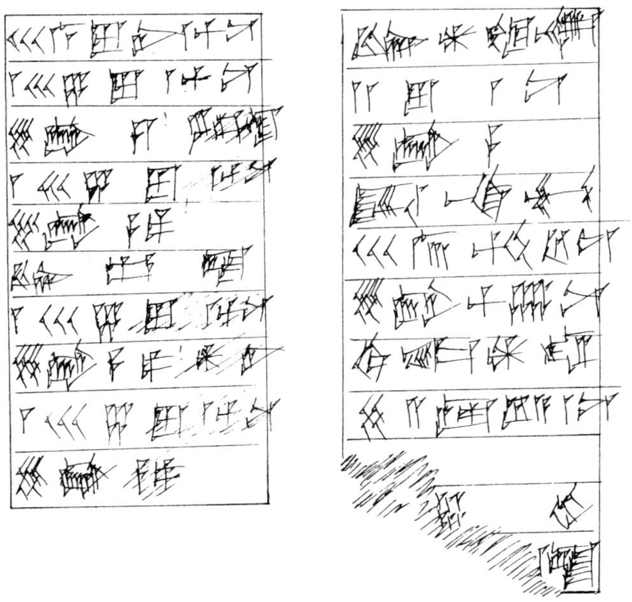

56

(IV/-/Š 40)

i. 1. 1 gur$_7$ 130.2.3 7⅔ sìla še gur lugal
★2. še gána-gu$_4$
3. gur ga-tum$_4$-dam
4. gur
★5. še gána-uru$_4$-lá
6. 4.3.4 5 sìla gur
7. še-numun-ta gur-ra
8. 0.4.3 še amar ba-ug$_7$
9. (BLANK)
10. šu+níĝin 1 gur$_7$ 136.0.5 2⅔ sìla gur
11. saĝ nì-gur$_{11}$-ra-kam
12. šà-bi-ta
13. 450.1.0 gur
14. kìšib Ur-ša$_6$-ga dumu É-úr-bi
15. 143.0.0 gur
ii. 16. kìšib L[ú-^{d}Ba]-ú dumu Na-ba-ša$_6$
17. 0.4.2 5 sìla gur
18. kìšib Ur-^{d}Nin-ĝír-su dumu Na-ba-ša$_6$
19. 153.1.0 gur
20. kìšib A-mu dumu Lugal-ḫé-ĝál
21. 0.1.0 gur
22. kìšib Ur-Nin-mar-ki dumu Lú-^{d}Utu
23. 173.2.0 gur
★24. kìšib Lú-bùluĝ-ĝá dumu Du$_{10}$-ga
25. 196.3.2 5 sìla gur
26. kìšib Ab-ba-mu má-laḫ$_5$-gal
27. (BLANK)
28. má-a si-ga
29. kìšib lú-ĝìr-ĝen-na-ke$_4$-ne
30. 1393.4.1 5 sìla gur
31. kìšib-bi 2-àm
32. kìšib Ur-dam dumu Ur-^{d}Nanše
33. 37.4.0 dabin gur
34. kìšib-bi 2-àm
35. kìšib Lú-^{d}Nin-šubur dumu Ur-ša$_6$-ga
36. 180.0.0 gur
iii. ★37. ì-dub a-šà a-saĝ-dù-du
38. 181.0.0 gur
★39. ì-dub a-šà Inim-ma-AN
★40. 128.0.1 2 sìla gur
41. 100.0.3 zíz gur
42. ì-dub a-šà Pú-du
43. 190.4.5 ⅓ sìla gur
44. ì-dub ki-tuš DA.AN.LA.KI
45. úgu-a ĝá-ĝá
46. ì-dub didli
47. kìšib Ur-diĝir-ra saĝa
48. 42.4.0 gur
49. še-ba ù Lú-^{d}Ba-ú dumu É-gal-mu-šár-ra-ni
★50. gu$_4$ é-gal-ke$_4$ íb-uru$_4$-a-šè
51. zi-ga
52. (BLANK)
53. šu+níĝin 1416.2.5 gur
54. má-a si-ga
55. kìšib lú-ĝìr-ĝen-na-ke$_4$-ne
56. šu+níĝin 1393.4.1 5 sìla gur
57. kìšib Ur-dam dumu Ur-^{d}Nanše
58. šu+níĝin 37.4.0 gur
59. kìšib Lú-^{d}Nin-šubur dumu Ur-ša$_6$-ga
iv. 60. šu+níĝin 780.0.3 2⅔ sìla gur
61. ì-dub didli
62. kìšib Ur-diĝir-ra saĝa
63. úgu-a ĝá-ĝá
64. šu+níĝin 52.4.0 gur
65. še-ba ù Lú-^{d}Ba-ú dumu É-gal-mu-šár-ra-ni
★66. gu$_4$ é-gal-ke$_4$ íb-uru$_4$-a-šè
67. zi-ga
68. (BLANK)
★69. šu+níĝin 1 gur$_7$ 81.0.3 7⅔ sìla gur
70. zi-ga
★71. lá-u$_x$ 55.0.1 5 sìla gur
72. (BLANK)
73. nì-ka$_9$-ak
74. Ur-diĝir-ra saĝa ^{d}Šul-gi
75. iti šu-numun
76. (BLANK)
77. mu-ús-sa é *Puzur$_4$-iš-^{d}Da-gan* ba-dù

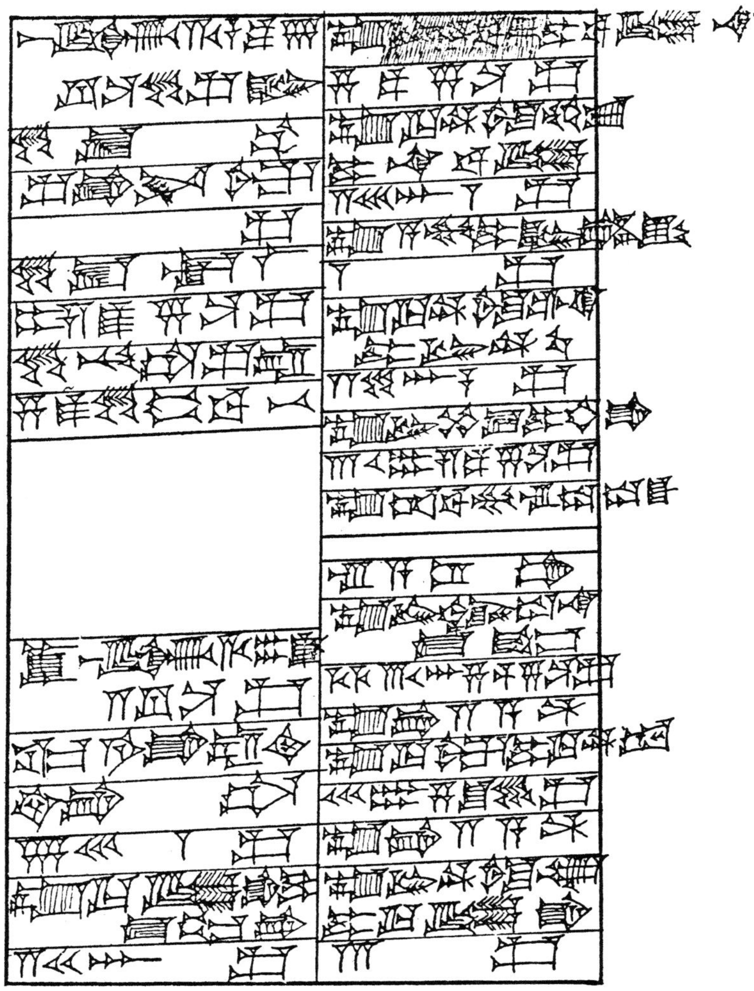

56 obverse

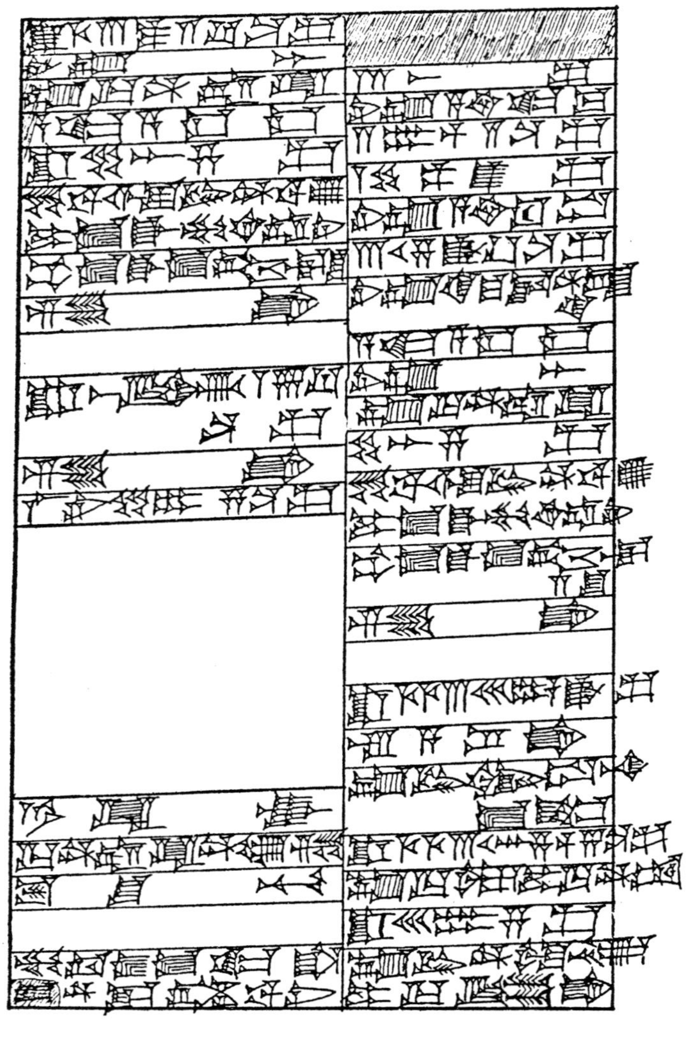

56 reverse

57

(-/-/Š 40)

i. 1. 1927.2.4 7 sìla še gur lugal
★2. še gána-gu$_4$
3. gur
★4. še gána-uru$_4$-lá
5. gur
6. še-numun-ta gur-ra
7. 1.2.3 gur
8. še amar ba-ug$_7$
9. (BLANK)
★10. šu+níĝin 1929.0.1 7 sìla še gur lugal
11. saĝ-nì-gur$_{11}$-ra-kam
12. šà-bi-ta
★13. 851.2.5 5 sìla gur
ii. ★14. gur zabar-ta
15. 190.0.0 7 sìla gur
16. gur še-ba-ta
17. kišib-bi 3 àm
18. kišib Ur-dam
19. dumu Ur-^{d}Nanše
★20. 265.1.5 5 sìla gur
21. kišib-bi 3 àm
22. kišib Ur-^{d}Lama
23. dumu Me-luḫ-ḫa
24. 84.3.5 gur
25. kišib Gù-dé-a
26. dumu Ur-^{d}Ba-ú
★27. 537.1.3 gur
28. mu ba-a-al-la-a-šè
29. kišib Ur-dam
iii. 30. dumu Ur-^{d}Nanše
31. úgu-a ĝá-ĝá
32. (BLANK)
★33. šu+níĝin 1578.4.3 2 sìla gur
★34. kišib Ur-dam dumu Ur-^{d}Nanše
★35. šu+níĝin 265.1.5 5 sìla gur
36. (BLANK)
★37. kišib Ur-^{d}Lama
★38. dumu Me-luḫ-ḫa
★39. šu+níĝin 84.3.5 gur
★40. kišib Gu-dé-a dumu Ur-^{d}Ba-ú
★41. úgu-a ĝá-ĝá
iv. 42. (BLANK)
43. šu+níĝin 1928.0.1 7 sìla še gur lugal
44. zi-ga
45. (BLANK)
46. nì-ka$_9$-ak
47. Lú-^{d}Šul-gi šabra
★48. še é-^{d}Nin-mar-ki
★49. mu-ús-sa é *Puzur$_4$-iš-^{d}Da-gan* ba-dù

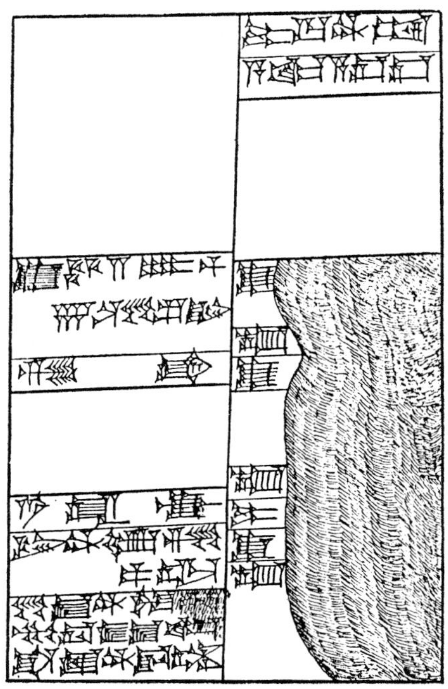

58

(-/-/Š 40)

OBV.

1. 20 da[bin gur]
2. si-ì-tum [ ]
3. šà-bi-ta
4. 22.2.0 gur
5. lú-ḪU.KU.BU kú-a
6. 3.3.0 lá-u$_x$ su-ga
7. ĝìr Ur-[d]Šul-pa-è gu-za-lá

REV.

8. (BLANK)
9. šu+níĝin 27.0.0 dabin gur
10. nì-ka$_9$-ak si-ì-tum
11. Nì-[d]Ba-ú dumu Ni-ba
12. mu-ús-sa é *Puzur$_4$-iš-Da-gan* ba-dù

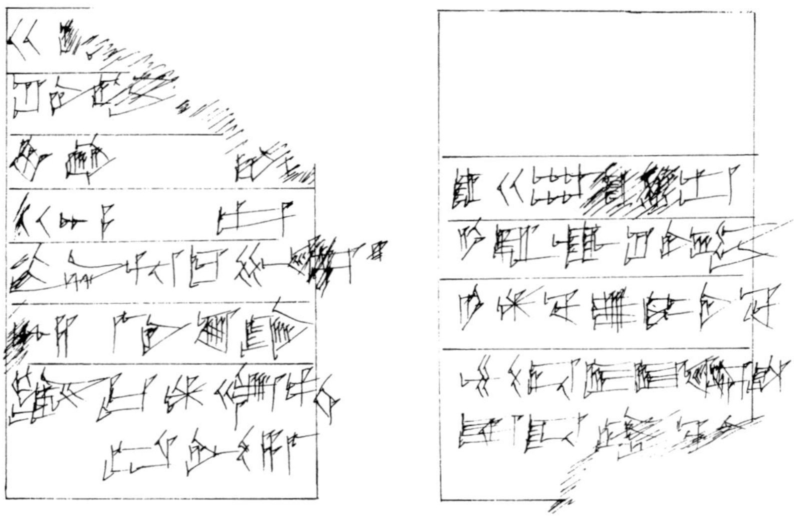

59

(-/-/Š 45)

OBV.

1. 2⅓ ma-na [ ]
2. ésir-é-a-bi [ ]
3. ki Ba-zi dum[u]
*4. 30 lá 1.0.0 ésir-é-[a gur] éns[i]
5. ki Lugal-nir-ĝá[l]
6. (BLANK)
*7. šu-niĝin 39.2.3 ésir-é-a gur
8. šà-bi-ta
9. ⅔ ša 8 gín kù
10. nì-ka$_9$ mu Si-mu-ur$_4$-ru-um^{ki} Lu-lu-bu^{ki} a-rá 10 lá 1-kam-aš ba-ḫul-a
11. úgu Lú-^{d}Nin-šubur ba-ĝar
*12. 2 gín lá 6 še kišib-bi ba-zi-ir
13. kišib énsi-ka
14. 17.3.5 7 sìla ésir-é-a
15. nì-ka$_9$ má lugal-mu [ ] mu-ĝál

REV.

16. 15 ésir-é-a gur
17. úgu Ur-^{d}Nanše ba-a-ĝar
18. 13.4.3 3 sìla ésir-é-a gur
19. úgu Nam-maḫ ba-a-ĝar
20. 14.1.3 6 sìla ésir-é-a gur
21. úgu Ur-^{d}Dumu-zi ba-a-ĝar
22. nì-ka$_9$ mu Si-mu-ur$_4$-ru-um^{ki} Lu-lu-bu^{ki} a-rá 10 lá 1-kam ba-ḫul mu-ĝál
23. 3.0.2 ésir-é-a gur
24. ĝìr Eš-àm
25. ⅓ ša kù ĝìr Ba-zi
26. nì-ka$_9$ mu Ur-bí-[lum^{ki} ba-ḫul]
27. úgu Eš-àm [ ]
28. (BLANK)
29. šu+níĝin 1 ma-na 10 gín [ ]
*30. ésir-é-a-bi 32+[ ]
31. šu+níĝin 64.0.2 6 sìla [ ]
32. zi-[ga]
33. lá-u$_x$ 0.2.0 9 sìla [ ]

L.E.

34. nì-ka$_9$-ak kù-ta sa$_{10}$-a
35. Eš-àm
36. mu Si-mu-ur$_4$-um^{ki} Lu-lu-bu^{ki} a-rá 10 lá 1-kam ba-ḫul

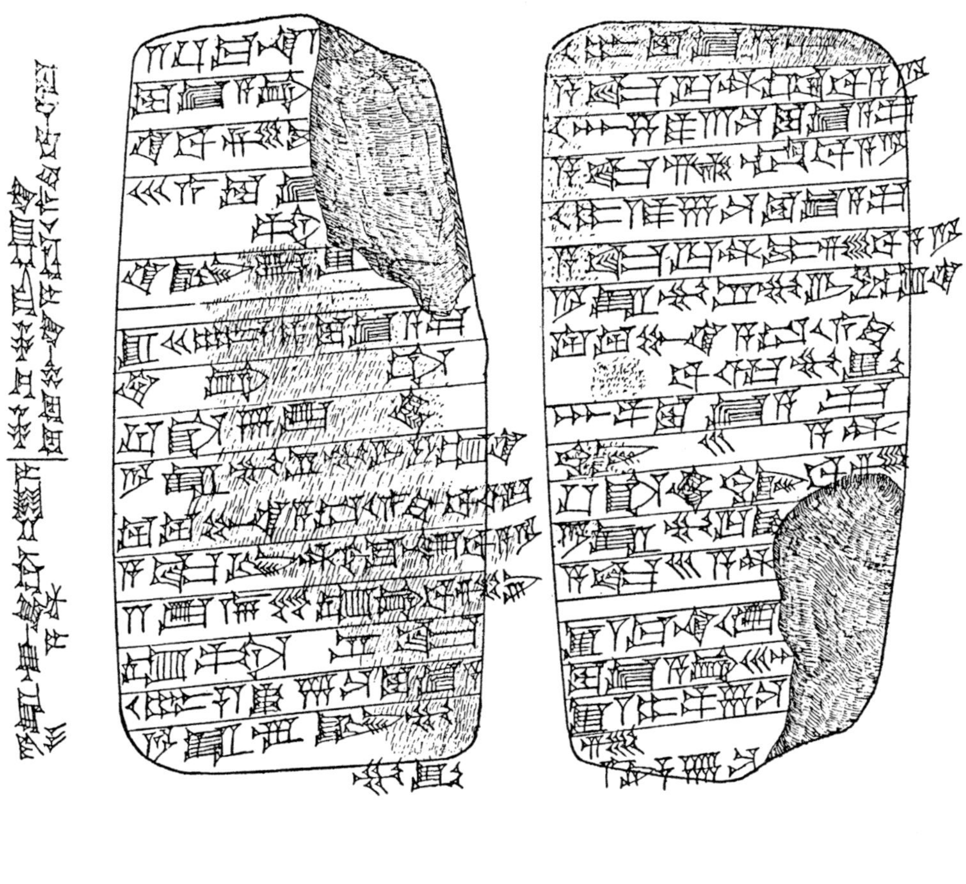

60

(-/-/Š 46)

i.
1. [ ] 6 sìla še gur lugal
2. [ ] ù
3. [2]+.2.1 5 sìla gur
4. 1gín lá igi-4-ĝál kù
5. mu Ur-bí-lum^{ki}
6. 1035.2.5 8⅓ sìla gur
7. 1⅚ ma-na 4½ gín 1 še kù
8. mu Ki-maš^{ki}
9. 2.3.0 lá-u$_{x}$ Ur-dam
*10. 5.0.3 6 sìla gur
11. lá-u$_{x}$ Ur-^{d}Nin-ĝeš-zi-da
12. ki Ur-^{d}En-ki-ta

ii.
13. 2.4.0 gur
14. ki Ur-mes gu-za-lá-ta
15. 8.0.0 gur
*16. ki Níg-^{d}Ba-ú ù Ka$_{5}$-a-ta
17. 3.0.0 še é-kin-a
18. ki Lugal-uru-da sa$_{12}$-du$_{5}$-ta
*19. 10.4.1 gur lá-u$_{x}$ su-ga
20. ki Nì-ú-rum-ta
21. (BLANK)
*22. šu+níĝin 1100.1.0 6⅓ sìla gur
*23. šu+níĝin 2 ma-<na> 5 gín igi-4-ĝál
    1 še <kù>

iii.
24. šà-bi-ta
*25. 1088.2.4 3 sìla gur
*26. kìšib Ur-^{d}Nin-ĝeš-zi-da dumu
    Lugal-kù-ga
*27. 2 ma-na 5 gín igi-4-ĝál 1 še
*28. 2½ gín kù
*29. še-bi 2.2.3 gur
*30. Nì-ú-rum šu ba-ti
31. (BLANK) *(erasure)*
32. mu-túm
*33. lá-u$_{x}$ 9.0.5 3⅓ sìla gur

iv.
34. (BLANK)
35. nì-ka$_{9}$-ak
*36. [l]á-u$_{x}$ è-a
*37. [ki Ur-^{d}E]n-ki-[ta]
38. [ ]
39. [ ] ši [šu]bur
40. [Ki]-maš^{ki} [ ]-ḫul

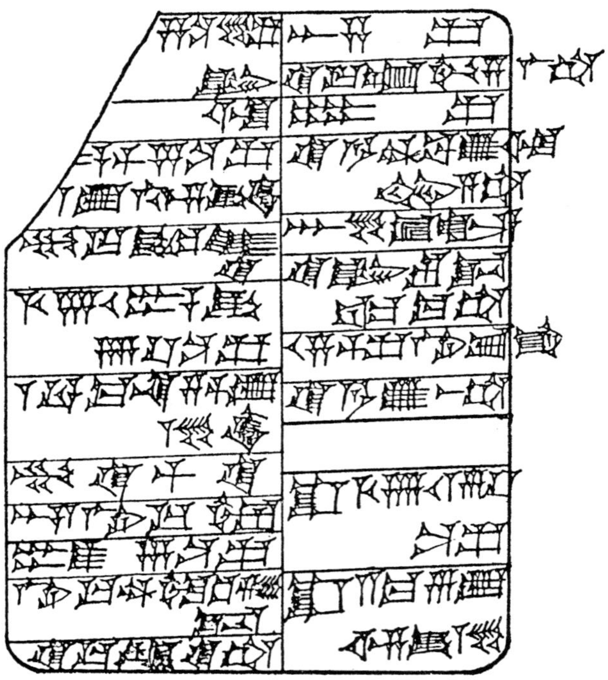

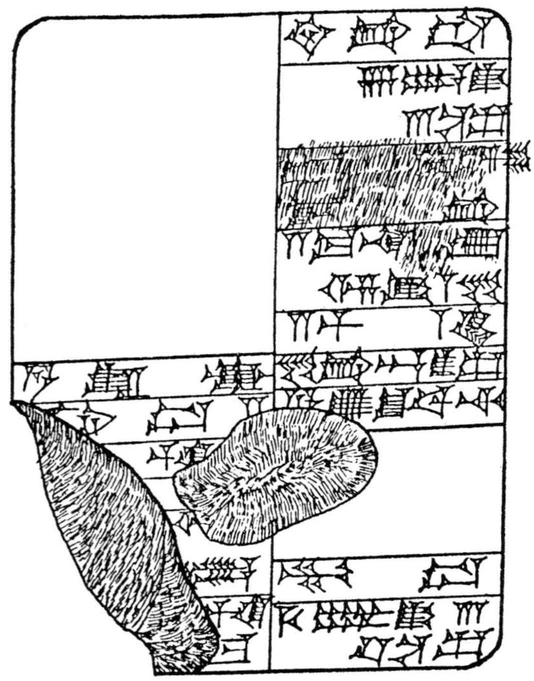

61

(X/-/Š 47)

OBV.

1. 30.0.0 še gur lugal
2. ĝìr Ur-^{ĝeš}gigir
3. ⸢20.0.0⸣ [gu]r ĝìr Lú-^{d}Inanna
4. a-šà gíd-da-ta
5. 11.0.0 gur ki Lú-^{d}Igi-ma-šè-ta
6. 3.0.0 gur ki Ur-^{d}Ig-alima-ta
7. ĝìr Lú-^{d}Utu
8. 4.0.0 gur ki Lú-^{d}Ba-ú-«a»-ta
9. (BLANK)
10. šu-niĝin 68 še gur
11. šà-bi-ta
12. 13.0.0 kaš sig$_5$ gur
13. 16.0.0 kaš ĝen gur
14. ĝìr Ur-mes
15. zi-ga lugal
16. 1.0.1 5 sìla še gur še-ba iti [x]
17. iti munu$_4$-kú-ta iti amar-[a-a-si-šè]
18. še-bi 6.1.3 ⸢še gur⸣
19. iti 6-kam
20. (BLANK)
21. šu-niĝin 13 kaš sig$_5$ gu[r]
22. [še-bi] 6.2.3 gur

REV.

23. šu-niĝin 16.0.0 kaš [ĝen lugal]
24. šu-niĝin 6.1.3 [ ]
25. (BLANK)
26. še-bi 41.4.0 gur
27. zi-ga-àm
28. 0.3.1 ninda-ár-ra ĝe[n]
29. 2.0.0 še gur
30. 0.0.4 5 sìla munu$_4$ še-bi 0.0.1 ⸢6⸣ [sìla]
31. 7.3.0 šim sig$_5$ gur
32. še-bala-bi 5.0.2 gur
33. 0.2.0 kaš ĝen
*34. še-bi 15.3.3 6⅔ sìla gur
35. é-a-bala-a
*36. šu-niĝin 57.2.3 6⅔ sìla gur
37. [z]i-ga-àm
38. [lá-u$_x$] 10.2.1 3⅔ sìla gur
39. (BLANK)
40. nì-ka$_9$-ak Ḫé-na-ti
41. iti amar-a-a-si
42. mu-ús-sa Ki-maš^{ki} ba-ḫul

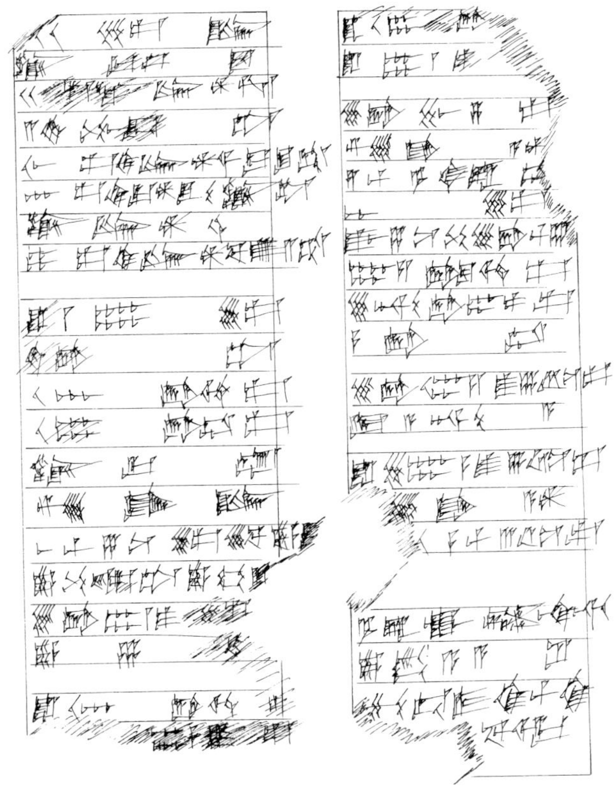

62

(XI/-/Š 47)

OBV.

1. 22.0.2 4⅓ [sìla še gur] lugal
2. si-ì-tum nì-ka$_9$-ak
3. 2.0.0 gur a-rá 1-kam
4. 4.0.0 gur a-rá 2-kam
5. ki Ur-^{d}En-líl-lá-ta
6. 3.0.0 gur mu Ur-^{d}Lama-[šè]
7. ki Ur-^{d}Ig-alima-ta
8. (BLANK)
9. šu+níĝin 31.0.2 4⅓ sìla še gur
10. šà-bi-t[a]
11. 18.0.0 kaš ĝen gur
12. [a]ga-ús A-la-a^{ki}-k[a]
13. 3.0.0 kaš ĝen aga-ús [x]-ù^{ki}
14. 0.1.0 kaš sig$_5$ énsi
15. ki Da-[x]
16. 0.1.4 kaš sig$_5$ NIM [ ]
17. [ ] kaš ĝen [ ]
18. [ ] ninda šà [ ]
19. [ ]

REV.

(top of reverse destroyed)

20. 0.4.0 še [ ]
21. (BLANK)
22. šu-niĝin 0.2.4 kaš sig$_5$ [ ]
23. še-bala-bi 0.1.2 [ ]
24. šu+níĝin 21.4.4 kaš ĝen gur
25. šu+níĝin 0.4.5 še [ ]
26. še-bi 23.3.3 [ ]
27. zi-ga
28. 6.1.5 4⅓ sìla še gu[r]
29. *nì-ĝál-la
30. (BLANK)
31. nì-ka$_9$-ak ka-lá-a
32. ĝìr ^{d}Ba-ú dumu *A-ḫu-a*
33. iti še-kin-ku$_5$ u$_4$ 15-kam
34. mu-ús-sa Ki-maš^{ki} ba-ḫul

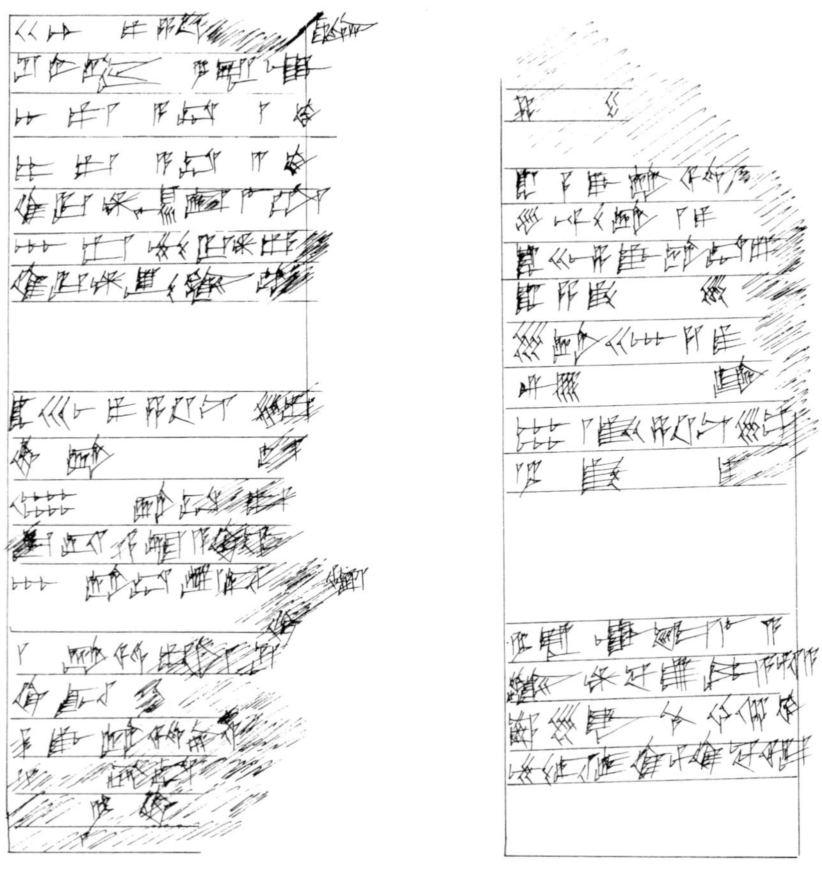

63 (XII/-/AS 1)

i. 1. 1 gú 30 ma-na 6⅓ gín síg ^{ĝeš}ga-ríg-ak túg lugal
2. 3⅔ ma-na síg ^{ĝeš}ga-ríg-ak túg-ús lugal
3. 9 ma-na 10 gín síg ^{ĝeš}ga-ríg-ak túg 3-kam-ús
4. 8 ma-na 2½ gín síg ^{ĝeš}ga-ríg-ak túg 4-kam-ús
5. 30⅓ ma-na gú-tar túg lugal
6. 8⅔ ma-na 8 gín síg gú-tar túg 3-kam-ús
7. 3 gú 44 ma-na síg mug
★8. 8495½ géme u$_4$ 1-šè
9. á túg tag-a-ra U.NU-a síg ^{ĝeš}ga-ríg-ak túg ĝeš-a-ĝál-la
10. ku$_4$-ra ugula uru-bi 424 ⅔ 5½ gín géme u$_4$ 1-šè
11. 42 ma-na síg za-rí-in túg-ús lugal
12. 1 gú 10 ma-na síg za-rí-in túg 3-kam-ús
13. (BLANK)
14. é-šu-šúm-ma
15. iti m[unu$_4$]-kú

ii. 16. 1 gú 48½ ma-na 1 gín síg túg lugal
17. 3 gú 23⅔ ma-na 8 gín síg túg-ús lugal
18. 4 gú 9⅚ ma-na 5 gín túg 3-kam-ús
19. 16 ma-na túg 4-kam-ús
20. (BLANK)
21. é-kišib-ba-ta
22. 191½ géme
23. šà kurum$_7$-ma
24. iti munu$_4$-kú-ta
25. iti še-íl-la-šè
26. iti-bi iti 8-àm
27. á-bi 45960 géme u$_4$ 1-šè
28. 8 géme lá-u$_x$ su-ga
29. iti ezen ^{d}Ba-ú-ta
30. iti še-íl-la-šè
31. iti-bi iti 5-àm
32. á-bi 1200 géme u$_4$ 1-šè
33. ⅔ ma-na 5 gín ŠID á 6-gín
34. á-bi 270 géme u$_4$ 1-šè
35. ku$_4$-ra ugula uru-bi 13½ u$_4$
36. ki Gu-za-ni-ta
37. 5⅔ ma-na 5 gín síg za-rí-<in> túg-ús lugal
38. ki Nì-ĝá-ni-ta
39. (BLANK)

iii. 40. (BLANK)
41. šu+níĝin 1 gú 51 ma-na 4⅔ gín síg ^{ĝeš}ga-ríg-ak túg lugal
42. šu+níĝin 1 gú 53⅓ ma-na 9 gín síg ^{ĝeš}ga-ríg-ak túg-ús lugal
43. šu+níĝin 2 gú 33⅓ ma-na 7½ gín síg ^{ĝeš}ga-ríg-ak túg 3-kam-ús
44. šu+níĝin 16 ma-na 2½ gín síg ^{ĝeš}ga-ríg-ak túg 4-kam-ús
45. šu+níĝin 34⅓ ma-na 2½ gín 18 še síg gú-tar túg lugal
46. šu+níĝin 21⅚ ma-na 7⅔ gín 24 še síg gú-tar túg-ús lugal
47. šu+níĝin 37½ ma-na 9½ gín síg gú-tar túg 3-kam-ús
48. šu+níĝin 1½ ma-na 6 gín síg gú-tar túg 4-kam-ús
49. šu+níĝin 6 gú 33⅓ ma-na 9⅓ gín 6 še síg mug

iv. 50. síg izi-kú-bi 1 gú 28 ma-na 17½ gín 2[+] še
51. šu+níĝin 1 gú 8 ma-na 5 gín síg túg lugal
52. šu+níĝin 31⅚ ma-na 5 gín túg-ús
53. šu+níĝin 31⅓ ma-na síg za-rí-in túg 3-kam-ús
54. šu+níĝin 56363⅔ 5½ gín géme u$_4$ 1-šè
55. (BLANK)
56. šu+níĝin 18 gú 32½ ma-na igi-4-ĝál 8 še nì ki-lá-a
57. saĝ nì-ĝar-ra
58. šà-bi-ta
59. 2 ^{túg}nì-lám lugal
60. 20 túg guz-za lugal
61. ki-lá-bi 1 gú 14½ ma-na 7 gín
62. 3 ^{túg}nì-lám-ús lugal
63. 7 túg guz-za gíd-a-ús lugal
64. 10 ^{túg}bar-si 3-ka[m]-ú[s]
65. 22 ^{túg}bar-[si 4-kam-ús]
66. ki-lá-bi 34[+ ma-na˺ 15[+ gín]
67. 30 ^{túg}nì-lám [3 kam]-ús
68. 5 túg guz-za 3-kam-ús

v. 69. ki-lá-bi 1 g[ú] ma-na 7 gín
70. 20 lá 1 ^{túg}<nì>-lám 4-kam-ús

71. 2 túg guz-[za 4]-kam-ús
72. 1 túg [ ]
73. 1 ^{túg}n[ì-lám]
74. 5 túg saĝ [ ]
75. ki-<lá>-bi 1 [gú] ma-na lá [ ]
76. 5 túg nì-[lám] [x]
77. ki-lá-bi 7 [ ]
78. 12 túg nì-[lám] túg [ ]
*79. ki-lá-bi 20 m[a-na]
80. 3 túg nì-lá[m] 3-kam-[ús]
81. (BLANK)
82. 1 túg gú-[x] 3-kam-ú[s]
83. ki-lá-bi 9⅔ [ma]-na 8 gín
84. á-bi 16[843] géme u$_4$-[1-šè]
85. [ ]
86. [ ] tag-ga
87. [ ] ma-na síg mug
88. (BLANK)
89. kìšib énsi

vi. 90. 6 ma-na 12 gín [x] DU.x.ĜAR
(several lines broken)
91. [ ] 17 [géme u$_4$] 1-šè
92. [gém]e u$_4$ 1-šè
93. [ ]SI-ka
94. [ma]-na gu túg lugal
95. á-bi 30
96. 4 ma-na 5 gín gú-tar 4-kam-ús
97. kìšib A-ba-ni-sì-gi
98. ⅚ ma-na síg za-rí-in túg lugal
99. *(erasure)* na ŠID túg 3-ka[m-ús]
100. á-bi *(erasure)*
101. kìšib Lú-du$_{10}$-ga [ ]
102. ⅓ ma-na síg ^{ĝeš}<ga>-ríg-[ak] túg lug[al]
103. 8 gín gu túg lu[gal]
104. á-bi 34
*105. [5] ma-na 5 gín síg za-rí-in túg l[ugal]
106. [kìšib] Al-la-kam
107. *(erasure)* 10 gín [ ] géme u$_4$ 1-šè
108. [ ] RA PA.KIN á [x] da 3 a [x] -ús
109. iti amar-a-a-si u$_4$ 24 ba-zal-ta
110. 4 géme iti še-[íl-la] u$_4$ 11+ [ ]
111. iti še-í[l-la]

vii. 112. iti-bi iti 2 u$_4$-6-àm á-bi 327+
113. á g[éme]
114. 3 gé[me]
115. iti [ ]
116. á [ ]
117. 7 gé[me] síg ak [ ]
118. (BLANK)
119. 3843 u$_4$ [1-šè]
120. u$_4$ KU-a géme saĝ-nì-gur$_{11}$-ra á 5-àm ì-íb-túm
121. 30 ma-na síg túg-ús lugal
122. kìšib Ur-^{d}Šul-gi
123. 1 ma-na síg ^{ĝeš}ga-ríg-ak túg 3-kam-ús
124. kìšib Nì-ĝá-ni
125. *(several lines broken)*
126. ½ m[a-na]
127. nì-gur$_{11}$ gé[me x]
128. 36 ma-na 15 gín síg ^{ĝeš}ga-ríg-ak túg 3-kam-ús
129. 50⅚ ma-na 4 gín síg ^{ĝeš}ga-ríg-ak túg 4-kam-ús

viii. 130. 7 ma-na 8 gín síg gú-tar túg lugal
131. 5⅓ ma-na 3 gín síg gú-tar túg-ús lugal
132. 13⅓ ma-na 5 gín síg gú-tar 3-kam-ús
133. 3 ma-na 16 gín síg gú-tar túg 4-kam-ús
134. 2 gú 10⅚ ma-na síg mug
135. 10350 géme u$_4$ 1-šè
136. á túg tag-a ŠID U.NU-a síg ^{ĝeš}ga-ríg-ak túg ĝeš-a-ĝál-la
137. ku$_4$-ra ugula uru-bi 517½ géme u$_4$ 1-šè
138. 1 gú 7 ma-na 15 gín síg túg lugal
139. 31⅓ ma-na síg túg 3-kam-ús
140. é-šu-šúm-ma
141. (BLANK)
142. [ ]2+ gú 2½ ma-na 1⅚ [g]ín síg ^{ĝeš}ga-ríg-ak túg lugal
143. šu+níĝin 34⅚ ma-na [ ] gín síg ^{ĝeš}ga-rí[g-ak] túg-ús lu[gal]
144. šu+níĝin 2 gú 8 ma-na 2 gín síg ^{ĝeš}ga-ríg-ak túg 3-kam-ús
145. šu+níĝin 2 gú 26 ma-na 1 gín síg ^{ĝeš}ga-ríg-ak túg 4-kam-ús

ix. 146. šu+níĝin 16 ma-na 7 gín síg gú-tar túg lugal
147. šu+níĝin 25 ma-na ⅓ gín síg gú-tar túg-ús lugal
148. [šu+níĝin] 23 ma-na 3 gín [síg gú]-tar túg 3-kam-ús
149. šu+níĝin 7⅓ ma-na 1 gín síg gú-tar túg 4-kam-ús
150. šu+níĝin 5 gú 50⅚ ma-na síg mug
151. izi-kú-bi 1 gú 35 ma-na 2 gín 20 še

152. šu+níĝin 1 gú 8 ma-na 5 gín síg za-rí-in túg lugal
153. šu+níĝin 31 ma-na 5 gín túg-ús
154. šu+níĝin 31⅓ ma-na síg za-[r]í-in túg 3-kam-ús
155. 16125⅔+ géme u_4 1-šè
156. (BLANK)
157. šu+níĝin 8 gú 1 ⌜ma⌝-na 19⅚ gín [níĝ] ki-lá-a
158. zi-ga-àm
159. lá-u_x 1 gú 18 [ma-n]a 5 gín síg ^{ĝeš}g[a-ríg-ak] túg-ús lugal
160. diri 11⅓ ma-na 6 gín igi-6-ĝál síg ^{ĝeš}ga-ríg-ak túg lugal
161. 25⅓ ma-na 4½ gín síg ^{ĝeš}ga-ríg-ak túg 3-kam-ús
162. diri 2 gú 20 ma-na 8 gín síg ^{ĝeš}ga-ríg-ak túg 4-kam-ús
163. 18 ma-na 15 gín 18 še ĝeš-tag túg lugal
164. diri 3 ma-na 12 gín igi-6-ĝál 6 še síg gú-tar túg-ús lugal

x. *165. šu+níĝin 4⅓ ma-na 6½ gín síg gú-tar 3-kam-ús
166. [x]
167. *(several lines broken)*
168. (BLANK)
169. nì-ka_9-ak
170. ugula Lú-^{d}Nanna
171. nu-bànda *A-ḫu-um*-diĝir
172. iti $munu_4$-kú-ta
173. iti še-íl-la-šè
174. iti-bi 8-àm
175. (BLANK)
176. mu ^{d}Amar-^{d}Suen lugal

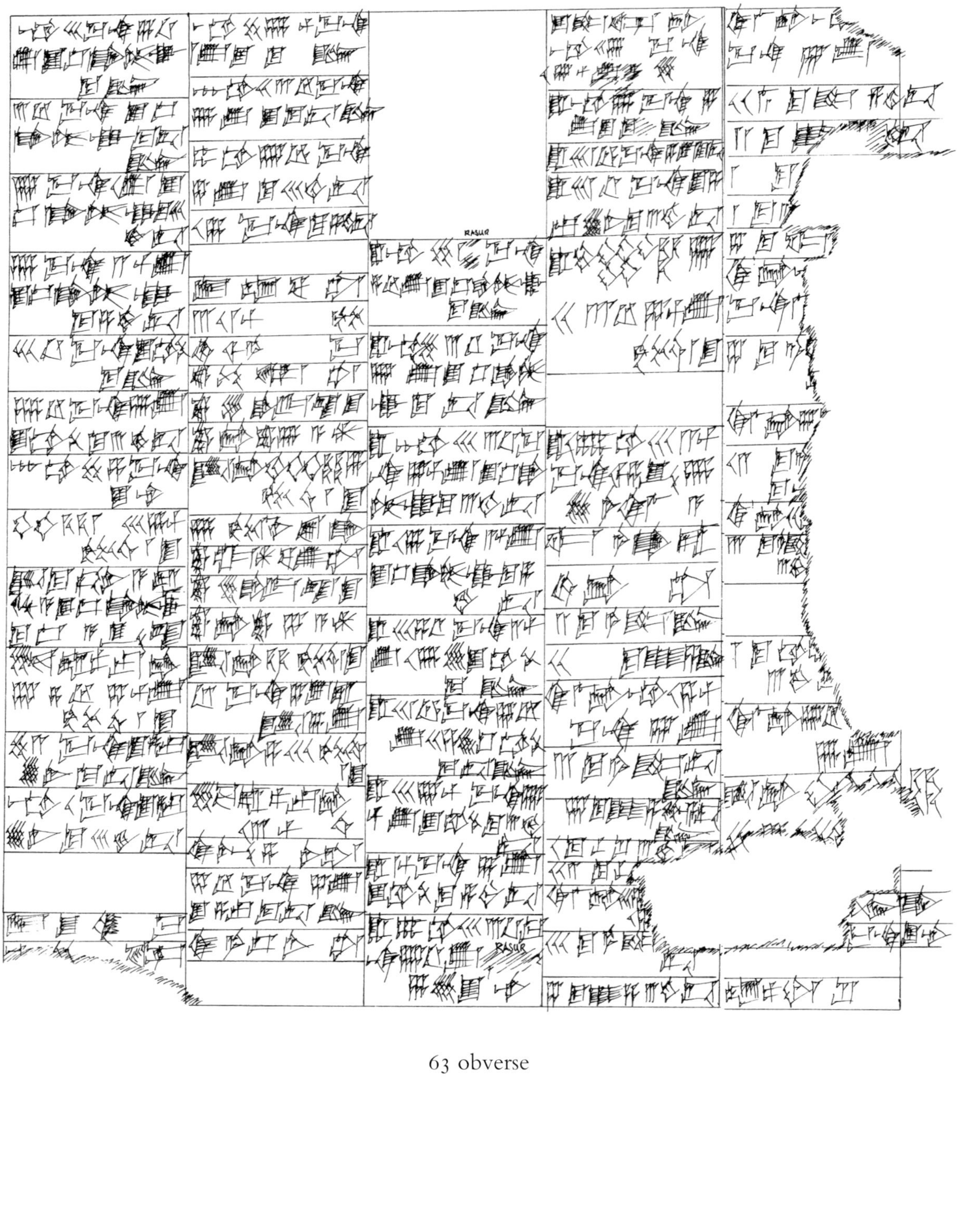

63 obverse

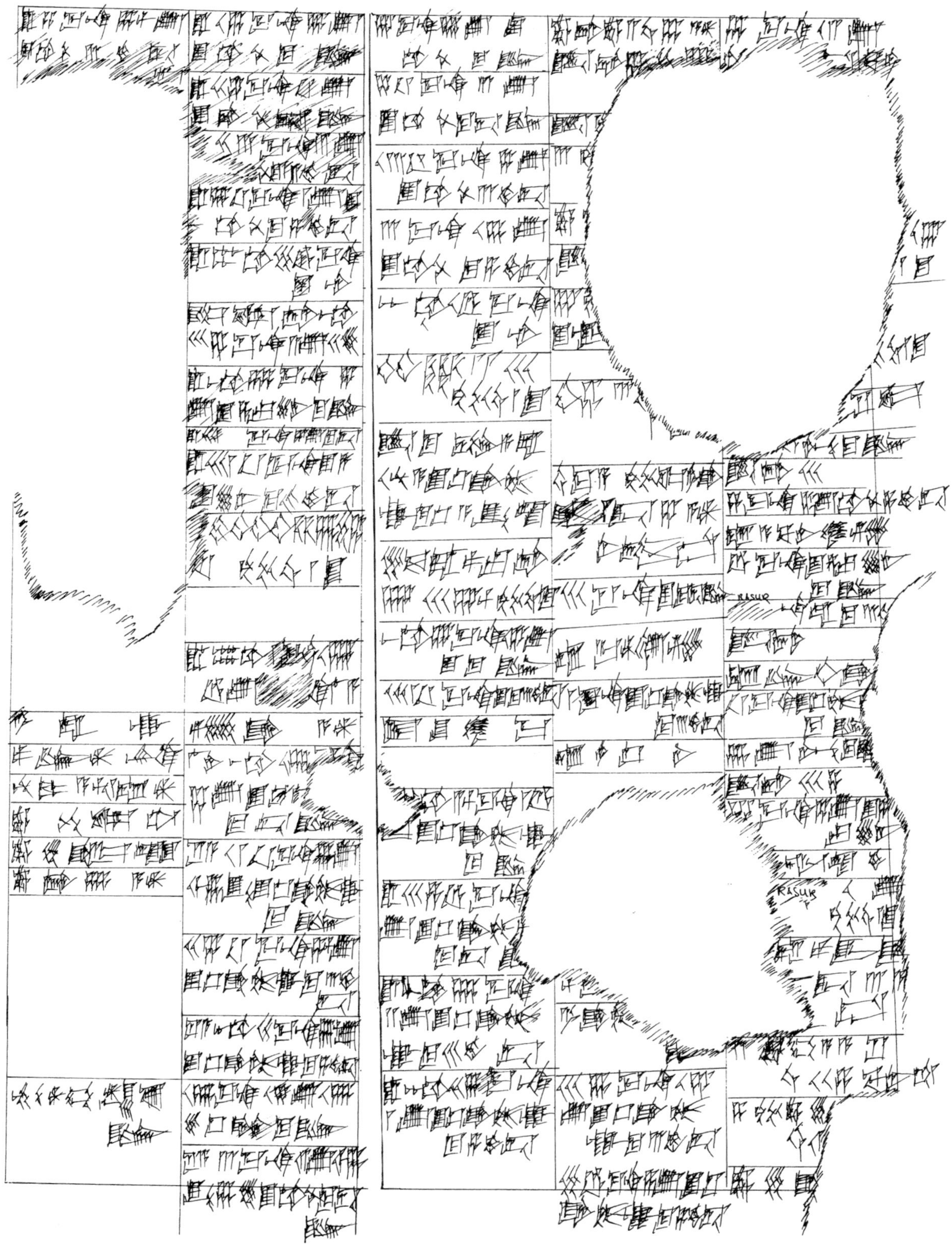

63 reverse

64

(-/-/AS 1)

i. 1. 16.2.0 zì-sig$_{15}$ gur lugal
2. má Šà-ba-na-ĝar
3. 40.0.0 dabin gur
4. má Lú-bala-ša$_{6}$-ga
5. 1.2.2 zì-sig$_{15}$ gur
6. 0.3.2 zì-gu
7. má Lú-^{d}Nin-šubur
8. 0.3.1 8 sìla dabin
9. má Lú-^{d}Nin-ĝír-su
10. ki Ur-é-ninnu dumu Du-du-ta
11. 15.1.1 zì-sig$_{15}$ gur
12. má Šà-ba-na-ĝar
13. ki Nam-zi-tar-ra-ta
14. 13.0.1 zì-sig$_{15}$ gur
15. má Šà-ba-na-ĝar
16. 27.0.0 dabin gur
17. má Lugal-ki-áĝ
18. ki Lú-^{d}Na-rú-a-ta
19. 14.1.2 zì-sig$_{15}$ gur
20. má Šà-ba-na-ĝar
21. [1+].0.0 dabin gur
22. [má Lu]gal-ki-áĝ
23. [x.x].2 zì-sig$_{15}$ gur
24. [x].2.0 1 sìla zì-gu

ii. 25. má Lú-^{d}Nin-[ ]
26. ki Lú-kal-la-ta
27. 1.1.1 ^{zì}ba-ba sig$_{5}$ gur
28. 1.2.5 zì a-saĝ gur
29. 11.4.3 zì-sig$_{15}$ gur
30. 0.4.0 eša
31. 0.1.5 zì-gu sig$_{5}$
32. 1.3.0 zì-gu-ús gur
33. 0.4.2 2 sìla dabin
34. 0.3.0 ^{zì}ba-ba še
35. ĝìr Ir$_{11}$-^{d}Ba-ú
36. ki Lú-^{d}Nin-ĝír-su dumu Ba-zi-ta
37. 1.1.1 ^{zì}ba-ba sig$_{5}$ gur 0.4.0 eša 0.1.5 zì-gu sig$_{5}$ 0.3.0 ^{zì}ba-ba-še 76.2.4 zì-sig$_{15}$ gur 84.0.5 5 sìla dabin
38. má u$_{4}$-zal-la
39. Ĝír-su^{ki}-ta
40. 1.3.5 2 sìla ^{zì}ba-ba sig$_{5}$
41. 0.1.0 6 sìla zì-gú-še
42. 29.2.4 1½ sìla zì-sig$_{15}$ gur
43. 1.0.2 zì-gu sig$_{5}$ lugal gur
44. 0.0.2 2 sìla eša

iii. 45. [ ]
*46. 0.1.0 3 [sìla gur]
47. 41.4.1 [ ]
48. kìšib Ur-ni$_{9}$-[ĝar]
*49. ki Ur-^{d}Ig-a[lima-ta] zì á [ ]
50. 1.1.0 še ku$_{6}$ x [ ]
51. ĝìr Ur-^{d}En-[ ]
52. 2.0.4 šà-gal lú-[kaš$_{4}$]
53. ĝìr Lú-Nina^{ki}
*54. 0.3.0 še ku$_{6}$ [ ]
55. ĝìr dam-gàr
56. 3.3.0 6 sìla gur
57. šà-gal gu$_{4}$-udu
58. ĝìr Lú-kal-la
59. ki Ur-^{d}En-líl-lá-ta
60. 0.1.2 ninda-ár-ra sig$_{5}$
61. ki lú-lunga-é-gibil-ta
62. (BLANK)
*63. šu+níĝin 3.0.0 2 sìla ^{zì}ba-ba sig$_{5}$
64. šu+níĝin 106.0.2 6 [sìla] zì-sig$_{15}$ gur
65. šu+níĝin 0.4.2 2 sìla e[ša]
66. šu+níĝin 1.2.1 zì [ ]
67. šu+níĝin 0.3.0 x [ ]

iv. *68. šu+níĝin 0.2.0 [ ] ninda-ár-[ ]
*69. šu+níĝin 130+.[x.x]
*70. šu+níĝin 6.2.4 5 [sìla]
*71. še-bi 420.3[.x] sìla g[ur]
*72. (BLANK)
*73. šà-bi-ta
*74. 3.0.2 3 sìla še-ba-ba sig$_{5}$ gur
*75. 91.4.5 3⅓ <sìla> gur
*76. 14.0.2 3 sìla zì-sig$_{15}$ gur
*77. 66.0.5 2 sìla dabin gur
*78. ninda sig$_{5}$
*79. 0.0.2 2 sìla zì-gu-nida
*80. 0.2.0 zì-sig$_{15}$ šuku-ì-da-a
*81. 0.4.0 zì-sig$_{15}$ šuku-kìšib-du$_{\star 8}$-ḫu-um
*82. 0.4.2 5 sìla šuku-mar-sa-ŠUM ^{zì}ba-ba-šè
*83. 0.1.0 zì-sig$_{15}$ [šuku] ĝeš-dù
*84. 1.0.1 zì-gu si[g$_{5}$]
*85. 3.4.0 ninda zì-g[u]
*86. 0.0.2 zì [ ]
*87. 7.0.3 1 sìla z[ì]
*88. 0.1.0 7 sìla [ ]
*89. 2 sìla [ ]

*90. 0.3.3 5 [sìla]
*91. [ ]
v. 92. 3.3.0 6 sìla gur
93. šà-gal gu$_{4}$-udu
*94. 0.2.0 šà-gal šidim
*95. še-bi 302.3.3 1½ sìla gur
*96. kaš-dé-a lugal
*97. 1.1.2 ⅔ sìla zì-sig$_{15}$ gur
*98. 1.2.0 ⅚ sìla dabin gur
*99. še-bi 3.3.4 6 sìla 10 gín gur
*100. igi-1-ĝál zì uru-ta-ḫi-DU-a
*101. (B L A N K)
*102. zi-ga
*103. 44.3.3 dabin gur
*104. úgu Ur-ninnu ĝál-la
*105. dub-sar zì-da ba-a-ĝar
*106. (B L A N K)
*107. šu+níĝin 352.1.4 7⅔ sìla gur
*108. zi-ga
*109. lá-u$_{x}$ 7.1.4 8⅓ sìla gur
vi. 110. (B L A N K)
111. nì-ka$_{9}$-ak
*112. zì kaš-dé-a lugal
113. Šeš-kal-la dumu Lú-du$_{10}$-ga
*114. ù Ur-ni$_{9}$-ĝar dumu Lú-^{d}Nanše
115. mu ^{d}Amar-^{d}Suen lugal

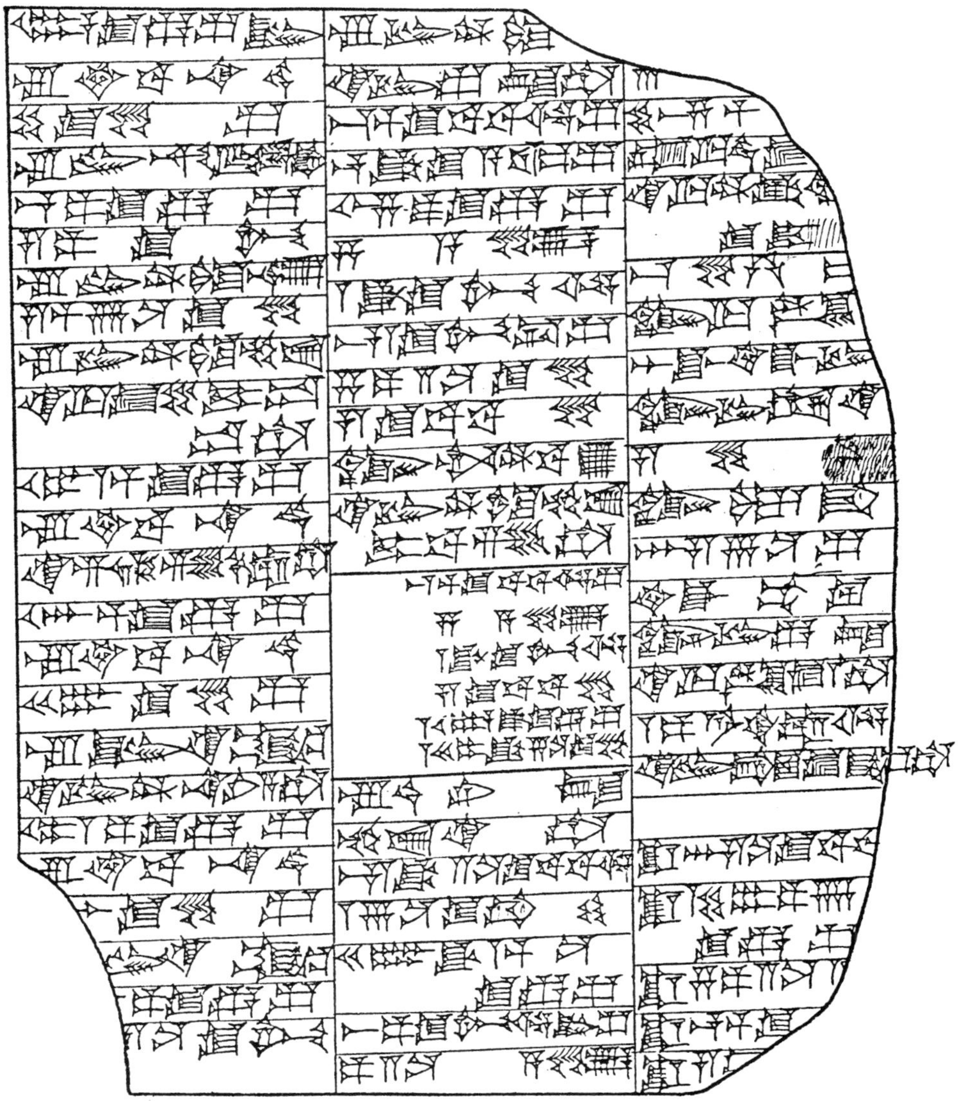

64 obverse

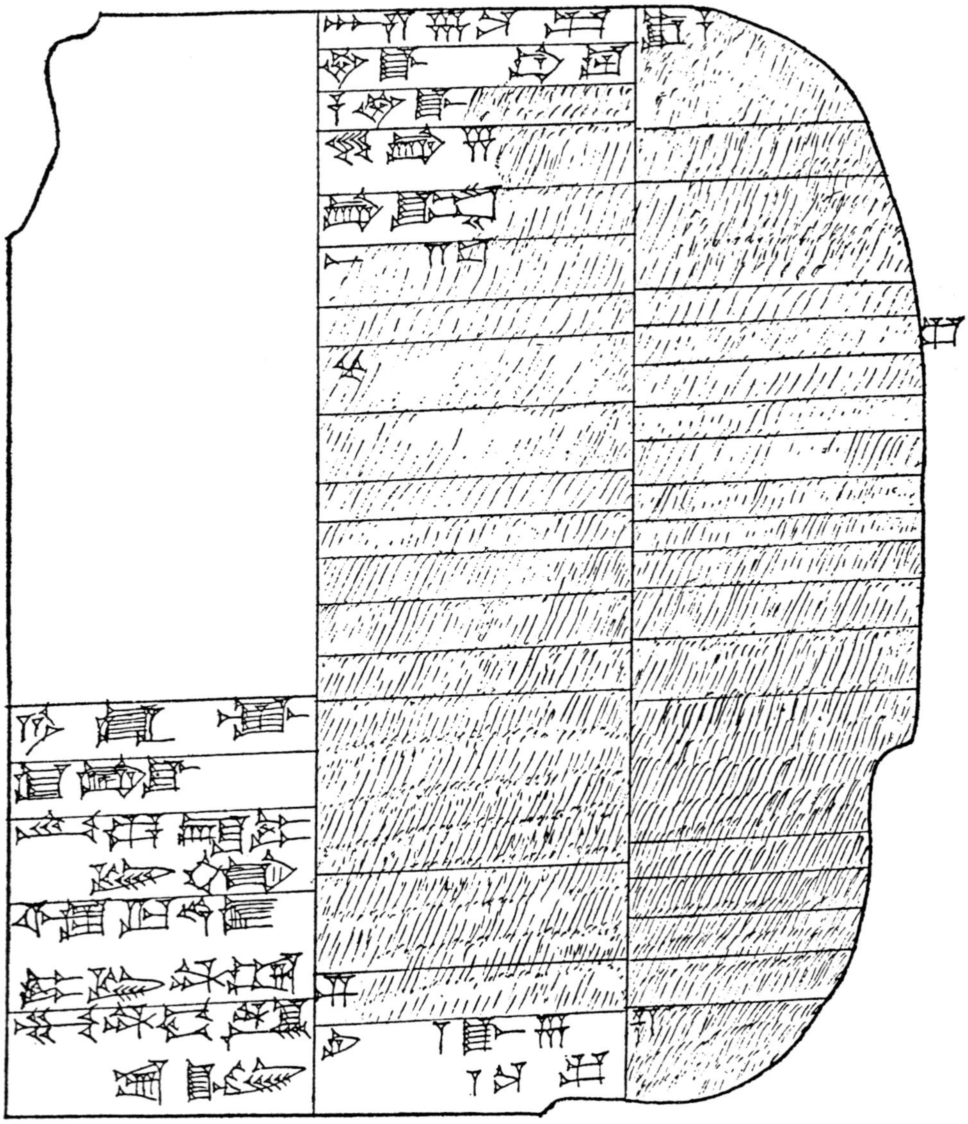

64 reverse

65

(IV/-/AS 2)

OBV.

1. 0.3.4 5 sìla še lugal
2. si-ì-tum nì-ka$_9$-ak
3. 14.0.0 gur Nin-á-zi-da-ta
4. 11.0.0 gur É-a-en-na-ta
5. 12.3.5 2½ sìla gur

*6. Nin-KWU543-ta

7. 17.0.0 gur še ^{d}En-líl-lá
8. 0.3.0 še máš-da-ru-a

*9. 0.3.0 Ur-mes-ta

10. (B L A N K)
11. šu+níĝin 56.3.3 7½ sìla lugal
12. šà-bi-ta
13. [ ] sìla kaš sig$_5$ gur
14. [ ] kaš ĝen gur

(*bottom of obverse broken*)

REV.

(*top of reverse broken*)

15. [ ] kišib Ur-^{ĝeš}gigir
16. 16 sìla ba-ba-munu$_4$

*17. 1 dida sig$_5$ kaš sig$_5$ á iti-da

*18. 7.0.0 zì gur kišib Inim-^{d}Inanna úgu ĝál

*19. 0.3.3 še-ba u$_4$ 1-kam iti še-kin-ku$_5$-ta

20. iti šu-numun-šè še-bi 4.1.0 gur
21. iti 6-kam
22. (B L A N K)
23. šu+níĝin 11.2.3 6 sìla kaš sig$_5$ gur
24. še bala-bi 5.3.4 8 sìla gur

*25. šu+níĝin 28.0.0 2 sìla kaš ĝen gur
šu+níĝin 9.1.0 še gur

26. šu+níĝin 0.0.1 6 sìla ba-ba-munu$_4$
27. še bala-bi 0.0.1 6 sìla gur
28. še-bi 54.2.5 8 sìla gur
29. zi-ga
30. lá-u$_x$ 2.0.3 lá 1 sìla gur
31. nì-ka$_9$-ak Bí-du$_{11}$-ì-ša$_6$
32. mu ^{d}Amar-^{d}Suen lugal-e Ur-bí-lum^{ki} ba-ḫul

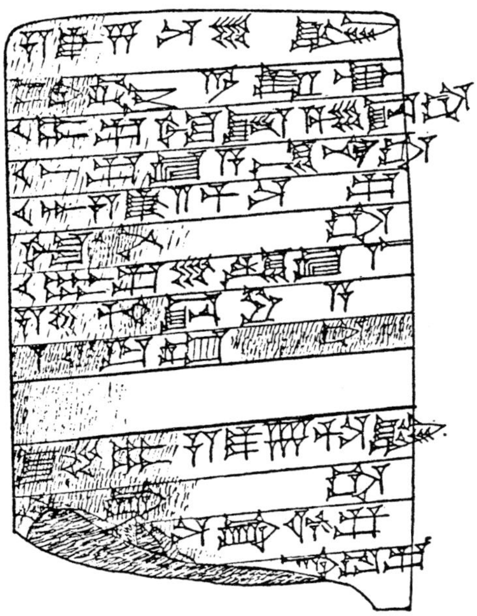

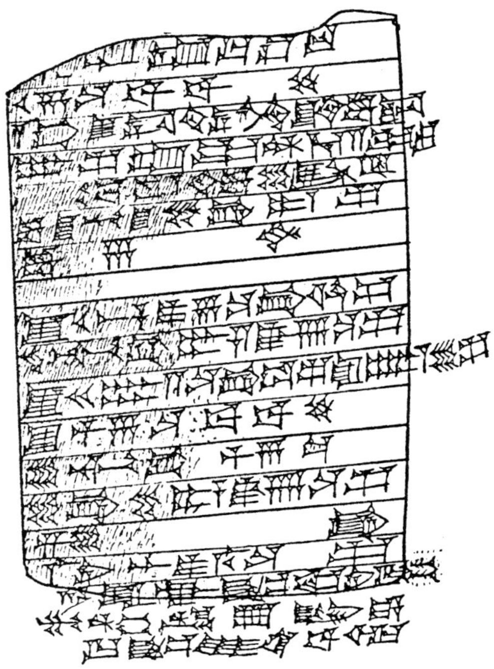

66

(-/-/AS 2)

OBV.

1. 480.0.0 [ ]
*2. kìšib Na-ba-[ša$_6$]
3. ki Ur-^{d}[ ]
*4. 575.0.0 [ ]
5. kìšib Ur-^{d}Ba-[ú]
6. ki Ur-^{d}Nanše-ta
7. 170.0.0 gur
*8. kìšib Na-ba-ša$_6$
9. ki Ur-^{d}Dumu-zi-ta
10. (BLANK)
11. šu+níĝin 1225 gur
12. šà-bi-ta
13. 1077.4.1 3½ [sìla] gur

REV.

14. na-kab-tum-ma ba-an-ku$_4$
15. Za-lí-a šu ba-ti
16. 21.2.2 5 sìla gur
17. úgu Ur-^{d}En-líl ba-a-ĝar
18. (BLANK)
19. šu+níĝin 1099.1.3 8½ sìla gur
20. mu-túm
*21. lá-u$_x$ 125.3.2 1½ sìla gur
22. (BLANK)
23. nì-ka$_9$-ak še má-a si-ga
*24. Na-⌜ba⌝-[ša$_6$] dub-sar mar-sa
25. ù Ur-^{d}Ba-ú dumu Lú-^{d}Nin-ĝír-su
26. mu ^{d}Amar-^{d}Suen lugal Ur-bí-[lum^{ki} ba-ḫul]

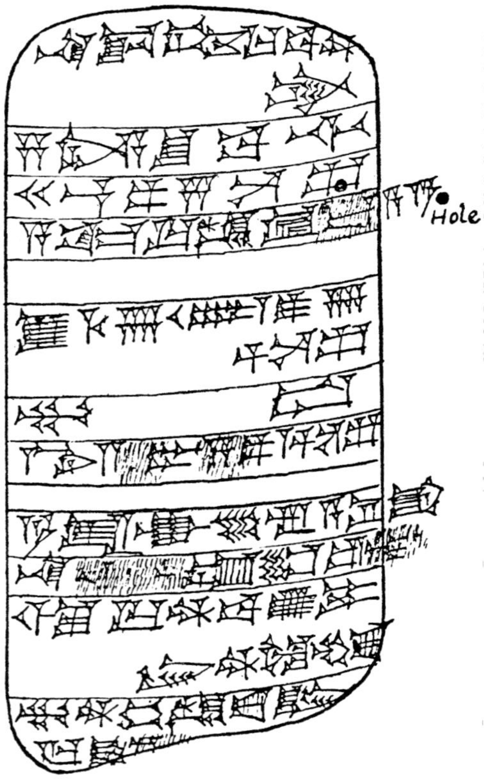

67 (XII/-/AS 4)

i. 1. 71 u$_8$
★2. [ ] 3 udu-níta
3. 4 sila$_4$
4. ki Gù-dé-a dumu Un-ĝa$_6$-ta
5. 18 udu-niga
6. ki Si-dù kurušda-ta
7. nì-ka$_9$-ta
★8. 70 lá 1 udu-máš
9. ki Ur-^{d}Lama dumu Ú-du-ku-ta
★10. 67 máš
11. ĝìr Ur-^{d}Ig-alima
★12. 34 máš
13. ĝìr Ḫu-wa-wa
14. ki Ur-^{d}Ig-alima-ta
15. [ ] udu 5 máš
16. [ki U]r-ab-ba dumu Ur-li-ta
★17. [ ] udu [^{d}B]a-ú-ta
18. [ ] 21 udu gukkal
19. [ ] NE
★20. [ki Gù-d]é-a-ta
21. [ ] ta
ii. 22. 482+[ ] u$_8$
23. 369 udu-níta
24. (BLANK)
25. šu+níĝin 905 udu-máš
26. šà-bi-ta
27. 30 udu sá-du$_{11}$
28. 1 udu nì-šà-te
29. 6 udu 2 máš
30. daḫ-ḫu lugal
31. èš-èš u$_4$-sakar u$_4$-15
32. iti 1-kam
33. iti še-kin-ku$_5$
34. mu gu-za ^{d}En-líl-lá ba-dím-ta
35. iti še-íl-la
36. mu en-maḫ-gal-an-na en ^{d}Nanna
ba-ḫun-šè
37. udu-bi 555
38. máš-bi 30
39. iti 15-kam
★40. iti diri 1-àm šà-ba ì-ĝál
iii. 41. 34 [udu]
42. 8 máš
43. iti še-kin-ku$_5$
44. ù iti še-íl-la
45. mu gu-za ^{d}En-líl-lá
★46. 103 udu
47. 32 máš
48. nì-ezen-ma iti 12-kam
49. mu en-maḫ-gal-an-na en ^{d}Nanna
ba-ḫun
50. sá-du$_{11}$ nì-ezen-ma
51. iti 15-kam
52. 21 udu-máš
53. diri nì-ka$_9$-ak
54. mu gu-za ^{d}En-líl-lá ba-dím
55. (BLANK)
★56. šu+níĝin 783 udu-máš
★57. zi-ga
★58. lá-u$_x$ 63 udu-máš
59. Ab-ba-kal-la
60. èš ^{d}Nanše
61. 247 u$_8$
62. [ ]6 udu-níta
iv. ★63. 5 [ ]
★64. ki Gù-dé-a dumu Un-ĝa$_6$-ta
65. 14 udu-niga
★66. ki Si-dù kurušda-ta
★67. 112 udu gukkal-gibil
68. ki Gù-dé-a-ta
★69. sig$_4$-ka-si-ta
70. (BLANK)
71. šu+níĝin 664 udu-máš
72. šà-bi-ta
★73. 3 udu ^{d}Nin-dar-a
74. 15 udu ^{d}Dumu-zi
75. 4 udu Ur-^{d}Nin-kára
76. ù Ur-^{d}Nanše
77. im-ma-gi-na
78. 4 udu 1 máš
★79. ^{d}Nin-dar-a
80. 4 udu 1 máš
81. ^{d}Dumu-zi
82. sízkur [ ]
83. èš-èš [ ]
v. ★84. [ ] ezen-m[a] [ ]
85. [ ]
86. šu+níĝin 30 udu
87. šu+níĝin 2 máš
88. iti še-kin-ku$_5$
89. mu gu-za ^{d}En-líl-lá ba-dím-ta
90. iti še-íl-la

91. mu en-maḫ-gal-an-na en ^{d}Nanna
ba-ḫun-šè
92. udu-bi 450
93. máš-bi 30
94. iti 15-kam
★95. iti diri 1-àm šà-ba ì-ĝál
★96. 53 udu
97. 11 máš
98. iti še-kin-ku$_5$
99. ù iti še-íl-la
100. mu gu-za ^{d}En-líl-lá ba-dím
101. 6 [ ]
102. 44 [ ]
103. 30 máš
vi. 104. [ ]
105. [ ]
106. [ ] x x x x [ ]
★107. Ur-^{d}Nin-[kára]
108. ù Ur-^{d}Nanše
109. nì-ezen-ma iti 12-kam
110. (BLANK)
111. šu+níĝin 664 udu-máš
112. zi-ga
113. Lú-^{d}Igi-ma-šè kurušda ^{d}Dumu-zi
114. (BLANK)
115. nì-ka$_9$-ak ka-lá-a
116. Ab-ba-kal-la
★117. ù Lú-^{d}Igi-ma-áš
★118. iti še-kin-ku$_5$
119. mu gu-za ^{d}En-líl-lá ba-dím-ta
120. iti še-íl-la
121. mu en-maḫ-gal-[an-na en] ^{d}Nanna
ba-ḫun-šè
122. [iti] 15-kam

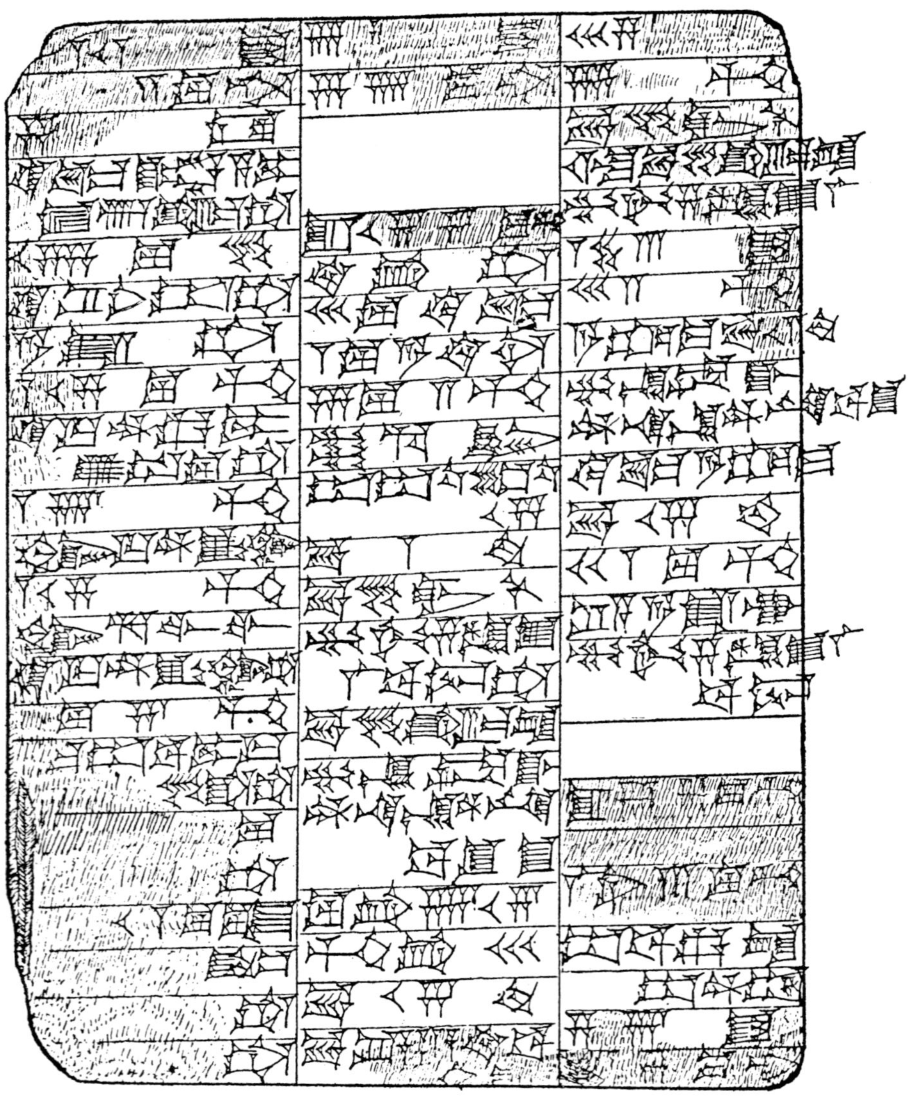

67 obverse

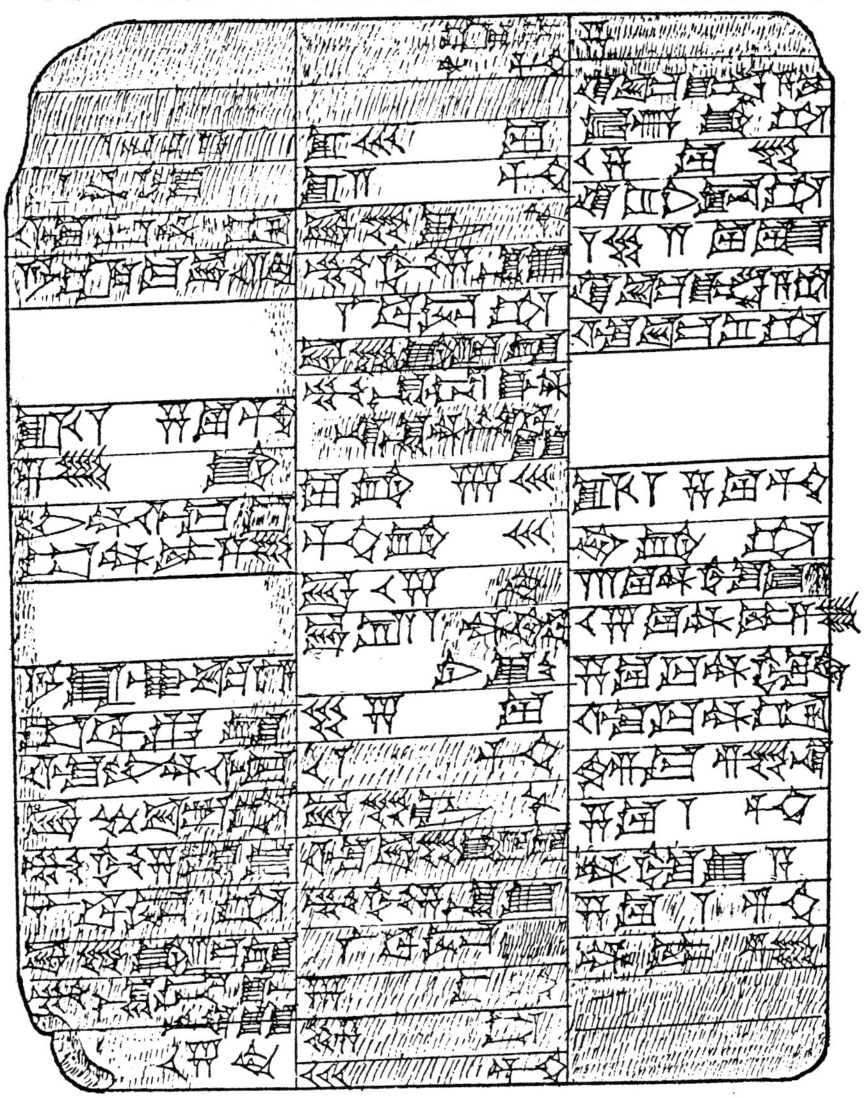

67 reverse

68

(IV/-/-)

OBV.

1. 1.0.0 x x munu$_4$ gur
2. 40.0.0 numun lugal gur
*3. 150.0.0 2 sìla kaš sig$_5$ gur
4. 6.0.0 ninda gur
*5. 40.0.0 [x] x gur
6. 157.3[.x] kaš ĝen
7. 65.3.2 [ ] še gur
8. šu+níĝin še-bi 340[+] še gur
9. ki Lugal-me-lám-ta
10. Ur-mes šu ba-ti
11. šà-bi-ta
12. 120.3.1 ⌜x sìla⌝ munu$_4$
*13. 102.1.2 1 sìla [ ] gur
14. še bala-bi 57.0.5 5½ sìla

(bottom of obverse broken)

REV.

(top of reverse broken)

15. [ ] ⌜16+.1.1 3 sìla x⌝
16. ki Lú-me-lám-ta
17. (BLANK)
18. úgu Ur-mes ĝá-ĝá-dam
19. (BLANK)
20. nì-ka$_9$-ak ka-lá
21. Ur-mes ù Lú-me-lám
22. (BLANK)
23. iti ezen ^{d}Li$_9$-si$_4$
24. iti šu-numun

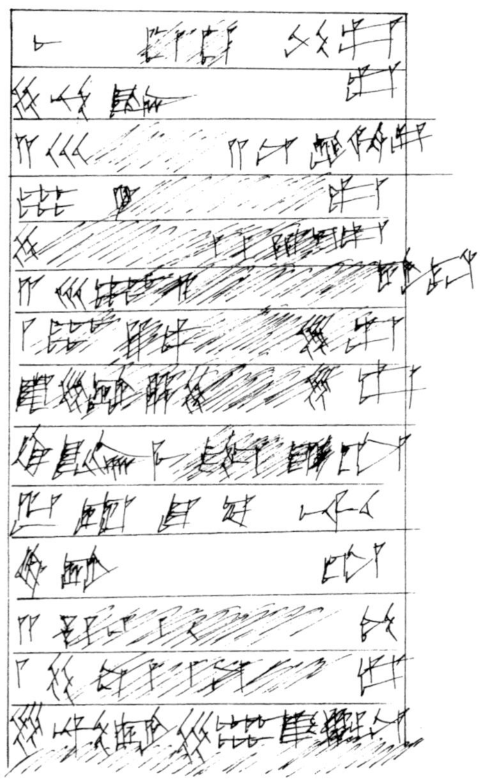

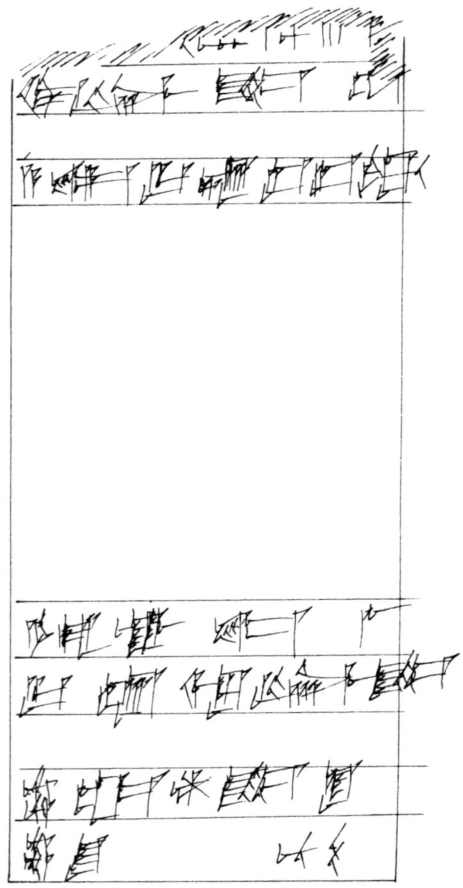

69 (date not preserved)

OBV.

1. [ ] 108+.0.3 5½ sìla še gur lugal
2. (B L A N K)
3. [sa]ĝ-nì-gur$_{11}$-ra-kam
4. šà-bi-ta
5. 144.0.0 kìšib Ur-^{d}Šul-pa-è
6. 60.1.2 kìšib šabra
7. 96.0.3 še-ba un-ĝa$_{6}$ ù á-lú-ḫun-ĝá a-šà
8. ĝìr Lú-gu-la nì-ka$_{9}$-bi ba-ak
9. 20.2.3 še šà-gu$_{4}$ nu-dab$_{5}$-me
10. 0.1.0 Úr-ra-ni
11. [ ] Da-a-mu
12. [ ]15+.0.0 Lú-uru-ki-ĝar-ra
13. [ ] bi ba [ ]

REV.

(*top half of reverse destroyed*)

14. [ ]
15. [ ] x
16. [ ] NIR
17. [ ] RA
18. [ ] NI RU
19. [ ] gur
20. [ ] DU
21. [ ] 328.1.1 5 sìla gur

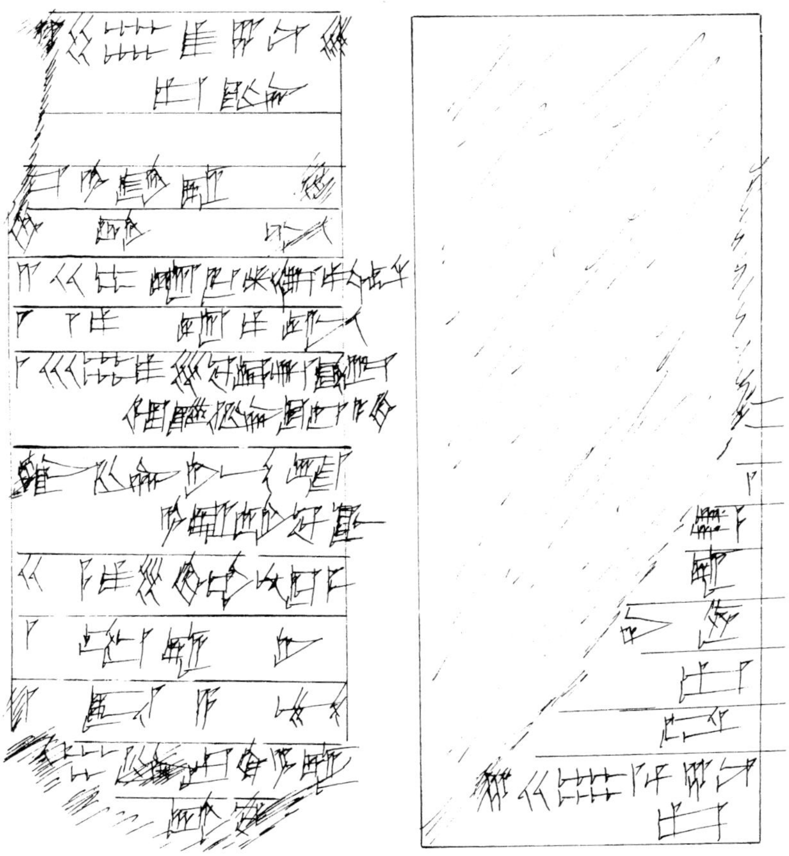

70

(-/-/Š 36)

OBV.

1. 25798 ⸢udu⸣
2. 21942 udu-níta
*3. 8767 kir$_{11}$
4. 9016 sila$_{4}$-níta
*5. 632 máš-saĝ
6. (BLANK)
7. šu+níĝin 66155
*8. udu-ḫi-a
9. gub-ba-àm
*10. 10 gú 56½ ma-na 10 lá 1 gín síg-ḫi-a túg-lugal
*11. [ ] gú 1½ ma-na 5 gín [síg-ḫi-a t]úg-ús-lugal
*12. [ ] 23 ma-na [ ] gín [ ]

(*bottom of obverse broken*)

REV.

(*top of reverse broken*)

13. [ ]-àm
14. 2770 u$_{8}$
15. 782 udu-níta
16. 60 sila$_{4}$
17. šu+níĝin 3612 udu-ḫi-a
*18. udu *ru-ub-ba-àm*
19. 2278 u$_{8}$
20. 1056 udu-níta
*21. 26 sila$_{4}$ 7 máš
22. šu+níĝin 3367 udu-ḫi-a
23. lá-u$_{x}$-àm
24. (BLANK)
25. udu gukkal niĝin-ba Ĝír-su^{ki}
26. mu ^{d}Šul-gi
27. nita kalag-ga
28. lugal Uri^{ki}-ma
29. lugal an-ub-da limmu-ba-ke$_{4}$
30. ^{d}Nanna Kar-zi-da é-a-ni ku$_{4}$

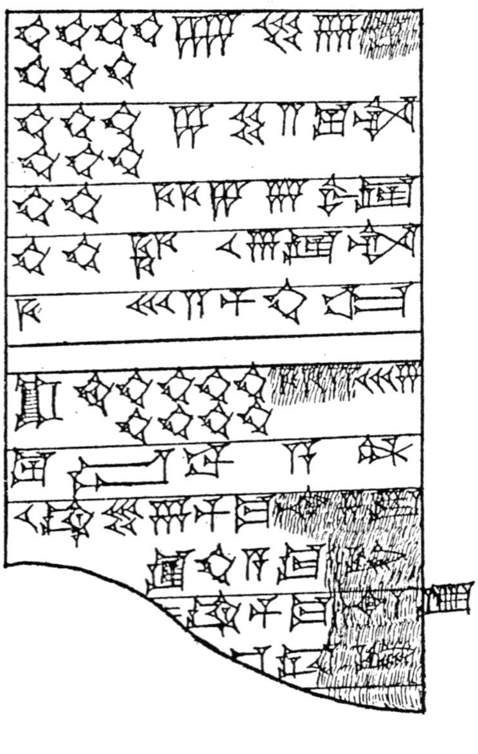

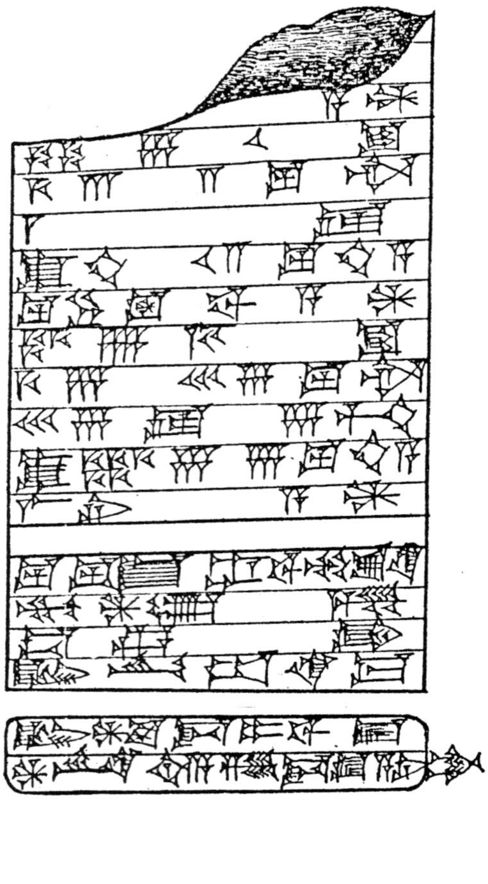

71

(-/-/Š 39)

OBV.

1. 25 gu[b-ba]
2. Da-da dumu AB-[ ]
3. 35 [gub-ba]
4. 3 zi-ga
5. 11 lá-u$_x$
6. Im-ta-diĝir
7. 65 gub-ba
8. 14 zi-ga
9. 30 lá-u$_x$
10. Ḫar-ra-ni-⸢ì⸣-ša$_6$
11. 11 gub-ba
12. ^{d}Nin-mar-ki-[ ]

(bottom of obverse destroyed)

rev.

(top of reverse destroyed)

13. [l]ú-kaš$_4$ [ ]
14. [z]i-g[a]
15. (B L A N K)
16. mu *Puzur$_4$-i*[*š*-^{d}*Da-gan*] é ^{d}Š[ul-gi] ba-dù

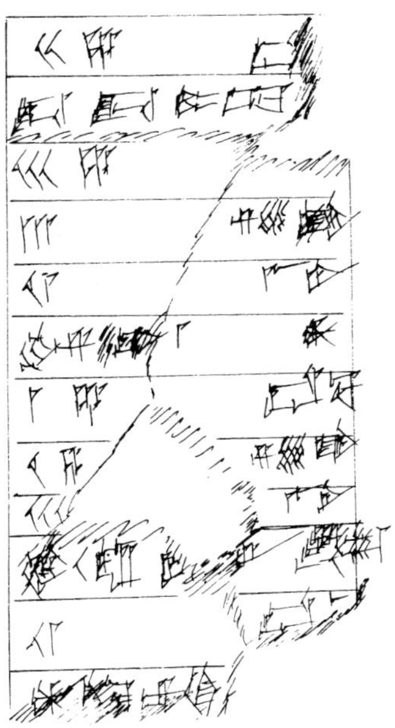

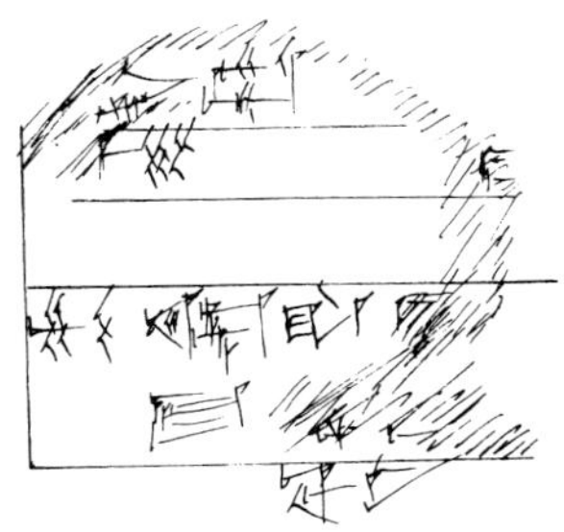

72

(-/-/Š 47)

OBV.

1. 53 [u$_8$]
2. 10 lá 1 udu [ ]
*3. 14 ki[r$_{11}$]
4. 12 sila$_4$-níta
*5. 2 máš s[aĝ]
*6. 1 sila$_4$-níta diri
7. (BLANK)
*8. mu-túm
9. 2 u$_8$-udu-[gukkal]
10. zi-ga
*11. 15 u$_8$ 10 lá 1 udu-níta
*12. sila$_4$

REV.

13. ri-ri-ga
14. u$_8$ udu
15. sila$_4$
16. lá-u$_x$-àm
17. (BLANK)
18. šu+níĝin 91 gub-ba
19. šu+níĝin 2 zi-ga
20. šu+níĝin 24 ri-ri
21. šu+níĝin lá-u$_x$
22. Nam-ḫa-ni na-gada
*23. ugula *Šar-[ru-um]-ì-[lí]*
24. [šà] Gú-ab-ba[ki]
25. [m]u-ús-sa Ki-m[aš[ki] ba-ḫul]

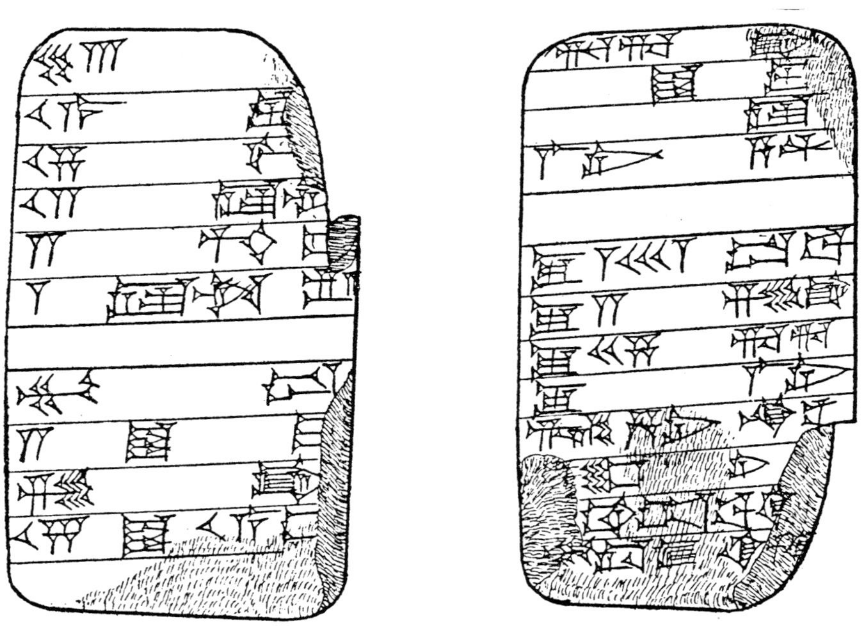

73

(-/4/Š 48)

i.
1. 13 u_8 20 udu-níta
2. 5 $sila_4$-ba-ur_4
3. libir-àm
4. 10 $sila_4$-ba-ur_4
5. lá-u_x su-ga
6. síg-bi
★7. ^{d}Utu-kam nagar 50 lá 2
★8. 62 u_8 5 udu-gal
9. 32 udu-níta
10. 1 udu bar-su
11. 10 lá 1 $sila_4$-ba-ur_4
12. síg-bi
13. Lugal-ab-ba 110 lá 1
14. 95 u_8 60 udu-gal
15. 126 udu-níta
16. 75 $sila_4$-ba-ur_4
17. libir-àm

ii.
18. 10 [ ]
19. 34 [ ]
20. SAĜ [ ]
21. síg-[bi]
22. Ur-[ ]
23. [ ]
24. 25 [ ]
25. 14 [ ]
26. síg-bi
27. Ir_{11}-m[u]
28. 36 [ ]
29. 27 [ ]
30. síg-bi
★31. Gú-[x]
32. 41 u_8 [ ]
33. 14 [ ]
★34. 13 $sila_4$ [ ]

iii.
35. síg-bi
★36. Ur-bára dumu Ḫu-ba 74
★37. 77 u_8 40 udu-gal
38. 160 lá 2 udu-níta
39. 60 $sila_4$-ba-ur_4
★40. Ur-^{d}Nin-sún 300[+35]
41. 26 u_8 13 udu-[gal]
42. 10 lá 1 $sila_4$-ba-ur_4
43. síg-bi
44. Ur-^{d}Ḫendur-saĝ [48]
45. 20 udu-gal 30 lá 1 sil[a_4]
46. 1 udu-níta bar-su
47. 20 $sila_4$-ba-ur_4
48. síg-bi
49. A-tu dumu Al-la 60[+10]
50. (BLANK)

iv.
51. (BLANK)
★52. šu+níĝin 1215 udu-ḫi-a
53. (BLANK)
54. udu ba-ur_4 u_4 4-kam
55. šà Gú-ab-ba^{ki}
★56. mu-ús-sa Ki-maš^{ki} ba-ḫul mu-ús-sa-a-bi

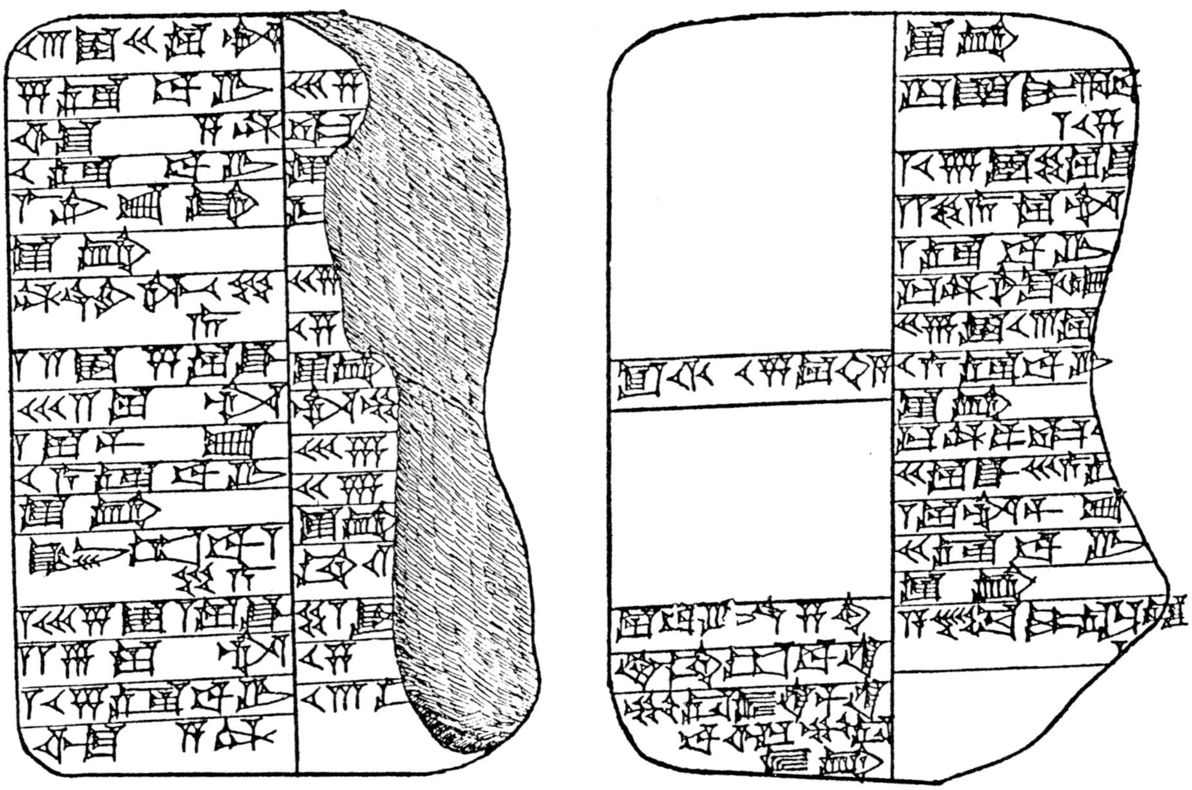

73

74

(-/4/AS 1)

i. *(top of column i destroyed)*

1. [ ] kam
2. [ ] Nina[ ] SAĜ-šè [ ] šubur
   [ ] ḪI-da bàd
3. [ ] 123+.1.0 gur
4. [ ] ^{d}Nanše
5. [^{ĝeš}ki]ri$_6$ ^{d}Nin-mar-ki gú a diri
6. 0.3.0 sig$_5$ 9.2.0
7. A-kal-la
8. ^{ĝeš}kiri$_6$ ^{d}Ištaran
9. (B L A N K)

ii.

10. (B L A N K)
11. ugula Ur-^{d}Ba-ú
12. 1.3.0 Lú-nita-gi-na lú-[x]
13. ^{ĝeš}kiri$_6$ a-ru-a Lú-^{d}Nanše
14. 0.1.0 sig$_5$ 5.1.0 gur
15. Ba-ga-zi-mu
16. ^{ĝeš}kiri$_6$ Lú-^{d}Nin-ĝír-su ša$_{13}$-dub-ba
17. 0.0.3 zù-lum DI

iii.

*18. 0.3.0 sig$_5$ 9.2.0 gur
19. Ì̀r-da-ni
20. ^{ĝeš}kiri$_6$ Ur-^{d}Nin-ĝír-su gu-la
21. (B L A N K)
22. ugula Gú-ù-mu
23. 1.0.0 sig$_5$ 56.0.0 gur
24. Lú-diĝir-ra-šè dumu Lú-du$_{10}$-ga
25. 1.0.0 sig$_5$ 65.1.0 gur
26. Ur-^{d}Li$_9$-si$_4$ dumu Ab-ba-mu
27. ^{ĝeš}kiri$_6$ gu-la šà uru

iv.

28. ugula Ab-ba-gi-na
29. (B L A N K)
30. u$_4$ 4-kam
31. mu ^{d}Amar-^{d}Suen lugal

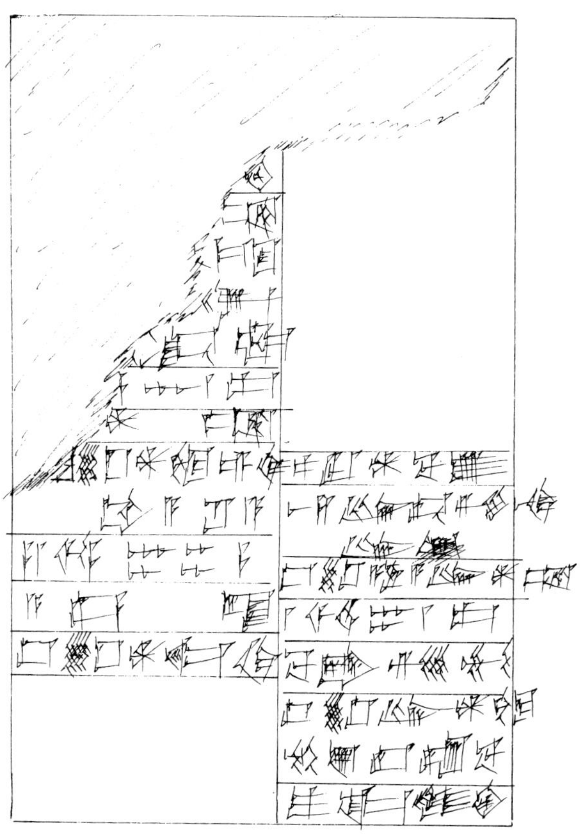

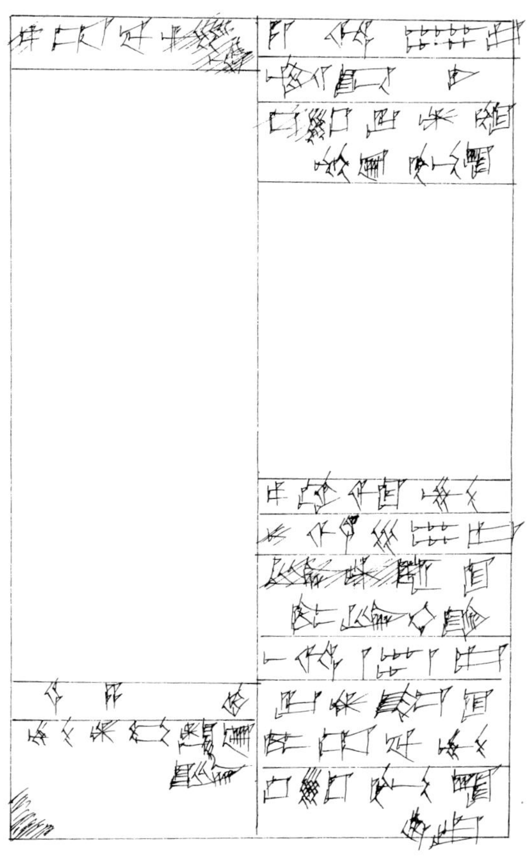

75

(-/5/AS 2)

OBV.

1. 1 KA gurdub tab-ba túg-ús lugal 5⅓ ma-na Ĝír-su^{ki}-šè
2. 1 gurdub síg 3-kam-ús 23[+ ma]-na
3. 3 gurdub [síg 4-kam]-ús [ ]-ta
4. (BLANK)
5. šu+níĝin 5 gurdub-ḫi-a
6. síg udu ^{d}Na-rú-a
7. šà Gú-ab-ba^{ki}-gu-la

REV.

8. 1 gurdub síg [ ]
9. 1 gurdub [ ]
10. 1 gurdub síg [x]

*11. 1 gurdub síg túg Nina^{ki}-t[a]

12. (BLANK)
13. šu+níĝin 4 gurdub síg-ĝen-ḫi-a
14. u_4 5-kam
15. šà Gú-ab-ba^{ki}
16. mu ^{d}Amar-^{d}Suen lugal-e Ur-bí-lum^{ki} mu-ḫul

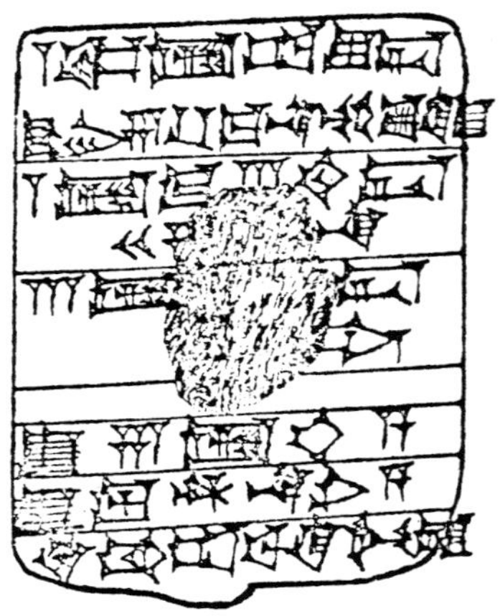

76

(-/8/AS 2)

i. 1. 16 m[a-na túg lugal]
2. [x m]a-na túg-ús lugal
3. [x] ma-na [túg] 3 kam-ús
4. 6+ [gú] 2 ma-na [túg] 4 kam-ús
5. 13 ma-na síg-ĝen
6. 11 gú 38⅔ ma-na
7. A-[ ] na-gada
8. 17½ ma-na túg lugal
9. 2[0+] ma-na túg-ús lugal
10. 2 gú 5½ ma-na <túg> 3 kam-ús
11. 7 gú 37 ma-na túg 4 kam-ús
12. 32 ma-na síg-ĝen
13. 11 gú 21½ ma-na
14. Ba-zi-zi na-gada
15. 15⅔ ma-na túg lugal
16. 27 ma-na túg-ús lugal
17. 1 gú 22⅓ ma-na túg 3 kam-ús

ii. 18. ⸢4⸣ gú ⸢5⸣ ma-na túg 4 kam-ús
19. 16 ma-na síg-ĝen
20. 6 gú 26 ma-na
21. Ur-^{d}Lugal-bàn-da
22. 8 ma-na 10 gín túg [lugal] 23⅓ ma-na túg-ús lugal
23. 1 gú 21½ ma-na túg 3 kam-ús
24. 4 gú 25 ma-na túg 4 kam-ús
25. 10 ma-na síg-ĝen
*26. 6 gú 28 ma-na
27. Lú-^{d}Ĝeš-bar-è
28. 4⅓ ma-na túg lugal
29. 14½ ma-na túg-ús lugal
30. 30 ma-na túg 3 kam-ús
31. 2 gú 30 ma-na túg 4 kam-ús
32. 5½ ma-na síg-ĝen
33. 3 gú 24⅓ ma-na
34. Ku-li-kal-la na-gada
35. 7⅔ ma-na túg lugal
36. 16 ma-na túg-ús lugal
37. 31 ma-na túg 3 kam-ús

iii. *38. 3 gú 35 ma-na 4 kam-ús
39. 11 ma-na síg-ĝen
40. 4 gú 40⅔ ma-na
41. Lú-ša$_6$-ga
42. 8½ ma-na túg lugal
43. 8½ ma-na túg-ús lugal
44. 29 ma-na 10 gín «na» túg 3 kam-ús
45. 1 gú 15 ma-na túg 4 kam-ús
46. 3 gú 1⅔ 10 gín ma-na síg-ĝen
47. (BLANK)
48. Lú-^{d}Nin-šubur na-gada
49. 7⅔ ma-na túg lugal
50. 14½ ma-na túg-ús
*51. 1 gú 6 ma-na túg 3 kam-ús
52. 5 gú 15 ma-na túg 4 kam-ús
53. 6 ma-na ma-na síg-ĝ[en]
54. 5 <gú> 49 ma-na
55. Ba-zi na-gada
56. *(erasure)*
57. *(erasure)*
58. *(erasure)*
59. *(erasure)*
60. *(erasure)*

iv. 61. *(erasure)*
62. *(erasure)*
63. *(erasure)*
64. šu+níĝin 1 gú 27⅔ ma-na túg lugal
65. šu+níĝin 3 gú 6⅚ ma-na túg-ús lugal
66. šu+níĝin 10 gú 28½ ma-na túg 3 kam-ús
67. šu+níĝin 36 gú 10 ma-na túg 4 kam-ús
68. šu+níĝin 1 gú 33½ ma-na síg-ĝen
69. 52 gú 46½ ma-na túg
70. túg ba-lá u$_4$ 8-kam
71. šà Ki-nu-nir^{ki}
72. mu ^{d}Amar-^{d}Suen lugal-e Ur-bí-lum^{ki} mu-ḫul

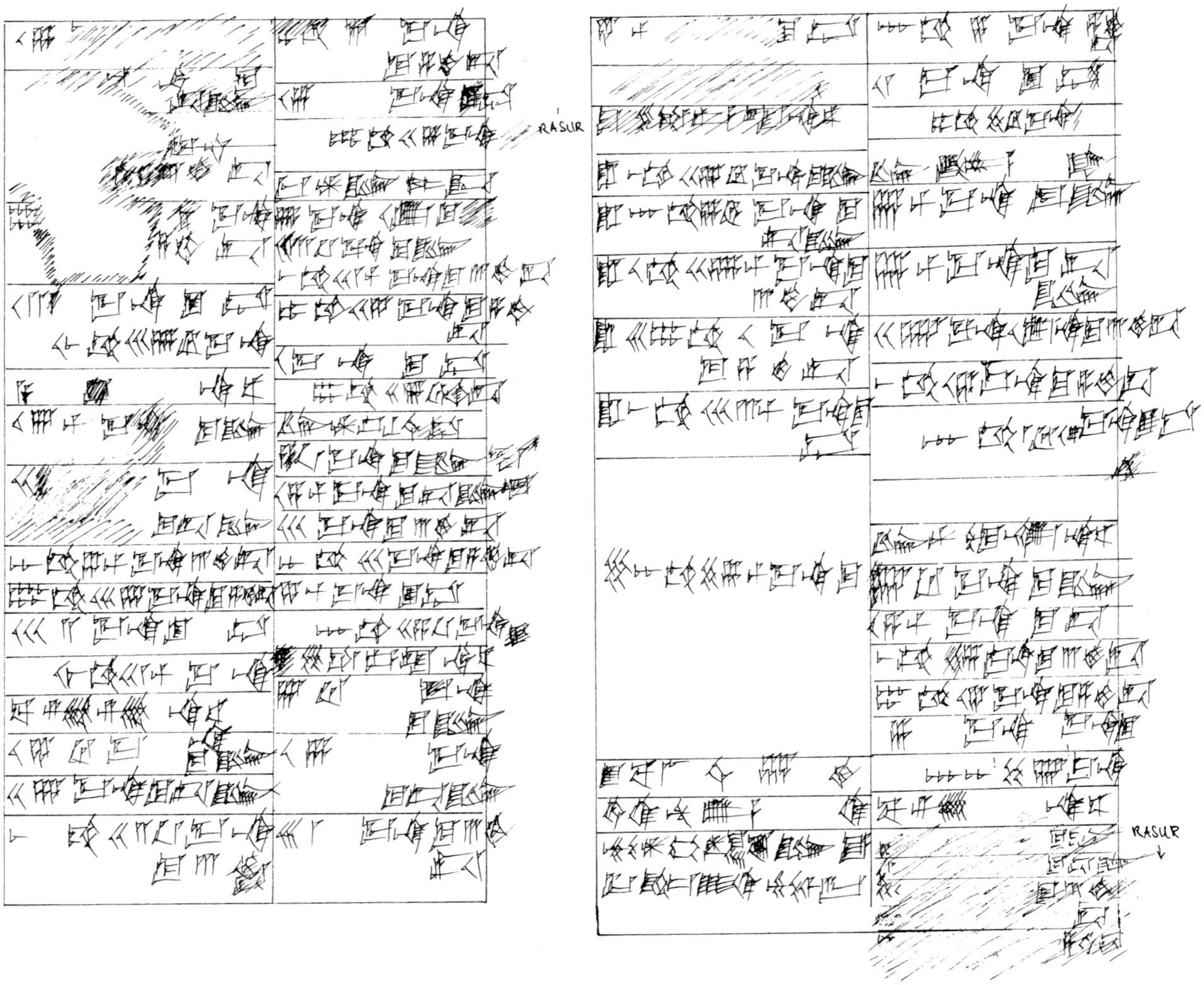

76

77

(-/10/AS 2)

OBV.

1. 4 gurdub síg lugal 30 ma-na-«gú»-ta
2. 6 gurdub síg-ús lugal 30 ma-na-ta
3. 2 gurdub síg nì-lám 3-kam-ús 1 gú-ta
*4. 15 [4]-kam-[ús]
5. 48 [ ]

REV.

6. gurdub síg guz-za 1 gú-ta
7. 2 gurdub síg-ĝen 1 gú-ta
*8. gurdub síg-$ĝi_6$ 1 gú-ta
9. (BLANK)
10. šu+níĝin 77 gurdub-ḫi-a
11. u_4 10-kam
12. šà Ki-nu-nir^{ki}
13. mu ^{d}Amar-^{d}Suen lugal Ur-bí-lum^{ki} mu-ḫul

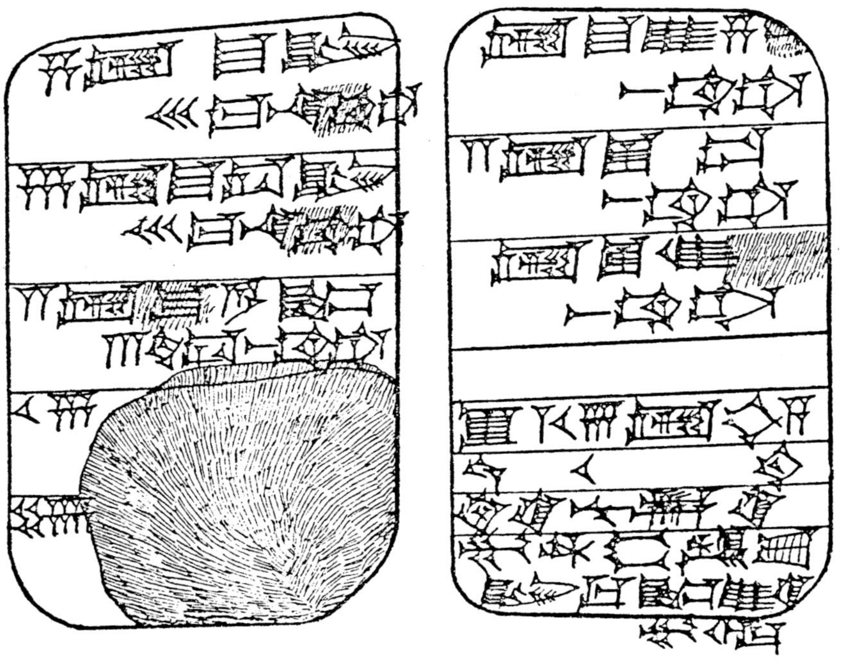

78

([ ]/AS 2 or 3)

OBV.

1. 30 udu-saĝ sila$_4$
2. 2 u$_8$ 3 kir$_{11}$
3. 3 sila$_4$-níta
4. 4 ud$_5$-máš-⸢ḫi⸣-a
5. 3 ^{mí}áš-gàr 20 máš-saĝ ud$_5$
6. 6 máš-tur gub-[ba]
7. 5 udu x [ ] URU ⸢ḫi⸣
8. 2 udu 10 lá 1 máš
9. ki Ur-^{d}Ba-ú dumu Ḫé-ša$_6$
10. 6 udu 8 máš
11. ki Lú-^{d}[ ]-ta
12. udu šuku-ra
13. 10 máš [lá]-u$_x$ su-ga
14. ki Nam-maḫ-ta
15. [ ] udu 1 máš lá-u$_x$ su-ga
16. [ki L]ú-^{d}Ba-ú dumu Lugal-[i$_7$]-ta
17. [ ] udu

REV.

18. [ ] 10 [ ]
19. [ ] 12 [ ] máš
20. Á-[ ] NI
21. 23 udu [ ] 2 [ ]
22. 3 sila$_4$ [ ]
23. 2 u[d$_5$]
24. 25 máš [ ]
25. 15 [ ]
26. L[ú-]
27. 2 [ ]
28. 12 [ ]
29. 2 [ ]
30. (BLANK)
31. é [ ]
32. iti [ ]
33. mu [ ] Ur-bí-[lum^{ki} mu-ḫul]

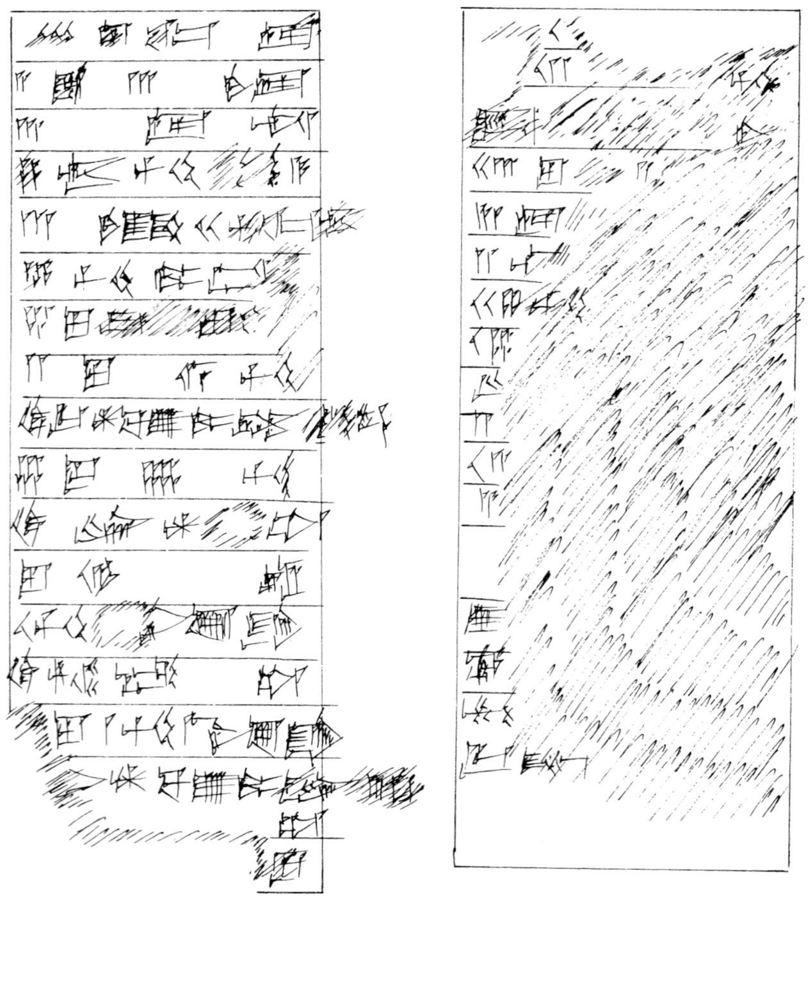

79

(XI/-/AS 8)

OBV.

1. 70 géme u_4-1-kam
2. 62 géme u_4-2-kam
3. 50 géme u_4-3-kam
4. gu bù-ra

REV.

5. ugula Ur-^{d}Nin-tu
6. kišib Ur-^{d}Ùr-bar-tab
7. iti še kin-ku_5
8. SEAL
9. mu-ús-sa Ḫu-ḫu-nu-ri^{ki} ba-ḫul

Seal: Ur-^{d}Ùr-bar-tab
dub-sar
dumu Diĝir-ra

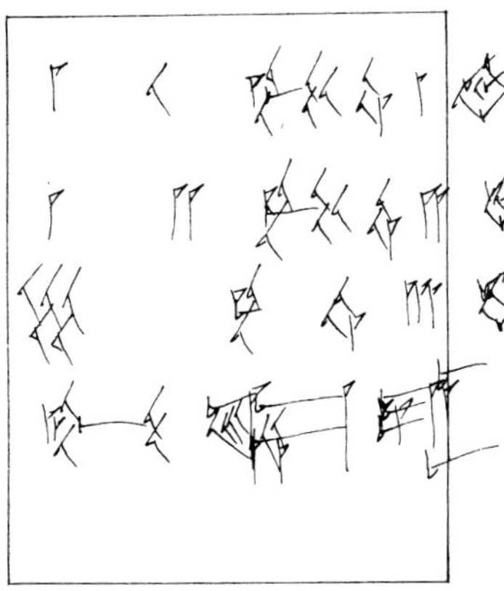

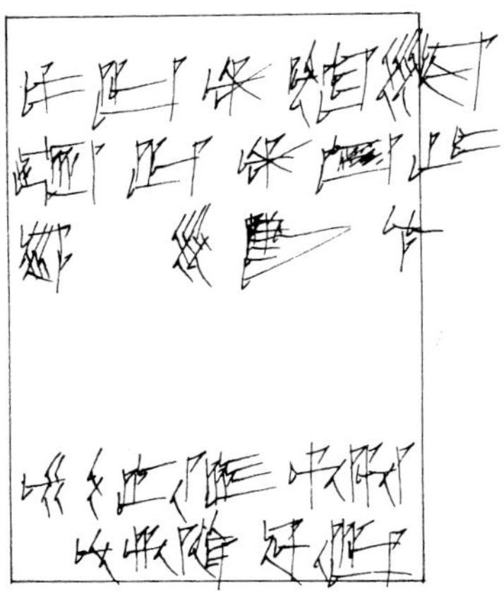

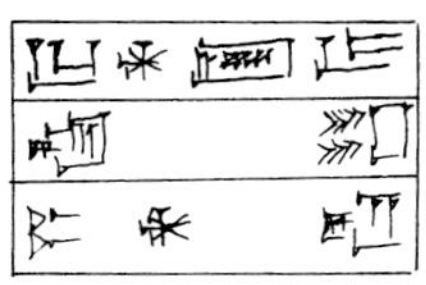

80

(-/-/ŠS 8)

OBV.

1. [ ] 3 aslag
★2. [nu-bànda] Lú-i[nim-ša$_6$-g]a
3. 5 géme 1 aslag
4. libir-àm
5. 11 géme 6 aslag
6. [nu]-bànda É-i$_7$-lú-ru
★7. 217 géme 3 aslag
8. nu-bànda Lú-nita-gi-na
9. 110 érin Nag-su^{ki}
10. ugula *Dah-hi-še-en*

REV.

11. 165 érin
12. ugula *Ib-ni*-^{d}Šul-gi
13. (BLANK)
★14. [šu+nígin] 275 géme
15. [šu+nígin] 13 aslag
16. [šu+nígi]n 275 érin
17. 583
18. [x] u$_4$ 3-kam
19. [šà] Gú-ab-ba^{ki}
★20. [mu má-gu]r$_8$-mah ba-dím

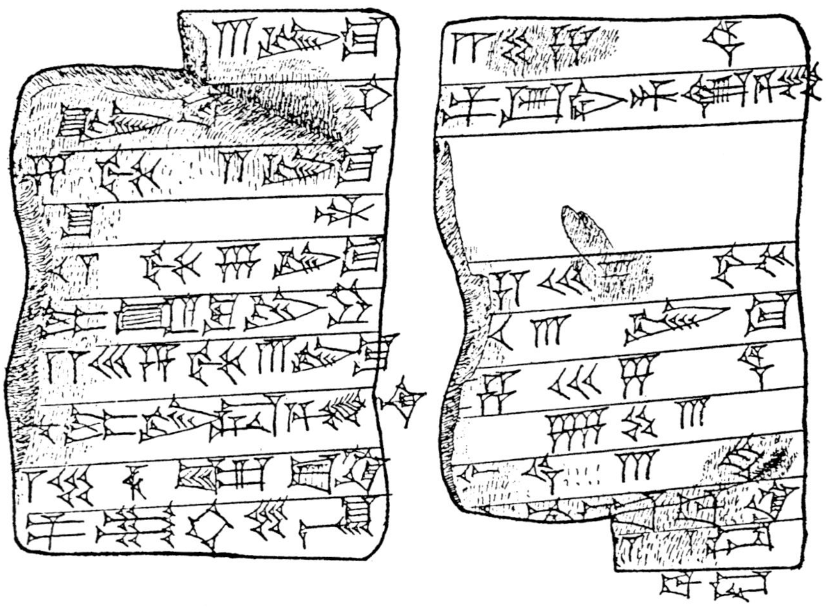

81

([ ]/ŠS 9)

OBV.

1. igi-3-ĝál kù-babbar
2. nì-sa$_{10}$-àm [ ]
3. Lugal-gi-^{d}Ba-ú-ka-šè
4. ki Nin-ĝál-[ ]

REV.

5. UŠ [ ]
6. úgu-[a ĝá-ĝá]
7. [ ]
8. mu é ^{d}Šára ba-dù

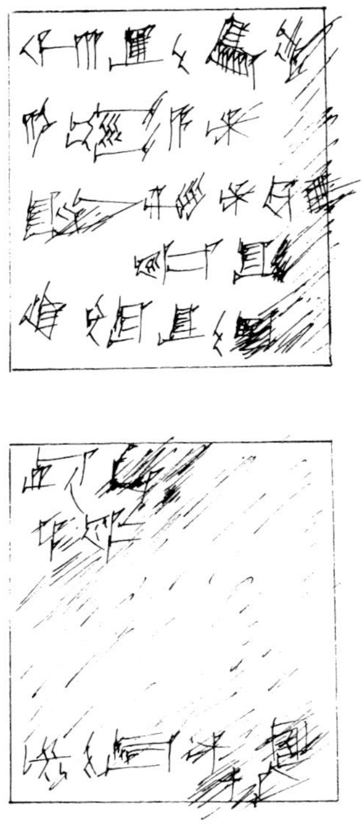

82 (XII/-/IS 1)

OBV.

(*top of obverse broken*)

1. u$_4$ 10[+ ba-zal]
★2. 1 túg-bar N[I]
3. u$_4$ 10[+ ba-za]l
★4. 1 túg-bar NI-[ ] é ^{d}Ba-⸢ú⸣
5. u$_4$ 12 ba-zal
★6. 1 túg-bar Šeš-ki-lu$_5$-la è [ ] ba-an-ku$_4$ nu-bànda Lú-K[A]
7. u$_4$ 24 ba-zal
8. 1 túg-bar Šeš-kal-la dumu Lugal-l[a]
★9. [é ^{d}]Nin-ĝír-su ba-an-ku$_4$
10. [u$_4$] ba-zal
★11. [x]-ma dumu *Ku-ku-um*

REV.

12. [ ] é gi [ ]
13. [x] ba-an-ku$_4$ [x x]
★14. [u$_4$ x]8 ba-zal
15. [ ] dumu Ur-mes
★16. [ ]^{d}Šul-pa-è Ka$_5$-a-mu ì-dab$_5$
★17. [ ] ^{d}Ba-ú [ ] ba ba-an-⸢ku$_4$⸣
★18. túg-bar ^{I}Ur-^{d}Nin-ĝeš-zi-[da] dam-a-⸢ni⸣
★19. túg-bar ^{I}Šà-ge gudu$_4$ é ^{d}Nin-[ ]
★20. túg-bar ^{I}Ur-igi-ĝál sipa énsi-k[a]
21. túg-bar ^{I}Ab-ba-gi-na dumu [ ]
★22. túg-bar ^{I}Lugal-zi-mu lú [é] ^{d}Nanše ba-an-ku$_4$
23. sumun ^{I}Ir$_{11}$ dumu *Ìr-ri-ib* [ ]
24. [ ] *Šu-Eš$_4$-tár* [ ]
25. [ ] é gu$_4$ diri

(*bottom of reverse broken*)

26. iti še-íl-la mu ^{d}*I-bí*-^{d}Suen lu[gal]

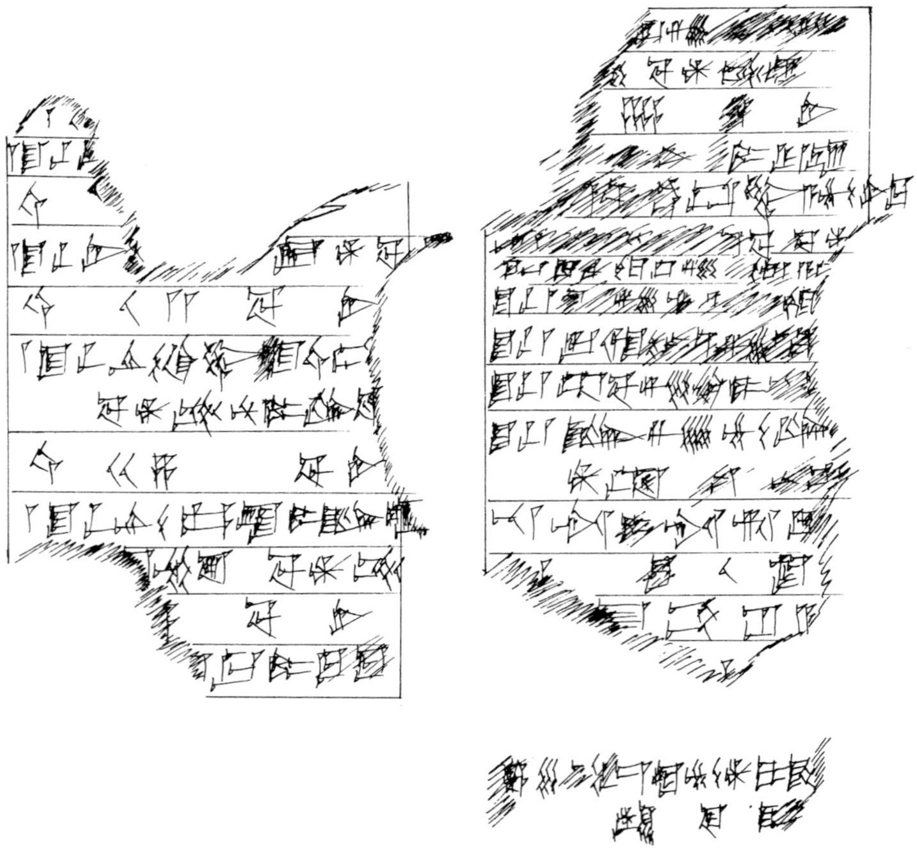

83

(I/[ ])

OBV.

1. 5 sìla [ ]
2. Al-la-m[u]
3. ra-gaba-šè mu:na-gi$_4$
4. (B L A N K)

REV.

5. (B L A N K)
6. i[ti buru$_x$(GÁN)]-maš
7. [ ]

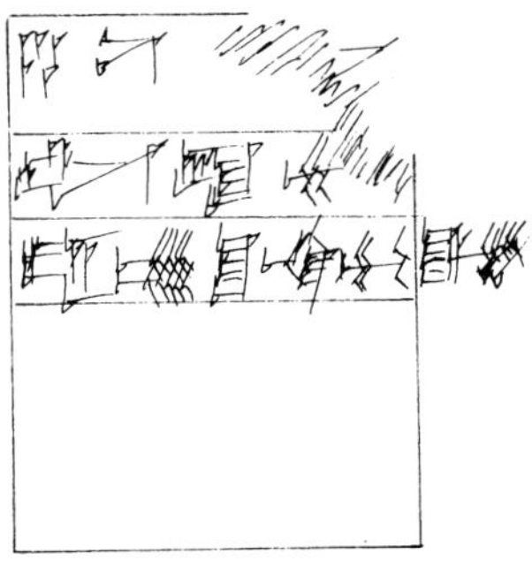

84

(II/[ ])

OBV.

1. 1 [ ]
2. 1 máš-ní[ta]
3. 2 [ ]
4. 1 ⸢sila$_4$⸣ AN [ ]
5. ĝìr [ ]
6. 1 ud$_5$ 1 máš
7. [x]

REV.

8. 1 sila$_4$ 1 máš
9. ki ^{d}Suen
10. 1 sila$_4$ ^{d}Šul-šà-ga-na kurušda
11. (B L A N K)
12. u$_4$ x kam iti gu$_4$-rá-b[í-mú-mú]
13. mu [ ]

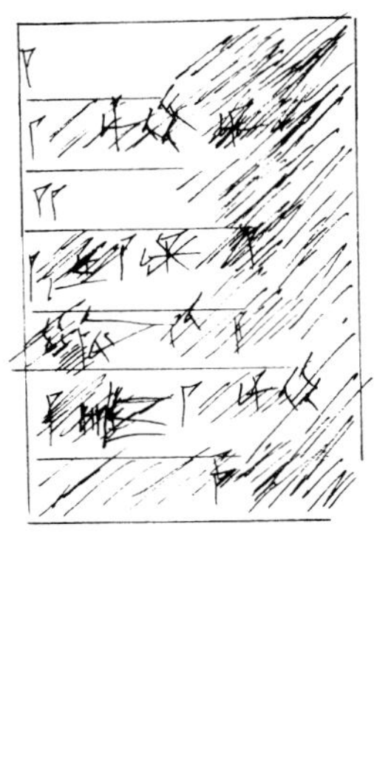

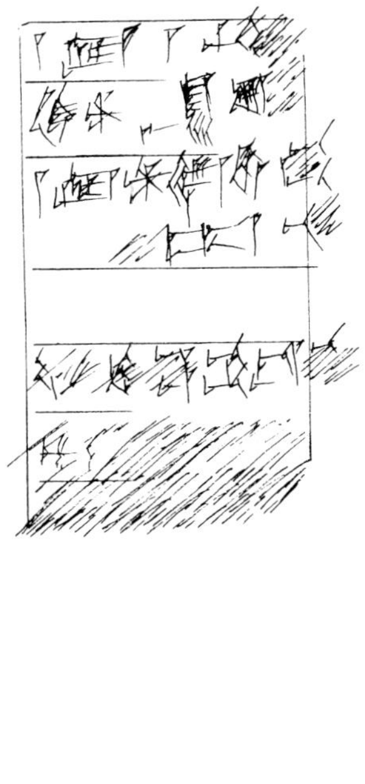

85

(date not preserved)

OBV.

(*top of obverse broken*)

1. [x]
2. (BLANK)
3. (BLANK)
4. mu-túm
5. 4 u$_8$ 2 udu 1 sila$_4$
6. zi-ga
7. 44 u$_8$ 16 udu-níta
8. 8 sila$_4$

REV.

9. ri-ri-ga
10. u$_8$ udu-níta
11. sila$_4$
12. lá-u$_x$-àm
13. (BLANK)
14. šu+nígin 585 gub-ba
15. šu+nígin 7 zi-ga
16. šu+nígin 68 ri-ri-ga
17. šu+nígin lá-u$_x$
18. Ur-^{d}Nin-ĝeš-z[i-da]
19. [ ] x [ ]

(*bottom of reverse broken*)

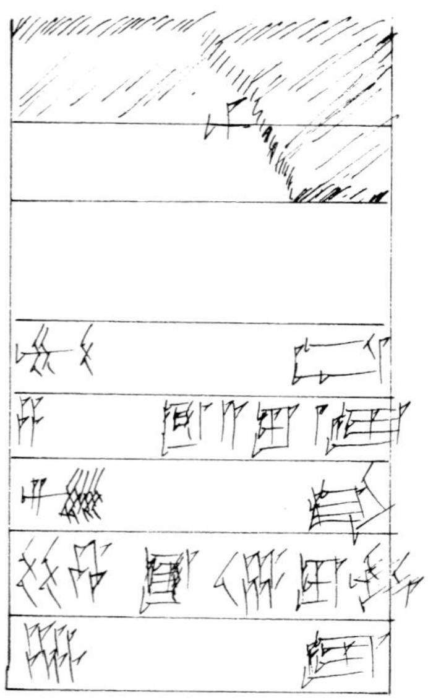

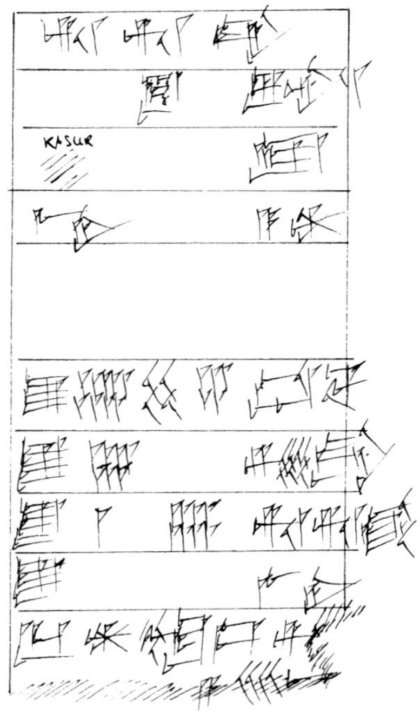

86 (date not preserved)

i. 1. 10.0.0 še gur lugal
2. ki Lú-kal-la-ta
3. 5.0.0 ki Lú-gi-na-ta
4. 4.3.0 zíz ki É-ambar-ta
5. 8.1.0 še 0.2.0 zíz
6. ki A-tu-ta
7. 3.0.0 ki Ur-[d]Nanše-ta
8. 4.1.3 3 sìla gur
9. ki Ur-[d]Dumu-zi-ta
10. 6.0.0 ki Ur-[d]Nin-ĝeš-zi-da-ta
11. 2.0.0 ki Ur-[d]Ba-ú dumu Ab-ba-uru-ta
12. 9.1.0 ki Ur-[d]Nin-piriĝ-ta
13. 9.2.0 Ĝír-ĝír-ta
14. 9.2.0 5 sìla gur
*15. [ki] Inim-[d]Inanna-ta
16. 9.0.0 a-rá 1-kam

ii. 17. [ ]
18. 20 [ ]
19. é-ba-ḪA[R]
20. (BLANK)

iii. *(top of column iii destroyed; bottom blank)*

iv. *(column iv blank)*

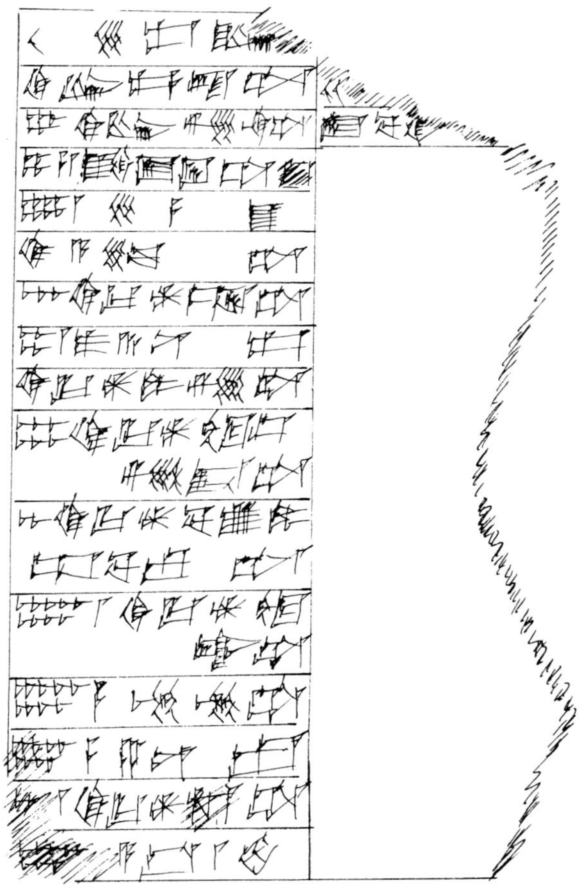

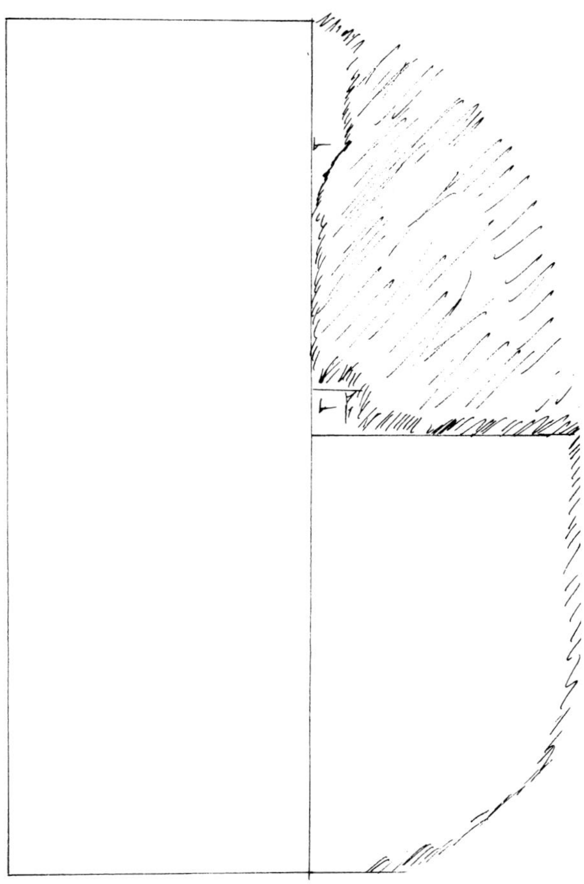

87

(date not preserved)

OBV.

1. 156.2.0 še ⸢gur⸣ lugal
2. (*erasure*) zì gur
3. naĝa-bi nu-dé
4. gána-gu$_4$ Lugal-dub-lal
5. ^{d}Utu-bar-ra engar
6. ugula Ur-^{d}Nin-mar-ki

REV.

7. (BLANK)
8. [d]a-a
9. [z]i-da
10. [ ]

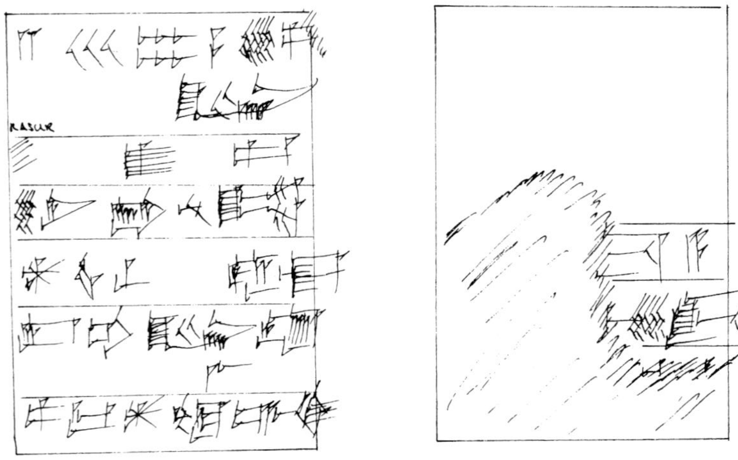

88 (date not preserved)

i. *(top of column i broken)*

1. šu+níĝin 1 gur$_7$ 156.2.5 še gur lugal
2. saĝ-nì-gur$_{11}$-ra-kam
3. šà-bi-ta
4. 184+.0.0 gur
5. [ ] mu
6. [ ]-ḫé-ĝál
7. [ ] x [ ]
8. [ ]
9. [ ] x

ii. *(top of column ii broken)*

10. [ ] Na-x [ ]
11. 2752.4.0 [ ]
12. 7.3.2 še mun gazi
13. kìšib Nì-^{d}Ba-ú
14. dumu Ni-ba
15. kìšib-bi 2-àm
16. 55.0.0 gur
17. kìšib Ur-^{ĝeš}gigir ka-gur$_7$
18. 20.0.0 gur

iii.

19. [ ] Ur-dam
20. [ ] ^{d}Nanše
21. [ ] gur
22. [ ] NI DU
23. [ ] saĝa
24. [ ]

(bottom of column iii broken)

iv. *(top of column iv broken)*

25. (BLANK)
26. šu+níĝin [ ]
27. [ ]

89 (date not preserved)

OBV.

(top of obverse broken)

1. 8⸢6⸣ ⸢gú⸣-[zì-sig$_{5}$ gur]
2. Ur-tur
3. 6.0.0 zì-sig$_{15}$ gur Šeš-kal-la
4. 23.0.0 zíz-gú-nida gur
5. 57.0.0 zì-sig$_{15}$ gur 101.0.0 zíz-sig$_{15}$ 23 gú-nida 86 gú-zì-sig$_{5}$ gur

*6. Lugal-igi-du$_{10}$-g[a]

REV.

7. 9.2.0 zì-sig$_{15}$ gur 20.0.0 zíz gur
8. Nin-ki-ḫar-ša$_{6}$
9. 9.1.0 zì-sig$_{15}$ 26.0.0 zíz gur
10. x-sila$_{4}$-ni
11. 8.0.3 zì-sig$_{15}$ 20.0.0 zíz gur
12. Géme-é-an-na
13. 9.2.0 zì gur 20 zíz gur
14. Inim-^{d}Ba-ú-ni?
15. [zì-s]ig$_{15}$ 20 zíz gur
16. [ ] x

(bottom of reverse broken)

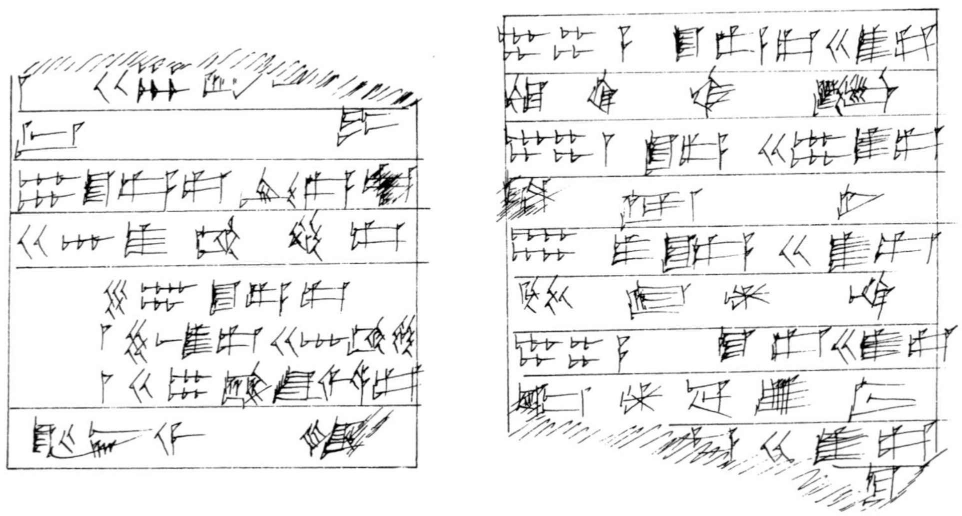

90

(date not preserved)

i. 1. 0.0.1 8 sìla 10 gín ì-nun
2. ki Lú-inim-ĝar-ša$_{6}$-ga-ta
3. 0.0.3 ì-nun
4. kišib Nam-m[aḫ]-^{d}Ba-ú
5. 0.0.3 2½ sìla ì-n[un]
6. ki Ir$_{11}$-x-[ ]-N[E]
7. ĝìr [A]
(bottom of column i broken)

ii. 8. 0.1.0 ì-[ ]
9. ĝìr U[r-]
*10. kišib N[u] Ma-x-[ ]
11. 4 sì[la]
12. kì[šib]
(bottom of column ii broken)
(reverse not preserved)

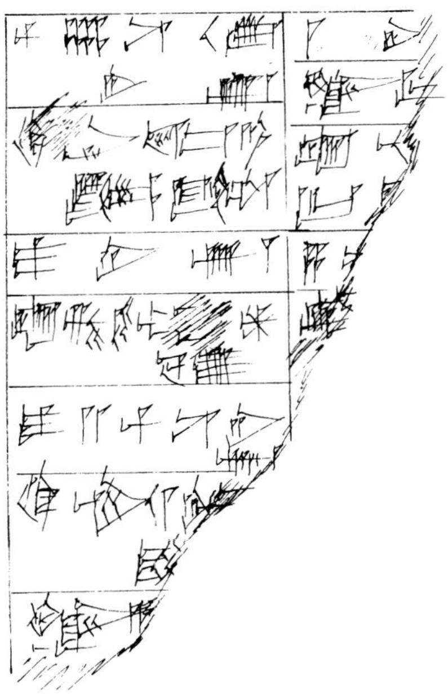

91 (date not preserved)

OBV.

*1. 56 áb-máḫ
2. Ur-^{d}Nanše
3. 4 Lú-^{d}Ba-ú
4. 12 Ìr-dam
5. 4 Lugal-nimgir
6. 2 Lú-^{d}Nin-ĝír-su
7. 1 Èš-ta-šu-š[a_6-ga]
8. 80 lá 1
9. [ ] x

REV.

10. [ ]
11. [ ]
12. [ ]
13. [ ] x [ ]
*14. [ ] Lugal-ezen
*15. iti [eze]n ^{d}Dum[u-zi]
16. [ ] x [ ]

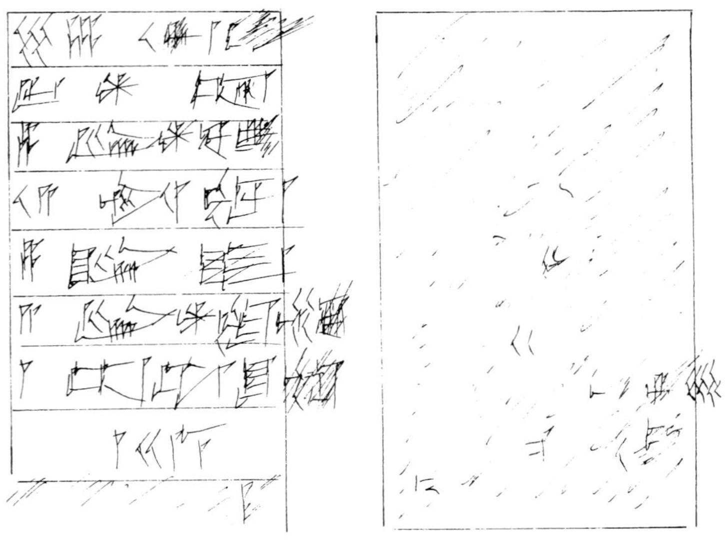

92 (date not preserved)

OBV.

(*top of obverse broken*)

1. [ ]
2. (*erasure*)
3. gub-ba-àm
4. lá-u$_x$ 1 anše-níta 20
5. 1 anše 10
6. lá-u$_x$-àm
7. Ab-ba-mu ba-kul

★8. 7 anše-níta

9. gub-ba-àm
10. Ka$_5$-a engar
11. 1 anše

REV.

12. 5 anše-níta
13. 1 anše-níta Zu-zu engar nu-bànda
14. gub-ba-àm

★15. (*erasure*)

16. Lugal-ma-du$_{10}$ engar

★17. ki Ur-ba-ga-ta

18. 1 áb-máḫ
19. 2 gu$_4$-ĝeš
20. 1 áb-2-ĝeš-šè

★21. 1 gu$_4$-ĝeš Su-ga engar

22. 1 áb-máḫ šu-gi$_4$
23. gub-ba-àm
24. [ ] engar

(*bottom of reverse broken*)

L.E.

25. ugula Ur-é-ninnu 5

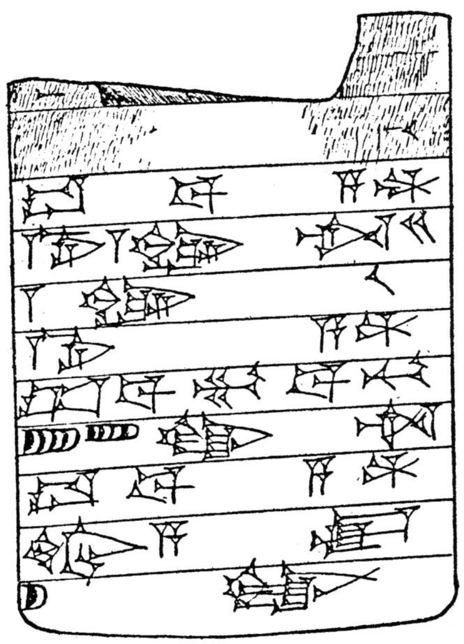

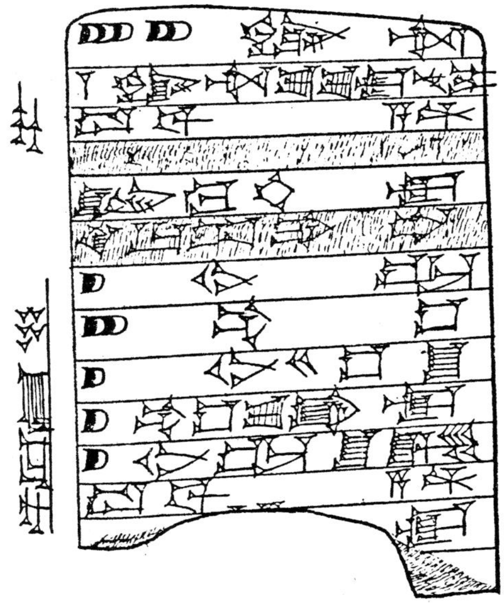

93 (date not preserved)

OBV.

i. *(top of column i broken)*

1. [x] gur
2. [x.x.]5 zì-sig$_{15}$ gur
3. [ ] sìla eša [U]Š gur [ ] NA gur
4. [s]ig$_5$ šà-gal [x] gur
5. [x] sig$_5$ [ ] gur
6. [ ] ús [ ] gur
7. [ ] še [ ] dabin [ ] gur
8. [ ] SA [ ] 10 kam [ ] mar [ ] gur
9. [x] sig$_5$ [ ] sig$_5$
10. [x] ⅚ [ ] gur
11. [ ] zì-sig$_{15}$ [ ] gur
12. [zì]-gu gur
13. [x.x.]5 1 sìla dabin gur
14. [ ] ŠI sig$_5$
15. [ ] eša gur
16. [x.x.]5 ½ sìla ar-za-na
17. [ ] sìla dabin é [ ] UŠ rá-gaba
18. [ ] šà é-gal
19. [g]a ĝar diri [ ] da x[ ]

(bottom of column i broken)

ii. *(top of column ii broken)*

20. ⌜iti še-ki⌝[n-ku$_5$]
21. (BLANK)
22. zi-ga lugal
23. 2.0.0 2 sìla zì-sig$_{15}$ gur
24. 18.4.5 3½ sìla dabin gur
25. igi-1-ĝál zì Ĝír-su^{ki}-ta de$_6$-a
26. 0.4.0 3 sìla nì-kú-a-géme-tur
27. kìšib Lugal-ki-gal-la
28. 0.3.0 zì-ba-ba sig$_5$
29. 3.0.1 5 sìla zì gur
30. 0.1.0 zì-gu sig$_5$ šà-gal lugal
31. 0.3.0 zì-gu ús
32. maš-da-ri-<a> ki lugal-šè
33. šà Nina^{ki}
34. kìšib Ur-mes
35. 6.0.0 šà-gal érin i$_7$-NE-tum-ma-al gub-ba
36. kìšib Á-ša$_6$-ga
37. zi-ga
38. 2.3.0 2 sìla zì-ba-ba sig$_5$ gur
39. 0.2.4 6 sìla zì-gú sig$_5$
40. 1.1.2 3 sìla nì-ù-du$_8$-ḫu-um gur
41. 42.2.1 2⅚ sìla zì-sig$_{15}$ [gur]
42. 0.0.1 [ ]
43. 0.4.3 [ ]
44. 0.2.2 [ ]

(bottom of column ii broken)

iii. *(top of column iii broken)*

45. [ ]
46. x [ ]
47. 4.0.0 zì-sig$_{15}$ gur
48. 0.2.0 zì-gu sig$_5$ šagina
49. 0.3.0 zì-g[u ús]
50. kaš-dé-a da[m]
51. (BLANK)
52. kaš-dé-a [ ] ma-a[l]
53. 74.[x.x] zì [ ]
54. kìšib Ma-[ ]
55. úgu-[a ĝá-ĝá]
56. 90+[.x.x]
57. 25+[.x.x] zì x[ ]
58. 5 [x]
59. kìšib [ ] du[mu]
60. 30+[ ]
61. 10+[ ]

(bottom of column iii broken)

REV.

iv. *(column iv not preserved)*

v. *(top of column v broken)*

62. kìšib 30 [ ]
63. 13 gín 20 [ ]
64. 2.0.0 lá 8 sìla [ ]
65. Šeš-kal-la [ ]
66. 10 gín x[ ]
67. Ba-zi šu b[a-ti]
68. úgu-a ĝá-[ĝá]
69. (BLANK)
70. [ ] na
71. [ ] gur

(bottom of column v broken)

vi. *(top of column vi broken)*

72. šu+níĝin [ ]
73. [ ] ar-za-[na] še bala-bi x [ ] 15 gín [ ]
74. [ ] 15.0.0 zì-gu sig$_5$ šà-gal lugal gur
75. [ ] zì-ba-ba še
76. [še bal]a-bi 3.0.1 2 sìla gur
77. [ ] 8.1.3 5 sìla [ ] sig$_5$ šagina gur
78. [še-bal]a-bi 2.4.0 9½ sìla gur

79. [1]24+.4.1 7⅔ sìla ninda zì-gu gur
80. [ ]2+.0.3 2 sìla zì gur
81. [1]42+.3.2 4 sìla dabin gur
82. [x.]2.1 7½ sìla dabin sa gur
83. [ ] 34+ [ ]

(bottom of column vi broken)

94

(not dated)

OBV.

1. 31.2.1 še gur lugal
2. 1.4.0 zì gur
3. ì-dub Gàr-šum^{ki}
4. 5.4.0 zíz gur
5. ĝìr Ab-ba-mu
6. 4.3.0 gur
7. ĝìr Lú-^{d}Na-rú-a

REV.

8. lá-u$_{x}$-àm
9. diri 10.1.0 5 sìla še gur
10. ĝìr Ur-^{d}Ba-ú dumu Ur-ša$_{6}$-ga
11. ì-dub U-ša-núm-ma

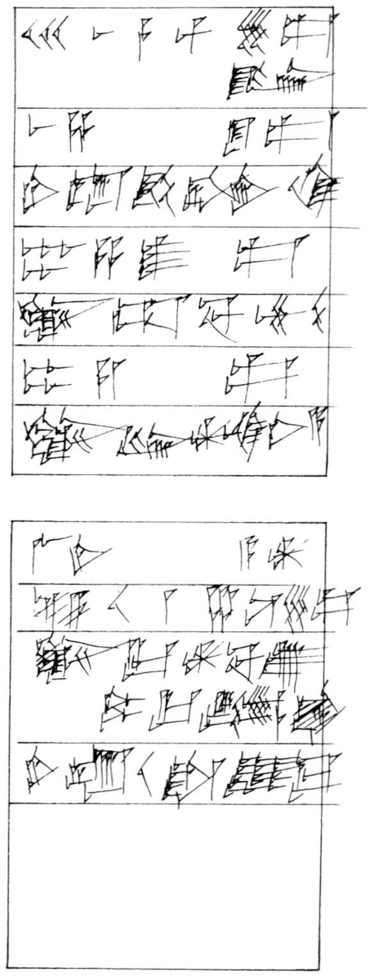

95

(not dated)

OBV.

1. [ ] 14.0.2 še gur lugal
2. [ĝ]ìr Lú-^{d}Nanše dumu U[r]-^{d}Ba-[ú]
3. [ ] še [ ] x DA [ ]
4. 302.2.0 [ ]
5. ki Lú-du$_{10}$-ga [ ]
6. (BLANK)
7. saĝ-nì-gur$_{11}$-ra-ka[m]
8. (BLANK)

(reverse uninscribed)

96 (not dated)

OBV.

i.

1. 183 udu Ì-du$_{10}$-ga
2. (B L A N K)
3. šà Gú-ab-ba^{ki}
*4. 50 lá 2 La-ni-mu 52
5. 3 Ur-^{d}Dumu-zi 4
6. 60 lá 1 Lú-kal-la 65
7. [ ] 5 A 40 lá 1 da
8. [ ] 5 Lú-^{d}Ba-ú 40 lá 1
9. [ ] 7 da
10. [ ] lá 1 x [ ]

(bottom of column i broken)

ii.

★11. 18 Nimgir-saĝ-ezen
★12. 24 Ku-li [ ] šeš-a-ni
13. 16 Nam-ḫa-ni dumu Ĝìri-ni
14. (B L A N K)
15. šà Ki-nu-nir^{ki}
16. ugula Du$_{11}$-ga-zi-da
17. *(erasure)* Nam-ḫa-ni
18. x [ ]

(bottom of column ii broken)

REV.

iii.

(top of column iii broken)

★19. ⌜šà Ĝír-su⌝$^{[ki]}$
20. 93 É-eze[n]
21. 10 Lú-^{d}Ba-ú
★22. 44 Lú-^{d}Ĝeš-bar-è
★23. 41 Lugal-šà-lá
24. 678 Nam-ḫa-ni
25. 4 Ab-ba-kal-la
26. 3 A-tu
★27. 8 Un-í[l]
28. 4 Ku-li-kal-la

iv.

(top of column iv broken)

29. [ ]
30. [ ] *Śar-ru-um-ì-[lí]*

OBV.

1. 15.0.0 zù-lum
2. šà-bi-ta
3. 9.0.0 gur
4. Ur-^{d}En-ki
5. 5.0.0 gur
6. Ka$_{5}$-a

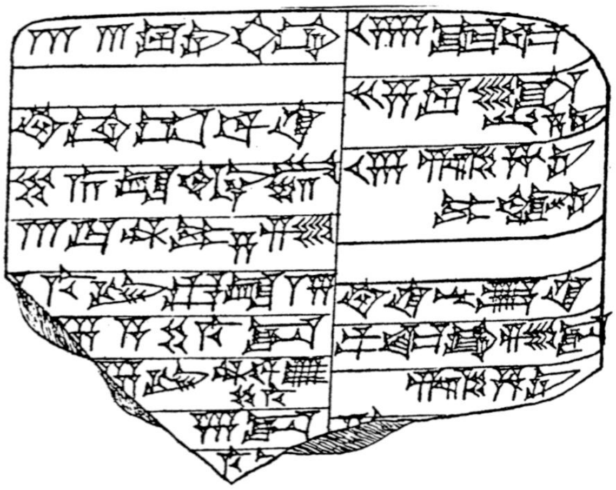

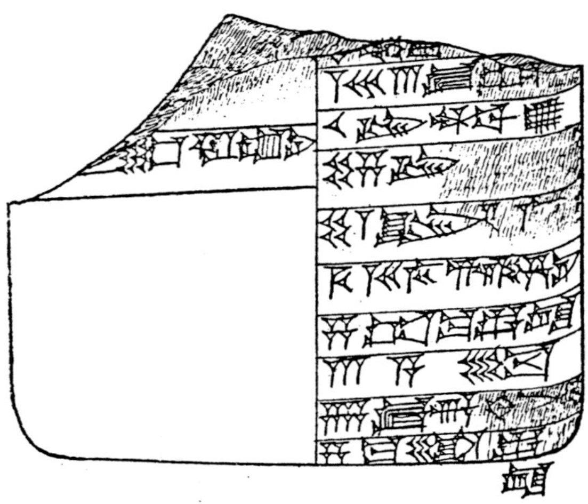

97

(not dated)

REV.

7. (BLANK)
8. kišib Ur-ab-ba
9. ugula Ka$_5$-a

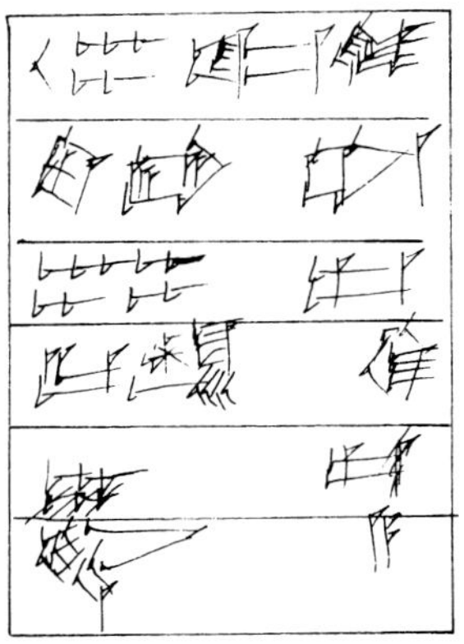

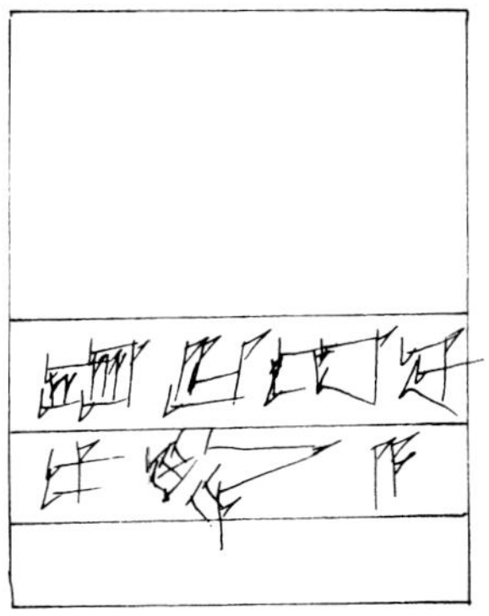

98

(not dated)

OBV.

1. 1 Ur-^{d}Ba-ú
2. A-ḫa-ba-la gudu$_4$ ^{d}Lama
3. im-e tak$_4$-a

REV.

4. daḫ-ḫu
5. Ni$_9$-ĝar-^{d}Ba-ú

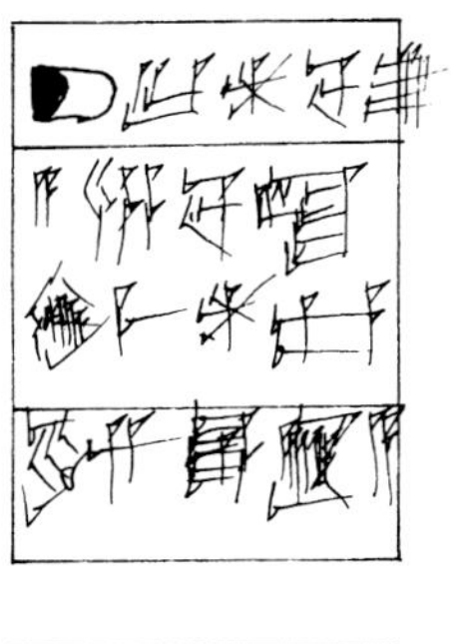

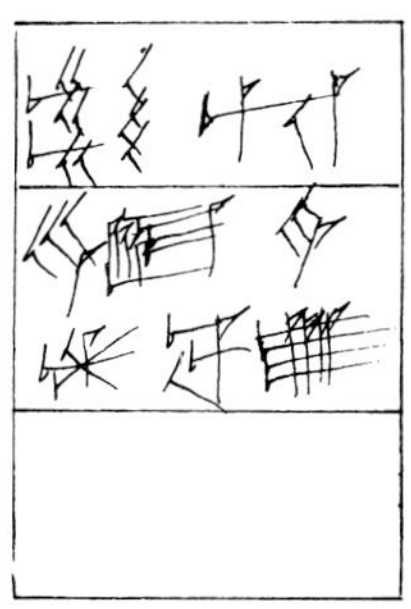

99

(I/-/Š 34)

OBV.

1. 3 túg nì-lám-ús lugal
2. ki-lá-bi 4⅔ ma-na 8 gín
3. 6 túg guz-za 4 kam-ús

REV.

4. ki-lá-bi 21 ma-na
5. mu-túm
6. Lú-gi-na
7. iti še-kin-ku$_5$
8. mu An-ša-an ba-ḫul

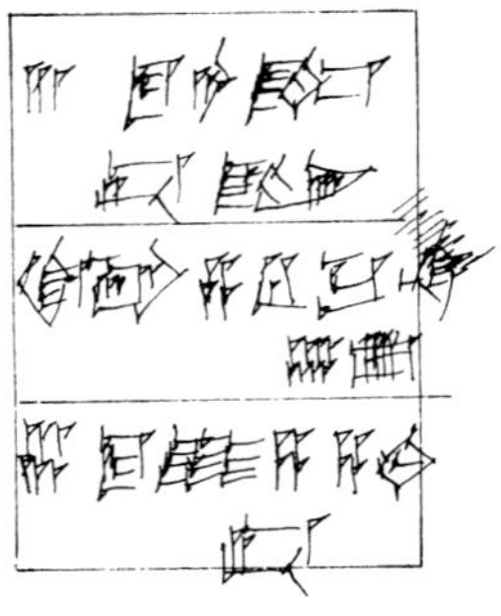

100

(not dated)

OBV.

*1. [ ] ½ ⸢sìla⸣ [ ] ì-nun-n[a]
2. Al-[ ]-šè
3. 24½ sìla ì-nun
4. Ur-^{d}Lama-[šè]

REV.

5. (BLANK)
6. mu-túm
7. mu Ur-ĝar énsi Lagaš^{ki}

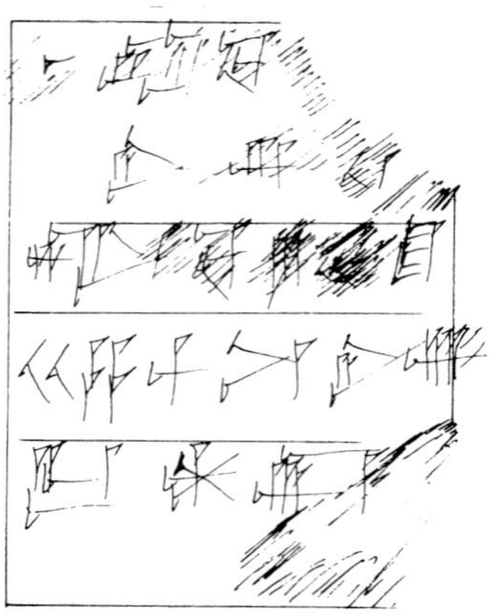

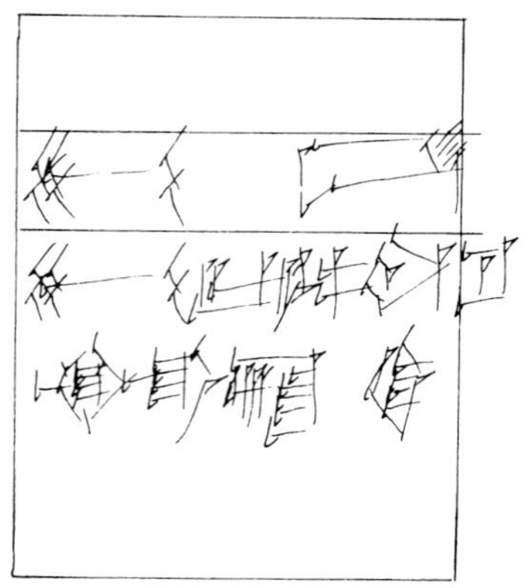

101 (not dated)

OBV.

1. [2 gín kù]-babbar
2. Nì-^{d}Ba-ú
3. 2 gín Ur-é-an-na
4. ½ gín Ur-^{d}Ba-ú
5. ⅔ (gín) Ur-^{d}Igi-zi-bar-ra
6. ⅔ (gín) Ur-^{d}Igi-zi-bar-ra dumu Nam-ḫa-ni
7. ½ gín ^{d}Inanna-ka

REV.

8. 1 gín ^{d}Utu-bar-ra
9. 1 gín Šeš-kal-la
10. (BLANK)
11. šu+níĝin 8 gín igi-3-ĝál
12. šu-ḫa-me
13. (BLANK)
14. mu-túm

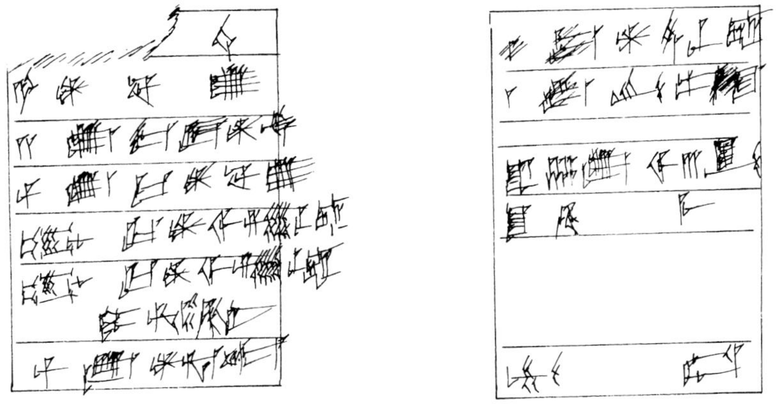

102 (XI/-/Š 27)

OBV.

1. 20 ^{dug}gir$_{16}$ ga-sig$_{7}$-a
2. é-gal lugal ba-an-ku$_{4}$
3. má u$_{4}$-zal-la

REV.

*4. ĝìr Ur-bàd-dúr-ra
5. (BLANK)
6. iti še-kin-ku$_{5}$
*7. mu Ḫa-ar-<ši>^{ki} ba-ḫul

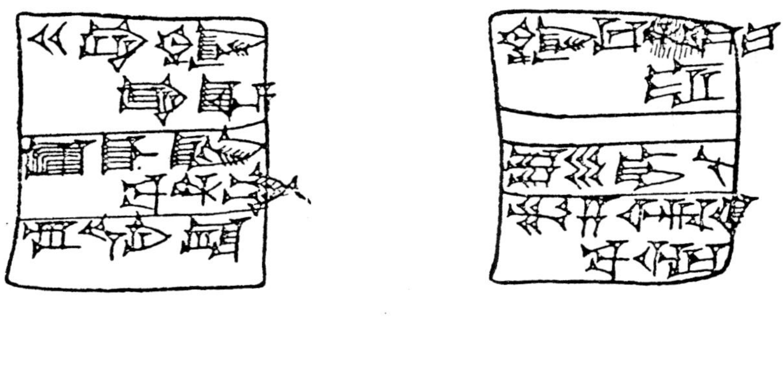

103

(V/-/Š 44)

obv.
1. 5 sìla kaš
2. lú ^{ĝeš}tukul-lugal
3. ka nimgir-an-ni-zu-šè im-ši-ĝen-na
4. Lú-kiri$_4$-zal maškim
5. ĝìr Ur-mes nu-bànda

REV.
6. (BLANK)
7. iti munu$_4$-kú
8. mu Si-mu-ru-um^{ki} Lu-lu-bu-um^{ki} a-rá 10 lá 1-kam-aš ba-ḫul

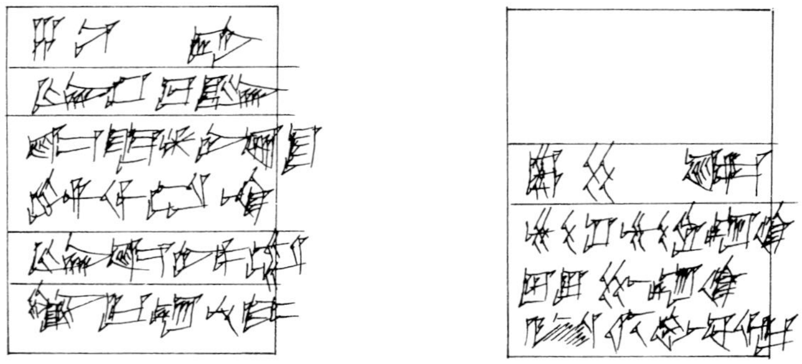

104

(-/-/ŠS 1)

OBV.
1. [ ]
2. [ ]-gi-na n[a-gada]
3. [ ]-kal-la dumu dab$_5$-[ba]
4. [A]-kal-la dumu dab$_5$-<ba>
5. [ ] dumu dab$_5$-ba
6. [ ] Al-la na-gada
7. 1.0.0 Ĝìri-ni-ì-ša$_6$ na-gada
8. 1.0.0 A-kal-la na-gada
9. 1.0.0 Ku$_5$-da na-gada
10. 1.0.0 A-tu na-gada dumu Al-la
11. 1.0.0 Ur-^{d}Lama <dumu> dab$_5$-<ba>
12. 1.0.0 Lú-^{d}Na-rú-a dumu dab$_5$-<ba>
13. 1.0.0 Gú-ù-mu dumu dab$_5$-<ba>
14. 1.0.0 Gu-za-na na-gada
15. 1.0.0 Ma-[ ] dumu dab$_5$-ba
16. 1.0.0 Mu-[du]mu dab$_5$-<ba>
17. a-ru-a [ ]-me
18. úr [ ] ù [ ]

REV.
19. 1.1.0 Lugal-ú-[ ]
20. 1.0.0 Da-da [ ]
21. 1.0.0 A-tu [ ]
22. 1.0.0 Lugal-má-gur$_8$-[re]
23. ĝìr Ú-du-[ ]
24. 1.0.0 ^{d}Nin-mar-ki-ka ⌜dumu dab$_5$⌝-<ba>
25. 1.0.0 Ur-^{d}Èš-du$_{10}$-nun má-gal
26. 1.0.0 Šà-kù-ge dumu dab$_5$-<ba>
27. 1.0.0 Lú-kal-la má-gal
28. 1.0.0 [du]mu dab$_5$-ba
29. 1.0.0 [ ] na-gada
30. [ ] má-gal
31. [x]-kù-ge dumu dab$_5$-<ba>
32. [^{d}Šu]l-pa-è na-gada
33. [ ] na-gada
34. [ ] dumu dab$_5$-<ba>
35. [ ] dumu dab$_5$-<ba>

36. [dumu] dab$_5$-<ba>
37. [ ] muš
38. [ ]
39. [ ] DU
40. [ ] NU
41. [x]
42. šu+níĝin 50 udu 3 máš dab$_5$-ba
43. mu-ús-sa en [d]Nanna Kar-zi-da ba-ḫun

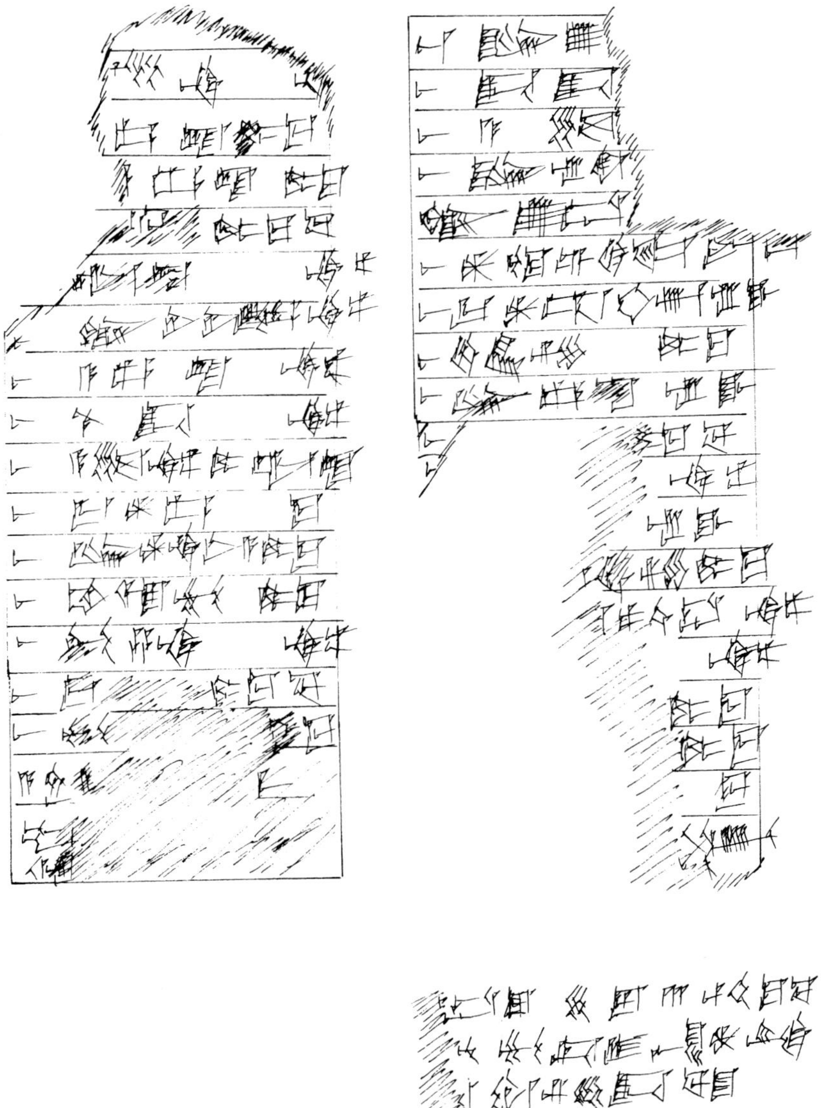

105

(I/-/ŠS 2)

OBV.

1. 5.0.0 zì-munu$_4$-ḫi-a gur lugal
2. má-a ĝar-ra
3. *En-um-ì-lí* rá-gaba

REV.

4. A-dam-šáḫ^{ki}-ta ĝen-na
5. ĝìr Al-la-mu
6. zi-ga
7. iti buru$_x$(GÁN)-maš
8. mu má dàra-abzu ba-ab-du$_8$

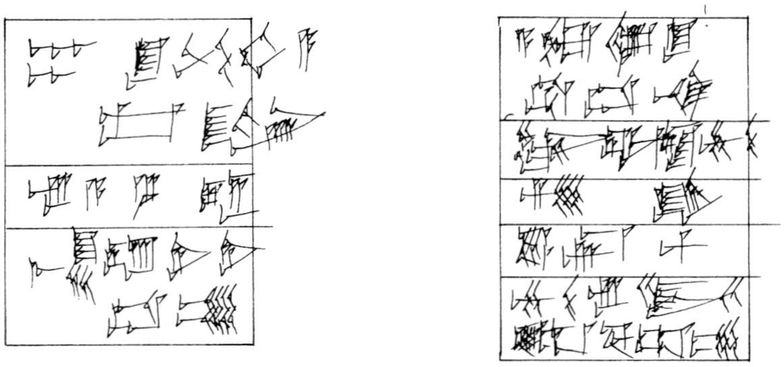

106

(V/-/[ŠS 8])

OBV.

1. 1.0.0 duḫ-a lugal
2. gu$_4$-šè
3. zi-ga

REV.

4. Nimgir-ra-[kam]
5. (*seal illegible*)
6. iti munu$_4$-kú
7. mu [ ]

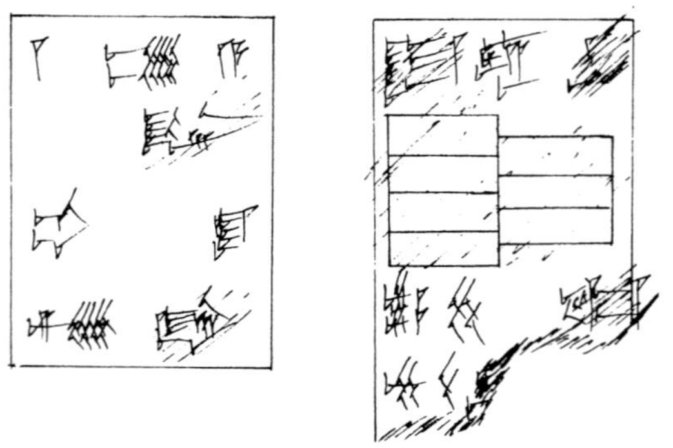

107 (X/-/ŠS 8)

OBV.

1. 0.1.0 duḫ-a
2. un-ĝa$_6$-me
3. zi-ga
4. [N]imgir-ra-kam

REV.

5. iti amar-a-a-si
6. *(seal illegible)*
7. mu má-gur$_8$-maḫ ba-dím

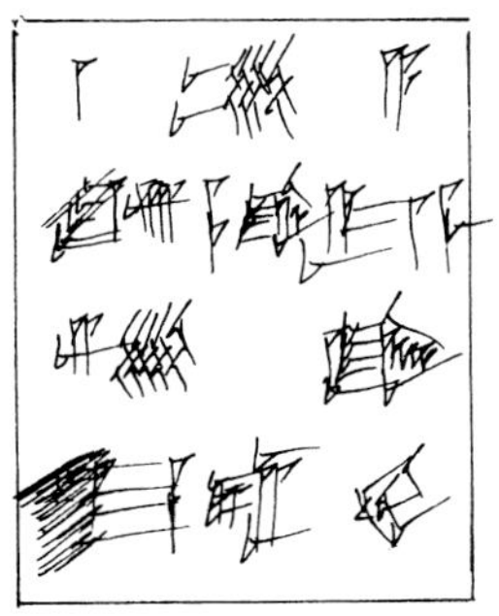

108 (XII/-/ŠS 8)

OBV.

1. [ ] duḫ
2. ĝìr en Lagaš^{ki}
3. zi-ga

REV.

4. Nimgir-ra-kam
5. iti še-íl-la
6. *(seal illegible)*
7. mu má-gur$_8$-[ma]ḫ ba-dím

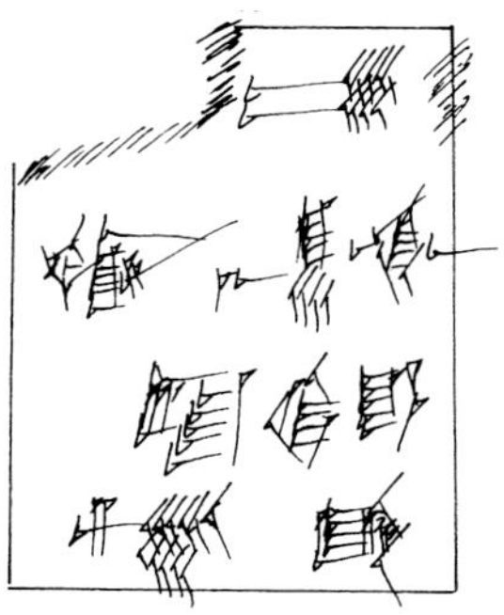

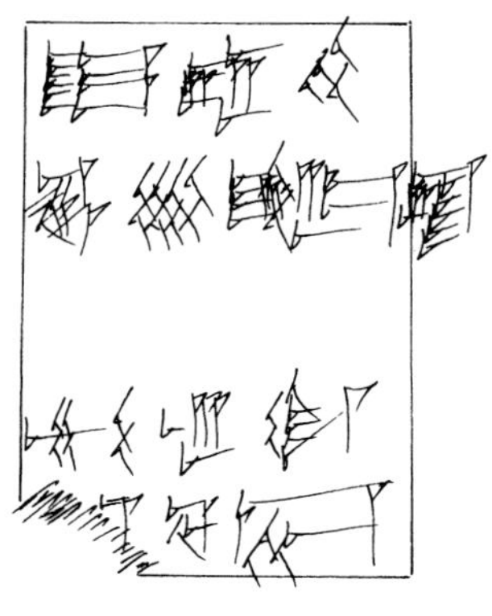

109 (I/-/-)

OBV.

*1. 0.2.1 zíz AN ša lugal-ta
2. dumu Lú-igi-ša$_6$-ša$_6$ ka-gur$_7$-me
3. Gú-ab-ba[ki]-ta

REV.

4. *Èr-ra-ba-ni* maškim
5. (BLANK)
6. zi-ga
7. iti buru$_x$(GÁN)-maš

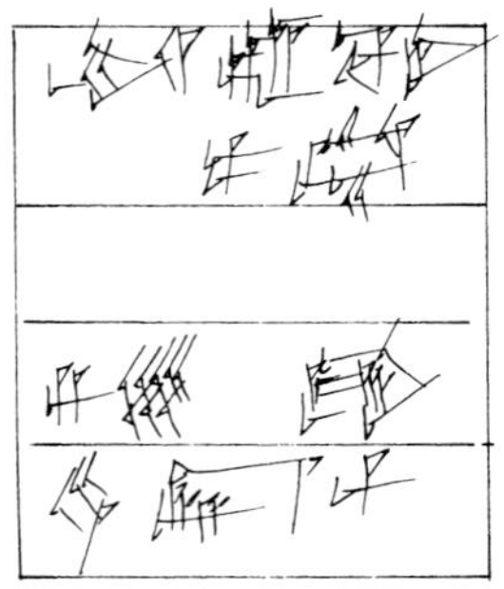

110 (IV/-/-)

OBV.

1. 0.0.1 kaš sig$_5$
2. èš-èš u$_4$-sakar u$_4$ 15-[kam]
3. 1 dida sig$_5$
4. [d]Šul-pa-è-é-gal
5. 1 dida sig$_5$
6. nì numun du$_{10}$-ga
7. [d]Šul-gi
8. 0.0.1 kaš sig$_5$
9. Gù-dé-a énsi

REV.

10. 0.2.0 kaš ĝen lugal
11. Diĝir-*á-lí-ik* Mar-tu
12. (BLANK)
13. iti šu-numun

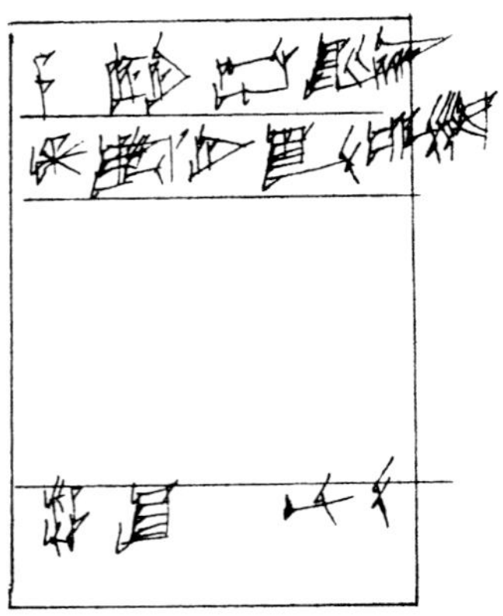

111 (VII/-/-)

OBV.

1. 0.0.1 zì-dub-dub
*2. 5 sìla ninda-àr-ra ŠU.AN
*3. balaĝ-u$_4$-da é Uru-kù^{ki}

REV.

4. ĝìr ^{d}Utu-bar-ra gala-maḫ
5. (BLANK)
6. zi-ga
7. iti ezen ^{d}Šul-gi

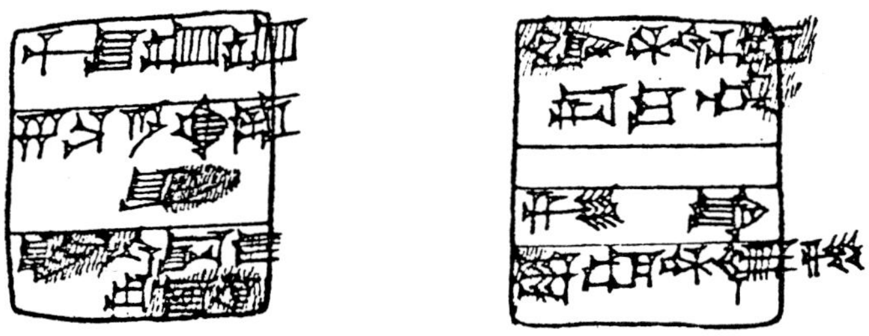

112 (VII/-/-)

OBV.

1. 10 gín ì-ĝeš
2. èš-èš u$_4$-sakar u$_4$ 15
3. ½ sìla ì lugal ki ^{d}Na-rú-a-šè ĝen-na
4. 1 sìla ì-ĝeš
5. Lugal-ezen-ma tuš-a

REV.

6. ^{d}Šul-gi
7. 1 sìla ì-ĝeš
8. Diĝir-ma-ì-ĝál
9. (BLANK)
10. iti ezen ^{d}Šul-gi

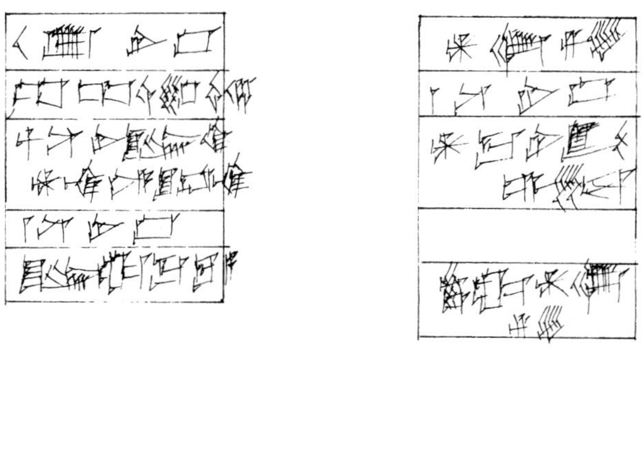

113 (XII/-/-)

OBV.

1. 1 dida ĝen
2. 0.0.1 zì-sig$_{15}$
3. 3 sìla zì-dub-dub
4. 2 sìla eša

REV.

5. ÁB.A.ŠI
6. An-ta-sur-ra
7. ĝìr ^{d}Utu-bar-ra gala-maḫ
8. zi-ga
9. iti še-íl-la

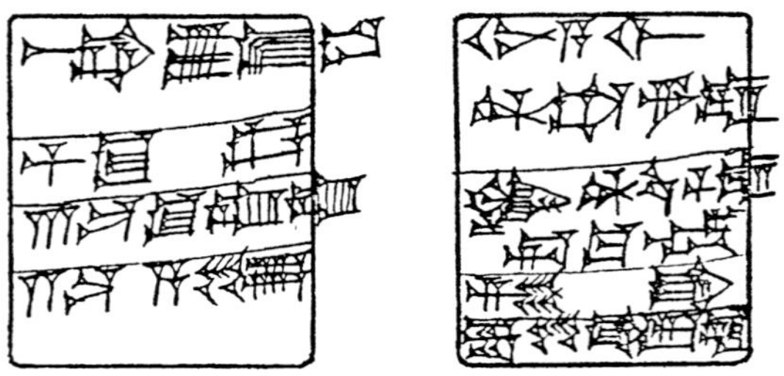

114 (XII/-/-)

OBV.

*1. 2.0.0 zì-munu$_{4}$-ḫi-a gur lugal
2. *I-din*-^{d}Suen dumu lugal

REV.

*3. Ka-si-šè ĝen-na
*4. *A-ḫu-a* sukkal maškim
5. zi-ga
6. iti še-íl-la

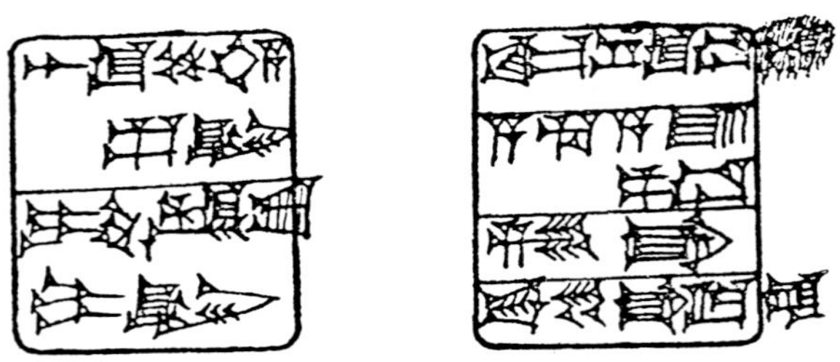

115

(XII/-/-)

OBV.

1. 2 dida ĝen
2. ĜIŠGAL.ĜIŠGAL gaba Má-gan-na
3. 2 dida ĝen
4. 2 sìla zì-sig$_{15}$
5. 3 sìla zì-gu

REV.

6. 2 sìla zì-dub-dub
7. 1 sìla eša
8. nì sízkur-ra má Má-gan-na
9. ĝìr Ur-ab-ba lú-kaš$_{4}$
10. zi-ga iti še íl-la

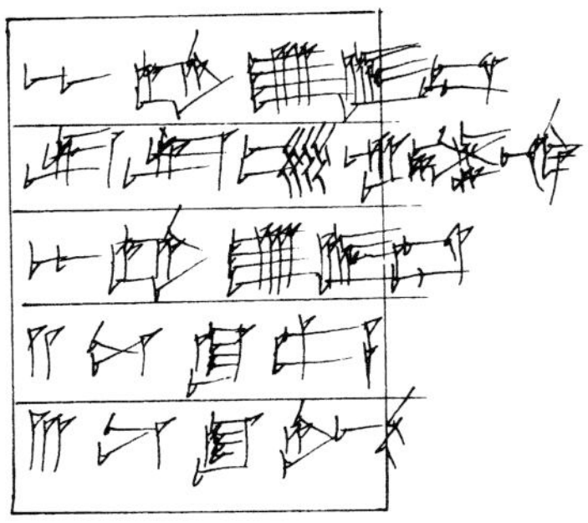

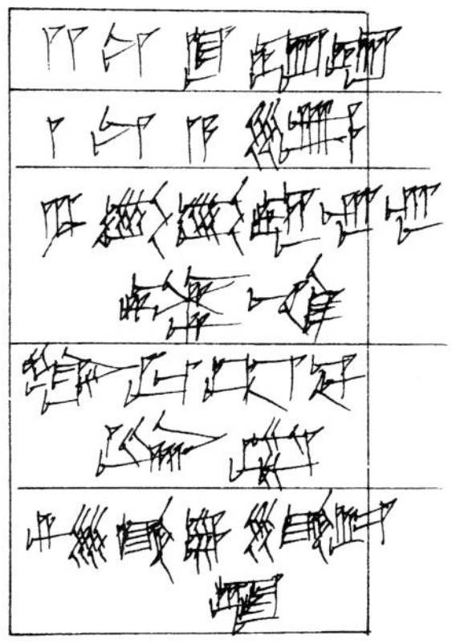

116

(XII/-/-)

OBV.

1. 1 dida sig$_{5}$
2. 0.0.1 zì-sig$_{15}$
3. 0.0.1 zì-gu
4. 3 sìla zì-dub-dub
5. 2 sìla eša
6. é ^{d}IM-šè
7. 2 dida sig$_{5}$

REV.

8. 0.0.1 zì-sig$_{15}$
9. 0.0.1 zì-gu
10. 0.0.1 zì-dub-dub
11. 5 sìla eša
12. An-ta-sur-ra-šè
13. Ga-kú-è-a
14. zi-ga
15. iti še-íl-la

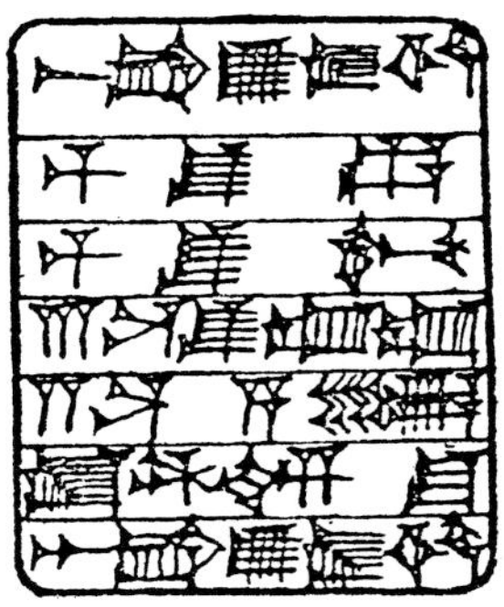

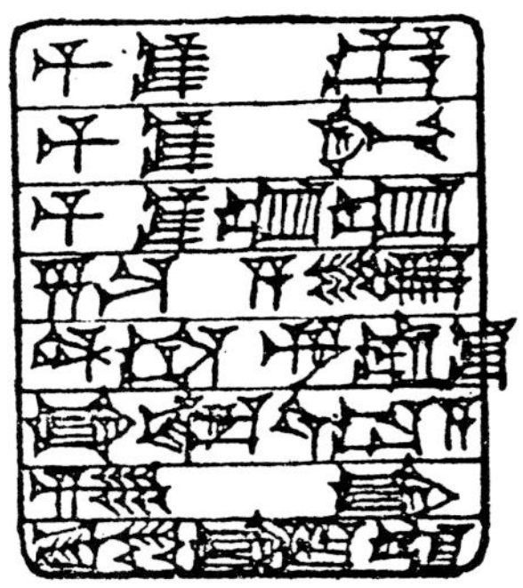

117 (XII/-/[ ])

OBV.

1. 0.0.1 kaš 0.0.3 z[ì]
2. 0.0.1 kaš-ĝi$_6$ gur
3. 0.0.1 zì-gu
4. 5 sìla zì-sig$_{15}$
5. 1 ½ sìla zì-dub-dub
6. 1 ½ sìla eša
7. sá-du$_{11}$ u$_4$-da íl
8. 5 ĝìr-[la]m 3 sìla
9. nì-dab$_5$ u$_4$-sakar
10. [ ] é-a GIŠ 0.0.3
11. [ ] 3 sìla

REV.

12. [ki-a]-naĝ
13. [ ] x a-šè
14. 2 ezen-ma 3 sìla
15. iti še-íl-l[a]
16. nì ezen x-šè
17. (BLANK)

*18. ^{d}Ḫendur-[sa]ĝ

19. mu ú[s-sa]

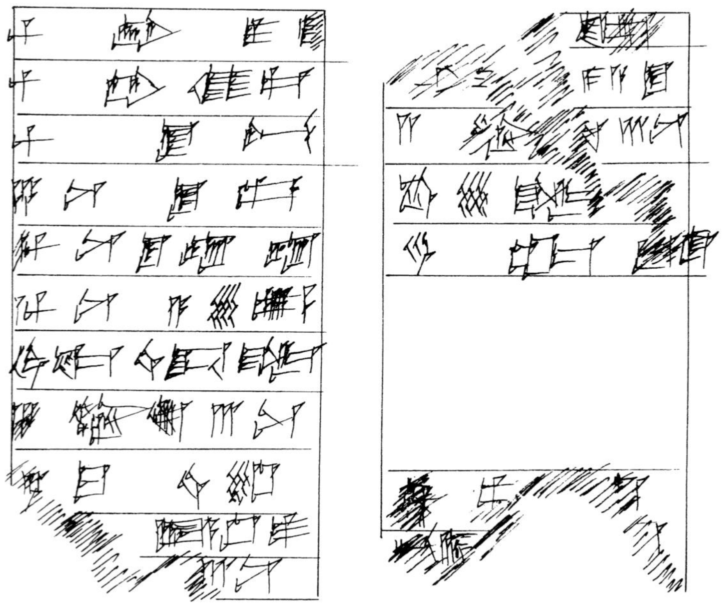

118 (date not preserved)

OBV.

1. 1 [ ]
2. Ur-[ ]
3. 1 [ ]
4. 1 *Šu*-[ ]
5. 1 NÌ [ ]
6. 1 [x]
7. 1 [x]
8. 1 [L]ú-uru-[ ]
9. 1 Lú-ḪAR-[ ]
10. 1 Ba-mu
11. 1 Ur-^{d}Šára
12. 1 Ur-^{d}Nanše
13. 1 Ur-^{d}Ba-ú
14. 1 Lú-kal-la
15. 1 Da-da

REV.

16. 1 Ka$_{5}$-a
17. (BLANK)
18. šu+nígin 15 túg da-ba-tum
19. ḫé-dab$_{5}$ ^{ĝeš}tukul-e dab$_{5}$-ba-me
20. é ^{d}Šul-gi-me
21. ki Lú-^{d}Nin-šubur dumu Ìr-mu-ta
22. (BLANK)
23. ugula Šeš-kal-la
24. ĝìr Ur-^{d}Nanše dumu NUN-[ ]
25. (BLANK)
26. iti ezen ^{d}[ ]
27. mu ĝeš[ ]

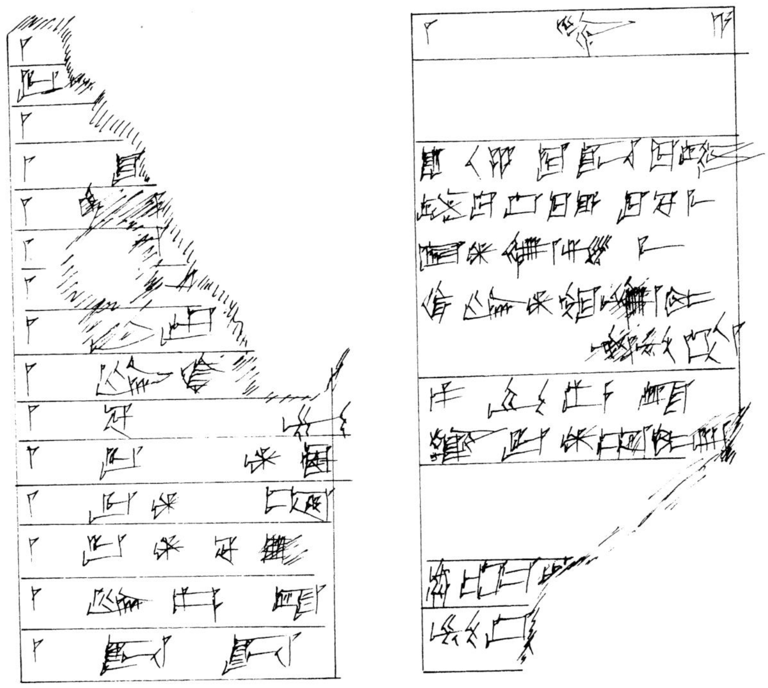

119 (date not preserved)

OBV.

1. [ ] sìla zù-lum [ ]
2. [ ] Ur-^{d}Dumu-zi
3. [ ] sìla a x
4. [x] x [ ]-mar-ki
5. [ ] x-x-pa-⌜è⌝
6. [ ]-^{d}Nin-ĝír-su ù
7. [x]-^{d}Ba-ú
8. [ ] še lugal
9. [ ]
10. [ ]

(reverse destroyed)

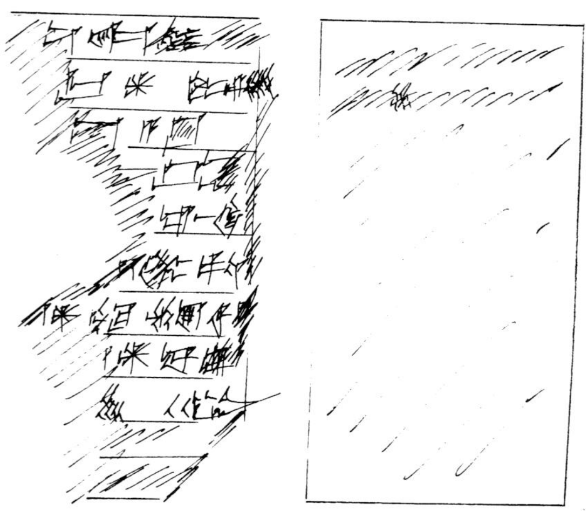

120 (-/-/Š 25)

OBV.

1. 4 dusu 0.0.1 5 sìla-ta
2. 6 dusu 0.0.1
3. 2 dusu 0.0.3
4. ki sukkal-maḫ-š⸢è⸣
5. 0.0.1 5 sìla ninda gu-la

*6. 0.3.3 ĝeš-da-didli

REV.

7. ki Lú-^{d}Na-rú-a-ta

*8. kìšib A-gu

9. *(seal illegible)*
10. mu Si-mu-ru-um^{ki} ba-ḫul

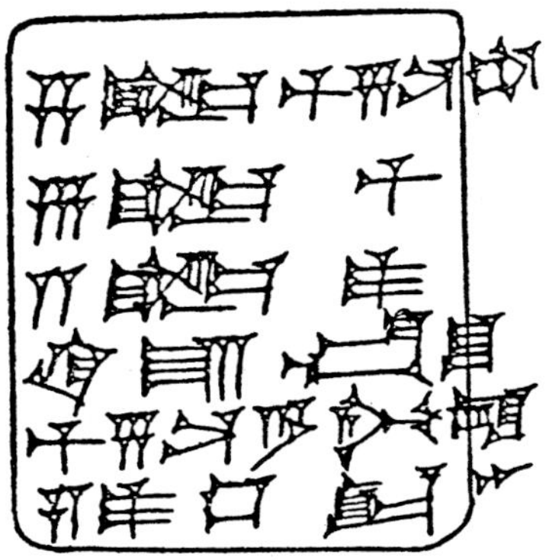

121 (IV/-/Š 42)

OBV.

(top of obverse broken)

1. 3.3.3 še [gur] luga[l]
2. ki Ur-^{d}Igi-[ ]
3. kìšib Nam-maḫ

REV.

4. SEAL
5. [it]i šu-numu[n]
6. [mu] Ša-aš-r[um-um^{ki}]

Seal: Nam-maḫ-^{d}Ba-ú
dumu Ab-ba-gi-na
ugula kíkken énsi-[ka]

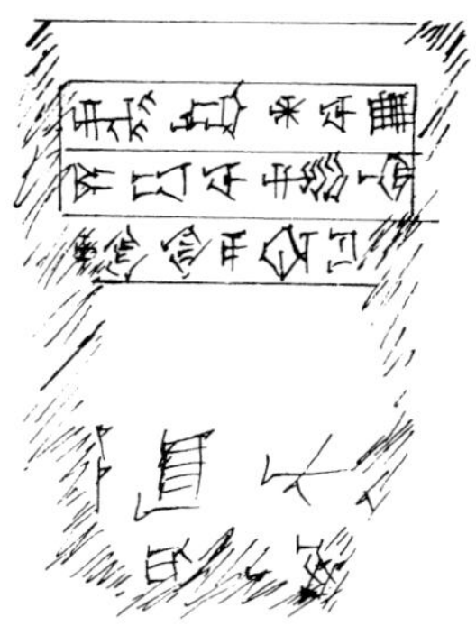

122

(-/-/Š 43)

OBV.

1. 0.0.3 8⅓ sìla ì-nun lugal
2. 1 gú 49½ ma-na síg ud$_5$
3. ki Ur-ab-ba-ta

REV.

4. Igi-an-na-ke$_4$-zu kuš$_7$ šu ba-ti
5. lá-u$_x$ mu-ús-sa é *Puzur$_4$-iš-^{d}Da-gan* ba-dù
6. mu en ^{d}Nanna maš-e ì-pàd

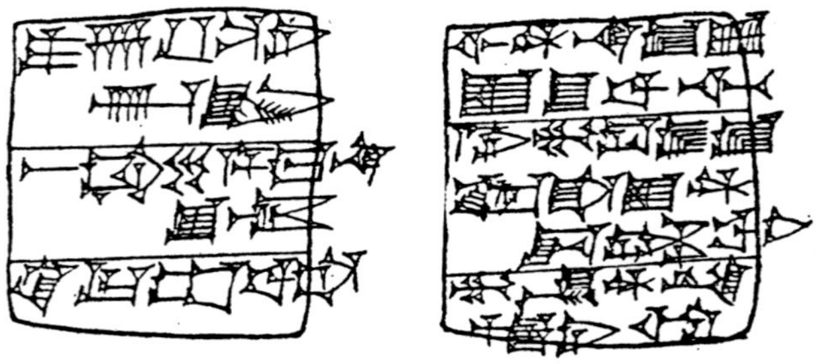

123

(V/-/Š 44)

OBV.

1. 30 ma-na [x]
2. 3 gín kù-babbar
3. ki Lú-^{d}Nin-ĝír-su-ta
4. Zu-dam-du$_{10}$

REV.

5. šu ba-ti
6. ĝìr Ìr-mu
7. iti munu$_4$-kú
8. mu a-rá 10 lá 1-kam Si-[m]u-<ru>-um^{ki} ba-ḫul

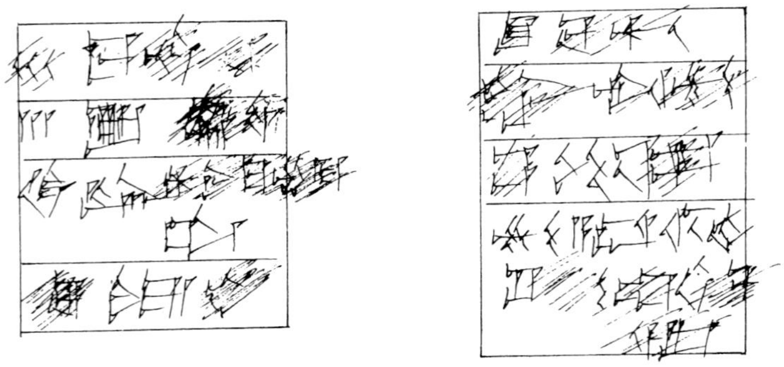

124 (I/-/Š 45)

OBV.

*1. 76.3.2 še gur lugal
2. ì-dub á-gul-ta
3. ki Ba-zi

REV.

4. Lú-^{d}Nin-tu
5. šu ba-ti
6. iti buru$_{x}$(GÁN)-maš
7. mu Ur-bí-lum^{ki} ba-ḫul

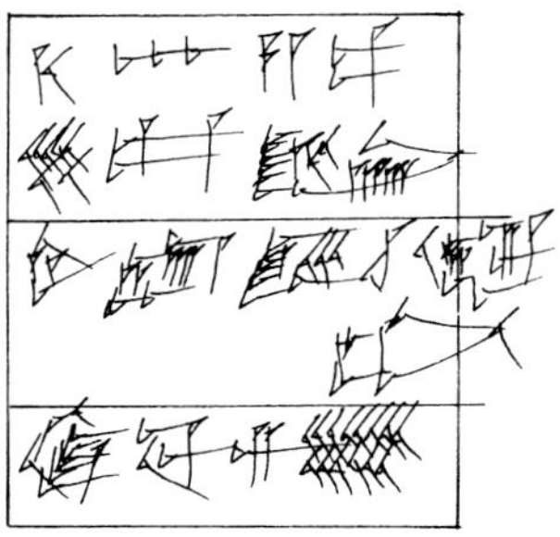

125 (V/-/Š 45?)

OBV.

1. 2 ḫu-bu-um umbin
2. ki-lá-bi 7 ma-na 10 gín urudu
3. ki Ur-^{d}Nin-ĝeš-zi-da-ta

REV.

*4. énsi-ke$_{4}$ ì-lá
5. (BLANK)
6. [iti munu$_{4}$]-kú
7. [mu U]r-bí-[lum^{ki} ba-ḫu]l

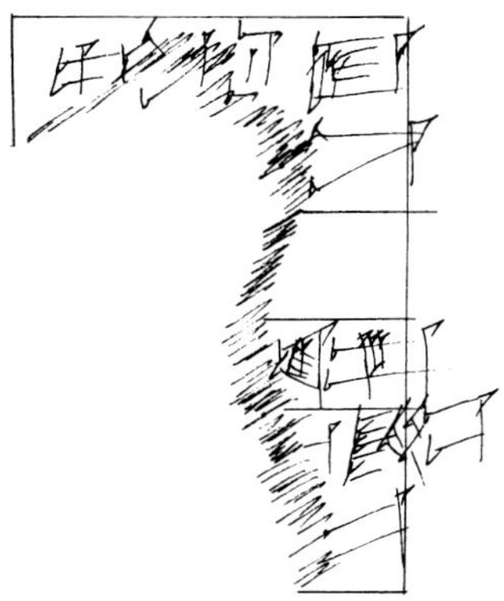

126

(VIII/-/Š 45)

OBV.

1. [ ]2 áb-máḫ
2. [x] gu$_4$ šà é-gal-ta
3. k[i x]-ta
4. Ur-^{d}Asal-lú-ḫi

REV.

5. ì-dab$_5$
6. (BLANK)
7. iti ezen ^{d}Ba-ú
8. mu Ur-bí-lum^{ki} ba-ḫul

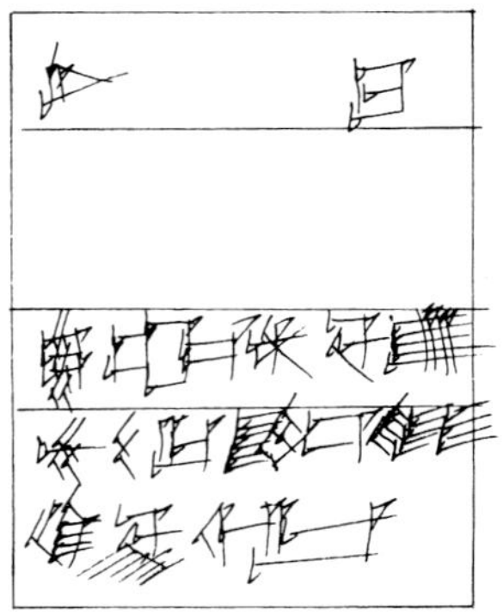

127

(X/-/Š 45)

OBV.

1. 211.3.0 še gur lugal
2. še-àr-ra ab-ba ab-ba ù engar nu-bànda-gu$_4$
3. ì-dub ELAM-ne-ta
4. ki Ba-zi-ta

REV.

5. Lú-bi-mu
6. šu ba-ti
7. šà Nina^{ki}
8. iti amar-a-a-si
9. mu Ur-bí-lum^{ki} ba-ḫul

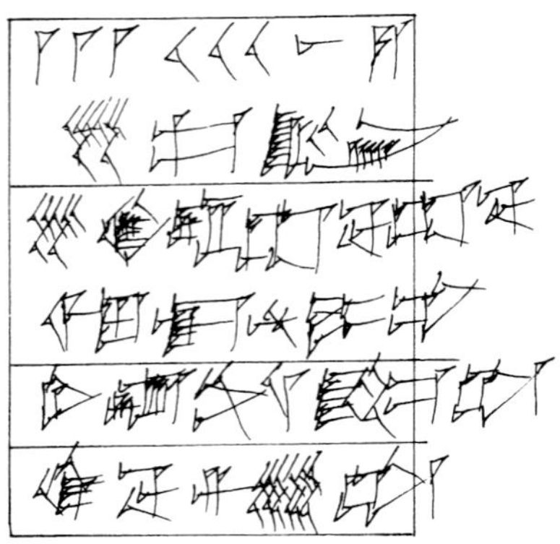

128 (IV/-/Š 46)

OBV.

1. 7.2.0 zíz gur lugal
2. zíz zì.KA-ta
3. ki Lú-diĝir-ra-ta
4. Lú-^{d}Nin-ĝír-su
5. šu ba-ti

REV.

6. iti šu-numun
7. (BLANK)
8. mu-ús-sa Ur-bí-lum^{ki} ba-ḫul

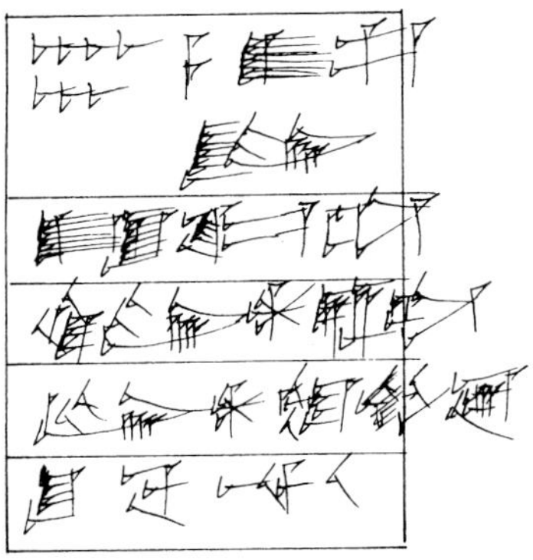

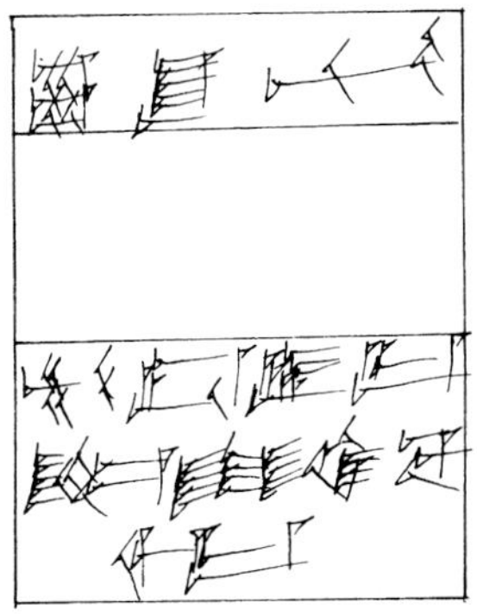

129 (-/-/Š 46)

OBV.

1. 5 gín kù-babbar
2. ki Ba-na-ti-ta
3. 7 gín lá igi-6-ĝál
4. ki Ur-^{d}Nanše dumu Ur-^{d}Ig-alima-ta
5. 3 gín lá igi-6-ĝál
6. ki Ur-^{d}Šu-an-na dumu Ur-^{ĝeš}gigir-ta
7. igi-3-ĝál 5 še

REV.

8. ki Lú-^{d}Utu ugula kíkken-ta
9. (BLANK)
10. šu+níĝin 15 gín 5 še
11. kišib énsi-ka
12. ĝìr Ur-^{d}Ba-ú dumu Si-dù
13. mu Ki-maš^{ki} ba-ḫul

(Note: še *is written on the left edge next to lines 1 and 3*)

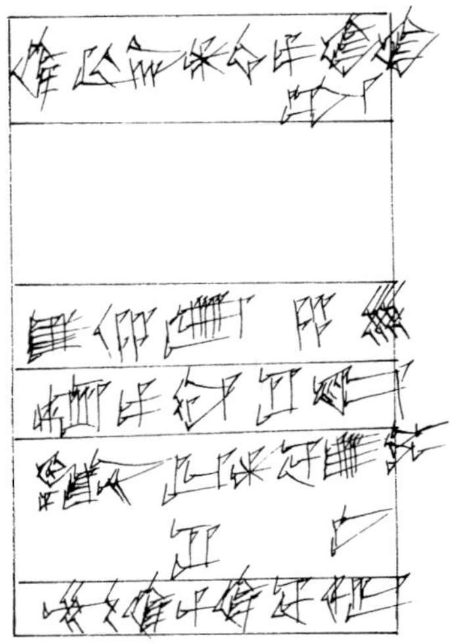

130 (VI/-/Š 47)

OBV.

1. 0.2.0 še lugal
2. ki Ur-^{d}Ba-ú-ta
3. še-ba kù-ta sa$_{10}$-a-šè
4. kìšib *Èr-ra-nu-id*

REV.

5. še Kù-^{d}Nanše
6. SEAL
7. iti ezen ^{d}Dumu-zi
8. mu-ús-sa Ki-maš^{ki} ba-ḫul

Seal: *Èr-ra-nu-id*
dub-sar
dumu Ur-ša$_{6}$-ga

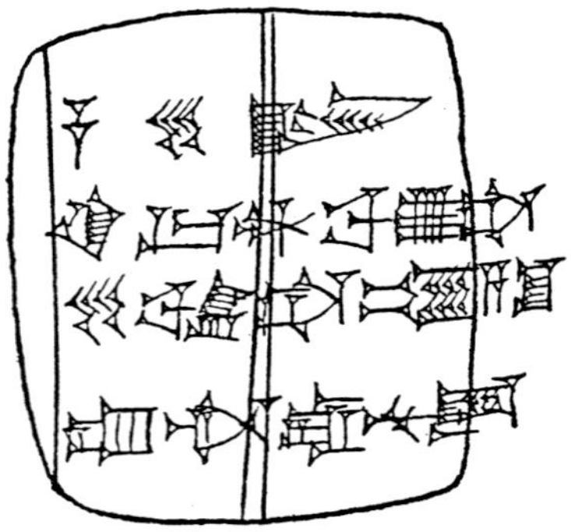

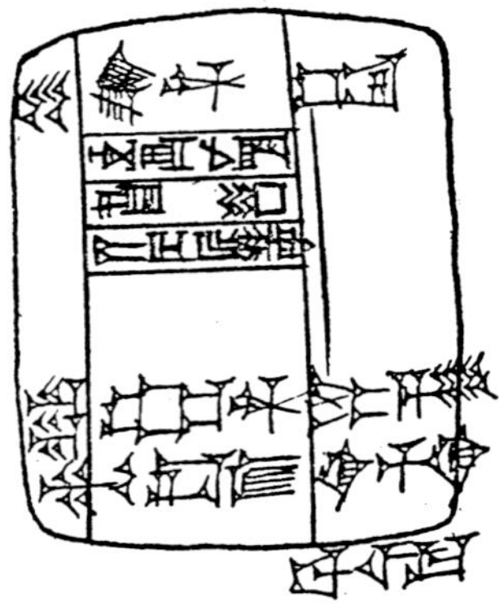

131 (III/-/Š 48)

OBV.

1. 10.2.3 nin[da]-à[r]-ra sig$_{5}$
2. 1.4.0 zì gur
3. 1.0.0 ⌜zì⌝ A.SI.GÚ
4. ki Ur-^{d}Ba-ú dumu Ur-ni$_{9}$-ĝar-ta

REV.

5. [x] dumu Da-gi

*6. šà Ki-sur-ra

7. iti ezen ^{d}Li$_{9}$-si$_{4}$
8. mu-ús-sa Ki-maš^{ki} b[a-ḫu]l mu-ús-[sa]-bi

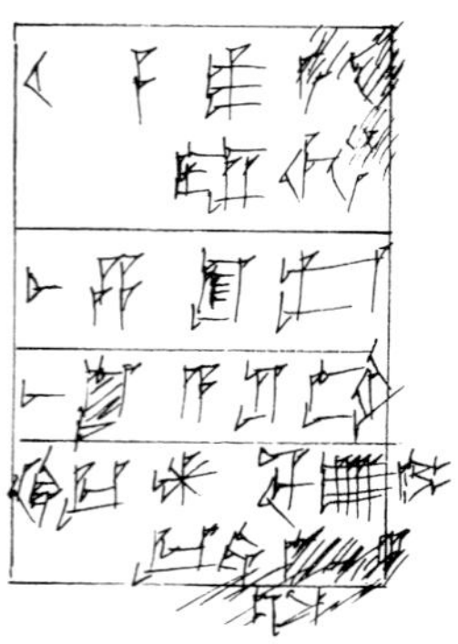

132

(-/-/Š 48)

OBV.

1. 3.0.0 dabin gur lugal
2. ki Ur-ba-ga-ta
3. Ur-^{d}Ba-ú

REV.

4. šu ba-ti
5. (B L A N K)
6. mu-ús-sa Ki-maš^{ki} mu-ús-sa-bi

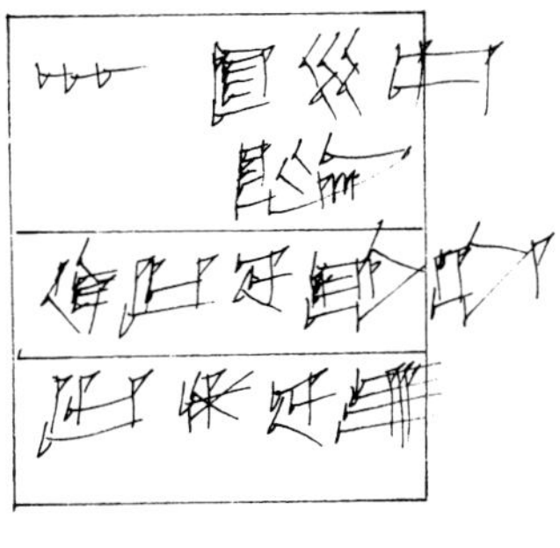

133

(II/-/AS 1)

OBV.

1. 6 gu$_{4}$ na-kab-tum
2. bala-šè
3. ki A-kal-la-ta

*4. Ba-a ì-dab$_{5}$

REV.

5. ĝìr Ur-^{d}-Šul-pa-è
6. iti gu$_{4}$-rá-bí-mú-mú
7. mu Amar-^{d}Suen lugal

134

(III/10/AS 1)

OBV.

1. 85.1.2 zì-sig$_{15}$ lugal
2. 432.0.1 1 sìla dabin
3. 4.2.1 ar-za-na [ninda-à]r-ra sig$_5$
4. [ ] da

REV.

5. [ki] ba [t]a
6. [x]-la
7. šu ba-ti
8. iti ezen ^{d}Li$_9$-si$_4$ u$_4$ 10 ba-zal
9. mu ^{d}Amar-^{d}Suen lugal

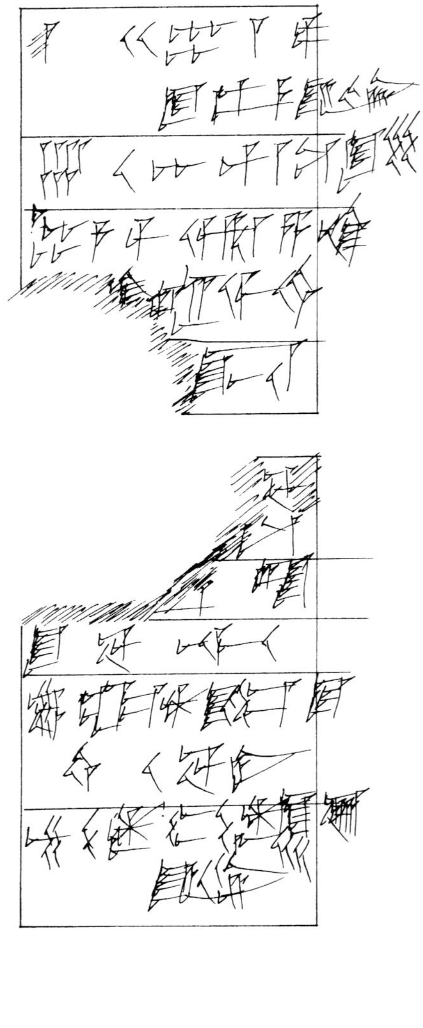

135

(V/-/AS 1)

OBV.

1. 20 urudu [ ]
2. ki-lá-bi 10 ma-na
3. ki Ur-^{d}Nin-ĝeš-z[i]-da-t[a]
4. ba-z[i]
5. Lugal-ti-ra-áš [ ]

REV.

6. šu ba-ti
7. ĝìr Lugal-ki-[x]
8. ĝìr Ur-^{d}Ba-[ú] dumu Lugal-NÍG [ ]
   nu-bànda
9. iti munu$_4$-kú
10. mu ^{d}Amar-^{d}E[N].ZU lug[al]

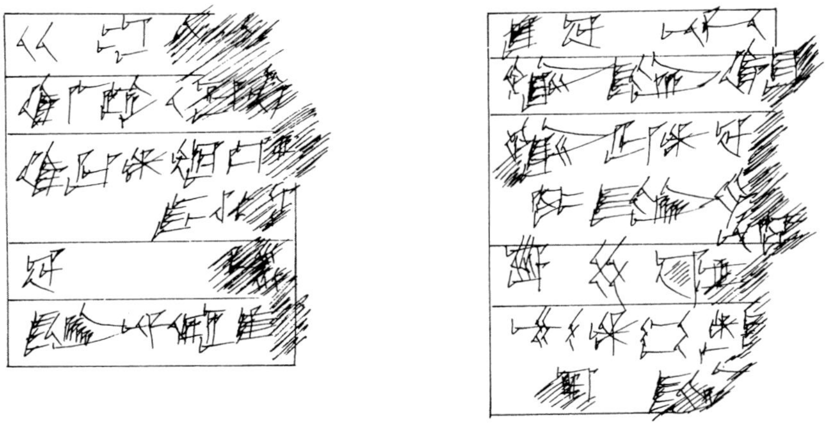

136

(X/-/AS 1)

OBV.

1. 0.3.0 še lugal
2. še ur$_5$-ra
3. ki saĝa ^{d}Nin-mar-ki-ta
4. Da-da

REV.

*5. en[gar]-gu-la
6. šu ba-ti
7. iti amar-a-a-si
8. mu ^{d}Amar-^{d}Suen lugal

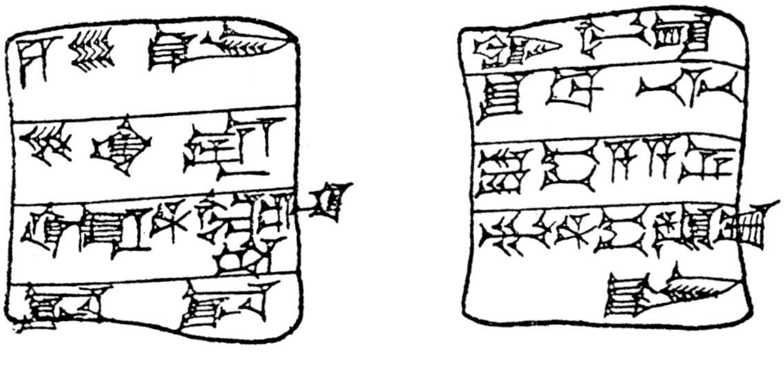

137

(-/-/AS 1)

OBV.

1. 0.2.0 še lugal
2. Ur-^{d}Lama dumu Un-ĝa$_6$
3. 0.2.0 Lú-^{d}Nin-ĝír-su dumu Lú-^{d}Igi-ma-šè
4. še ur$_5$-ra su-su-dam
5. ì-dub a-šà ḫi-ĝál-ta

REV.

6. ki saĝa ^{d}Nin-mar-ki-ta
7. kišib Lú-kiri$_4$-zal dumu Ur-^{d}Ba-ú
8. (BLANK)
9. mu ^{d}Amar-^{d}Suen lugal

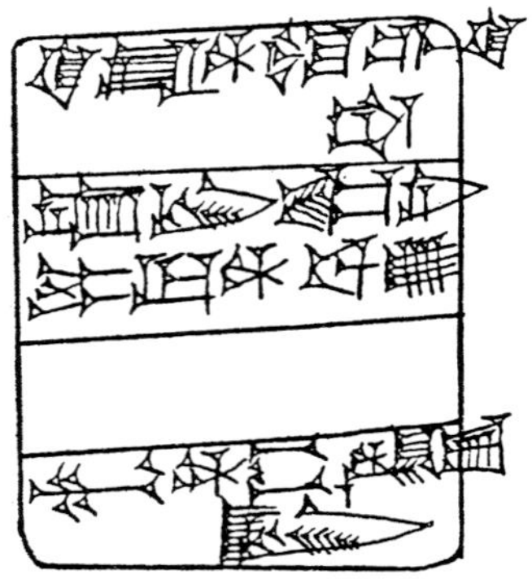

138

(-/-/AS 1)

OBV.

1. 91.2.3 še gur lugal
2. še ur$_5$-ra dumu dab$_5$-[ba]
3. še ^{d}En-líl-lá
4. Ur-mes dumu Ba-ad-da

REV.

5. šu ba-ti
6. (BLANK)
7. mu ^{d}Amar-^{d}Suen lugal

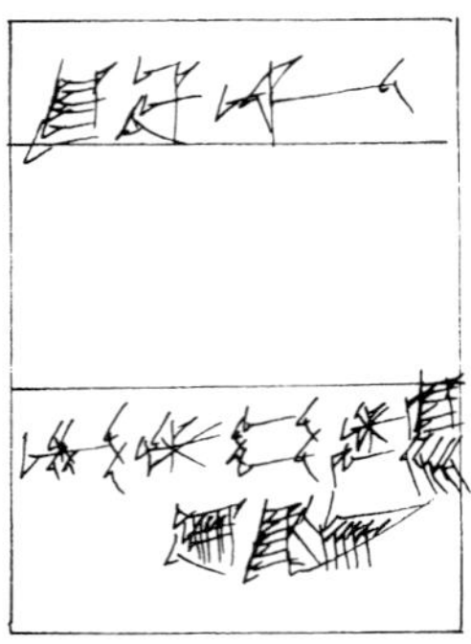

139 (IV/-/AS 2)

OBV.

(top of obverse broken)

1. [ ]
2. 0.2.0 ninda-àr-ra sig$_5$ má Ur-^{d}Išta⸢ran-ta⸣
3. 5.0.0 gur ki Ur-^{d}Šul-pa-è-ta
4. 5.0.0 gur ki Lú-^{d}Na-rú-a-ta
5. 5.0.0 gur ki Bí-du$_{11}$-ì-ša$_6$-ta
6. 0.0.3 kaš ĝen ki È-a-mu-ta
7. 3.0.0 gur na-kab-tum-ta
8. 0.2.0 maš-da-ri-a
9. 0.0.2 kaš ĝen ki *Pù-du-uš*-<*ki*>-*in*-ta
10. (BLANK)
11. [ ] x

(bottom of obverse broken)

REV.

(top of reverse broken)

12. [ ] ⸢UŠ.ME⸣
13. 1.1.3 4 sìla kaš sig$_5$ 0.3.4 kaš ĝen
14. *Na-ab-da-núm* úgu-a ĝá-ĝá
15. ĝìr Ur-^{d}Ba-ú dumu Na-mu
16. iti šu-numun
17. 1.1.3 kaš sig$_5$ gur 3.1.4 kaš ĝen gur
18. [ ] Lugal-ú-šim-e
19. [x] zì-sig$_{15}$-la Ur-^{d}Ig-alima
20. [x] kìšib Lú-^{d}Na-rú-a
21. [ ] kìšib Lú-^{d}Inanna
22. [ ] kaš ĝen kìšib Ur-^{d}Ba-ú <dumu> Na-di
23. [ ] kìšib ì-rá-rá
24. ⸢ĝìr⸣ Ur-^{d}Šul-pa-è
25. [^{d}]Šul-gi-*ì-lí* Mar-tu
26. [ ] x

(bottom of reverse broken)

27. iti ezen ^{d}[Li$_9$-si$_4$]
28. ù iti šu-[numun]
29. mu-^{d}Amar-[^{d}Suen] Ur-bí-l[um^{ki}]

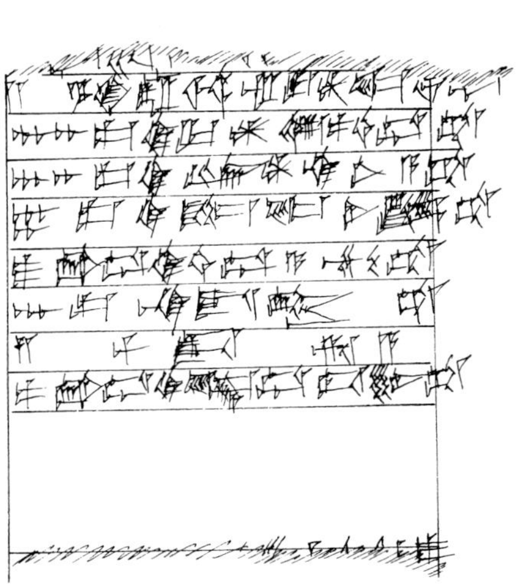

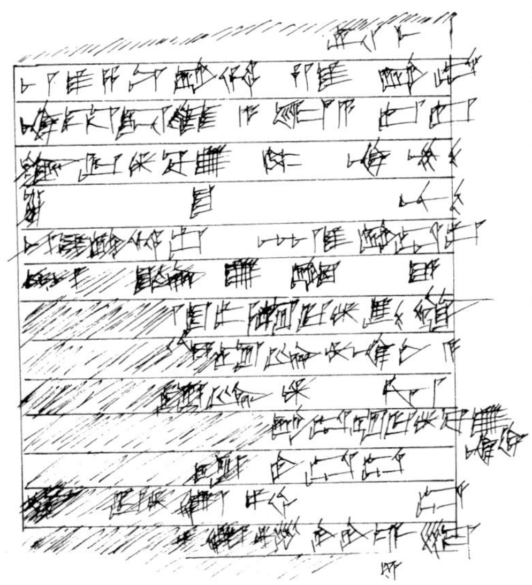

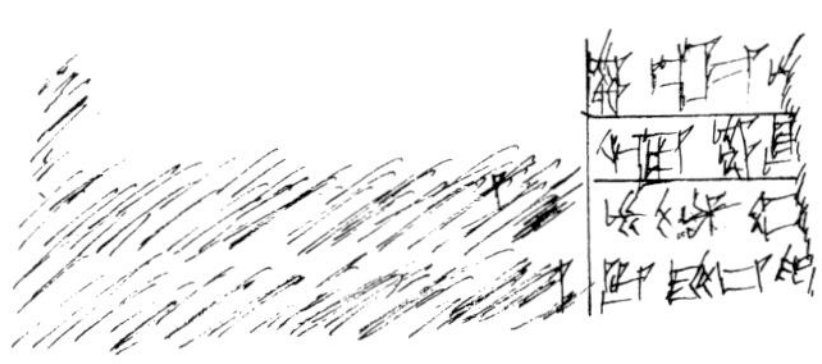

140 (VI/-/AS 2)

OBV.

1. ⅔ ša lá igi-4-ĝál kù-babbar
2. kù ĝeš-ì-ka
3. ki Da-da dumu Ur-^{ĝeš}gigir-ta
4. ĝìr Lú-^{d}Nin-ĝír-su

REV.

5. dumu Ì-kal-la
6. é-gal-la ba-an-ku$_4$ šà Uri$_5^{ki}$-ma
7. (BLANK)
8. iti ezen ^{d}Dumu-zi
9. mu ^{d}Amar-^{d}Suen lugal-e Ur-bí-lum^{ki} mu-ḫul

141 (X/-/AS 2)

OBV.

1. 1 sìla làl
2. ki A-gi$_4$-ta
3. ⋆3. šuku saĝ-sè-ga
4. u$_4$-sakar iti amar-a-a-si-šè

REV.

5. kišib Lugal-gú-gal
6. SEAL
7. iti amar-a-a-si
8. mu ^{d}Amar-^{d}Suen lugal-e Ur-bí-lum^{ki} mu-ḫul

Seal: Lugal-gú-gal
dub-sar
dumu Lú-^{d}En-líl

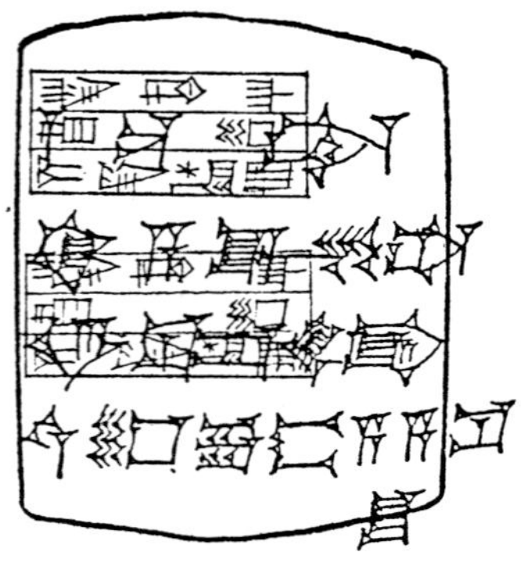

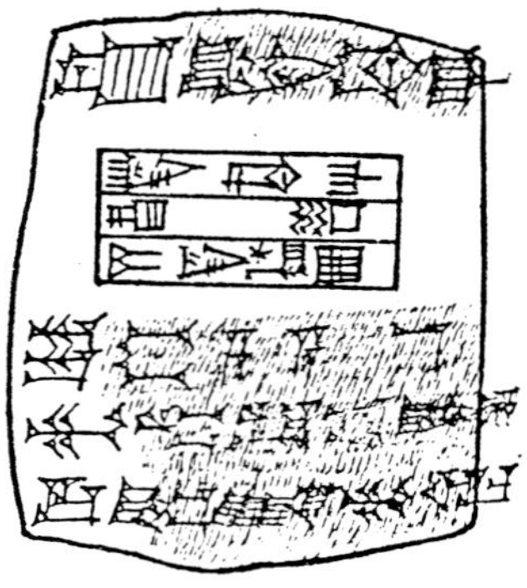

142

(-/-/AS 2)

OBV.

1. 2 áb-máḫ
2. 13 gu$_4$-ĝeš
3. gu$_4$ na-kab-tum
4. É-nì-bi ì-dab$_5$
5. ugula Du-du
6. é [d]Nanše

REV.

7. (B L A N K)
8. ŝà é-gibil-le
9. mu-ús-sa [d]Amar-[d]Suen lugal

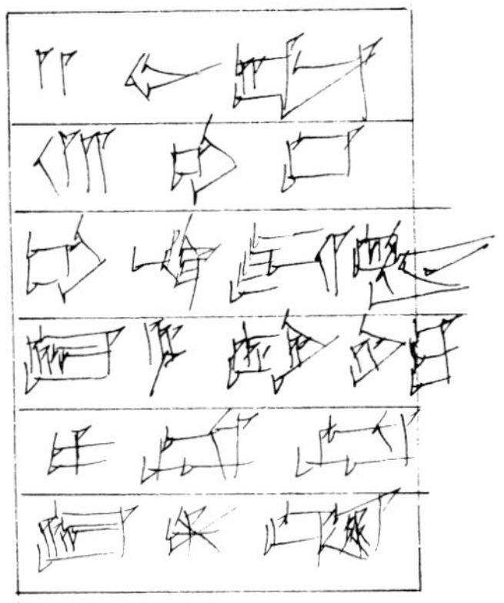

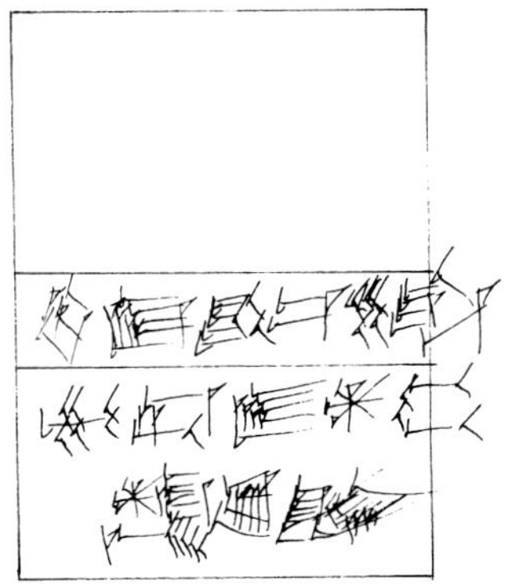

143

(-/-/AS 2)

OBV.

1. 11⅔ ma-na 6 gín igi-6-ĝál 5 še kù-babbar
2. kù saĝ-tuk
3. maš-da-ri-a ezen-maḫ-šè
4. é-gal-la ba-an-ku$_4$

REV.

5. ĝìr Ur-[d]Nun-gal
6. ù Lú-[d]Nin-tu dumu Ì-kal-la
7. (B L A N K)
8. mu [d]Amar-[d]Suen lugal-e Ur-bí-lum[ki] mu-ḫul

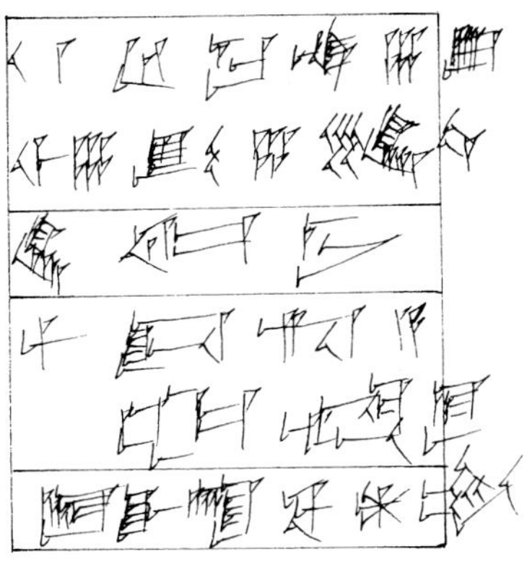

144

(II/-/AS 3)

OBV.

1. 0.1.5 8 sìla ku$_6$ 4-kam-ús
2. ki Ur-šu-ga-lam-ma-ta
3. (BLANK)
4. kìšib Lú-nita-gi-na
5. ĝìr Lú-ki-nu-nir

REV.

6. iti gu$_4$-rá-bí-mú-mú
7. SEAL
8. mu $^{\hat{g}e\check{s}}$gu-za ^{d}En-líl-lá ba-dím

Seal: Lú-nita-gi-na
dumu I-ta-è-a

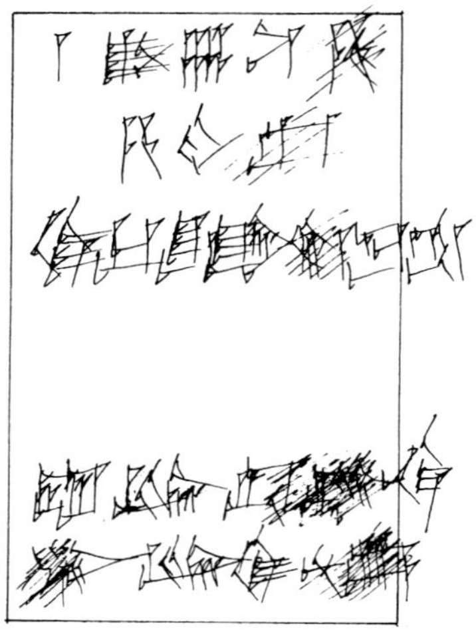

145

(IV/-/AS 3)

OBV.

1. 1 áb-máḫ ka-a
2. (BLANK)
3. é-gal gú-túl-ta

REV.

4. engar ^{d}Šul-gi
5. Lugal-da-ga ì-dab$_5$
6. (BLANK)
7. iti šu-numun
8. mu $^{\hat{g}e\check{s}}$gu-za ^{d}En-líl-lá ba-dím

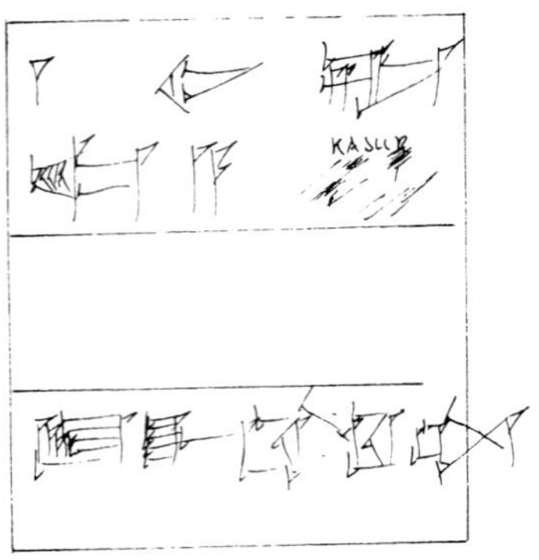

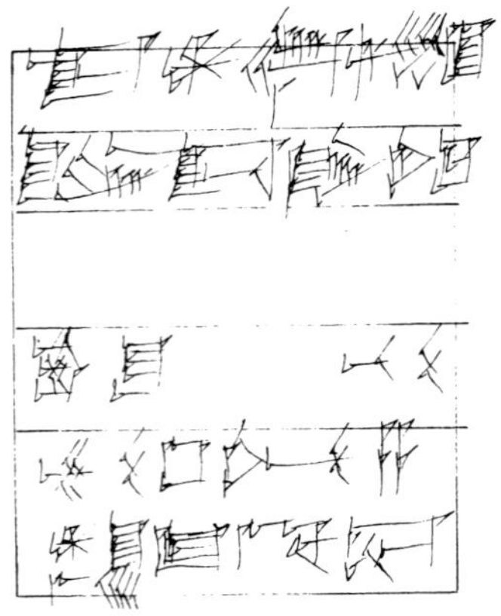

146

(V/-/AS 3)

OBV.

1. šim 6 dug du$_{10}$

*2. šim zì ká-a ^{d}Nin-ĝír-su-ka

3. ki Nì-bi-ta

4. Ur-^{d}Nin-ĝeš-zi-da

REV.

5. šu ba-ti

6. iti munu$_{4}$-kú

7. (B L A N K)

8. mu ^{ĝeš}gu-za ^{d}En-líl ba-dím

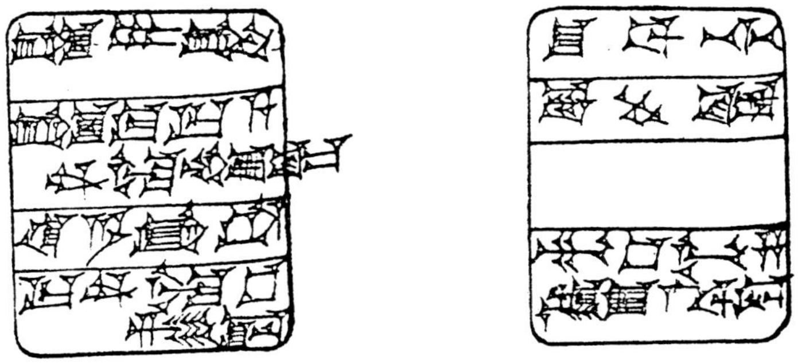

147

(V/-/AS 3)

OBV.

1. ½ ma-na kù-babbar

2. kù šà Nina

3. ki Ur-^{d}Lama saĝa ^{d}Nin-šubur-ta

4. é-gal-la ba-ku$_{4}$

5. kišib énsi

REV.

6. ĝìr Ur-^{d}Lama

7. šà Nibru^{ki}

8. (B L A N K)

9. iti munu$_{4}$-kú

10. mu ^{ĝeš}gu-za ^{d}En-líl-lá ba-dím

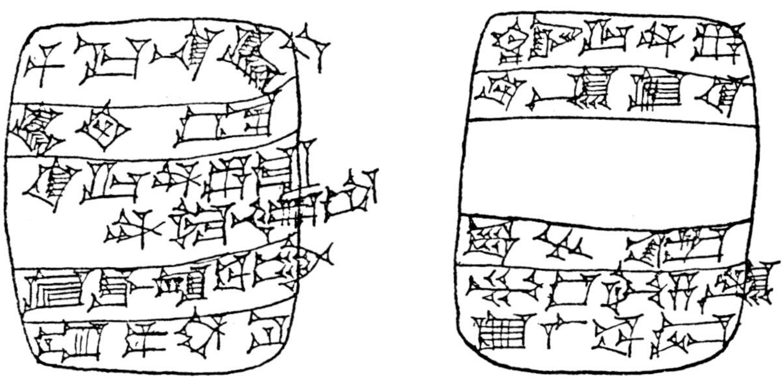

148

(X/-/AS 3)

OBV.

1. 49.1.0 še gur lugal
2. má-a si-ga
3. ì-dub A.K[A] muš-bi-ed[in]
4. ki Ur-mes-[ta]

REV.

5. Ur-^{d}En-líl-lá
6. šu ba-ti
7. (BLANK)
8. iti amar-a-a-si
9. mu $^{\langle\text{ĝeš}\rangle}$gu-za ^{d}En-líl-lá ba-dím

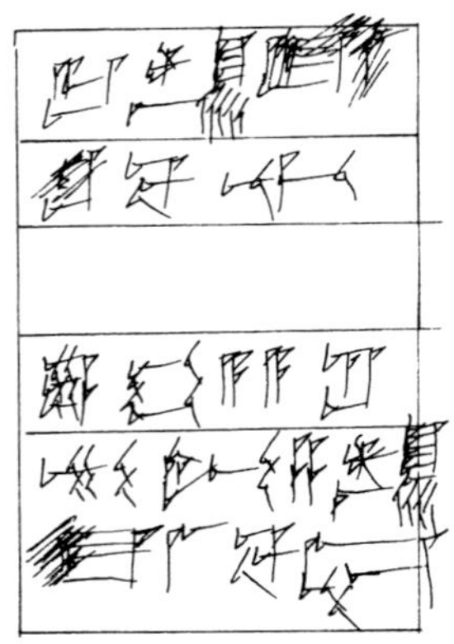

149

(X/-/AS 3)

OBV.

1. [ ] 2+ ma-na síg-gi
2. nu-bànda
3. [ ] 5 ma-na síg PA [ ]
4. [x] a-šà a-NÍĜ.ḪU ⌜síg⌝ ki ka
5. [z]i-ga é-gal-šè

REV.

6. [í]b-uru$_{4}$-a-šè
7. ki Lú-^{d}Nin-ĝír-su-ta
8. Lú-^{d}Ba-ú dumu Na-ba-ša$_{6}$
9. šu ba-ti
10. iti amar-a-a-si
11. mu $^{\langle\text{ĝeš}\rangle}$gu.za ^{d}En-líl-lá ba-dím

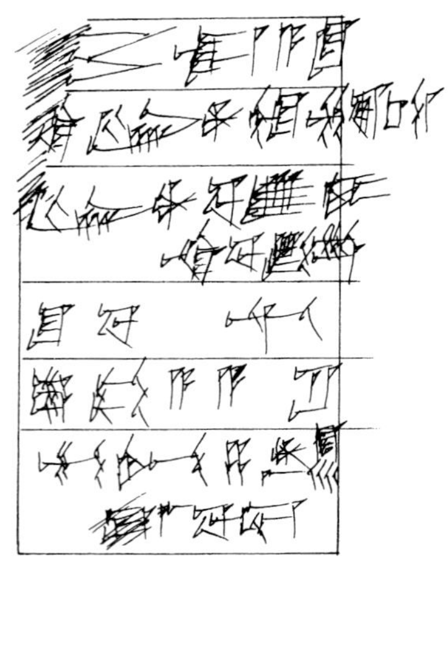

150

(diri/-/AS 3)

OBV.

1. 5.4.0 še gur lugal
2. še ur$_5$-ra
3. ì-dub URU×GÁNA*tenû*^{ki}-ta
4. ki Lú-^{d}Nin-šubur ù Lú-^{d}Dumu-zi-ta

REV.

5. Lú-diĝir-ra ugula
6. šu ba-ti
7. mu Ur-^{d}Nin-<ĝír>-su-šè
8. kišib Lú-diĝir-ra
9. iti diri še-kin-ku$_5$
10. mu gu-za ^{d}En-líl-lá ba-dím
11. nu-bànda Ur-^{d}Nin-ĝír-su

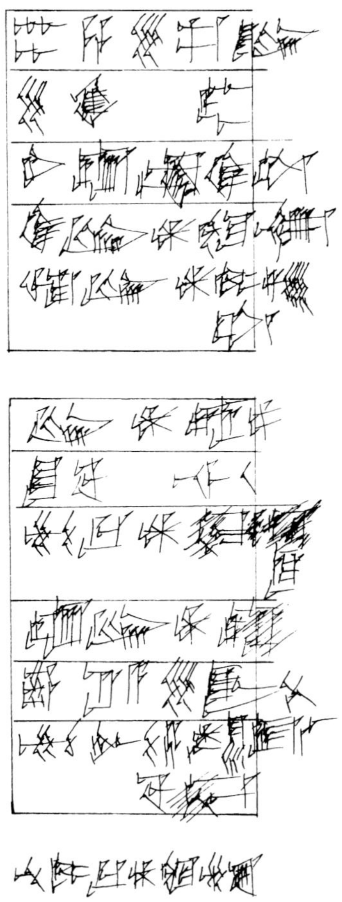

151

(-/-/AS 3)

OBV.
1. ½ ma-na šim
2. 1 sìla še-li
*3. ki A-gi$_4$-ta
4. kaš ú-sa-a-da
5. bappir ba-ab-tag

REV.
6. kišib Lú-^{d}Nin-ĝír-su dumu Ba-zi
7. SEAL
8. mu gu-za maḫ ba-dím

Seal: Lú-^{d}Nin-ĝír-su
dub-sar
dumu Ba-zi

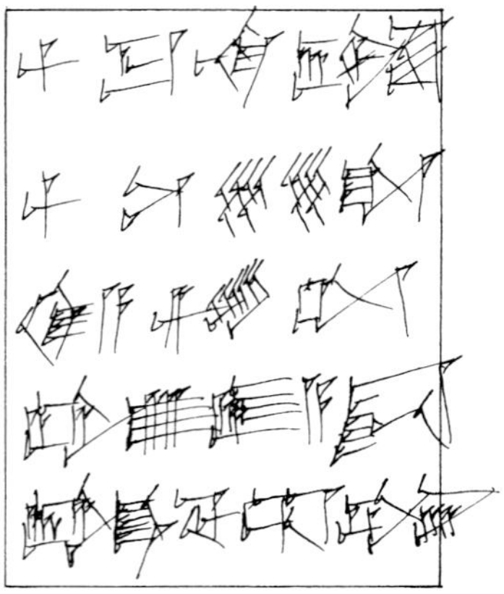

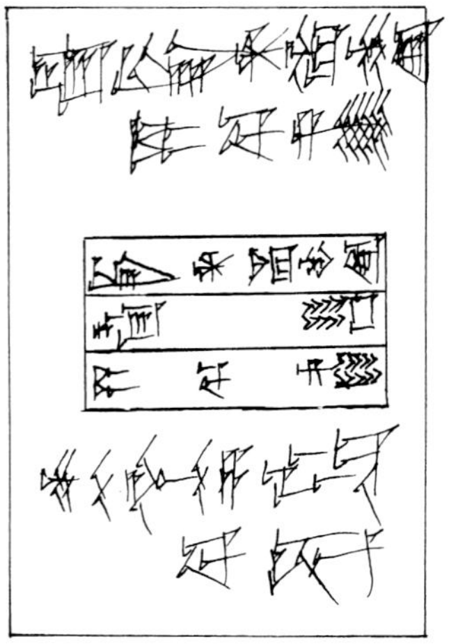

152

(-/-/AS 3)

OBV.
1. 25.3.0 ⌜še gur⌝ lugal
2. še é kin-ĝá
3. ì-dub me-si-za
4. še ur$_5$-ra

REV.
5. ki Šeš-ka[l-l]a-ta
6. Lú-^{d}Lama dumu Ga-ni [ ]
7. šu ba-ti
8. m[u g]u-za [^{d}En-líl-lá ba]-d[ím]

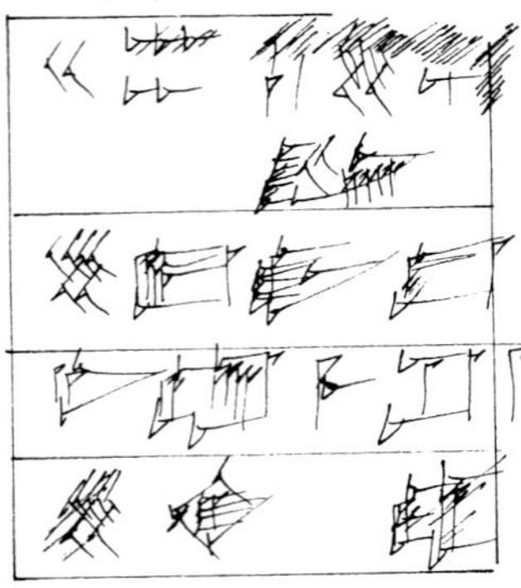

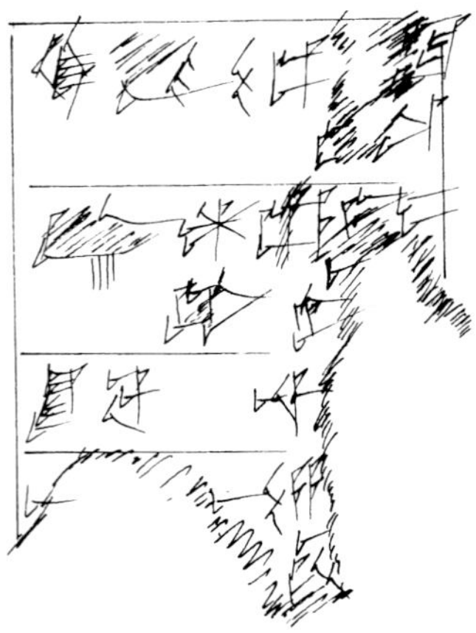

153

(-/-/AS 3)

OBV.

1. 296 ad$_x$ udu ba-ug$_7$
2. 60 ad$_x$ sila$_4$ ba-ug$_7$
3. ki Ur-^{d}Ig-alima-ta
4. Lugal-uru-da

REV.

5. šu ba-ti
6. mu géme uš-bar-šè
7. (BLANK)
8. mu gu-za ^{d}En-líl-lá ba-dím

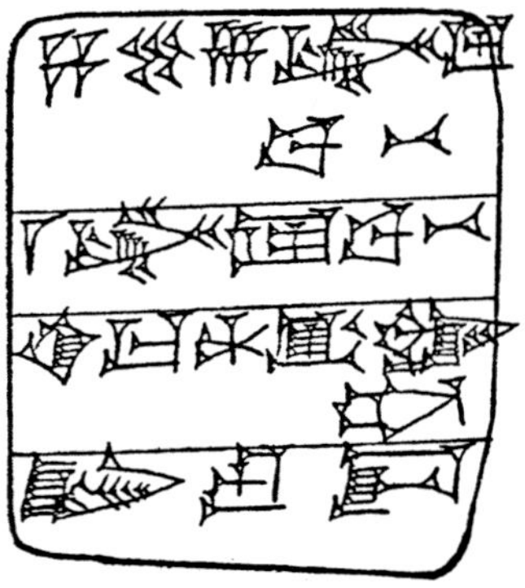

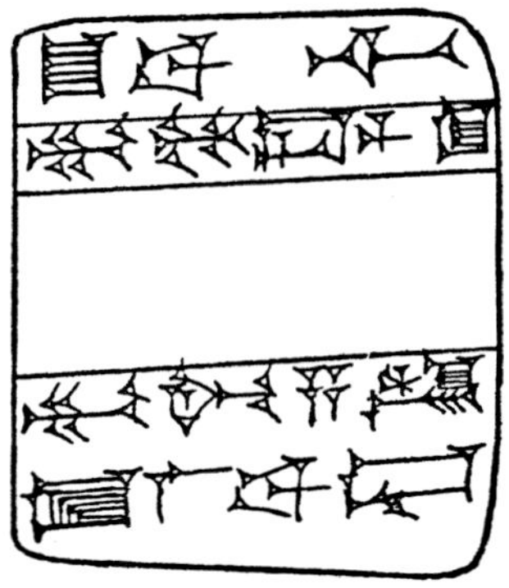

154

(-/-/AS 3)

OBV.

1. 165 ad$_x$ udu
2. 118 ad$_x$ udu
3. mu géme uš-bar-šè
4. ki Ur-^{d}Ig-alima-ta
5. Lugal-uru-da

REV.

6. šu ba-ti
7. egir KA.SI.KA-ta
8. (BLANK)
9. mu gu-za ^{d}En-líl-lá ba-dím

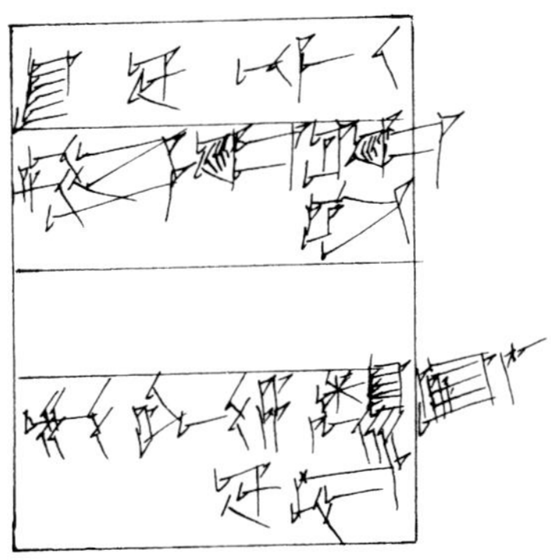

155

(-/-/AS 3)

OBV.

1. 25 ma-na sí[g]
2. é-udu é-gal-ta
3. 26 ma-na síg
4. lá-u$_x$ su-ga sipa-didli
5. 40 ma-na é-nìĝin-ta
6. ĝìr Ur-ša$_6$-ga
7. 1 gú 20 ma-na síg

REV.

8. [é]-nì-gur$_{11}$ dam-[gàr]
9. ĝìr Ur-ab-ba
10. é-lugal-šè
11. Ur-^{d}Ba-ú šu-zi
12. šu ba-ti
13. (BLANK)
14. mu ^{ĝeš}gu-za ^{d}En-líl-lá ba-dím

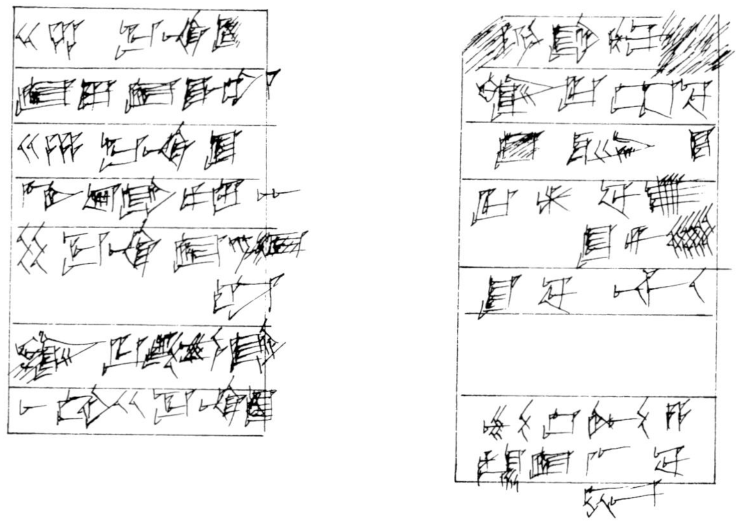

156

(-/-/AS 3)

OBV.

1. šim-ì 0.4.0 lugal
2. 4 sìla-ta
3. ki Ur-é-gal-ta
4. Lugal-^{d}Nin-ĝír-su
5. šu ba-ti

REV.

6. ì-ba diĝir-re-ne-šè
7. (BLANK)
8. mu ^{ĝeš}gu-za maḫ ^{d}En-líl-lá ba-dím

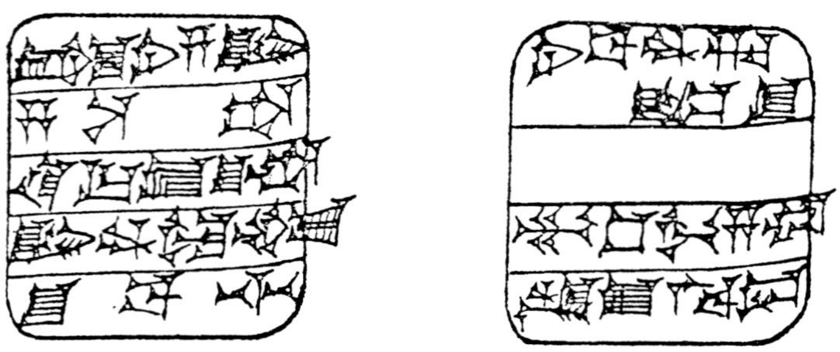

157

(II/-/AS 4)

OBV.

1. 1 še gur lugal
2. ki Túl-ta-ta
3. Ur-^{d}En-líl-lá
4. šu ba-ti
5. [ ] da a[b]

REV.

6. [(BLANK)]
7. iti gu$_4$-rá-bí-mú-mú
8. mu en-maḫ-gal-an-na en ^{d}Nanna ba-ḫun

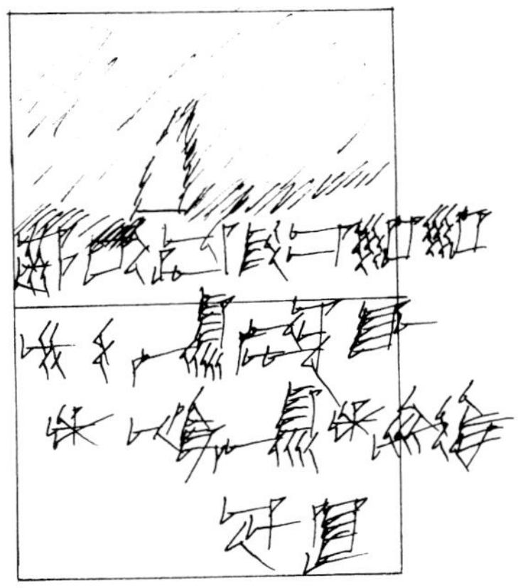

158

(-/-/AS 4)

OBV.

1. 1707.0.0 še gur lugal
2. [x] ri [ ] ĝen-na
3. ki L[ú-diĝir]-ra šabra

REV.

4. Ur-ezen-ma
5. mu zabar-d[ab$_5$-šè]
6. šu ba-ti
7. bala ezen-maḫ Naĝ-su$^{[ki]}$
8. Gi$_4$-gi$_4$-ba mu lugal-bi ì-pàd
9. mu en-maḫ-gal-an-na en ^{d}Nanna^{ki} ba-ḫun

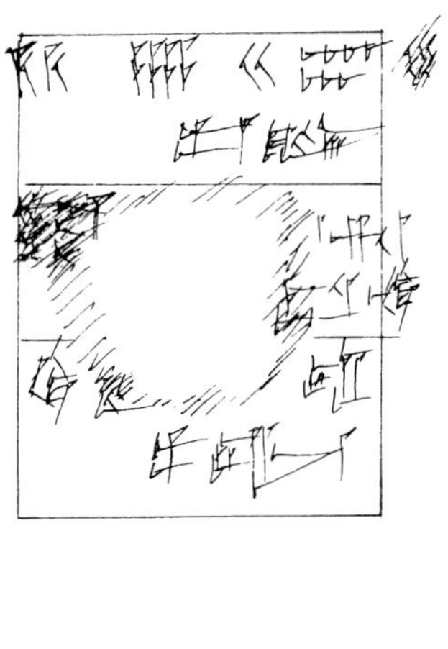

159

(-/-/AS 4)

OBV.

1. 6 dug dida
2. mar-sa-ta
3. ki Nam-maḫ-ta
4. mu Ur-^{d}Ba-ú dumu Ba-zi-šè

REV.

5. SEAL
6. mu en-maḫ-<gal>-an-na ^{d}Nanna
   ba-ḫun

Seal: Ur-^{d}Ba-ú
dub-sar
dumu Lú-[ ]

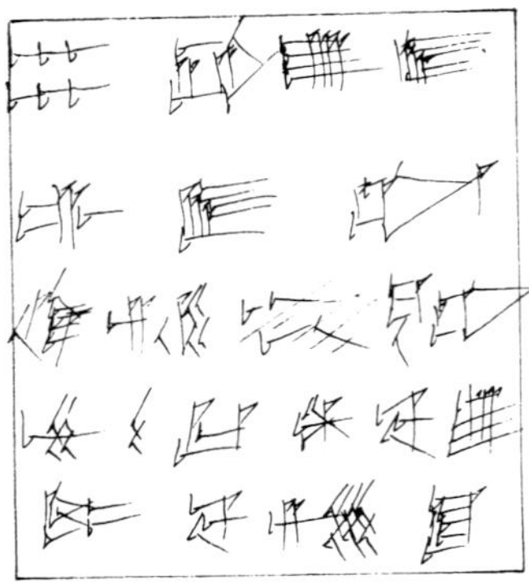

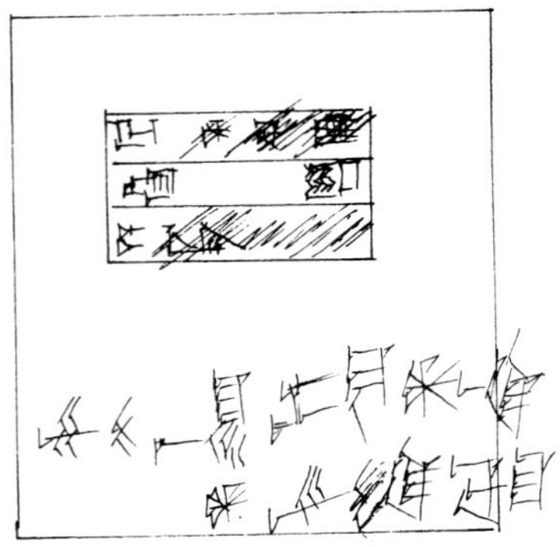

160

(II/-/AS 5)

OBV.

1. 0.4.0 še-ĝeš-ì lugal
2. ki Ur-ab-ba-ta
3. numun a-šà ḫi-ĝál-šè
4. Lú-diĝir-ra

REV.

5. šu ba-ti
6. (BLANK)
7. iti gu$_4$-rá-bí-mú-mú
8. mu-ús-sa en-maḫ-gal-an-na ba-ḫun

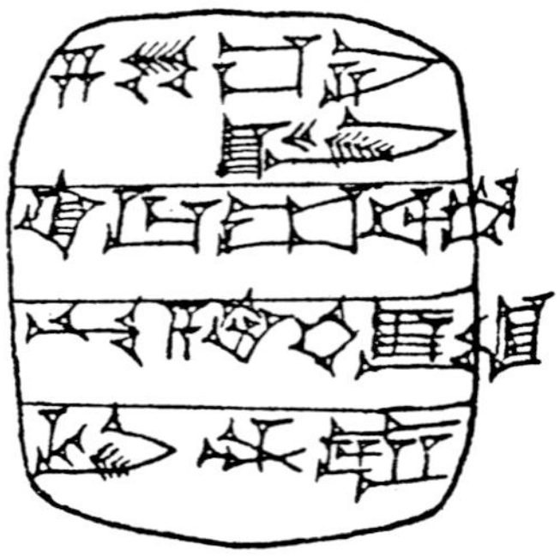

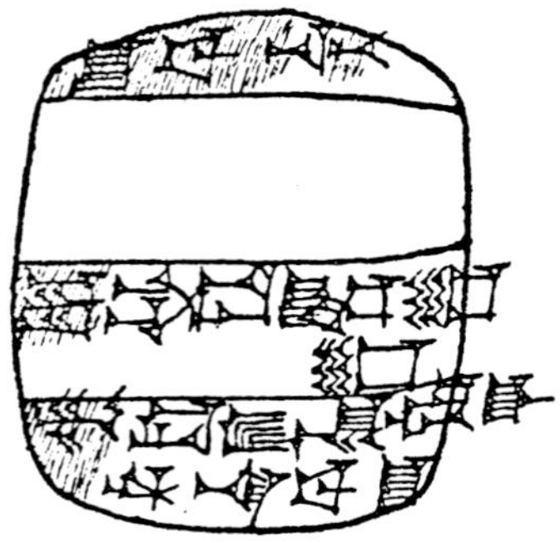

161 (XI/-/AS 5)

OBV.

1. 52 ma-na 10 gín síg-ud$_5$
2. ki Lú-^{d}Nin-ĝír-su dumu Ìr-mu-ta
3. kìšib Lú-^{d}Nin-ĝír-su dumu Ba-zi

REV.

4. iti še-kin-ku$_5$
5. (*seal illegible*)
6. mu En-unu$_6$-gal ^{d}Inanna ba-ḫ[un]

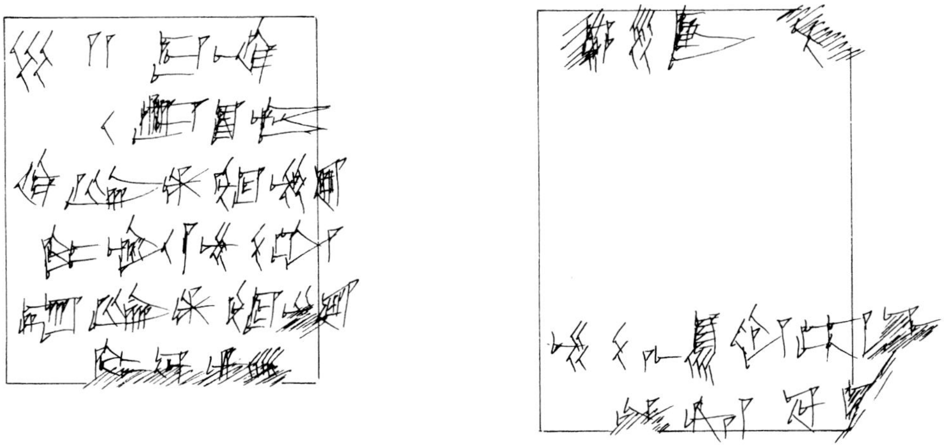

162 (-/-/AS 5)

OBV.

1. 1.0.0 gú-gal gur lugal
2. mu a-šà ú-sar-du$_8$-gíd-da
3. ki Šà-da-ta
4. Ur-^{d}Ba-ú

REV.

5. šu ba-ti
6. mu Ur-^{d}Ba-ú-šè
7. kìšib Má-gur$_8$-re íb-<rá>
8. šabra Šeš-kal-la
9. mu en-unu$_6$-gal ^{d}Inanna ba-a-ḫun

163

(III/-/AS 6)

OBV.

1. 2 ma-na duḫ-ĝen-⸢ta⸣
2. ki Lú-ki-nu-nir^{ki}-ta
3. kìšib Lú-^{d}Nin-ĝír-su dumu Ba-zi

REV.

4. iti ezen ^{d}Li$_{9}$-si$_{4}$
5. SEAL
6. mu ^{d}Amar-^{d}Suen lugal-e Ša-aš-ru-um^{ki} mu-ḫul

Seal: Lú-^{d}Nin-ĝír-su
dub-sar
dumu Ba-zi

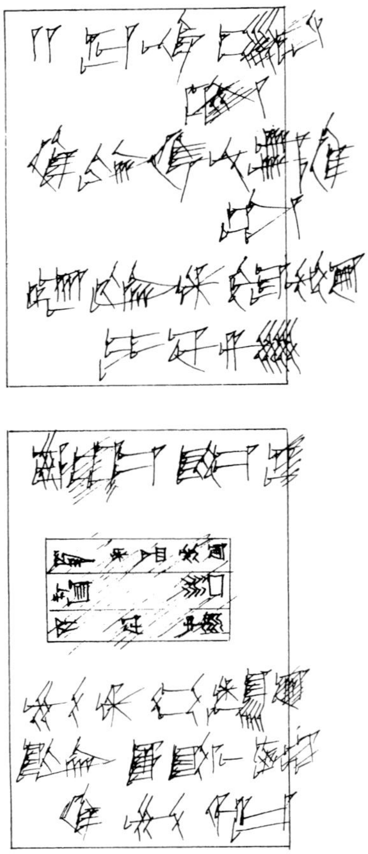

164

(VI/-/AS 6)

TABLET

OBV.

1. 10 ad$_{x}$ udu
2. ĝeš-e-dab$_{5}$-ba
3. šu ba-ti
4. ĝìr *A-ḫu-a*
5. ki Lugal-inim-gi-na-ta

REV.

6. šà Ki-nu-nir^{ki}
7. (BLANK)
8. iti ezen ^{d}Dumu-zi
9. mu Ša-aš-ru^{ki} ba-ḫul

CASE

OBV.

1. 10 ad$_{x}$ [ ]
2. kìšib ĝeš [ ]

Seal: Ur-^{d}[ ]
dub-[sar]
* dumu Lú-[ ]-ḫi-[x]

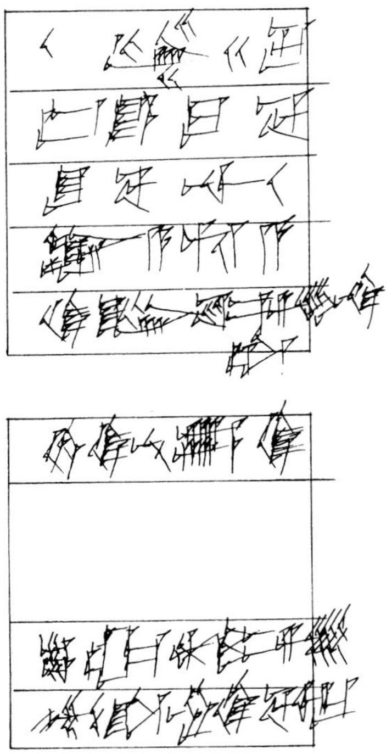

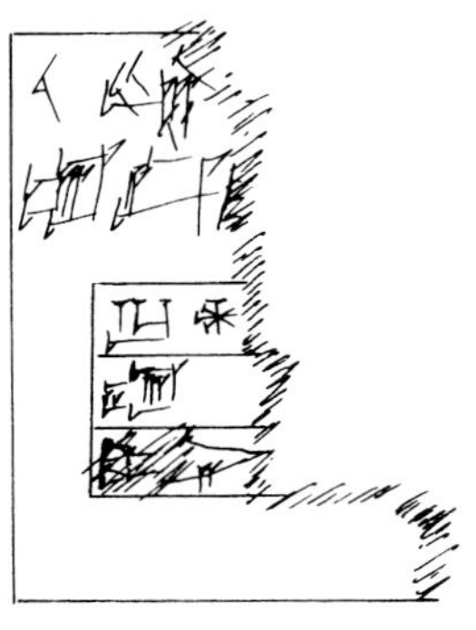

165 (IX/-/AS 7)

OBV.

1. 510 ^{ĝeš}eme-sig má 60.0.0 gur
2. 90 ^{ĝeš}eme-sig má 30.0.0 gur
3. 100 sa ^{ĝeš}ma-nu

REV.

4. ĝeš-dù má-šè
5. é-kišib-ba mar-sa-ta
6. Nam-maḫ šu ba-ti
7. (BLANK)
8. iti mu-šu-du$_7$
9. mu Ḫu-ḫu-nu-ri^{ki} ba-ḫul

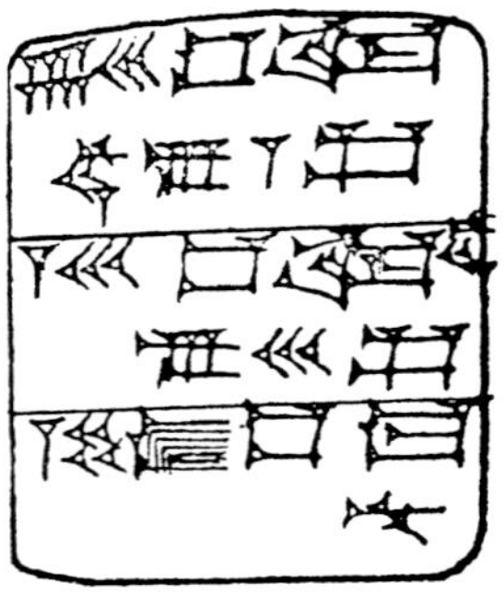

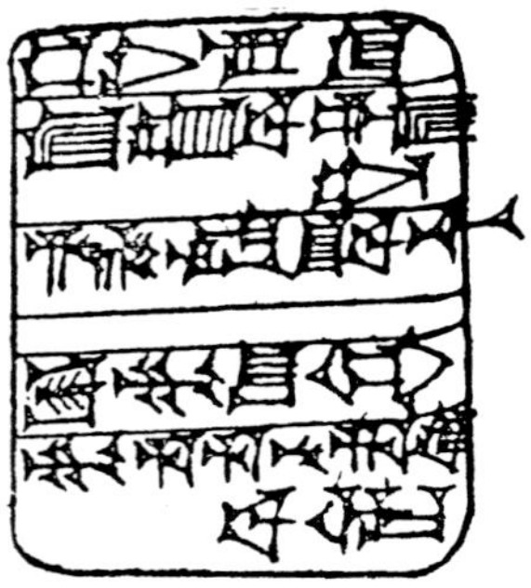

166 (IX/-/AS 7)

OBV.

1. 72 dug-KIN
2. é-kišib-ba énsi-gal-ta
3. ki Lú-kiri$_4$-zal-ta
4. Lú-tur-šè

REV.

5. šu ba-ti
6. (BLANK)
7. iti mu-šu-du$_8$
8. mu Ḫu-ùḫ-nu-ti^{ki} ba-ḫul

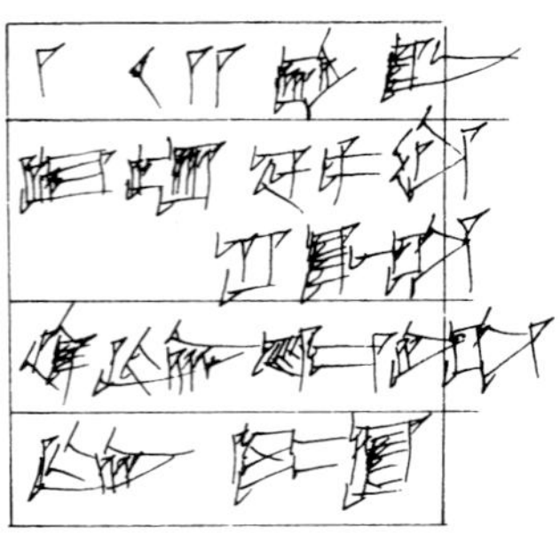

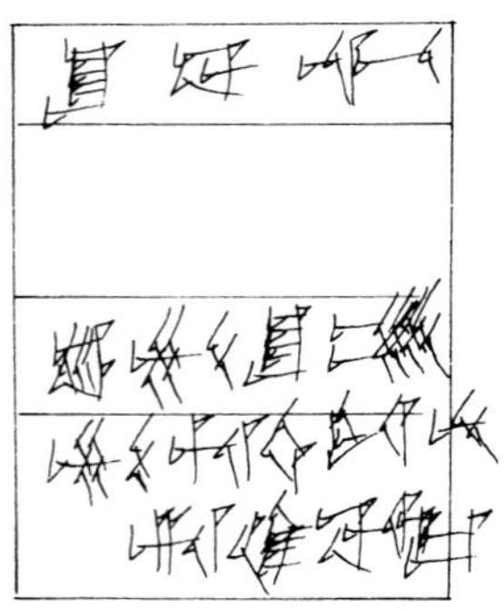

167

(-/-/AS 7)

OBV.
1. 0.0.3 5 sìla dabin lugal
2. ki A-a-kal-la-ta

REV.
3. kìšib Šà-kù-ge
4. ĝìr Ba-zi
5. SEAL
6. mu Ḫu-ḫu-nu-ri

Seal: Šà-kù-ge
dub-sar
dumu Lú-kal-la

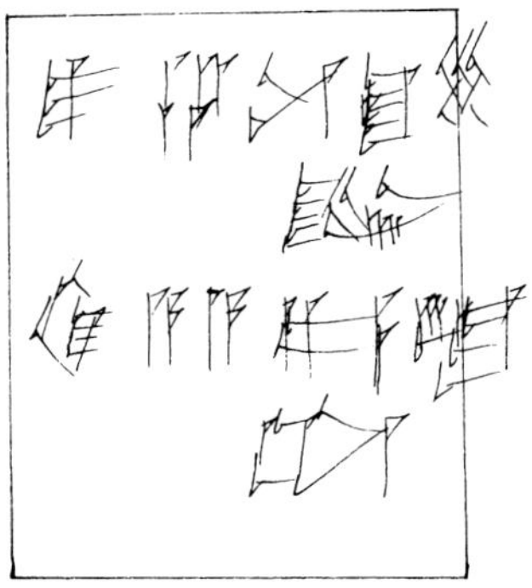

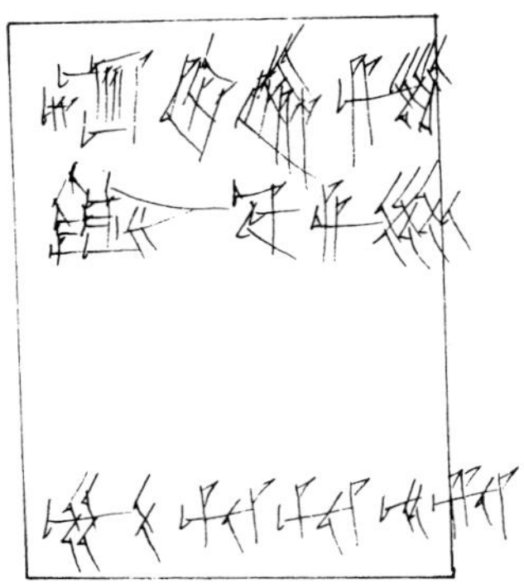

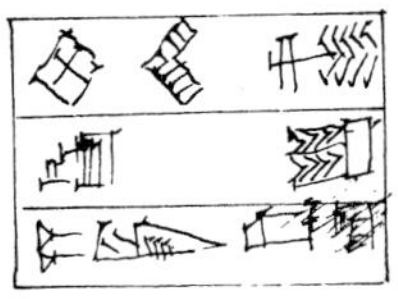

168

(X/-/ŠS 5)

OBV.

1. 3.4.0 še gur lugal
2. ì-dub ḫi-ĝál-ta
3. ki Al-la-mu-ta
4. Lú-diĝir-ra ugula mušen-dù-ke$_4$
5. šu ba-ti

REV.

6. še ur$_5$-ra su-su-dam
7. (BLANK)
8. iti amar-a-a-si
9. mu-ús-sa ^{d}*Šu*-^{d}Suen lugal-e bàd Mar-tu mu-dù

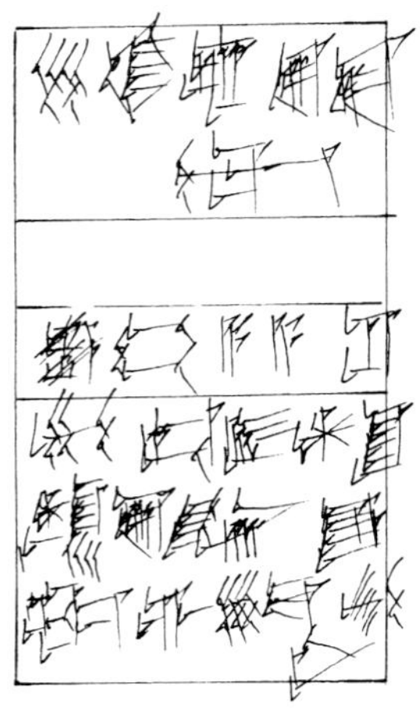

169

(-/-/ŠS 5)

OBV.

1. 2 gín 20 lá 2 <še> kù-babbar
2. Ur-^{d}En-líl-lá-ta
3. Lugal-im-ru-a
4. su-su-dam
5. šà-bala-a

REV.

6. si-ì-tum
7. úgu-a ĝá-ĝá
8. (*seal illegible*)
9. mu-ús-sa bàd Mar-tu ba-dù

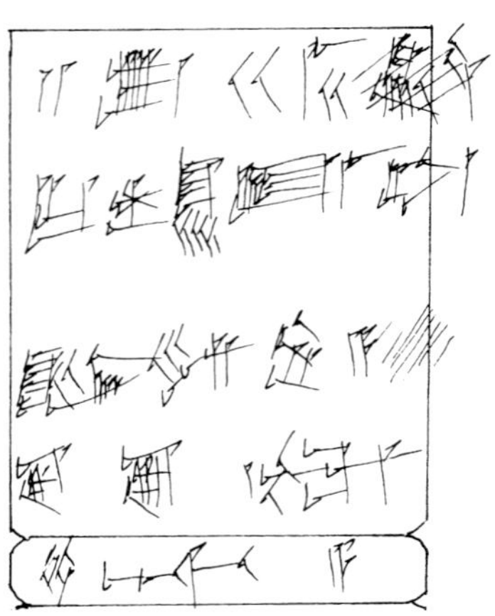

170 (-/-/ŠS 5)

OBV.

1. 1 gín lá 12 še kù-babbar
2. 0.3.0 še lugal
3. ki Ur-^{d}En-líl-lá-ta

REV.

4. kìšib ^{d}En-líl-lá
5. su-su-dam
6. (*seal illegible*)
7. mu-ús-sa bàd ⌜Mar⌝-tu ba-dù

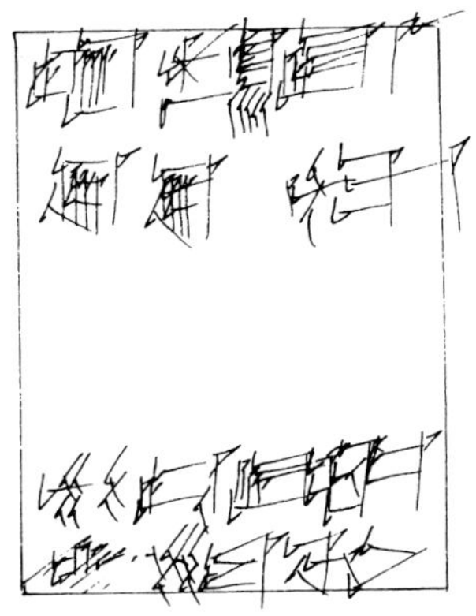

171 (VIII/3/ŠS 6)

OBV.

(*top of obverse broken*)

1. ki Ur-ba-[x-ta]
2. 2 udu-ì 2 udu-niga
3. ki Lú-kal-la-ta
4. 2 udu-ì 4 udu-ni[ga]
5. ki Ur-^{d}Ba-ú-[ta]
6. é-udu ĝá-nun-ĝeš-[x]

REV.

7. sízkur [ ]
8. [ ] iti [ ]
9. [ ] ⌜x⌝ [ ]
10. (B L A N K)
11. [iti] ezen ^{d}Ba-[ú]
12. u_4 3 ba-zal
13. [mu n]a-rú-a maḫ [ ]

(*bottom of reverse broken*)

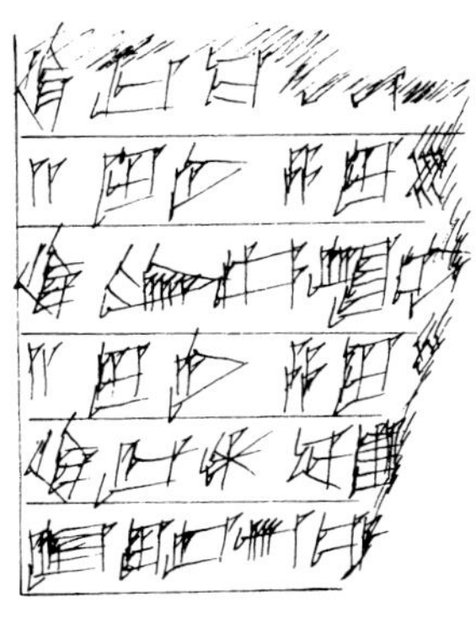

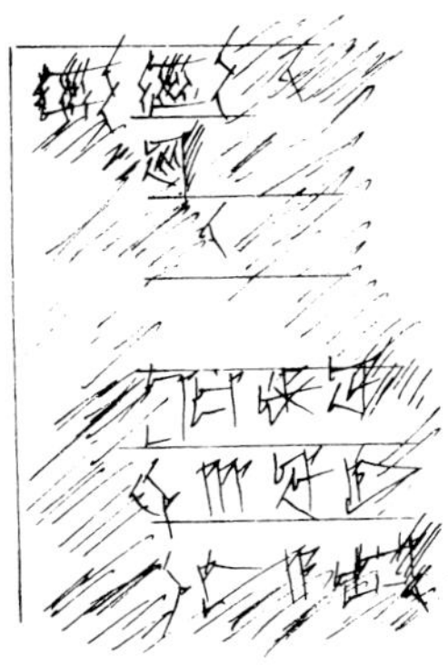

172

(IV/-/IS 1?)

OBV.

(*top of obverse broken*)

1. [ ] 4 sìla ì [ ]
2. ki Na-ba-ša$_6$-[ta]
3. kišib Nam-maḫ-^{d}[ ]
4. ⌜iti ezen⌝-an-na

REV.

5. SEAL
6. [i]ti šu-num[un]
7. mu ^{d}*I*-[*bí*-^{d}Suen]

(*bottom of reverse broken*)

Seal: Ur-[ ]
dub-[sar]
dumu Ur-[ ]

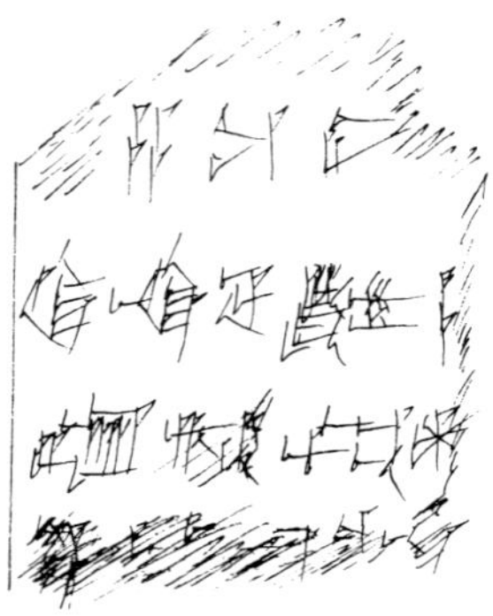

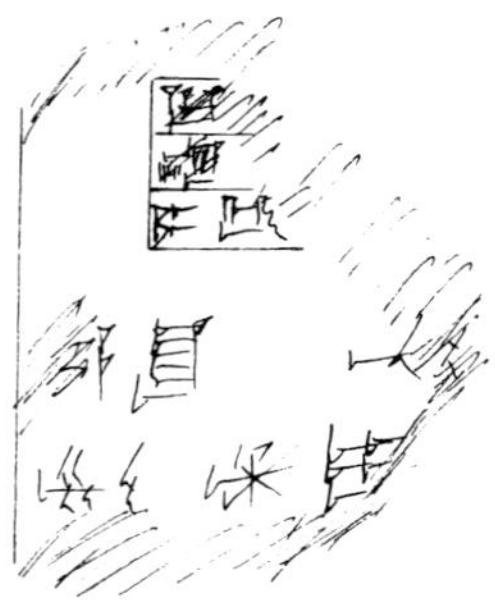

173

(XII/-/IS 1)

OBV.

1. 1.1.0 še gur
2. še ur$_5$-ra dumu dab$_5$-ba
3. ì-dub a-šà uru-ul-ta
4. ki Lú-diĝir-ra-ta
5. Lugal-Unug^{ki}-šè
6. šu ba-ti
7. mu Lugal-Unug^{ki}-šè

REV.

8. kìšib Un-ĝa$_6$
9. dumu dab$_5$-ba íb-ra
10. SEAL
11. iti še-íl-la
12. mu ^{d}I-bí-^{d}Suen lugal

Seal: Un-ĝa$_6$
* dumu *Nu-úr-ì-lí*
[ ]

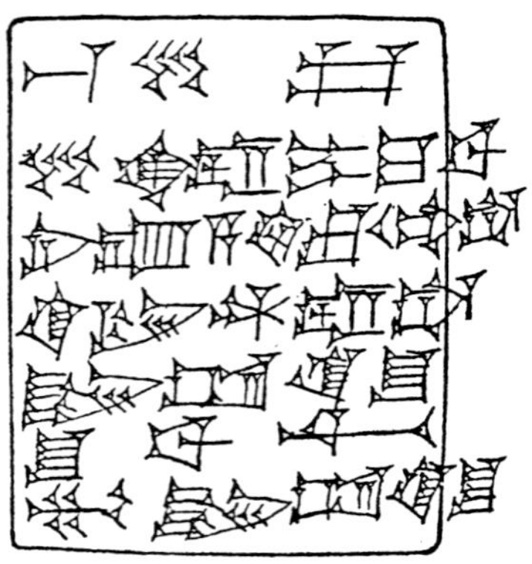

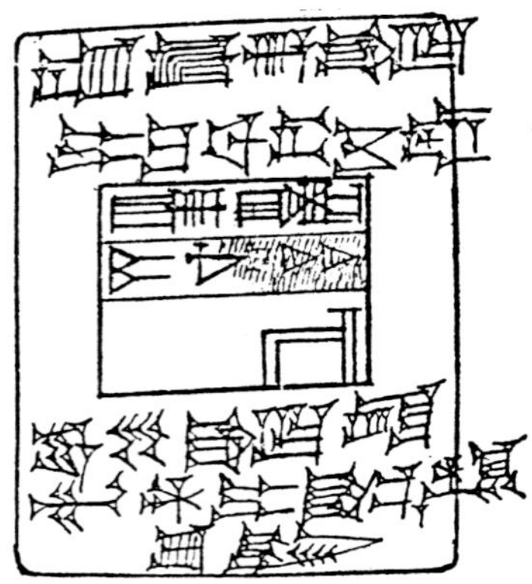

174

(-/-/IS 1)

TABLET

OBV.

1. 3.4.0 še gur
2. 2.0.0 gur še engar-e sàg-ga
3. a-šà ^{d}Ba-ú-tùr-sù-ta
4. ki Ur-^{d}Saḫar-^{d}Ba-ú-ta

REV.

5. Ur-^{d}Nin-mar-ki
6. šu ba-ti
7. (BLANK)
8. mu ^{d}I-bí-^{d}Suen lugal

CASE

OBV.

1. 3.4.0 še gur
2. 2.0.0 gur še engar-e sàg-ga
3. SEAL
4. [a-šà ^{d}]Ba-ú-tùr-sù-ta

REV.

5. ki Ur-^{d}Saḫar-^{d}Ba-ú-ta
6. kišib Ur-^{d}Nin-mar-ki
7. SEAL
8. mu ^{d}*I-bí*-^{d}Suen lugal

Seal: Ur-^{d}Nin-mar-ki
dub-sar
dumu Lugal-ušumgal

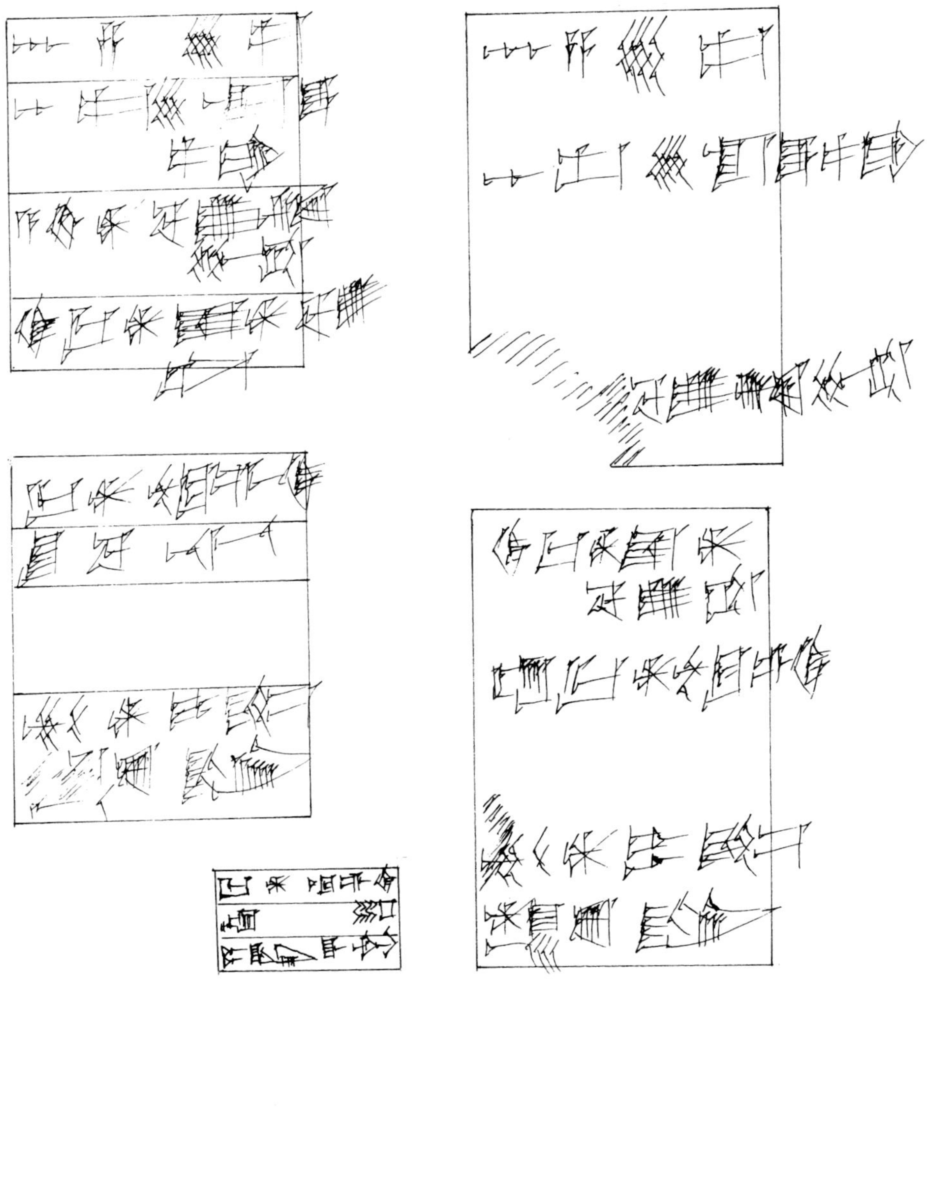

175 (IV/-/-)

OBV.

1. 24 še gur lugal
2. ki Lú-gi-na-ta
3. Lú-^{d}Ba-ú dumu Lú-kal-la

REV.

4. šu ba-ti
5. (BLANK)
6. a-rá 4-kam
7. iti šu-numun

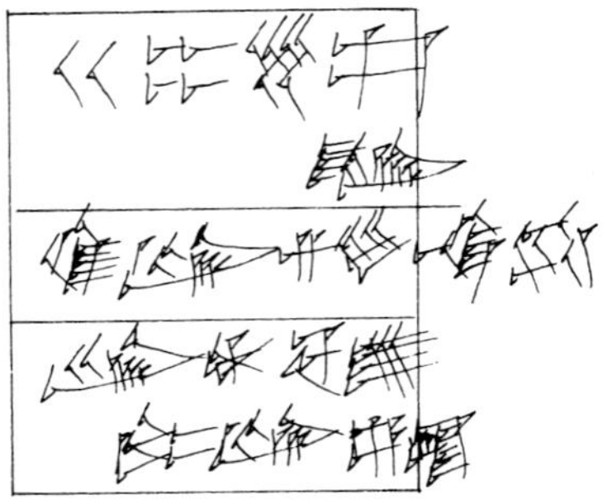

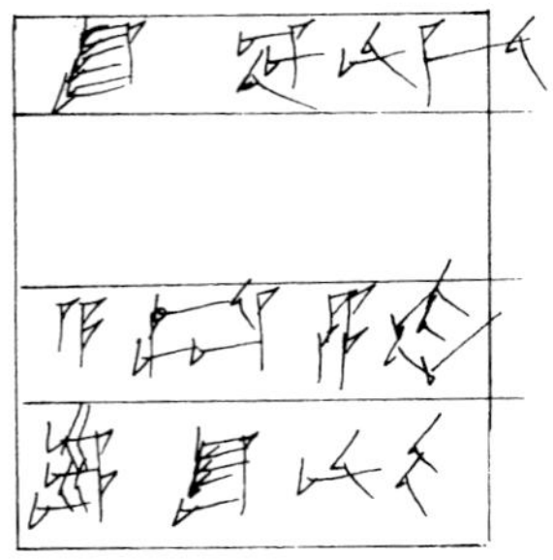

176 (V/-/-)

OBV.

1. 2.0.0 zú-lum gur
2. ki Gú-mu-ta
3. Nam-maḫ-^{d}Ba-ú
4. šu ba-ti

REV.

5. iti munu$_4$-kú
6. SEAL

Seal: Nam-maḫ-^{d}Ba-ú
dub-sar
dumu [x x]
[ ]

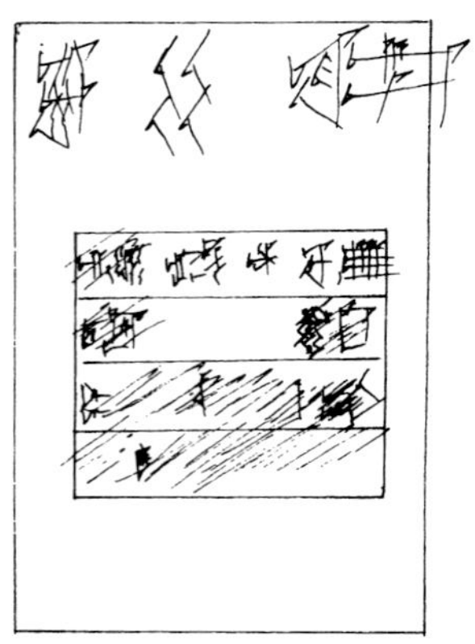

177 (VIII/7/-)

OBV.

1. 4.0.0 dabin gur lugal
2. nì numun-šè
3. ki Lú-mar-sa-ta
4. kìšib Lú-^{d}Nin-ĝír-su

REV.

5. ĝìr Kur-ta-mu-gi$_4$
6. iti ezen ^{d}Ba-ú u$_4$ 7 ba-zal

Seal: Lú-^{d}Nin-ĝír-su
dub-sar
dumu Ìr-mu

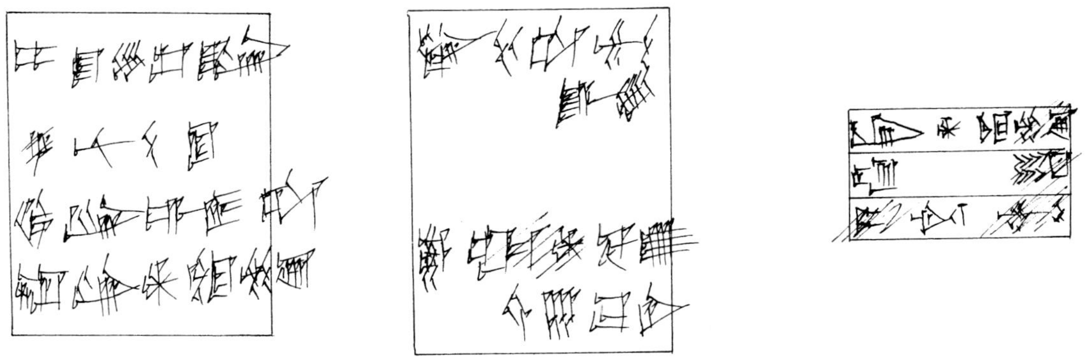

178 (IX/-/-)

OBV.

1. 1 dida
2. [ki] Lú-má-gur$_8$-ra-ta
3. [síz]kur a-šà nin
4. [x] érim-e-šè
5. [Á]-na-mu
6. [š]u ba-ti

REV.

7. [it]i mu-šu-du$_7$
8. SEAL

Seal: [Á]-na-[mu]
dub-[sar]
dumu Ur-$^{[d]}$Ba-[ú]

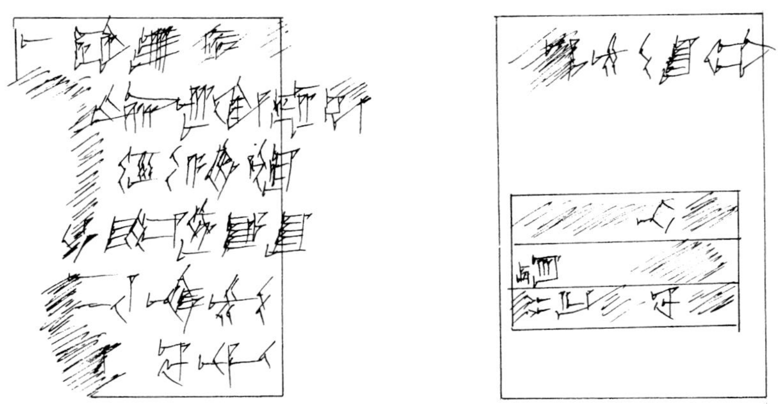

179

(X/-/-)

OBV.

1. 6.0.0 munu$_4$ [x]
2. érin še kin
3. (B L A N K)

REV.

4. (B L A N K)
5. iti amar-a-a-si

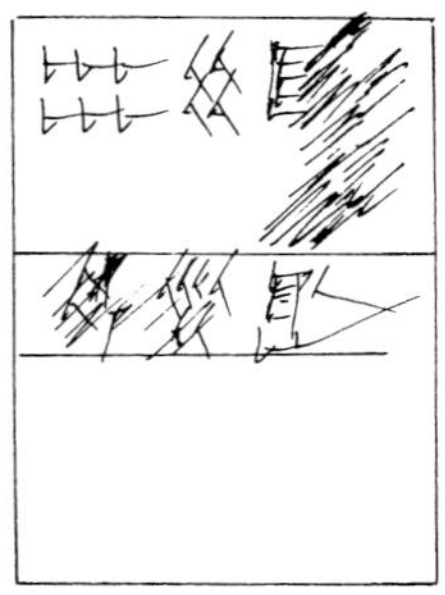

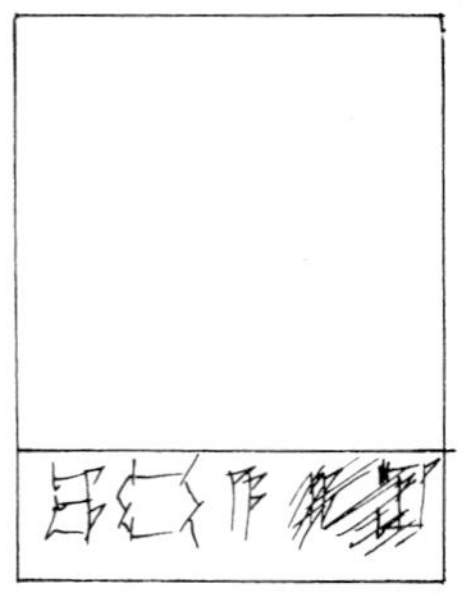

180

(-/-/Š 38)

OBV.

1. ša$_{13}$-dub-ba
2. še-érin-e šu-ti-a
3. nì-ka$_9$-šu SU-ba
4. mu An-ša-an^{ki} ba-ḫul-ta
5. mu bàd ma-da ba-dù-šè
6. mu 4-kam

REV.

7. gú-un de$_6$-a
8. mu en Eridu^{ki}-ta
9. mu-ús-sa bàd ma-da ba-dù-šè
10. mu 10-kam
11. (B L A N K)
12. ì-ĝál

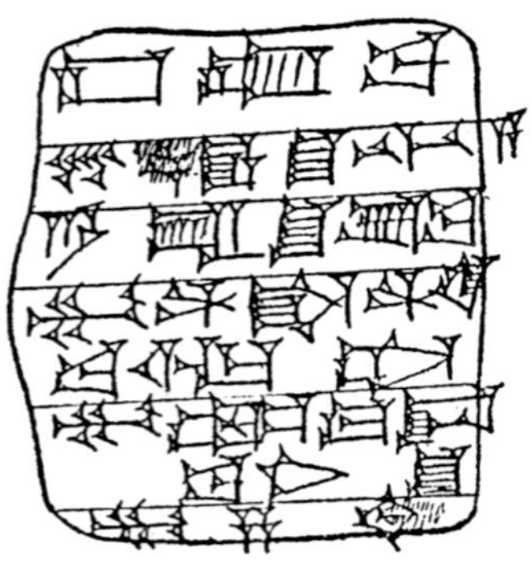

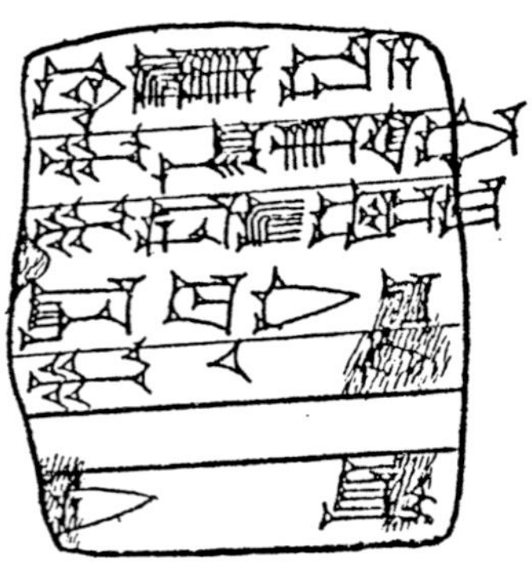

181

(-/-/Š 41)

OBV.

1. bisaĝ-dub-ba
2. bisaĝ ambar-sur-ra
3. ĝìr Lú-diĝir-ra
4. dumu A-ba-šu-na

REV.

5. (BLANK)
6. mu-ús-sa é *Puzur*$_{4}$-*iš*-^{d}*Da-gan* mu-ús-sa-bi

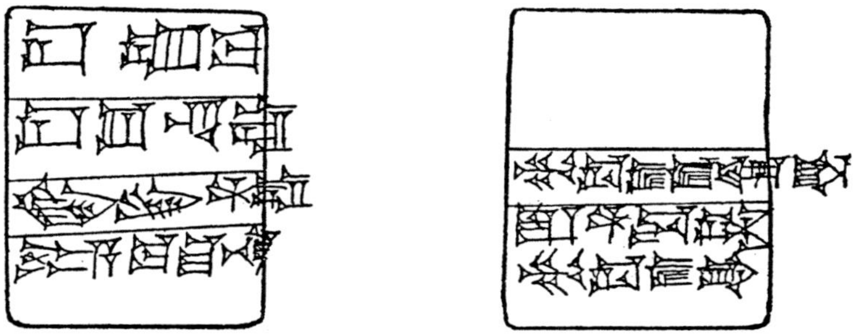

182

(-/-/Š 46)

OBV.

1. bisaĝ-dub-ba
2. dub-gíd-da

*3. Lú-bi-mu dumu Ur-^{d}Ig-al[ima]

4. ì-ĝál

REV.

5. (BLANK)
6. mu Ki-maš^{ki} ba-ḫul

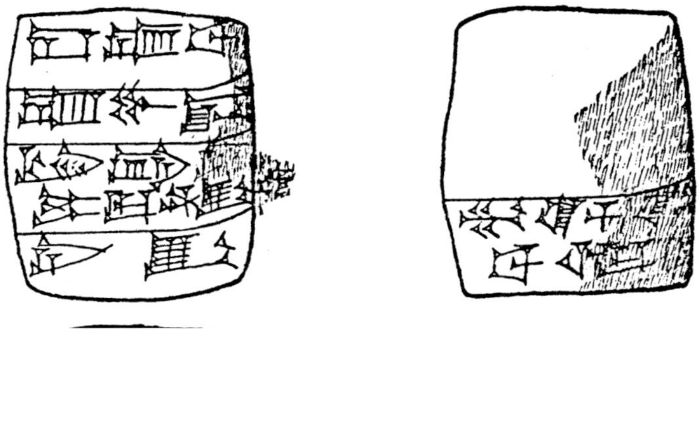

183

(-/-/Š 48)

OBV.

1. bisaĝ-dub-ba
2. dub-gíd-da ì-dub
3. ĝìr Ur-^{d}Nanše dumu Lú-du$_{10}$-ga
4. ì-ĝál

REV.

5. (BLANK)

*6. mu Ḫa-ar$^{!}$-˹ši˺^{ki} Ki-maš^{ki} Ḫu-ur$_{5}$-ti^{ki}
ba-ḫul

184

(-/-/AS 2)

OBV.

1. ša$_{13}$-dub-ba
2. kurum$_{7}$-ak simug
3. dub-sar é-kìšib-ba
4. gala Nina^{ki}
5. nu-bànda Ur-^{d}Nanše
6. nu-bànda Ur-^{d}Utu
7. nu-bànda Lú-kal-la
8. sagi
9. ab-ba-uru
10. dam-gàr
11. lú ĝeš-ì

REV.

12. é-kurušda Ĝír-su^{ki}
13. nu-bànda *A-ḫu-a*
14. é ^{d}Nanše
15. kurušda didli-bi
16. é-muḫaldim
17. gala Gú-ab-ba^{ki}
18. Ú-du-lu dub-sar gu$_{4}$-udu
*19. lú-kaš$_{4}$ sa$_{12}$-du$_{5}$
20. šu-ḫa mušen-dù
21. géme kíkken énsi
22. ù ĝeš-túg ga-ru-[dam]
23. mu ^{d}Amar-^{d}Suen Ur-bí-lum^{ki} mu-ḫul

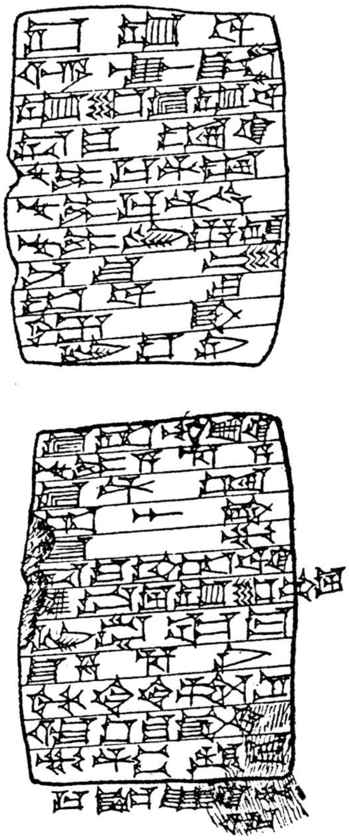

185

(I/4/-)

OBV.

1. 5 sìla kaš 5 sìla zì
2. 1 ì á-gam
3. Bí-ti-ti sukkal
4. érin še-kin-šè ĝen-na
5. 5 sìla kaš 3 sìla zì
6. 1 ì á-gam
7. Ì-kal-la muḫaldim
8. Nam-maḫ ĝen-na
9. 3 sìla kaš 2 sìla zì
10. 1 ì á-gam

REV.

11. [ ]
12. A[ ] ĝen-na
13. 5 sìla kaš 3 sìla <zì>
14. 1 ì á-gam
15. Ur-^{d}Nanna sukkal
16. A.GÍN^{ki}-šè ĝen-na
17. 3 sìla kaš 2 sìla <zì>
18. 1 ì á-gam
19. Lú-^{d}Nanna lú-kaš$_4$
20. Ur-^{d}Ba-ú dumu Ab-ba-mu-šè ĝen-na
21. zi-ga u_4 4-kam
22. iti buru$_x$(GÁN)-maš

186

(I/8/-)

OBV.

1. 5 sìla kaš 5 sìla zì
2. 1 ì á-gam
3. Bí-ti-ti sukkal
4. érin še-kin ĝen-na
5. 3 sìla kaš 2 sìla zì
6. 1 ì á-gam
7. E-šu-a-núm lú-kaš$_4$

★8. zì-má-a-si-gi$_4$ ĝen-na

REV.

9. 3 sìla kaš 2 sìla zì
10. 1 ì á-gam

★11. Lú-^{d}[Utu] muḫaldim

12. má-a-si ĝen-na
13. 3 sìla kaš 2 sìla <zì>
14. 1 ì á-gam
15. Ur-^{d}Nanše Mar-tu
16. zi-ga u$_4$ 8-kam
17. iti buru$_x$(GÁN)-maš

187

(I/17/-)

OBV.

1. 0.0.1 kaš 5 sìla zì
2. 1 ì á-gam
3. Ur-Šul-pa-è lú-mu$_{13}$-mu$_{13}$
4. sízkur Nina^{ki}-šè ĝen-na
5. 5 sìla kaš 3 sìla zì
6. 1 ì á-gam
7. *Á-bí-lí* sukkal

REV.

8. 5 sìla kaš 5 sìla <zì>
9. 1 ì á-gam
10. Bí-ti-ti sukkal
11. 3 sìla kaš 2 sìla <zì>
12. 1 ì á-gam
13. *A-da-làl* lú-kaš$_4$
14. Šušina^{ki}-ta ĝen-na
15. zi-ga u$_4$ 20 lá 3
16. iti buru$_x$(GÁN)-maš

188 (I/29/-)

OBV.

1. 3 sìla kaš 2 sìla ninda
2. 2 gín ì
3. *Puzur*$_4$*-ì-lí* a-šà-šè-ne ĝen-na
4. 3 sìla kaš 2 sìla ninda
5. 2 gín ì

REV.

6. I-ti-a lú ^{ĝeš}tukul gu-la
7. 3 <sìla> kaš 2 sìla <ninda>
8. 2 gín ì
9. Lú-diĝir-ra šim anše-šè ĝen-na
10. 3 sìla kaš 2 sìla ninda
11. 2 gín ì

*12. *A-mur-*^{d}Utu lú-kaš$_4$

13. zi-ga u$_4$ 30 lá 1
14. iti buru$_x$(GÁN)-maš

189

(I/-/-)

OBV.

1. 5 sìla kaš 5 sìla ninda
2. 1 ì-ĝeš á-gam
3. *Bí-bí* sukkal
4. 5 sìla kaš 5 sìla ninda
5. *Puzur*$_4$-^{d}Inanna sukkal
6. 5 sìla kaš 5 sìla ninda
7. 1 ì-ĝeš á-gam

*8. *Puzur*$_4$*-ab-bi* sukkal

9. 5 sìla kaš 5 sìla ninda
10. ^{d}Nanna-ì-ša$_6$ sukkal

REV.

11. 5 sìla kaš 5 sìla ninda
12. 1 ì-ĝeš á-gam
13. *Ì-lí*-^{d}Lama sukkal
14. 3 dida
15. 0.0.4 dabin lugal
16. 5 ì-ĝeš á-gam
17. NIM Za-ul^{ki}-ke$_4$ šu ba-ti
18. ĝìr *Ì-lí*-^{d}Lama sukkal

*19. An-ša-an^{ki}-ta ù Nibru^{ki}-ta ĝen-[na]

20. iti buru$_x$(GÁN)-maš

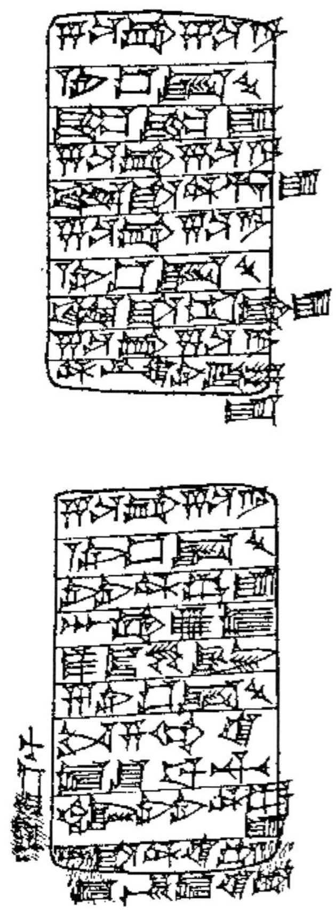

190

(I/-/-)

OBV.

1. 5 sìla kaš 5 sìla ninda
2. 1 ì-ĝeš á-gam
3. *A-bí-a* sukkal
4. 5 sìla kaš 5 sìla ninda
5. 1 ì-ĝeš á-gam
6. Lugal-diĝir-mu sukkal
7. 5 sìla kaš 5 sìla ninda
8. 1 ì-ĝeš á-gam
9. Še-lu$_5$ sukkal
10. 5 sìla kaš 5 sìla ninda

REV.

11. 1 ì-ĝeš á-gam
12. I-ti-a sukkal
13. 5 sìla kaš 5 sìla ninda
14. *Šu*-^{d}Utu sukkal
15. 2 dida
16. 0.0.4 zì ù ninda lugal
17. 3 ì-ĝeš á-gam
18. NIM Ši-ma-aš-ki šu ba-ti
19. 5 sìla kaš 5 sìla ninda
20. ĝìr *Š*[*u*]-^{d}[Utu sukkal]
21. [ ]
22. iti buru$_x$(GÁN)-maš

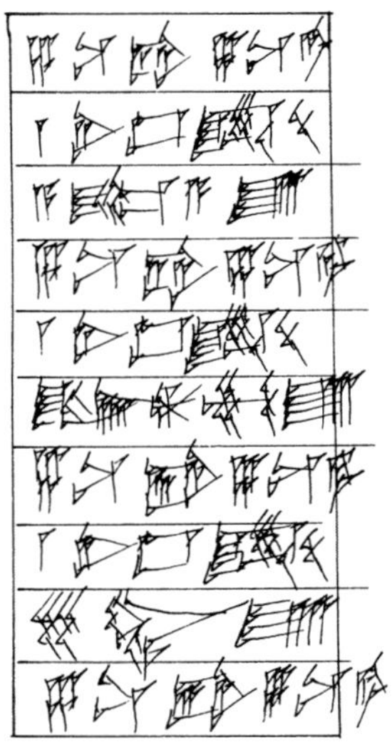

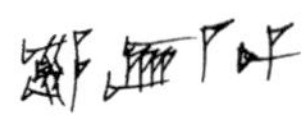

191

(I/-/-)

OBV.

1. 2 sìla ninda Inim-ša$_6$-ša$_6$ lú-kaš$_4$
2. 0.0.3 ninda NIM Si-ù^{ki}-me
3. ĝìr Inim-ša$_6$-ša$_6$ lú-kaš$_4$
4. Si-ù^{ki}-ta ĝen-né
5. 3 sìla ninda Lú-Suen sukkal
6. mu ki$^{!}$-^{d}En-líl-lá-ka-šè ĝen-na
7. 8 sìla ninda u$_4$ 4-kam
8. *Á-pil-lí-a* sukkal
9. mu túg-gada-šè ĝen-na

REV.

10. 8 sìla u$_4$ 4-kam
11. Lugal-[Ma]r-tu
12. ĝeš [x] i$_7$ [ĝ]en-na
13. 4 sì[la]
14. *A-ḫu-*[ ]
15. érin i$_7$ [ ] è-dè ĝen-na
16. 4 sìla ninda u$_4$ 2-kam
17. *Puzur$_4$*-è-a lú-kaš$_4$
18. [ ] érin NE.DU-a-è-$^{[d]}$è ĝen-na
19. iti buru$_x$(GÁN)-maš

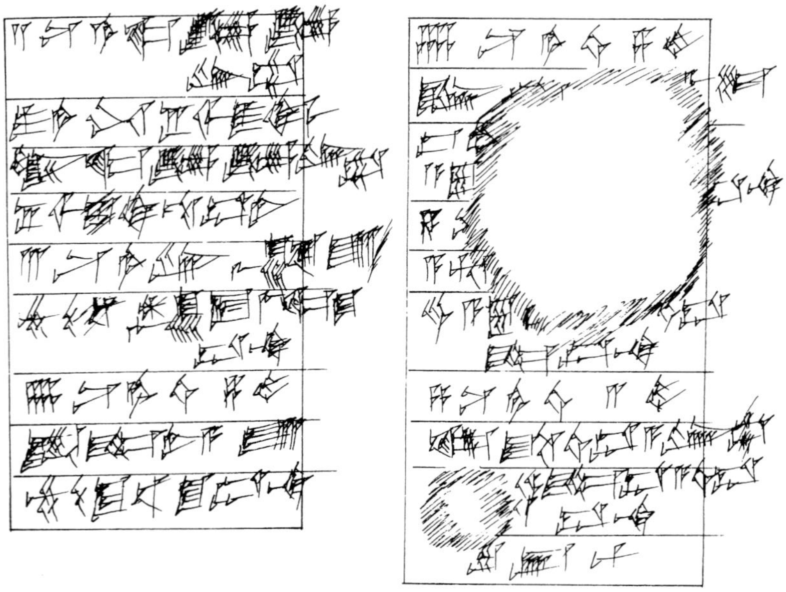

192

(I/-/-)

OBV.

1. 5 sìla kaš 5 sìla ninda
2. 1 ì-ĝeš á-gam
3. I-ti-a sukkal
4. 5 sìla kaš 5 sìla ninda
5. 1 ì-ĝeš á-gam
6. Ga-lu$_5$ sukkal
7. 5 sìla kaš 5 sìla ninda
8. 1 ì-ĝeš á-gam
9. Ur-kù-nun sukkal
10. 3 sìla kaš 2 sìla ninda

REV.

11. 1 ì-ĝeš á-gam
*12. Ur-^{ĝeš}gigir lú-kaš$_4$
13. 5 sìla kaš 5 sìla ninda
14. 1 ì-ĝeš á-gam
15. La-lu$_5$-lum sukkal
16. 3 dida
17. 0.0.5 zì 0.0.2 ninda lugal
18. ½ sìla ì-ĝeš
19. NIM Du$_8$-du$_8$-lí^{ki} šu ba-ti
20. ĝìr ^{d}IM-*ba-ni* sukkal

L.E.

*21. An-ša-an^{ki}-ta ù Nibru^{ki}-šè ĝen-na
22. iti buru$_x$(GÁN)-maš

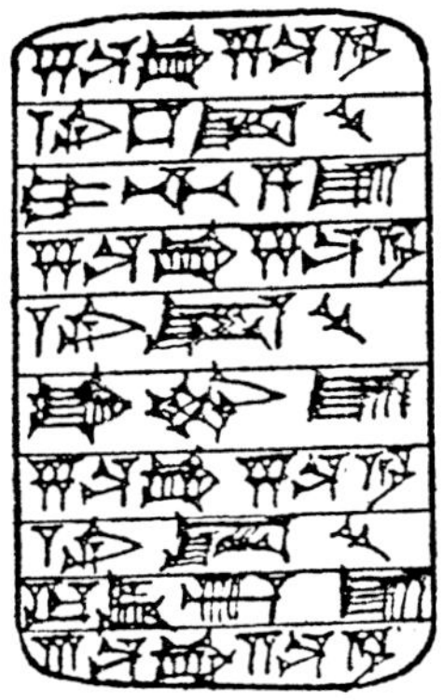

193

(I/-/-)

OBV.

1. 3 sìla ninda šà-uru
2. 5 sìla ninda kaskal-šè
*3. I-zu-a sukkal
4. 0.0.4 ninda šà uru
5. 0.1.0 ninda lugal kaskal-šè
6. NIM Za-ul^{ki}-me
7. ĝìr I-[zu-a sukkal]
8. Šušina^{ki} [ĝ]en
9. 2 sìla [x]
10. Sa-b[u-um^{ki}] ĝen
11. 3 sìl[a x]
12. ĝìr [ ]
13. 4 [ ]
(*bottom of obverse broken*)

REV.

14. 2 sìla ninda [ ]
15. 5 sìla ninda kaskal-šè
16. Ši-a-a lú-kaš$_4$
17. 0.1.0 ninda lugal šà uru
18. 0.0.4 ninda kaskal-šè
19. NIM An-ša-an^{ki}-me
20. ĝìr Ši-a-a lú-kaš$_4$
21. An-ša-an^{ki}-šè ĝen-né
22. 3 sìla ninda A-da-a sukkal
23. Šušina^{ki}-ta ĝen-né
24. 2 sìla ninda *Šu*-^{d}Šubur lú-kaš$_4$
25. Ú.URU×A^{ki}-ta ĝen-né
26. 3 sìla ninda šà uru
27. 5 sìla ninda kaskal-šè *I-din*-^{d}Utu sukkal
28. 0.1.0 ninda lugal šà uru
29. 0.1.0 ninda kaskal-šè
30. NIM Za-ul^{ki}-me
31. ĝìr *I-din*-^{d}Utu sukkal
32. Za-ul^{ki}-šè ĝen-né
33. iti buru$_x$(GÁN)-maš

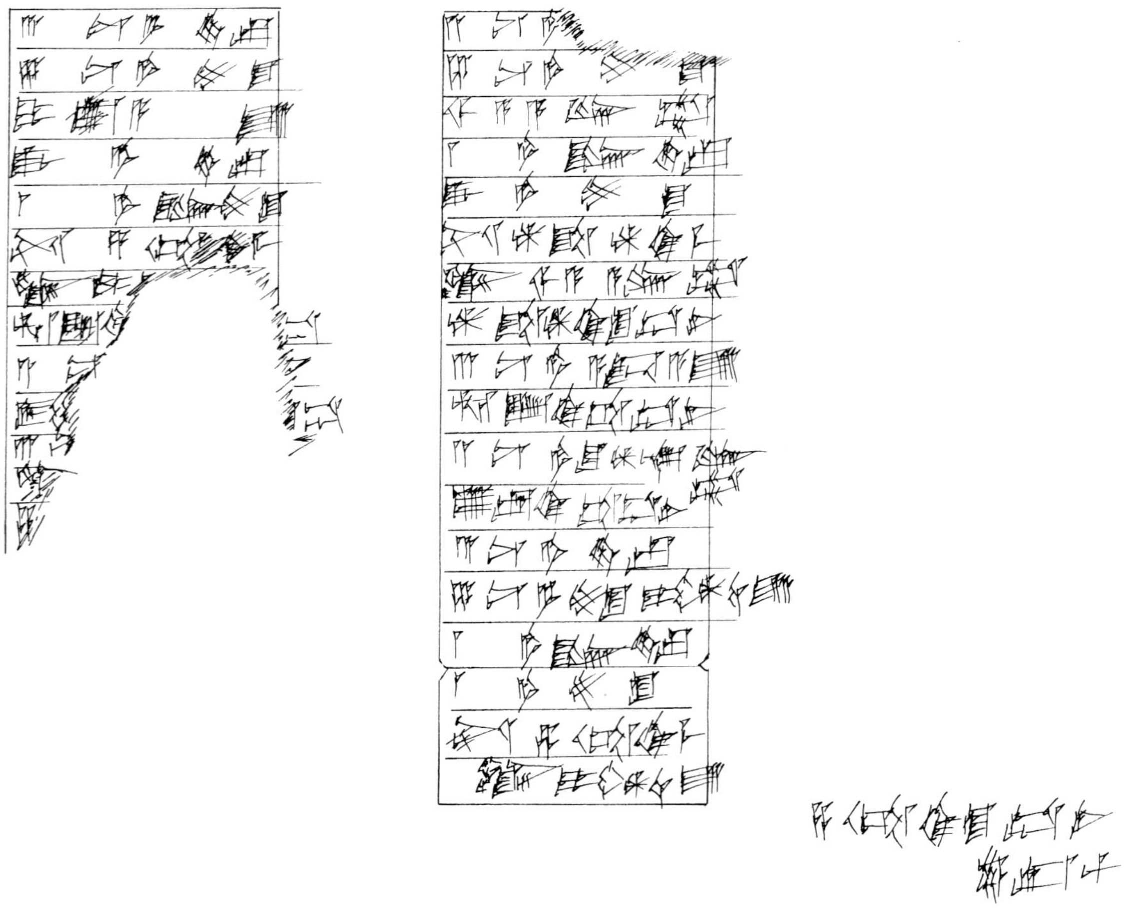

194

(II/13/-)

OBV.

1. 0.0.1 kaš 5 sìla zì
2. 1 ì á-gam
3. Bí-ti-ti sukkal
4. érin še-kin-šè ĝen-na
5. 5 sìla kaš 3 sìla <zì>
6. 1 dida-ĝen
7. 0.0.1 dabin
8. Lú-^{d}Da-mu sukkal
9. še sukkal uru-KU-šè ĝen-na

REV.

10. 3 sìla kaš 2 sìla <zì>
11. 1 ì á-gam
12. Lugal-an-na-túm
*13. [sí]zkur Lagaš$^{\langle ki \rangle}$ ĝen-na
14. 3 sìla kaš 2 sìla <zì>
*15. 1 ì á-gam
16. Ur-^{d}Ba-[ú suk]kal
17. A-NE.N[E] ĝen-<na>
18. zi-ga u$_4$ 13-kam
19. iti gu$_4$-rá-bí-mú-mú

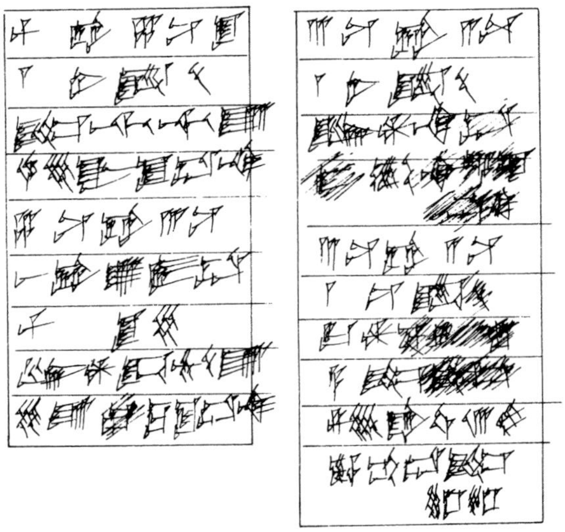

195

(II/-/-)

OBV.

1. 2 á-gam ì-ĝeš
2. u_4 2-kam
3. Lugal-an-na-túm sukkal
4. Šušina^{ki}-šè ĝen-né
5. 2 á-gam ì-ĝeš
6. *Bí-bí-a* aga-ús-gal
7. ù ^{d}Lama sukkal
8. A-dam-šáḫ^{ki}-šè ĝen-na
9. 2 á-gam ì u_4 2-kam
10. *I-ti-šu-ni-im* aga-ús-gal

REV.

11. Ḫu-ḫu-nu-ri^{ki}-šè ĝen-né
12. 2 á-gam ì u_4 1-kam
13. Lú-^{d}Nanše sukkal
14. ù *Nu-úr-*^{d}Suen aga-ús
15. Ki-maš^{ki}-šè ĝen-né
16. (BLANK)
17. iti gu_4-rá-bí-mú-mú

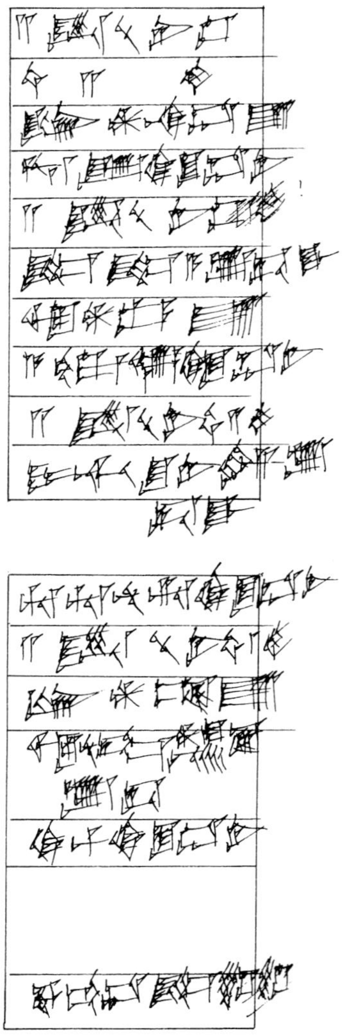

196

(II/-/-)

OBV.

1. 1 á-gam ì-ĝeš
2. *I-šem-*^{d}Šul-gi lú-kaš$_{4}$
3. ½ sìla ì-ĝeš
4. NIM Si-ù-na^{ki}-me

REV.

5. ĝìr *I-šem-*^{d}Šul-gi lú-kaš$_{4}$
6. Si-ù-na-ta ĝen-né
7. (BLANK)
8. iti gu$_{4}$-rá-bí-mú-mú

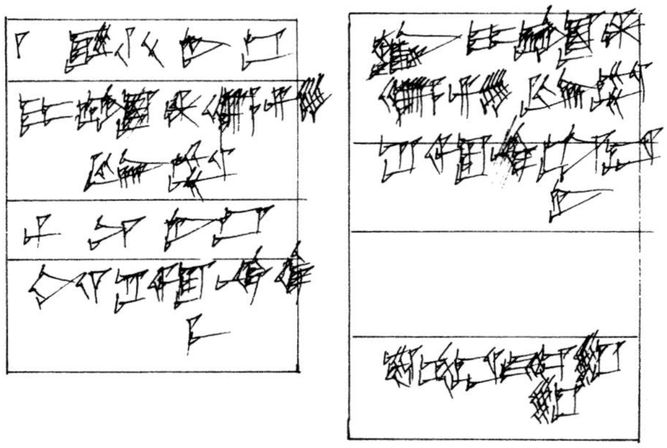

197

(II/-/-)

OBV.

1. 35.1.5 7½ sìla še gur lugal
2. 0.1.0 6⅚ sìla 6 gín ì-ĝeš
3. zi-ga lugal
4. 9 sìla kaš 9 sìla ninda
5. 6 gín ì-ĝeš
6. aga-ús énsi-me
7. 2 sìla kaš 2 gín ì
8. lú Lú-diĝir-ra
9. 5 sìla kaš 2 sìla ninda

REV.

10. 4 gín ì-ĝeš
11. lú *Ì-làl-lum*
12. še-bi 0.0.2 7 sìla
13. ì-bi 12 gín
14. zi-ga didli
15. (B L A N K)

*16. dub-ba ^{kuš}du$_{10}$-gan ĝar-ĝar
17. Ur-^{d}Nanše dumu Ur-é-an-na
18. iti buru$_{x}$(GÁN)-maš-ta
19. iti gud-rá-bí-mú-[mú]
20. iti 2-kam

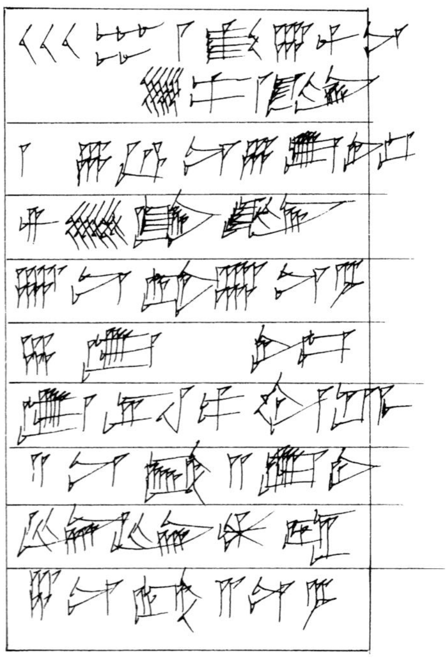

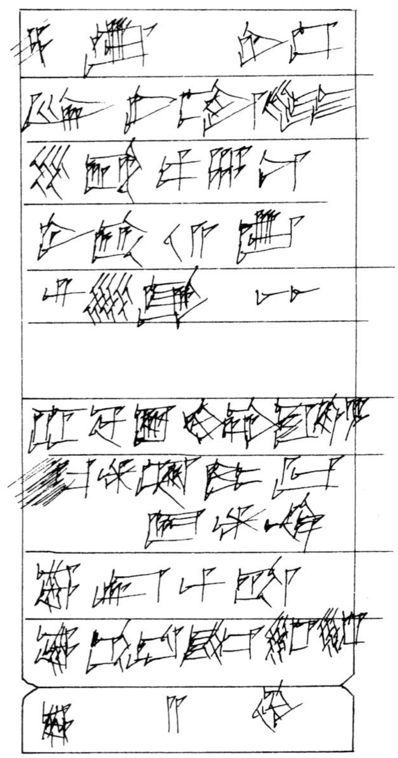

198

(III/14/-)

OBV.

1. 5 sìla kaš 5 sìla zì
2. 1 ì á-gam
3. é-DÙ.DÙ ĝeš-šè ĝen-na
4. 3 sìla kaš 2 sìla zì
5. 1 ì á-gam
6. Da-a-a gi-šul-ḫi-šè ĝen-na
7. 5 sìla kaš 3 sìla zì
8. 2 ì á-gam
9. *I-šar-pá-dan* lú ^{ĝeš}tukul gu-la
10. 3 sìla kaš 2 sìla <zì>

REV.

11. 1 ì á-gam
12. U-bar-NI lú-kaš$_4$
13. nar-da ĝen-na
14. 3 sìla kaš 2 sìla <zì>
15. 1 ì á-gam
16. Ur-ma-ni lú-kaš$_4$
17. 3 sìla kaš 2 sìla <zì>
18. 1 ì á-gam
19. Lú-^{d}Šára lú-kaš$_4$
20. 3 sìla kaš 2 sìla <zì>
21. 1 ì á-gam
22. Lugal-ezen lú-kaš$_4$
23. 5 sìla Kù-^{d}Nanna sukkal
24. zi-ga u$_4$ 14-kam
25. iti ezen ^{d}Li$_9$-si$_4$

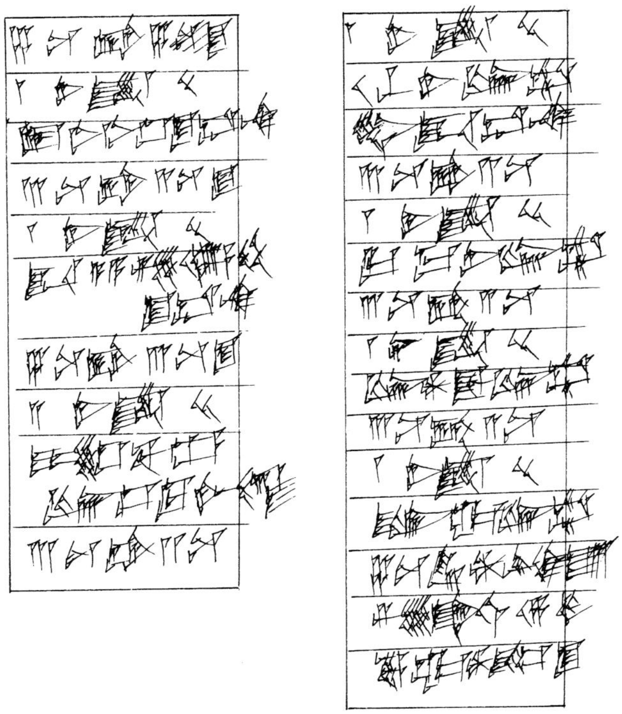

199

(III/-/-)

OBV.

1. 3 sìla ninda
2. *A-ḫu-a* sukkal
3. 0.2.3 NIM bí-ra-aš-ak Ki-maš^{ki}-me
4. ĝìr *A-ḫu-a* sukkal

REV.

5. Ki-maš^{ki}-ta ĝen-né
6. (BLANK)
7. iti ezen $^{\langle d\rangle}$Li$_{9}$-si$_{4}$

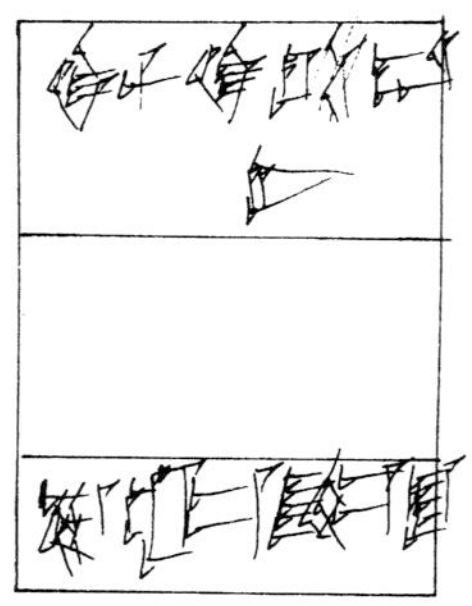

200

(III/-/-)

OBV.

*1. 0.0.1 kaš *A-gu-a* lú ^{ĝeš}tukul gu-la
2. Šušina^{ki}-ta ĝen-né
3. 5 sìla kaš *Nu-úr-ì-lí* aga-ús-gal
4. Šušina^{ki}-ta ĝen-né
5. 0.0.1 kaš šà uru
6. 1 dida kaskal-šè
7. *Bur-Ma-ma* lú ^{ĝeš}tukul gu-la
8. 0.0.1 kaš šà uru
9. 1 dida kaskal-šè
10. Lugal-á-zi-da lú ^{ĝeš}tukul gu-la
11. Šušina^{ki}-šè ĝen-né
12. 0.0.1 kaš

REV.

13. *Puzur*$_4$-M[a-ma]
14. Šušina^{ki}-š[è]
15. 5 sìla kaš D[a-]
16. Šušina^{ki}-ta ĝen-né
17. 0.0.1 kaš šà uru
18. 1 dida kaskal-šè
19. Lugal-nisaĝ-e lú ^{ĝeš}tukul gu-la
20. 0.0.1 kaš *A-gu-a* lú ^{ĝeš}tukul gu-<la>
21. Šušina^{ki}-šè ĝen-né
22. 0.0.1 kaš
23. Ad-da-na-bi
24. lú ^{ĝeš}tukul gu-la
25. [Šu]šina^{ki}-ta ĝen-né
26. iti ezen ^{d}Li$_9$-si$_4$

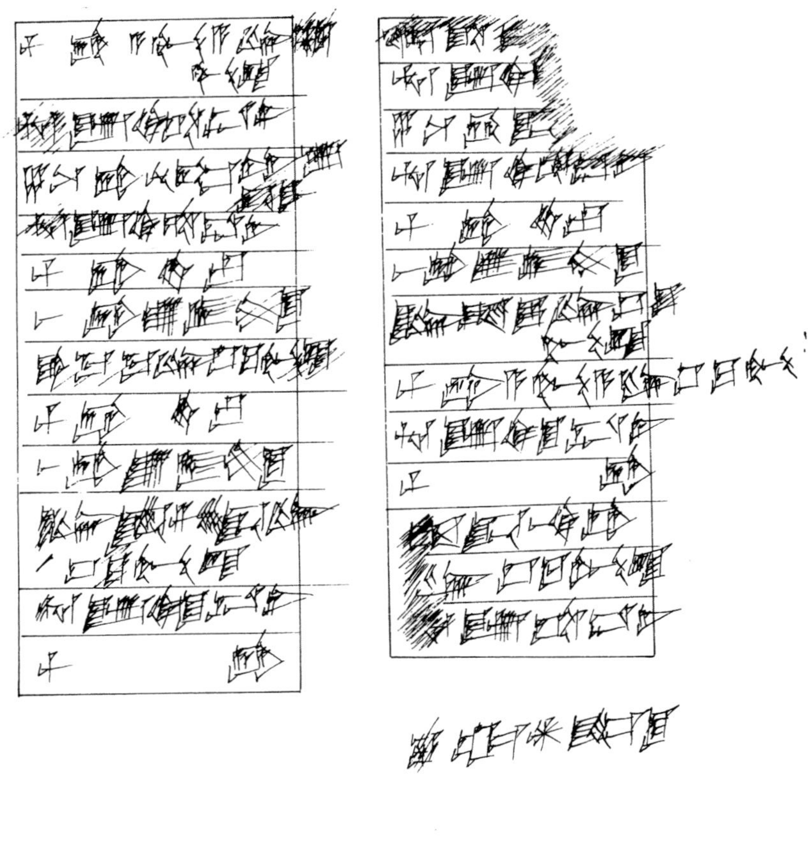

201

(III/-/AS 8)

OBV.

1. 5 sìla kaš 3 sìla ninda
2. 2 gín ì
3. *Puzur$_4$-ḫa-ià*
4. 3 sìla kaš 2 sìla ninda
5. 2 gín ì
6. Nu-ḫa-lum

REV.

7. 5 sìla kaš 3 sìla ninda
8. 2 gín ì
9. Še-e-a
10. 3 sìla kaš [ ]
11. 2 gín ì
12. E-NE.NE
13. iti ezen ^{d}Li$_9$-si$_4$
14. mu en Eridu^{ki} ba-ḫun

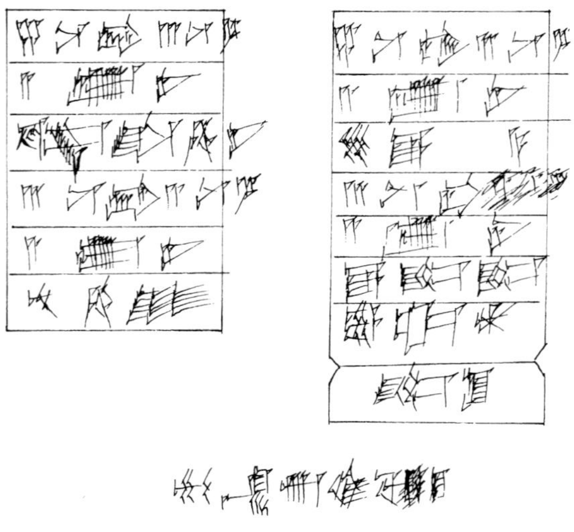

202

(IV/18/-)

OBV.

1. 5 sìla kaš 3 sìla zì
2. 2 ì á-gam
3. Ur-^{d}Šul-pa-è lú ^{ĝeš}tukul gu-la
4. 2 sìla zì 1 ì á-gam
5. lú-kaš$_{4}$ Ù-ba-a
6. 3 sìla kaš 2 sìla zì

REV.

7. 1 ì á-gam
8. Diĝir-*ba-ni* lú-kaš$_{4}$
9. 3 sìla kaš 2 sìla zì
10. 1 ì á-gam
11. *Na-bí*-^{d}Suen
12. Šušina^{ki}-ta ĝen-na
13. zi-ga u$_{4}$ 18
14. iti šu-numun

203 (IV/27/-)

OBV.

1. 5 sìla kaš 3 sìla zì
2. 1 ì á-gam
3. An-né-ba-du$_7$ sukkal
4. 3 sìla kaš 2 sìla zì
5. 1 ì á-gam
6. Diĝir-*ba-ni* saĝ-šè ĝen-na
7. 3 sìla kaš 2 sìla zì
8. 1 ì á-gam
9. Šà-da túg-šè ĝen-na
10. 3 sìla kaš 2 sìla zì

REV.

11. zi-zi-ig
12. 3 sìla kaš 2 sìla z[ì]
13. 1 ì á-gam
14. Èr-ra-nu-sar [ ]
15. lú-má-saĝ ĝen-na
16. 5 sìla kaš 3 sìla [zì]
17. 1 ì á-gam
18. Lú-an-na-túm sukkal
19. Sa-bu-um^{ki}-šè ĝen-na
20. zi-ga u$_4$ 27
21. iti šu-numun

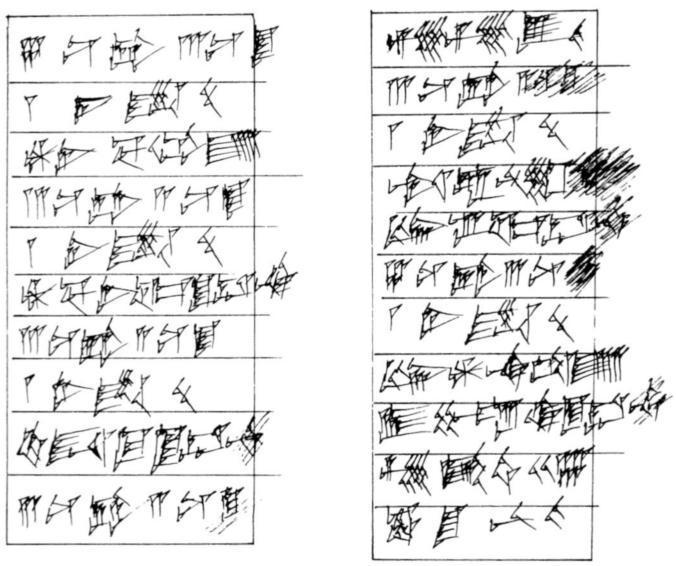

204 (IV/29/-)

OBV.

1. 5 sìla kaš 5 sìla zì
2. 2 ì á-gam
3. Ur-^{d}Šul-pa-è lú ^{ĝeš}tukul gu-la
4. 5 sìla kaš 3 sìla zì
5. 1 ì á-gam
6. Ĝi$_{6}$-da-a lú ^{ĝeš}tukul gu-la
7. 2 sìla zì 1 ì á-gam
8. NIM Ši-ma-aš-gi$_{4}^{ki}$

REV.

9. 5 sìla kaš 3 sìla zì
10. 1 ì á-gam
11. An-né-ba-du$_{7}$ sukkal
12. šabra ^{d}Šul-gi-*a-bí*-da ĝen-na
13. 3 sìla kaš 2 sìla zì
14. 1 ì á-gam
15. Diĝir-*ba-ni* saĝ-šè ĝen-na
16. 3 sìla kaš 2 sìla zì
17. 1 ì á-gam
18. Šà-da túg-šè ĝen-na
19. zi-ga u$_{4}$ 30 lá 1
20. iti šu-numun

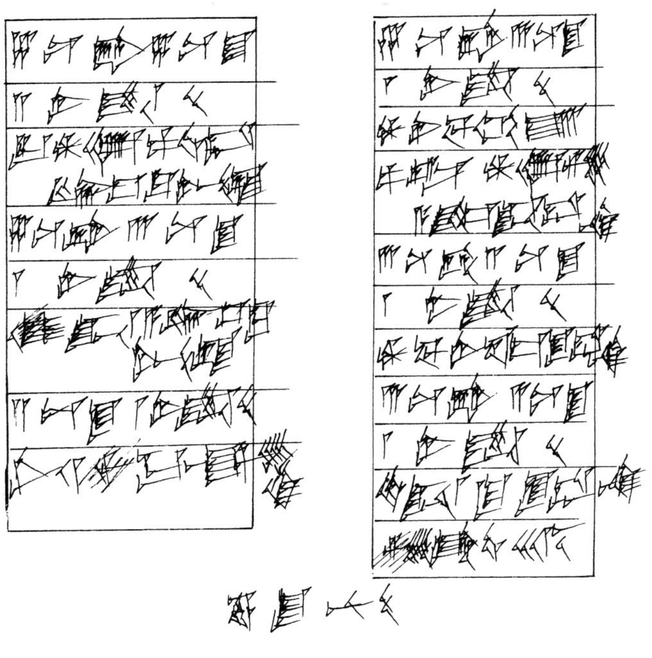

205

(IV/-/-)

OBV.

1. 1 udu NIM Ki-maš^{ki}-me
2. ĝìr ^{d}IM-*ba-ni* sukkal
3. Ki-maš^{ki}-ta ĝen-né
4. 1 máš NIM Gi-ša^{ki}-me
5. ĝìr *Puzur$_4$-šu* sukkal
6. [G]i-ša^{ki}-šè ĝen-na
7. [1] udu NIM Ḫu-bu-la^{ki}-me

REV.

8. ĝìr Ma-ma-kešda lú-kaš$_4$
9. Ḫu-bu-la^{ki}-šè ĝen-né
10. (BLANK)
11. iti šu-numun

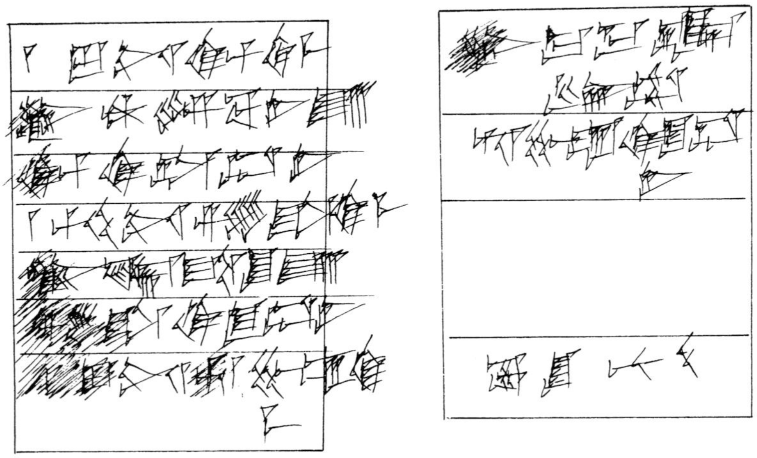

206

(IV/-/-)

OBV.

1. 5 sìla kaš 5 sìla ninda
2. 1 ì-ĝeš á-gam
3. Lú-ma-an-du$_{11}$ sukkal
4. Inim-inim-ma-šè ĝen-na
5. 5 sìla kaš 5 sìla ninda
6. 1 ì-ĝeš á-gam
7. *Še-li-ma-núm* sukkal
8. túg-gibil-šè ĝen-n[a]
9. 5 sìla kaš 5 sìla ninda
10. 1 ì-ĝeš á-gam
11. Ur-^{d}[ ]

REV.

12. Gù-dé-a TAG.TUKU
13. 5 sìla kaš 5 sìla ninda
14. 1 ì-ĝeš á-gam
15. Ur-^{d}Lama sukkal
16. 5 sìla kaš 5 sìla ninda
17. 1 ì-ĝeš á-gam
18. É-dar-gi$_{4}$-ni lú ^{ĝeš}tukul gu-la

*19. 0.1.0 kaš 0.1.0 ninda 0.4.0 dabin

20. 1 sìla ì-ĝeš
21. NIM Ši-ma-aš-ki šu ba-ti
22. 5 sìla kaš 5 sìla ninda

*23. ĝìr ZA.SÁ.A sukkal

24. 3 sìla kaš 2 sìla ninda
25. [x]-DU.BUR.DU$_{8}$-ta

*26. An-ša-an^{ki}-ta ĝen-na

*27. ù Nibru^{ki}-šè ĝen-na

*28. iti šu-numun

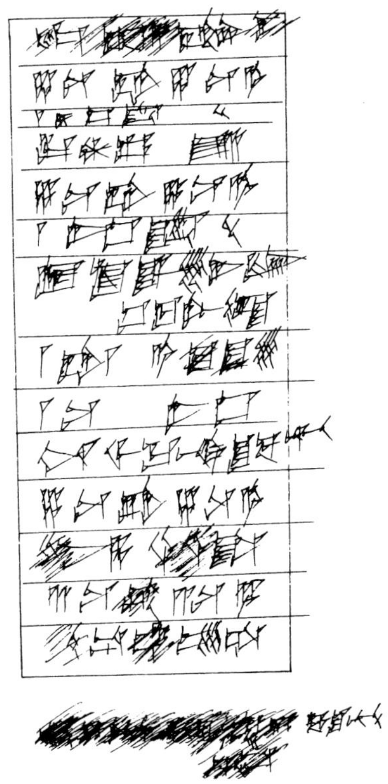

207

(IV/-/-)

OBV.

1. 1 á-gam ì
2. *En-núm-mi-lí* sukkal
3. A-dam-šáḫ^{ki}-šè ĝen-né
4. 1 á-gam ì
5. *A-gu-a* sukkal
6. Šušina^{ki}-šé ĝen-né
7. 2 á-gam ì
8. Si-mu lú ^{ĝeš}tukul gu-la
9. 1 á-gam ì
10. Lú-šùd

REV.

11. ĝìr Si-mu lú ^{ĝeš}tukul gu-la
12. Šušina^{ki}-ta ĝen-né
13. 1 á-gam ì
14. I-ba-ni-ni lú ^{ĝeš}tukul gu-la
15. Šušina^{ki}-šè ĝen-né
16. 1 á-gam ì
17. Im-ti-da sukkal
18. Šušina^{ki} ĝen-né
19. 1 á-gam ì
20. *Á-pil-lí-a* dumu nu-bànda Ḫu-ḫu-nu-ri^{ki}-šè ĝen-<na>
21. iti šu-numun

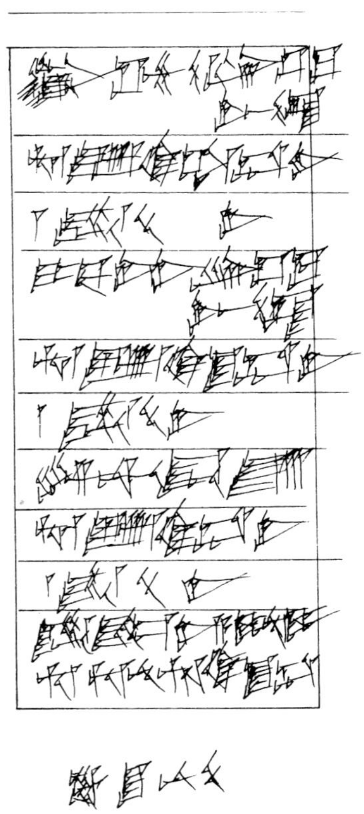

208

(IV/-/-)

OBV.

1. 5 sìla kaš 5 sìla ninda
2. 1 ì-ĝeš á-gam
3. *Šu-Eš$_{11}$-tár* sukkal
4. 5 sìla kaš 5 sìla ninda
5. 1 ì-ĝeš á-gam
6. *A-bù-ṭá-ab*
7. 5 sìla kaš 5 sìla ninda
8. 1 ì-ĝeš á-gam

REV.

9. *Pù-zur$_{x}$*-Ma-ma
10. 5 sìla kaš 5 sìla ninda
11. 1 ì-ĝeš á-gam
12. *Šu*-^{d}IM sukkal
13. An-ša-an^{ki}-ta ù Nibru^{ki}-ta ĝen-na
14. iti šu-numun

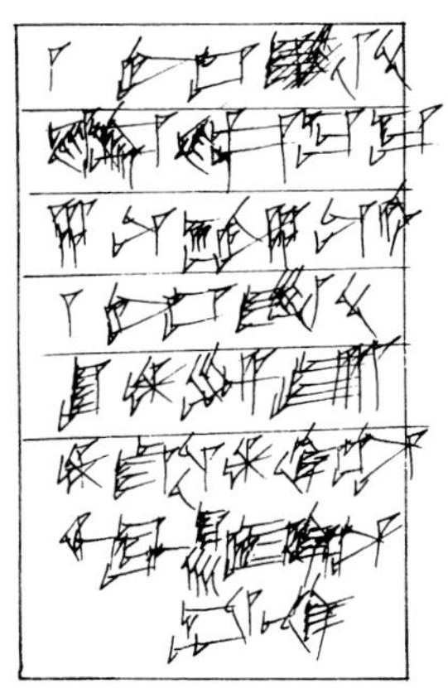

209

(IV/-/-)

OBV.

1. 1 á-gam ì
2. *A-ḫu-a* sukkal
3. Šušina^{ki}-šè ĝen-né
4. 1 á-gam ì
5. *Šu-Eš-tár* lú-kaš$_4$
6. Šušina^{ki}-ta ĝen-né
7. 1 á-gam ì
8. I-ti-a lú-kaš$_4$
9. 2 sìla ì-ĝeš
10. NIM Ú-lum-ma^{ki}-me

REV.

11. ĝìr I-ti-a lú-kaš$_4$
12. Ú-lum^{ki}-šè ĝen-né
13. 1 á-gam ì
14. *I-din*-diĝir sukkal
15. Šušina^{ki}-ta ĝen-né
16. 1 á-gam ì
17. *A-bu-ni* sukkal
18. Ú.URU×A^{ki}-ta ĝen-né
19. (BLANK)
20. iti šu-numun

210 (V/2/-)

OBV.

1. 6 sìla kaš 4 sìla ninda
2. 4 gín ì
3. *Bur*-^{d}IM Ga-eš-šè ĝen-na
4. 6 sìla kaš 4 sìla ninda
5. 10 gín ì
6. Diĝir-*ba-ni* ki-zabar-dab$_5$-ta ĝen-na
7. 3 sìla kaš 2 sìla ninda
8. 2 gín ì
9. *Nu-úr-Eš*-*tár* sukkal
10. 0.0.4 kaš sig$_5$ 0.1.2 kaš ĝen
11. 0.2.0 dabin 2 sìla ì-ĝeš

REV.

12. NIM Ši-ma-aš-gi$_4$ ù Du$_8$-du$_8$-lí^{ki} Nibru^{ki}-ta
13. ĝìr *Nu-úr-Eš*-*tár* sukkal
14. 3 sìla kaš 2 sìla ninda
15. 2 gín ì
16. Lú-^{d}En-ki gu$_4$-da ĝen-na
17. 3 sìla kaš 2 sìla ninda
18. 2 gín ì
19. Ur-^{d}Nanna sukkal
20. 3 sìla kaš 2 sìla ninda
21. 2 gín ì
22. *Ša-ra-ì-lí* Sa-bu-um^{ki}-šè ĝen-na
23. zi-ga u$_4$ 2-kam
24. iti munu$_4$-kú

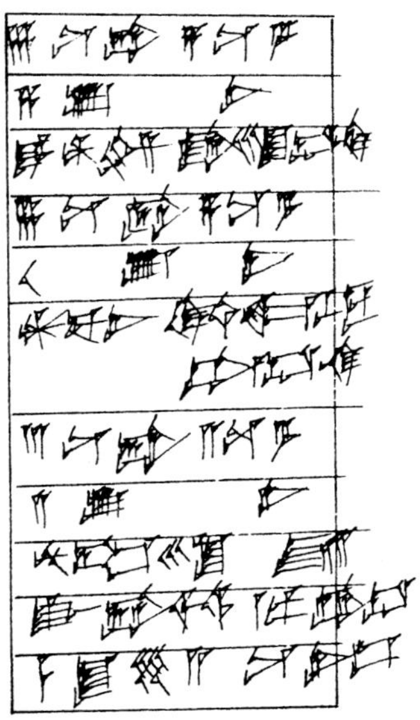

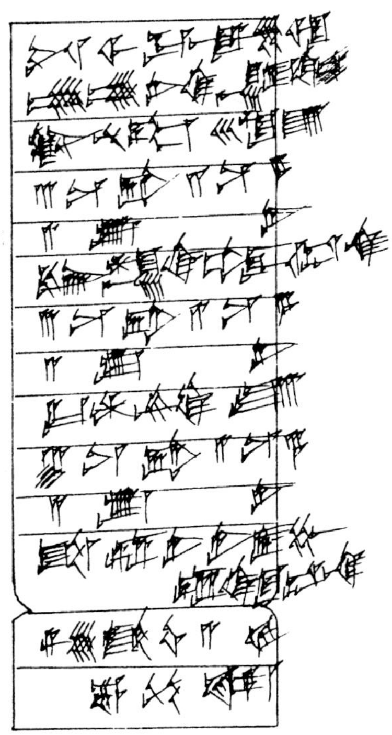

211

(V/22/-)

OBV.

1. 5 sìla kaš 5 sìla zì
2. 1 ì á-gam
3. Lú-^{d}Da-mu sukkal
4. 4 sìla kaš 3 sìla zì
5. 1 ì á-gam
6. Ḫa-ar-ši lú-kaš$_4$
7. 3 sìla kaš 2 sìla zì
8. 1 ì á-gam
9. *A-ḫu*-a-gàr lú-kaš$_4$
10. 3 sìla kaš 2 sìla zì
11. 1 ì á-gam
12. An-gàr lú-kaš$_4$

REV.

13. gu$_4$-re zi-ga-me
14. 0.0.1 kaš sig$_5$ 5 sìla zì
15. 1 ì á-gam
16. Da-da sukkal
17. 5 sìla kaš 3 sìla zì
18. 1 ì á-gam
19. Lú-*ša-lim* lú Sa-<bu>-um-šè ĝen-na
20. 5 sìla kaš 3 sìla zì
21. 1 ì á-gam
22. Ĝìri-ni-ì-ša$_6$ sukkal
23. 3 sìla kaš 2 sìla <zì>
24. 1 ì á-gam
25. Ur-^{d}Nun-gal Mar-tu
26. zi-ga u$_4$ 22-kam
27. iti munu$_4$-kú

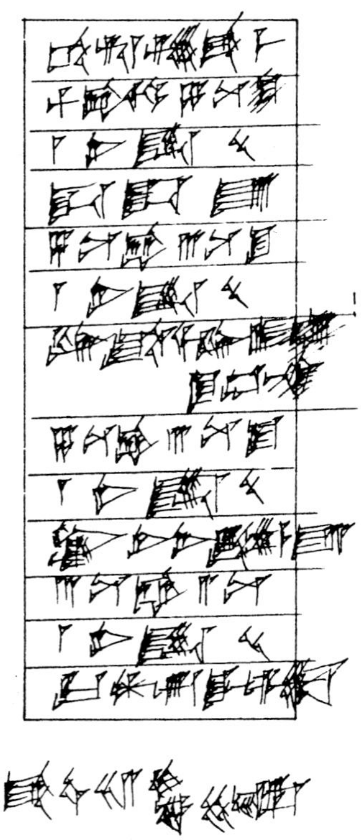

212 (V/24/-)

OBV.

1. 3 sìla kaš 2 sìla ninda
2. 2 gín ì
3. Lugal-á-zi-da lú ^{ĝeš}tukul gu-la
4. 3 sìla kaš 2 sìla ninda
5. 2 gín ì
6. *A-ḫu-ni* Gú-ab-ba^{ki}-šè ĝen-na
7. 3 sìla kaš 2 sìla ninda
8. 2 gín ì

REV.

9. *Šu-Èr-ra* Šušina^{ki}-[šè]
10. 3 sìla kaš 2 sìla ninda
11. 2 gín ì
12. *Šu-ì-lí* má ĝeš-<ì>-šè ĝen-na
13. 0.0.2 4 sìla kaš u$_4$ 23-kam
14. 0.0.2 4 sìla kaš u$_4$ 24-kam
15. dub-sar Lú-diĝir-ra-me
16. 0.0.1 8 sìla kaš 0.0.1 zì u$_4$ 23
17. 0.0.1.8 sìla kaš 0.0.1 zì u$_4$ 24
18. dub-sar ^{d}Šára-kam-me
19. zi-ga u$_4$ 24-kam
20. iti munu$_4$-kú

213

(V/-/-)

OBV.

1. 2 sìla ninda
2. *Šu*-^{d}Utu lú-kaš$_{4}$
★3. 0.1.1 dabin NIM Ši-ma-aš-ki-me
4. ĝìr *Šu*-^{d}Utu lú-kaš$_{4}$
5. Ši-ma-aš-ki-ta ĝen-né
6. 3 sìla ninda šà uru
7. 5 sìla ninda kaskal-šè
8. La-ni-mu sukkal
9. Šušina^{ki}-šè ĝen-né

REV.

10. 20 sìla ninda Na-di lú-kaš$_{4}$
11. 35 ĝuruš 2 sìla zì-ta
★12. bí-ra-aš-ak Ki-maš^{ki}-me
13. ĝìr Na-di lú-kaš$_{4}$
14. Ú.URU.A^{ki}-ta ĝen-né
15. 3 sìla ninda šà uru
16. 5 sìla ninda kaskal-šè
17. *Iš-me-a-ni* sukkal
18. 0.0.4 dabin šà uru
19. 0.1.0 dabin kaskal-šè
★20. NIM Ḫu-lí-bar-me

L.E.

21. ĝìr *Iš-me-a-ni* sukkal
22. Du$_{8}$-du$_{8}$-lí^{ki}-šè ĝen-né iti munu$_{4}$-kú

214 (V/-/-)

OBV.

1. 5 sìla kaš 5 sìla ninda
2. 1 ì-ĝeš á-gam
3. Lugal-má-gur$_8$-re sukkal
4. 0.1.3 kaš 0.1.3 ninda lugal
5. ½ sìla ì-ĝeš
6. NIM A-dam-šáḫ^{ki} šu ba-ti
7. 5 sìla kaš 5 sìla ninda
8. 1 ì-ĝeš á-gam
9. ĝìr *Puzur$_4$-ra-bí* sukkal
10. ⸢5 sìla kaš⸣ 5 sìla ninda

REV.

11. 1 ì-ĝeš á-gam
12. Lú-^{d}Nanna sukkal
13. 3 sìla kaš 2 sìla ninda
14. 1 ì-ĝeš á-gam
15. Ga-du lú-kaš$_4$
16. 5 sìla kaš 5 sìla ninda
17. 1 ì-ĝeš á-gam
18. *Šu*-^{d}IM sukkal
19. An-ša-an^{ki}-ta ù Nibru^{ki}-ta
20. iti munu$_4$-kú

215

(V/-/-)

OBV.

1. 1 á-gam ì-ĝeš
2. Kal-ši-a aga-ús-gal
3. Sa-bu-um^{ki}-šè ĝen-né
4. 1 á-gam ì
5. *Ìl-ma-zu* lú-kaš$_4$
6. Ši-ma-aš-ki-ta ĝen-né
7. 4 á-gam ì u$_4$ 2-kam
8. *Puzur$_4$-šu* ù-gúl
9. ù *Á-pil-lí* šeš-ba

REV.

10. A-dam-šáḫ^{ki}-šè ĝen-né
11. 4 á-gam ì u$_4$ 2-kam
12. *Šu*-^{d}Utu sukkal
13. ù <*Ìl*>-*ma-zu* šeš-ba
14. Šušina^{ki}-šè ĝen-né
15. (BLANK)
16. iti munu$_4$-kú

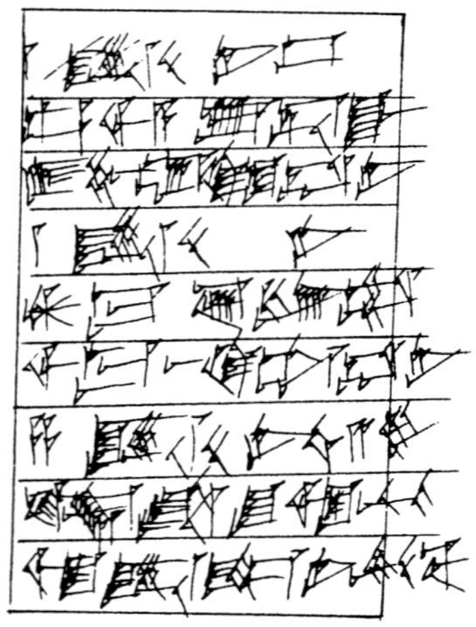

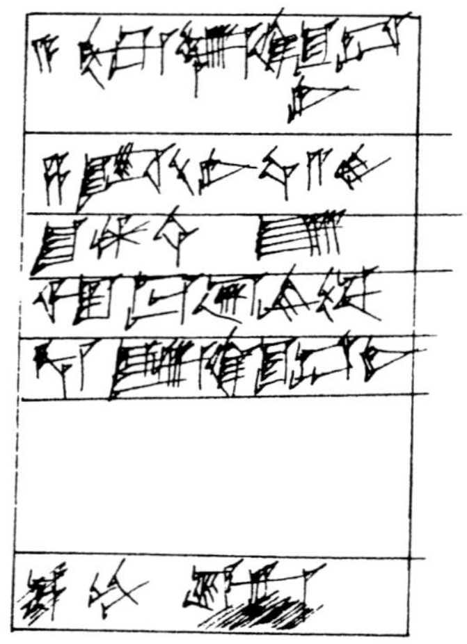

216

(V/-/-)

OBV.

1. 5 sìla kaš 5 sìla ninda
2. 1 á-gam ì-ĝeš
3. Lú-^{d}Da-mu lú ^{ĝeš}tukul gu-la
4. Gú-a-ab-ba-ta^{ki} énsi-ta ĝen-[na]
5. 5 sìla kaš ⸢5⸣ sìla ninda
6. 1 á-gam ì-ĝeš
7. U.RU.BE-gin$_{7}$ sukkal
8. 5 sìla kaš ⸢5 sìla ninda⸣
9. 1 á-gam ì-ĝeš

REV.

10. I-ti-a sukkal
11. Inim-inim-ma^{ki}-šè ĝen-na
12. 5 sìla kaš 5 sìla ninda
13. 1 á-gam ì-ĝeš
14. Ur-ba-ga sukkal
15. 5 sìla kaš 5 sìla ninda
16. 1 á-gam ì-ĝeš
17. É-sa-ra-du$_{10}$ sukkal
18. urudu-<ḫa>-bù-da ĝen-na
19. 3 sìla kaš 2 sìla ninda
20. 1 á-gam ì-ĝeš
21. Inim-inim lú-kaš$_{4}$

L.E.

22. Nibru^{ki}-ta ĝen-na
23. iti munu$_{4}$-kú

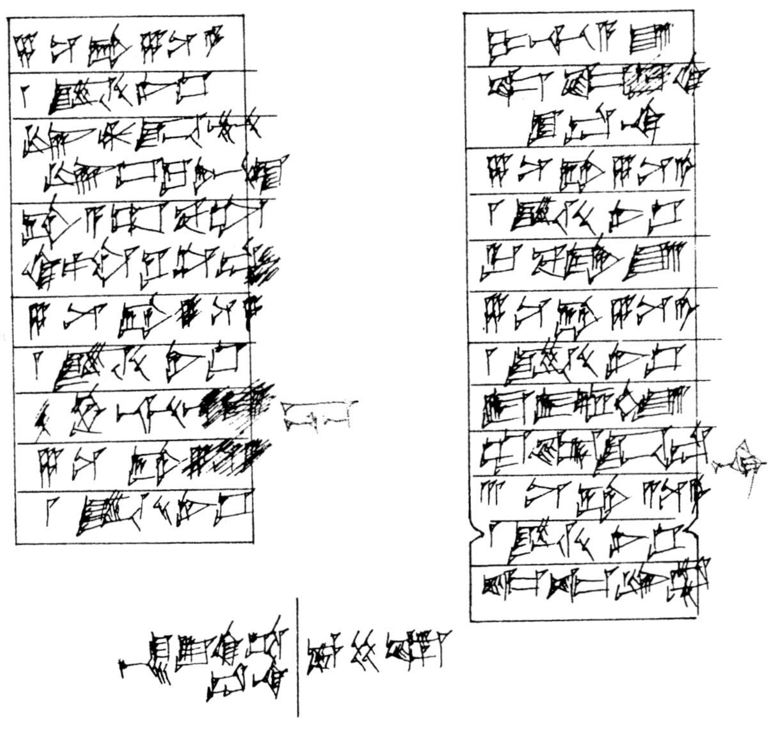

217

(V/-/-)

OBV.

1. 2 dida ĝen
2. 0.0.2 5 sìla zì lugal
3. 12 gín ì-ĝeš
4. NIM An-ša-an^{ki}-me
5. 5 sìla kaš

REV.

6. 3 sìla [zì]
7. 5 gín ì
8. *A-bu-ni* sukkal
9. Uri$_5^{ki}$-šè ĝen-né
10. iti munu$_4$-kú

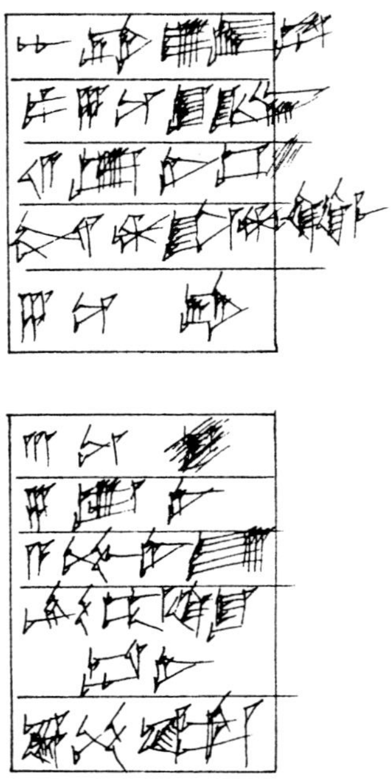

218 (V/-/-)

OBV.

1. 2 sìla ninda
2. *Šu-ì-lí* lú-kaš$_4$
3. Šušina^{ki}-ta ĝen-né
4. 3 sìla ninda šà uru
5. 5 sìla ninda kaskal-šè
6. *Na-bí-*^{d}Suen sukkal
7. Šušina^{ki}-ta ĝen-né
8. 2 sìla ninda Šu-^{d}Nin-šubur lú-kaš$_4$
9. Šušina^{ki}-ta ĝen-né

REV.

10. 3 sìla ninda šà uru
11. 5 sìla ninda kaskal-šè
12. Lú-^{d}Nanna sukkal
13. Sa-bu-um^{ki}-šè ĝen-né
14. 3 sìla ninda
15. ^{d}Suen-*ba-ni* sukkal
16. 0.1.0 dabin NIM Ki-maš^{ki}-me
17. ĝìr ^{d}Suen-*ba-ni* sukkal
18. Ki-maš^{ki}-ta ĝen-né
19. iti munu$_4$-kú

219

(V/-/-)

OBV.

1. 3 sìla kaš 2 sìla ninda
2. 4 gín ì-ĝeš
3. *Ì-lí*-^{d}Lama lú-kaš$_{4}$
4. 5 sìla kaš 5 sìla ninda
5. 4 gín ì-ĝeš
6. *A-ḫu-a* sukkal
7. 5 sìla kaš 5 sìla ninda
8. A-kal-la aga-ús-gal-gal
9. 5 sìla kaš 5 sìla ninda
10. 4 gín ì-ĝeš

REV.

*11. *Íl-ma-zu* sukkal
12. 5 sìla kaš 5 sìla ninda
13. Ga-du sukkal
14. 0.0.2 kaš 0.0.3 ninda lugal
15. NIM Gi-ša^{ki}
16. šu ba-ab-ti
17. 5 sìla kaš 5 sìla ninda
18. 4 gín ì-ĝeš
19. ĝìr Da-bu-ma sukkal
20. Urí^{ki}-šè ĝen-né
21. iti munu$_{4}$-kú

220 (V/-/-)

OBV.

1. 5 sìla kaš 5 sìla ninda
2. 1 ì-ĝeš á-gam
3. *Šu*-^{d}Nanna sukkal
4. 5 sìla kaš 5 sìla ninda
5. 1 ì-ĝeš á-gam
6. Lugal-^{d}Utu sukkal
7. 5 sìla kaš 5 sìla ninda
8. 1 ì-ĝeš á-gam
9. Nì-du$_{7}$-pa-è sukkal

REV.

10. 5 sìla kaš 5 sìla ninda
11. 1 ì-ĝeš á-gam
12. *Šu*-^{d}Nisaba sukkal
13. 5 sìla kaš 5 sìla ninda
14. 1 ì-ĝeš á-gam
15. ^{d}Nanna-a-ki-ág sukkal
16. An-ša-an^{ki}-ta ĝen-né
17. Nibru^{ki}-ta ĝen-né
18. iti munu$_{4}$-kú

221

(VI/5/-)

OBV.

1. 3 sìla kaš 2 sìla zì
2. 1 ì á-gam
3. Lukur-*be-lí* lú-kaš$_4$
4. 3 sìla kaš 2 sìla zì
5. 1 ì á-gam
6. Šu-PAP.PAP lú-kaš$_4$
7. lú-nin-diĝir-^{d}Ba-ú-da ĝen-na
8. 5 sìla kaš 3 sìla <zì>
9. 1 ì á-gam
10. *A-ḫu-ni* sukkal

REV.

11. Saḫar^{ki}-ta ĝen-na
12. 5 sìla kaš 5 sìla zì
13. 1 ì á-gam
14. Lugal-an-na-túm
15. anše zi-gúm-ma-šè ĝen-na
16. 3 sìla kaš 2 sìla zì
17. 1 ì á-gam
18. Lugal-^{d}Utu lú-kaš$_4$
19. 1 dida 0.0.1 dabin
20. Lú-diĝir-ra dub-sar
21. zi-ga u$_4$ 5-kam
22. iti ezen ^{d}Dumu-zi

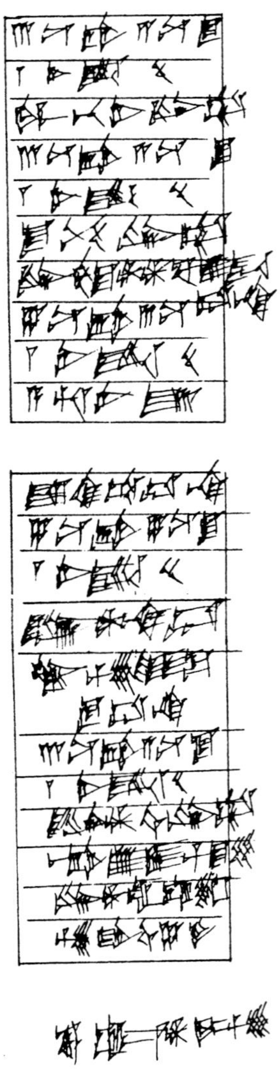

222 (VI/16/-)

OBV.

1. 5 sìla kaš 5 sìla zì
2. 1 ì á-gam
3. Lú-^{d}Da-mu sukkal
4. 5 sìla kaš ^{d}Nin-šubur sukkal
5. 5 sìla kaš 3 sìla <zì>
6. 1 ì á-gam
7. Ur-^{d}En-líl-lá lú-kaš$_{4}$
8. 5 sìla kaš 3 sìla <zì>
9. 1 ì á-gam
10. ½ sìla ì-ĝeš

*11. Ur-^{d}Utu sukkal Gáraš^{ki}

REV.

12. 5 sìla kaš 2 sìla <zì>
13. 1 ì á-gam
14. *Še-li-lu*$_{5}$

*15. 3 sìla kaš 2 sìla <zì>

16. 1 ì á-gam
17. Ur-^{d}Lama Mar-tu
18. 3 sìla kaš 2 sìla [zì]
19. 1 ì á-gam
20. *A-bí-a* lú-kaš$_{4}$
21. 3 sìla kaš *A-ḫu-ma*
22. zi-ga u$_{4}$ 16-kam
23. iti ezen ^{d}Dumu-zi

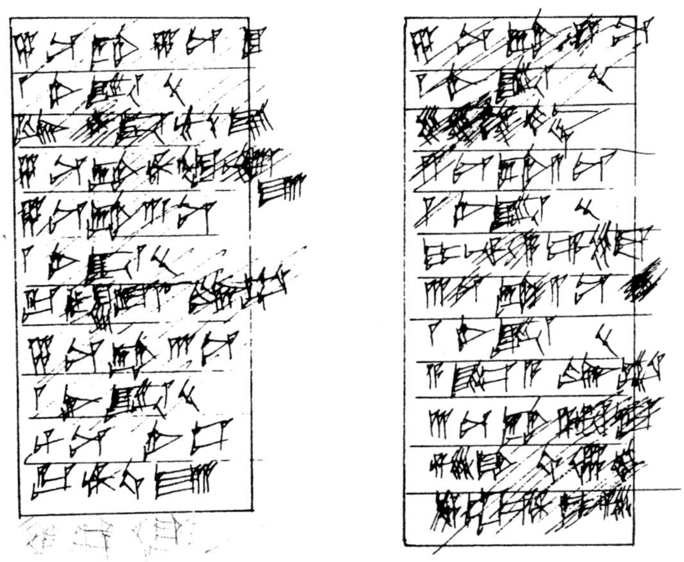

223

(VI/-/-)

OBV.

1. 0.0.1 5 sìla zì-gu
2. Na-ba-ša$_6$ Mar-tu
3. lú má-saĝ-ĝá-ke$_4$-ne-šè ĝen-na
4. 5 sìla zì šà uru
5. 5 sìla zì kaskal-šè
6. Lú-*ì-lí* lú-kaš$_4$
7. Šušina^{ki}-šè ĝen-né
8. 5 sìla zì-gu

REV.

9. Lú-bàn-da sukkal
10. 0.1.0 dabin lugal
11. *Še-li-bu-um* énsi
12. Sa-bu-um^{ki}-ta ĝen-né
13. ĝìr Lú-bàn-da sukkal
14. 5 sìla zì-gu
15. *Á-pil-la-núm* sukkal
16. Šušina^{ki}-ta ĝen-né
17. iti ezen ^{d}Dumu-zi-da

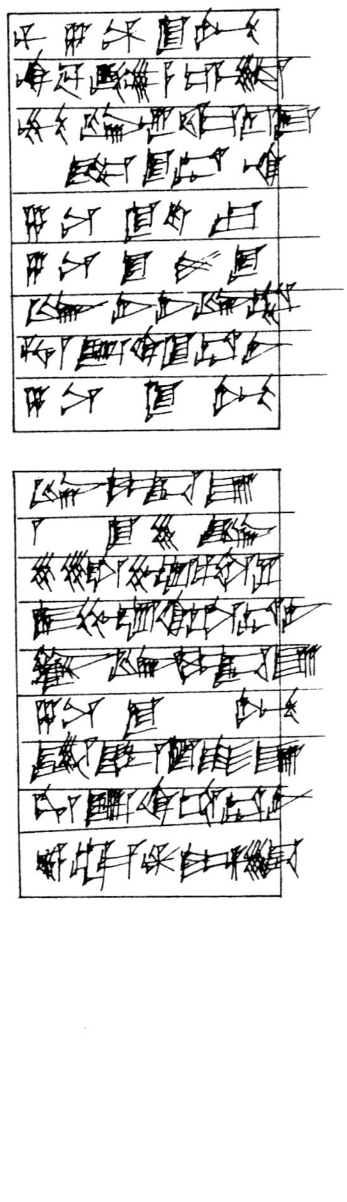

224 (VI/-/-)

OBV.

1. 5 sìla kaš ĝen
2. 5 sìla dabin
3. 1 á-gam ì
4. *Ú-ṭúl*-Ma-ma (*erasure*)
5. lú ^{ĝeš}tukul gu-la
6. Šušina^{ki}-ta ĝen-né
7. 5 sìla kaš 5 sìla dabin

REV.

8. 1 á-gam ì
9. Ur-^{d}Lama sukkal
10. 0.1.0 kaš ĝen lugal
11. 0.1.0 dabin lugal
12. lú-dab$_5$-ba uru didli-me
13. ĝìr Ur-^{d}Lama sukkal
14. Šušina^{ki}-ta ĝen-né
15. iti ezen ^{d}Dumu-zi-da

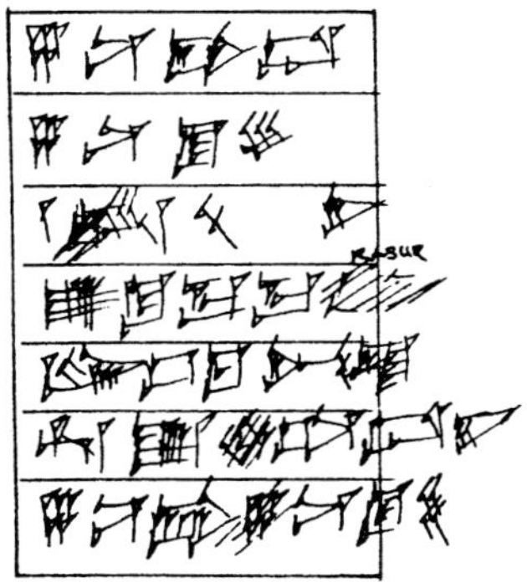

225

(VI/-/AS 8)

OBV.

1. 5 sìla kaš 3 sìla ninda
2. 2 gín ì
3. [d]Utu-*be-lí*
4. 2 sìla kaš 2 sìla ninda
5. 2 gín ì
6. [d]Šul-gi-[d]Suen

REV.

7. 3 sìla kaš 3 sìla ninda
8. 2 gín ì
9. *I-ti-šu* sukkal
10. iti ezen [d]Dumu-zi
11. mu en Eridu[ki] ba-a-ḫun

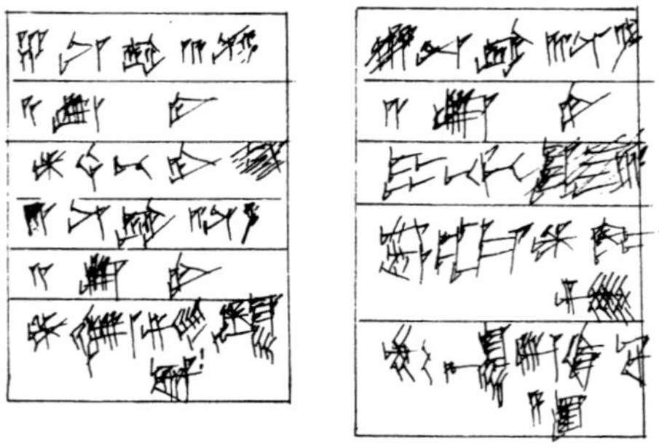

226

(VII/8/-)

OBV.

1. 3 sìla kaš 2 sìla ninda
2. 4 gín ì
3. *A-da-làl* lú ^{ĝeš}tukul gu-la
4. 3 sìla kaš 2 sìla ninda
5. 2 gín ì
6. *Šu-Èr-ra* lú-kaš$_4$
7. Saḫar^{ki}-ta ĝen-na
8. 3 sìla kaš 2 sìla ninda

REV.

9. 2 gín ì
10. Ur-^{d}Šul-pa-è
11. dub-sar Lugal-da-DU
12. 3 sìla kaš 2 sìla ninda
13. 2 gín ì
14. ša dub *Ì-lí-ḫa-za-núm* é-^{d}ĜEŠ.BAR-è-
    ta ĝen-na
15. 3 sìla kaš 2 sìla ninda
16. 2 gín ì
17. Lú-^{d}Nanna
18. 3 sìla kaš 2 sìla ninda
19. 2 gín ì
20. *Šu-nu-Eš-tár* A-dam-šáḫ^{ki}-šè ĝen-na

L.E.

21. zi-ga u$_4$ 8 iti ezen ^{d}Šul-gi

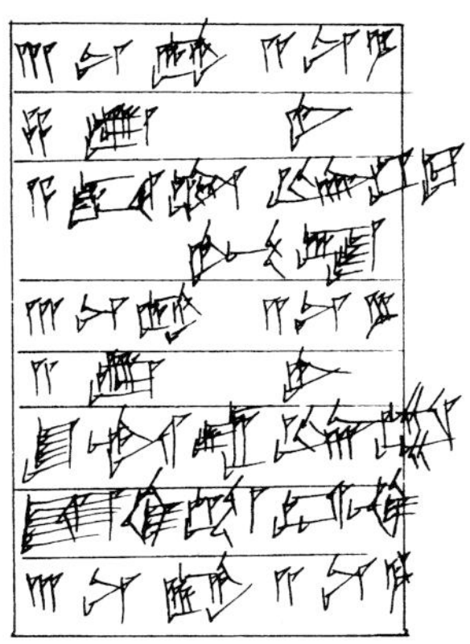

227

(VII/-/-)

OBV.

1. 0.0.1 zì u$_4$ 2-kam
2. *A-ḫu*-du$_{10}$ ù ti
3. Ú.URU×A.A^{ki}-ta ĝen-né
4. 2 sìla zì Da-a lú-kaš$_4$
5. 5 sìla zì *Šu*-Ma-ma sukkal
6. Šušina^{ki}-ta ĝen-né
7. 0.0.2 zì u$_4$ 2-kam *Šu*-^{d}Utu sukkal
8. ù *Nu-úr-ì-lí* aga-ús-gal
9. Sa-bu-um^{ki}-ta ĝen-né
10. 0.0.1 5 sìla zì u$_4$ 3-kam
11. Ma-ma-kešda šeš-ba (*written over erasure*)

REV.

12. Ú.URU×A.A^{ki}-ta ĝen-né
13. 5 sìla zì *Iš-du*$_{11}$-gin$_7$ aga-ús-gal
14. 0.1.1 zì NIM Za-ul^{ki}-šè ĝen-né
15. ĝìr *Iš-du*$_{11}$-gin$_7$ aga-ús-gal
16. Za-ul^{ki}-ta ĝen-né
17. ⸢0.0.2⸣ zì u$_4$ 2-kam šà uru
18. 0.0.1 zì kaskal-šè Šu-na-gi$_4$
19. ù Lu$_5$-lí-lí sukkal
20. Ki-maš^{ki}-šè ĝen-né
21. 0.0.1 5 sìla zì u$_4$ 3-kam
22. AN.EN.TUM-šè šeš-ba

L.E.

23. Ú.URU×A.A^{ki}-ta ĝen-né
24. iti ezen ^{d}Šul-gi

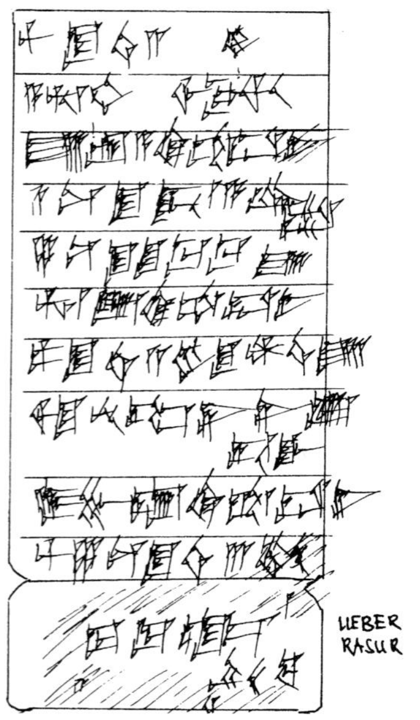

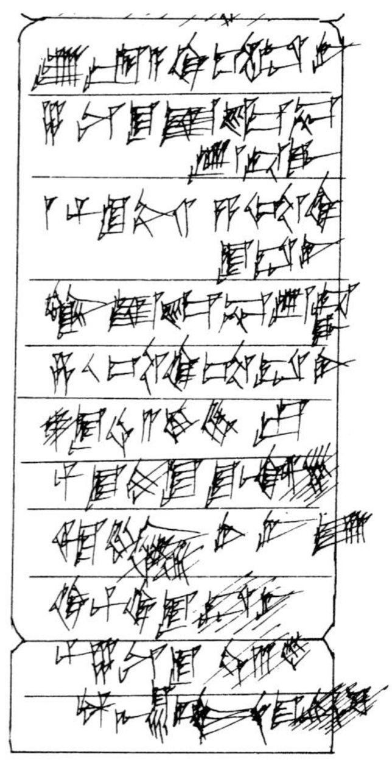

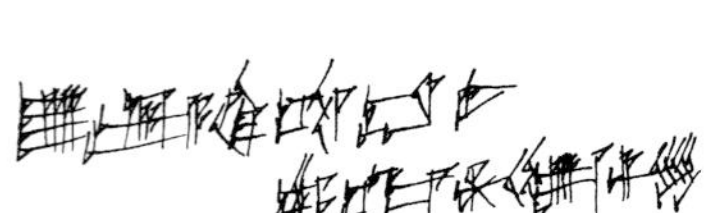

228 (VII/-/-)

OBV.

1. 5 sìla kaš ĝen
2. I-<x?>-^{d}Suen lú-kaš$_4$
3. Šušina^{ki}-ta ĝen-né
4. 0.0.1 5 sìla u$_4$ 3-kam
5. Ur-bàd-KU-a sukkal
6. 0.0.2 5 sìla kaš u$_4$ 5-kam
7. Ú-du NIM
8. Gi-gi-li^{ki}-ta ĝen-ne-ne

REV.

9. ĝìr Ur-bàd-KU-a sukkal
10. 0.0.2 kaš u$_4$ 4-kam
11. 0.1.0 kaš ĝen kaskal-šè
12. *A-da-làl* lú-kaš$_4$
13. in NIM-ne ĝen-na
14. 5 sìla kaš ĝen
15. *Šu-íb-tum* ra-gaba
16. Sa-<bu>-um^{ki}-ta ĝen-né
17. 5 sìla Šu-bí ra-gaba NIM
18. Šušina^{ki}-ta ĝen-né
19. zi-ga iti ezen ^{d}Šul-gi

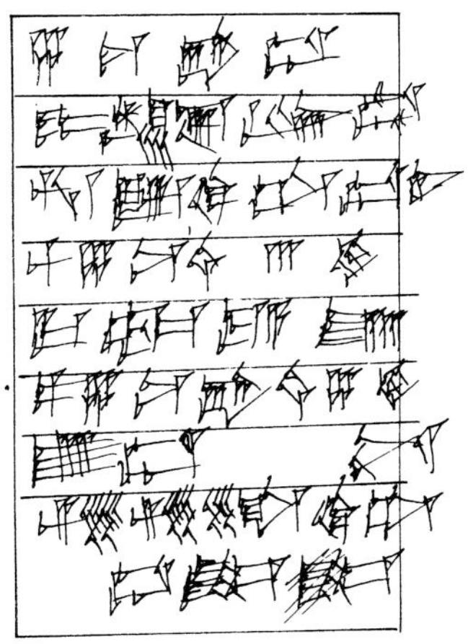

229

(VII/-/-)

OBV.

1. 4 sìla zì-gu šà uru
2. 0.0.1 zì kaskal-šè
3. Ba-ša$_6$-ga lú ^{ĝeš}tukul gu-la
4. A-dam-šáḫ^{ki}-šè ĝen-né
5. 0.0.2 zì u$_4$ 2-kam šà uru
6. 0.0.1 zì kaskal-šè
7. A-a-kal-la dumu nu-bànda
8. ù *A-mur*-diĝir sukkal
9. Šušina^{ki}-šè ĝen-né
10. 0.0.2 zì u$_4$ 2-kam šà uru
11. 0.0.1 zì kaskal-šè
12. *Šu-ni-tum* aga-ús-gal

REV.

*13. ù Lú-^{d}Alammuš dumu nu-bànda
14. 5 sìla zì-gu šà uru
15. 5 sìla zì kaskal-šè
16. [Ì]r-ra-šum šeš-ba
17. [A-d]am-šáḫ^{ki}-šè ĝen-ne-ne
18. 0.0.1 zì Da-da dumu nu-bànda
19. ù Lugal-si-sá sukkal
20. Ú.URU×A.A^{ki}-ta ĝen-né
21. 0.0.1 zì Lú-gu-la šeš-ba
22. ù Èr-ra-ur-saĝ sukkal
23. 0.1.0 zì NIM Ši-ma-aš-ki-me
24. ĝìr Lú-gu-la šeš-ba
25. Ši-ma-aš-ki-ta ĝen-né

L.E.

26. iti ezen ^{d}Šul-gi

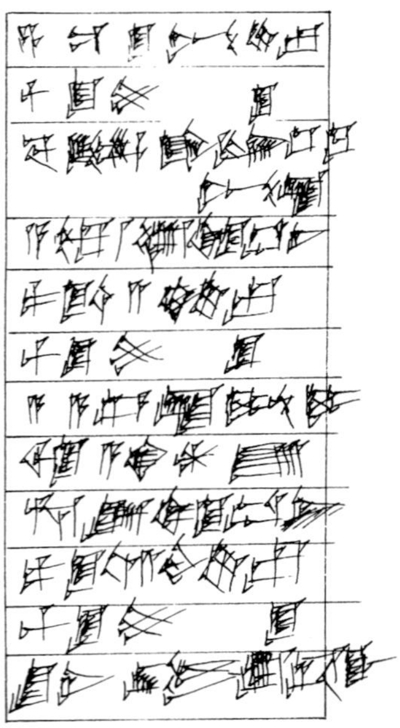

230 (VII/-/-)

OBV.

1. 5 sìla kaš ĝen šà uru
2. 1 dida ĝen kaskal-šè
*3. *Ta-ri-bu-um* sukkal
4. Šušina^{ki}-šè ĝen-né
5. 3 sìla kaš *Šu*-^{d}IM lú-kaš$_{4}$
6. 3 sìla kaš Im-ti-da lú-kaš$_{4}$
7. Ú.URU×A.A^{ki}-ta ĝen-né
8. 5 sìla kaš šà uru
9. 1 dida-ĝen kaskal-šè
10. *Šu-Èr-ra* sukkal

REV.

11. 0.1.0 kaš ⸢šà⸣ ur[u]
12. 0.1.1 kaš kaskal-[šè]
13. NIM An-ša-an^{ki}-me
14. ĝìr *Šu-Èr-ra* sukkal
15. An-ša-an^{ki}-šè ĝen-né
16. 3 sìla kaš Ni$_{9}$-ĝar-ki-du$_{10}$ lú-kaš$_{4}$
17. Šušina^{ki}-ta ĝen-né
18. 5 sìla kaš ^{d}Nanna-dalla sukkal
19. Sa-bu-um^{ki}-ta ĝen-né
20. iti ezen ^{d}Šul-gi

231

(VII/-/-)

OBV.

1. 5 sìla kaš 5 sìla ninda
2. *Šu*-^{d}IM sukkal
3. 5 sìla kaš 5 sìla ninda
4. 1 ì á-gam
5. E-ma-àm sukkal
6. 5 sìla kaš 5 sìla ninda
7. 1 ì á-gam
8. *Á-pil-la-núm* sukkal
9. 5 sìla kaš 5 sìla ninda
10. 1 ì á-gam

REV.

11. [B]U sukkal
12. [ ] sìla ninda
13. [ ]
14. [suk]kal
15. [ ] kaš lugal
16. [ ]
17. 5/6 sìla ì-ĝeš
18. NIM Ši-ma-aš-ki
19. šu ba-ab-ti
20. ĝìr Na-na sukkal
21. An-ša-an^{ki}-ta
22. Nibru^{ki}

L.E.

23. iti ezen ^{d}[Šul]-g[i]

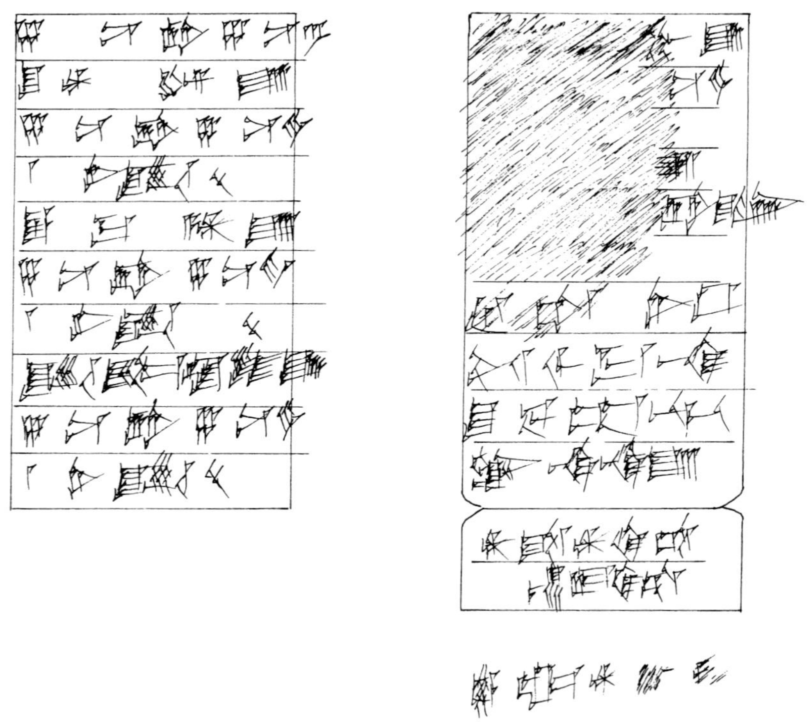

232 (VIII/2/-)

1. 5 sìla zì-gu šà uru
2. 0.0.1 zì kaskal-šè
3. *Èr-ra-dan* lú ^{ĝeš}tukul gu-la
4. Ki-maš^{ki}-šè ĝen-né
5. 0.0.1 5 sìla zì u_4 3-kam
6. Ši-a-a ù-gúl
7. Šušina^{ki}-ta ĝen-né
8. 0.0.2 zì u_4 2-kam šà uru
9. 0.0.1 zì kaskal-šè
10. ^{d}Utu-*ši-la-at* sukkal
11. ù ^{d}Nanna-du_{10} aga-ús-gal

REV.

12. Sa-bu-um^{ki}-šè ĝen-né
13. 5 sìla zì šà uru
14. 5 sìla zì kaskal-šè
15. *Ì-lí-a-núm* sukkal
16. 0.1.2 zì šà uru
17. 0.1.3 zì kaskal-šè
18. NIM Gi-ša^{ki}-me
19. ĝìr *Ì-lí-a-núm* sukkal
20. Gi-ša^{ki}-šè ĝen-né
21. 0.0.1 zì u_4 2-kam
22. *Šu-na-a* aga-ús-gal
23. Šušina^{ki}-ta ĝen-né

L.E.

24. iti ezen ^{d}Ba-ú

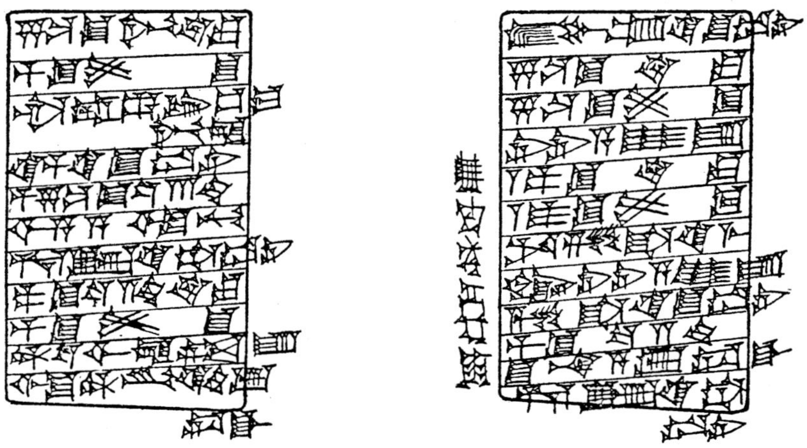

233 (VIII/2/-)

OBV.

1. 5 sìla zì-gu
2. Da-da-ni ù-gúl
3. 5 sìla zì *Šu-na-a* šeš-ba
4. Ú.URU×A.A^{ki}-ta ĝen-né
5. 0.0.2 zì u$_4$ 2-kam šà uru
6. 0.0.1 zì kaskal-šè
7. Ba-za-mu aga-ús-gal
8. ù I-dará-ki-ni šeš-ba
9. Sa-bu-um^{ki}-ta ĝen-né
10. 2 sìla zì *Šu*-^{d}Utu lú-kaš$_4$
11. 5 sìla zì *Á-pil-lí* aga-ús-gal

REV.

12. Šušina^{ki}-ta ĝen-né
13. 0.0.2 zì u$_4$ 2-kam šà uru
14. 0.0.1 zì kaskal-šè
15. Gu-ub-^{d}Utu sukkal
16. ù Ìr-^{d}Nanna aga-ús-gal
17. A-dam-šáḫ^{ki}-šè ĝen-né
18. 0.0.1 5 sìla zì u$_4$ 3-kam
19. Da-gu-nir aga-ús-gal
20. 0.0.1 5 sìla zì u$_4$ 3-kam
21. *Šu*-^{d}Utu sukkal
22. Šušina^{ki}-ta ĝen-né
23. 0.0.1 zì u$_4$ 2-kam
24. *A-ḫu*-du$_{10}$ ù-gúl
25. Ú.URU×A.A^{ki}-ta ĝen-né

L.E.

26. iti ezen ^{d}Ba-ú

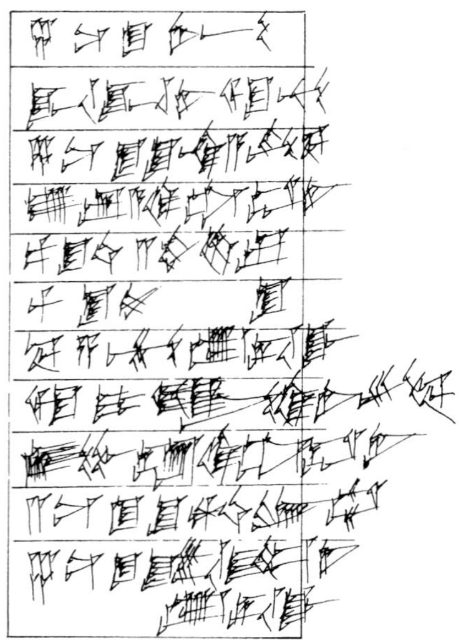

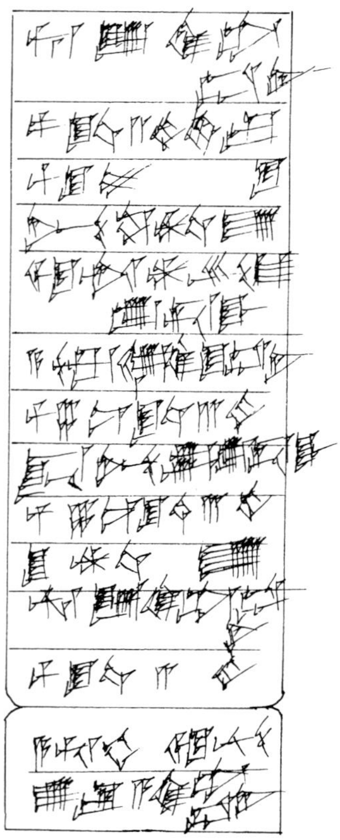

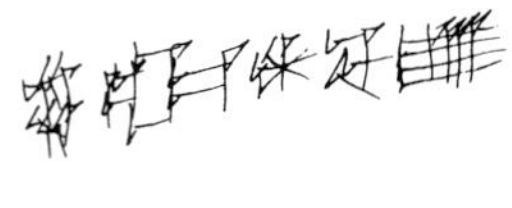

234

(VIII/30/-)

OBV.

1. 3 sìla kaš 2 sìla zì
2. 1 ì á-gam
3. U[r lú-ka]š$_4$
4. 3 sìla kaš 2 sìla z[ì]
5. 1 ì ⸢à-g⸣am
6. *Ś*[*u*]-^{d}Utu lú-kaš$_4$
*7. kur-šè ĝen-na
8. 3 sìla kaš 2 sìla zì
9. 1 ì á-gam

REV.

10. Ìr-[m]u Mar-tu
11. ĜEŠ-ab-ba-šè ĝen-na
12. 5 sìla kaš 3 sìla zì
13. 1 ì á-gam
14. *Nu-úr*-^{d}IM sukkal
15. Gú-ab-ba^{ki}-šè ĝen-na
*16. 1 dida 1.1.0 dabin
17. ĝìr *Ì-lí*-ša$_6$ sukkal
18. [l]ú Nin-kal-la
19. zi-ga u$_4$ 30-kam
20. iti ezen ^{d}Ba-ú

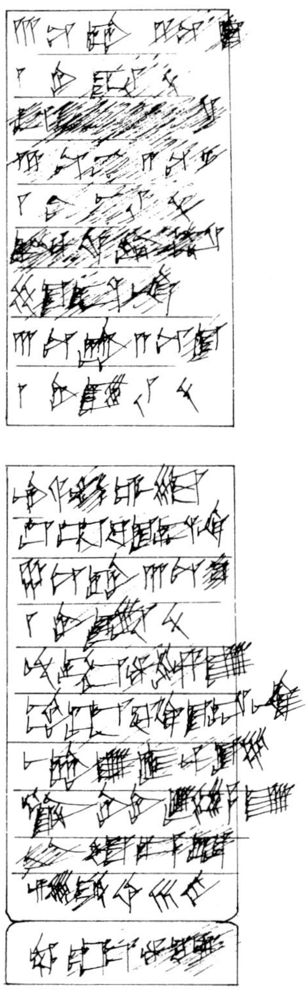

235

(VIII/30/-)

OBV.
1. 0.2.0 kaš ĝen lugal
2. 0.1.0 dabin
3. 1 sìla ì-ĝeš
4. Diĝir-á-ì-ĝál Mar-tu

REV.
5. (BLANK)
6. u_4 30-kam
7. iti ezen [d]Ba-ú

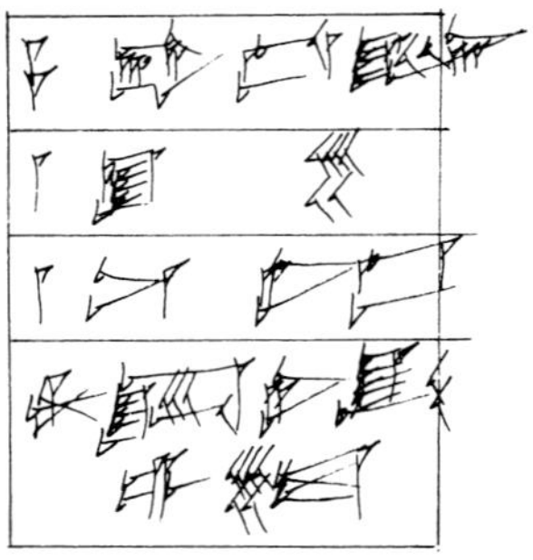

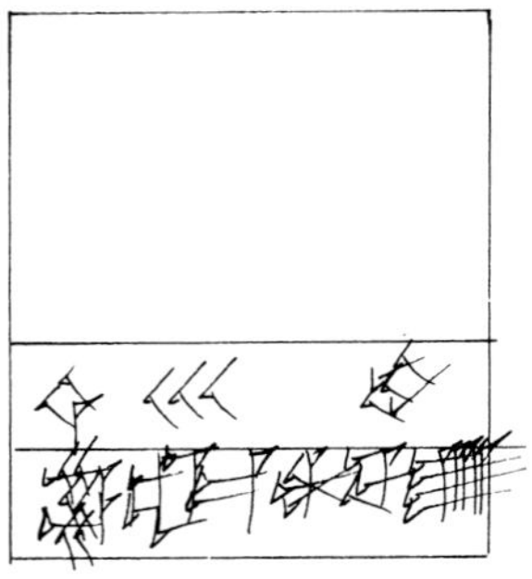

236

(VIII/-/-)

OBV.

1. 0.0.1 kaš 0.0.1 ninda [lugal]
2. 2 ì á-gam
3. sá-du$_{11}$ u$_{4}$ 2-kam
4. Ur-^{ĝeš}gigir sukkal KA?
5. inim-ma uru ĝen-na
6. 0.0.1 kaš 0.0.1 ninda lugal
7. 2 ì á-gam
8. sá-du$_{11}$ u$_{4}$ 2-kam
9. Lugal-^{ĝeš}gigir-re sukkal
10. še ^{d}En-líl-lá má-a
11. si-gi$_{4}$-dè ĝen-na

REV.

12. [5] sìla kaš 5 [sìla ninda]
13. 1 ì á-gam
14. a-rá 1-kam
15. 5 sìla kaš 5 sìla ninda
16. 1 ì á-gam
17. Ur-^{d}Da-mu sukkal
18. 5 sìla kaš 5 sìla ninda
19. 1 ì á-gam
20. Lú-bàn-da sukkal
21. 0.0.1 5 sìla <kaš> 0.0.1 5 sìla ninda lugal

*22. NIM [An]-ša-an[^{ki} x] Ni[bru^{ki}-ta]

L.E.

23. ĝìr La-lí An-ša-an^{ki}-ta ĝen-na
24. iti ezen ^{d}Ba-ú

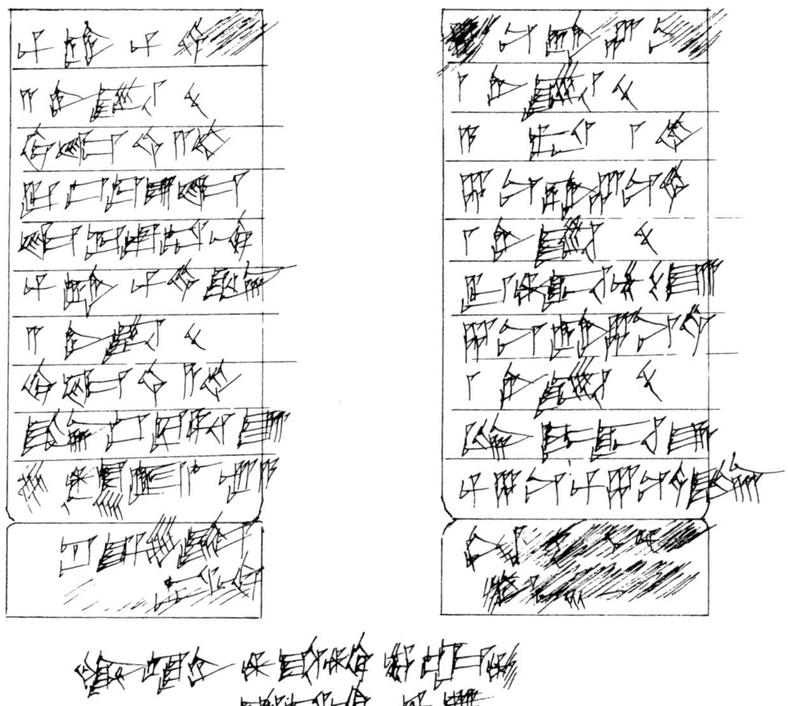

237

(IX/5/-)

OBV.

1. 3 sìla kaš 2 sìla zì
2. 1 ì á-gam
3. *Nu-úr-ì-lí*
4. 3 sìla kaš 2 sìla zì
5. 1 ì á-gam
6. Ur-^{d}En-líl sagi
7. kù-sig$_{17}$ gur$_{7}$-a ĝen-na

REV.

8. 3 sìla kaš 2 sìla zì
9. 1 ì á-gam
10. *Šu-Èr-ra* lú-kaš$_{4}$
11. 3 sìla kaš 2 sìla zì
12. 1 ì á-gam
13. *Šu-ì-lí* lú-kaš$_{4}$
14. 3 sìla kaš 2 sìla zì
15. 1 ì á-gam
16. *Ša-ì-lí* lú-kaš$_{4}$
17. 3 sìla kaš 2 sìla zì
18. 1 ì á-gam Lú-^{d}Nin-šubur

L.E.

19. zi-ga u$_{4}$ 5-kam iti mu-šu-du$_{7}$

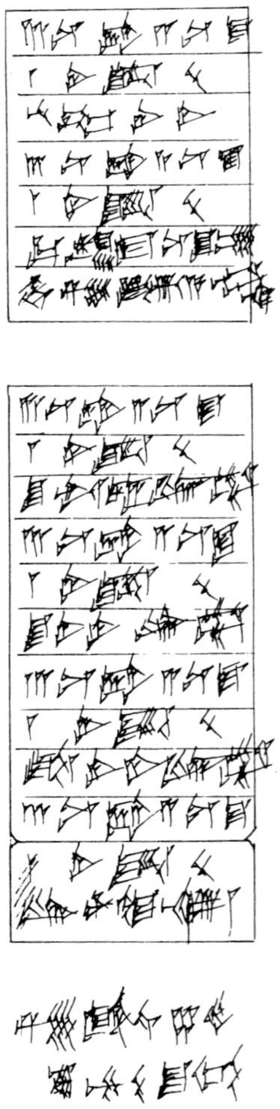

238

(IX/13/-)

OBV.

1. 3 sìla kaš 2 sìla ninda
2. 4 gín ì
3. *I-ti-lum* lú [ĝeš]tukul gu-la
4. 3 sìla kaš 2 sìla ninda
5. 2 gín ì
6. Da-a-a šabra an-na-šè ĝen-na

REV.

7. 3 sìla kaš 2 sìla ninda
8. 2 gín ì
9. Du-du ki-énsi-ta ĝen-na
10. 3 sìla kaš 2 sìla ninda
11. 2 gín ì
12. *Šu-ga-tum* nu-bànda dumu-dab_5-ba-šè ĝen-na
13. zi-ga u_4 13-kam
14. iti mu-šu-du_7

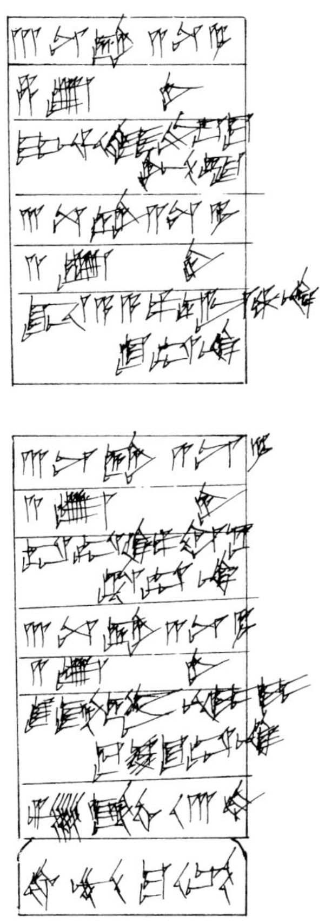

239

(IX/21/-)

OBV.

1. 5 sìla kaš 3 sìla zì
2. 1 ì á-gam
3. Bí-ti-ti sukkal
4. 5 sìla kaš 5 sìla zì
5. 1 ì á-gam
6. Ba-ša$_{6}$-ga sukkal
7. má ĝeš-ì-šè ĝen-na
8. 5 sìla kaš 3 sìla zì
9. 1 ì á-gam
10. Lú-*ša-lim* sukkal
11. ^{ĝeš}ĝanun-šè ĝen-na
12. 5 sìla kaš 5 sìla zì
13. 1 ì á-gam
14. Ur-^{d}Nin-mug sukkal

REV.

15. 3 sìla kaš 2 sìla zì
16. [1 ì á]-gam
17. [M]ar-tu
18. [ ] ĝen-na
19. 5 sìla kaš 5 sìla zì
20. 1 [ì á]-gam
21. Ur-^{d}[ ] lú-kaš$_{4}$
22. a-[z]i ĝen-na
23. 2 sìla [kaš 2] sìla zì
24. 1 ì á-gam
25. *Puzur$_{4}$-ì-lí* lú-kaš$_{4}$
26. 5 sìla kaš 3 sìla zì
27. 1 ì á-gam
28. ĝìr *Ì-lí*-ša$_{6}$ sukkal
29. Saḫar^{ki}-šè ĝen-na
30. zi-ga u$_{4}$ 21

L.E.

31. iti mu-šu-du$_{7}$

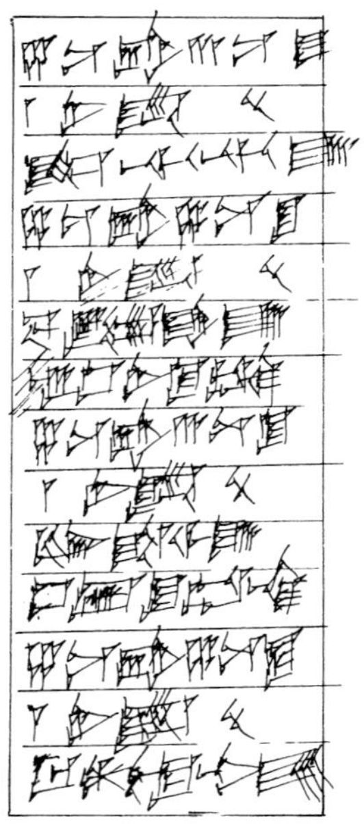
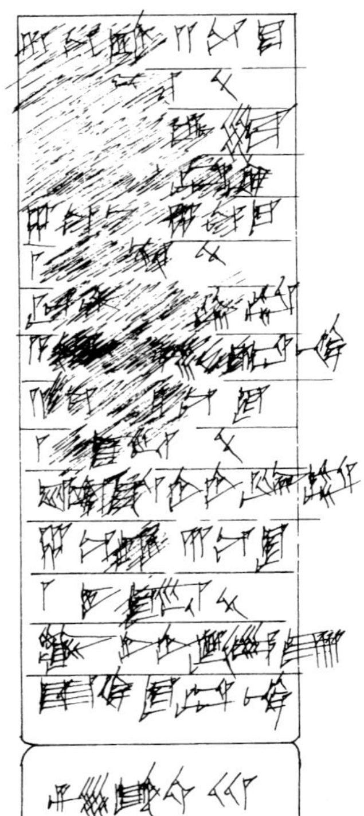
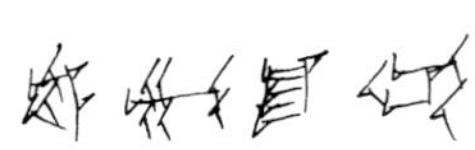

240 (IX/24/-)

OBV.

*1. 3 sìla kaš 2 sìla zì
2. 1 ì á-gam
3. [*I*]*p-qú-ša* lú-kaš$_4$
4. 5 sìla kaš 2 sìla zì
5. 1 ì á-gam
6. A-kal-la lú ^{ĝeš}tukul gu-la
7. 2 sìla kaš 2 sìla zì
8. 1 ì á-gam
9. Lú-^{d}Utu Mar-tu

REV.

*10. 3 sìla kaš 2 sìla zì
11. 1 ì á-gam
12. Ur-ba-ga Mar-tu
13. 5 sìla kaš 3 sìla zì
14. 1 ì á-gam
15. *Šu*-^{d}Nisaba sukkal
16. ⸢ab-ba⸣-da ĝen-na
17. 3 sìla kaš 2 sìla zì
18. 1 ì á-gam
19. *Šu*-^{d}Suen lú-kaš$_4$
20. zi-ga u$_4$ 24-kam
21. iti mu-šu-du$_7$

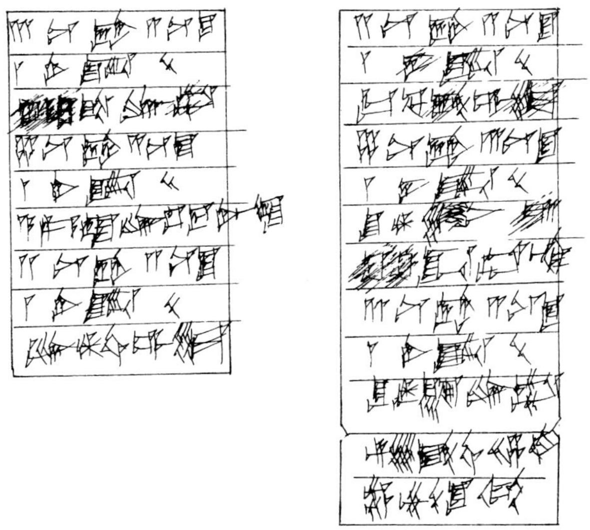

241 (IX/-/-)

OBV.

*1. ⌜5⌝ sìla kaš 5 sìla ninda
2. ⌜1⌝ ì-ĝeš á-gam
3. *Bí-bí*-DU
4. 5 sìla kaš 5 sìla ninda
5. 1 ì-ĝeš á-gam
*6. Šu-da-ba sukkal
7. 5 sìla kaš 5 sìla ninda
8. 1 ì-ĝeš á-gam
9. Éš-la-a sukkal

REV.

10. 1 dida
11. 0.0.2 kaš 0.0.2 ninda lugal
12. 2 sìla ì-ĝeš
13. NIM Ši-ma-aš-ki-ke$_4$ šu ba-ti
14. 5 sìla kaš 5 sìla ninda
15. 1 ì-ĝeš á-gam
16. ⌜Pù⌝-pù-da sukkal
*17. An-ša-an^{ki}-[ta] ĝen-na ù Ni[bru^{ki}]

L.E.

18. iti mu-šu-du$_7$

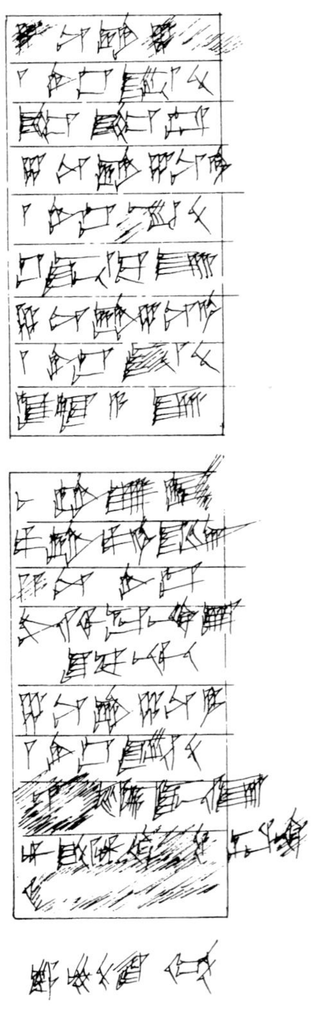

242 (IX/-/-)

OBV.

1. 5 sìla kaš 5 sìla ninda
2. 1 ì-ĝeš á-gam
3. Ba-lu$_5$-lu$_5$ sukkal
4. 5 sìla kaš 5 sìla ninda
5. 1 ì-ĝeš á-gam

REV.

6. Lugal-mas-su sukkal
7. iti mu-šu-du$_7$

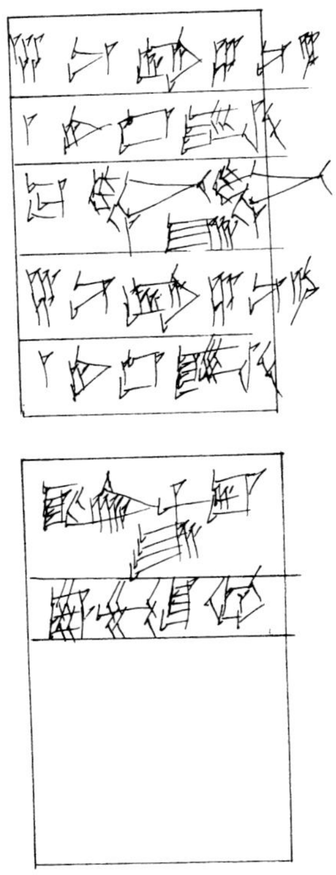

243 (X/7/-)

OBV.

1. 5 sìla kaš 3 sìla zì
2. 1 ì á-gam
3. Ur-ša$_6$-ga sukkal
4. 0.1.0 kaš ĝen lugal
5. 0.1.0 dabin 1 sìla ì-ĝeš
6. NIM Sa-bu-um^{ki} Nibru^{ki}-ta ĝen-na
7. ĝìr Ur-ša$_6$-ga sukkal
8. 5 sìla kaš 3 sìla zì
9. 1 ì á-gam
10. A-gu-a-ti sukkal

REV.

*11. ⸢An-ša-an^{ki}⸣ [x rá]-gaba-da ĝen-na
12. 5 sìla kaš 3 sìla zì
*13. 1 ì á-gam
*14. *Ì-lí-ti* lú ^{ĝeš}tukul ⸢gu-la⸣
15. 5 sìla kaš 3 sìla zì
16. 1 ì á-gam
*17. *La-qí-pu-um* sukkal
*18. [x x].AB.A-šè ĝen-na
19. 2 sìla kaš 2 sìla zì
20. 1 ì á-gam
*21. *I-ti-lum* lú-kaš$_4$
22. 3 sìla kaš 2 sìla zì
23. 1 ì á-gam
24. *Bur*-Ma-ma lú-kaš$_4$
25. 3 sìla kaš 2 sìla <zì>
26. 1 ì á-gam
27. A-da-làl

L.E.

28. zi-ga u$_4$ 7-kam iti amar-a-a-⸢si⸣

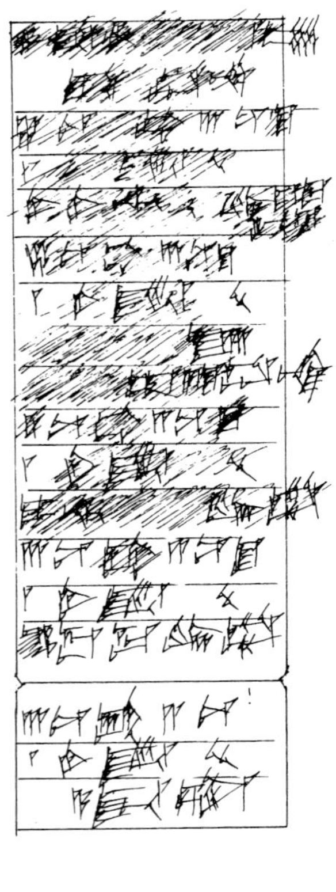

244

(X/8/-)

OBV.

1. 5 sìla kaš 3 sìla zì
2. 2 ì á-gam
3. Ur-dun lú ^{ĝeš}tukul gu-la
4. 6 sìla dabin aga-ús lugal-bi
5. 3-àm ḪU Sa-bu-um^{ki}-ta ĝen-na
6. ĝìr Ur-dun sukkal
7. 3 sìla kaš 2 sìla zì
8. 1 ì á-gam
9. *I-ti-ì-lum*
10. Ur-^{ĝeš}gigir rá-gaba ĝen-na

REV.

11. 3 sìla kaš 2 sìla zì
12. 1 ì á-gam
13. *Nu-úr*-^{d}Suen
14. ki Lú-^{d}Nin-ĝír-su-šè ĝen-na
15. 5 sìla kaš 3 sìla zì
16. 1 ì á-gam
17. Lú-^{d}Da-mu
18. má ĝeš-ì-ka-šè ĝen-na
19. zi-ga u$_{4}$ 8-kam
20. iti amar-a-a-si

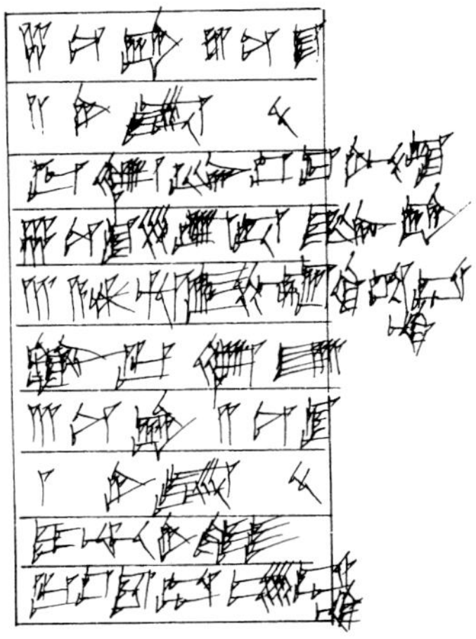

245

(X/18/-)

OBV.

1. 3 sìla kaš 2 sìla ninda
2. 3 gín ì
3. ⌜A⌝-da-a Ur-^{d}Ba-ú-mu-da ĝen-na
4. 3 sìla kaš 2 sìla ninda
5. 2 gín ì-ĝeš 1 gín ì-udu
6. Ḫu-lí-lí lú ^{ĝeš}tukul gu-la
7. 3 sìla kaš 2 sìla ninda
8. 2 gín ì
9. Nì-^{d}IM má ĝeš-ì-šè ĝen-na
10. 3 sìla kaš 2 sìla ninda

REV.

11. 2 gín ì
12. TE D[Ù] [ ]
13. 3 sìla [kaš 2 sìla ni]nda
14. 1 g[ín] ⌜ì⌝
15. *A-bu-[um* n]ir NI DA [ ]^{ki} ĝen-na
16. 3 sìla kaš sig$_5$ ur
17. 1 sìla zì anše
18. zi-[g]a u$_4$ 18-kam
19. iti amar-a-a-si

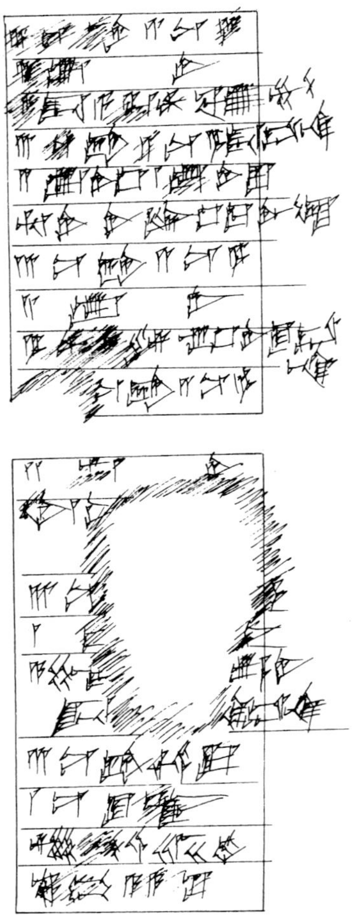

246 (X/20/-)

OBV.

1. [sìl]a kaš 3 sìla zì
2. [ ] ì á-gam
3. Lugal-nisaĝ-e sukkal
4. 5 sìla kaš 3 sìla zì
5. 1 ì á-gam
6. A-da-a sukkal
7. 3 sìla kaš 2 sìla zì
8. 1 ì á-gam

*9. *En-ú-mi-ì-lí* lú má-gal-gal-šè ĝen-<na>

REV.

10. 5 sìla kaš 5 sìla zì
11. 1 ì á-gam
12. *I-šar-ba-ni* sukkal
13. 3 sìla kaš 3 sìla zì
14. 1 ì á-gam
15. U-bar lú-kaš$_4$
16. 3 sìla kaš 3 sìla zì
17. 1 ì á-gam
18. I-ti-ì-lum
19. [z]i-ga u$_4$ 20-kam
20. [it]i amar-a-a-s[i]

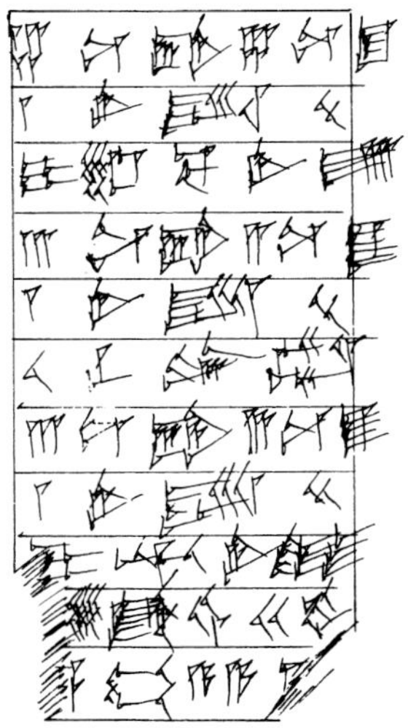

247

(X/-/-)

OBV.

1. 5 sìla kaš ĝen
2. 3 sìla ninda
3. 1 á-gam ì
4. Diĝir-*dan* dumu nu-bànda

REV.

5. Šušina^{ki}-ta ĝen-né
6. zi-ga
7. iti amar-a-a-si

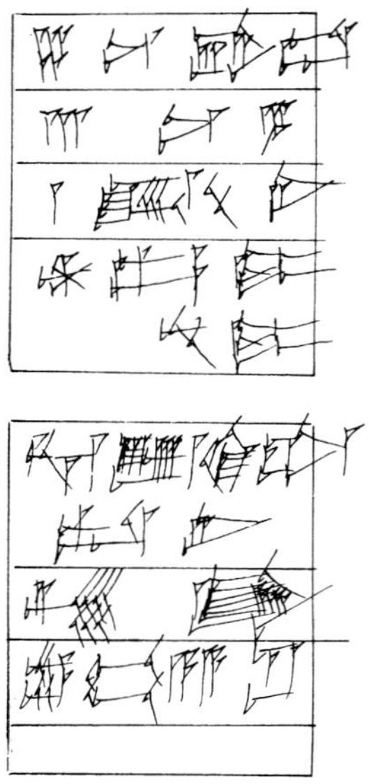

248

(X/-/-)

OBV.

1. 5 sìla kaš 5 sìla ninda
2. 1 ì-ĝeš á-gam
3. *A-bí-a* sukkal
4. 5 sìla kaš 5 sìla ninda
5. 1 ì-ĝeš á-gam
6. Na-na-a sukkal
7. 5 sìla kaš 5 sìla ninda
8. 1 ì-ĝeš á-gam
9. *Bur*-ma-àm lú ^{ĝeš}tukul gu-la

REV.

10. 5 sìla kaš 5 sìla ninda
11. 1 ì-ĝeš á-gam
12. Šu-nir-um sukkal
13. 5 sìla kaš 5 sìla ninda
14. 1 ì-ĝeš á-gam
15. Bur-ra sukkal
16. 5 sìla kaš 5 sìla ninda
17. *Ì-lí-a-núm* sukkal
18. An-ša-an^{ki}-ta ù Nibru^{ki}

L.E.

19. iti amar-a-a-si

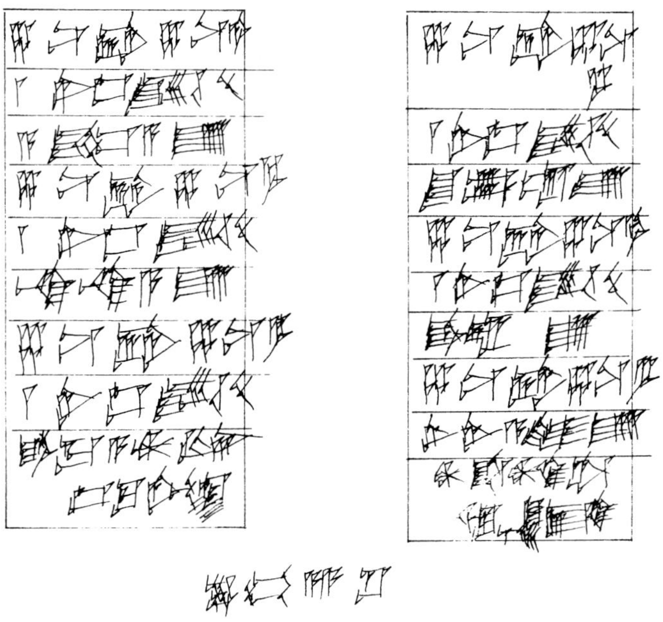

249

(X/-/-)

OBV.

1. 0.0.3 [kaš si]g_5 lugal
2. 2 di[da] sig_5
3. 0.2.0 [x]
*4. Ur-[d]Mes-[x]-è
5. ĝìr Lú-[d]Nin-ĝír-su
6. 4.0.0 [ka]š ĝen gur
7. 1.0.0 kaš sig_5 gur
8. é-gidri-šè
9. ĝìr Ur-ba-ga

REV.

10. 0.0.1 kaš sig_5
11. 1 dida sig_5
12. [d]Šul-gi-*ì-lí*
13. 0.0.1 kaš sig_5
14. ĝìr NE-li
15. 0.1.0 kaš sig_5
16. 0.2.0 kaš ĝen
17. Ḫu-ba-a
18. 0.0.1 kaš sig_5
19. 0.0.1 kaš ĝen
20. dumu Ḫu-ba-a
21. iti amar-a-a-si

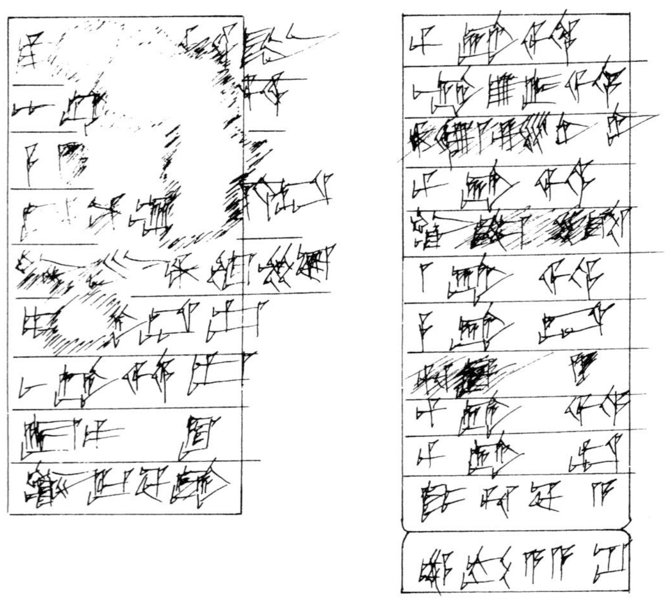

250 (XI/19/-)

OBV.

1. 5 sìla kaš 3 sìla zì
2. 2 ì á-gam
3. *Šu-Eš-tár* lú ^{ĝeš}tukul gu-la
4. 5 sìla kaš 3 sìla zì
5. 2 ì á-gam
6. ^{d}Šul-gi-*ì-lí* lú ^{ĝeš}tukul gu-la
7. 5 sìla kaš 3 sìla zì
8. 2 ì á-gam
9. *Šu-ì-lí* lú ^{ĝeš}tukul gu-la
10. 3 sìla kaš 2 sìla zì
11. 1 ì á-gam

REV.

12. 5 sìla kaš 3 sìla zì
13. 1 ì á-gam
14. A-gu-a-ti sukkal
15. 5 sìla kaš 3 sìla zì
16. 1 ì á-gam
17. *En-ú-mi-za* sukkal
18. túg-šè ĝen-na
19. 3 sìla kaš 2 sìla zì
20. 1 ì á-gam
21. *Nu-úr-ì-lí* lú-kaš$_4$
22. 5 sìla kaš 3 sìla zì
23. 1 ì á-gam
24. *A-bu-da*-du$_{10}$ sukkal
25. Sa-bu-um^{ki} ĝen-na
26. zi-ga u$_4$ 20 lá 1-kam
27. iti še-kin-ku$_5$

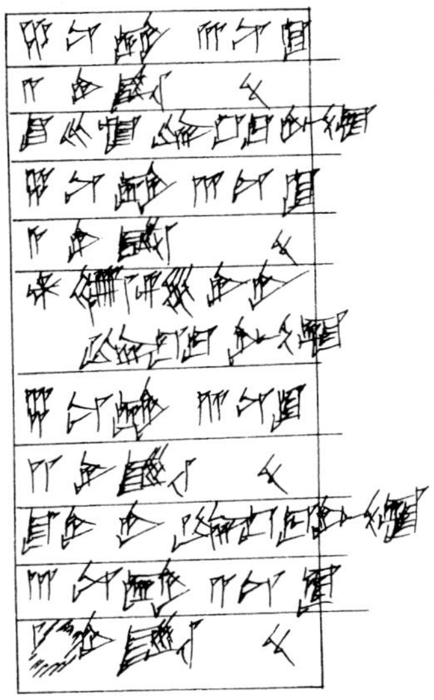

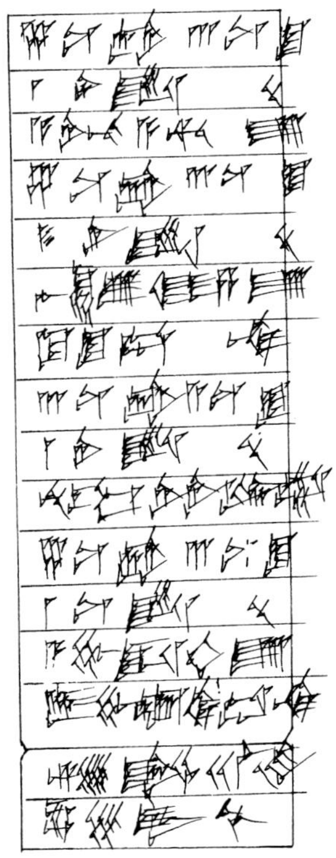

251

(XI/-/-)

OBV.

1. 0.0.3 3 sìla kaš lugal
2. 0.0.2 2 sìla ninda lugal
3. 11 ì á-gam
4. sá-du$_{11}$ u$_{4}$ 11-kam
5. ^{d}Šul-gi-*ì-lí* sukkal
6. 0.0.2 kaš 0.0.2 zì lugal
7. 4 ì á-gam
8. sá-du$_{11}$ u$_{4}$ 4-kam
9. Nì-^{d}Ba-ú sukkal

REV.

10. lú-kin-gi$_{4}$-a saĝ-sipa-Lugal-nir-ĝál-ka gub-ba-me
11. 5 sìla kaš 5 sìla ninda
12. 1 ì á-gam
13. *A-da-làl* lú ^{ĝeš}tukul gu-[la]
14. 5 sìla kaš 5 sìla ninda
15. 1 ì á-gam
16. Èr-ra-nu-ke$_{4}$ sukkal
17. 5 sìla kaš 5 sìla ninda
18. 2 ì á-gam
19. *Śu-e-li* lú ^{ĝeš}tukul
20. An-ša-an^{ki}-ta

L.E.

21. iti še-kin-ku$_{5}$

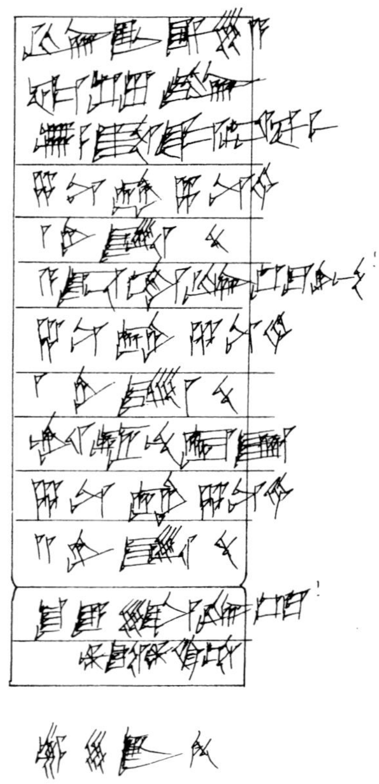

252

(XI/-/-)

OBV.

1. 5 sìla kaš 5 sìla ninda
2. 1 ì á-gam
3. *Šu*-^{d}En-ki sukkal
4. 5 sìla kaš 3 sìla ninda
5. 1 ì á-gam
6. Lú-^{d}Nanna sukkal
7. 5 sìla kaš 3 sìla ninda
8. 1 ì á-gam
9. Lú-diĝir lú ^{ĝeš}tukul gu-la
10. 5 sìla kaš 3 sìla ninda

REV.

11. 1 ì á-gam
12. Ur-^{d}En-líl-lá sukkal
13. 5 sìla kaš 3 sìla ninda
14. 1 ì á-gam
15. E-ib-éš-gàr sukkal
16. 5 sìla kaš 3 sìla ninda
17. 1 ì á-gam
18. An-e-ba-ab-du$_{7}$ sukkal
19. An-ša-an^{ki}-ta ù
20. Nibru^{ki}-ta ĝen-na

L.E.

21. iti še-kin-ku$_{5}$

253

(XI/-/-)

OBV.

1. 5 sìla kaš 5 sìla ninda
2. 1 ì-ĝeš á-gam
3. Kù-[d]Nanna sukkal
4. 0.1.0 kaš lugal
5. 0.1.0 ninda du_8-a lugal
6. 1 sìla ì-ĝeš
7. NIM Ki-maš[ki]-ke_4 šu ba-ti

REV.

8. 5 sìla kaš 5 sìla ninda
9. 1 ì-ĝeš á-gam
10. ĝìr *$Puzur_4$*-[d]Inanna sukkal
11. 5 sìla kaš 5 sìla ninda
12. 1 ì-ĝeš á-gam

*13. Diĝir-*dan* lú zi-gúm-ma ŠU.ĜÁ×ZA
14. Nibru[ki]-ta ù URU×A[ki]

L.E.

15. iti še-kin-ku_5

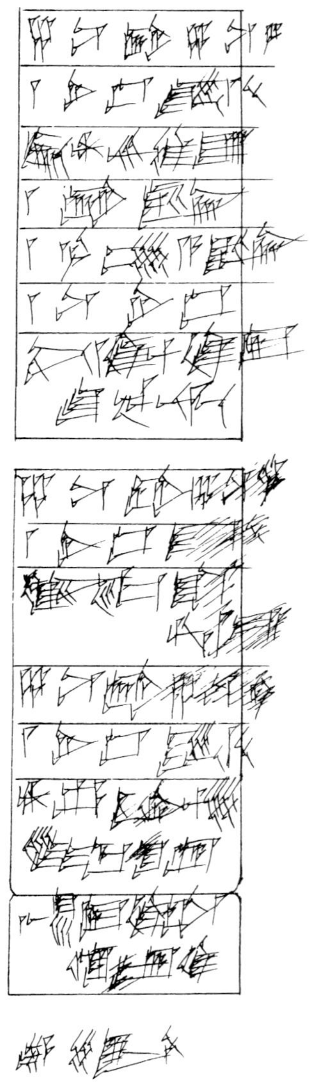

254

(XI/-/-)

OBV.

1. 5 sìla kaš ĝen
2. 3 sìla zì-gu
3. 1 á-gam ì šà uru
4. 1 dida ĝen
5. 5 sìla zì kaskal-šè
6. Kù-^{d}Nanna sukkal
7. Šušina^{ki}-šè ĝen-né
8. 5 sìla kaš ĝen

REV.

9. 3 sìla zì-gu
10. 1 á-gam ì
11. Maš-um sukkal
12. Šušina^{ki}-ta ĝen-né
13. 3 sìla kaš ĝen
14. 2 sìla zì-gu
15. 1 á-gam ì
16. Šu-ba-nir-ĝál lú-kaš$_{4}$
17. Šušina^{ki}-ta ĝen-né
18. iti še-kin-ku$_{5}$

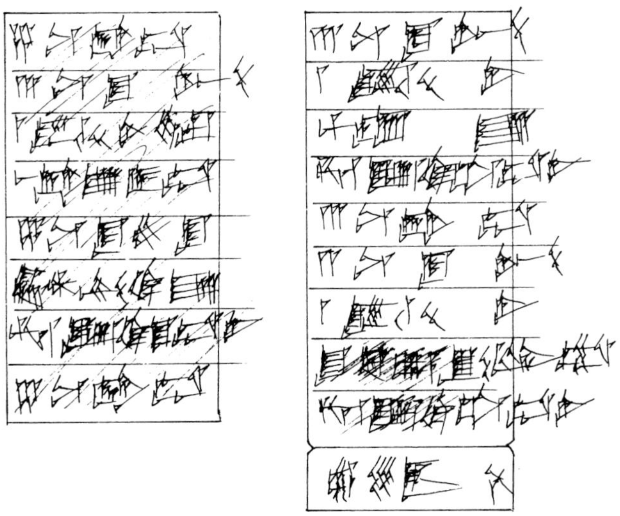

255

(XII/9/-)

OBV.

1. 5 sìla kaš 3 sìla zì
2. 1 ì á-gam
3. 1 dida 0.0.1 dabin
4. Lú-kiri$_4$-zal sukkal
5. 5 sìla kaš 3 sìla zì
6. 1 ì á-gam
7. Lú-*ša-lim* lú ^{ĝeš}tukul gu-la
8. 5 sìla kaš 5 sìla zì
9. 1 ì á-gam
10. Ḫa-la-a lú-kaš$_4$

REV.

11. 5 sìla kaš 5 sìla zì
12. 1 ì á-gam
13. Èr-ra-a lú-kaš$_4$
14. érin še-kin-šè ĝen-na
15. 3 sìla kaš 2 sìla zì
16. 1 ì á-gam
17. Ur-ba-ga Mar-tu
18. 3 sìla kaš 2 sìla zì
19. 1 ì á-gam
20. U-bar-ni lú-kaš$_4$
21. 5 sìla kaš 3 sìla zì
22. 1 ì á-gam
23. Lugal-agrig-zi
24. 3 sìla kaš 2 sìla zì
25. Da-da-bu-ni

L.E.

26. zi-ga u$_4$ 10 lá 1-kam iti še-íl-la

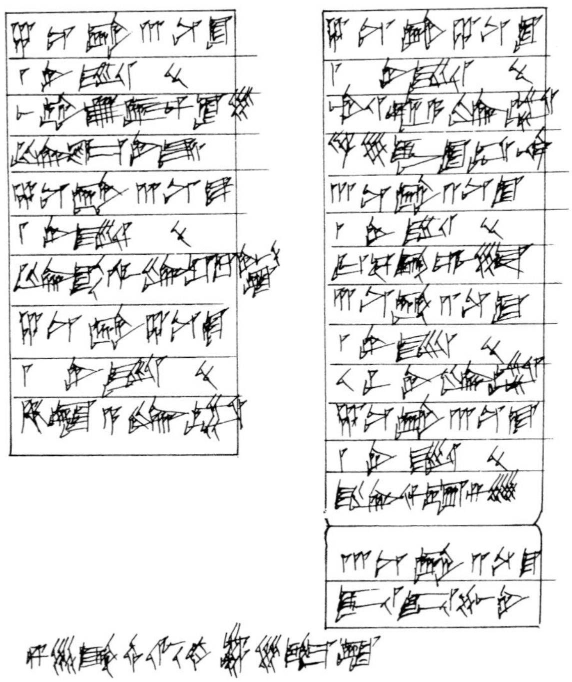

256 (XII/10/-)

OBV.

1. 5 sìla kaš 3 sìla zì
2. 2 ì á-gam
3. *Šu-Eš₄-tár* lú ^{ĝeš}tukul gu-la
4. 5 sìla kaš 3 sìla zì
5. 1 ì á-gam
6. Lú-^{d}Nanna sukkal
7. 5 sìla kaš 3 sìla zì
8. 1 ì á-gam
9. *Il-ma-su* sukkal
10. é Ur-^{d}Ig-alima-šè ĝen-na
11. 3 sìla kaš 2 sìla zì
12. 1 ì á-gam
13. Ur-^{d}Nin-ĝeš-zi-da
14. 3 sìla kaš 2 sìla zì
15. 1 ì á-[gam]
16. Lugal-t[i Mar-t]u

(*bottom of obverse broken*)

(*top of reverse broken*)

REV.

17. ⌜2⌝ [ ]
18. 1 ì ⌜á⌝-[gam]
19. *Nu-úr-su* sukkal
20. a-šà Mar-tu kur-ba ĝen-n[a]
21. 3 sìla kaš 2 sìla zì
22. 1 ì á-gam
23. Ùr-re-ba-du$_7$ Mar-tu
24. 3 sìla kaš 2 sìla zì
25. 1 ì á-gam
26. Ur-^{d}Nanše Mar-tu
27. 3 sìla kaš 2 sìla zì
28. 1 ì á-gam
29. *Šu*-^{d}IM lú-kaš$_4$
30. 3 sìla kaš 2 sìla zì
31. 1 ì á-gam
32. *A-bu-da-dí* lú-kaš$_4$
33. 0.0.1 kaš 5 sìla zì
34. 1 ì á-gam
35. Ìr-^{d}Nanna sukkal
36. ugula uš-bar-šè ĝen-na

L.E.

37. zi-ga u$_4$ 10-kam iti še-íl-la

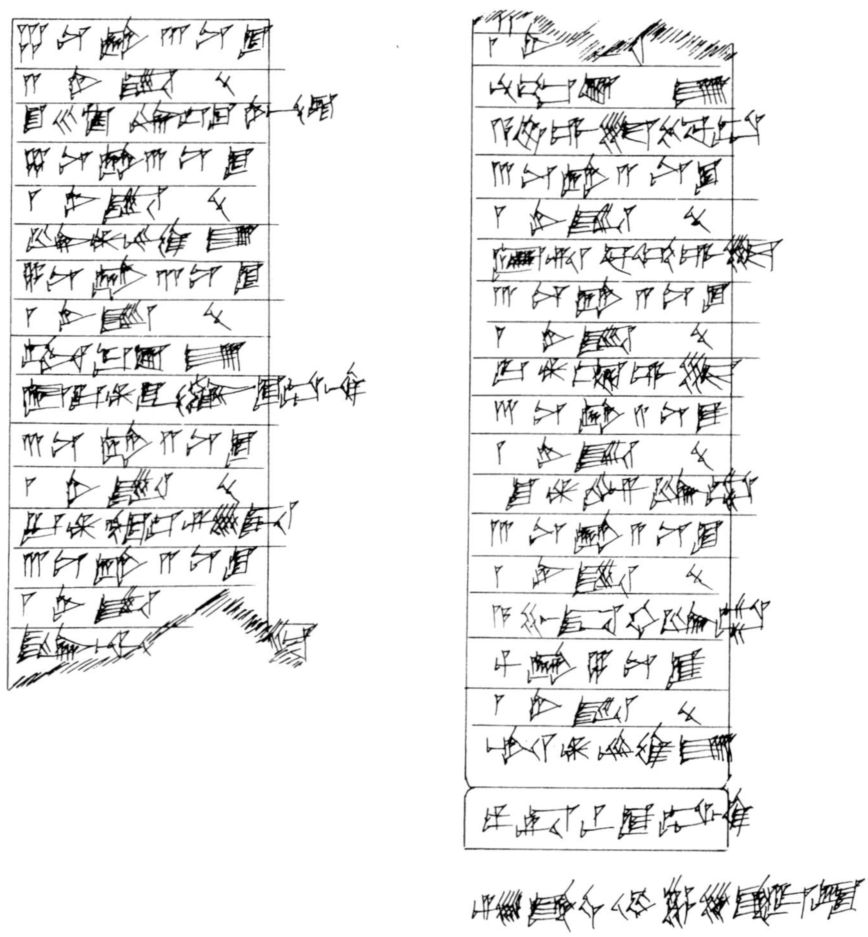

256

257

(XII/24/-)

OBV.

1. 3 sìla kaš 2 sìla zì
2. 1 ì á-gam
3. *Nu-úr-su*
4. 3 sìla kaš 2 sìla zì
5. 1 ì á-gam
6. Ùr-re-ba-du$_7$
7. ú-bù-re-dè ĝen-na-me
8. 3 sìla kaš 2 sìla zì

REV.

9. 1 ì á-gam
10. Al-la Mar-tu
11. lú-maḫ ^{d}Inanna-šè ĝen-na
12. 3 sìla kaš 2 sìla zì
13. 1 ì á-gam
14. *La-qì-ip*
15. Sa-bu-um^{ki}-ta ĝen-na
16. u$_4$ 24-kam

L.E.

17. iti še-íl-la

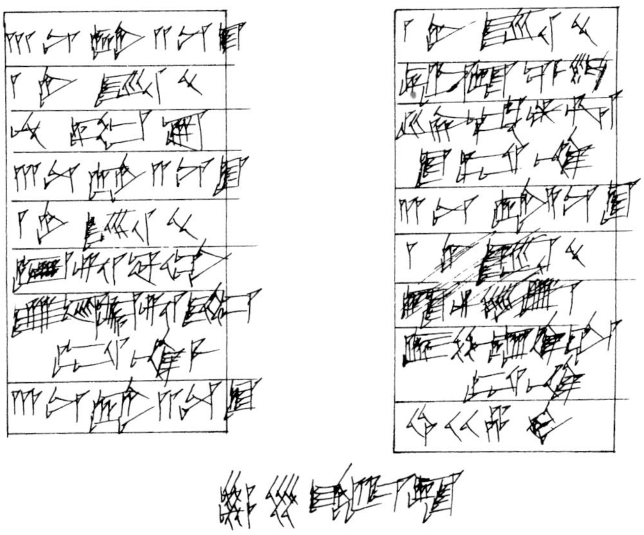

258

(XII/29/-)

OBV.

1. ⸢0.0.2 kaš⸣ sig$_5$ 0.0.2 kaš ĝen
2. [ ] ì
3. [L]ú-^{d}En-líl
4. 0.0.1 kaš sig$_5$ 0.0.1 kaš ĝen
5. 0.0.2 ninda
6. *Puzur$_4$-Eš$_4$-tár*
7. 3 sìla kaš 2 sìla ninda
8. 1 gín ì
9. [^{d}Aš]-da-bára ĝen-na
10. 0.0.3 kaš 0.0.3 ninda lugal

REV.

11. ½ sìla ì-ĝeš
12. ^{d}Nanna-ša$_6$-ga érin še-kin-šè ĝen-na
13. 3 sìla kaš 3 sìla ninda
14. 1 gín ì
15. Lú-^{d}En-ki sukkal
16. 3 sìla kaš 2 sìla ninda
17. 2 gín ì
18. *Šu-Eš$_4$-tár* lú-kaš$_4$
19. 3 sìla kaš 2 sìla ninda
20. 2 gín ì
21. Ur-^{d}Da-mu
22. 1 sìla kaš Ur-é-maḫ
23. u$_4$ 30 lá 1-kam

L.E.

24. iti še-íl-la

259

(XII/-/-)

OBV.

1. 3 [ ]
2. 2 gí[n] ⸢ì⸣
★3. *Šu*-^{d}IM [ ]
4. 3 sìla kaš 2 sìla [ ]
5. 2 gín ì
6. Lú-^{d}En-ki Gú-ab-[ba]^{ki}-šè ĝen-na
7. 3 sìla kaš 2 sìla zì
8. 2 gín ì

REV.

★9. *Šu-ì-lí* Sa-bu-um [ ]
10. 6 sìla kaš lú-[ ]
11. 3 sìla kaš 2 sìla ninda
12. 2 gín ì
13. Lú-^{d}Nanna
14. Šušina^{ki}-ta ĝen-na
★15. 0.0.2 1 sìla kaš 0.0.2 1 sì[la ninda]
16. dub-sar ĝìr [Lú]-^{d}Ĝeš-bar-è
17. zi-ga u$_4$ [ ]
18. iti še-í[l-la]

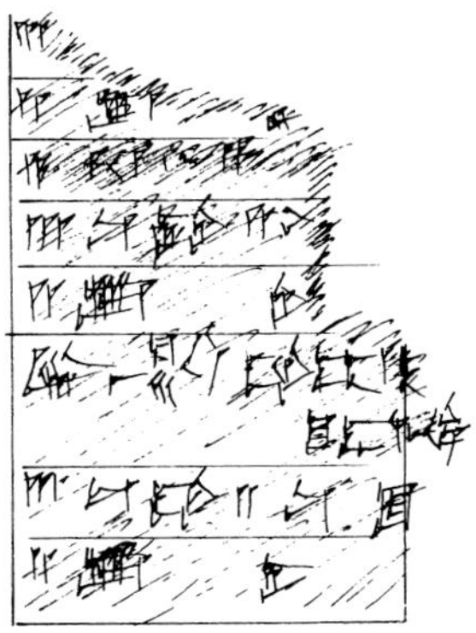

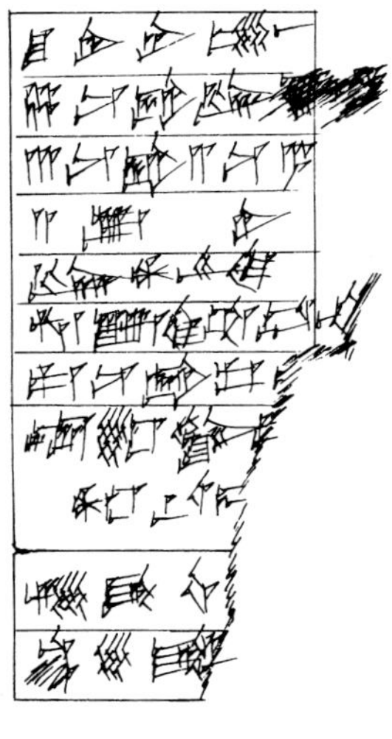

260

(XII/-/-)

OBV.

1. 5 sìla kaš 3 sìla ninda
2. 1 ì á-gam
3. *Šu*-^{d}Dumu-zi sukkal
4. 5 sìla kaš 3 sìla ninda
5. 1 ì á-gam
6. Da-da-a sukkal
7. 5 sìla kaš 3 sìla ninda
8. 1 ì á-gam
9. *Šu*-^{d}Utu sukkal
10. 5 sìla kaš 3 sìla ninda
11. Ur-^{ĝeš}gigir sukkal

REV.

12. 5 sìla kaš 3 sìla ninda
13. *Šu-É-a* sukkal
14. 5 sìla kaš 3 sìla ninda
15. 1 ì á-gam
16. Ga-du sukkal
17. 5 sìla kaš 5 sìla ninda
18. 1 ì á-gam
19. U-bar sukkal
20. 5 sìla kaš 5 sìla ninda
21. 1 ì á-gam
22. *A-a-ni-šu* sukkal
23. An-ša-an^{ki}-ta ĝen-na

L.E.

24. iti še-íl-la

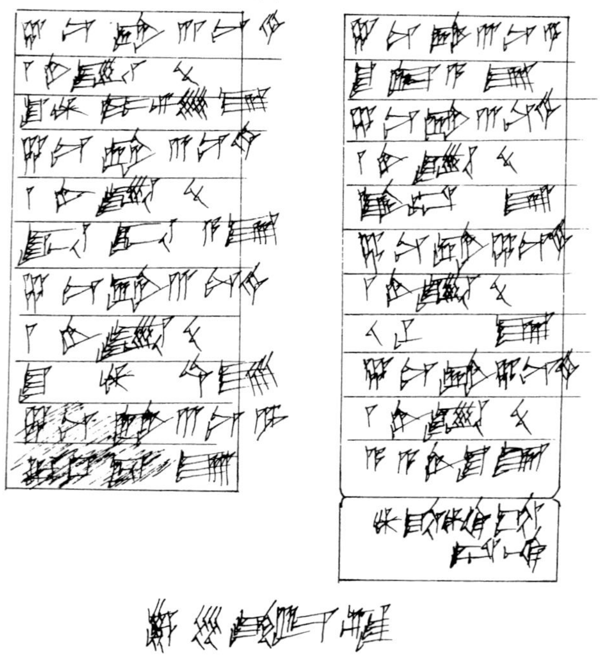

261

(XII/-/-)

OBV.

1. 5 sìla kaš 3 sìla ninda
2. 1 ì á-gam
3. *Šu*-^{d}Nin-šubur sukkal
4. 5 sìla kaš 3 sìla ninda
5. 1 ì á-gam
6. *Šu-Eš$_4$-tár* sukkal
7. 5 sìla kaš 3 sìla ninda
8. 1 ì á-gam
9. Šu-ša$_6$-ga sukkal
10. 5 sìla kaš 3 sìla ninda
11. 1 ì á-gam

REV.

12. Du$_{11}$-ga-li sukkal
13. 5 sìla kaš 3 sìla ninda
14. NE.NE sukkal
15. 5 sìla kaš 3 sìla ninda
16. 1 ì á-gam
17. *A-ḫu-a* sukkal
18. 5 sìla kaš 5 sìla ninda
19. 1 ì á-gam
20. Ur-^{d}Nanna aga-ús-gal-gal
21. 5 sìla kaš 5 sìla ninda
22. *Šu*-^{d}Nanna sukkal
23. An-ša-an^{ki}-ta «ĝeš» ĝen-na

L.E.

24. iti še-íl-la

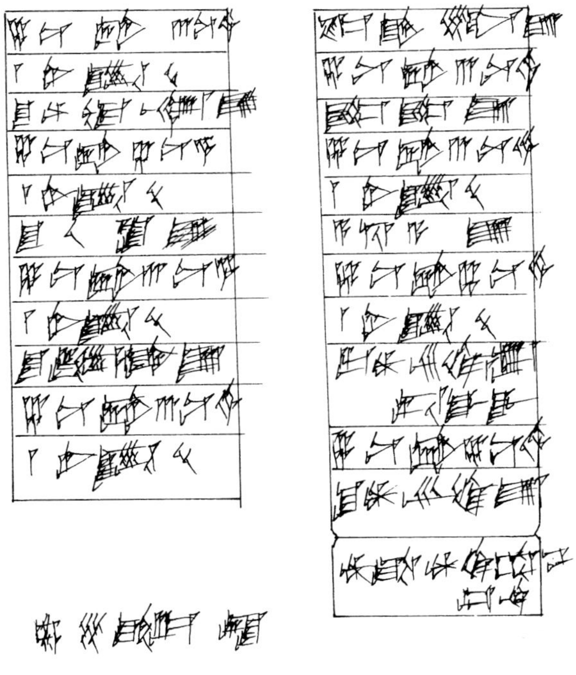

262

(XII/-/-)

OBV.

1. 0.2.0 kaš ninda lugal
2. šà uru
3. 0.3.2 dabin kaskal-šè
4. aga-ús-bi 40-àm
5. 1 dida sig_5

REV.

6. ugula alan-da ĝen-na
7. aga-ús alan-da ĝen-na-me
8. (BLANK)
9. zi-ga
16. iti še-íl-la

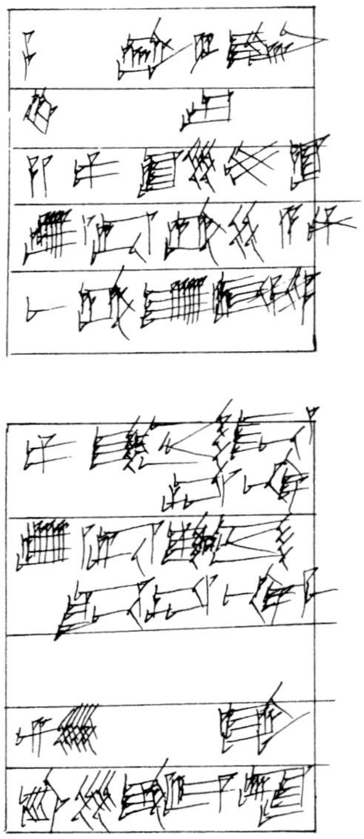

263 (XII/-/-)

OBV.

1. 5 sìla kaš 5 sìla zì 1 á-gam ì
2. A-na-ti dumu nu-bànda
3. 5 sìla kaš 5 sìla zì 1 á-gam ì
4. *A-ḫu-a* šeš lukur
5. Šušina^{ki}-ta ĝen-[né]
6. 3 sìla kaš 2 sìla zì [ ]
7. I-ti lú-ka[š$_4$]
8. 5 sìla kaš 5 sìla zì 1 [á-gam ì]

*9. Bur-ra-bi aga-ús [ ]

(*bottom of obverse broken*)

REV.

(*top of reverse broken*)

10. ⸢5 sìla kaš 5 sìla zì⸣ [ ]
11. NÌ.ŠE Diĝir-*ra-bí* l[ú]
12. Šušina^{ki}-ta ĝen-né
13. 5 sìla kaš 5 sìla zì 1 á-gam [ì]
14. *Šu*-^{d}Utu aga-ús-gal
15. Šušina^{ki}-ta ĝen-né
16. 5 sìla kaš 5 sìla zì 1 á-gam <ì>
17. Ur-^{d}Nanna sukkal
18. Šušina^{ki}-šè ĝen-né
19. iti še-íl-la

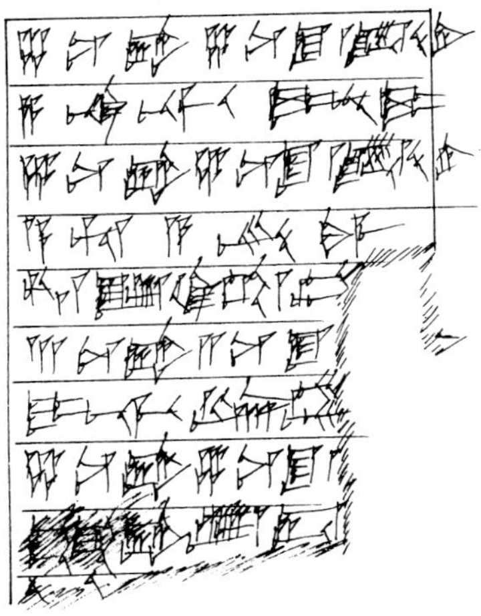

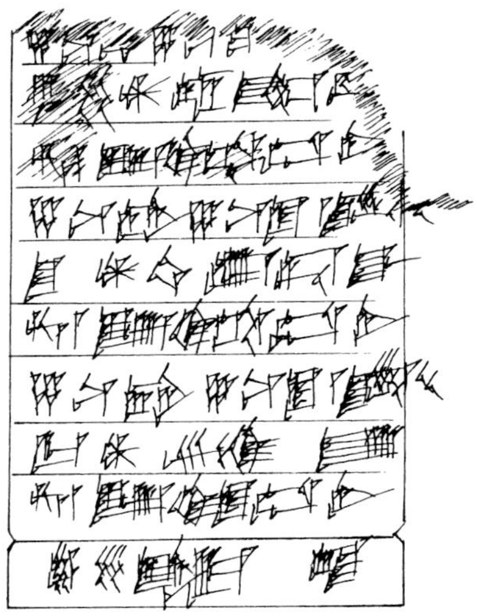

264 (XII/-/-)

OBV.

1. 3 sìla kaš
2. 2 sìla ninda
3. 4 gín ì
4. Ìr-^{d}Nanna lú ^{ĝeš}tukul
5. 3 sìla kaš
6. 2 sìla ninda
7. 4 gín ì

REV.

8. *Nu-ḫi-lum* lú-[ ]
9. [ ] sìla kaš 3 sìl[a]
10. [ ] gín ì-ĝeš
11. Lú-^{d}Šul-gi lú ^{ĝeš}tukul gu-la
12. zi-ga
13. iti še-íl-la

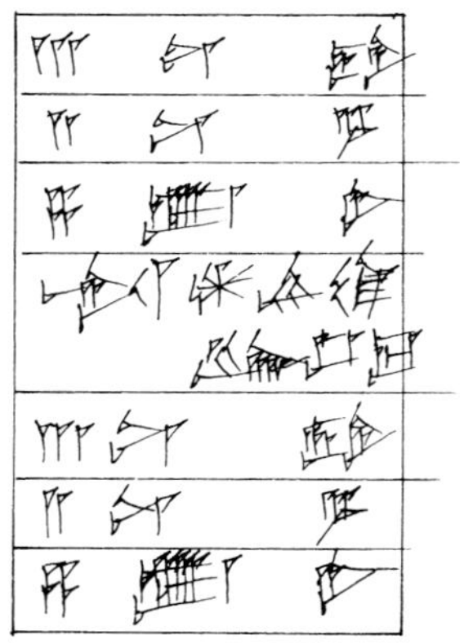

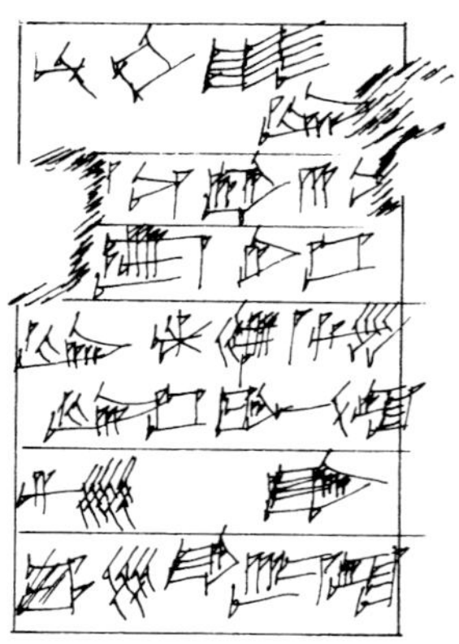

265 (XII/-/-)

OBV.

1. 3 sìla kaš ĝen
2. 2 sìla ninda du$_8$-a
3. 4 gín ì-ĝeš
4. *I-ti*-^{d}Suen
5. 3 sìla kaš 2 sìla ninda
6. 4 gín ì-ĝeš
7. *Šu-Eš-tár*

REV.

8. 3 sìla kaš ĝen
9. 2 sìla ninda 4 gín ì-ĝeš
10. *Šu*-^{d}IM
11. 3 sìla kaš 2 sìla ninda
12. 4 gín ì-ĝeš
13. A-li gudu$_4$
14. 0.2.0 dabin lugal šà-gal aga-ús
15. iti še-íl-la

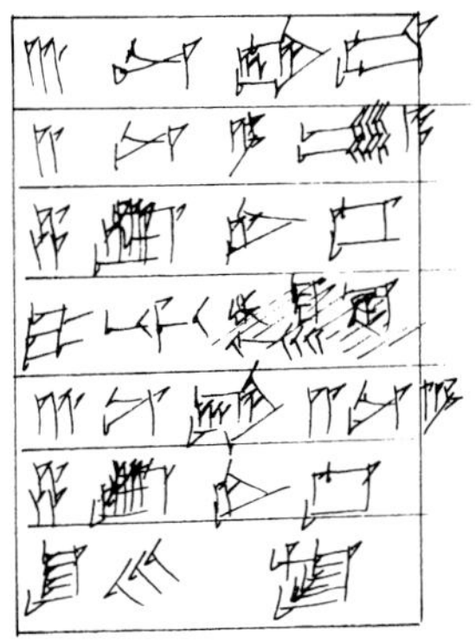

266 (date not preserved)

OBV.

1. [ ] ⸢sìla⸣ [ ]
2. [ ] à [ ]
3. [*A-d*]*a-làl* sukkal
4. [s]ìla kaš 3 sìla zì
5. [ ] ì á-gam
6. Lú-^{d}En-ki sukkal
7. 3 sìla kaš 2 sìla zì
8. 1 ì á-gam
9. *A-gu-a* lú-kaš$_4$
10. gu$_4$-ĝeš-šè ĝen-na
11. 5 sìla kaš 3 sìla zì

REV.

12. 2 ì [á-gam]
13. Ur-kisal ⸢lú ^{ĝeš}tukul⸣ gu-la
14. 3 sìla kaš 2 sìla zì
15. 1 ì á-gam
16. A-la-a lú-kaš$_4$
17. 3 sìla kaš 2 sìla zì
18. 1 ì á-gam
19. U-bar lú-kaš$_4$
20. [ ] sìla kaš 2 sìla zì
21. [ ] ì á-gam
22. [ ] lú-kaš$_4$
23. [ ]-šè ĝen [ ]
24. [ ]

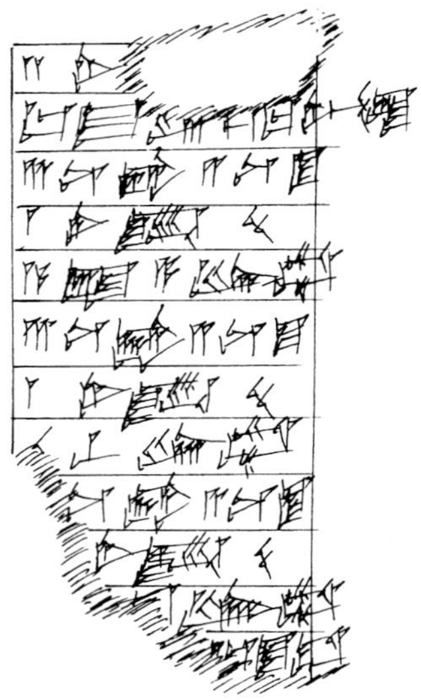

267 (date not preserved)

OBV.

(top of obverse broken)

1. 9 [ ]
2. 5 [ ]
3. 4 [ ]
*4. zàḫ-me
5. 36 saĝ-ḫi-a
6. 14 gu$_4$-ĝeš-ḫi-a
7. 10 anše-ĝeš-ḫi-a
8. gu$_4$-apin-bi 3
9. 13 áb-é-tùr-ḫi-a
10. 180 lá 1 udu-gukkal-ḫi-a
11. 291 udu-eme-gi-ḫi-a
12. 9 udu-máš-niga
13. 3 anše-bar
14. 2½ iku ^{ĝeš}kiri$_6$
15. 1 má-gur$_8$ kù-babbar tur
16. [ ] za-lum zabar-ḫi-a
17. [ ] zabar u[r]

(bottom of obverse broken)

REV.

(top of reverse broken)

18. [ ] x du$_{10}$-ga [ ]
19. [ ]x ì-du$_{10}$ [ ]
20. [ ] làl [ ]
21. [ ] sìla ga-àr
22. [ ] sìla zù-lum
23. [ ] ma-na ^{ĝeš}erin
24. [ ] ^{ĝeš}gu-za sig$_5$-ḫi-a
25. [ ] ^{ĝeš}gu-za-ḫi-a
26. [ ] ĝeš-nud sig$_5$
27. 5 ĝeš-nud-ḫi-a
28. 1 ^{ĝeš}ĝìr-gub sig$_5$
29. 1 ^{ĝeš}ĝìr-gub
30. 5 ^{ĝeš}banšur sig$_5$-ḫi-[a]
31. 2 ^{ĝeš}banšur-ḫi-a
32. 9 ^{ĝeš}ma-[ ]
33. 4 ^{ĝeš}[ ]

(bottom of reverse broken)

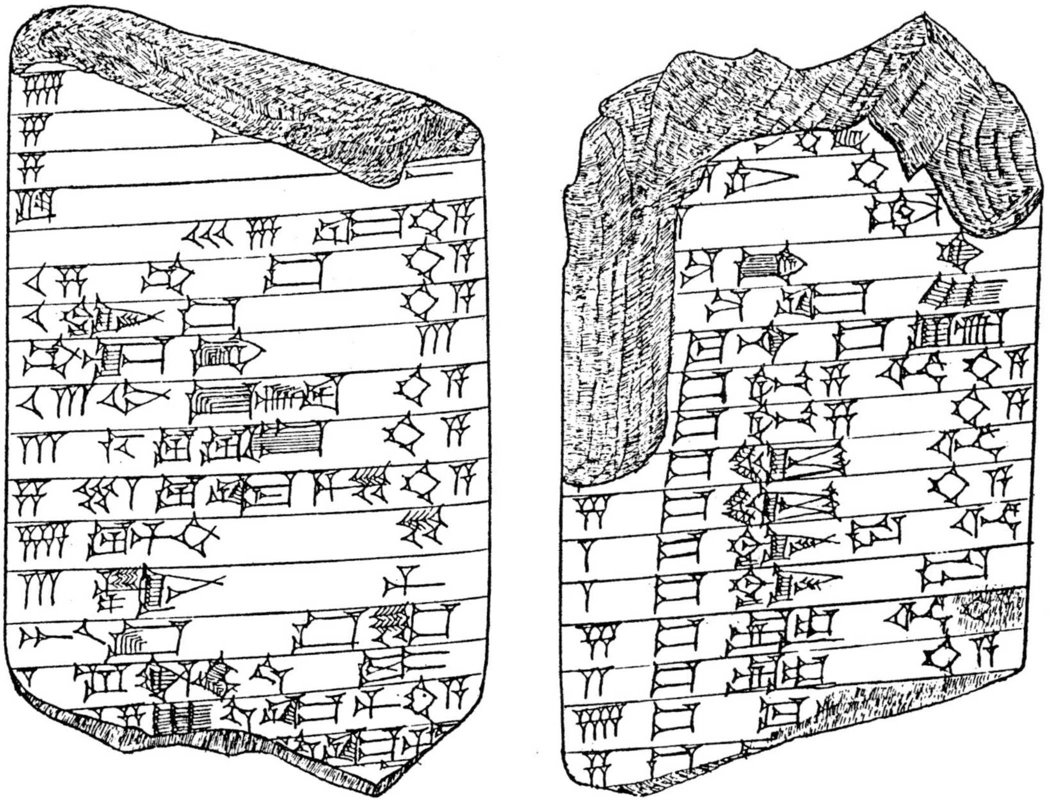

268

(not dated)

BULLA WITH SEAL

1. [ ] ma
2. [lu]gal-an-ub-[da-lí]mmu-ba
3. x UD x [ ] ḪI
4. dam-su

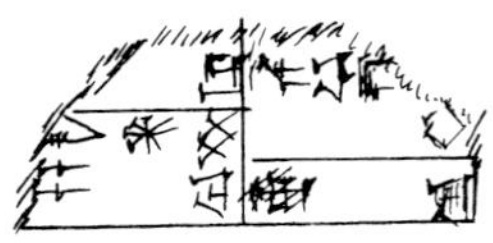

269

(date not preserved)

OBV.

(*top of obverse broken*)

1. 1 (eše) Lugal-⸢šà⸣-l[á]
2. 1 túg bar Ur-^{d}NE.ZI x ZI ZI x
3. 1 (eše) Ur-^{d}Gù-dé-a
4. iti u_4 8 ba-zal
5. 1 (eše) Da-gu-ù
6. 1 (eše) Ur-è-a
*7. 1 (eše) Gi_4-da

REV.

8. 1 (bur) Kù-x-sá-NE
9. iti u_4 10 ba-zal
10. 1 (eše) 1 Lú-LU[M]
11. 1 (eše) 1 Lú-diĝir-ra [dumu] Ur-^{ĝeš}[ ]
12. 1 (eše) En-AB.DI rá-gaba
13. ša Unug[^{ki}]

(*bottom of obverse broken*)

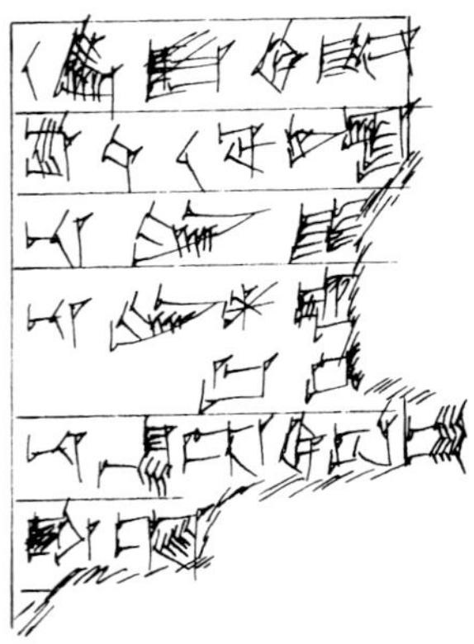

270

(I/-/AS 1)

OBV.
1. [x] duḫ
2. [x]-la
3. [ ] ^{d}Ìr-[eze]n KU

REV.
4. (BLANK)
5. iti [b]uru$_x$(GÁNA)-maš
6. mu [^{d}A]mar-^{d}Suen lugal

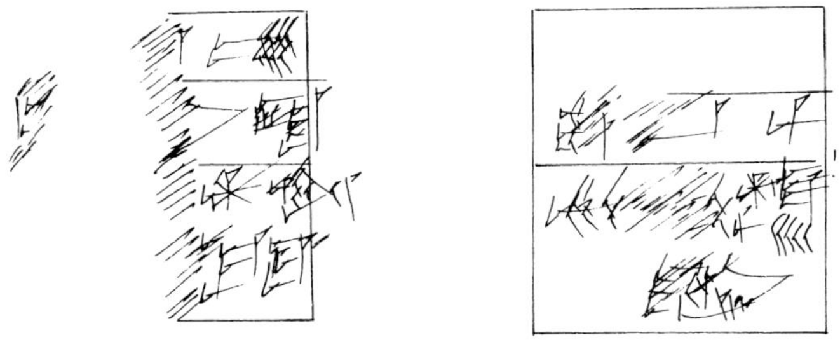

271

(XI/-/[ ])

OBV.
(*obverse destroyed*)

REV.
1. (*seal illegible*)
2. iti še-kin-ku$_5$
3. mu [ ] en [ ]

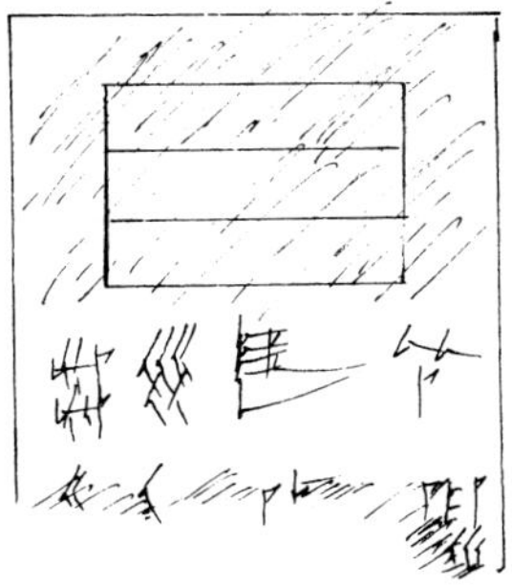

272

(-/-/AS 8)

OBV.

1. 20 sar sum [ ]
2. 25 sar sum ĝeš ḪI-[da]
3. sar-a igi-saĝ ⅔ sìla-ta
4. ĝeš 2⅚-ta
5. igi-saĝ-bi 0.0.3
6. ĝeš-sum-numun-bi 56⅔
7. ĝeš-sum ĝeš ḪI-da-bi 70⅔
8. Ka$_{5}$-àm nu-^{ĝeš}kiri$_{6}$
9. 10 sar sum-numun 20 sar sum ĝeš ḪI-da
10. [igi-saĝ] ⅔ sìla ĝeš 2⅚-ta
11. [igi-saĝ]-bi 0.0.1 3⅓ sìla
12. [ĝeš-sum]-numun-bi 28⅓ [ ]
13. [ĝeš-sum] ĝeš ḪI-da-bi 28[⅓]
14. [ ] sig$_{5}$ UM [ ]
15. [ ] sar-sum [ ]
16. [s]ar-sum ĝeš ḪI-[da]

(bottom of obverse broken)

REV.

(top of reverse broken)

17. [ ] ⌜3⌝
18. [ ] x GA UM
19. [ ] igi-saĝ 1 sìla-ta ĝeš 6-ta
20. igi-saĝ-bi 0.0.2 7 sìla ĝeš-bi 2 [x]
21. Ú-ma-ni dumu Lú-ga [ ]
22. 20 sar sum-numun 40 sar sum ĝeš ḪI-d[a]
23. igi-saĝ ⅔ sìla-ta ĝeš 4⅔-ta
24. igi-saĝ-bi 0.0.4 [ ]
25. ĝeš-sum-numun-bi 93⅓
26. ĝeš-sum ĝeš ḪI-da-bi 186⅔
27. Inim-^{d}Šára dumu Da-a-ga
28. duḫ a-šà ^{d}Šul-pa-è
29. (BLANK)
30. šu+níĝin 1.1.1 9 sìla igi-saĝ gur
31. šu+níĝin 942⅔ ĝeš sum-numun
32. šu+níĝin 987⅔ ĝeš sum ĝeš ḪI-da
33. igi-saĝ nì-sur-bi 0.1.1 5⅔ sìla 8 gín
34. ĝeš-sum-numun nì-sur-bi 188½.0.0 3 gín
35. ĝeš-sum ĝeš ḪI-da nì-sur-bi 198+[.0].1 2 g[ín]

L.E.

36. sum kú-du$_{11}$-ga
37. šà A-pi$_{4}$-sal$_{4}$^{ki}
38. mu en Eridu^{ki} ba-ḫun

272

273

(-/30/-)

OBV.

1. 0.0.1 šim 3 sìla mun
2. 110 sa-gi 24 gú ^{ĝeš}ásal
3. 36 gú gi-ru-uš 10 sa-gi-ku$_6$
4. u$_4$ 21-kam
5. 0.0.1 3 sìla [šim] 4 sìla mun
6. 110 sa-gi [ ] ^{ĝeš}ásal
7. 34 gú gi-ru-uš 10 sa-gi-ku$_6$-šè
8. u$_4$ 22-kam
9. 0.0.1 3 sìla mun
10. 90 sa-gi 22 gú ^{ĝeš}ásal
11. 32 gú gi-ru-uš u$_4$ 23-kam
12. 8 sìla [ši]m 2 sìla mun
13. 20+[sa-g]i [x] ⸢g⸣ú ^{ĝeš}ásal
14. 21 gú gi-ru-uš 10 sa-gi u$_4$ 24-kam
15. 0.0.1 šim 3 sìla mun
16. 100 sa-gi 21 gú ^{ĝeš}ásal
17. 37 gú gi-ru-uš 10 sa-gi-ku$_6$
18. u$_4$ 25-kam
19. 0.1.0 ninda àr-ra sig$_5$ 4 sìla še-lú
20. 3 sìla gazi 5 sìla mun tu$_7$ si-šè
21. 0.0.1 šim 0.0.1 mun nì u$_4$-sakar

REV.

22. [ ] 2 gú ^{ĝeš}ásal
23. 33 gú gi-ru-uš 10 sa-gi-ku$_6$
24. u$_4$ 26-kam
25. 6 sìla šim 1 sìla mun
26. 20 gi-kaskal 60 ^{gi}kid
27. 90 sa-gi 24 gú ^{ĝeš}ásal
28. 32 gú gi-ru-uš 10 sa-gi-ku$_6$-šè
29. u$_4$ 27-kam
30. 8 sìla šim 3 sìla mun
31. 100 sa-gi 24 gú ^{ĝeš}ásal
32. 34 gú gi-ru-uš 10 sa-gi-ku$_6$-šè
33. u$_4$ 28-⸢kam⸣
34. 7 sìla šim 3 sìla mun
35. 90 sa-gi 21 gú ^{ĝeš}ásal
36. 32 gú gi-ru-uš 10 sa-gi u$_4$ 30 lá 1-kam
37. 6 sìla šim 2 sìla mun
38. 100 sa-gi 21 gú ^{ĝeš}ásal
39. 28 gú gi-ru-uš 10 sa-gi-ku$_6$-šè
40. u$_4$ 30-kam

*41. šu+nîĝin 0.1.5 8 sìla šim šu+nîĝin 0.0.3 lá 1 sìla mun

42. šu+nîĝin 0.1.0 ninda àr-ra šu+nîĝin 1060 sa-gi
43. šu+nîĝin 234 gú ^{ĝeš}ásal šu+nîĝin 338 gú gi-ru-uš
44. šu+nîĝin 4 sìla še-lú šu+nîĝin 3 sìla gazi
45. šu+nîĝin 0.2.0 ^{gi}kid šu+nîĝin 40 gi-kaskal
46. u$_4$ 30-kam

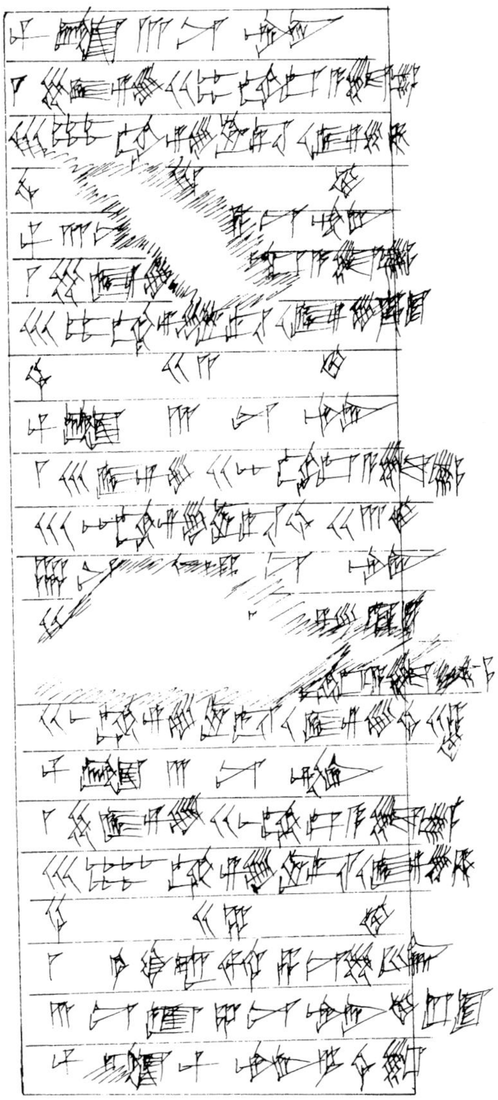

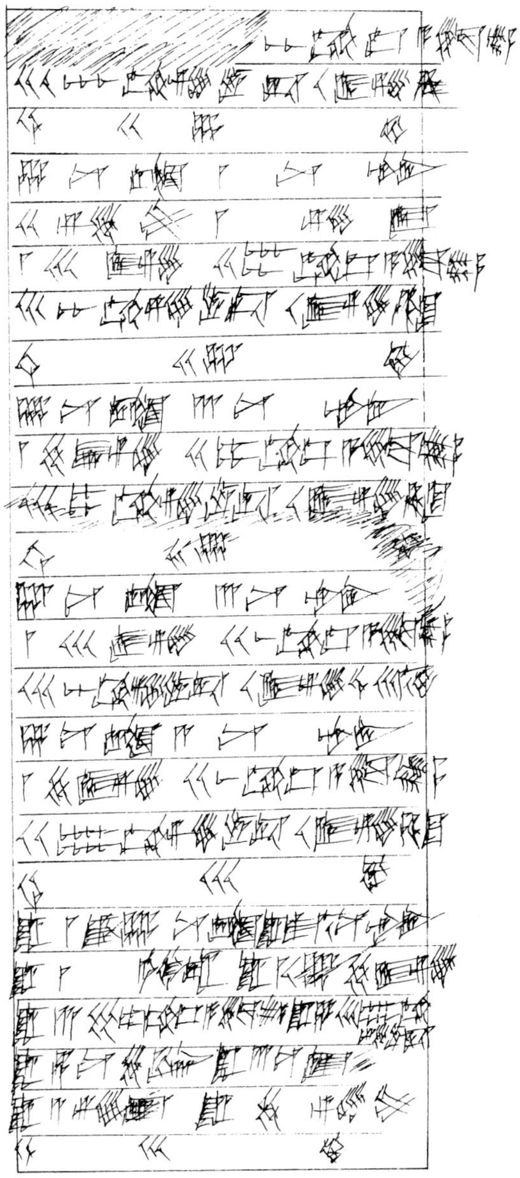

274

(date not preserved)

OBV.

(*top of obverse broken*)

1. 0.0.4 5 sìla [ ]
2. [ ] Ir$_{11}$-dam [dumu N]a-ba-ša$_{6}$-ke$_{4}$
3. [ ] gur kaš

REV.

4. ⸢Šeš⸣-šeš šu ba-ti
5. kaš Ni$_{9}$-a
6. (BLANK)

(*bottom of reverse broken*)

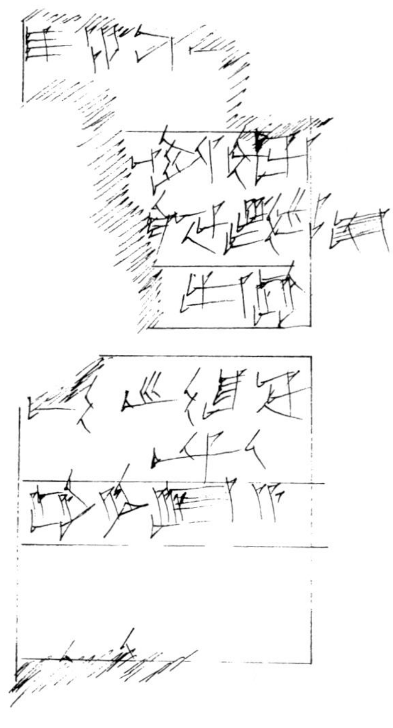

275

(III/-/ŠS 8)

OBV.

1. 1.0.0 gur ^{ĝeš}ḫašḫur-a
2. ki ^{d}Šára-kam-ta
3. kìšib Lú-^{d}Nin-šubur
4. šà-bi-ta
5. 0.1.4 ^{ĝeš}ḫašḫur-a
6. Lú-^{d}Nin-šubur

(bottom edge of obverse contains several unrelated notations)

REV.

7. 0.1.2 Ab-ba-kal-la
8. 0.1.5 8 sìla Du$_{11}$-ga-zi-da
9. šu+níĝin 0.4.5 8 sìla ^{ĝeš}ḫašḫur-a
10. zi-ga-àm
11. iti še-kar-a-ra-ĝál-la
12. mu ^{d}*Šu*-^{d}Suen lugal Urí^{ki}-ma má-gur$_8$-maḫ é

L.E.

13. ^{d}En-líl ^{d}Nin-líl-ra mu-ne-dím

276 (XII/-/-)

OBV.

1. 8.2.1 8 sìla še
2. iti ezen ^{d}Šul-gi
3. 3.0.3 4 sìla še gur
4. iti pa$_4$-ú-e
5. (BLANK)

REV.

6. 20.2.3 še gur
7. iti ^{d}Dumu-zi
8. 11.2.3 5 sìla gur
9. zi-ga kaš-dé-a
10. ĝìr La-mu
11. šà é-temen-na

277 (not dated)

OBV.

1. 65 aslag
2. 80 lá 2 kuš-ḫi-a
★3. Ur-^{d}Lama
4. 55 kuš udu
5. 61 kuš-ḫi-a
6. Ì-kal-la
7. 24 aslag

REV.

★8. [x] kuš
9. Al-la
10. (BLANK)
★11. šu+níĝin 90 lá 1 aslag
★12. šu+níĝin 170 lá 1 kuš udu
13. zi-ga
★14. 175 ad$_x$ [ ]
15. 10 kuš udu
16. Lú-^{d}Nin-šubur

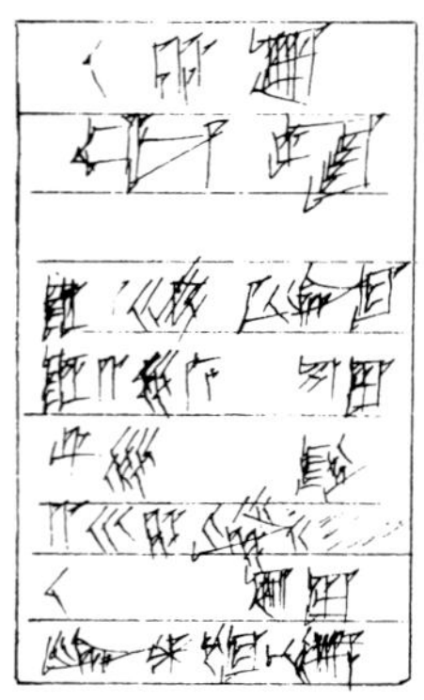

278

(-/-/Š 48)

OBV.

1. 6 gu$_4$-ĝeš
2. 1 anše
3. 5 anše-níta šu-gi$_4$
4. engar-bi 2 àm
5. gu$_4$ gibil-ka
6. kéš-rá

REV.

7. ki Ur-gu-la-ta
8. Lú-kiri$_4$-zal ì-dab$_5$
9. mu-ús-sa Ki-maš^{ki} ba-ḫul mu-ús-sa-bi

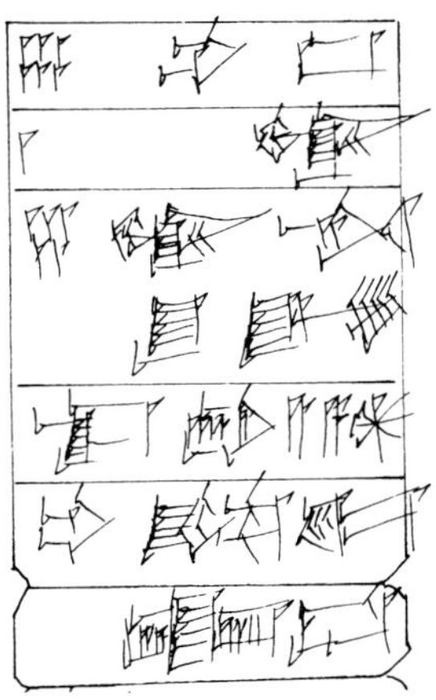

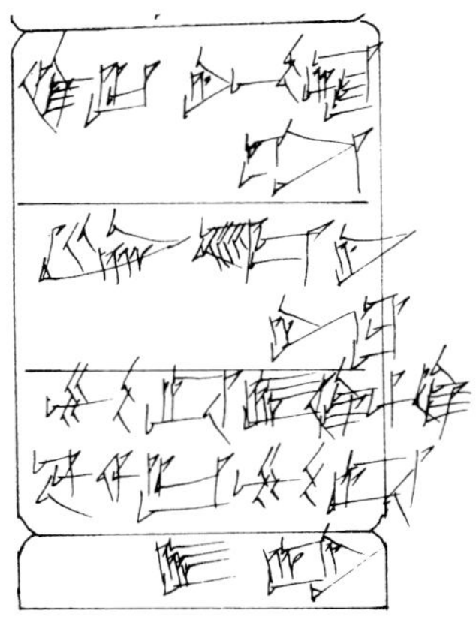

279

(X/-/AS 5)

OBV.

1. 2 ^{kuš}a-ĝá-lá
2. ki A-kal-la-[ta]
3. kišib Lu[gal]
4. šà [ ]

REV.

5. iti ⸢ezen ^{d}Šul⸣-gi
6. *(seal illegible)*
7. mu en-unu$_6$-gal-an-[na] ba-[ḫun]

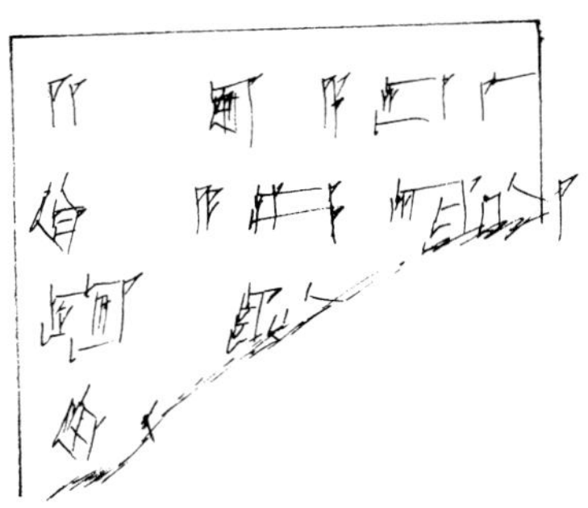

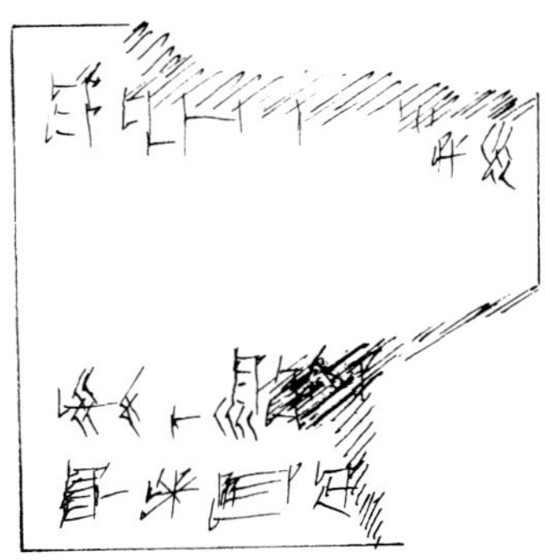

280

(XI/-/AS 7)

OBV.

1. 18 ^{ĝeš}a-ra má 60.0.0 gur
2. 10 lá 1 ^{ĝeš}a-da má 120.0.0 gur
3. 3 ^{ĝeš}a-da má 60.0.0 gur
4. ki Lugal-usar-ta

REV.

5. 1 ^{ĝeš}a-da má 120.0.0 gur
6. 1 ^{ĝeš}a-da má 60.0.0 gur
7. ki Gur_7-ta
8. kìšib Lú-$ša_6$-ì-zu
9. iti pa_4-ú-e
10. SEAL
11. mu Ḫu-ùḫ-nu-ri^{ki} ba-ḫul

Seal: Lú-$ša_6$-[ì-zu]
dub-sar
dumu A-kal-la

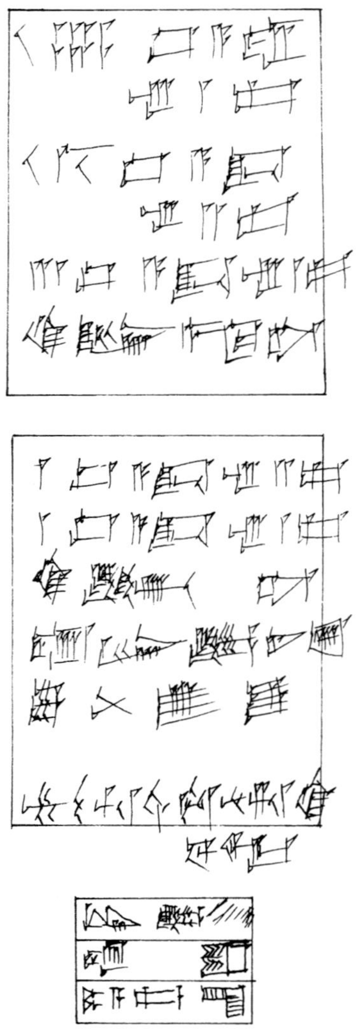

281 (X/-/-)

OBV.

1. 2 peš-murgu
2. ki A-tu-ta
3. kìšib Lú-^{d}Nin-šubur

REV.

4. (BLANK)
5. iti ezen ^{d}Šul-gi

Seal: Lú-^{d}Nin-šubur
dub-sar
dumu Lú-^{d}Ba-ú

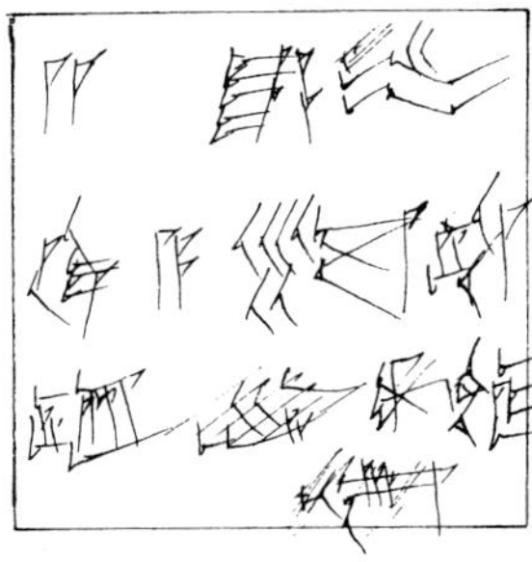

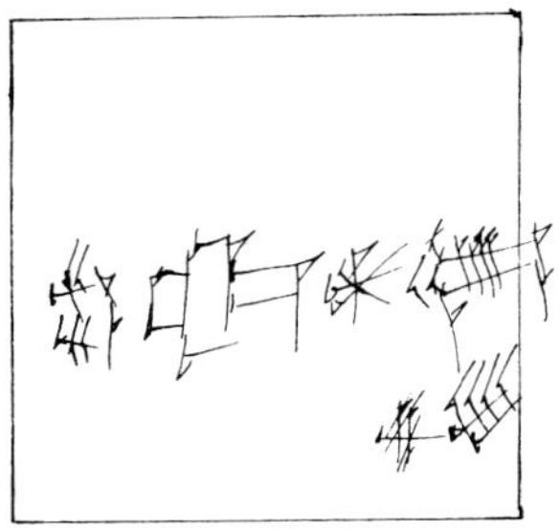

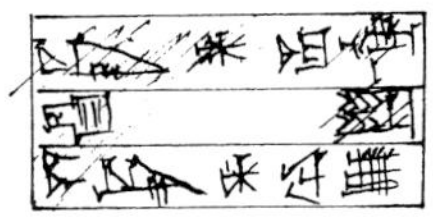

282 (IX/-/IS 1)

OBV.

1. ⅓ ma-na 4½ gín kù-babbar
2. lá-u$_{x}$ su-ga
3. ĝìr *Ì-lí*-ša$_{6}$ ugula uš-bar
4. á-lú-ḫun-ĝá

REV.

5. ambar a-šà [ ] maš
6. ma-da Unug^{ki}
7. a-ta-tùm-dè
8. É-úr-šum
9. šu ba-an-ti
10. iti šu-eš-ša
11. mu ^{d}*I-bí*-^{d}Suen lugal

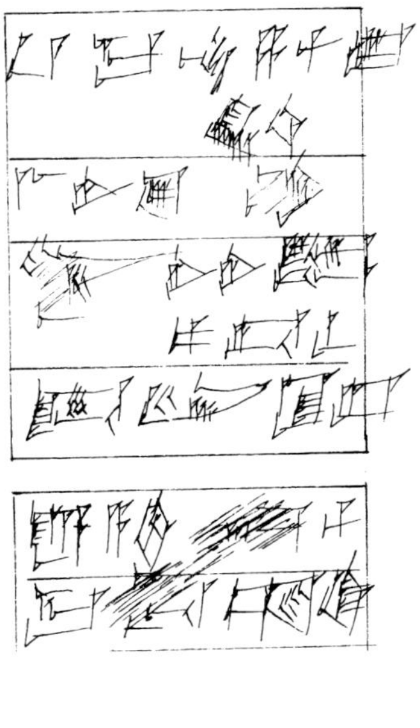

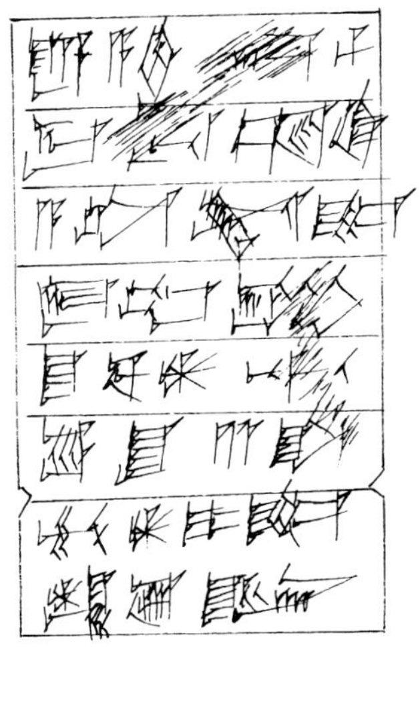

283 (I/30/IS 7)

OBV.

1. 5 sìla ninda sá-du$_{11}$ ^{d}En-[ki]
2. 3 sìla sá-du$_{11}$ ^{d}Nanše
3. u$_{4}$ 1-kam u$_{4}$-30-šè
4. ninda-bi 0.4.0
5. iti še-kin-ku$_{5}$
6. 2½ sìla sá-du$_{11}$ ^{d}En-ki
7. 1½ sìla sá-du$_{11}$ ^{d}⌜Nanše⌝
8. u$_{4}$ 1-kam u$_{4}$-30-šè
9. ninda-bi 0.2.0
10. iti maš-dù-kú
11. (BLANK)
12. ⌜šu+níĝin⌝ 1.1.0 ninda gur
13. saĝ-nì-gur$_{11}$-ra-kam šà-bi-ta

REV.

14. 0.0.1 2½ sìla šà ninda ì-du$_{8}$
15. 0.0.1 5 (sìla) Ur-^{d}En-ki-ke$_{4}$ sukkal
16. 0.0.1 5½ (sìla) Ì-ba-ab-du$_{7}$ nar sig$_{7}$-a
17. 0.0.1 2½ sìla Ù-tur géme-kíkken
18. ĝìr érin-bi ^{d}En-ki sá mu-ra-du$_{11}$-me
19. 0.0.2 2½ sìla KU [ ] na x géme ù [ ]
*20. ĝìr érin-[ ] $^{[d]}$Nanše ĝá-dù-[x]
*21. 0.0.1 1½ sìla šagina ar-za-n[a]
22. iti še-kin-ku$_{5}$ u$_{4}$ 15 [ ]
23. (BLANK)
24. šu+níĝin 0.1.3 ninda še-bi 0.3.0 gur
25. [x] [ ] 0.0.2
26. nì-ka$_{9}$-ak ninda èš-ta-gur-[ra]
27. sá-du$_{11}$ ^{d}En-ki ù ^{d}Nanše
28. ezen ^{d}Nanna iti-kam
29. [it]i še-kin-ku$_{5}$ ù iti maš-dù-kú
30. mu-ús-sa bàd-gal ba-dù

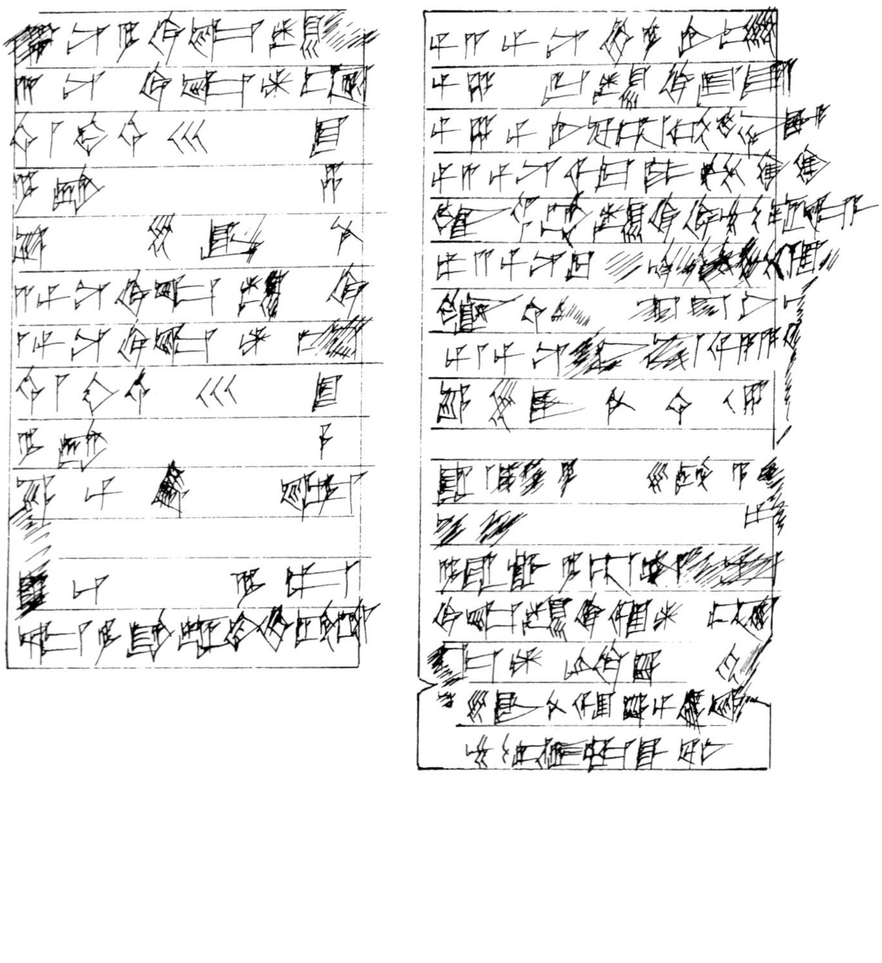

284 (-/xii/ŠS 1)

OBV.

i. *(top third of column i broken)*

1. [iti š]e-kin-ku$_5$ ba-zal
2. [mu ^{d}]*Šu*-^{d}Suen lugal
3. [ ] áb 1
4. 25 gu$_4$ 1
5. ù-tu-da
6. 2.2.4 ì-nun gur
7. 2.2.4 ga gur
8. áb a-rá 2
9. 2 áb 2
10. ĝìr Ur-kù-nun-na
11. k[i]NI a-SU-ta
12. [mu] má dàra-ZU.[AB]
13. [ ] 5 [ ]
14. [ ] x [ ]

ii.

15. [ ]
16. [ ] gu$_4$ 1
17. [ ] 14
18. nì-ka$_9$-ak
19. [m]u ^{d}*Šu*-^{d}Suen lugal
20. [1] áb 3
21. mu Ù.AMAR.BA.ŠU-šè
22. 2 áb 3
23. 11 gu$_4$ 2
24. mu SU.ḪU.ÚḪ-šè
25. 6 áb-máḫ šu-gíd
26. igi sig$_5$
27. [ì]-⌜bi⌝ 0.0.3
28. ga-bi 0.0.3
29. 22.0.0
30. gur ga ì-dab$_5$
31. 2 áb-m[áḫ]
32. igi [x]
33. ì-bi [ ]
34. ga-bi [ ]
35. 1 áb-má[ḫ]
36. [3] áb 1+[ ]
37. [ ] áb 1+ [ ]
38. [ ]
39. 23

REV.

iii.

40. [ba]-ug$_7$ šà si[g$_5$]
41. [ba]-ug$_7$ šà si[g$_5$]
42. *(erased line)*
43. 2.2.1 ì-[nun gur]
44. 0.0.1 8 sìla ga [gur]
45. 2.1.3 3 sìla ga [ ]
46. mu-túm
47. *Nu-úr*-^{d}Suen šu ba-t[i]
48. (BLANK)
49. zi-ga-àm
50. 165 áb-máḫ
51. 20 lá 1 áb 3
52. 40 lá 1 áb 2
53. 1 áb 2 SU
54. 23+ áb 1
55. 4 gu$_4$-áb
56. 11 gu$_4$-gal
57. 16+ gu$_4$ 3
58. 3 gu$_4$ 3 mu-gu$_4$-2-šè
59. 28 gu$_4$ 2
60. 26+ gu$_4$ 1
61. [ ] 376+ [ ]
62. [ ] ba šu [ ]

iv.

63. [ ]
64. [zi-ga]-àm
65. [ ] 5 [ ]
66. diri [zi]-ga-àm

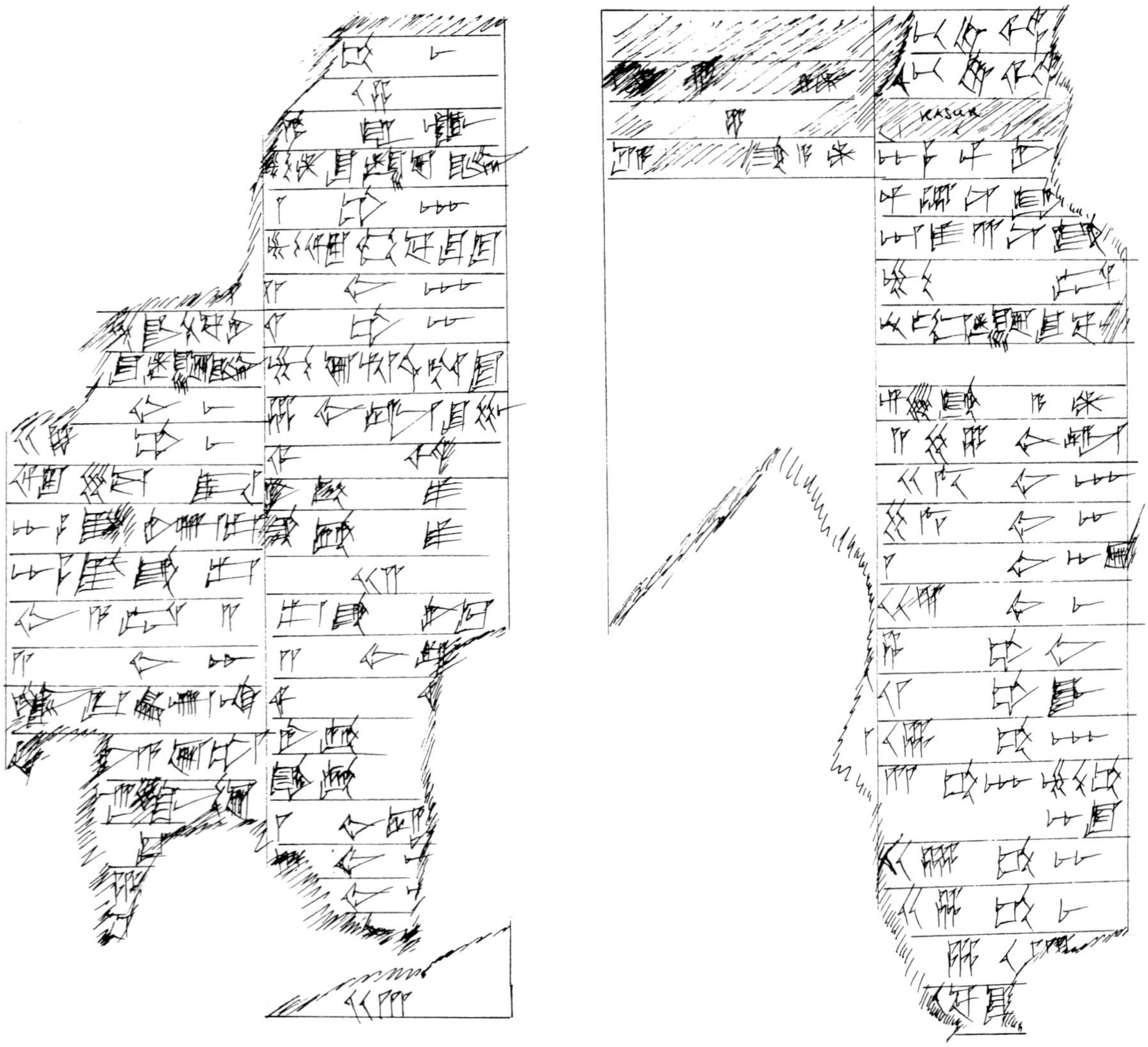

284

285 ([-/-]/ŠS 9)

OBV.

1. 20 lá 1 ud$_5$
2. 5 ^{mí}áš-gàr
3. 3 máš-gal
4. 2 máš-níta
5. 8 máš-šà-du$_{10}$
6. Lú-^{d}Dumu-zi
7. 37

REV.

(most of reverse destroyed)

8. [ ] ki x [ ]
9. mu é ^{d}Šára Umma^{ki} ba-dù

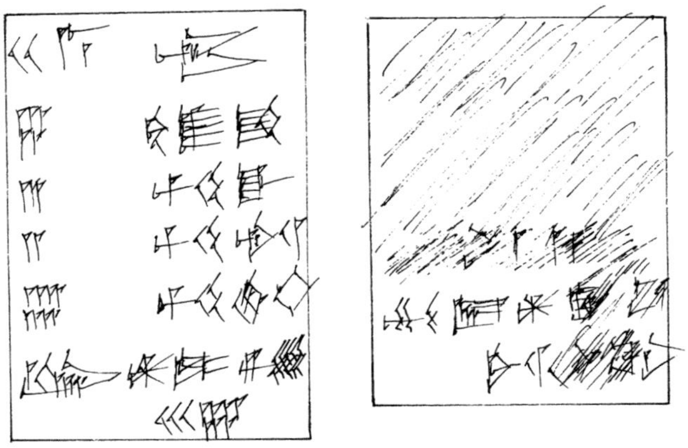

286 (date not preserved)

OBV.

1. 10 gu$_4$ 80 [ ]
2. ĝìr šagina x
3. 146 udu LAL.SAR.BAR [ ]
4. 22 udu En-e-šu-d[u$_7$]
5. a-rá 1-kam
6. mu énsi-[šè]
7. x [ ]

REV.

(reverse not preserved)

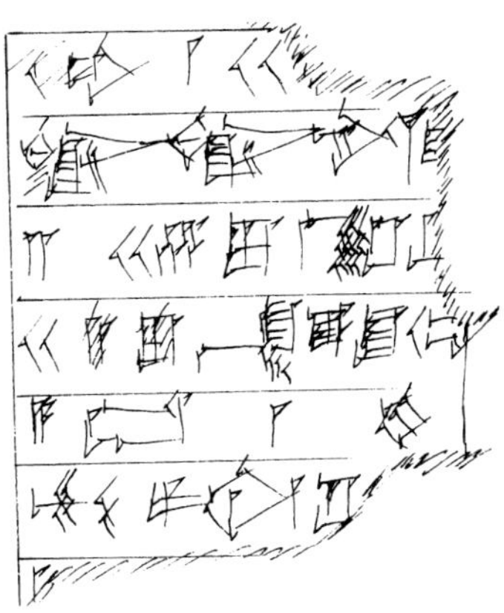

287

([ ]/12/-)

OBV.

1. 1 ud$_5$-niga ^{d}En-líl
2. 1 ud$_5$-niga ^{d}Nin-líl
3. mu-túm *Ṣe-lu-uš-*^{d}*D*[*a-gan*]
4. 1 sila$_4$ ^{d}Nusku
5. 1 sila$_4$ ^{d}Nin-urta
6. mu-túm énsi Nibru^{ki}
7. Zabar-dab$_5$ maškim
8. 1 u$_8$-sila$_4$-nú-a niga
9. mu a-ga-am$_6$ u$_8$-sila$_4$-nú niga ba-ḫ̮ul-a-šè

REV.

10. A-a-kal-la muḫ̮aldim [ ]
11. é-uz-ga [ ]
12. Ur-^{d}Ba-ú maškim
13. 3 gu$_4$ 3 áb
14. 2 áb mu-2
15. šu-gíd é-muḫ̮aldim-šè
10. ĝìr Lú-diĝir-ra
11. [u$_4$] 12-kam
12. [ ]

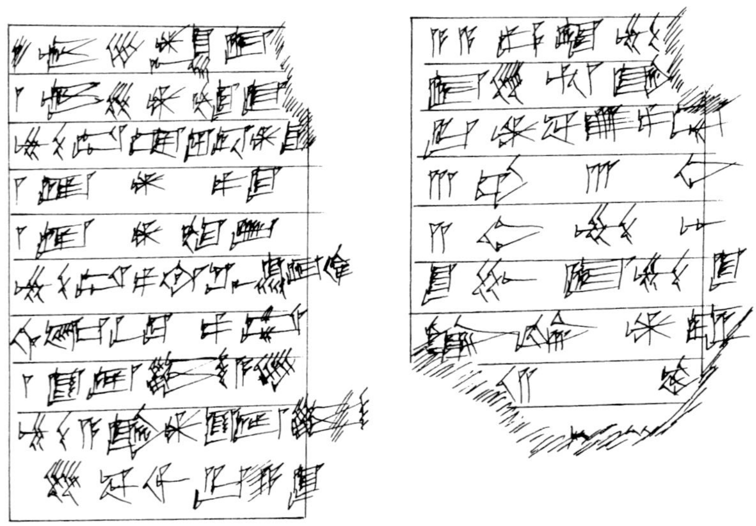

288

(XII/-/Š 33)

OBV.

i.

1. 5 áb-máḫ ba-ug$_7$
2. 1 amar-PEŠ mu-1 ba-ug$_7$
3. 2 gu$_4$-gal ba-ug$_7$
4. 1 amar-gu$_4$ mu-1 ba-ug$_7$
5. ki Ur-^{d}Lama utul-ta
6. 4 áb-máḫ
7. 2 áb mu-3
8. 2 gu$_4$-gal
9. 5 gu$_4$ mu-2
10. 4 amar-gu$_4$ mu-1
11. ki Lugal-im-ru-a-ta
12. 8 áb-máḫ
13. 1 áb mu-3
14. 2 áb mu-2
15. 1 gu$_4$ mu-3
16. 2 gu$_4$ mu-2
17. 6 amar-gu$_4$ mu-1
18. ki Ur-iti-ma-ta
19. 6 áb-máḫ
20. 3 áb mu-3
21. 1 áb mu-2
22. 2 gu$_4$-gal
23. 2 gu$_4$ mu-3
24. ki Du$_{10}$-*ì-lí*-ta
25. 2 áb-máḫ
26. [ ] gu$_4$ mu-2
27. [ki U]r-ig-alima-ta
28. [ ]

ii.

29. 2 áb mu-1
30. 2 amar-PEŠ mu-1
31. 1 amar-gu$_4$ mu 1
32. ki Ur-^{d}Nin-da-ta
33. 2 áb-máḫ
34. 1 áb mu-3
35. 1 gu$_4$ [ ]
36. 2 amar-gu$_4$ [ ]
37. ki Bu-zu-[ ]
38. 5 áb [ ]
39. 4 gu$_4$ [ ]
40. ki Lú-[ ]
41. 1 áb [ ]
42. 1 gu$_4$ [ ]
43. 2 gu$_4$-gal
44. 1 gu$_4$ mu-2
45. ki Ur-^{d}Nanna-ta
46. 3 áb-máḫ
47. ki ^{d}Inanna-ur-saĝ-ta
48. 8 áb-máḫ
49. 2 áb mu-3
50. 2 áb mu-2
51. 8 amar-PEŠ mu-1
52. 7 gu$_4$ mu-3
53. 5 gu$_4$ mu-2
54. 7 amar-gu$_4$ mu-1
55. ki Diĝir-*ra-bí*-ta
56. 8 áb-máḫ

★57. [ ] áb mu-3

58. [ ] gu$_4$ áb
59. [ ]-^{d}Utu-ta

REV.

iii.

60. [áb]-máḫ
61. [m]u-3
62. [ ] áb
63. [ ] mu-2
64. k[i]x-ta
65. 2 [áb]-máḫ
66. 1 [á]b mu-2
67. 1 gu$_4$ mu-3
68. 1 amar-gu$_4$ mu-1
69. ki Ur-^{d}Ba-ú-ta
70. 4 áb-máḫ
71. 2 áb mu-2
72. 2 amar-gu$_4$ mu-1
73. ki Ur-engur-ka-ta
74. (BLANK)
75. é-kišib-ba-šè Lugal-u$_4$-sù-šè šu ba-ti
76. 3 áb-máḫ
77. 1 áb mu-2
78. 2 amar-PEŠ mu-1
79. 6 amar-gu$_4$ mu-1
80. ki Lugal-ma-ta
81. 7 áb-máḫ
82. 1 áb mu-3
83. 1 amar-PEŠ mu-1
84. 5 gu$_4$ mu-2
85. 1 amar-gu$_4$ mu-1

★86. ki I-ba-ni-ta

87. (BLANK)
88. mu géme un-ĝa$_6$-šè
89. Du-du šu ba-ti
90. 2 áb-máḫ

91. 1 amar-PEŠ mu-1
92. 1 gu_4-gal
93. 1 amar-gu_4 mu-1
94. ki Ur-ni_9-ĝar-ta

iv. *(top of column iv broken)*

95. [ḫ]i-ĝál-ta
96. [á]b-máḫ
97. [ ] amar-PEŠ mu-1
98. 2 gu_4 mu-2
99. 2 amar-gu_4 mu-1
100. ki Ur-saĝ-na-ra-ta
101. (BLANK)
102. mu géme Mar-tu-ne-šè
103. En-diĝir-mu šu ba-ti
104. (BLANK)
105. šu+níĝin 92 áb-máḫ ba-ug_7
106. šu+níĝin 12 áb mu-3 ba-ug_7
107. šu+níĝin 14 áb mu-2 ba-ug_7
108. šu+níĝin 20 amar-PEŠ mu-1 ba-ug_7
109. šu+níĝin 4 gu_4-áb ba-ug_7
110. šu+níĝin 10 lá 1 gu_4-gal ba-ug_7
111. šu+níĝin 12 gu_4 mu-3 ba-ug_7
112. šu+níĝin 24 gu_4 mu-2 ba-ug_7
113. šu+níĝin 35 amar-gu_4 mu-1 ba-ug_7
114. gu_4 ba-ug_7
115. (BLANK)
116. zi-ga
117. iti še-kin-ku_5
118. mu-ús-sa a-rá 3-kam Si-mu-ru-um[ki] ba-ḫul

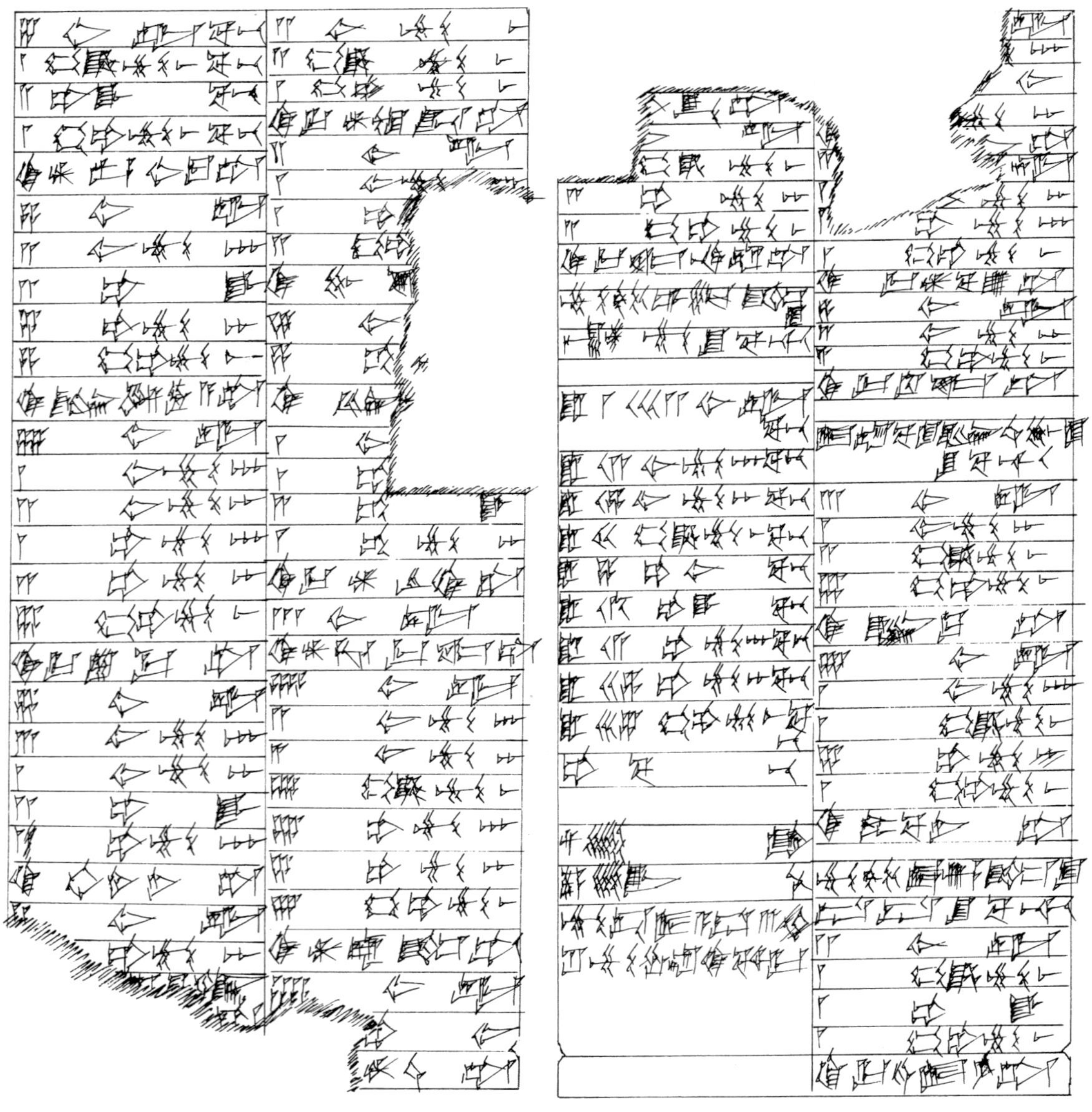

289

(IV/-/Š 39)

OBV.

1. 4 udu-níta
2. 2 máš 2 sila$_4$
3. iti šeš-da-kú
4. 2 u$_8$ 2 ud$_5$
5. 3 máš 1 sila$_4$
6. iti u$_5$-bí-kú
7. 6 udu-níta

REV.

8. [x] máš
9. iti ki-síg ^{d}Nin-a-zu

*10. sá-du$_{11}$ ^{d}*Be-la-at-šuḫ-ni-ir*

*11. ù ^{d}*Be-la-at-dar-ra-[b]a-an*

12. *An-nu-ni-tum*
13. ù ^{d}*Ul-ma-ši-tum*
14. iti 3-kam

L.E.

15. mu é *Puzur$_4$-iš-^{d}Da-gan* ba-dù

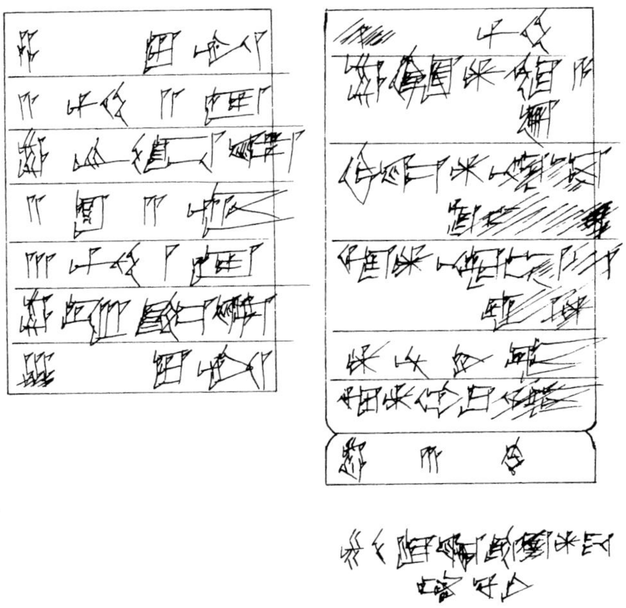

290

(VIII/-/Š 42)

OBV.

1. 2 u$_8$ 1 sila$_4$
2. 1 udu 2 máš
3. sá-du$_{11}$ ^{d}*Be-la-at-suḫ-ne-er*
4. ^{d}*Be-la-at-dar-ra-ba-an*

REV.

5. *An-nu-ni-tum*
6. ù ^{d}*Ul-ma-si-tum*
7. iti šu-eš-ša
8. mu Ša-aš-ru^{ki} ba-ḫul-a

291 (II/-/Š 48)

OBV.

i. *(top of column i broken)*

1. [mu]^{ki} ù Ki-maš^{ki} ba-ḫul
2. 142 gu$_4$
3. 72 áb
4. iti maš-dù-kú
5. 13 gu$_4$
6. iti šeš-da-kú
7. 11 gu$_4$
8. 1 áb
9. iti u$_5$-bí-kú
10. 3 gu$_4$
11. iti ki-síg ^{d}Nin-a-zu
12. 18 gu$_4$
13. 2 áb
14. iti ezen ^{d}Nin-a-zu
15. 8 gu$_4$
16. 2 áb
17. iti á-ki-ti
18. 7 gu$_4$
19. iti ezen ^{d}Šul-gi
20. 225 gu$_4$
21. 38 áb
22. iti šu-eš-ša

ii. *(top of column ii broken)*

23. mu-túm lugal
24. 7 gu$_4$
25. 6 áb
26. šu-gíd
27. ki Zabar-dab$_5$-ta
28. iti maš-dù-kú
29. 1 gu$_4$
30. 1 áb
31. ki *Ṣe-lu-uš*-^{d}*Da-gan*-ta
32. 1 gu$_4$
33. ki Ur-^{d}Suen dumu Ù-ša$_6$-a-ta
34. iti ki-síg ^{d}Nin-a-zu
35. 1 gu$_4$
36. 1 áb
37. ki Lú-URU×GÁNA*tenû*^{ki}-ta
38. iti ezen ^{d}Nin-a-zu
39. 18
40. mu-ús-sa Ki-maš^{ki} ba-ḫul
41. 15 gu$_4$
42. 1 áb
43. ki Al-la-[ ]

iii. *(top of column iii broken)*

44. 5 [ ]
45. iti ezen [ ]
46. ki Ur-^{d}[ ]
47. 1 [ ]
48. ki *Śar-ru-um*-[ ]
49. iti ezen ^{d}[ ]
50. 70+[ ]
51. mu Ḫa-ar-[ši]^{ki} Ki-maš^{ki} [ba-ḫul]
52. 40 [ ]
53. ki Al-l[a]
54. iti šeš-da-[kú]
55. 60 [ ]
56. 35 [ ]
57. ki Zaba[r-dab$_5$]
58. 3 [ ]
59. ki Diĝir-a-[x]
60. 1 [ ]
61. ki Ur-^{d}En-[ ]
62. iti u$_5$-bí-[kú]
63. 10 lá 1 [ ]
64. 1 á[b]
65. ki Lú[ ]
66. iti [ ]

REV.

iv.

67. [ ]
68. 5 [ ]
69. iti ezen [ ]
70. 6 [ ]
71. iti ezen me-k[i-ĝál]
72. kišib *Puzu*[*r*$_4$ x]
73. 32 [ ]
74. 10 lá 1 [ ]
75. kišib *Ar-ši*-[*aḫ*] énsi Bab[ili^{ki}]
76. 22 [ ]
77. 4 [ ]
78. kišib Ka$_5$-a-[ ] mu énsi-[šè]
79. a-rá 1-[kam]
80. 1 gu$_4$ ḫal-ḫal [ ]
81. mu *Dan*-^{d}Š[ul]-g[i]
82. *1 gu$_4$ ḫal [ ]
83. ĝìr K[a$_5$-a]
84. a-rá [ ]
85. 3 [ ]
86. ⌜ĝìr⌝ [ ]

(bottom of column iv broken)

v. 87. 1 gu$_4$ kìšib Ab-ba
88. 1 gu$_4$ [ ]-ḪI sukkal
89. 3 g[u$_4$] ⌜kìšib⌝ ⌜x⌝-bi
90. 1 gu$_4$
91. kìšib Sú-li-li
92. 2 gu$_4$ kìšib-bi 2-àm
93. kìšib *Èr-ra-ba-ni*
94. 1 gu$_4$
95. kìšib *Šu*-Ma-ma
96. 4 gu$_4$ kìšib ^{d}Šul-gi-uru-mu
97. lú Lú-^{d}Nin-šubur šabra-an-na
98. 1 gu$_4$
99. kìšib *I-ti-su*
100. 2 gu$_4$
101. kìšib *A-bu-um*-diĝir
102. 1 gu$_4$
103. kìšib *Šu-ku-bu-um*
104. 1 gu$_4$
105. kìšib Ur-^{d}Suen dumu Ù-ša$_6$-a
106. a-rá 2-kam
107. iti šeš-da-kú
108. 11 gu$_4$
109. 2 áb
110. kìšib B[i-]
(*bottom of column v broken*)
vi. 111. 3330
112. zi-ga-àm

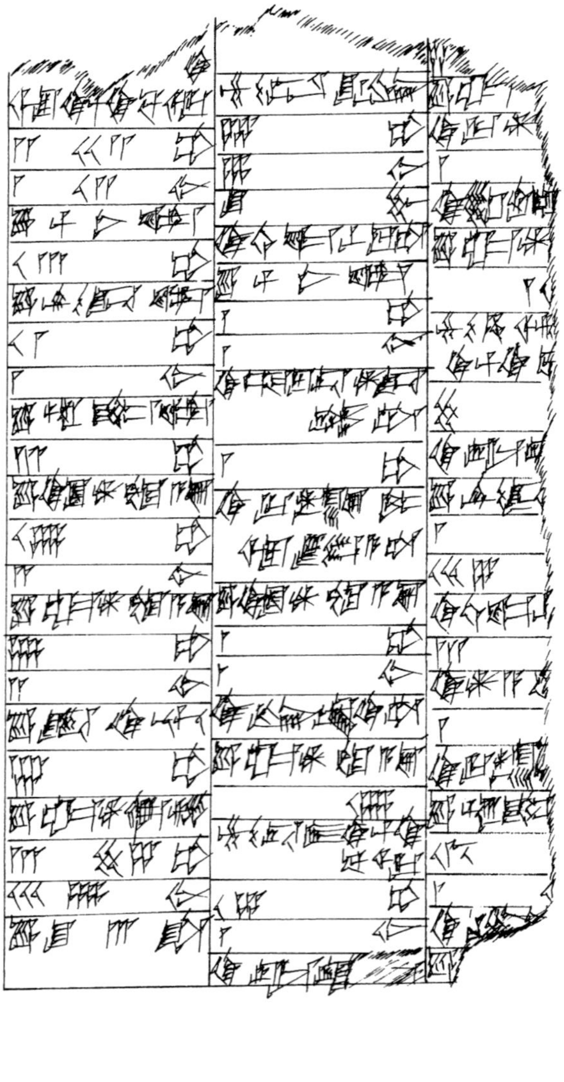

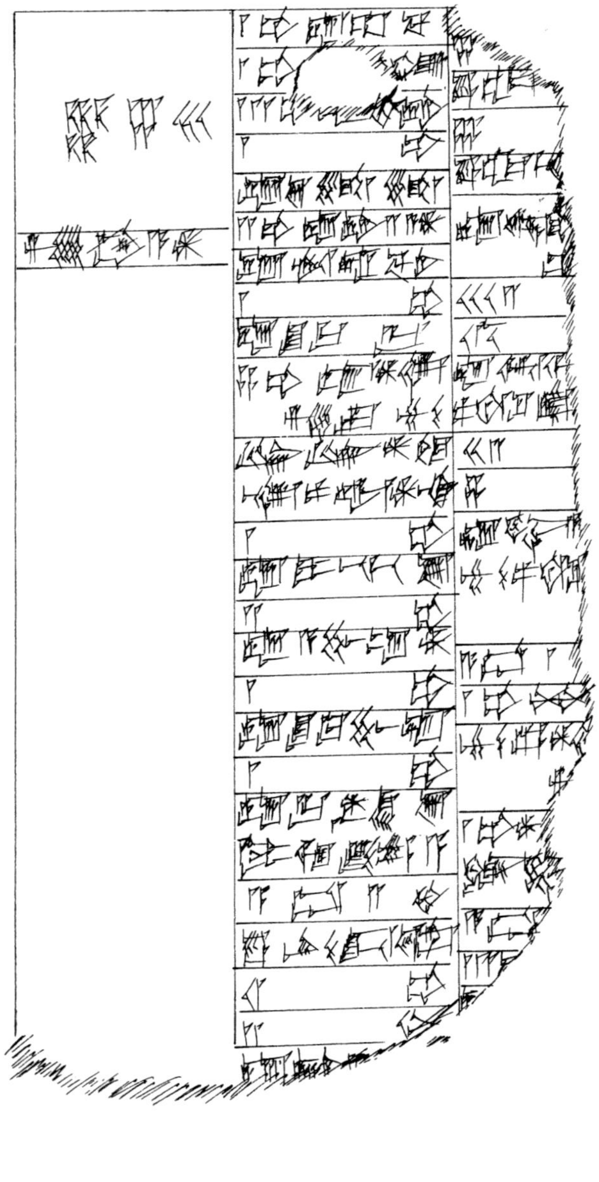

292 (XI/16/AS 5)

OBV.

1. 1 sila$_4$ ká-ĝi$_6$-[par$_4$]
2. 1 sila$_4$ ĜÁ [x]
3. 1 sila$_4$ ^{d}Na-na-a
4. u$_4$ 3-kam
5. 1 sila$_4$ ^{d}Inanna
6. 1 sila$_4$ ^{d}Lú[-làl]
7. 1 sila$_4$ máš-[šu-gíd]
8. 1 sila$_4$ ^{d}[x]
9. 1 sila$_4$ ká-g[i$_6$-par$_4$]
10. TÚG.ŠÈ lúgud-da [ ]
11. u$_4$ 5-[kam]
12. 1 sila$_4$ ká-ĝ[i$_6$-par$_4$]
13. 1 sila$_4$ ^{d}N[in]
14. u$_4$ 7-kam
15. 1 sila$_4$ ká-ĝi$_6$-par$_4$
16. 1 sila$_4$ ^{d}Muš-a-igi-ĝál
17. 1 sila$_4$ ^{d}Si-ĝar-an-na
18. 1 sila$_4$ ^{d}Nin-ḫur-saĝ
19. 1 sila$_4$ ^{d}Lugal-bàn-da
20. [u]$_4$ 10-kam

REV.

21. [1 sila]$_4$ é-gu$_4$
22. [1 sila$_4$] ká-ĝi$_6$-par$_4$
23. [u$_4$ x] kam
24. [1 sila$_4$ x] gal DU.DU
25. [u$_4$ x] kam
26. [1 sila$_4$ k]á-ĝi$_6$-par$_4$
27. [1 sila$_4$] gu-la
28. [u$_4$ x] kam
29. [1 sila$_4$ è]š ^{d}Inanna
30. [1 sila$_4$ g]u-za-an-na
31. 1 [sila$_4$ k]á-ĝi$_6$-par$_4$
32. 1 sila$_4$ ^{d}Nin-sún
33. u$_4$ 16-kam
34. ĝìr A-tu sagi
35. (BLANK)
36. šu+níĝin 24 sila$_4$
37. zi-ga šà Unug^{ki}-ga
38. bala énsi Sippar^{ki}
39. iti ezen ^{d}Me-ki-ĝál
40. mu en ^{d}Inanna Unug^{ki}-[ga] máš-e [ì-pàd]

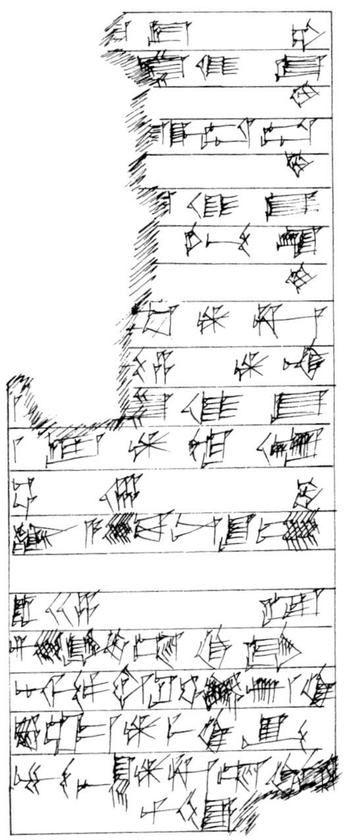

293

(VIII/-/ŠS 5)

OBV.

1. 15 túg uš-b[ar]
2. nar a-ru-a dŠu-dSuen-ka-me
3. 11 nar a-ru-a dAmar-dSuen-ka-me
4. (*erased line*)

REV.

5. (*erased line*)
6. (*erased line*)
7. ì-ba-eš
8. iti šu-eš-ša
9. mu-ús-sa bàd M[ar-tu] ba-dù

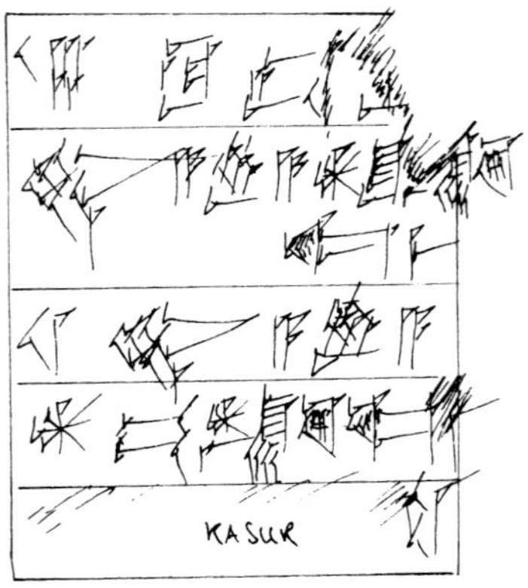

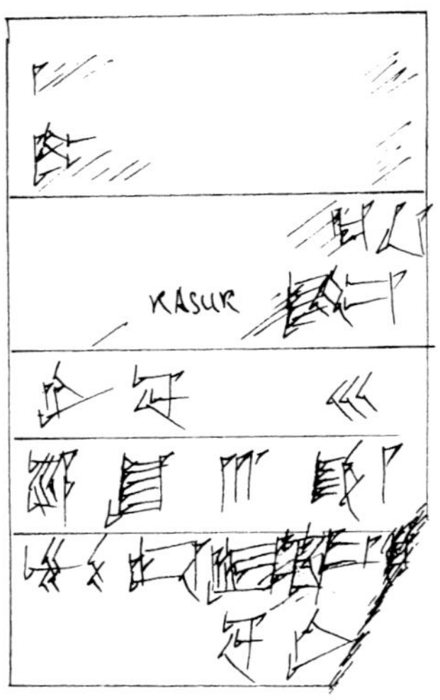

294

(XI/-/-)

OBV.

1. [ ] MU.LUM
2. [x] Èr-ra
3. 0.0.2 E-la-ra-ak
4. 0.0.2 *Šu*-x-kù
5. 0.0.2 Mi-na-NI
6. 0.0.2 Nam-ḫa-ni ⸢x⸣
7. 0.0.2 A-[x]-du$_{10}$-⸢x⸣
8. 0.0.2 *A-ḫa-ni-šu*

REV.

9. 0.0.2 [^{d}]Utu-*illat*
10. 0.0.2 [x] x ša x ul
11. 0.0.2 Èš-gal [x]
12. 0.0.2 [E]n-^{d}Nisaba
13. 0.0.2 *A-mur*-diĝir
14. 0.0.2 *A-bu*-du$_{10}$
15. 0.0.2 *Ib-ni*-^{d}Suen
16. [0.0.2] *Nu-úr-ì-lí*
17. [ ] še [ ]
18. [*b*]*í-ì-lí* kaš$_4$
19. [iti ezen] me-ki-ĝál

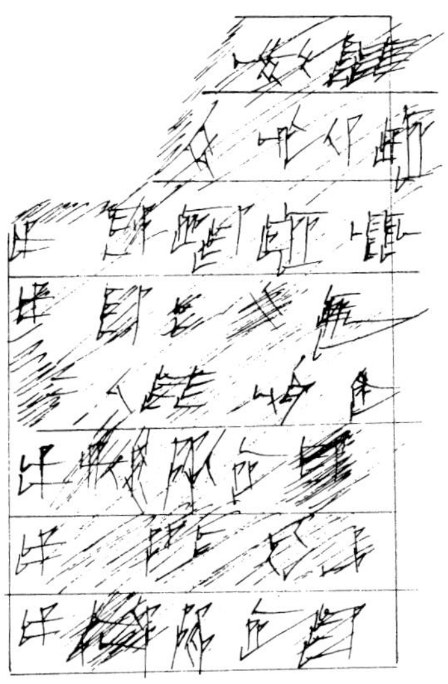

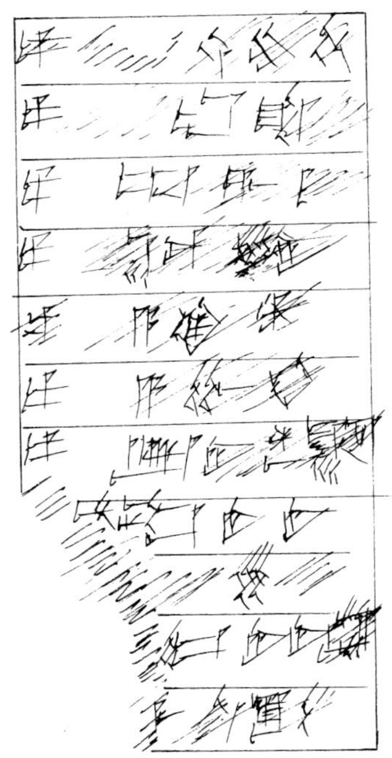

295 (date not preserved)

OBV.

i. *(top of column i broken)*

1. ⸢1⸣ $sila_4$ énsi [Ni]bru^{ki}
2. [ ] 20
3. u_4 22-kam
4. 2 $sila_4$ Ur-^{d}x-ra
5. 1 $sila_4$ énsi ÚR×$Ú^{ki}$ 1 máš Gú-dé-a dam-gàr
6. 1 $sila_4$ Kù-^{d}Nin-gal
7. [g]u_4 niga

ii. *(bottom of column i broken)*

(top of column ii broken)

8. x [ ]
9. 0.0.2 síg a [ ]
10. 2 gu_4
11. 10 lá 1 máš
12. *Á-píl-lum* Mar-tu
13. 1 máš
14. Ur-^{d}En-líl-lá
15. 1 $sila_4$
16. [ ] me

(bottom of column ii broken)

iii. *(top of column iii broken)*

17. 1 [ ]
18. 1 [ ]
19. L[ú]
20. 10 [ ]
21. 1[ ]

(bottom of column iii broken)

REV.

(reverse not preserved)

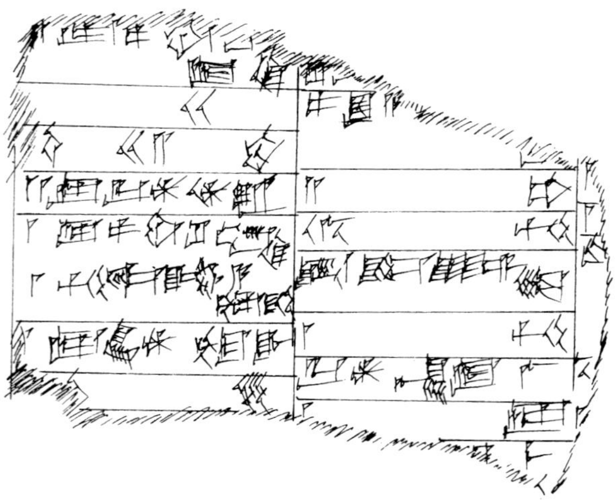

296 (XI/11/AS 2)

OBV.

1. 1 máš-gal-niga
*2. kìšib ḪU.KIN lú Ḫa-ar-ši^{ki}
3. Ir$_{11}$-mu maškim
4. iti u$_4$ 11 ba-zal

REV.

5. ki ^{d}Šul-gi-a-a-mu-ta
6. ba-zi
7. iti ezen me-ki-ĝál
8. mu ^{d}Amar-^{d}Suen lugal-e Ur-bí-lum^{ki} mu-ḫul

L.E.

9. 1

297 (V/-/ŠS 4)

OBV.

1. 1 udu-niga zà-gú-<lá>
2. šà é-gal
3. šà mu-er$_{10}$-ra-ta
4. u$_4$ 11-kam
5. ki In-ta-è-a-ta

REV.

6. ba-zi
7. ĝìr *Nu-úr*-^{d}Suen dub-sar
8. iti ki-síg ^{d}Nin-a-zu
9. mu-ús-sa Si-ma-núm^{ki} ba-ḫul

L.E.

10. 1 udu

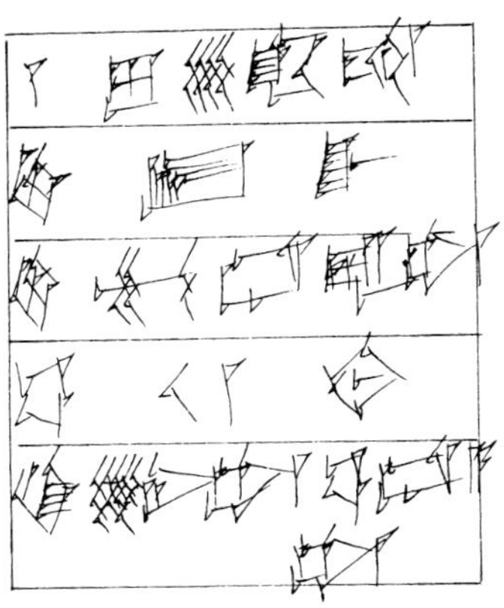

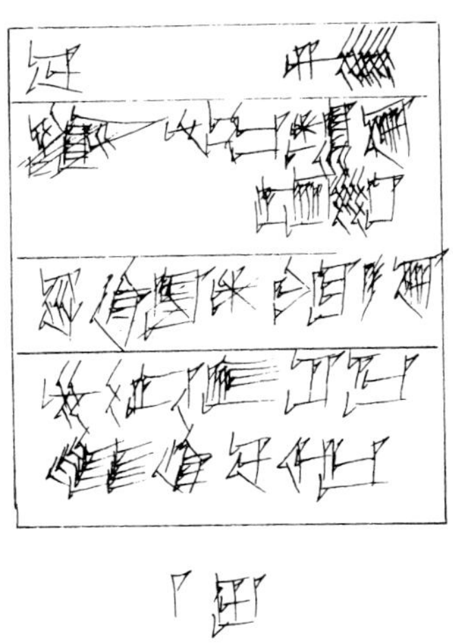

298 (I/29/ŠS 7)

OBV.

1. 1 amar-mašda níta
2. ^{d}En-líl
3. Lú-ku$_{4}$-ra
4. šà mu-er$_{10}$-ra-ta
5. u$_{4}$ 29-kam
6. ki In-ta-è-a-ta ba-zi

REV.

7. ĝìr ^{d}Nanna-ma-ba dub-sar
8. iti še-kin-ku$_{5}$
9. mu ^{d}*Šu*-^{d}Suen lugal Urí^{ki}-ma-ke$_{4}$
10. ma-da Za-ab-ša-li^{ki}
11. mu-ḫul

L.E.

12. 1 mašda

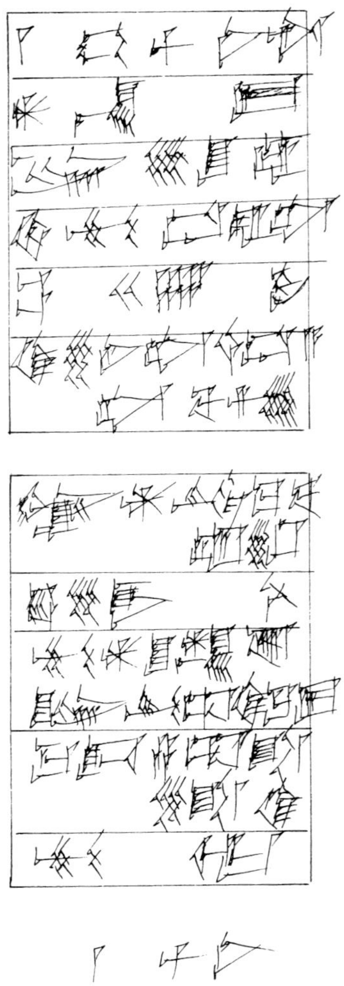

299 (VI/-/Š 39)

OBV.

(*top of obverse broken*)

- ⋆1. ki ⌜Na-ša$_6$⌝-[ta]
- 2. Lugal-[ ]
- 3. šu-ba-ti

REV.

- 4. SEAL
- 5. iti á-ki-t[i]
- ⋆6. mu é ^{d}*P*[*uzur*$_4$ ba-d]ù

⋆Seal: Lugal-[ ]
dumu NI

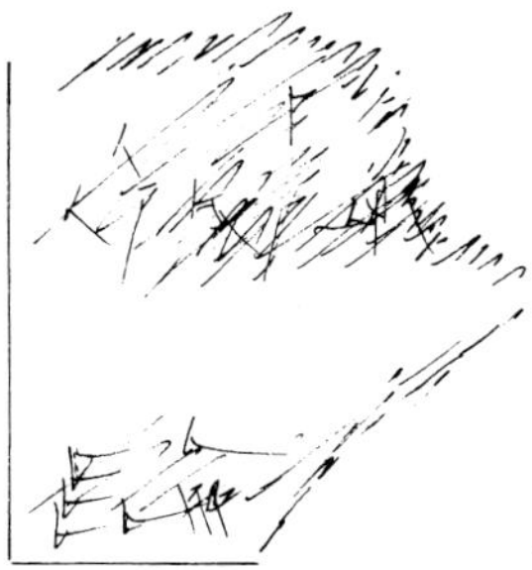

300 (VII/-/Š 45)

OBV.

- 1. 3 gu$_4$ ba-ug$_7$
- 2. ki Na-ša$_6$-ta
- 3. Ur-ni$_9$-ĝar
- 4. šu ba-ti

REV.

- 5. (BLANK)
- 6. iti ezen ^{d}Šul-gi
- 7. mu ^{d}Šul-gi lugal-e
- 8. Ur-bí-lum Lu-lu-bu
- 9. Si-mu-ru-um^{ki} ù Kára-ḫar^{ki}
- 10. 1-šè saĝ-du-bi šu-tibir-a bí-ra-a

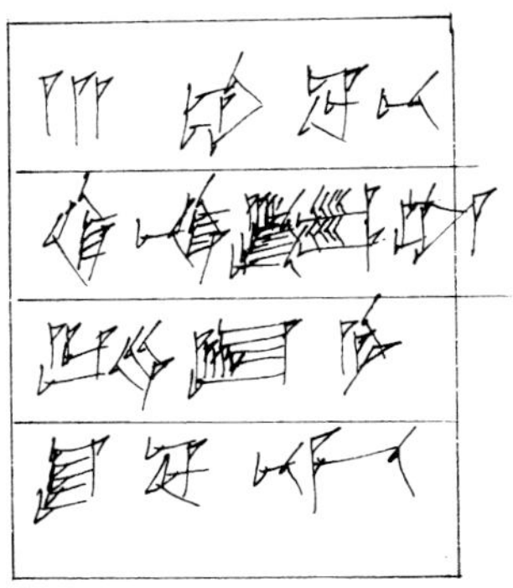

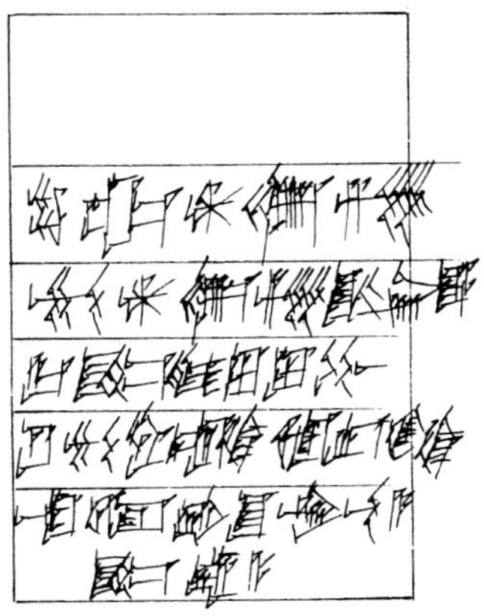

301

(II/-/AS 2)

OBV.

1. 1 alim-níta
2. 1 amar alim-níta-ga
3. 1 amar alim-SAL-ga
4. 1 máš-a-síg
5. 1 máš-ga-a-síg
6. ba-ug$_7$ u$_4$ 27-kam

REV.

7. ki Lú-diĝir-ra-ta
8. Ur-ni$_9$-ĝar
9. šu ba-ti
10. iti šeš-da-kú
11. mu ^{d}Amar-^{d}Suen lugal-e Ur-bí-lum^{ki} mu-ḫul

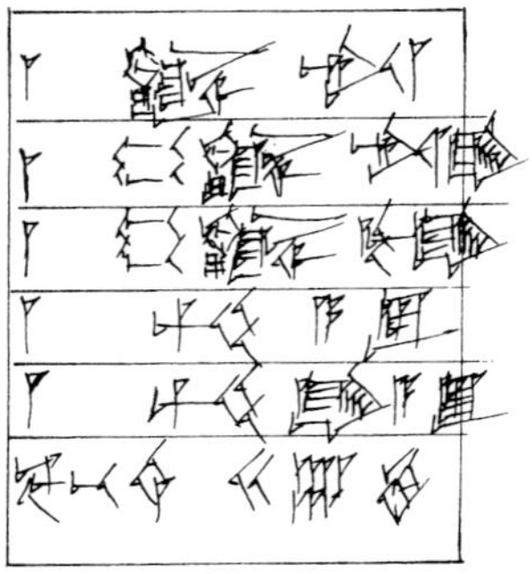

302

(XI/-/AS 2)

OBV.

1. 2 sila$_4$-ga
2. 1 kir$_{11}$-ga
3. 2 máš-ga
4. ù-tu-da
5. u$_4$ 16-kam

REV.

6. ^{d}Šul-gi-a-a-mu ì-dab$_5$
7. iti ezen me-ki-ĝál
8. mu ^{d}Amar-^{d}Suen lugal-e Ur-bí-lum^{ki} mu-ḫul

L.E.

9. 5

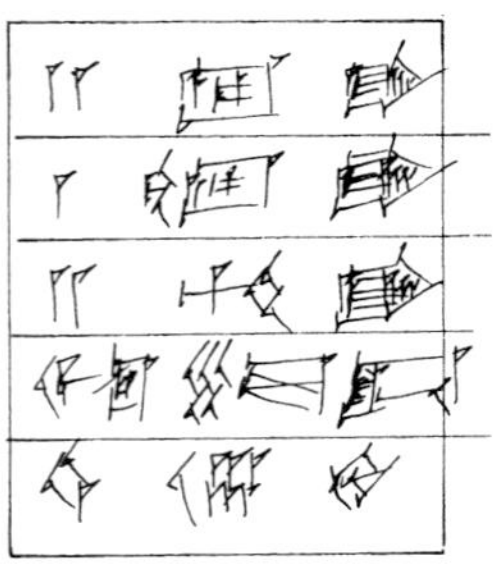

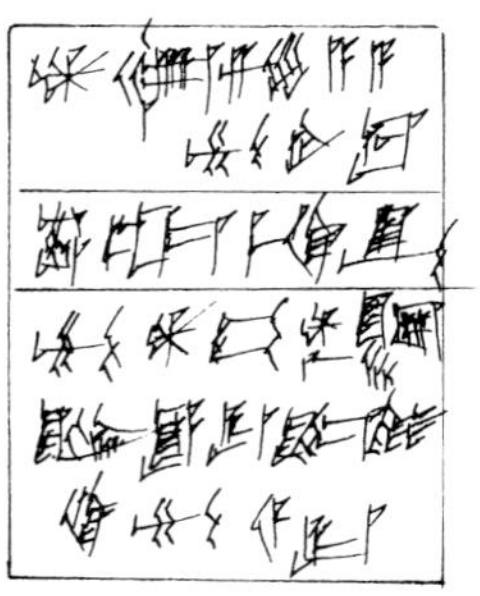

303 (II/9/AS 4)

OBV.

1. 1 [u]du
2. 1 máš
3. SI.A-a nu-bànda
4. 10 lá 1 udu 1 máš
5. *Ṣe-lu-uš*-^{d}*Da-gan*
6. 3 udu 1 máš-gal
7. 1 máš
8. *Á-píl-lí* ù-gúl
9. 2 udu niga 1 kir$_{11}$
10. Zabar-dab$_5$
11. 5 máš-gal 1 máš
12. kišib *Ṣe-lu-uš*-^{d}*Da-gan*
13. 1 gu$_4$-niga 10 lá 1 udu
14. 1 sila$_4$
15. In-nu-ri
16. 2 gu$_4$-niga 20 udu
17. 1 máš dam Nu-ì-da

REV.

18. iti-ta u$_4$ 6 ba-ra-zal
19. 2 gu$_4$-niga 20 udu
20. 1 máš Nu-ì-da
21. 1 gu$_4$-niga 10 udu
22. ^{d}Šára-kam
23. 4 udu 1 máš
24. Ur-^{d}En-líl-lá dam-gàr
25. iti-ta u$_4$ 7 ba-ra-zal
26. [ ] udu-niga Gal-la-àm-a šabra
27. iti-[t]a u$_4$ 8 ba-ra-zal
28. 2 udu-⌜niga⌝ 1 ^{mí}áš-gàr
29. *I-mi-it*-^{d}[*Eš*$_4$]-*t*[*ár*] kuš$_7$
30. 1 sila$_4$-niga 1 si[la$_4$]
31. iti-ta u$_4$ 10 lá 1 ba-ra-zal
32. nì ezen è-lu-lum šà É-saĝ-da-na^{ki}-ka
33. mu-túm ^{d}Šul-gi-*sí-im-tum*
34. *Á-píl-la-tum* ì-dab$_5$
35. [iti š]eš-da-kú
36. [m]u en ^{d}Nanna maš-e ì-pàd-da

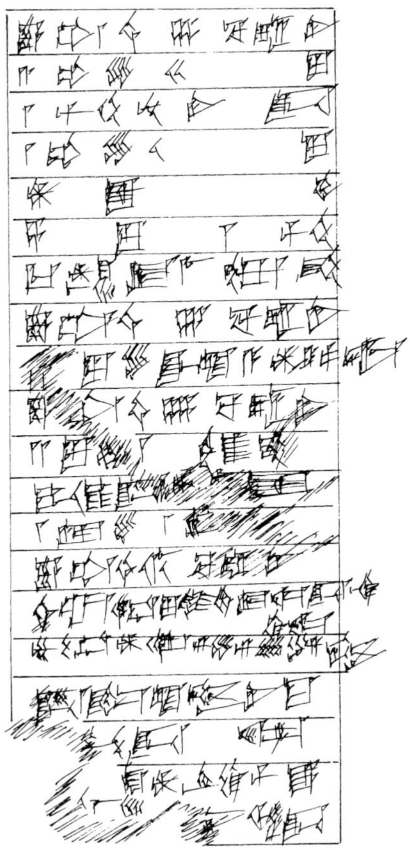

304

(II/-/AS 4)

OBV.

1. 1 máš-gal-babbar
2. u$_4$ *wa-da-al-tum*
3. 1 sila$_4$ amar
4. ba-ug$_7$ u$_4$ 8-kam
5. ki ^{d}Šul-gi-a-a-mu-ta

REV.

6. ^{d}Šul-gi-uru-mu
7. šu ba-ti
8. iti šeš-da-kú
9. mu en ^{d}Nanna ba-ḫun

L.E.

10. 2

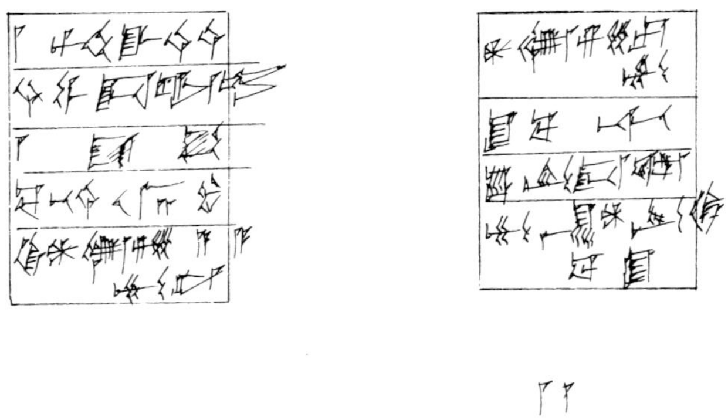

305

(XI/-/ŠS 4)

OBV.

1. 30 kuš gu$_4$-ḫi-a síg-sar
2. mu gu$_4$-si-aš-šè
3. 10 kuš gu$_4$-ḫi-a še-gín
4. 20 kuš anše-ḫi-a še-gín
5. mu še-gín-šè
6. 5 kuš udu-ḫi-a nì-kú-a

REV.

7. nì gù-dé-šè
8. é-kišib-ba-ta
9. Ur-^{d}Šul-pa-è
10. šu ba-an-ti
11. iti ezen ^{d}Me-ki-ĝál
12. mu bàd Mar-tu ba-dù

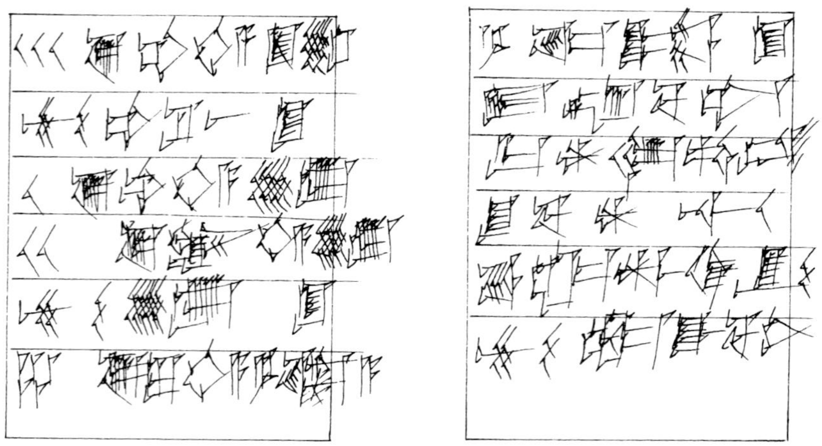

306 (VIII/21/AS 8)

OBV.
1. 0.0.1 5 sìla šim sig$_5$ kum
2. 4 sìla mun
3. 3 uzu gu$_4$ niga-šè
4. 10 sa-gi
5. 48 gú gi-ru-uš

REV.
6. é-gu$_4$-gaz
7. 10 sa-gi
8. šà nì-du$_{10}$ sila$_4$-šè
9. (BLANK)
10. u$_4$ 21-kam
11. iti šu-eš-ša
12. mu en Eridu^{ki} ba-ḫun

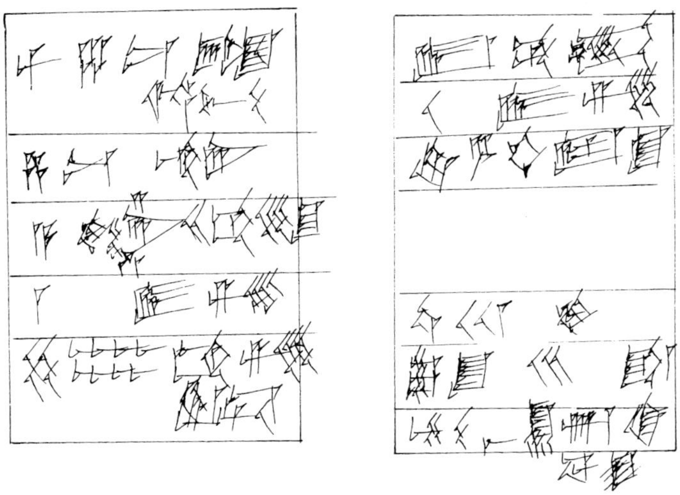

307

(-/-/Š 40)

OBV.

1. 1.2.3 zì-sig$_{15}$ gur
2. kišib Ur-zu-a
3. ki *I-la-ak-nu-id*

*4. Amar-šúba

REV.

5. SEAL
6. mu-ús-sa é ba-dù-a

Seal: Ḫa-ba-lu$_5$-gé
énsi Adab^{ki}
* Amar-šúba
dub-sar ir$_{11}$-zu

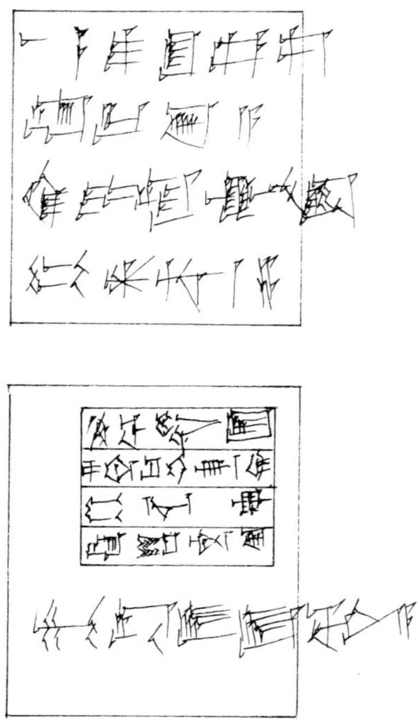

308 (date not preserved)

OBV.

(top of obverse broken)

1. [ ] x x [ ]
2. ⸢mu⸣ [ ]
3. lá-u$_x$ 5 sìla [ ] NE A [ ]
4. Lugal-si-[ ]
5. 0.0.2 8⅓ sìla ì [ ]
*6. A-kal-la kuš$_7$ [ ]
7. 0.0.1 7½ sìla ì [ ]
8. Lú-^{d}Šul-gi
9. 9 sìla ì [ ]
10. Ur-^{d}Ba-ú [ ] GAN [ ]
11. 6⅔ sìla ba [ ] x [ ]

REV.

(top of reverse broken)

12. [ ] SUR.BA [ ]
13. [x] UM [ ]
14. [ ] ba-zi [ ]
15. [ ] x [ ]
16. (BLANK)
17. [ ] DU [ ]

(bottom of reverse broken)

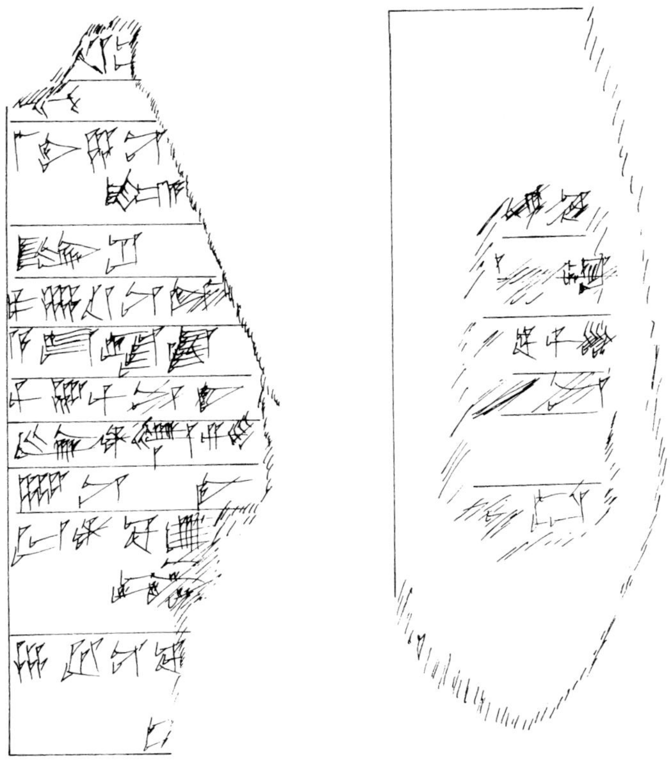

309 (date not preserved)

OBV.

1. 10 gín lá igi-6-ĝál kù-babbar
2. ki Ur-^{d}Nanše dumu Ur-ḫé-ĝál
3. igi-3-ĝál kù-[babbar]
4. Ur-ki-gu-la [dumu] Lugal-ezen
5. ki [ ]-e-la
6. 2½ gín lá 10 še k[ù-babbar]
7. ki Gu-la
8. x x [ ]

REV.

9. [ ] du[mu]
10. 5 [ ]
11. [ ]
12. [ ]
13. [ ] ^{d}Ut[u]
14. [ ] 1 sìla [ ]
15. [ ] 2 sìla [ ]
16. [ ]

310 (not dated)

OBV.

1. (*erasure*) [ ] A
2. 10.0.0 gur [ ]
3. 43+.[0.0] ⸢su⸣-ga
4. 11+.[0.0] ^{d}En-líl-lá dumu Al-[rá]-gaba
5. [ ] gur 0.1.0 zì
6. kìšib Ur-lugal santana
7. 18.2.3 5 sìla gur
8. kìšib Ni$_{9}$-ĝar-ki-du$_{10}$ GU$_{4}$ IN
9. 0.1.2 lá 1 sìla zíz [ ]
10. kìšib Lugal-kù-zu dum[u]
11. 181.3.3 4+ [sìla]
12. 57.3.2 2½ [sìla]
13. kìšib Lú-K[A]

REV.

14. 94.0.5 1 [sìla]
15. kìšib La-ni [ ]
16. 143.2.3 7+ [sìla]
17. 60.1.5 8½ sìla [ ]
18. kìšib Lú-bala-[ ]
19. 4.2.0 gur šà-dub [ ]
20. 9.3.2 4 sìla lá-u$_{x}$ še zi-ga
21. kìšib Lugal-diĝir-ra
22. 16.4.1 5 sìla lá-u$_{x}$ še zi-ga
23. kìšib Lugal-usar
24. (BLANK)

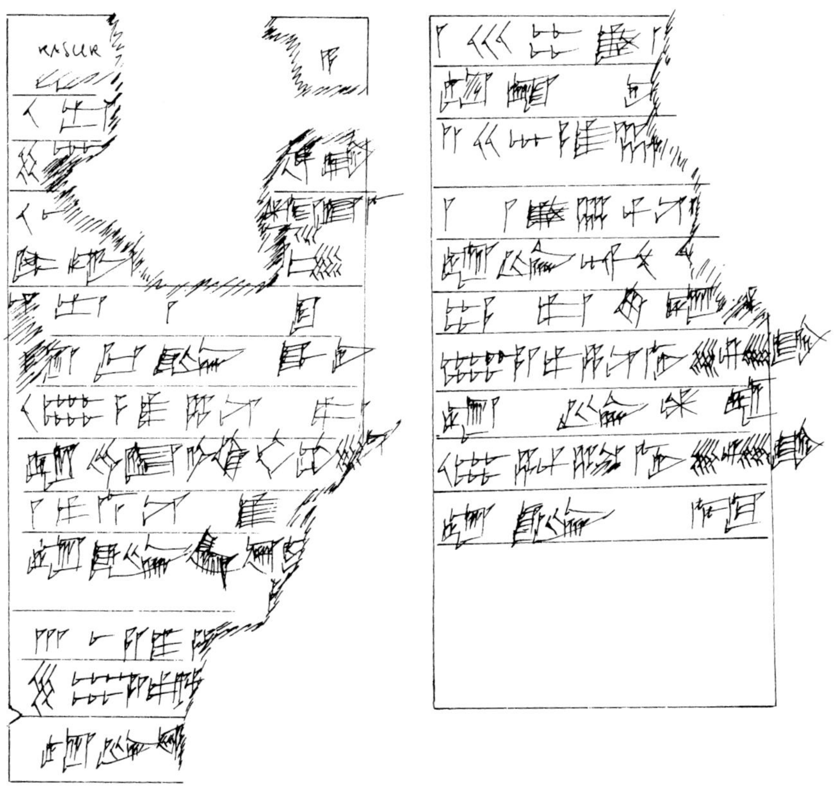

311 (not dated)

OBV.

1. 20 UŠ
2. ka-i$_7$-zi-luḫ-da
3. uru Bàd-an-na-šè
4. 10 U-bar utul
5. 1 Gu-ur$_4$
6. 1 Èr-ra-a
7. utul lugal-me
8. 1 *Nu-ḫi-lum*
9. 1 Ur-^{d}Saḫar-^{d}Ba-ú
10. 1 Lú-gín
11. 1 Gi-na
12. 1 A-a-kal-la
13. šabra Gú-⸢u$_4$-x-ka⸣-me

REV.

14. šà-ba-ni 1 gi 30
15. ù ki še-ĝeš-ì šà-ba ì-ĝál
16. 440 UŠ
17. uru Bàd-an-na-ta
18. ka-mun-ambar-ta
19. UR bu-um-šè 5 UŠ
20. 1 La-ni
21. 1 Ba-an-zi-gi
22. 1 Ur-^{d}En-líl-lá
23. 2 ^{d}Utu-me-lám
24. utul lugal-me
25. 1 Ur-^{d}Li$_9$-si$_4$ utul *Na-ra-am-ì-lí*
26. šà-ba-ni nu-KU
27. 6 UŠ na-bu-la-ta gi-luḫ-da-ta

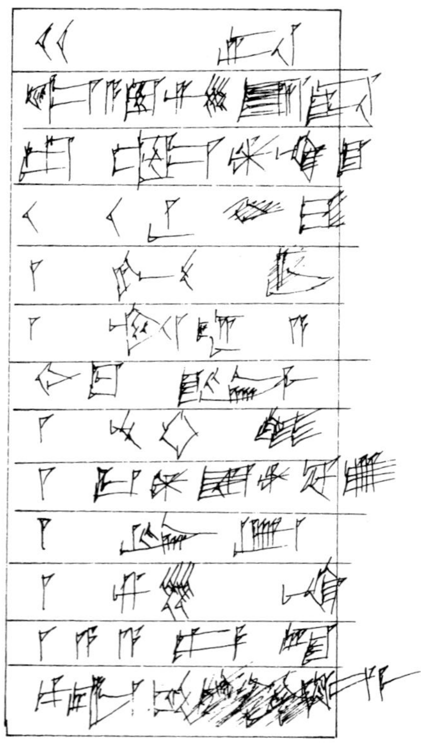

312 (date not preserved)

OBV.

(*top of obverse broken*)

1. [gì]n kù-⌜babbar⌝
2. [x] inim ma [ ]
*3. Ur-ud-da-x diĝir-x
4. dumu N[i$_{9}$]
5. Ur-^{d}Ba[ ]
6. zi lugal ⌜x x⌝
7. dam Ur-ud-da-[x]
8. lú-Ur-x-x [ ]
9. šu du$_{8}$-a-bi in-[ ]
10. Ba-ba-mu nar [ ]
11. [ ] lú [x]
12. [ ]
13. [ ] šu x x [ ]
14. [ ] ni [ ]

REV.

15. Ur-šu-ga [ ]
16. x lú [ ]
17. [ ] x [ ]
18. x SAL [ ]
19. [ ] LA [ ]
20. (B L A N K)

(*bottom of reverse broken*)

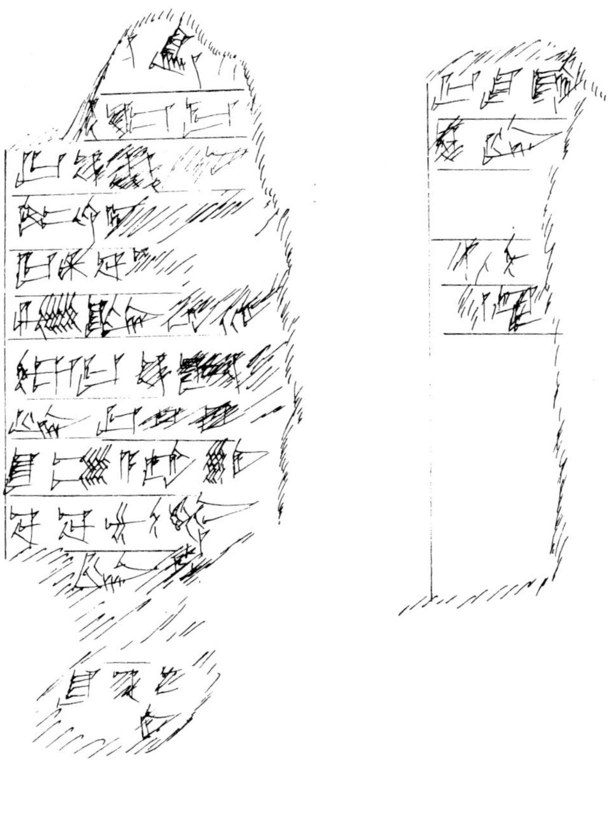

313

(date not preserved)

OBV.

1. 15 nindan uš
2. ab-sín-bi 90
3. še-bi 0.0.2 2½ sìla
4. 11 nindan uš ab-sín-bi 15
5. še-bi 3⅔ sìla 5 gín
6. 1 nindan uš ab-sín-bi 4 *(erasure)*
7. še-bi 4 sìla
8. *A-da-làl* engar dumu Im-ti-dam

*9. 1 nindan uš ab-sín-bi 18

10. [ ] 5½ sìla

(bottom half of the obverse is broken)

REV.

(top half of the reverse is broken)

11. [nindan uš] a[b-sín-bi]
12. še-bi 3⅓ sìla
13. i-ri-ib
14. (BLANK)

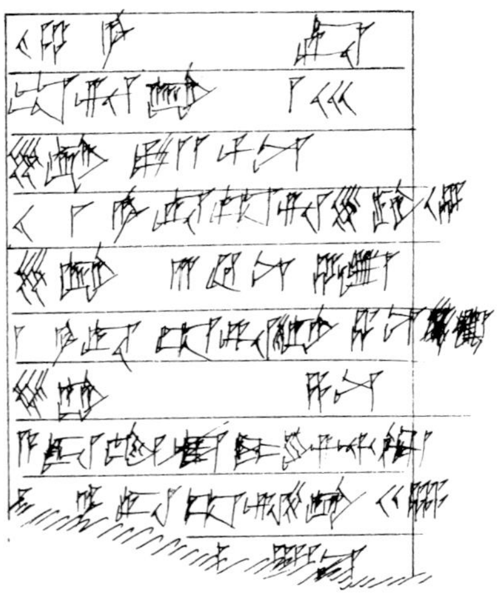

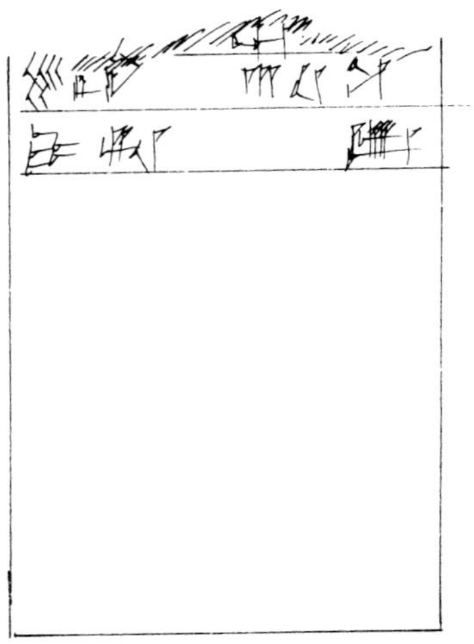

314 (date not preserved)

OBV.

i. *(top of column i broken)*

1. [ĝur]uš sig$_7$ [ ]
2. [ ] ĝuruš-sig$_7$-a 0.0.3-[ta]
3. 2 ĝuruš 0.0.2-ta
4. 7 ĝuruš sig$_7$-a 0.0.3-ta
5. 1 géme sig$_7$-a 0.0.3
6. 1 dumu 0.0.1
7. nar-me
8. 5 ĝuruš 0.1.0-ta
9. 1 ĝuruš 0.0.5
10. 1 ĝuruš 0.0.4
11. 2 ĝuruš 0.0.3-ta
12. 1 dumu 0.0.2
13. 4 dumu 0.0.1 5 (sìla)-ta
14. 4 dumu 0.0.1-ta
15. 1 ĝuruš šu-g[i$_4$]

(bottom of column i broken)

ii. *(top of column ii broken)*

16. [ ]
17. 1 [ ]
18. 1 dum[u]
19. é-íl [ ]
20. 4 ĝuruš [ ]
21. 1 ĝuruš [ ]
22. bur-saĝ [ ]
23. 1 ĝuruš [ ]
24. 1 dumu 0.0.1 [ ]
25. ga-íl-me
26. 4 géme 0.0.3-ta
27. 1 dumu 0.0.2
28. [ ] x [ ]

(bottom of column ii broken)

rev.

(reverse not preserved)

315 (date not preserved)

OBV.

(*top of obverse broken*)

1. [x]
2. [ ] 4⅓ sìla x [ ]
3. [L]ú-SI.ĜAR [ ]
4. [ ] A-kal-la
5. [ ] ⅓ sìla ì-nun
*6. [ ] Na-ba-ša$_6$
7. [x] Nin-gu-la
8. [ ]

REV.

(*top of reverse broken*)

9. [ ]
10. [ ] x [ ]
11. [x] sìla [ ]
12. [ ] x [ ]
*13. [ ] sízkur kam [ ]
14. [x]
15. [ ] 6 [ ]

(*bottom of reverse broken*)

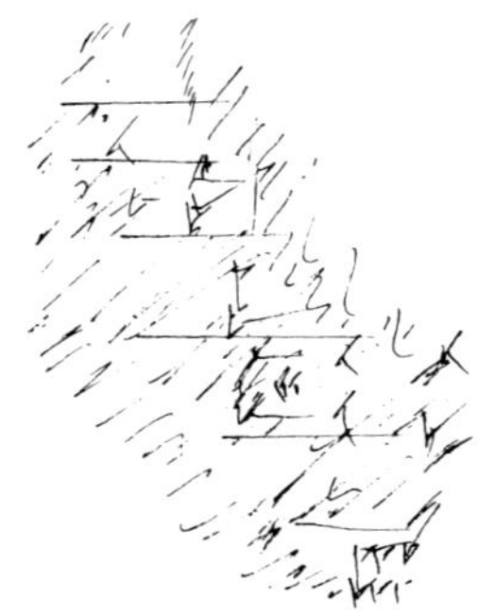

316 (date not preserved)

OBV.

1. 1 Ur-^{d}Namma dumu Da-a-mu
2. [ ] ^{d}Lama-ra DU [ ] x ŠEŠ.KI.A x
3. [Lu]gal-gú-tuku ugula
4. [Ša-a]l-maḫ šeš [ ] ⌜x x x⌝
5. [ ] ^{d}Inanna

REV.

(*top of reverse destroyed*)

*6. [ ] ḫi-a [ ]
7. [l]ú-ma
8. [ ] A [ ]
*9. é-kìšib-ba [ ]
10. na-kab-tum

317 (date not preserved)

OBV.

(top of obverse broken)

1. [ ] še zi [ ]
2. [ ] En-líl-lá [ ]
3. [ ] ḫa-na [ ]
4. (BLANK)
5. [ ] dam Ur-ša$_6$-[ga]
6. [ ] BI LUL [x]
7. [ ] gu lugal [x]
8. [ ] máš x [ ]
9. [x] ḫa [x]
10. [ ] x [ ]

(bottom of obverse broken)

REV.

(reverse not preserved)

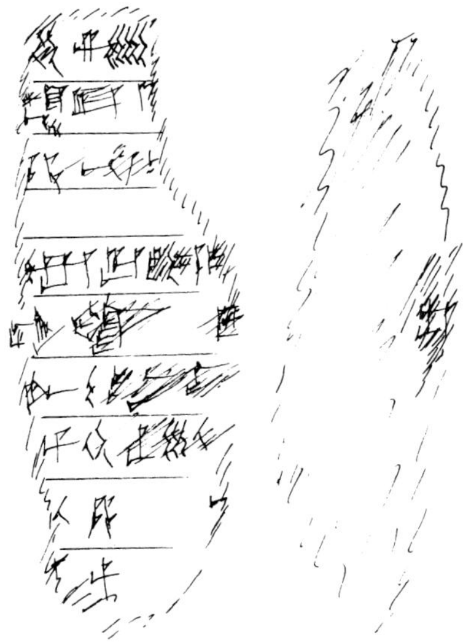

318 (date not preserved)

OBV.
i. *(top of obverse broken)*

1. [ ] x [ ]
2. [ ] kù [ ]
3. [ ] ĝál-la [ ]
4. [ ] ḪAR^{ki} [ ]
5. [ ]ki [ ]

(bottom of obverse broken)

REV.
ii. *(top of reverse broken)*

6. A [ ]
7. x [ ]

iii. 8. [x]

9. [ ] gal
10. [ ] šè
11. [ ] me

(bottom of reverse broken)

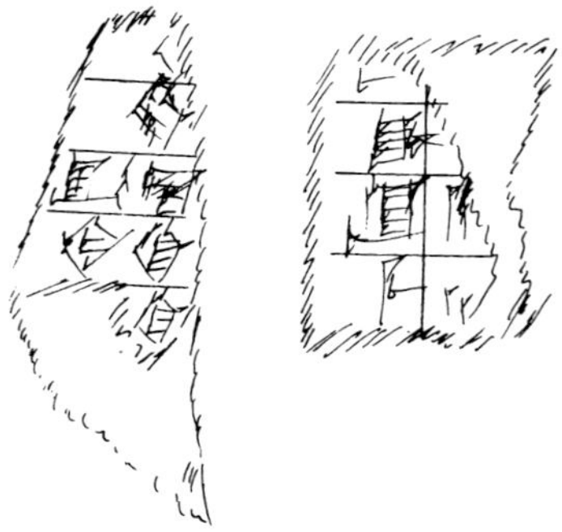

Glossary of Selected Terms

(*passim* indicates 4 or more occurrences in the text)

-A-

^{ĝeš}a-da *plank*
- ^{ĝeš}a-da má 120 gur: 280: 2, 5
- ^{ĝeš}a-da má 60 gur: 280: 3, 6

^{kuš}a-ĝá-lá *leather sack*
- ^{kuš}a-ĝá-lá: 279: 1

a-ĝál-la
- túg ĝeš-a-ĝál-la: 63: 9

^{ĝeš}a-ra *part of a boat*
- ^{ĝeš}a-ra má 60 gur: 280: 1

a-rá *times, "1st time," "2nd time," etc.*
- a-rá 1-kam: 1: *passim*; 62: 3; 86: 16; 236: 14; 286: 5; 291: 79
- a-rá 2-kam: 1: *passim*; 62: 4; 291: 106
- a-rá 4-kam: 175: 6
- a-rá [ ]: 291: 84
- áb a-rá 2: 284: 8

a-ru-a *gift, donation*
- 104: 17
- ^{ĝeš}kiri$_6$ a-ru-a Lú-^{d}Nanše: 74: 13
- nar a-ru-a ^{d}Amar-^{d}Suen-ka-me: 293: 3
- nar a-ru-a ^{d}*Šu*-^{d}Suen-ka-me: 293: 2

a-saĝ *a designation of flour*
- zì-a-saĝ: 64: 28

a-šà *field*
- (For individual fields, see index)
- a-šà: 188: 3; 282: 5
- še-ba un-ĝa$_6$ ù á-lú-ḫun-ĝá a-šà: 69: 7

á *side, strength, wage, work*
- 34: 5
- á-bi: 14: *passim*; 63: *passim*
- á géme uš-bar Nina^{ki}: 30: 2
- á-gul-la: 14: 187, 194
- á-ḫun-ĝá: 1: *passim*; 282: 4
- á iti-da: 65: 17
- á še-kéš-rá: 10: 6
- á še-kin-ku$_5$: 10: 3
- á túg tag-a-ra U.NU-a ^{ĝeš}ga-ríg-ak túg ĝeš-a-ĝál-la: 63: 9, 136
- á u$_4$-te-na-bi: 45: 11
- še-ba un-ĝa$_6$ ù á-lú-ḫun-ĝá a-šà: 69: 7

á-gam *measure of liquid capacity*
- ì á-gam (see under ì)

á-u$_4$-te-na *evening*
- 45:11

ab-ba *father, elder*
- še-kíkken ab-ba ab-ba ù engar nu-bànda-gu$_4$: 127: 2
- ab-ba-uru: 184: 9

ab-sín *furrow*
- níg-ús ab-sín: 313: *passim*

áb *cow*
- 284: 36, 37; 291: *passim*
- áb 1: 284: 1, 54
- áb 2/ mu-2: 284: 9, 52
- áb 2/ mu-2 ba-ug$_7$: 288: *passim*
- áb 2/ mu-2 šu-gíd: 287: 14
- áb-2-ĝeš-šè: 92: 20
- áb 2 SU: 284: 53
- áb 3: 284: 20, 22, 51
- áb 3/ mu-3 ba-ug$_7$: 288: *passim*
- áb a-rá 2: 284: 8
- áb-é-tur-ḫi-a: 267: 9
- áb-máḫ: 91: 1; 92: 18; 126: 1; 142: 1; 145: 1; 284: 31, 35, 50
  - áb-máḫ ba-ug$_7$: 288: *passim*
  - áb-máḫ šu-gi$_4$: 92: 22
  - áb-maḫ šu-gíd: 284: 25
- áb šu-gíd: 287: 13; 291: 25
- gu$_4$-áb: 284: 55
- gu$_4$-áb ba-ug$_7$: 288: 58, 109

ad-gub$_5$ *reed-worker*
- 19: 30, 36, 46; 20: 27, 33, 41

ad$_x$ (lú-*šeššig*) *carcass*
- ad$_x$ [ ]: 277: 14
- ad$_x$ sila$_4$ ba-ug$_7$: 153: 2
- ad$_x$ udu: 38: 10; 154: 1, 2; 164: 1
- ad$_x$ udu ba-ug$_7$: 153: 1

aga-ús *soldier*
- 195: 14; 262: 4, 7
- aga-ús énsi: 197: 6
- aga-ús GN: 62: 12, 13
- aga-ús-gal: 195: 6, 10; 200: 3; 215: 2; 227: 8, 13, 15; 229: 12; 232: 11, 22; 233:

passim; 261: 20; 263: 9, 14
aga-ús saĝa: 3: 74, 75
aga-ús šabra: 19: 12; 20: 12
dabin aga-ús lugal: 244: 4
šà-gal aga-ús: 265: 14

ak *to do*
al ak: 7: 2, 8
nì-gul ak: 7: 4, 10

al *hoe*
al ak: 7: 2, 8

alan *statue, image*
aga-ús alan-da: 262: 7
ugula alan-da: 262: 6

alim *bison*
alim-níta ba-ug_7: 301: 1
amar alim-níta-ga ba-ug_7: 301: 2
amar-alim-SAL-ga ba-ug_7: 301: 3
šà-gal alim: 45: 6

amar *calf*
1: *passim*; 52: 22; 53: 19
amar alim-níta-ga ba-ug_7: 301: 2
amar-alim-SAL-ga ba-ug_7: 301: 3
amar ba-ug_7: 1: 124;
amar-gu_4 mu-1 ba-ug_7: 288: *passim*
amar-mašda níta DN: 298: 1
amar-PEŠ mu-1 ba-ug_7: 288: *passim*
še-amar-e kú-a: 46: 3; 56: 8; 57: 8

ambar *marsh, reed-bed*
bisaĝ ambar-sur-ra: 180: 2
en-nu-da-ambar-a: 3: 68
ka-mun-ambar-ta: 311: 18

anše *donkey*
92: 5, 11; 188: 9; 278: 2
anše-bar: 267: 13
anše-ĝeš-ḫi-a: 267: 7
anše-níta: 92: *passim*
anše-níta šu-gi_4: 278: 3
anše zi-gúm-ma-šè ĝen-na: 221:15
kuš anše-ḫi-a še-gín: 305: 4
šà-gal anše zi-gúm-ma: 44: 16

apin *plow*
apin-a: 14: 165
gána-apin-a: 1: *passim*; 9: 23; 12: *passim*
iku apin-a: 14: 162

ar-za-na *barley groats*
93: 16, 73
ar-za-na ninda-àr-ra sig_5: 134: 3
šagina ar-za-na: 283: 21

àr *milled, ground*
ninda-àr-ra: 45: 1, 7: 61: 28; 64: 60; ; 111: 2; 273: 42; 131: 1; 134: 3; 139: 2; 273: 19
še-àr-ra: 127: 2

^{ĝeš}ásal *poplar*
273: *passim*

aslag *fuller*
19: 14, 21; 20: 20; 80: *passim*; 277: 1, 7, 11

^{mí}áš-gàr *young female goat*
78: 5; 285: 2; 303: 28

-B-

ba *rations, share, to give*
ì-ba diĝir-re-ne: 156: 6
ì-ba-eš: 293: 7
síg-ba (see under síg)
še-ba (see under še)

^{zì}ba-ba *porridge*
^{zì}ba-ba še: 64: *passim*; 93: 75
^{zì}ba-ba sig_5: 64: *passim*; 93: 28, 38

ba-ba-$munu_4$ *porridge of malt-soaked grain*
65: 16, 26

ba-ug_7 *dead*
ba-ug_7 šà sig_5: 284: 40, 41
dumu ba-ug_7: 14: 32, 80
ad_x $sila_4$ ba-ug_7: 153: 2
ad_x udu ba-ug_7: 153: 1
(also see under áb, alim, amar, gu_4, máš, $sila_4$, udu)

baḫar *potter*
19: 26; 20: 25

bala *period of office, turn*
bala énsi Sippar[ki]: 292: 38
bala ezen-maḫ Naĝ-su[ki]: 158: 7
bala gub-ba: 14: *passim*; 24: 2; 25: 9; 26: 3; 27: 3
bala-šè: 133: 2
bala tuš-a: 14: *passim*; 31: 3
é-a-bala-a: 61: 35
mu ba-a-al-la-a-šè: 57: 28
šà-bala: 61: 32; 62: 23; 65: 24, 27; 68: 14; 93: 73, 76, 78; 169: 5
túg ba-lá u_4-8-kam: 76: 70

balaĝ *lyre* or *harp*
balaĝ-u_4-da é GN: 111: 3

^{ĝeš}banšur *table*
^{ĝeš}banšur-ḫi-a: 267: 31
^{ĝeš}banšur sig$_5$-ḫi-a: 267: 30

bappir *beer bread*
bappir ba-ab-tag; 151: 5

bar *outer(?) (garment)*
túg-bar: 82: *passim*

^{túg}bar-si *type of garment*
^{túg}bar-si 3-kam-ús: 63: 64
^{túg}bar-si 4-kam-ús: 63: 65

bar-su *plucked*
udu-níta bar-su: 73: 46

bisaĝ *basket*
bisaĝ ambar-sur-ra: 180: 2
bisaĝ-dub-ba: 180: 1; 181: 1; 182: 1; 183: 1
bisaĝ má-gur$_8$-ra: 45: 3

bur-saĝ *a type of offering?*
314: 22

-D-

da-ba-tum a textile
túg da-ba-tum: 118: 18

dab$_5$ *to hold, seize, take, hire, receive*
ì-dab$_5$: 5: 12; 8: 3, 6; 82: 16; 126: 5; 133: 4; 142: 4; 145: 5; 278: 8; 284: 30; 302: 6; 303: 34
lú-dab$_5$-ba (see lú-dab$_5$-ba)
mu mušen-šè dab$_5$-ba: 44: 9
ḫé-dab$_5$ ^{ĝeš}tukul-e dab$_5$-ba: 118: 19
ĝeš-e-dab$_5$-ba: 164: 2
^{ĝeš}tukul-e dab$_5$-ba-me: 8: 9; 19: 42
še šà-gu$_4$ nu-dab$_5$-me: 69: 9

dabin *barley flour*
24: 1; 30: 1; 44: 1, 8; 56: 33; 58: 1, 9; 64: *passim*; 93: *passim*; 132: 1; 134: 2; 167: 1; 177: 1; 189: 15; 194: 7; 206: 19; 213: 3; 218: 16; 221: 19; 224: 2, 7, 11; 234: 16; 235: 2; 243: 5; 244: 4; 255: 3; 265: 14
dabin kaskal-šè: 213: 19; 262: 3
dabin šà uru: 213: 18

daḫ-ḫu *substitute?*
98: 4
daḫ-ḫu lugal: 67: 30

dam *wife, spouse*
303: 17
dam-a-ni: 82: 18
dam-ni: 21: 8
dam-su: 268: 4

dam-gàr *merchant*
14: 115; 19: 38, 45; 20: 35, 40; 64: 55; 184: 10; 295: 5; 303: 24
é-nì-gur$_{11}$ dam-gàr: 155: 8

dé *to pour, winnow*
naĝa-bi nu-dé: 87: 3

de$_6$ *to bring, to carry*
gú-un de$_6$-a 180: 7
zì Ĝír-su^{ki}-ta de$_6$-a: 93: 25

dida *beer, an ingredient in beer*
178: 1; 189: 14; 190: 15; 192: 16; 221: 19; 234: 16; 241: 10; 255: 3
dida ĝen: 113: 1; 115: 1, 3; 194: 6; 217: 1
dida ĝen kaskal-šè: 230: 2
dida kaskal-šè: 200: 6, 9, 18
dida sig$_5$: 65: 17; 110: 3, 5; 116: 1, 7; 249: 2, 11; 262: 5
dug dida: 159: 1

didli *assorted, various, separately*
ì-dub didli: 56: 46, 61
ku$_4$-ra didli: 7: 11
kurušda didli-bi: 184: 15
lá-u$_x$ su-ga sipa didli: 155: 4
lú-dab$_5$-ba uru didli-me: 224: 12

diri *excess, addition*
47: 21; 55: 18; 63: 160, 162, 164; 72: 6; 82: 25; 93: 19; 94: 9
diri-àm: 1: 337
diri nì-ka$_9$-ak: 67: 53
diri zi-ga: 284: 66
iti diri 1-àm a-ba ì-ĝál: 67: 40, 95

du$_8$ *to bake*
ninda du$_8$-a: 253: 5; 265: 2

du$_8$-ḫu-um
šuku-kišib-du$_8$-ḫu-um: 64: 81
nì-ù-du$_8$-ḫu-um 93: 40

^{kuš}du$_{10}$-gan *leather bag*
dub-ba ^{kuš}du$_{10}$-gan ĝar-ĝar: 197: 16

dub *clay tablet*
dub-ba ^{kuš}du$_{10}$-gan ĝar-ĝar: 197: 16
dub-gíd-da: 182: 2
dub-gíd-da ì-dub: 183: 2
ša dub: 226: 14
šà dub: 310: 19

dub-dub *a heap (of flour)*
zì-dub-dub: 44: 3; 111: 1; 113: 3; 115: 6; 116: 4, 10; 117: 5
dub-nagar
4: 6
dub-sar *scribe*
3: 61; 10: seal; 21: seal; 30: seal; 43: seal; 46: seal; 79: seal; 130: seal; 141: seal; 151: seal; 159: seal; 163: seal; 164: seal; 167: seal; 172: seal; 174: seal; 176: seal; 177: seal; 178: seal; 221: 20; 259: 17; 280: seal; 281: seal; 297: 7; 298: 7; 307: seal
dub-sar a-šà érin-na: 3: 72
dub-sar é-kišib-ba: 184: 3
dub-sar érin-na: 3: 70
dub-sar gu$_4$-apin: 3: 60
dub-sar gu$_4$-udu: 184: 18
dub-sar mar-sa: 66: 24
dub-sar PN: 212: 15, 18; 226: 11
dub-sar-tur-tur: 38: 4
dub-sar zì-da ba-ĝar: 64: 105
dug *jar, vessel*
dug dida: 159: 1
dug-KIN: 166: 1
^{dug}gir$_{16}$ ga-sig$_7$-a: 102: 1
duḫ *bran, residue*
45: 8; 106: 1; 107: 1; 108: 1; 270: 1
duḫ a-šà ^{d}Šul-pa-è: 272: 28
duḫ-babbar: 45: 2
duḫ-ĝen: 163: 1
duḫ-ĝi$_6$: 45: 9
dumu *son*
dumu PN (see personal name index)
dumu ba-ug$_7$: 14: *passim*
dumu (géme): 34: *passim*; 35 *passim*; 36: *passim*; 314: *passim*
dumu (ĝuruš): 314: *passim*
dumu lú-didli: 41: 23
dumu nu-bànda (see under nu-bànda)
dumu sipa ^{anše}kunga$_2$: 41: 11
dumu-šeš-a-ni: 19: 22
dumu-da-ba *cf.* dumu dab$_5$-ba
dumu-da-ba: 14: *passim*
dumu dab$_5$-ba *a type of field worker*
dumu dab$_5$-ba: 104: *passim*; 173: 9
nu-bànda dumu-dab$_5$-ba: 238: 12
še ur$_5$-ra dumu dab$_5$-ba: 138: 2; 173: 2
cf. dumu-da-ba: 14: *passim*
dusu *transportation basket*
dusu: 120: 1, 2, 3

-E-

é *house, household, temple*
1: *passim*; 28: 2; 78: 31
é DN: 1: *passim*; 11: 5; 14: *passim*; 21: 11; 24: 3; 26: 8; 57: 48; 82: *passim*; 142: 6; 184: 14; 226: 14
é GN: 111: 3
é PN: 1: 215; 256: 10
é-a-bala-a: 61: 35
é-gibil: 142: 8
é-gidri: 249: 8
é gu-zal-lá: 27: 3
é-gu$_4$: 292: 21
é-gu$_4$-gaz: 306: 6
é-íl: 314: 19
é-kaš$_4$: 41: 13
é-kin-a: 60: 17
é-kin-ĝá: 152: 2
é kurušda: 184: 12
é-la-la: 34: 13
é-lugal: 155: 10
é-nì-gur$_{11}$ dam-gàr: 155: 8
é-niĝin: 155: 5
é-nun saĝa: 6: 4
é šu-ga-lam-ma: 1: 109
é-šu-šúm-ma: 63: 14, 140
é temen-na: 276: 11
é-tukul: 41: 8
é udu: 10: 9; 37: 5; 155: 2
é-udu-ĝá-nun-ĝeš: 171: 6
é-gal *palace*
93: 18; 155: 2
é-gal-la ba-ku$_4$: 147: 4
é-gal-la ba-an-ku$_4$: 143: 4
é-gal-la ba-an-ku$_4$ šà Urí^{ki}-ma: 140: 6
é-gal gú-túl-ta: 145: 3
é-gal lugal ba-an-ku$_4$: 102: 2
gu$_4$ é-gal-ke$_4$ íb-uru$_4$-a-šè: 56: 50, 66
zi-ga é-gal-šè íb-uru$_4$-a-šè 149:5–6
lú-ḫun-ĝá é-gal-la: 13: 5
šà é-gal: šà é-gal: 93: 18; 126: 2; 297: 2

é-kíkken *mill*
19: 57; 20: 46

é-kišib-ba *storeroom*
é-kišib-ba: 4: 7; 63: 21; 184: 3; 288: 75; 305: 8; 316: 9
é-kišib-ba énsi-gal: 166: 2
é-kišib-ba mar-sa: 165: 5

é-muḫaldim *kitchen*
é-muḫaldim: 184: 16; 287: 15

é-uz-ga
é-uz-ga: 287: 11

è *to go out*
še ĝeš è-a: 3: 49; 15: 25; 16: 9; 17: 7
uru-ta nu-è: 14: *passim*

è-lu-lum *a festival*
ezen è-lu-lum šà É-saĝ-da-na^{ki}-ka: 303: 32

egir *after*
egir KA.SI.KA-ta: 154: 7

eme-gi *(a breed of sheep)*
udu-eme-gi-ḫi-a: 267: 11

^{ĝeš}eme-sig *plank*
^{ĝeš}eme-sig má: 165: 1, 2

en *priest*
en Lagaš^{ki}: 108: 2

en-nu *to watch, guard*
en-nu-da-ambar-a: 3: 68
lú-dab$_5$-ba en-nu: 37: 8

engar *farmer*
9: 15, 18, 21; 14: *passim*; 15: *passim*; 16: 2, 6; 17: 2; 18: *passim*; 87: 5; 92: *passim*; 174:2; 278: 4; 313: 8
engar-búr: 14: 99, 151
engar gu-la: 136: 5
engar ĝeš-ì: 3: 73
engar nu-bànda: 92: 13; 127: 2
engar ^{d}Šul-gi: 145: 4
še engar-e sàg-ga 174:2

énsi *governor*
59: 4; 110: 9; 216: 4; 223: 11; 238: 9; 286: 6; 291: 78
énsi-ke$_4$ ì-lá: 125: 4
énsi Adab^{ki}: 307: seal
énsi Babili^{ki}: 291: 75
énsi Lagaš^{ki}: 100: 7
énsi Nibru^{ki}: 287: 6; 295: 1
énsi ÚR×Ú^{ki}: 295: 5
aga-ús énsi: 197: 6
bala énsi Sippar^{ki}: 292: 38
é-kišib-ba énsi-gal: 166: 2
géme-kíkken énsi: 184: 21
kaš sig$_5$ énsi: 62: 14
kišib énsi: 59: 13; 63: 89; 129: 11; 147: 5
ní énsi: 14: 46, 102
sipa énsi: 82: 20
šà énsi: 39: 22; 40: 23
ugula kíkken énsi-ka: 121: seal

erēbu *to enter*
i-ri-ib: 313: 13

^{ĝeš}erin *cedar*
^{ĝeš}erin: 267: 23

érin *people, troops*
12: 22; 14: *passim*; 26: 1; 31: 1; 80: 11, 16; 191: 15, 18
dub-sar a-šà érin-na: 3: 72
dub-sar érin-na: 3: 70
érin bala gub-ba: 24: 2
érin bala-tuš-a: 31: 3
érin-bi ^{d}En-ki sá mu-ra-du$_{11}$-me: 283: 18
érin [ ] ^{d}Nanše ĝá-dù-[ ]: 283: 20
érin é DN: 24: 3
érin é-tukul: 41: 8
érin ḫun-ĝá: 13: 7
érin ḫun-ĝá bala-tuš-a: 14: *passim*
érin i$_7$-NE-tum-mal gub-ba: 93: 35
érin Naĝ-su^{ki}: 80: 9
érin šà-gu$_4$: 11: 2, 7
érin še kin: 179: 2; 185: 4; 186: 4; 194: 4; 255: 14; 258: 12
šà-gal érin-na: 22: 3
šà-gal érin bala gub-ba: 24: 2; 25: 9; 26: 3; 27: 3
šà-gal érin i$_7$-NE-tum-mal gub-ba: 93: 35
še-érin: 180: 2

ésir *bitumen*
ésir-é-a: 59: *passim*

éš-gàr *assignment*
šà-gal éš-gàr: 42: 2

èš *shrine*
èš ^{d}Inanna: 292: 29
èš ^{d}Nanše: 67: 60

èš-èš *festival day*
67: 83

èš-èš u$_4$-sakar u$_4$-15: 67: 31; 110: 2; 112: 2

èš-ta-gur-ra *redistribution center*
283: 26

eša *emmer wheat flour*
64: *passim*; 93: 3, 15; 113: 4; 115: 7; 116: 5, 11; 117: 6

ezen *festival*
passim in month names; 117: 14
ezen è-lu-lum šà É-saĝ-da-na^{ki}-ka: 303: 32
ezen-maḫ: 142: 3; 158: 7
ezen ^{d}Nanna: 283: 28
nì ezen x-šè: 117: 16
nì-ezen-ma: 67: 48, 50, 109

-G-

ga *milk*
284: *passim*
ga (see under kir$_{11}$, máš, sila$_4$)

ga-àr *cream*
267: 21

^{ĝeš}ga-ríg-ak *comb*
síg ^{ĝeš}ga-ríg-ak: 63: *passim*

ga-ru *for* ĝar
ĝeš-túg ga-ru-dam: 184: 22

gab-ús *shepherd*(?) [cf. ePSD: ga-ab-ús]
géme Mar-tu gab-ús udu-gukkal-me: 29: 3

gada *flax* or *linen*
túg-gada: 191: 9

gala *lamentation priest*
14: 113; 19: 8; 20: 8
gala-maḫ: 111: 4; 113: 7
gala Gú-ab-ba^{ki}: 184: 17
gala Nina^{ki}: 184: 4

gána *field*
gána-apin-a: 1: *passim*; 9: 23; 12: *passim*
gána-gu$_4$: 16: 3, 7; 17: 2; 56: 2; 87: 4
še gána-gu$_4$: 56: 2
še gána-uru$_4$-lá: 56: 5

gazi *a spice, possibly mustard*
88:12; 273: 20, 44

géme *female slave, servant*
19: 49, 54; 20: 43; 33: 4, 5, 14; 34: *passim*; 35: 1, 2; 63: *passim*; 80: *passim*; 283: 19; 314: 26
géme-kíkken: 23: 7; 283: 17
géme-kíkken énsi: 184: 21
géme Mar-tu: 288: 102
géme Mar-tu gab-ús udu-gukkal-me: 29: 3
géme sig$_7$-a: 314: 5
géme u$_4$ 1-šè: 63: *passim*
géme u$_4$-x-kam: 79: 1, 2, 3
géme un-ĝa$_6$: 288: 88
géme uš-bar: 30: 2; 32: 2; 34: 11; 153: 6; 154: 3
nì-kú-a-géme-tur: 93: 26

géme-kar-kid (géme-kar-^{kid}kid★) *prostitute*
19: 1; 20: 1; 36: 5★, 6★

gi *reed*
gi-kaskal: 273: 26, 45
^{gi}kid: 273: 26, 45
sa-gi: 273: *passim*; 306: 4, 7
sa-gi-ku$_6$: 273: *passim*

gi-na *straight, reliable*
im-ma-gi-na: 67: 77

gi-tab-ba *labor involving reeds*
14: 166

gi-ru-uš *a type of reed*
273: *passim*; 306: 5

gi$_4$ *to return, come back*
gi$_4$: 83: 3
gi$_4$-gi$_4$-BA mu lugal-bi ì-pàd: 158: 8
gibil *new*
é-gibil: 142: 8

gín *shekel, measure of weight*
9, 12, 29; 60: *passim*; 63: *passim*; 70: 10, 11, 12; 76: 22, 44, 46; 90: 1; 93: 63, 66; 99: 2; 101: *passim*; 112: 1; 123: 2; 125: 2; 129: *passim*; 143: 1; 161: 1; 169: 1; 170: 1; 272: 33, 34, 35; 282: 1; 309: 1, 6; 312: 1
gín ì 188: *passim*; 197: *passim*; 201: *passim*; 210: *passim*; 212: *passim*; 217: 3, 7; 219: *passim*; 225: 2, 5, 8; 226: *passim*; 238: *passim*; 245: *passim*; 258: *passim*; 259: *passim*; 264: 3, 7, 10; 265: *passim*

^{dug}gir$_{16}$ *jar*
^{dug}gir$_{16}$ ga-sig$_7$-a: 102: 1

gu-la *great, large*
74: 20, 27

^{ĝeš}gu-za *chair, throne*
^{ĝeš}gu-za-ḫi-a: 267: 25
^{ĝeš}gu-za sig$_5$-ḫi-a: 267: 24

gu-za-lá *chair-bearer, throne-bearer*
gu-za-lá: 27: 6; 58: 7; 60: 14
gú *talent, measure of weight*, = 30 ma-na
63: *passim*; 70: 10, 11; 76: *passim*; 77: *passim*; 122: 2; 273: *passim*
gú *edge or shore*
é-gal gú-túl-ta: 145: 3
gú-gal *chick-pea*
162: 1
gú-nida *a type of emmer wheat*
89: 23
zíz-gú-nida: 89: 4
gú-tar *back of the head*
síg gú-tar: 63: *passim*
gú-un *tribute*
gú-un de$_6$-a: 180: 7
gù-dé
nì gù-dé-šè: 305: 7
gu$_4$ *ox*
2: 13; 12: 22; 46: 1; 47: 23, 24; 48: 10, 11; 49: 20, 21; 50: 17, 18; 51: 19, 20; 52: 19, 20; 53: 17, 18; 54: 11, 12; 82: 25; 106: 2; 126: 2; 210: 16; 286: 1; 291: *passim*; 295: 10
gu$_4$ DN: 17: 9
gu$_4$ 1: 284: 16, 60
gu$_4$ 1 ù-tu-da: 284: 4
gu$_4$ 2: 284: 23, 59
gu$_4$ 2/ mu-2 ba-ug$_7$: 288: *passim*
gu$_4$ 3: 284: 57
gu$_4$ 3/ mu-3 ba-ug$_7$: 288: *passim*
gu$_4$ 3 mu-gu$_4$-2-šè: 284: 58
gu$_4$-áb: 284: 55
gu$_4$-áb ba-ug$_7$: 288: 58, 109
gu$_4$-apin-bi: 267: 8
gu$_4$ ba-ug$_7$: 300; 1
gu$_4$ é-gal-ke$_4$ íb-uru$_4$-a-šè: 56: 50, 66
gu$_4$-gal: 284: 56
gu$_4$-gal ba-ug$_7$: 288: *passim*
gu$_4$ gibil-ka: 278: 5
gu$_4$-ĝeš: 92: 19, 21; 142: 2; 266: 10; 267: 6; 278: 1
gu$_4$-ĝeš-ùr: 11: 1, 6
gu$_4$ ḫal-ḫal: 291: 80, 82
gu$_4$ na-kab-tum: 133: 1; 142: 3
gu$_4$ niga: 295: 7; 303: *passim*
gu$_4$-numun: 12: *passim*; 13: *passim*
gu$_4$-re zi-ga-me: 211: 13
gu$_4$ šu-gíd: 287: 15; 291: 24
dub-sar gu$_4$-apin: 3: 60
dub-sar gu$_4$-udu: 184: 18
gána-gu$_4$: 16: 3, 7; 56: 2; 87: 4
kuš gu$_4$-ḫi-a síg-sar: 305: 1
kuš gu$_4$-ḫi-a še-gín: 305: 3
nu-bànda gu$_4$: 3: 20; 15: 5, 10, 15; 16, 3, 7; 17: 2
šà-gal gu$_4$: 45: 10
šà-gal gu$_4$-udu: 64: 57, 93
uzu gu$_4$ niga-šè: 306: 3
gub-ba *standing, "serving"*
10: 7; 37: 9; 71: *passim*; 72: 18; 85: 14; 251: 10
gub-ba-àm: 70: 9; 92: *passim*
bala gub-ba: 14: *passim*; 24: 2; 25: 9; 26: 3; 27: 3
é-kíkken-a gub-ba: 19: 57; 20: 46
érin i$_7$-NE-tum-mal gub-ba: 93: 35
máš-tur gub-ba: 78: 6
gudu$_4$ *priest*
gudu$_4$ DN: 98: 2
gudu$_4$ é DN: 82: 19
gukkal *fat-tailed* (sheep)
udu gukkal: 67: 18, 267: 10
udu gukkal-gibil: 67: 67
udu gukkal níĝin-ba Ĝír-su^{ki}: 70: 25
gur *measure of capacity* = 300 sìla
1: *passim*; 3: *passim*; 14: *passim*; 15: *passim*; 16: 5; 18: 8; 22: 2; 23: 27; 25: 8; 26: 2; 27: 2; 30: 1; 31: 2; 44: 10, 12, 14; 46: 2; 54: 9; 56: *passim*; 57: *passim*; 58: 4, 9; 59: *passim*; 60: *passim*; 61: *passim*; 62: *passim*; 64; *passim*; 65: *passim*; 66: *passim*; 68: *passim*; 74: *passim*; 86: 8, 14; 87: 2; 88: *passim*; 89: *passim*; 93: *passim*; 94: *passim*; 97: 3, 5; 131: 2; 139: *passim*; 173: 1; 174: 1, 2; 176: 1; 249: 6, 7; 272: 30; 274: 3; 275: 1; 276: 3, 6, 8; 280: *passim*; 284: *passim*; 307: 1; 310: *passim*
gur lugal: 1: 1; 3: 49; 6: 1; 14: 14; 16: 1; 17; 1; 18: 1; 24: 1; 28: 1; 32: 1; 34: 10; 43: 1; 56: 1; 57: 1, 10, 43; 60: 1; 61: 1; 62: 1; 64: 1; 69: 1; 86: 1; 87: 1; 88: 1; 94: 1; 95: 1; 105: 1; 114: 1; 121: 1; 124: 1; 127: 1; 128: 1; 132: 1; 138: 1; 148: 1; 150: 1; 152: 1; 157: 1; 158: 1; 162: 1; 168: 1; 175: 1; 177: 1; 197: 1; 283: 12
gur-saĝ-ĝál: 15: 1, 17

má x gur: 165: 1, 2; 280: *passim*
še-numun-ta gur-ra: 56: 7; 57: 6

gur$_7$ *silo*
56: 1, 10, 69; 88: 1

gurdub *reed basket*
75:*passim*; 77: *passim*

-Ĝ-

ĝá-ĝá *to place, establish*
si-ì-tum úgu-a ĝá-ĝá: 169: 7
úgu ĝá-ĝá (see úgu)
še ĝeš è-a ĝá-ĝá-dam: 18: 12

ĝá-nun *storehouse*
ĝá-nun-ĝeš: 37: 9; 45: 5
ĝá-nun saĝa: 27: 5
ĝá-nun-da-tuš-a: 41: 4
é-udu-ĝá-nun-ĝeš: 171: 6

ĝál *to be*
úgu PN ĝál-la: 64: 104
ì-ĝál: 67: 40, 95; 180: 12; 182: 4; 183: 4; 311: 15

^{ĝeš}ĝanun *storehouse*
239: 11

ĝar *to establish, place*
úgu PN ba-ĝar: 59: *passim*; 66: 17
dub-sar zì-da ba-ĝar: 64: 105
má-a-ĝar-ra: 105: 2
dub-ba ^{kuš}du$_{10}$-gan ĝar-ĝar: 197: 16

ĝen *ordinary quality*
dida ĝen (see under dida)
kaš ĝen (see under kaš)
ninda-àr-ra ĝen (see under ninda)
síg-ĝen (see under síg)

ĝen-na/ ĝen-né *going, coming*
ĝen-na: 158: 2
GN-ta ĝen-na: 105: 4
ĝeš-šè ĝen-na: 41: 21
ka nimgir-an-ni-zu-šè im-ši-ĝen-na: 103: 3
ki ^{d}Na-rú-a-šè ĝen-na: 112: 3
sízkur-šè ĝen-na: 38: 11

Destinations and points of origin in the messenger texts – Texts 185–266:
A-dam-šaḫ^{ki}-šè ĝen-na/né: 195: 8; 207: 3; 215: 10; 226: 20; 229: 4, 17; 233: 17
A-GÍN^{ki}-šè ĝen-na: 185: 16
A-NE.NE ĝen-na: 194: 17
a-šà-šè ĝen-na: 188: 3
a-šà Mar-tu kur-ba ĝen-na: 256: 20
ab-ba-da ĝen-na: 240: 16
[ ] AB.A-šè ĝen-na: 243: 18
aga-ús alan-da ĝen-na-me: 262: 7
An-ša-an^{ki}-šè ĝen-né: 193: 21; 230: 15
An-ša-an^{ki}-ta ĝen-na/né: 220: 16; 236: 23; 251: 20; 260: 23; 261: 23
An-ša-an^{ki}-ta Nibru^{ki}: 231: 21; 248: 18
An-ša-an^{ki}-ta ù Nibru^{ki}-ta ĝen-na: 189: 19; 208: 13; 214: 19; 241: 17; 252: 19
An-ša-an^{ki}-ta ù Nibru^{ki}-šè ĝen-na: 192: 21; 206: 26
An-ša-an^{ki} [rá]-gaba-da ĝen-na: 243: 11
anše zi-gúm-ma-šè ĝen-na: 221: 15
^{d}Aš-da-bára ĝen-na: 258: 9
Du$_8$-du$_8$-lí-^{ki}-šè ĝen-né: 213: 22
é-DÙ.DÙ ĝeš-šè ĝen-na: 198: 3
é ^{d}Ĝeš-bar-è-ta ĝen-na: 226: 14
é Ur-^{d}Ig-alima-šè ĝen-na: 256: 10
érin i$_7$ [ ] ĝen-na: 191: 15
érin NE.DU-a-è-dè ĝen-na: 191: 18
érin še-kin-šè ĝen-na: 185: 4; 186: 4; 194: 4; 255: 14; 258; 12
Ga-eš-šè ĝen-na: 210: 3
^{ĝeš}ĝanun-šè ĝen-na: 239: 11
Gi-gi-li^{ki}-ta ĝen-ne-ne: 228: 8
Gi-ša^{ki}-šè ĝen-na/né: 205: 6; 232: 20
gi-šul-ḫi-šè ĝen-na: 198: 6
[ ] ĝen-na: 239: 18, 22
[ ]^{ki} ĝen-na: 245: 15
Gú-a-ab-ba^{ki} énsi-ta ĝen-na: 216: 4
Gú-ab-ba^{ki}-šè ĝen-na: 212: 6; 234: 15; 259: 6
gu$_4$-da ĝen-na: 210: 16
gu$_4$-ĝeš-šè ĝen-na: 266: 10
ĜEŠ-ab-ba-šè ĝen-na: 234: 11
^{urudu}<ḫa>-bù-da ĝen-na: 216: 18
Ḫu-bu-la^{ki}-šè ĝen-né: 205: 9
Ḫu-ḫu-nu-ri^{ki}-šè ĝen-né: 195: 11; 207: 20
in NIM-ne ĝen-na: 228: 13
Inim-inim-ma^{ki}-šè ĝen-na: 206: 4; 216: 11
Inim-inim-ma uru ĝen-na: 236: 4
Iš^{ki}-šè ĝen-na: 239: 29
Iš^{ki}-ta ĝen-na: 226: 7

Ka-si-šè ĝen-na: 114: 3
Ki-maš^{ki}-šè ĝen-né: 195: 15; 199: 5; 227: 20; 232: 4
Ki-maš^{ki}-ta ĝen-né: 205: 3; 218: 18
ki-énsi-ta ĝen-na: 238: 9
ki Lú-^{d}Nin-ĝír-su-šè ĝen-na: 244: 14
ki-zabar-dab$_{5}$-ta ĝen-na: 210: 6
kù-sig$_{17}$ gur$_{7}$-a ĝen-na: 237: 7
kur-šè ĝen-na: 234: 7
lú má-gal-gal-šè ĝen-na: 246: 9
lú má-saĝ ĝen-na/ lú má-saĝ-ĝá-ke$_{4}$-ne-šè ĝen-na: 203: 15; 223: 3
lú-maḫ ^{d}Inanna-šè ĝen-na: 257: 11
lú-nin-diĝir-^{d}Ba-ú-da ĝen-na: 221: 7
má-a-si ĝen-na: 186: 12
má ĝeš-ì-ka-šè ĝen-na: 212: 12; 239: 7; 244: 18; 245: 9
mu ki!-^{d}En-líl-lá-ka-šè ĝen-na: 191: 6
mu túg-gada-šè ĝen-na: 191: 9
nar-da ĝen-na: 198: 13
Nibru^{ki}-ta ĝen-na/né: 216: 22; 220: 17; 243: 6
Nibru^{ki}-ta ù URU×A^{ki}: 253: 14
nu-bànda dumu-dab$_{5}$-ba-šè ĝen-na: 238: 12
PN ĝen-na: 185: 8, 20; 244: 10
rá-gaba ĝen-na: 244: 10
Sa-bu-um^{ki} ĝen-na: 193: 10; 250: 25; 259: 10
Sa-bu-um^{ki}-šè ĝen-na: 203: 19; 210: 22; 211: 19; 215: 3; 218: 13; 232: 12
Sa-bu-um^{ki}-ta ĝen-né: 223: 12; 227; 9; 228: 16; 230: 19; 233: 9; 244: 5; 257: 15
saĝ-šè ĝen-na: 203: 6; 204: 15
Saḫar^{ki}-ta ĝen-na: 221: 11
si-gi$_{4}$-dè ĝen-na: 236: 11
Si-ù^{ki}-ta ĝen-né: 191: 4
Si-ù-na-ta ĝen-né: 196: 6
sízkur Lagaš^{ki} ĝen-na: 194: 13
sízkur Nina^{ki}-šè ĝen-na: 187: 4
šabra-an-na-šè ĝen-na: 238: 6
šabra ^{d}Šul-gi-a-bí-da ĝen-na: 204: 12
še sukkal uru-KU-šè ĝen-na: 194: 9
Ši-ma-aš-ki-ta ĝen-né: 213: 5; 215: 6; 229: 25
šim anše-šè ĝen-na: 188: 9
Šušina^{ki} ĝen-né: 207: 18
Šušina^{ki}-šè ĝen-né: 195: 4, 200: 11, 14, 21; 207: 6, 15; 209: 3; 212: 9; 213: 9; 215: 14; 223: 7; 229: 9; 230: 4; 254: 7; 263: 18
Šušina^{ki}-ta ĝen-na/-né: 187: 14; 193: 23; 200: 2, 4, 25; 202: 12; 207: 12; 209: 6, 15; 218: 3, 7, 9; 223: 16; 224: 6, 14; 227: 6; 228: 3, 18; 230: 17; 232: 7, 23; 233: 12, 22; 247: 5; 255: 12, 17; 259: 15; 263: 5, 12, 15
túg-gibil-šè ĝen-na: 206: 8
túg-šè ĝen-na: 203: 9; 204: 18; 250: 18
ú-bù-re-dè ĝen-na-me: 257: 7
Ú-lum^{ki}-šè ĝen-né: 209: 12
ugula alan-da ĝen-na: 262: 6
ugula uš-bar-šè ĝen-na: 256: 36
Ur-^{d}Ba-ú-mu-da ĝen-na: 245: 3
URU×A^{ki}(*with variants*)-ta ĝen-né: 193: 25; 209: 18; 213: 14; 227: 3, 12, 23; 229: 20; 230: 7; 233: 4, 25
Urí^{ki}-šè ĝen-né: 217: 9; 219: 20
Za-ul^{ki}-šè ĝen-né: 193: 32; 227: 14
Za-ul^{ki}-ta ĝen-né: 227: 16
zì-má-a-si-gi$_{4}$ ĝen-na: 186: 8

ĝeš *wood*
ĝeš-šè ĝen-na: 41: 21
ĝeš-da-didli: 120: 6
ĝeš-e-dab$_{5}$-ba: 164: 2
ĝeš x-ta: 272: *passim*
ĝá-nun-ĝeš: 37: 9; 45: 5

ĝeš-a-ĝál-la
túg ĝeš-a-ĝál-la: 63: 9

ĝeš-dù *wood for building*
ĝeš-dù má-šè: 165: 4

ĝeš-ì *sesame seeds, sesame oil*
(see also ì)
3: 10
engar ĝeš-ì: 3: 73
kù ĝeš-ì-ka: 140: 2
lú ĝeš-ì: 184: 11
še ĝeš-ì: 160: 1

ĝeš-nud *bed*
ĝeš-nud-ḫi-a: 267: 27
ĝeš-nud sig$_{5}$: 267: 26

ĝeš-tag *an offering*
63: 163

ĝeš-túg ĝar *to listen*
ĝeš-túg ga-ru-dam: 184: 22

ĝi$_6$-par$_4$

292: 1, 9 12, 15 22 26 31

ĝìr *conveyed by, guaranteed by*

1: 59, 63; 8: 10; 14: 117; 15: 18, 24; 19: 6, 43; 20: 6, 38; 32: 6; 33: 17; 36: 12; 37: 11; 38: 8; 39: 17, 20; 40: 8, 18, 21; 41: 21, 22, 24; 42: 4; 58: 7; 59: 24, 25; 61: *passim*; 62: 32; 64: *passim*; 67: 11, 13; 69: 8; 84: 5; 90: 7, 9; 94: 5, 7, 10; 95: 2; 102: 4; 103: 5; 104: 23; 105: 5; 108: 2; 111: 4; 113: 7; 115: 9; 118: 24; 123: 6; 129: 12; 133: 5; 135: 7, 8; 139: 15, 24; 140: 4; 143: 5; 144: 5; 147: 6; 155: 6, 9; 164: 4; 167: 4; 177: 5; 180: 3; 183: 3; 189: 18; 190: 20; 191: 3; 192: 20; 193: *passim*; 196: 5; 199: 4; 205: 2, 5, 8; 206: 23; 207: 11; 209: 11; 210: 13; 213: 4, 13, 21; 214: 9; 218: 17; 219: 19; 223: 13; 224: 13; 227: 15; 228: 9; 229: 24; 230: 14; 231: 20; 232: 19; 234: 17; 236: 23; 239: 28; 243: 7; 244: 6; 249: 5, 9, 14; 253: 10; 259: 17; 276: 10; 282: 3; 283: 18, 20; 284: 10; 286: 2; 287: 10; 291: 83, 86; 292: 24; 297: 7; 298: 7

ĝìr-ĝen-na *library*

lú-ĝìr-ĝen-na-ke$_4$ 56: 29, 55

^{ĝeš}ĝìr-gub *footstool*

267: 29

^{ĝeš}ĝìr-gub sig$_5$: 267: 28

ĝìr-lam *basket*

117: 8

ĜIŠGAL

ĜIŠGAL.ĜIŠGAL gaba Má-gan-na: 115: 2

ĝuruš *worker, dependent laborer*

7: *passim*; 9: *passim*; 10: 1, 4; 13: 2; 14: *passim*; 19: 54; 20: 43; 22: 1; 23: *passim*; 25: *passim*; 27: 1; 213: 11; 314: *passim*

ĝuruš ḫé-dab$_5$: 9: 1

ĝuruš lú-ḫun-ĝá: 12: *passim*; 13: 7

ĝuruš sig$_7$-a: 314: *passim*

ĝuruš šu-gi$_4$: 314: 15

-Ḫ-

^{urudu}ḫa-bù-da *hoe*

216: 18

^{ĝeš}ḫašḫur *apple tree*

275: 1, 5, 9

ḫé-dab$_5$ *worker*

3: 67; 7: 13; 9: 1, 9; 19: 52, 55; 20: 44; 35: 11; 36: 9

ḫé-dab$_5$ ^{ĝeš}tukul-e dab$_5$-ba: 118: 19

ĝuruš ḫé-dab$_5$: 9: 1

ḫu-bu-um *wheel*

ḫu-bu-um umbin: 125: 1

ḪU.KU.BU *worker*

1: *passim*

lú ḪU.KU.BU: 58: 5

ḫul *to destroy*

passim in year names

mu a-ga-am$_6$ u$_8$-sila$_4$-nú-a niga ba-ḫul-a: 287: 9

ḫun *to choose, hire, rent*

passim in year names

á-ḫun-ĝá (see under á)

lú-ḫun-ĝá (see lú-ḫun-ĝá)

-I-

ì *oil*

172; 1; 188: *passim*; 197: 7, 13; 201: *passim*; 210: *passim*; 212: *passim*; 217: 7; 225: 2, 5, 8; 226: *passim*; 238: *passim*; 245: *passim*; 258: *passim*; 259: *passim*; 264: 3, 7; 308: 5, 7, 9

ì á-gam:185: *passim*; 186: *passim*; 187: *passim*; 194: 2, 11, 15; 198: *passim*; 202: *passim*; 203: *passim*; 204: *passim*; 211: *passim*; 221: *passim*; 222: *passim*; 231: 4, 7, 10; 234: *passim*; 236: *passim*; 237: *passim*; 239: *passim*; 240: *passim*; 243: *passim*; 244: *passim*; 246: *passim*; 250: *passim*; 251: *passim*; 252: *passim*; 255: *passim*; 256: *passim*; 257: *passim*; 260: *passim*; 261: *passim*; 266: *passim*

ì-du$_{10}$: 267: 19

ì lugal: 112: 3

á-gam ì: 195: 9, 12; 207: *passim*; 209: *passim*; 215: 4, 7, 11; 224: 3, 8; 247: 3; 254: 10, 15; 263: *passim*

á-gam ì šà uru: 254: 3

ì-ba *oil allotment*

ì-ba diĝir-re-ne: 156: 6

ì-du$_8$ *doorkeeper*

ì-du$_8$ é-la-la: 34: 13

ì-dub *granary, storehouse*

ì-dub (for individual storehouses, see index)

ì-dub didli: 56: 46, 61

ì-ĝeš *sesame oil*

112: 1, 4, 7; 192: 18; 196: 3; 197: 2, 5, 10;

206: 20; 209: 9 ; 210: 11; 214: 5; 217: 3; 219: *passim*; 222: 10; 231: 17; 235: 3; 241: 12; 243: 5; 245: 5; 253: 6; 258: 11; 264: 10; 265: *passim*

ì-ĝeš á-gam: 189: *passim*; 190: *passim*; 192: *passim*; 206: *passim*; 208: *passim*; 214: *passim*; 220: *passim*; 241: *passim*; 242: 2, 5; 248: *passim*; 253: 2, 9, 12

á-gam ì-ĝeš: 195: 1, 5; 196: 1; 215: 1; 216: *passim*

ì-nun *butter*

90: 1, 3, 5; 100: 1, 3; 122: 1; 284: 6, 43; 315: 5

ì(-nun): 284: 27, 33

ì-udu *mutton fat*

245: 5

igi-x-ĝál *used to express fractions: ⅓, ¼, etc..*

60: 4, 23, 27; 63: 56; 64: 100; 81: 1; 93: 25; 101: 11; 129: 3, 5, 7; 140: 1; 143: 1; 309: 1, 3

igi-saĝ *to sort, choose*(?)

272: *passim*

igi sig_5

284: 26

iku *measure of area* = to 100 sar

1: *passim*; 3: *passim*; 4: 1; 14: *passim*

iku $^{ĝeš}kiri_6$: 267: 14

íl *to raise, lift*

ga-íl: 314: 25

un-$ĝa_6$ (see un-$ĝa_6$)

im *clay*

im-du_8-a: 14: 170

im-e tak_4-a: 8: 7; 35: 6; 98: 3

imĝaĝa$_3$ *emmer*

44: 4

ìr *male slave*

19: 35; 20: 32

ir_{11} *male slave*

ir_{11}-zu: 307: seal

iti *month*

passim in month names; 269: 4, 9; 283: 28; 296: 4

iti-bi iti x-àm: 63: *passim*

iti-ta: 14: *passim*; 303: *passim*

iti x-kam: 61: 19; 65: 21; 67: *passim*; 197: 20; 289: 14

-K-

ka *mouth*

ka-i_7-zi-luḫ-da: 311: 2

ka-mun-ambar-ta: 311: 18

ka-gur_7 *granary official*

3: 25, 56; 88: 17; 109: 2

ka-lá-a *remainder*

nì-ka_9-ak ka-lá-a: 62: 31; 67: 115; 68: 20

KA.SI

egir KA.SI.KA-ta: 154: 7

ká *gate*

$sila_4$ ká-$ĝi_6$-par: 292: *passim*

šim zì ká-a ^{d}Nin-ĝír-su-ka: 146: 2

kar-kid (see géme-kar-kid)

karadin *pile of sheaves*

9: *passim*

kaskal *journey, road*

kaskal-šè (see under dabin, dida, kaš, ninda, zì)

kaš *beer*

39: 1, 16; 40: 1, 17; 103: 1; 117: 1; 185: *passim*; 186: *passim*; 187: *passim*; 188: *passim*; 189: *passim*; 190: *passim*; 192: *passim*; 194: *passim*; 197: 4, 7, 9; 198: *passim*; 200: *passim*; 201: *passim*; 202: 1, 6, 9; 203: *passim*; 204: *passim*; 206: *passim*; 208: *passim*; 210: *passim*; 211: *passim*; 212: *passim*; 214: *passim*; 216: *passim*; 217: 5; 219: *passim*; 220: *passim*; 221: *passim*; 222: *passim*; 224: 7; 225: 1, 4, 7; 226: *passim*; 228: 6, 10; 230: *passim*; 231: *passim*; 234: *passim*; 236: *passim*; 237: *passim*; 238: *passim*; 239: *passim*; 240: *passim*; 241: *passim*; 242: 1, 4; 243: *passim*; 244: *passim*; 245: *passim*; 246: *passim*; 248: *passim*; 250: *passim*; 251: *passim*; 252: *passim*; 253: 1, 8, 11; 255: *passim*; 256: *passim*; 257: *passim*; 258: *passim*; 259: *passim*; 260: *passim*; 261: *passim*; 263: *passim*; 264: 1, 5, 9; 265: 5, 11; 266:*passim*; 274: 3, 5

kaš-$ĝi_6$: 117: 2

kaš ĝen: 61: 13, 23, 33; 62: *passim*; 65: 14, 25; 68: 6; 110: 10; 139: *passim*; 210: 10; 224: 1, 10; 228: 1, 14; 243: 4; 247: 1; 249: 6, 16, 19; 254: 1, 8, 13; 258: 1, 4; 265: 1, 8

kaš ĝen kaskal-šè: 228: 11

kaš ĝen lugal: 235: 1

kaš ĝen šà uru: 230: 1
kaš kaskal-šè: 230: 12
kaš lugal: 231: 15; 251: 1; 253: 4
kaš ninda lugal šà uru: 262: 1
kaš sig$_5$: 61: 12, 21; 62: 14, 16, 22; 65: *passim*; 68: 3; 139: 13, 17; 210: 10; 211: 14; 245: 16; 249: *passim*; 258: 1, 4
kaš šà uru: 200: 5, 8, 17; 230: 8, 11
kaš ú-sa-a-da: 151: 4

kaš-dé-a *beer offering, libation*
276: 9
kaš-dé-a lugal: 64: 96, 112; 93: 50, 52

kaš$_4$ *to run, a courier*
é-kaš$_4$: 41: 13
(see also under lú-kaš$_4$)

kéš-rá *to bind*
278: 6
á še-kéš-rá: 10: 6

ki *from*
1: *passim*; 5: 11; 10: 10; 14: *passim*; 19: *passim*; 20: *passim*; 22: 5; 24: 4; 25: 11; 26: 5; 27: 4; 28: 5; 32: 3; 42: 3; 43: 3; 44: 11; 59: 3, 5; 60: *passim*; 61: 5, 6, 8; 62: 5, 7: 15; 63: 36, 38; 64: *passim*; 66: 3, 6, 9; 67: *passim*; 68: 9; 78: *passim*; 81: 4; 84: 9; 86: *passim*; 90: 2, 6; 92: 17; 95: 5; 118: 21; 120: 4, 7; 122: 3; 123: 3; 124: 3; 125: 3; 126: 3; 127: 4; 128: 3; 129: *passim*; 130: 2; 131: 4; 132: 2; 133: 3; 135: 3; 136: 3; 137: 6; 139: *passim*; 140: 3; 141: 2; 144: 2; 146: 3; 147: 3; 148: 4; 149: 7; 150: 4; 151: 3; 152: 5; 153: 3; 154: 4; 156: 3; 157: 2; 158: 3; 159: 3; 160: 2; 161: 2; 162: 3: 163: 2; 164: 5; 166: 3; 167: 2; 168: 3; 170: 3; 171: 1, 3, 5; 172: 2; 173: 4; 174: 4; 175: 2; 177: 3; 178: 2; 275: 2; 278: 7; 279: 2; 280: 4, 7; 281: 2; 284: 11; 288: *passim*; 291: *passim*; 296: 5; 297: 5; 298: 6; 299: 1; 300: 2; 301: 7; 304: 5; 307: 3; 309: 2, 5, 7; 310: *passim*
ki zabar-dab$_5$-ta: 210: 6

ki *place*
ki énsi: 238: 9
ki Lú-^{d}Nin-ĝír-su-šè ĝen-na: 244: 14
ki ^{d}Na-rú-a-šè ĝen-na: 112: 3

ki-a-naĝ *offering*
117: 12

ki-lá *weight*
nì ki-lá-a: 63: 56
ki-lá-bi: 63: *passim*; 99: 2, 4; 125: 2; 135: 2

ki-sar *vegetable plot*
7: 5

kíkken *miller*
é-kíkken-a: 19: 57; 20: 46
géme-kíkken: 23: 7; 283: 17
géme-kíkken énsi: 184: 21; 121: seal
ugula kíkken-ta 129: 8

KIN *a type of vessel*
dug-KIN: 166: 1

kir$_{11}$ *female lamb*
70: 3; 72: 3; 78: 2; 303: 9
kir$_{11}$-ga: 302: 2

^{ĝeš}kiri$_6$ *garden*
(for individual gardens, see index): 8: 2; 74: *passim*
iku ^{ĝeš}kiri$_6$: 267: 14

kišib *seal, sealed by PN*
2: 2; 10: 11; 30: 4; 43: 5; 46: 4; 56: *passim*; 57: *passim*; 60: 26; 63: *passim*; 64: 48; 65: 15, 18; 66: 2, 5, 8; 69: 5; 79: 6; 88: 13, 17; 90: 4, 10, 12; 93: *passim*; 97: 8; 120: 8; 121: 3; 130: 4; 137: 7; 139: 20, 21, 22; 141: 5; 144: 4; 150: 8; 151: 6; 161: 3; 162: 7; 163: 3; 167: 3; 170: 4; 172: 3; 174: case 6; 177: 4; 275: 3; 279: 3; 280: 8; 281: 3; 291: *passim*; 296; 2; 303: 12; 307: 2
kišib-bi ba-zi-ir: 59: 12
kišib-bi 2-àm: 56: 31, 34; 88: 15; 291: 92
kišib-bi 3-àm: 57: 17, 21
kišib énsi: 59: 13; 63: 89; 129: 11; 147: 5
kišib ì-rá-rá: 139: 23
kišib íb-ra: 162: 7; 173: 8
kišib šabra: 69: 6

kú *to eat*
kú-a: 58: 5
še-amar-e kú-a: 46: 3

kù *silver, precious*
59: 9, 25; 60: *passim*
kù ĝeš-ì-ka: 140: 2
kù saĝ-tuk: 143: 2
kù šà Nina: 147: 2
še-ba kù-ta sa$_{10}$-a-šè: 130: 3

kù-babbar *silver*
81: 1; 101: 1; 123: 2; 129: 1; 140: 1; 143: 1; 147: 1; 169: 1; 170: 1; 282: 1; 309: 1, 3, 6; 312: 1
má-gur$_8$ kù-babbar tur: 267: 15

kù-sig$_{17}$ *gold*
kù-sig$_{17}$ gur$_7$-a: 237: 7

ku$_4$ *to enter, bring, deliver*
ku$_4$-ra didli: 7: 11
ku$_4$-ra ugula uru-bi: 63: 10, 35, 137
ba-an-ku$_4$: 82: *passim*
é-gal-la ba-ku$_4$: 147: 4
é-gal-la ba-an-ku$_4$: 143: 4
é-gal-la ba-an-ku$_4$ šà Urí^{ki}-ma: 140: 6
é-gal lugal ba-an-ku$_4$: 102: 2
na-kab-tum-ma ba-an-ku$_4$: 66: 14

ku$_6$ *fish*
ku$_6$ 4-kam-ús: 144: 1

kul *to collect*
92:7

^{anše}kúnga *donkey, mule*
dumu sipa ^{anše}kúnga: 41: 11

kur *mountain*
234: 7

kurum$_7$ *inspection*
šà kurum$_7$-ma: 63: 23
kurum$_7$-ak simug: 184: 2

kurušda *fattener*
67: 6, 66; 84: 10
é kurušda: 184: 12
kurušda ^{d}Dumu-zi: 67: 113
kurušda didli-bi: 184: 15

kuš *skin, hide*
277: 2, 5, 8
kuš anše-ḫi-a še-gín: 305: 4
kuš gu$_4$-ḫi-a síg-sar: 305: 1
kuš gu$_4$-ḫi-a še-gín: 305: 3
kuš udu-ḫi-a nì-kú-a: 305: 6

kuš$_7$ *valet, groom*
122: 4; 303: 29; 308: 6

-L-

lá *minus, less*
60: 4; 65: 30; 67: 8; 72: 2, 11; 73: *passim*; 78: 8; 91: 8; 93: 64; 96: 4, 7, 8; 129: 3, 5; 140: 1; 169: 1; 170: 1; 187: 15; 188: 12; 204: 19; 250: 26; 255: 26; 258: 23; 267: 10; 273: 36; 277: 2, 11, 12; 280: 2; 284: 51, 52; 285: 1; 288: 110; 291: 63, 74; 295: 11; 303: 4, 13, 31; 309: 1, 6

lạ́ *to weigh*
énsi-ke$_4$ ì-lá: 125: 4

lá-u$_x$(NI) *deficit, arrears*
1: 213, 56: 71; 59: 33; 60: 33, 36; 61: 38; 63: 159; 64: 109; 65: 30; 66: 21; 67: 58; 71: 5, 9; 72: 21; 85: 17; 92: 4; 308: 3; 310: 20, 22
lá-u$_x$-àm: 1: 335; 70: 23; 72: 16; 85: 12; 92: 5; 94: 8
lá-u$_x$ è-a: 60: 36
lá-u$_x$ su-ga: 1: 229, 279; 43: 2; 58: 6; 60: 19; 63: 28; 73: 5; 78: 13, 15; 282: 2
lá-u$_x$ su-ga sipa didli: 155: 4
lá-u$_x$ PN: 60: 9, 11
lá-u$_x$ YN: 122: 5

làl *honey*
lál: 141: 1; 267: 20

libir *old, former*
libir-àm: 19: 20; 20: 19; 73: 3, 17; 80: 4

lú *man*
82: 22; 312: 16; 316: 3
lú [ ]: 264: 8; 312: 8, 11
lú gi-gúm-ma: 253: 13
lú ĝeš-ì: 184: 11
lú Ḫa-ar-ši^{ki}: 296: 2
lú ḪU.KU.BU: 58: 5
lú-kisal: 39: 4; 40: 4
lú-maḫ DN: 257: 11
lú PN: 197: 8, 11; 234: 18; 291: 97
lú-šuku-ra é-a-me: 3: 11, 21, 28
dumu lú-didli: 41: 23

lú-dab$_5$-ba *conscripted worker?*
lú-dab$_5$-ba en-nu: 37: 8
lú-dab$_5$-ba ĝá-nun-ĝeš: 37: 9
lú-dab$_5$-ba uru didli-me: 224: 12

lú-ĝìr-ĝen-na-ke$_4$ *librarian*
56: 29, 55

lú-ḫun-ĝá *hired man*
11: 3; 12: *passim*; 13: 6; 69: 7
lú-ḫun-ĝá é-gal-la: 13: 5
á-lú-ḫun-ĝá: 282: 4

lú-kaš$_4$ *courier, messenger*
64: 52; 71: 13; 115: 9; 185: 19; 186: 7; 187: 13; 188: 11; 191: 1, 3, 17; 192: 12; 193:

16, 20, 24; 196: 2, 5; 198: *passim*; 202: 5, 8; 205: 8; 209: 5, 8, 11; 211: 6, 9, 12; 213: *passim*; 214: 15; 215: 5; 216: 21; 218: 2, 8; 219: 3; 221: 3, 6, 18; 222: 7, 20; 223: 6; 226: 6; 227: 4; 228: 2, 12; 230: 5, 6, 16; 233: 10; 234: 3, 6; 237: 10, 13, 16; 239: 21, 25; 240: 3, 19; 243: 21, 24; 246: 15; 250: 21; 254: 16; 255: 10, 13, 20; 256: 39, 32; 258: 18; 263: 7; 266: *passim*; 294: 18

lú kaš$_4$ sa$_{12}$-du$_5$: 184: 19

šà-gal lú-kaš$_4$: 64: 52

lú-kin-gi$_4$ *craftsman*

lú-kin-gi$_4$-a saĝ-sipa Lugal-nir-ĝál-ka gub-ba-me: 251: 10

lú-lunga *brewer*

lú-lunga-é-gibil: 64: 61

lú-má *boatman*

lú-má-gal-gal: 246: 9

lú-má-saĝ: 203: 15; 223: 3

lú-mu$_{13}$-mu$_{13}$ *incantation priest*

187: 3

lú-mušen-dab$_5$ *bird-catcher*

37; 10

lú ^{ĝeš}tukul *soldier*

36: 12; 251: 19; 264: 4

lú ^{ĝeš}tukul gu-la: 188: 6; 198: 9; 200: *passim*; 202: 3; 204: 3, 6; 206: 18; 207: 8, 11, 14; 212: 3; 216: 3; 224: 5; 226: 3; 229: 3; 232: 3; 238: 3; 240: 6; 243: 14; 245: 6; 248: 9; 250: 3, 6, 9; 251: 13; 252: 9; 255: 7; 256: 3; 264: 11; 266: 13

lú ^{ĝeš}tukul-lugal: 103: 2

lugal *king, royal*

317: 7

lugal-an-ub-da-limmu-ba: 268: 2

aga-ús lugal: 244: 4

daḫ-ḫu lugal: 67: 30

dumu lugal: 114: 2

é-gal lugal ba-an-ku$_4$: 102: 2

gur lugal (see gur)

(gur) lugal: 22: 1; 25: 1; 26: 1; 27: 1; 31: 1; 42: 1; 44: 1; 65: 1; 106: 1; 119: 8; 122: 1; 130: 1; 134: 1; 136: 1; 137: 1; 156: 1; 160: 1; 167: 1; 170: 2; 189: 15; 190: 16; 192: 17; 193: 5, 17, 28; 214: 4; 217: 2; 219: 14; 225: 10, 11; 236: 6, 21; 241: 11; 243: 4; 251: 2, 6; 253: 5; 258: 10; 265; 14

kaš-dé-a lugal: 64: 96, 112

kaš ĝen lugal: 110: 10

mu lugal-bi ì-pàd: 158: 8

sagi lugal: 3: 83

šà-gal lugal: 93: 74

utul lugal: 311: 7, 24

zi-ga lugal (see under zi)

zi lugal: 312: 6

lúgud

TÚG.ŠÈ lúgud-da: 292: 10

lukur *priestess*

263: 4

-M-

ma-da *land*

ma-da Unug^{ki}: 282: 6

ma-na *measure of weight*

59: 1, 29; 60: *passim*; 63: *passim*; 70: 10, 11, 12; 75: 1; 76: *passim*; 77: 1, 2; 99: 2, 4; 122: 2; 123: 1; 125: 2; 135: 2; 143: 1; 147: 1; 149: 1, 3; 151: 1; 155: *passim*; 161: 1; 267: 23; 282: 1

^{ĝeš}ma-nu *willow*(?)

165: 3

má *boat*

30: 3

má PN: 64: *passim*; 139: 2

má 60 gur: 280: 3, 6

má 120 gur: 280: 2, 5

má-a ĝar-ra: 105: 2

má-a si: 56: 28, 54; 66: 23; 148: 2; 186: 8, 12

má-gal: 104: 25, 27, 30; 246: 9

má ĝeš-DN: 191: 6

má ĝeš-ì-ka: 212: 12; 239: 7; 244: 18; 245: 9

má-gur$_8$-ra: 45: 3

má-gur$_8$ kù-babbar tur: 267: 15

má Má-gan-na: 115: 8

má-saĝ :203: 15; 223: 3

má u$_4$-zal-la: 64: 38; 102: 3

ĝeš-dù má-šè: 165: 4

^{ĝeš}eme-sig má: 165: 1, 2

še ^{d}En-líl-lá má-a: 236: 10

má-gín *boat builder*

38: 6

má-laḫ$_5$ *sailor*
má-laḫ$_5$-gal: 56: 26
mar-sa *depot*
159: 2
é-kišib-ba mar-sa: 165: 5
dub-sar mar-sa: 66: 24
šuku-mar-sa-ŠUM: 64: 82
Mar-tu *Amorite, westerner*
géme Mar-tu: 29: 3; 288: 102
PN Mar-tu: 44: 2; 110: 11; 139: 25; 186: 15; 191: 11; 211: 25; 222: 17; 223: 2; 234: 10; 235: 4; 239: 17; 240: 9, 12; 255: 17; 256: 16, 23, 26; 257: 10; 295: 12
Mar-tu-mí: 37: 7; 38: 5; 41: 20
maš-da-ri-a (see máš-da-ri-a)
máš *goat*
55: 15; 67: *passim*; 70: 21; 78: *passim*; 84: 6, 8; 205: 4; 289: 2, 5, 8; 290: 2; 295: 5, 11; 303: *passim*
máš-a-síg ba-ug$_7$: 301: 4
máš-ga: 302: 3
máš-ga-a-síg ba-ug$_7$: 301: 5
máš-gal: 285: 3; 303: 6, 11
máš-gal-babbar: 304: 1
máš-gal-niga: 296: 1
máš-níta: 84: 2; 285: 4
máš-saĝ: 70: 5; 72: 5; 78: 5
máš-šà-du$_{10}$: 285: 8
máš-tur: 78: 6
udu-máš: 67: *passim*
udu máš dab$_5$-ba: 104: 42
máš-da-ri-a *animal offering*
maš-da-ri-a ki lugal: 93: 32; 139: 8
máš-da-ri-a ezen-maḫ: 143: 3
máš-da-ru-a *animal offering*
še máš-da-ru-a: 65: 8
mašda *gazelle*
298: 12
amar-mašda níta DN: 298: 1
maškim *inspector, bailiff, sheriff*
103: 4; 109: 4; 114: 4; 287: 7; 296: 3
mu *year*
passim in year names
mu-ús-sa: *passim* in year names
mu x kam: 180: 6, 10
mu *name*
mu lugal-bi ì-pàd: 158: 8
mu PN: 100: 7
mu ... šè *on behalf of*
19: *passim*; 20: *passim*; 62: 6; 150: 7; 153: 6; 154: 3; 158: 5; 159: 4; 162: 6; 173: 7; 284: 21, 24; 286: 6; 287: 9; 288: 88, 102; 291: 78
mu bala-šè: 57: 28
mu gu$_4$-si-aš-šè: 305: 2
mu mušen-šè dab$_5$-ba: 44: 9
mu še-gín-šè: 305: 5
mu pàd *to take an oath*
mu lugal-bi ì-pàd: 158: 8
mug *low-quality wool*
síg mug: 63: *passim*
muḫaldim *cook, baker*
19: 34; 20: 31; 185: 7; 186: 11; 287: 10
é-muḫaldim: 184: 16; 287: 15
mun *salt*
273: *passim*; 306: 2
mun tu$_7$ si: 273: 20
še mun gazi: 88: 12
munu$_4$ *malt*
61: 30; 68: 1, 12; 179: 1
ba-ba-munu$_4$: 65: 16, 26
zì-munu$_4$-ḫi-a: 105: 1; 114: 1
mur-gu$_4$ *fodder*
mur-gu$_4$ ḪU.KU.BU: 1: *passim*
mušen-dù *fowler*
44: 8; 184: 20
ugula mušen-dù: 168: 4

-N-

na-gada *chief shepherd*
29: 4; 72: 22; 76: *passim*; 104: *passim*
na-kab-tum *a place for fattening cattle*
139: 7; 316: 10
gu$_4$ na-kab-tum: 133: 1; 142: 3
na-kab-tum-ma ba-an-ku$_4$: 66: 14
nagar *carpenter*
39: 16; 40: 17; 73: 7
naĝa *potash, soap*
naĝa-bi nu-dé: 87: 3
nar *singer*
19: 4; 20: 4; 312: 10; 314: 7

nar a-ru-a ^{d}Amar-^{d}Suen-ka-me: 293: 3
nar a-ru-a ^{d}*Šu*-^{d}Suen-ka-me: 293: 2
nar sig$_{7}$-a: 283: 16

nì *thing, property*
nì ezen x-šè: 117: 16
nì-ezen-ma: 67: 48, 50, 109
nì ezen è-lu-lum šà É-saĝ-da-na^{ki}-ka: 303: 32
nì gù-dé-šè: 305: 7
nì ki-lá-a: 63: 56
nì numun du$_{10}$-ga: 110: 6
nì numun-šè: 177: 2
nì sízkur-ra má Má-gan-na: 115: 8
nì-ù-du$_{8}$-ḫu-um 93: 40
nì u$_{4}$-sakar: 273: 21

nì-dab$_{5}$ *requisitions*
nì-dab$_{5}$ u$_{4}$-sakar: 117: 9

nì-du$_{10}$ *well-being*
šà nì-du$_{10}$ sila$_{4}$-šè: 306: 8

nì-ĝál-la *possessions*
62: 29

nì-gul *hatchet*
nì-gul ak: 7: 4, 10

nì-gur$_{11}$ *property*
63: 127
é-nì-gur$_{11}$: 155:8
saĝ nì-gur$_{11}$-ra: 56: 11; 57: 11; 63: 57, 120
saĝ-nì-gur$_{11}$-ra-kam: 69: 3; 88: 2; 95: 7; 283: 13

nì-ka$_{9}$-ak *balanced account*
nì-ka$_{9}$ YN: 59: 10, 26; 284: 19
nì-ka$_{9}$ YN mu-ĝál: 59: 22
nì-ka$_{9}$-ak: 56: 73; 57: 46; 60: 35; 63: 169; 64: 110
nì-ka$_{9}$-ak PN: 61: 40; 65: 31
nì-ka$_{9}$-ak gána-gána-a: 1: 340; 14: 204
nì-ka$_{9}$-ak ka-lá-a: 62: 31; 67: 115; 68: 20
nì-ka$_{9}$-ak kù-ta sa$_{10}$-a: 59: 34
nì-ka$_{9}$-ak si-ì-tum: 58: 10
nì-ka$_{9}$-ak še má-a si-ga: 66: 23
diri nì-ka$_{9}$-ak: 67: 53
nì-ka$_{9}$ má lugal-mu [ ] mu-ĝál: 59: 15
nì-ka$_{9}$-ak ninda: 283: 26
nì-ka$_{9}$-bi ba-ak: 69: 8
nì-ka$_{9}$-šu SU-ba: 180: 3
nì-ka$_{9}$-ta: 67: 7
si-ì-tum nì-ka$_{9}$-ak: 62: 2; 65: 2

nì-kú-a *food*
kuš udu-ḫi-a nì-kú-a: 305: 6
nì-kú-a-géme-tur: 93: 26

nì-lám *a type of garment*
síg nì-lám: 77: 3
^{túg}nì-lám: 63: *passim*
^{túg}nì-lám lugal: 63: 59
^{túg}nì-lám-ús lugal: 63: 62; 99: 1
^{túg}nì-lám 3-kam-ús: 63: 67, 80
^{túg}nì-lám 4-kam-ús: 63: 70

nì-sa$_{10}$ *price*
nì-sa$_{10}$-àm: 81: 2

nì-sur *filtered beer*(?)
nì-sur-bi: 272: 33–35

nì-šà-te *cool*
udu nì-šà-te: 67: 28

nì-ù-du$_{8}$-ḫu-um
93: 40

niga *fattened*
(see under gu$_{4}$, máš, u$_{8}$, ud$_{5}$, and udu)

niĝin *entirety*
udu gukkal niĝin-ba Ĝír-su^{ki}: 70: 25

nìĝin
é-nìĝin: 155: 5

NIM *Elamite, easterner*
NIM A-dam-šáḫ^{ki}: 214: 6
NIM An-ša-an^{ki}: 193: 19; 217: 4; 230: 13; 236: 22
NIM bí-ra-aš-ak Ki-maš^{ki}: 199: 3; 213: 12
NIM Du$_{8}$-du$_{8}$-lí^{ki}: 192: 19
NIM Gi-ša^{ki}: 205: 4; 219: 15; 232: 18
NIM Ḫu-bu-la^{ki}: 205: 7
NIM Ḫu-li-bar-me: 213: 20
NIM Ki-maš^{ki}: 205: 1; 218: 16; 253: 7
NIM Sa-bu-um^{ki}: 243: 6
NIM Si-ù^{ki}: 191: 2
NIM Si-ù-na^{ki}: 196: 4
NIM Ši-ma-aš-ki/ Ši-ma-aš-gi$_{4}^{ki}$: 190: 18; 204: 8; 206: 21; 213: 3; 229: 23; 231: 18; 241: 13
NIM Ši-ma-aš-ki ù Du$_{8}$-Du$_{8}$-lí^{ki}: 210: 12
NIM Ú-lum-ma^{ki}: 209: 10
NIM Za-ul^{ki}: 189: 17; 193: 6; 227: 14
PN NIM: 228: 7, 17
kaš sig$_{5}$ NIM: 62: 16

ninda *bread*

37: 1, 3; 38: 1, 7, 9; 39: *passim*; 40: *passim*; 41: 1, 21; 62: 18; 68: 4; 188: *passim*; 189: *passim*; 190: *passim*; 191: *passim*; 192: *passim*; 193: 14, 22, 24; 197: 4, 9; 199: 1; 201: 1, 4, 7; 206: *passim*; 208: *passim*; 210: *passim*; 212: *passim*; 213: 1, 10; 214: *passim*; 216: *passim*; 218: 1, 8, 14; 219: *passim*; 220: *passim*; 225: 1, 4, 7; 226: *passim*; 231: *passim*; 236: *passim*; 238: *passim*; 241: *passim*; 242: 1, 4; 245: *passim*; 247: 2; 248: *passim*; 251: *passim*; 252: *passim*; 253: 1, 8, 11; 258: *passim*; 259: 12; 260: *passim*; 261: *passim*; 264: 2, 6; 265: 5, 9, 11; 283: *passim*

ninda-àr-ra: 45: 1, 7: 111: 2; 273: 42

ninda-àr-ra ĝen: 61: 28

ninda-àr-ra sig_5: 64: 60; 131: 1; 134: 3; 139: 2; 273: 19

ninda du_8-a: 253: 5; 265: 2

ninda gu-la: 120: 5

ninda kaskal-šè: 193: *passim*; 213: 7, 16; 218: 5, 11

ninda sig_5: 64: 78

ninda šà uru: 193: *passim*; 213: 6, 15; 218: 4, 10

ninda zì-gu: 64: 85

kaš ninda lugal šà uru: 262: 1

nindan *a measure of length*

14: 167

nindan-gíd: 14: 166

nindan uš ab-sín: 313: *passim*

nu-bànda *an officer*

3: 27; 14: *passim*; 19: 33; 20: 30; 24: 6; 25: 7; 26: 6; 27: 6; 31: 4; 35: 4; 63: 171; 80: 2, 6, 8; 82: 6; 103: 5; 135: 8; 149: 2; 150: 11; 184: *passim*; 303: 3

nu-bànda dumu-dab_5-ba: 238: 12

nu-bànda gu_4: 3: 20; 15: 5, 10, 15; 16, 3, 7; 17: 2

nu-bànda ku_5-da: 22: 8

dumu nu-bànda: 207: 20; 229: 7, 13, 18; 247: 4; 263: 2

engar nu-bànda: 92: 13; 127: 2

nu-$^{ĝeš}kiri_6$ *gardener*

19: 3; 20: 3; 272: 8

numun *seed*

68: 2; 160: 3

nì numun du_{10}-ga: 110: 6

nì numun-šè: 177: 2

sum numun (see under sum)

-P-

pàd *to swear*

mu lugal-bi ì-pàd: 158: 8

PEŠ

amar-PEŠ mu-1 ba-ug_7: 288: *passim*

peš-murgu *a quantity of figs*

281: 1

-R-

ra-gaba / rá-gaba *courier*

ra-gaba: 228: 15, 17

rá-gaba: 41: 22; 83: 3; 93: 17; 105: 3; 243: 11; 244: 10; 269: 12; 310; 4

rá-gaba sipa ur-gi_7: 33: 12

rá-rá [var.(?) for kišib ra-ra, "to seal"]

kišib ì-rá-rá: 139: 23

ri-ri-ga *dead (said of cattle)*

ri-ri-ga: 72: 13; 85: 9, 16

ri-ri: 72: 20

-S-

sa-gi *reed bundle*

sa-gi: 273: *passim*; 306: 4, 7

sa-gi-ku_6: 273: *passim*

sá-du_{11} *regular offering*

49: 19; 52: 18

sá-du_{11}-diĝir-ra: 55: 17

sá-du_{11} DN: 283: *passim*; 289: 10; 290: 3

sá-du_{11} nì-ezen-ma: 67: 50

sá-du_{11} u_4-da íl: 117: 7

sá-du_{11} u_4 x-kam: 236: 3, 8; 251: 4, 8

udu sá-du_{11}: 67: 27

sa_{10} *to buy*

nì-ka_9-ak kù-ta sa_{10}-a: 59: 34

nì-sa_{10}-àm: 81: 2

še-ba kù-ta sa_{10}-a-šè: 130: 3

sa_{12}-du_5 *land recorder*

60: 18

sàg *to scatter*

174: 2

saĝ *head*

saĝ nì-gur_{11}-ra: 56: 11; 57: 11; 63: 57, 120

saĝ-nì-gur_{11}-ra-kam: 69: 3; 88: 2; 95: 7; 283: 13

saĝ-ḫi-a: 267: 5

saĝ-sè-ga
  šuku saĝ-sè-ga: 141: 3
saĝ-tuk
  kù saĝ-tuk: 143: 2
sagi *cup-bearer*
  3: 43; 184: 8; 237: 6; 292: 34
  sagi lugal: 3: 83
saĝa *priest*
  3: 6, 50; 56: 47, 62; 88: 23
  saĝa ^{d}Nin-mar-ki: 136: 3; 137: 6
  saĝa ^{d}Nin-šubur: 147: 3
  saĝa ^{d}Šulgi: 56: 74
  aga-ús saĝa: 3: 74, 75
  é-nun saĝa: 6: 4
  ĝá-nun saĝa: 27: 5
  saĝa URU×gána*tenû*^{ki}: 1: 5
  ugula saĝa ^{d}Gá-tùm-du$_{10}$: 31: 6
santana *gardener, orchard worker*
  310: 6
sar *surface measure*
  14: 163; 272: *passim*
si *to load (onto a boat)*
  má-a si: 56: 28, 54; 66: 23; 148: 2; 186: 8, 12
si
  mun tu$_7$ si: 273: 20
si-ì-tum *remainder, balance carried forward*
  58: 2
  si-ì-tum úgu-a ĝá-ĝá: 169: 7
  si-ì-tum nì-ka$_9$-ak: 62: 2; 65: 2
  nì-ka$_9$-ak si-ì-tum: 58: 10
síg *wool*
  63: *passim*; 70: 10, 11; 149: 3, 4; 155: 1, 3, 7; 295: 9
  síg 3-kam-ús: 75: 2
  síg 4-kam-ús: 75: 3
  síg-ba: 35: 8
  síg-bi: 73: *passim*
  síg ^{ĝeš}ga-ríg-ak: 63: *passim*
  síg-gi: 149: 1
  síg gú-tar: 63: *passim*
  síg guz-za: 77: 6
  síg-ĝen: 76: *passim*; 75: 13; 77: 7
  síg-ĝi$_6$: 77: 8
  síg izi-kú-bi: 63: 50, 151
  síg lugal: 77: 1
  síg-ús lugal: 77: 2
  síg mug: 63: *passim*
  síg nì-lám: 77: 3
  síg túg Nina^{ki}: 75: 11
  síg ud$_5$: 122: 2; 161: 1
  síg udu ^{d}Na-rú-a: 75: 6
  síg za-rí-in: 64: *passim*
sig$_4$ *brick*
  sig$_4$-ka-si-ta: 67: 69
sig$_5$ *good, of good quality*
  74: *passim*; 93: *passim*; 272: 14
  ^{zì}ba-ba sig$_5$: 64: *passim*; 93: 28, 38
  dida sig$_5$ (see under dida)
  ĝeš-nud sig$_5$: 267: 26
  ^{ĝeš}banšur sig$_5$-ḫi-a: 267: 30
  ^{ĝeš}gu-za sig$_5$-ḫi-a: 267: 24
  ^{ĝeš}ĝìr-gub sig$_5$: 267: 28
  kaš sig$_5$ (see under kaš)
  ninda sig$_5$ (see under ninda)
  ninda-àr-ra sig$_5$ (see under ninda)
  šim sig$_5$ (see under šim)
  zì-gu sig$_5$ (see under zì-gu)
sig$_7$-a *reaping, pruning*
  8: 1; 23: 5; 314: *passim*
  (see also under géme and ĝuruš)
sìla *measure of capacity*
  1: *passim*; 14: 90; 37: *passim*; 38: *passim*; 39: *passim*; 40: *passim*; 41: *passim*; 42: 1; 44: 3, 4; 45: 1; 47: *passim*; 48: *passim*; 49: *passim*; 50: *passim*; 51: *passim*; 52: *passim*; 53: *passim*; 54: *passim*; 55: *passim*; 56: *passim*; 57: *passim*; 59: *passim*; 60: *passim*; 61: *passim*; 62: 9, 28; 64: *passim*; 65: *passim*; 66: *passim*; 68: *passim*; 69: 1, 21; 83: 1; 86: 8, 14; 90: 1, 5, 11; 93: *passim*; 94: 9; 100: 1, 3; 103: 1; 111: 2; 112: 3, 4, 7; 113: 3, 4; 115: *passim*; 116: 4, 5, 11; 117: *passim*; 119: 1, 3; 120: 1, 5; 122: 1; 134: 2; 139: 13; 141: 1: 144: 1; 151: 2; 156: 2; 167: 1; 172: 1; 185: *passim*; 186: *passim*; 187: *passim*; 188: *passim*; 189: *passim*; 190: *passim*; 191: *passim*; 192: *passim*; 193: *passim*; 194: *passim*; 196: 3; 197: *passim*; 198: *passim*; 199: 1; 200: 3, 15; 201: *passim*; 202: *passim*; 203: *passim*; 204: *passim*; 206: *passim*; 208: *passim*; 209: 9; 210: *passim*; 211: *passim*; 212: *passim*; 213: *passim*; 214: *passim*; 216: *passim*; 217: 2, 5, 6; 218: *passim*; 219: *passim*; 220: *passim*; 221: *passim*; 222: *passim*; 223: *passim*; 224: *passim*; 225:

passim; 226: *passim*; 227: *passim*; 228: *passim*; 229: 1, 14, 15; 230: *passim*; 231: *passim*; 232: *passim*; 233: *passim*; 234: *passim*; 235: 3; 236: *passim*; 237: *passim*; 238: *passim*; 239: *passim*; 240: *passim*; 241: *passim*; 242: *passim*; 243: *passim*; 244: *passim*; 245: *passim*; 246: *passim*; 247: 1, 2; 248: *passim*; 250: *passim*; 251: *passim*; 252: *passim*; 253: *passim*; 254: *passim*; 255: *passim*; 256: *passim*; 257: *passim*; 258: *passim*; 259: *passim*; 260: *passim*; 261: *passim*; 263: *passim*; 264: *passim*; 265: *passim*; 266: *passim*; 267: 21, 22; 272: *passim*; 273: *passim*; 274: 1; 275: 8, 9; 276: 1, 3, 8; 283: *passim*; 284: 44, 45; 306: 1, 2; 308: *passim*; 309: 14, 15; 310: *passim*; 313: *passim*; 315: 2, 5, 11

sila$_4$ *male lamb*
55: 18; 70: 16, 21; 72: 12, 15; 73: 34, 45; 78: 1, 22; 84: 4, 8, 10; 85: 5, 8, 11; 289: 2, 5; 290: 1; 292: *passim*; 295: *passim*; 303: 14, 30; 306: 8
sila$_4$ DN: 287: 4, 5; 292: *passim*
sila$_4$ amar ba-ug$_7$: 304: 3
sila$_4$-ba-ur$_4$: 73: *passim*
sila$_4$-ga: 302: 1
sila$_4$ ká-ĝi$_6$-par$_4$: 292: *passim*
sila$_4$ máš-šu-gíd: 292: 7
sila$_4$-niga: 303: 30
sila$_4$-níta: 70: 4; 72: 4; 78: 3
sila$_4$-níta diri: 72: 6
ad$_x$ sila$_4$ ba-ug$_7$: 153: 2

simug *smith*
kurum$_7$-ak simug: 184: 2

sipa *shepherd*
lá-u$_x$ su-ga sipa didli: 155: 4
rá-gaba sipa ur-gi$_7$: 33: 12
sipa énsi: 82: 20
sipa ^{anše}kunga$_2$: 41: 11
sipa ur-me: 39: 15; 40: 16

sízkur *offering, sacrifice*
38: 11; 67: 82; 171: 7; 315: 13
sízkur a-šà nin: 178: 3
sízkur GN: 187: 4; 194: 13
nì sízkur-ra má Má-gan-na: 115: 8

su-ga *to replace*
[ ] su-ga: 310: 3
lá-u$_x$ su-ga (see lá-u$_x$)

su-su *to return, give back*
su-su-dam: 169: 4; 170: 5
še ur$_5$-ra su-su-dam: 137: 4; 168: 6

sukkal *messenger*
41: 5; 114: 4; 185: 3, 15; 186: 3; 187: 7, 10; 189: *passim*; 190: *passim*; 191: 5, 8; 192: *passim*; 193: *passim*; 194: *passim*; 195: 3, 7, 13; 198: 23; 199: 2, 4; 203: 3, 18; 204: 11; 205: 2, 5; 206: *passim*; 207: 2, 5, 17; 208: 3, 12; 209: 2, 14, 17; 210: 9, 13, 19; 211: 3, 16, 22; 213: 8, 17, 21; 214: *passim*; 215: 12; 216: *passim*; 217: 8; 218: *passim*; 219: *passim*; 220: *passim*; 221: 10; 222: 3, 4, 11; 223: 9, 13, 15; 224: 9, 13; 225: 9; 227: 5, 7, 19; 228: 5, 9; 229: 8, 19, 22; 230: *passim*; 231: *passim*; 232: 10, 15, 19; 233: 15, 21; 234: 14, 17; 236: *passim*; 239: *passim*; 240: 15; 241: 6, 9, 16; 242: 3, 6; 243: *passim*; 244: 6; 246: 3, 6, 12; 248: *passim*; 250: 14, 17, 24; 251: 5, 9, 16; 252: *passim*; 253: 3, 10; 254: 6, 11; 255: 4; 256: *passim*; 258: 15; 260: *passim*; 261: *passim*; 263: 17; 266: 3, 6; 283: 15; 291: 88
sukkal-maḫ: 120: 4

sum *onion*
272: *passim*
sum ĝeš ḪI-da: 272: *passim*
sum kú-du$_{11}$-ga: 272: 36
sum-numun: 272: 9, 22
ĝeš-sum ĝeš ḪI-da: 272: *passim*
ĝeš-sum-numun: 272: *passim*

sumun *old*
sumun PN: 82: 23

sur
bisaĝ ambar-sur-ra: 180: 2

-Š-

ša *unit of weight*
ša (kù-babbar): 140: 1

ša-dub
226: 14

šà *from, inside*
62: 18; 67: 40; 142: 8; 279: 4
šà GN: 2: 10, 12; 9: 25; 19: 58; 20: 47; 23: 30; 29: 6; 32: 7, 44: 13, 15; 72: 24; 73: 55; 75: 7, 15; 76: 71; 77: 12; 80: 19; 93: 33; 96: 3, 15, 19; 127: 7; 131: 6; 140: 6; 147: 2, 7; 164: 6; 269: 13; 272: 37; 283: 14; 292: 37; 303: 32; 306: 8
šà-ba: 311: 14, 15, 26

šà-bala: 169: 5
šà-bi-ta: 1: *passim*; 56: 12; 57: 12; 58: 3; 59: 8; 60: 24; 61: 11; 62: 10; 63: 58; 64: 73; 65: 12; 66: 12; 67: 26, 72; 68: 11; 69: 4; 88: 3; 97: 2; 275: 4; 283: 13
šà-dub: 310: 19
šà é-gal: 93: 18; 126: 2; 297: 2
šà é-temen-na: 276: 11
šà énsi: 39: 22; 40: 23
šà kurum$_7$-ma: 63: 22
šà mu-er$_{10}$-ra-ta: 297: 3; 298: 4
šà uru: 74: 27

ša$_{13}$-dub-ba *archivist*
3: 52; 40: 18; 74:16; 184:1

šà-gal *fodder*
93: 4
šà-gal aga-ús: 265: 14
šà-gal alim: 45: 6
šà-gal anše zi-gúm-ma: 44: 16
šà-gal érin-na: 22: 3
šà-gal érin bala gub-ba: 24: 2; 25: 9; 26: 3; 27: 3
šà-gal érin i$_7$-NE-tum-mal gub-ba: 93: 35
šà-gal éš-gàr: 42: 2
šà-gal gu$_4$: 45: 10
šà-gal gu$_4$-udu: 64: 57, 93
šà-gal lú kaš$_4$: 64: 52
šà-gal lugal: 93: 74
šà-gal šidim: 64: 94
šà-gal udu: 43: 4

šà-gu$_4$ *ox-driver*
érin šà-gu$_4$: 11: 2, 7
še šà-gu$_4$ nu-dab$_5$-me: 69: 9

šabra *temple administrator*
14: 119; 21: seal; 57: 47; 158: 3; 162: 8; 204: 12; 238: 6; 291: 97; 303: 26; 311: 13
aga-ús šabra: 19: 12; 20: 13
kišib šabra: 69: 6

šagina *general*
93: 48, 77; 286: 2
šagina ar-za-na: 283: 21

šár-ra-ab-du *inspector*
3: 58

še *barley, grain*
1: *passim*; 6: 1; 14: *passim*; 16: 1; 17: 1; 18: 1, 8; 22: 1; 23: 1; 25: 1, 8; 26: 1, 2; 27: 1, 2; 28: 1; 31: 1; 32: 1; 33: 1; 42: 1; 43: 1; 44: 10, 12, 14; 45: 4; 46: 1, 2; 47: *passim*; 48: *passim*; 49: *passim*; 50: *passim*; 51: *passim*; 52: *passim*; 53: *passim*; 54: *passim*; 55: *passim*; 57: 1; 60: 1, 29; 61: *passim*; 62: *passim*; 64: 95, 99; 65: *passim*; 68: *passim*; 69: 1; 86: 1, 5; 87: 1; 88: 1; 94: 1, 9; 95: 1; 119: 8; 121: 1; 124: 1; 127: 1; 130: 1; 136: 1; 137: 1; 138: 1; 148: 1; 150: 1; 152: 1; 157: 1; 158: 1; 168: 1; 170: 2; 173: 1; 174: 1, 2; 175: 1; 194: 9; 197: 1, 12; 276: 1, 3, 6; 283: 24; 310: 20, 22; 313: *passim*; 317; 1
še (as a unit of weight): 60: 7, 23, 27; 63: *passim*; 129: 10; 143: 1; 170: 1; 309: 6
še PN: 130: 5
še-amar-e kú-a: 46: 3
še-kíkken: 127: 2
še-ba: 1: 115, 168; 28: 2; 31: 2; 32: 2; 34: 10, 11, 13; 56: 49, 65; 57: 16; 65: 19
še-ba iti x: 61: 16
še-ba kù-ta sa$_{10}$-a-šè: 130: 3
še-ba un-ĝa$_6$ ù á-lú-ḫun-ĝá a-šà: 69: 7
še-bala: 61: 32; 62: 23; 65: 24, 27; 68: 14; 93: 73, 76, 78
še é-kin-a: 60: 17
še é-kin-ĝá: 152: 2
še é-^{d}Nin-mar-ki: 57: 48
še ^{d}En-líl-lá: 138: 3; 236: 10
še-érin: 180: 1
še gána-gu$_4$: 56: 2; 57: 2
še gána-uru$_4$-lá: 56: 5; 57: 2
še ĝeš è-a: 3: 49; 15: 25; 16: 9; 17: 7; 18: 12
še ĝeš-ì: 160: 1; 311: 15
še gur-saĝ-ĝál-la: 15: 1, 17
še ì-dè-a: 18: 10
še in-bi nu-dè: 17: 4
še-kéš-rá: 10: 6
še-kin-ku$_5$: 10: 3;
še ku$_6$: 64: 50, 54
še-li: 151: 2
še-lú: 273: 19, 44
še má-a si-ga: 66: 23
še mun gazi: 88: 12
še-numun: 1: 123; 6: 2
še-numun-ta gur-ra: 56: 7; 57: 6
še šu nu-ti-a: 14: *passim*
še ur$_5$-ra (see ur$_5$-ra)

šeg$_9$-bar *deer or mountain goat(?)*
47: 26; 48: 13; 49: 22; 50: 20; 51: 21; 52: 21; 53: 20; 54: 13

šeš *brother*
4: 9; 19: 17; 20: 16; 36: 2
šeš-a-ni: 96: 24
šeš lukur: 263: 4
dumu-šeš-a-ni: 19: 22
šeš-ba 215: 9, 13; 227: 11, 22; 229: 16, 21, 24; 233: 3, 8

ŠID
63: 99
ŠID á 6-gín: 63: 33

šidim *mason*
šà-gal šidim: 64: 94

šim *resin, aromatic*
3: 3, 9, 77; 151: 1; 273: *passim*
šim anše: 188: 9
šim dug du$_{10}$: 146: 1
šim-ì: 156: 1
šim sig$_5$: 61: 31; 306: 1
šim zì ká-a ^{d}Nin-ĝír-su-ka: 146: 2

šu du$_8$ *guarantor*
šu du$_8$-a-bi: 312: 9

šu-gi$_4$ *old (said of cattle or workers)*
áb-máḫ šu-gi$_4$: 92: 22
anše-níta šu-gi$_4$: 278: 3
géme šu-gi$_4$: 34: 6

šu-gíd *dues, obligation*
5: 10
(see also under áb, gu$_4$, and sila$_4$)

šu-ḫa *fisherman*
19: 2; 20: 2; 184: 20
šu-ḫa-me: 101: 12

šu ḫar
šu ḫar-re-me: 21: 9

šu+níĝin *total*
1: *passim*; 3: *passim*; 14: *passim*; 15: 17; 18: 8; 23: *passim*; 56: *passim*; 57: *passim*; 58: 9; 59: 7, 29, 31; 60: 22, 23; 61: *passim*; 62: *passim*; 63: *passim*; 64: *passim*; 65: *passim*; 66: 11, 19; 67: *passim*; 68: 8; 70: 7, 17, 22; 72: *passim*; 73: 52; 75: 5, 13; 76: *passim*; 77: 10; 80: 14, 15, 16; 85:*passim*; 88: 1, 26; 93: 72; 101: 11; 104: 42; 118: 18; 129: 10; 272: 30, 31, 32; 273: *passim*; 275: 9; 277: 11, 12; 283: 12, 24; 288: *passim*; 292: 36

šu ... ti *to receive, to take in hand*
šu ba-ab-ti: 219: 16; 231: 19
šu ba-ti: 6: 6; 22: 7; 26: 7; 27: 7; 28: 7; 30: 6; 32: 5; 37: 10; 42: 5, 60: 30; 66: 15; 68: 10; 93: 67; 122: 4; 123: 5; 124: 5; 127: 6; 128: 5; 132: 4; 134: 7; 135: 6; 136: 6; 138: 5; 146: 5; 148: 6; 149: 9; 150: 6; 152: 7; 153: 5; 154: 6; 155: 12; 156: 5; 157: 4; 158: 6; 160: 5; 162: 5; 164: 3; 165: 6; 166: 5; 168: 5; 173: 6; 174: 6; 175: 4; 176: 4; 178: 6; 189: 17; 190: 18; 192: 19; 206: 21; 214: 6; 241: 13; 253: 7; 274: 4; 284: 47; 288: 75, 89, 103; 299: 3; 300; 4; 301: 9; 304: 7
šu ba-an-ti: 282: 9; 305: 10
še-érin-e šu-ti-a: 180: 2
še šu nu-ti-a: 14: *passim*

šu-zi
155: 11

šuku *allotment*
[šuku]-ĝeš-dù: 64: 83
šuku-ì-da-a: 64: 80
šuku-kišib-du$_8$-ḫu-um: 64: 81
šuku-mar-sa-ŠUM: 64: 82
šuku saĝ-sè-ga: 141: 3
udu šuku-ra: 78: 12

šul-ḫi *outer wall*
gi-šul-ḫi-šè ĝen-na: 198: 6

-T-

tab-ba
gurdub tab-ba: 75: 1

tag *to weave*
á túg tag-a-ra U.NU-a: 63: 9, 136

tak$_4$ *to set aside*
im-e tak$_4$-a: 8: 7; 35: 6; 98: 3

tu$_7$ *soup*
mun tu$_7$ si: 273: 20

túg *article of cloth*
201: 9; 204: 18; 250: 18
túg 3-kam-ús: 63: *passim*; 76: *passim*
túg 4-kam-ús: 63: *passim*; 76: *passim*
túg ba-lá u$_4$-8-kam: 76: 70
túg-bar: 82: *passim*
túg da-ba-tum: 118: 18
túg-gada: 191: 9
túg-gibil: 206: 8
túg guz-za lugal: 63: 60

túg guz-za gíd-a-ús lugal: 63: 63
túg guz-za 3-kam-ús: 63: 68
túg guz-za 4-kam-ús: 63: 71; 99: 3
túg ĝeš-a-ĝál-la: 63: 9
túg lugal: 63: *passim*; 70: 10; 76: *passim*
túg-ús lugal: 63: *passim*; 70: 11; 75: 1; 76: *passim*
TÚG.ŠÈ lúgud-da: 292: 10
túg uš-bar: 293: 1

túg-íl *a profession*
19: 18; 20: 17

^{ĝeš}tukul *weapon*
^{ĝeš}tukul-e dab$_5$-ba-me: 8: 9; 19: 42; 36: 11
é-tukul: 41: 8
lú ^{ĝeš}tukul (see under lú ^{ĝeš}tukul)

túl *fountain, pond, or channel*
é-gal gú-túl-ta: 145: 3

túm *to bring, carry*
ì-íb-tum: 63: 120
mu-túm: 60: 32; 66: 20; 72: 8; 85: 4; 99: 5; 100: 6; 101: 14; 284: 46; 303: 33
mu-túm énsi Nibru^{ki}: 287: 6
mu-túm lugal: 291: 23
mu-túm *Ṣe-lu-uš*-^{d}Da-gan: 287: 3

tùm *to bring, carry*
a-ta-tùm-dè: 282: 7

tum$_4$ *to carry*
ga-tum$_4$-dam: 56: 3
tum$_4$-dam: 46: 6

tur
19: 15; 20: 14; 23: 25, 26

tuš *to sit*
tuš-a: 112: 5
bala tuš-a: 14: *passim*; 31: 3
ĝá-nun-da-tuš-a: 41: 4

-U-

U.NU-a *thread*(?)
á túg tag-a-ra U.NU-a: 63: 9, 136

ù
nì-ù-du$_8$-ḫu-um 93: 40

ù-gúl *overseer*
215: 8; 232: 6; 233: 2, 24; 303: 8

ù-tu-da *newborn*
302: 4
gu$_4$ 1 ù-tu-da: 284: 4

u$_4$ *day*
13: 20; 67: 31; 187: 15; 188: 12; 202: 13; 203: 20; 204: 19; 226: 21; 239: 30; 259: 18; 283: 22
u$_4$ x ba-zal (see under zal)
u$_4$ 1-kam u$_4$-30-šè: 283: 3, 8
u$_4$ x-kam: 11: 12; 12: 27; 19: 59; 20: 49; 37: 12; 38: 12; 39: 21; 40: 22; 41: 25; 45: 12; 47: 29; 48: 16; 49: 25; 50: 23; 51: 25; 52: 25; 53: 23; 54: 18; 55: 20; 62: 33; 65: 19; 73: 54; 74: 30; 75: 14; 76: 70; 77: 11; 79: 1, 2, 3; 80: 18; 84: 12; 141: 4; 185: 21; 186: 16; 191: 7, 16; 194: 18; 195: 2, 9, 12; 198: 24; 210; 23; 211: 26; 212: *passim*; 215: 7, 11; 221: 21; 222: 22; 227: *passim*; 228: 4, 6, 10; 232: 5, 8, 21; 233: *passim*; 234: 19; 235: 6; 237: 19; 238: 13; 240: 20; 243: 28; 244: 19; 245: 18; 246: 19; 250: 26; 251: 4, 8; 255: 26; 256: 37; 257: 16; 258: 23; 273: *passim*; 287: 11; 292: *passim*; 295: 3; 297: 4; 298: 5; 301: 6; 302: 5; 304: 4; 306: 10
u$_4$-KU-a: 19: 56; 63: 120
u$_4$ x-šè: 7: *passim*; 10: 2, 5; 14: *passim*; 63: *passim*
u$_4$ *wa-da-al-tum*: 304: 2
má u$_4$-zal-la: 64: 38; 102: 3

u$_4$-sakar *new moon*
èš-èš u$_4$-sakar u$_4$-15: 67: 31; 110: 2
nì-dab$_5$ u$_4$-sakar: 117: 9
nì u$_4$-sakar: 273: 21
u$_4$-sakar iti amar-a-a-si: 141: 4

u$_8$ *ewe*
67: 1, 22, 61; 70: 14, 19; 72: 1, 11, 14; 73: *passim*; 78: 2; 85: 5, 7, 10; 289: 4; 290: 1
u$_8$-sila$_4$-nú-a niga: 287: 8, 9
u$_8$-udu-gukkal: 72: 9

ud$_5$ *female goat*
78: 5, 23; 84: 6; 285: 1; 289: 4
ud$_5$-máš-ḫi-a: 78: 4
ud$_5$-niga DN: 287; 1, 2
síg ud$_5$: 122: 2; 161: 1

udu *sheep*
41: 12, 13, 21; 47: *passim*; 48: *passim*; 49: *passim*; 50: *passim*; 51: *passim*; 52: *passim*; 53: *passim*; 54: *passim*; 55: *passim*; 67: *passim*; 70: 1; 72: 2, 14; 73: 52; 78: *passim*; 85: 5; 96: 1; 205: 1, 7; 286: 3, 4; 290: 2; 297: 10; 303: *passim*
udu DN: 67: 73, 74, 81; 75: 6

udu ba-ur$_4$: 73: 54
udu bar-su: 73: 10, 46
udu-eme-gi-ḫi-a: 267: 11
udu-gal: 73: 8, 14, 41
udu gukkal (see gukkal)
udu-ì: 171: 2, 4
udu-máš: 67: *passim*
udu máš dab$_5$-ba: 104: 42
udu-máš-niga: 267: 12
udu nì-šà-te: 67: 28
udu-niga: 67: 5, 65; 171: 2, 4; 303: 9, 26, 28
udu-niga zà-gú-<lá>: 297: 1
udu-níta: 67: 2, 23, 62; 70: 2, 15, 20; 72: 11; 73: *passim*; 85: 7, 10; 289: 1, 7
udu-níta bar-su: 73: 46
udu *ru-ub-ba-àm*: 70: 18
udu sá-du$_{11}$: 67: 27
udu-saĝ sila$_4$: 78: 1
udu šuku-ra: 78: 12
ad$_x$ udu: 38: 10; 154: 1, 2; 164: 1
ad$_x$ udu ba-ug$_7$: 153: 1
dub-sar gu$_4$-udu: 184: 18
é udu: 10: 9; 37: 5
é-udu-ĝá-nun-ĝeš: 171: 6
kuš udu: 277: 4, 12, 15
kuš udu-ḫi-a nì-kú-a: 305: 6
šà-gal gu$_4$-udu: 64: 57, 93
šà-gal udu: 43: 4

úgu (A.KA) *account*
úgu-a ĝá-ĝá: 56: 45, 63; 57: 31, 41; 81: 6; 93: 55, 68; 139: 14
úgu PN ĝá-ĝá-dam: 68: 18
úgu PN ba-ĝar: 59: *passim*; 66: 17
úgu PN ĝál-la: 64: 104
si-ì-tum úgu-a ĝá-ĝá: 169: 7
PN úgu ĝál: 65: 18

ugula *overseer*
3: 41; 9: 3, 5, 7; 14: 44; 16: 10; 17: 8; 19: *passim*; 20: *passim*; 22: 6; 25: 3, 6; 31: 6; 34: 12; 36; 1; 63: 170; 72: 23; 74: 11, 22, 28; 79: 5; 80: 10, 12; 87: 6; 92: 25; 96: 16; 97: 9; 118: 23; 142: 5; 150: 5
ugula alan-da: 262: 6
ugula ḫé-dab$_5$: 3: 67
ugula kíkken: 129: 8
ugula kíkken énsi-ka: 121: seal
ugula mušen-dù: 168: 4
ugula uru-bi: 63: 10, 35, 137
ugula uš-bar: 256: 36; 282: 3

un-ĝa$_6$ *porter, laborer*
3: 63, 64, 65; 14: *passim*
un-ĝa$_6$-me: 107: 2
géme un-ĝa$_6$: 288: 88
še-ba un-ĝa$_6$ ù á-lú-ḫun-ĝá a-šà: 69: 7

um-mi-a *craftsman, specialist*
um-mi-a é-kišib-ba: 4: 7

umbin *wheel*
ḫu-bu-um umbin: 125: 1

ur *dog*
sipa ur-me: 39: 15; 40: 16

ur-gi$_7$ *dog*
rá-gaba sipa ur-gi$_7$: 33: 12; 41: 12
ur-gi$_7$: 39: 8, 9; 40: 9, 10
ur-gi$_7$-gal-gal: 38: 8

ur$_4$ *to pluck, shear*
sila$_4$-ba-ur$_4$: 73: *passim*

ur$_5$-ra *interest-bearing loan*
še ur$_5$-ra: 136: 2; 150: 2; 152: 4
še ur$_5$-ra dumu dab$_5$-ba: 138: 2; 173: 2
še ur$_5$-ra su-su-dam: 137: 4; 168: 6

uru *city*
9: 25; 194; 9; 236: 4
uru Bàd-an-na: 311: 3, 17
ab-ba-uru: 184: 9
šà uru: 74: 27 (see also under dabin, ì, kaš, ninda, and zì)
igi-1-ĝál zì uru-ta-ḫi-DU-a: 64: 100
lú-dab$_5$-ba uru didli-me: 224: 12
ugula uru-bi: 64: 10, 35, 137
uru-ta nu-è: 14: *passim*

uru$_4$ *to plow*
gu$_4$ é-gal-ke$_4$ íb-uru$_4$-a-šè: 56: 50, 66
zi-ga é-gal-šè íb-uru$_4$-a-šè 149:5–6

urudu *copper*
125: 2; 135: 1

UŠ *measure of length?*
311: *passim*

uš-bar *weaver*
19: 7; 20: 7; 35: 3
géme uš-bar: 30: 2; 32: 2; 34: 11; 153: 6; 154: 3
túg uš-bar: 293: 1
ugula uš-bar (see under ugula)

utul *herdsman, shepherd*
288: 5; 311: 4
utul lugal: 311: 7, 24

uzu *cut of meat*
uzu gu$_4$ niga-šè: 306: 3

-Z-

za-rí-in *ordinary quality*
síg za-rí-in: 64: *passim*

zabar *bronze*
267: 17
gur zabar: 57: 14
za-lum zabar-ḫi-a: 267: 16

zabar-dab$_5$
38: 7; 158: 5
ki zabar-dab$_5$-ta: 210: 6

zaḫ *to flee*
zaḫ-me: 267: 4

zal *to pass*
ba-zal: 8: 11; 9: 24; 63: 109; 284: 1
zal-la: 14: 192, 200
má u$_4$-zal-la: 64: 38; 102: 3
u$_4$ x ba-zal: 5: 1, 5; 82: *passim*; 134: 8; 171: 12; 177: 6; 269: 4, 9; 296: 4; 303: *passim*

zi *to disburse*
ba-zi: 36: 9; 135: 4; 296: 6; 297: 6; 298: 6; 308: 14
zi-ga: 1: *passim*; 14: 181; 37: 12; 38: 12; 39: 21; 40: 22; 41: 25; 56: 51, 67, 70; 57: 44; 59: 32; 61: 27, 37; 62: 27; 63: 158; 64: 102, 108; 65: 29; 67: 57, 112; 71: 4, 8, 14; 72: 10, 19; 85: 6, 15; 93: 37; 105: 6; 106: 3; 107: 3; 108: 3; 109: 6; 111: 6; 113: 8; 114: 5; 115: 10; 116: 14; 149: 5; 185: 21; 186: 16; 187: 15; 188: 12; 194: 18; 198: 24; 202: 13; 203: 20; 204: 19; 210: 23; 211: 13, 26; 212: 19; 221: 21; 222: 22; 226: 21; 234: 19; 237: 19; 238: 13; 239: 30; 240: 20; 243: 28; 244: 19; 245: 18; 246: 19; 247; 6; 250: 26; 255: 26; 256: 37; 259: 18; 262: 9; 264: 12; 275: 10; 276: 9; 277: 13; 284: 49, 64; 288: 116; 291: 112; 292: 37; 310: 20, 22
zi-ga didli: 197: 14
zi-ga lugal: 61: 15; 93: 22; 197: 3
zi-lugal: 312: 6
diri zi-ga: 284: 66

zi-gúm-ma *messenger hostel*
lú zi-gúm-ma: 253: 13
šà-gal anše zi-gúm-ma: 44: 16
anše zi-gúm-ma-šè ĝen-na: 221:15

zi-ir *to break*
kišib-bi ba-zi-ir: 59: 12

zì *flour*
65: 18; 87: 2; 93: 29, 80; 94: 2; 117: 1; 131: 2, 3; 185: *passim*; 186: *passim*; 187: *passim*; 190: 16; 192: 17; 194: 1; 198: *passim*; 202: 1, 6, 9; 203: *passim*; 204: *passim*; 211: *passim*; 213: 11; 217: 2, 6; 221: *passim*; 222: 1; 227: *passim*; 229: *passim*; 232: 21; 233: *passim*; 234: *passim*; 237: *passim*; 239: *passim*; 240: *passim*; 243: *passim*; 244: *passim*; 246: *passim*; 250: *passim*; 251: 6; 255: *passim*; 256: *passim*; 257: *passim*; 263: *passim*; 266: *passim*; 310: 5
zì-a-saĝ: 64: 28
zì anše: 245: 17
zì-dub-dub: 44: 3; 111: 1; 113: 3; 115: 6; 116: 4, 10; 117: 5
zì Ĝír-su^{ki}-ta DU-a: 93: 25
zì kaskal-šè: 223: 5; 227: 18; 229: *passim*; 232: *passim*; 233: 6, 14; 254: 5
zì kaš-dé-a lugal: 64: 112
zì má-a-si-gi$_4$: 186: 8
zì šà uru: 223: 4; 227: 17; 229: 5, 10; 232: 8, 13, 16; 233: 5, 13
gú-zì-sig$_5$: 89: 1, 5
ninda zì-gu: 64: 85; 93: 79
šim zì ká-a ^{d}Nin-ĝír-su-ka: 146: 2

zì-gu *a type of flour*
44: 6; 64: 6, 31; 93: 12; 115: 5; 116: 3, 9; 117: 3; 223: 1, 8; 233: 1; 254: 2, 9
zì-gu nida: 64: 79
zì-gu sig$_5$: 64: *passim*; 93: 30, 39, 48; 223: 1, 14
zì-gu šà uru: 229: 1, 14; 232: 1
zì-gu-še: 64: 41
zì-gu-ús: 64: 32; 93: 31, 49

zì-munu$_4$ *type of ration*
zì-munu$_4$-ḫi-a: 105: 1; 114: 1

zì-sig$_{15}$ a type of flour
64: *passim*; 89: *passim*; 93: *passim*; 113: 2; 115: 4; 116: 2, 8; 117: 4; 134: 1; 139: 19; 307: 1

zíz *emmer wheat*
56: 41; 86: 4, 5; 89: *passim*; 94: 4; 109: 1; 128: 1, 2; 310: 9
zíz-gú-nida: 89: 4
zíz-kal: 89: 5

zù-lum *dates*
74: 17; 97: 1; 176: 1; 267: 22

Personal Names

-A-

A-[ ]
76: 7 (na-gada)

A-a-kal-la
167: 2; 229: 7 (dumu nu-bànda); 287: 10 (muḫaldim); 311: 12

A-a-ni-šu
260: 22 (sukkal)

A-ab-ba
16: 10 (ugula)

A-ba-ni-sì-gi
63: 97

A-ba-šu-na
181: 4 (father of Lú-diĝir-ra)

A-bí-a
190: 3 (sukkal); 222: 20 (lú-kaš$_4$); 248: 3 (sukkal)

A-bu-[ ]
245: 15

A-bu-a
33: 9

A-bu-da-dí
256: 32 (lú-kaš$_4$)

*A-bu-da-*du$_{10}$
250: 24 (sukkal)

*A-bu-*du$_{10}$
294: 14

A-bu-ni
19: 6; 20: 6; 209: 17 (sukkal); 217: 8 (sukkal)

*A-bu-um-*diĝir
291: 101

A-bù-ṭá-ab
208: 6

A-da-a
193: 22 (sukkal); 245: 3; 246: 6 (sukkal)

A-da-làl
187: 13 (lú-kaš$_4$); 226: 3 (lú ^{ĝeš}tukul gu-la); 228: 12 (lú-kaš$_4$); 243: 27; 251: 13 (lú ^{ĝeš}tukul gu-la); 266: 3 (sukkal); 313: 8 (engar, dumu Im-ti-dam)

A-[ ]-du$_{10}$
294: 7

A-gi$_4$
141: 2; 151: 3

A-gu
120: 8

A-gu-[ ]
2: 5

A-gu-a
200: 1, 20 (lú ^{ĝeš}tukul gu-la); 207: 5 (sukkal); 266: 9 (lú-kaš$_4$)

A-gu-a-ti
243: 10 (sukkal); 250: 14 (sukkal)

A-ḫa-ba-la
98: 2 (gudu$_4$ ^{d}Lama)

A-ḫa-ni-šu
294: 8

A-ḫu-[ ]
191: 14

A-ḫu-a
4: 2; 14: 11, 40, 83 (nu-bànda); 33: 8; 62: 32 (father of ^{d}Ba-ú); 114: 4 (sukkal maškim); 164: 4; 184: 13 (nu-bànda); 199: 2, 4 (sukkal); 209: 2 (sukkal); 219: 6 (sukkal); 261: 17 (sukkal); 263: 4 (šeš lukur)

*A-ḫu-*a-gàr
211: 9 (lú-kaš$_4$)

*A-ḫu-*du$_{10}$
227: 2; 233: 24 (ù-gúl)

A-ḫu-ma
222: 21

A-ḫu-ni
212: 6; 221: 10 (sukkal)

*A-ḫu-um-*diĝir
63: 171

A-kal-la
1: 126, 214; 3: 17 (nu-bànda gu$_4$), 47; 13: 10; 21: 4; 74: 7; 104: 4 (dumu dab$_5$-ba), 8 (na-gada); 133: 3; 219: 8 (aga-ús-gal-gal); 240: 6 (lú ^{ĝeš}tukul gu-la); 279: 2; 280: seal (father of Lú-ša$_6$-ì-zu); 308: 6 (kuš$_7$); 315: 4

A-la-a
266: 16 (lú-kaš$_4$)

A-li
265: 13 (gudu$_4$)

A-li-šà-ge
41: 19 (Mar-tu-mí)
A-lum-ma
23: 15 (father of Lú-diĝir-ra)
A-mu
39: 16 (nagar); 40: 17 (nagar); 56: 20 (dumu Lugal-ḫé-ĝál)
A-mur-diĝir
229: 8 (sukkal); 294: 13
A-mur-^{d}Utu
188: 11 (lú-kaš$_4$)
A-na-ti
263: 2 (dumu nu-bànda)
A-tu
19: 25 (father of Nam-tar-íb-gu-ul); 20: 24 (father of Nam-tar-íb-gu-ul); 34: 13; 73: 49 (dumu Al-la); 86: 6; 96: 26; 104: 10 (na-gada, dumu Al-la), 21; 281: 2; 292: 24 (sagi)
Á-[ ]
78: 20
Á-bí-lí
187: 7 (sukkal)
Á-na-mu
41: 5 (sukkal); 49: 17; 51: 16; 52: 16; 53: 14; 55: 14; 178: 5, seal (dub-sar, dumu Ur-^{d}Ba-ú)
Á-<na>-mu: 47: 18
Á-pil-la-núm
223: 15 (sukkal); 231: 8 (sukkal)
Á-pil-la-tum
303: 34
Á-pil-lí
215: 9 (šeš-ba); 233: 11 (aga-ús-gal); 303: 8 (ù-gúl)
Á-pil-lí-a
191: 8 (sukkal); 207: 20 (dumu nu-bànda)
Á-pil-lum
295: 12 (Mar-tu)
Á-ša$_6$-ga
93: 36
AB-[ ]
71: 2 (father of Da-da)
Ab-ba
15: 20 (engar); 291: 87
Ab-ba-[ ]
3: 36
Ab-ba-gi-na
5: 6; 18: 5; 74: 28 (ugula); 82: 21 (dumu [ ]); 121: seal (father of Nam-maḫ-^{d}Ba-ú)
Ab-ba-kal-la
19: 12 (aga-ús šabra); 20: 12 (aga-ús šabra); 67: 59, 116; 96: 25; 275: 7
Ab-ba-mu
56: 26 (má-laḫ$_6$-gal); 74: 26 (father of Ur-^{d}Li$_9$-si$_4$); 92: 7 (ba-NUMUN); 94: 5; 185: 20 (father of Ur-^{d}Ba-ú)
Ab-ba-uru
3: 79; 86: 11 (father of Ur-^{d}Ba-ú)
Ad-da
38: 2
Ad-da-na-bi
200: 23 (lú ^{ĝeš}tukul gu-la)
Ad-da-uru
1: 115, 168; 39: 12; 40: 13
Ad-du-EN
29: 1
Ad-mu-a
41: 15 (Mar-tu-mí)
Al-[ ]
3: 45; 100: 2; 310: 4 (rá-gaba, father of ^{d}En-líl-lá)
Al-la
73: 49 (father of A-tu); 104: 6 (na-gada), 10 (father of A-tu); 257: 10 (Mar-tu); 277: 9
Al-la-[ ]
291: 43, 53
Al-la-kam
63: 106
Al-la-mu
21: seal (šabra, father of Nam-zi-tar-ra); 83: 2; 105: 5; 168: 3
Al-lí-ga
8: 6
Al-mu
3: 27 (nu-bànda gu$_4$)
Amar-ka$_5$-a
8: 1 (father of Ur-^{d}IM)
Amar-šúba
307: 4, seal (dub-sar, ir$_{11}$ énsi Adab^{ki})
An-e-ba-ab-du$_7$
252: 18 (sukkal)
AN.EN.TUM
227: 22 (šeš-ba)

An-gàr
211: 12 (lú-kaš$_4$)
An-né
47: 12; 49: 11; 50: 9; 51: 9; 52: 9; 53: 8; 54: 7; 55: 8
An-né-ba-du$_7$
203: 3 (sukkal); 204: 11 (sukkal)
Ar-ši-aḫ
291: 75 (énsi Babili[ki])

-B-

Ba-a
133: 4
Ba-ad-da
138: 4 (father of Ur-mes)
Ba-an-zi-gi
311: 21 (utul lugal)
Ba-ba-mu
312: 10 (nar)
Ba-ga-zi-mu
74: 15
Ba-lu$_5$-lu$_5$
242: 3 (sukkal)
Ba-mu
118: 10 (ḫé-dab$_5$ [ĝeš]tukul-e dab$_5$-ba)
Ba-na-ti
129: 2
Ba-ša$_6$-ga
19: 14 (dumu [d]Nin-mar-ki-ka), 26 (father of Lú-[d]Nin-šubur); 20: 25 (father of Lú-[d]Nin-šubur); 25: 3 (ugula); 229: 3 (lú [ĝeš]tukul gu-la); 239: 6 (sukkal)
[d]Ba-ú
62: 32 (dumu *A-ḫu-a*)
Ba-za-mu
233: 7 (aga-ús-gal)
Ba-zi
19: 31 (father of Lú-[d]Nin-ĝír-su); 20: 28 (father of Lú-[d]Nin-ĝír-su); 25: 11; 26: 4; 59: 3, 25; 64: 36 (father of Lú-[d]Nin-ĝír-su); 76: 55 (na-gada); 93: 67; 124: 3; 127: 4; 151: 6, seal (father of Lú-[d]Nin-ĝír-su); 159: 4 (father of Ur-[d]Ba-ú); 161: 3 (father of Lú-[d]Nin-ĝír-su); 163: 3, seal (father of Lú-[d]Nin-ĝír-su); 167: 4
Ba-zi-zi
76: 14 (na-gada)
Bi-[ ]
291: 110
Bí-bí
189: 3 (sukkal)
Bí-bí-a
195: 6 (aga-ús-gal)
Bí-bí-DU
241: 3
Bí-du$_{11}$-ì-ša$_6$
65: 31; 139: 5
Bí-ti-ti
185: 3 (sukkal); 186: 3 (sukkal); 187: 10 (sukkal); 194: 3 (sukkal); 239: 3 (sukkal)
Bu-zu-[ ]
288: 37
Bur-[d]IM
210: 3
BUR.LU-ma-al-gi$_4$
38: 11
Bur-ma-àm
248: 9 (lú [ĝeš]tukul gu-la)
Bur-Ma-ma
200: 7 (lú [ĝeš]tukul gu-la); 243: 24 (lú-kaš$_4$)
Bur-ra
248: 15 (sukkal)
Bur-ra-bi
263: 9 (aga-ús)

-D-

Da-[ ]
62: 15
Da-a
227: 4 (lú-kaš$_4$)
Da-a-a
198: 6; 238: 6
Da-a-mu
69: 11; 316: 1 (father of Ur-[d]Namma)
Da-an-ni-núm
35: 5
Da-bu-ma
219: 19 (sukkal)
Da-da
71: 2 (dumu AB-[ ]); 104: 20; 118: 15 (ḫé-dab$_5$ [ĝeš]tukul-e dab$_5$-ba); 136: 4 (engar gu-la); 140: 3 (dumu Ur-[ĝeš]gigir); 211: 16 (sukkal); 229: 18 (dumu nu-bànda)
Da-da-a
36: 3 (dumu Ur-[d]Ḫendur-saĝ); 260: 6 (sukkal)

Da-da-bu-ni
255: 25

Da-da-ni
19: 37 (ugula); 20: 34 (ugula); 233: 2 (ù-gúl)

Da-gi
131: 5 (father of [ ])

Da-gu-nir
233: 19 (aga-ús-gal)

Da-gu-ù
269: 5

Da-rí-ša
41: 16 (Mar-tu-mí)

Daḫ-ḫi-še-en
80: 10 (ugula)

Dan-^{d}Šul-gi
291: 81

Diĝir-a-[ ]
291: 59

Diĝir-á-ì-ĝál
235: 4 (Mar-tu)

Diĝir-*á-lí-ik*
44: 2 (Mar-tu); 110: 11

Diĝir-*ba-ni*
202: 8 (lú-kaš$_{4}$); 203: 6; 204: 15; 210: 6

Diĝir-*dan*
247: 4 (dumu nu-bànda); 253: 13 (lú zi-gúm-ma)

Diĝir-ĝá-ì-ša$_{6}$
21: 3

Diĝir-ma-ì-ĝál
112: 8

Diĝir-ra
79: seal (father of Ur-^{d}Ùr-bar-tab)

Diĝir-*ra-bí*
263: 11; 288: 55

Du-du
64: 10 (father of Ur-é-ninnu); 142: 5 (ugula); 238: 9; 288: 89

Du-šu-sig$_{7}$-a
37: 6

Du-ú-du
33: 6

Du$_{10}$-ga
56: 24 (father of Lú-bùluĝ-ĝá)

Du$_{10}$-*ì-lí*
288: 24

Du$_{11}$-ga
36: 9

Du$_{11}$-ga-li
261: 12 (sukkal)

Du$_{11}$-ga-zi-da
96: 16 (ugula); 275: 8

-E-

E-[ ]
35: 9 (father of Šeš-kal-la)

E-ib-éš-gàr
252: 15 (sukkal)

E-la-ra-ak
294: 3

E-ma-àm
231: 5 (sukkal)

E-NE.NE
201: 12

É-a-en-na
65: 4

É-a-mu
139: 6

É-ambar
86: 4

É-dar-gi$_{4}$-ni
206: 18 (lú ^{ĝeš}tukul gu-la)

É-ezen
96: 20

É-gal-mu-šár-ra-ni
56: 49, 65 (father of Lú-^{d}Ba-ú)

É-ḫi-li
35: 7 (dumu ^{d}En-líl-í[l])

É-i$_{7}$-lú-ru
80: 6 (nu-bànda)

É-^{d}IM
21: 6

É-nì-bi
142: 4

É-sa-ra-du$_{10}$
216: 17 (sukkal)

É-šu-a-núm
186: 7 (lú-kaš$_{4}$)

É-úr-bi
56: 14 (father of Ur-ša$_{6}$-ga)

É-úr-šum
282: 8

En-AB.DI
269: 12 (rá-gaba)

En-diĝir-mu
288: 103
En-e-šu-du$_7$
286: 4
En-ĝá-a
13: 11
^{d}En-líl-í[l]
35: 7 (father of É-ḫi-li)
^{d}En-líl-lá
65: 7; 170: 4; 310: 4 (dumu Al-[ ])
En-^{d}Nisaba
294: 12
En-nu-da[ ]
3: 40
En-núm-mi-lí
207: 2 (sukkal)
En-ša-kù-ge
5: 2
En-ša-saĝ
8: 4 (dumu eren-da)
En-ú-mi-ì-lí
246: 9
En-ú-mi-za
250: 17 (sukkal)
En-um-ì-lí
105: 3 (rá-gaba)
Ér-è-a
38: 7
Èr-ra-a
255: 13 (lú-kaš$_4$); 311: 6 (utul lugal)
Èr-ra-ba-ni
109: 4 (maškim); 291: 93
Èr-ra-dan
232: 3 (lú ^{ĝeš}tukul gu-la)
Èr-ra-nu-id
130: 4, seal (dub-sar, dumu Ur-ša$_6$-ga)
Èr-ra-nu-ke$_4$
251: 16 (sukkal)
Èr-ra-nu-sar
203: 14
Èr-ra-ur-saĝ
229: 22 (sukkal)
Eren-da
8: 4 (father of En-ša-saĝ)
Eš-àm
59: 24, 27, 35
Éš-la-a
241: 9 (sukkal)
Èš-gal
294: 11
Èš-ta-šu-ša$_6$-ga
91: 7
Eš$_4$-tár-um-ni
41: 18 (Mar-tu-mí)

-G-

Ga-du
214: 15 (lú-kaš$_4$); 219: 13 (sukkal); 260: 16 (sukkal)
Ga-kú-è-a
116: 13
Ga-lu$_5$
192: 6 (sukkal)
Ga-ni
152: 6 (father of Lú-^{d}Lama)
Gal-la-àm-a
303: 26 (šabra)
Géme-ba
19: 7 (uš-bar, mother of Ur-^{d}Nin-ĝeš-zi-da); 20: 7 (uš-bar, mother of Ur-^{d}Nin-ĝeš-zi-da)
Géme-^{d}Ba-ú
19: 50
Géme-é-an-na
89: 12
Géme-GU
26: 5 (mother of Šeš-kal-la, géme kar-ak-kid)
Géme-^{d}Lama
19: 1 (géme kar-kid, mother of Lú-^{d}Na-rú-a); 20: 1 (géme kar-kid, mother of Lú-^{d}Na-rú-a)
Gi-na
311: 11
Gi$_4$-da
269: 7
Gi$_4$-gi$_4$-ba
158: 8
Gi$_4$-ni-mu
4: 3 (father of Ur-^{ĝeš}gigir)
Gu-la
309: 7
Gu-na-ri
29: 2
Gu-ub-^{d}Utu
233: 15 (sukkal)

Gu-ur$_4$
 311: 5 (utul lugal)

Gu-za-na
 104: 14 (na-gada)

Gu-za-ni
 63: 36

Gú-[ ]
 73: 31

Gú-mu
 176: 2

Gú-ù-mu
 74: 22 (ugula); 104: 13 (dumu dab$_5$-ba)

Gú-u$_4$-[ ]-ka
 311: 13 (šabra)

Gù-dé-a
 35: 10; 44: 7; 57: 25, 40 (dumu Ur-^{d}Ba-ú); 67: 4 (dumu Un-íl), 20, 64 (dumu Un-íl), 68; 110: 9 (énsi); 206: 12 (TAG.TUKU); 295: 5 (dam-gàr)

Gu$_4$-[ ]
 23: 2

Gur$_7$
 280: 7

-Ĝ-

Ĝi$_6$-da-a
 204: 6 (lú ^{ĝeš}tukul gu-la)

Ĝír-ĝír
 86: 13

Ĝír-nun
 1: 119, 170, 224, 274

Ĝìri-ni
 96: 13 (father of Nam-ḫa-ni)

Ĝìri-ni-ì-dab$_5$
 19: 35 (ìr Ur-ab-ba); 20: 32 (ìr Ur-ab-ba)

Ĝìri-ni-ì-ša$_6$
 19: 23; 20: 22; 104: 7 (na-gada); 211: 22 (sukkal)

-Ḫ-

Ḫa-ar-ši
 211: 6 (lú-kaš$_4$)

Ḫa-ba-lu$_5$-gé
 307: seal (énsi Adab^{ki})

Ḫa-la-a
 255: 10 (lú-kaš$_4$)

Ḫar-ra-ni-ì-ša$_6$
 71: 10

Ḫé-na-a-a
 16: 6 (engar)

Ḫé-na-ti
 61: 40

Ḫé-ša$_6$
 78: 9 (father of Ur-^{d}Ba-ú)

Ḫu-ba
 73: 36 (father of Ur-bára)

Ḫu-ba-a
 249: 17, 20

ḪU.KIN
 296: 2 (lú Ḫa-ar-ši^{ki})

Ḫu-la-al
 33: 10

Ḫu-lí-lí
 245: 6 (lú ^{ĝeš}tukul gu-la)

Ḫu-wa-wa
 67: 13

-I-

I-ba-ni
 288: 86

I-ba-ni-ni
 207: 14 (lú ^{ĝeš}tukul gu-la)

I-dará-ki-ni
 233: 8 (šeš-ba)

I-din-diĝir
 209: 14 (sukkal)

I-din-^{d}Suen
 114: 2 (dumu lugal)

I-din-^{d}Utu
 193: 27, 31 (sukkal)

I-la-ak-nu-id
 307: 3

I-mi-it-^{d}*Eš$_4$-tár*
 303: 29 (kuš$_7$)

I-šar-ba-ni
 246: 12 (sukkal)

I-šar-pá-dan
 38: 8, 11; 198: 9 (lú ^{ĝeš}tukul gu-la)

I-šem-^{d}Šul-gi
 196: 2, 5 (lú-kaš$_4$)

I-ta-è-a
 I-ta-è-a: 144: seal (father of Lú-uš-gi-na)

I-ti
 263: 7 (lú-kaš$_4$)

I-ti-a
188: 6 (lú ^{ĝeš}tukul gu-la); 190: 12 (sukkal); 192: 3 (sukkal); 209: 8, 11 (lú-kaš$_4$); 216: 10 (sukkal)

I-ti-ì-lum
244: 9; 246: 18

I-ti-lum
238: 3 (lú ^{ĝeš}tukul gu-la); 243: 21 (lú-kaš$_4$)

I-ti-su
291: 99

I-ti-^{d}Suen
265: 4

I-ti-šu
225: 9 (sukkal)

I-ti-šu-ni-im
195: 10 (aga-ús-gal)

I-zu-a
193: 3, 7 (sukkal)

I-<x?>-^{d}Suen
228: 2 (lú-kaš$_4$)

Ì-ba-ab-du$_7$
283: 16 (nar sig$_7$-a)

Ì-du$_{10}$-ga
96: 1

Ì-kal-la
15: 18 (šeš Ur-Lama); 140: 5 (father of Lú-^{d}Nin-ĝír-su); 143: 6 (father of Lú-^{d}Nin-tu); 185: 7 (muḫaldim); 277: 6

Ì-làl-lum
197: 11

Ì-lí-a-núm
232: 15, 19 (sukkal); 248: 17 (sukkal)

Ì-lí-ḫa-za-núm
226: 14

Ì-lí-^{d}Lama
189: 13, 18 (sukkal); 219: 3 (lú-kaš$_4$)

*Ì-lí-*ša$_6$
41: 21; 234: 17 (sukkal); 239: 28 (sukkal); 282: 3 (ugula uš-bar)

Ì-lí-ti
243: 14 (lú ^{ĝeš}tukul gu-la)

Ib-ni-^{d}Suen
294: 15

Ib-ni-^{d}Šul-gi
80: 12 (ugula)

Igi-an-na-ke$_4$-zu
122: 4 (kuš$_7$)

Il-ma-su
256: 9 (sukkal)

Íl-ma-zu
219: 11 (sukkal)

Ìl-ma-zu
215: 5 (lú-kaš$_4$), 13 (šeš-ba)

^{d}IM-*ba-ni*
192: 20 (sukkal); 205: 2 (sukkal)

Im-ta-diĝir
71: 6

Im-ti-da
207: 17 (sukkal); 230: 6 (lú-kaš$_4$)

Im-ti-dam
313: 8 (father of *A-da-làl*)

In-nu-ri
303: 15

In-ta-è-a
297: 5; 298: 6

^{d}Inanna-ka
101: 7 (šu-ḫa)

^{d}Inanna-ka-[ ]
23: 18 (dumu Ur-dun)

^{d}Inanna-ur-saĝ
288: 47

Inim-^{d}Ba-ú-ni?
89: 14

Inim-^{d}Ba-ú-ì-gi
23: 16

Inim-^{d}Inanna
65: 18; 86: 15

Inim-inim
216: 21 (lú-kaš$_4$)

Inim-ma-ni-zi
16: 2 (engar)

Inim-ša$_6$-ša$_6$
191: 1, 3 (lú-kaš$_4$)

Ip-qú-ša
240: 3 (lú-kaš$_4$)

Ìr
12: 5

Ìr-da-ni
74: 19

Ìr-dam
91: 4

Ìr-mu
118: 21 (father of Lú-^{d}Nin-šubur); 123: 6; 161: 2 (father of Lú-^{d}Nin-ĝír-su); 177: seal (father of Lú-^{d}Nin-ĝír-su); 234: 10 (Mar-tu)

Ìr-^{d}Nanna
233: 16 (aga-ús-gal); 256: 35 (sukkal); 264: 4 (lú ^{geš}tukul)
Ìr-ra-šum
229: 16 (šeš-ba)
Ìr-ri-ib
82: 23 (father of Ir$_{11}$)
Ir$_{11}$
82: 23 (dumu *Ìr-ri-ib*)
Ir$_{11}$-[ ]
90: 6
Ir$_{11}$-^{d}Ba-ú
64: 35
Ir$_{11}$-da-ni
36: 3 (dumu Ur-^{d}Ḫendur-saĝ)
Ir$_{11}$-dam
274: 2 (dumu Na-ba-ša$_{6}$)
Ir$_{11}$-mu
73: 27; 296: 3 (maškim)
Iš-du$_{11}$-gin$_{7}$
227: 13, 15 (aga-ús-gal)
Iš-me-a-ni
213: 17, 21 (sukkal)

-K-

Ka$_{5}$-a
60: 16; 92: 10 (engar); 97: 6, 9 (ugula); 118: 16 (ḫé-dab$_{5}$ ^{geš}tukul-e dab$_{5}$-ba)
Ka$_{5}$-a-[ ]
291: 78, 83
Ka$_{5}$-a-mu
4: 5; 82: 16
Ka$_{5}$-àm
272: 8 (nu-^{ĝeš}kiri$_{6}$)
Kal-ši-a
215: 2 (aga-ús-gal)
Ku-ku-um
82: 11 (father of [ ]-ma)
Ku-li
10: 11, seal (dub-sar, son of Lú-kiri$_{4}$-zal); 30: 5 (father of Ur-^{d}Nanše)
Ku-li-[ ]
96: 12 (brother of Nimgir-saĝ-ezen)
Ku-li-kal-la
76: 34 (na-gada); 96: 28
Kù-^{d}Nanna
19: 39 (dumu Urí^{ki}); 20: 36 (dumu Urí^{ki}); 198: 23 (sukkal); 253: 3 (sukkal); 254: 6 (sukkal)
Kù-^{d}Nin-gal
295: 6
Kù-^{d}Nin-ĝír-su
28: 6
Kù-x-sá-NE
269: 8
Ku$_{5}$-da
38: 3; 104: 9 (na-gada)
Kur-ta-mu-gi$_{4}$
177: 5

-L-

La-lí
236: 23
La-lu$_{5}$-lum
192: 15 (sukkal)
La-mu
276: 10
La-ni
310: 15; 311: 20 (utul lugal)
La-ni-mu
96: 4; 213: 8 (sukkal)
La-qì-ip
257: 14
La-qí-pu-um
243: 17 (sukkal)
^{d}Lama
195: 7 (sukkal)
^{d}Lama-ì-dab$_{5}$
42: 4
Li-bur-^{d}Šul-gi
33: 2
Lú-[ ]
9: 12; 14: 150 (nu-bànda); 34: 14; 159: seal (father of Ur-^{d}Ba-ú); 164: seal (father of Ur-^{d}[ ])
Lú-^{d}[ ]
78: 11
Lú-^{d}Ab-Ú
18: 2 (engar)
Lú-aga
23: 9
Lú-^{d}Alammuš
229: 13 (dumu nu-bànda)
Lú-an-na-túm
203: 18 (sukkal)
Lú-ba-ni-da
39: 18; 40: 19

Lú-^{d}Ba-ú
19: 28 (father of Ur-^{d}Ḫendur-saĝ); 23: 6; 25: 6 (ugula); 56: 16 (dumu Na-ba-ša$_{6}$), 49(dumu É-gal-mu-šár-ra-ni), 65 (dumu É-gal-mu-šár-ra-ni); 61: 8; 78: 16 (dumu Lugal-i$_{7}$); 91: 3; 96: 8, 21; 149: 8 (dumu Na-ba-ša$_{6}$); 175: 3 (dumu Lú-kal-la); 281: seal (father of Lú-^{d}Nin-šubur)

Lú-bala-[ ]
310: 18

Lú-bala-ša$_{6}$-ga
64: 4

Lú-bàn-da
223: 9, 13 (sukkal); 236: 20 (sukkal)

Lú-bi-mu
127: 5; 182: 3 (dumu Ur-^{d}Ig-alima)

Lú-bùluĝ-ĝá
56: 24 (dumu Du$_{10}$-ga)

Lú-da-gi-na
9: 3 (ugula)

Lú-^{d}Da-mu
194: 8 (sukkal); 211: 3 (sukkal); 216: 3 (lú ^{ĝeš}tukul gu-la); 222: 3 (sukkal); 244: 17

Lú-diĝir-ra
4: 9 (šeš [ ]); 9: 7 (ugula); 19: 47 (ugula); 20: 42 (ugula); 23: 5 (dumu Ur-^{ĝeš}gigir), 15 (dumu A-lum-ma); 41: 10 (dumu sipa kunga$_{x}$); 74: 24 (dumu Lú-du$_{10}$-ga); 128: 3; 150: 5 (ugula); 8; 158: 3 (šabra); 160: 4; 168: 4 (ugula mušen-dù); 173: 4; 181: 3 (dumu A-ba-šu-na); 188: 9; 197: 8; 212: 15; 221: 20 (dub-sar); 252: 9 (lú ^{ĝeš}tukul gu-la); 269: 11 (dumu Ur-^{ĝeš}[ ]); 287: 10; 301: 7

Lú-du-du
9: 5 (ugula)

Lú-du$_{10}$-ga
1: 222 (father of Ur-^{d}Nanše); 63: 101; 64: 113 (father of Šeš-kal-la); 74: 24 (father of Lú-diĝir-ra); 95: 5; 183: 3 (father of Ur-^{d}Nanše)

Lú-^{d}Dumu-zi
35: 10; 150: 4; 285: 6

Lú-^{d}En-ki
19: 10; 20: 10; 210: 16; 258: 15 (sukkal); 259: 6; 266: 6 (sukkal)

Lú-^{d}En-líl-lá
41: 3 (ĝá-nun-da-tuš-a); 141: seal (father of Lugal-gú-gal); 258: 3

Lú-ga-[ ]
272: 21 (father of Ù-ma-ni)

Lú-gi-na
86: 3; 99: 6; 175: 2

Lú-gín
311: 10

Lú-gu-la
37: 11 (father of Lú-ša$_{6}$-ga); 69: 8; 229: 21, 24 (šeš-ba)

Lú-^{d}Ĝeš-bar-è
9: 13; 76: 27; 96: 22; 259: 17 (dub-sar)

Lú-ḪAR-[ ]
118: 9 (ḫé-dab$_{5}$ ^{ĝeš}tukul-e dab$_{5}$-ba)

Lú-*ì-lí*
223: 6 (lú-kaš$_{4}$)

Lú-^{d}Igi-ma-šè
61: 5; 67: 113 (kurušda ^{d}Dumu-zi), 117; 137: 3 (father of Lú-^{d}Nin-ĝír-su)

Lú-igi-ša$_{6}$-ša$_{6}$
16: 3 (nu-bànda gu$_{4}$); 109: 2 (ka-gur$_{7}$, father of [ ])

Lú-^{d}Inanna
19: 46 (ad-gub$_{5}$); 20: 41 (ad-gub$_{5}$); 61: 3; 139: 21

Lú-inim-ĝar-ša$_{6}$-ga
90: 2

Lú-inim-ša$_{6}$-ga
80: 2 ([nu-bànda])

Lú-K[A]
82: 6 (nu-bànda)

Lú-kal-la
12: 12; 47: 8; 48: 7; 49; 7; 50: 6; 51: 6; 52: 6; 53: 5; 54: 5; 55: 6; 64: 26, 58; 86: 2; 96: 6; 104: 27 (má-gal); 118: 14 (ḫé-dab$_{5}$ ^{ĝeš}tukul-e dab$_{5}$-ba); 167: seal (father of Šà-kù-ge); 171: 3; 175: 3 (father of Lú-^{d}Ba-ú); 184: 7 (nu-bànda)

Lú-ki-nu-nir^{ki}
144: 5; 163: 2

Lú-kiri$_{4}$-zal
10: seal (father of Ku-lí); 14: 50, 64; 103: 4 (maškim); 137: 7 (dumu Ur-^{d}Ba-ú); 166: 3; 255: 4 (sukkal); 278: 8

Lú-ku$_{4}$-ra
298: 3

Lú-ku$_{5}$-da-mu
1: 5 (dumu saĝa URU×gána*tenû*^{ki})

Lú-^{d}Lama
152: 6 (dumu Ga-ni)

Lú-LUM
269: 10
Lú-ma-an-du$_{11}$
206: 3 (sukkal)
Lú-má-gur$_{8}$
30: 3; 178: 2
Lú-mar-sa
177: 3
Lú-me-lám
19: 53 (ugula); 20: 45 (ugula); 68: 16, 21
Lú-^{d}Na-rú-a
19: 1 (dumu Géme-^{d}Lama), 18 (túg-íl), 43; 20: 1 (dumu Géme-^{d}Lama), 17 (túg-íl), 38; 64: 18; 94: 7; 104: 12 (dumu dab$_{5}$-ba); 120: 7; 139: 4, 20
Lú-^{d}Nanna
9: 15(?) (engar); 63: 170 (ugula); 185: 19 (lú-kaš$_{4}$); 214: 12 (sukkal); 218: 12 (sukkal); 226: 17; 252: 6 (sukkal); 256: 6 (sukkal); 259: 14
Lú-^{d}Nanše
64: 114 (father of Ur-ni$_{9}$-ĝar); 74: 13; 95: 2 (dumu Ur-^{d}Ba-ú); 195: 13 (sukkal)
Lú-nì-šul
47: 16
Lú-nimgir
14: 44, 85 (father of Ur-^{d}Ba-ú)
Lú-^{d}Nin-[ ]
64: 25
Lú-^{d}Nin-ĝír-su
14: 31, 55, 75, 91 (nu-bànda); 19: 31 (ugula, dumu Ba-zi); 20: 28 (ugula, dumu Ba-zi); 23: 14 (father of Ur-^{d}En-gal-du-du); 41: 24; 64: 9, 36 (dumu Ba-zi); 66: 25 (father of Ur-^{d}Ba-ú); 74: 16 (ša$_{13}$-dub-ba); 91: 6; 123: 3; 128: 4; 137: 3 (dumu Lú-^{d}Igi-ma-šè); 140: 4 (dumu Ì-kal-la); 149: 7; 151: 6, seal (dub-sar, dumu Ba-zi); 161: 2 (dumu Ìr-mu), 3 (dumu Ba-zi); 163: 3 (dumu Ba-zi), seal (dub-sar, dumu Ba-zi); 177: 4, seal (dub-sar, dumu Ìr-mu); 244: 14; 249: 5
Lú-^{d}Nin-šubur
19: 26 (baḫar, dumu Ba-ša$_{6}$-ga); 20: 25 (baḫar, dumu Ba-ša$_{6}$-ga); 49: 14; 50: 12; 51: 13; 52: 13; 53: 11; 55: 11; 56: 35, 59 (dumu Ur-ša$_{6}$-ga); 59: 11; 64: 7; 76: 48 (na-gada); 118: 21 (dumu Ìr-mu); 150: 4; 237: 18; 275: 3, 6; 277: 16; 281: 3, seal (dub-sar, dumu Lú-^{d}Ba-ú); 291: 97 (šabra)
Lú-^{d}Nin-tu
37: 5; 124: 4; 143: 6 (dumu Ì-kal-la)
Lú-Nina^{ki}
64: 53
Lú-nita-gi-na
46: 5, seal (dub-sar); 74: 12 (lú-[x]); 80: 8 (nu-bànda); 144: 4, seal (dumu I-ta-è-a)
Lú-sar
3: 32
Lú-SI.ĜAR
315: 3
Lú-^{d}Suen
191: 5 (sukkal)
Lú-šùd
207: 10
Lú-^{d}Šul-gi
308: 8
Lú-*ša-lim*
211: 19; 239: 10 (sukkal); 255: 7 (lú ^{ĝeš}tukul gu-la)
Lú-ša$_{6}$-ga
37: 11 (dumu Lú-gu-la); 76: 41
Lú-ša$_{6}$-ì-zu
280: 8, seal (dub-sar, dumu A-kal-la)
Lú-^{d}Šára
198: 19 (lú-kaš$_{4}$)
Lú-^{d}Šul-gi
57: 47 (šabra); 264: 11 (lú ^{ĝeš}tukul gu-la)
Lú-tur-šè
166: 4
Lú-tùr-[ ]
9: 11
Lú-uru-[ ]
118: 8 (ḫé-dab$_{5}$ ^{ĝeš}tukul-e dab$_{5}$-ba)
Lú-URU×gána*tenû*^{ki}
291: 37
Lú-uru-ki-ĝar-ra
69: 12
Lú-^{d}Utu
56: 22 (father of Ur-^{d}Nin-mar-ki); 61: 7; 129: 8 (ugula kíkken); 186: 11 (muḫaldim); 240: 9 (Mar-tu)
Lú-^{d}Utu-bar-ra
9: 18 (engar)
Lu$_{5}$-lí-lí
227: 19 (sukkal)

Lugal-[ ]
191: 11 (Mar-tu); 279: 3; 299: 2, seal (dumu NI-[ ])
Lugal-á-zi-da
200: 10 (lú ^{ĝeš}tukul gu-la); 212: 3 (lú ^{ĝeš}tukul gu-la)
Lugal-ab-ba
73: 13
Lugal-agrig-zi
255: 23
Lugal-an-na-túm
194: 12; 195: 3 (sukkal); 221: 14
Lugal-ba-ša$_6$
23: 10
Lugal-da-DU
226: 11
Lugal-da-ga
145: 5
Lugal-diĝir-mu
190: 6 (sukkal)
Lugal-diĝir-ra
310: 21
Lugal-dub-lal
87: 4
Lugal-ezen
8: 5 (father of Na-ba-ša$_6$); 19: 29; 21: 2; 91: 14; 112: 5; 198: 22 (lú-kaš$_4$); 309: 4 (father of Ur-ki-gu-la)
Lugal-gi-^{d}Ba-ú
81: 3
Lugal-^{ĝeš}gigir-re
236: 9 (sukkal)
Lugal-gú-gal
43: 5, seal (dub-sar, dumu Ur-^{d}Ba-ú); 141: 5, seal (dub-sar, dumu Lú-^{d}En-líl)
Lugal-gú-tuku
316: 3 (ugula)
Lugal-ḫé-ĝál
23: 11 (dumu Nin-inim-gi-na); 56: 20 (father of A-mu)
Lugal-i$_7$
78: 16 (father of Lú-^{d}Ba-ú)
Lugal-igi
14: 2, 16 (father of Ur-ša$_6$-ga)
Lugal-igi-du$_{10}$-ga
89: 6
Lugal-im-ru-a
169: 3; 288: 11
Lugal-inim-gi-na
16: 7 (nu-bànda gu$_4$); 164: 5
Lugal-inim-silim-ma
23: 4 (dumu [ ])
Lugal-ki-[ ]
135: 7
Lugal-ki-áĝ
64: 17, 22
Lugal-ki-gal
93: 27
Lugal-kù-ga
60: 26 (father of Ur-^{d}Nin-ĝeš-zi-da)
Lugal-kù-zu
310: 10 (dumu [ ])
Lugal-l[a]
82: 8 (father of Šeš-kal-la)
Lugal-ma
288: 80
Lugal-ma-du$_{10}$
92: 16 (engar)
Lugal-má-gur$_8$-re
35: 2; 104: 22; 214: 3 (sukkal)
Lugal-mas-su
242: 6 (sukkal)
Lugal-me-lám
68: 9
Lugal-NÍĜ-[ ]
135: 8 (father of Ur-^{d}Ba-ú, nu-bànda)
Lugal-nimgir
91: 5
Lugal-^{d}Nin-ĝír-su
156: 4
Lugal-nir-ĝál
59: 5; 251: 10
Lugal-nisaĝ-e
200: 19 (lú ^{ĝeš}tukul gu-la); 246: 3 (sukkal)
Lugal-pa-è
19: 11; 20: 11
Lugal-si-[ ]
308: 4
Lugal-si-sá
229: 19 (sukkal)
Lugal-síg-gíd
1: 67, 121, 172, 226, 276; 15: 23 (engar)
Lugal-šà-lá
96: 23; 269: 1

Lugal-ti-[ ]
256: 16 (Mar-tu)
Lugal-ti-ra-áš
135: 5
Lugal-ú-[ ]
104: 19
Lugal-ú-šim-[ ]
23: 3
Lugal-ú-šim-e
139: 18
Lugal-u$_4$-šù-šè
288: 75
Lugal-Unug^{ki}-šè
19: 9; 20: 9; 173: 5, 7
Lugal-uru-da
60: 18 (sa$_{12}$-du$_5$); 153: 4; 154: 5
Lugal-usar
280: 4; 310: 23
Lugal-^{d}Utu
220: 6 (sukkal); 221: 18 (lú-kaš$_4$)
Lugal-ušumgal
174: seal (father of Ur-^{d}Nin-mar-ki)
Lugal-zà-ge-zi
17: 8 (ugula)
Lugal-zi-mu
82: 22 (lú [ ])
Lukur-*be-lí*
221: 3 (lú-kaš$_4$)

-M-

Ma-[ ]
93: 54; 104: 15 (dumu dab$_5$-ba)
Ma-an-sì-na
30: 4 (father of Ur-^{d}Ba-ú)
Ma-an-sum
1: 160, 209; 23: 1
Ma-ma-kešda
205: 8 (lú-kaš$_4$); 227: 11 (šeš-ba)
Ma-ni
1: 116, 169, 228, 278
Má-gur$_8$-re
162: 7
Maš-um
254: 11 (sukkal)
Me-luḫ-ḫa
57: 23, 38 (father of Ur-^{d}Lama)
Mi-na-NI
294: 5
Mu-[ ]
104: 16 (dumu dab$_5$-ba)
Mu-mu
3: 18 (nu-bànda gu$_4$)

-N-

Na-ab-da-núm
139: 14
Na-ba-ša$_6$
1: 65 (father of Ur-^{d}Nanše); 8: 5 (dumu Lugal-ezen); 14: 106 (nu-bànda); 46: 4; 56: 16 (father of Lú-^{d}Ba-ú), 18 (father of Ur-^{d}Nin-ĝír-su); 66: 2, 8, 24 (dub-sar mar-sa); 149: 8 (father of Lú-^{d}Ba-ú); 172: 2; 223: 2 (Mar-tu); 274: 2 (father of Ir$_{11}$-dam); 315: 6
Na-bi-^{d}Suen
202: 11; 218: 6 (sukkal)
Na-bù-gu
33: 7
Na-di
139: 22 (father of Ur-^{d}Ba-ú); 213: 10, 13 (lú-kaš$_4$)
Na-mu
139: 15 (father of Ur-^{d}Ba-ú)
Na-na
231: 20 (sukkal)
Na-na-a
248: 6 (sukkal)
Na-ra-am-ì-lí
311: 25
^{d}Na-rú-a-palil
19: 34 (muḫaldim); 20: 31 (muḫaldim)
Na-ša$_6$
299: 1; 300: 2
Nam-ḫa-ni
29: 4 (na-gada); 72: 22 (na-gada); 96: 13 (dumu Ĝìri-ni), 17, 24; 101: 6 (father of Ur-^{d}Igi-zi-bar-ra); 294: 6
Nam-maḫ
25: 7 (nu-bànda); 59: 19; 78: 14; 159: 3; 165: 6; 172: 3; 185: 8;
Nam-maḫ-^{d}Ba-ú
90: 4; 121: 3, seal (dumu Ab-ba-gi-na ugula kíkken énsi-ka); 176: 3, seal (dub-sar, dumu [ ])
Nam-tar-íb-gu-ul
19: 25 (dumu A-tu); 20: 24 (dumu A-tu)

Nam-zi-tar-ra
2: 2; 21: seal (dub-sar, dumu Al-la-mu); 64: 13
^{d}Nanna-a-ki-áĝ
220: 15 (sukkal)
^{d}Nanna-dalla
230: 18 (sukkal)
^{d}Nanna-du$_{10}$
232: 11 (aga-ús-gal)
^{d}Nanna-ì-ša$_{6}$
189: 10 (sukkal)
^{d}Nanna-ma-ba
298: 7 (dub-sar)
^{d}Nanna-si-sá
54: 10
^{d}Nanna-ša$_{6}$-ga
258: 12
NE-li
249: 14
NE.NE
261: 14 (sukkal)
NI-[ ]
299: seal (father of Lugal-[ ])
Ni-ba
58: 11 (father of Nì-^{d}Ba-ú); 88: 14 (father of Nì-^{d}Ba-ú)
Nì -^{d}Ba-ú
19: 22 (nephew of Ur-^{d}Nin-ĝeš-zi-da); 20: 21 (dumu dumu-ni Ur-^{d}Nin-ĝeš-zi-da); 58: 11 (dumu Ni-ba); 60: 16; 88: 13 (dumu Ni-ba); 101: 2 (šu-ḫa); 251: 9 (sukkal)
Nì-bi
146: 3
Nì-du$_{7}$-pa-è
220: 9
Nì-ĝá-ni
63: 38, 124
Nì-^{d}IM
245: 9
Nì-kal-la
47: 4; 49: 4; 50: 3; 51: 3; 52: 3; 53: 3; 54: 3; 55: 3
Nì-ú-rum
39: 3 (lú-kisal); 40: 3 (lú-kisal); 60: 20, 30
Ni$_{9}$-[ ]
312: 4 (father of Ur-ud-da-[ ])
Ni$_{9}$-a
274: 5
Ni$_{9}$-ĝar-^{d}Ba-ú
98: 5
Ni$_{9}$-ĝar-ki-du$_{10}$
230: 16 (lú-kaš$_{4}$); 310: 8
Nimgir-di-ne
41: 7 (érin é-tukul)
Nimgir-ra-kam
106: 4; 107: 4; 108: 4
Nimgir-saĝ-ezen
96: 11 (brother of Ku-li-[ ])
Nin-a-ì-ša$_{6}$
36: 6 (mother of Ur-^{d}En-ki, géme kar-kid)
Nin-á-zi-da
65: 3
Nin-ĝál-[ ]
81: 4
Nin-gu-la
315: 7
Nin-inim-gi-na
23: 12 (mother of Lugal-ḫé-ĝál)
Nin-ki-ḫar-ša$_{6}$
19: 48; 89: 8
Nin-KWU543
65: 6
^{d}Nin-mar-ki-[ ]
71: 12
^{d}Nin-mar-ki-ka
19: 14 (aslag, father of Ba-ša$_{6}$-ga); 104: 24 (dumu dab$_{5}$-ba)
^{d}Nin-mar-ki-ka-ì-ša$_{6}$
21: 5
^{d}Nin-šubur
222: 4 (sukkal)
Nu-[ ]
90: 10
Nu-ḫa-lum
201: 6
Nu-ḫi-lum
264: 8 (lú [ ]); 311: 8
Nu-ì-da
Nu-ì-da: 303: 20
dam Nu-ì-da: 303: 17
Nu-úr-^{d}Eš-tár
210: 9, 13 (sukkal)

Nu-úr-ì-lí
173: seal (father of Un-íl); 200: 3 (aga-ús-gal); 227: 8 (aga-ús-gal); 237: 3; 250: 21 (lú-kaš$_4$); 294: 16
Nu-úr-^{d}IM
234: 14 (sukkal)
Nu-úr-su
256: 19 (sukkal); 257: 3
Nu-úr-^{d}Suen
195: 14 (aga-ús); 244: 13; 284: 47; 297: 7 (dub-sar)
NUN-[ ]
118: 24 (father of Ur-^{d}Nanše)

-P-

Pa-ne-ZA
5: 11
Pi-mi-rí
39: 7; 40: 7
Pi-mu
39: 11; 40: 12
Pu-ga
44: 8 (mušen-dù)
Pù-du-uš-ki-in
139: 9
Pù-pù-da
241: 16 (sukkal)
Pù-zur$_x$-Ma-ma
208: 9
Puzur$_4$-[ ]
Puzur$_4$-[ ]: 291: 72
Puzur$_4$*-ab-bi*
189: 8 (sukkal)
Puzur$_4$*-è-a*
191: 17 (lú-kaš$_4$)
Puzur$_4$*-Eš*$_4$*-tár*
39: 14; 40: 15; 258: 6
Puzur$_4$*-ḫa-ià*
201: 3
Puzur$_4$*-ì-lí*
33: 11; 188: 3; 239: 25 (lú-kaš$_4$)
Puzur$_4$-^{d}Inanna
189: 5 (sukkal); 253: 10 (sukkal)
Puzur$_4$-Ma-ma
200: 13
Puzur$_4$*-ra-bí*
214: 9 (sukkal)
Puzur$_4$*-šu*
205: 5 (sukkal); 215: 8 (ù-gúl)

-S-

SI.A-a
303: 3 (nu-bànda)
Si-dù
4: 4; 67: 6, 66 (kurušda); 129: 12 (father of Ur-^{d}Ba-ú)
Si-mu
207: 8, 11 (lú ^{ĝeš}tukul gu-la)
Su-ga
92: 21 (engar)
Sú-li-li
291: 91
^{d}Suen-*ba-ni*
218: 15, 17 (sukkal)

-Ṣ-

Ṣe-lu-uš-^{d}Da-gan
33: 16; 287: 3; 291: 31; 303: 5, 12

-Š-

Ša-al-maḫ
316: 4
Ša-ì-lí
237: 16 (lú-kaš$_4$)
Ša-il-tum
41: 14 (Mar-tu-mí)
Ša-lim-mi
41: 17 (Mar-tu-mí)
Ša-ra-ì-lí
210: 22
Šà-ba-na-ĝar
64: 2, 12, 15, 20
Šà-da
162: 3; 203: 9; 204: 18
Šà-ga-na
19: 49 (géme)
Šà-ge
17: 2 (engar); 82: 19 (gudu$_4$ é ^{d}Nin-[ ])
Šà-kù-ge
10: 10; 104: 26 (dumu dab$_5$-ba); 167: 3, seal (dub-sar, dumu Lú-kal-la)
Šar-ru-ru
39: 6; 40: 6
Šar-ru-um-[ ]
291: 48
Šar-ru-um-ì-lí
72: 23 (ugula); 96: 30

^{d}Šára-kam
212: 18; 275: 2; 303: 22
Še-e-a
201: 9
Še-li-bu-um
223: 11 (énsi)
Še-li-lu$_{5}$
222: 14
Še-li-ma-núm
206: 7 (sukkal)
Še-lu$_{5}$
190: 9 (sukkal)
Šeš-a-ni
35: 3 (dumu [ ])
Šeš-kal-la
9: 22; 13: 4; 35: 1, 9 (dumu E-[ ]); 36: 5 (dumu Géme-GU); 64: 113 (dumu Lú-du$_{10}$-ga); 82: 8 (dumu Lugal-l[a]); 89: 3; 93: 65; 101: 9 (šu-ḫa); 118: 23 (ugula); 152: 5; 162: 8 (šabra)
Šeš-ki-lu$_{5}$-la
82: 6
Šeš-šeš
274: 4
Ši-a-a
193: 16, 20 (lú-kaš$_{4}$); 232: 6 (ù-gúl)
Ši-ba-la-nim
39: 13; 40: 14
Šu-[ ]
118: 4 (ḫé-dab$_{5}$ ^{geš}tukul-e dab$_{5}$-ba)
Šu-ba-nir-ĝál
254: 16 (lú-kaš$_{4}$)
Šu-bí
228: 17 (ra-gaba NIM)
Šu-da-ba
241: 6 (sukkal)
Šu-^{d}Dumu-zi
260: 3 (sukkal)
Šu-e-li
251: 19 (lú ^{geš}tukul)
Šu-É-a
260: 13 (sukkal)
Šu-^{d}En-ki
252: 3 (sukkal)
Šu-Èr-ra
212: 9; 226: 6 (lú-kaš$_{4}$); 230: 10, 14 (sukkal); 237: 10 (lú-kaš$_{4}$)
Šu-Eš-tár
256: 3 (lú ^{geš}tukul gu-la); 258: 18 (lú-kaš$_{4}$); 265: 7
Šu-Eš$_{4}$*-tár*
82: 24; 209: 5 (lú-kaš$_{4}$); 250: 3 (lú ^{geš}tukul gu-la); 261: 6 (sukkal)
Šu-Eš$_{11}$*-tár*
208: 3 (sukkal)
Šu-ga-tum
238: 12
Šu-ì-lí
212: 12; 218: 2 (lú-kaš$_{4}$); 237: 13 (lú-kaš$_{4}$); 250: 9 (lú ^{geš}tukul gu-la); 259: 9
Šu-íb-tum
228: 15 (ra-gaba)
Šu-^{d}IM
39: 2 (lú-kisal); 40: 2 (lu-kisal); 208: 12 (sukkal); 214: 18 (sukkal); 230: 5 (lú-kaš$_{4}$); 231: 2 (sukkal); 256: 29 (lú-kaš$_{4}$); 259: 3; 265: 10
Šu-ku-bu-um
291: 103
Šu-[ ]-kù
294: 4
Šu-la-núm
33: 3
Šu-Ma-ma
227: 5 (sukkal); 291: 95
Šu-na-a
232: 22 (aga-ús-gal); 233: 3 (šeš-ba)
Šu-na-gi$_{4}$
227: 18
Šu-^{d}Nanna
220: 3 (sukkal); 261: 22 (sukkal)
Šu-ni-tum
229: 12 (aga-ús-gal)
Šu-^{d}Nin-šubur
218: 8 (lú-kaš$_{4}$); 261: 3 (sukkal)
Šu-nir-um
248: 12 (sukkal)
Šu-^{d}Nisaba
Šu-^{d}Nisaba: 220: 12; 240: 15 (sukkal)
Šu-nu-Eš-tár
226: 20
Šu-PAP.PAP
221: 6 (lú-kaš$_{4}$)
Šu-^{d}Suen
240: 19 (lú-kaš$_{4}$)

Šu-ša$_6$-ga
261: 9 (sukkal)

Šu-šim-a
31: 4 (nu-bànda)

Šu-^{d}Šubur
193: 24 (lú-kaš$_4$)

Šu-^{d}Utu
190: 14, 20 (sukkal); 213: 2, 4 (lú-kaš$_4$); 215: 12(sukkal); 227: 7 (sukkal); 233: 10 (lú-kaš$_4$), 21 (sukkal); 234: 6 (lú-kaš$_4$); 260: 9 (sukkal); 263: 14 (aga-ús-gal)

^{d}Šul-gi-a-a-mu
296: 5; 302: 6; 304: 5

^{d}Šul-gi-*a-bí*
204: 12 (šabra)

^{d}Šul-gi-*dan*
33: 13

^{d}Šul-gi-ḫa-ma-ti
33: 1, 17; 39: 5; 40: 5

^{d}Šul-gi-*ì-lí*
139: 25 (Mar-tu); 249: 12; 250: 6 (lú ^{ĝeš}tukul gu-la); 251: 5 (sukkal)

^{d}Šul-gi-*sí-im-tum*
303: 33

^{d}Šul-gi-^{d}Suen
225: 6

^{d}Šul-gi-uru-mu
291: 96; 304: 6

Šul-lu$_5$
19: 3 (nu-^{ĝeš}kiri$_6$); 20: 3 (nu-^{ĝeš}kiri$_6$)

^{d}Šul-pa-è-é-gal
110: 4

^{d}Šul-šà-ga-na
84: 10 (kurušda)

-T-

Ta-ri-bu-um
230: 3 (sukkal)

Túl-ta-ta
156: 2

-U-

U-bar
246: 15 (lú-kaš$_4$); 260: 19 (sukkal); 266: 19 (lú-kaš$_4$); 311: 4 (utul)

U-bar-ni
255: 20 (lú-kaš$_4$)

U.RU.BE-gin$_7$
216: 7 (sukkal)

Ú-du
228: 7 (NIM)

Ú-du-[ ]
104: 23

Ú-du-ku
67: 9 (father of Ur-^{d}Lama)

Ú-du-lu
184: 18 (dub-sar gu$_4$-udu)

Ú-ṭúl-Ma-ma
224: 4 (lú ^{ĝeš}tukul gu-la)

Ù-ba-a
202: (lú-kaš$_4$)

Ù-ma-ni
272: 21 (dumu Lú-ga-[ ])

Ù-ṣe-mu-pe-li
33: 15

Ù-ša$_6$-a
291: 33, 105 (father of Ur-^{d}Suen)

Ù-tur
283: 17 (géme-kíkken)

Un-ĝa$_6$
8: 10; 18: 6 (engar); 67: 4 (father of Gù-dé-a); 96: 27; 137: 2 (father Ur-^{d}Lama); 173: 8 (dumu dab$_5$-ba), seal (dumu *Nu-úr-ì-lí*)

Ur-[ ]
73: 22; 118: 2 (ḫé-dab$_5$ ^{ĝeš}tukul-e dab$_5$-ba); 172: seal (dub-sar, dumu Ur-[ ]); 234: 3 (lú-kaš$_4$)

Ur-^{d}[ ]
14: 110; 15: 13 (engar); 36: 1 (ugula); 66: 3; 164: seal (dub-sar, dumu Lú-[ ]); 206: 11; 239: 21 (lú-kaš$_4$); 291: 46

Ur-^{ĝeš}[ ]
269: 11 (father of Lú-diĝir-ra)

Ur-ab-ba
19: 35; 20: 32; 67: 16 (dumu Ur-li); 97: 8; 115: 9 (lú-kaš$_4$); 122: 3; 155: 9; 160: 2

Ur-^{d}Asal-lú-ḫi
126: 4

Ur-ba-[ ]
171: 1

Ur-ba-ga
92: 17; 132: 2; 216: 14 (sukkal); 240: 12 (Mar-tu); 249: 9; 255: 17 (Mar-tu)

Ur-^{d}Ba-ú

2: 1; 5: 3; 6: 3; 13: 3; 14: 44, 85 (ugula, dumu Lú-nimgir); 19: 8 (gala), 17 (šeš Ur-^{d}Nin-šar), 36 (ad-gub$_{5}$), 40 (dumu Ur-mes), 44, 45 (dam-gàr); 20: 8 (gala), 16 (šeš Ur-^{d}Nin-šar), 33 (ad-gub$_{5}$), 37 (dumu Ur-mes), 39, 40 (dam-gàr); 23: 17; 27: 4; 30: 4 (dumu Ma-an-sì-na); 32: 6; 41: 6 (érin é-tukul); 43: seal (father of Lugal-gú-gal); 57: 26, 40 (father of Gù-dé-a); 66: 5, 25 (dumu Lú-^{d}Nin-ĝír-su); 74: 11 (ugula); 78: 9 (dumu Ḫé-ša$_{6}$); 86: 11 (dumu Ab-ba-uru); 94: 10 (dumu Ur-ša$_{6}$-ga); 95: 2 (father of Lú-^{d}Nanše); 98: 1; 101: 4 (šu-ḫa); 118: 13 (ḫé-dab$_{5}$ ^{ĝeš}tukul-e dab$_{5}$-ba); 129: 12 (dumu Si-dù); 130: 2; 131: 4 (dumu Ur-ni$_{9}$-ĝar); 132: 3; 135: 8 (dumu Lugal-NÍG-[ ]); 137: 7 (father of Lú-kiri$_{4}$-zal); 139: 15 (dumu Na-mu), 22 (<dumu> Na-di); 155: 11 (šu-zi); 159: 4 (dumu Ba-zi), seal (dub-sar, dumu Lú-[ ]); 162: 4, 6; 171: 5; 178: seal (father of Á-na-mu); 185: 20 (dumu Ab-ba-mu); 194: 16 (sukkal); 245: 3; 288: 73; 308: 10

Ur-bàd-dúr-ra

102: 4

Ur-bàd-KU-a

228: 5, 9 (sukkal)

Ur-bar-NI

198: 12 (lú-kaš$_{4}$)

Ur-bára

73: 36 (dumu Ḫu-ba)

Ur-^{d}Da-mu

19: 30 (ad-gub$_{5}$); 20: 27 (ad-gub$_{5}$); 32: 4; 34: 12 (ugula); 37: 2; 41: 1 (ĝá-nun-da-tuš-a); 236: 17 (sukkal); 258: 21

Ur-dam

56: 32, 57 (dumu Ur-^{d}Nanše); 57: 18, 29, 34 (dumu Ur-^{d}Nanše); 60: 9; 88: 19

Ur-diĝir-ra

1: 230, 280; 56: 47, 62, 74 (saĝa ^{d}Šul-gi)

Ur-^{d}Dumu-zi

4: 6 (dub-nagar); 59: 21; 66: 9; 86: 9; 96: 5; 119: 2

Ur-dun

23: 18 (father of ^{d}Inanna-ka-[ ]); 244: 3 (lú ^{ĝeš}tukul gu-la), 6 (sukkal)

Ur-é-[ ]

2: 4; 3: 84

Ur-é-an-na

101: 3 (šu-ḫa); 197: 17 (father of Ur-^{d}Nanše)

Ur-é-dar-a

38: 6 (má-gín)

Ur-é-gal

156: 3

Ur-é-maḫ

40: 8; 258: 22

Ur-é-ninnu

14: 15, 41, 60, 94, 129; 26: 6 (nu-bànda); 64: 10 (dumu Du-du); 92: 25 (ugula)

Ur-è-a

269: 6

Ur-^{d}En-[ ]

64: 51; 291: 61

Ur-^{d}En-gal-du-du

23: 13 (dumu Lú-^{d}Nin-ĝír-su)

Ur-^{d}En-ki

12: 18; 36: 6 (dumu Nin-a-ì-ša$_{6}$), 8 (nar ^{d}Ba-ú, dumu Ur-^{d}SAR-da); 60: 12, 37; 97: 4; 283: 15 (sukkal)

Ur-^{d}En-líl-lá

62: 5; 64: 59; 66: 17; 148: 5; 157: 3; 169: 2; 170: 3; 222: 7 (lú-kaš$_{4}$); 237: 6 (sagi); 252: 12 (sukkal); 295: 14; 303: 24 (dam-gàr); 311: 22 (utul lugal)

Ur-engur-ka

288: 73

Ur-^{d}Èš-du$_{10}$-nun

104: 25 (má-gal)

Ur-ezen-ma

158: 4

Ur-ĝar

14: 20, 54 (father of Ur-^{d}Lama), 205; 17: 2 (nu-bànda gu$_{4}$); 39: 20; 40: 21; 100: 7 (énsi Lagaš^{ki})

Ur-^{ĝeš}gigir

4: 3 (dumu Gi$_{4}$-ni-mu); 23: 5 (father of Lú-diĝir-ra); 35: 4 (nu-bànda, father of Ur-saĝ-ku$_{5}$); 41: 9 (dumu sipa ^{anše}kunga$_{2}$); 43: 3; 61: 2; 65: 15; 88: 17 (ka-gur$_{7}$); 129: 6 (father of Ur-^{d}Šu-an-na); 140: 3 (father of Da-da); 192: 12 (lú-kaš$_{4}$); 236: 4 (sukkal); 244: 10; 260: 11 (sukkal)

Ur-gu-la

14: 172 (father of Ur-ša$_{6}$-ga); 22: 6 (ugula); 278: 7

Ur-^{d}Gù-dé-a

269: 3

Ur-^{d}Ĝeš-bar-è

14: 9, 25, 79, 98 (nu-bànda)

Ur-^{d}Ḫé-ĝál

309: 2 (father of Ur-^{d}Nanše)

Ur-^{d}Hendur-saĝ

19: 4 (nar), 28 (dumu Lú-^{d}Ba-ú); 20: 4 (nar); 36: 4 (father of Da-da-a and Ir$_{11}$-da-ni); 42: 3; 73: 44

Ur-^{d}Ig-alima

1: 318; 6: 5; 9: 20; 19: 38 (dam-gàr); 20: 35 (dam-gàr); 41: 22 (rá-gaba); 61: 6; 62: 7; 64: 49; 67: 11, 14; 129: 4 (father of Ur-^{d}Nanše); 139: 19; 153: 3; 154: 4; 182: 3 (father of Lú-bi-mu); 288: 27

Ur-^{d}Igi-[ ]

121: 2

Ur-igi-ĝál

82: 20 (sipa énsi)

Ur-^{d}Igi-zi-bar-ra

19: 32; 20: 29; 101: 5 (šu-ḫa), 6 (šu-ḫa, dumu Nam-ḫa-ni)

Ur-^{d}IM

8: 1 (dumu Amar-ka$_{5}$-a); 18: 3 (engar)

Ur-^{d}Inanna

8: 3

Ur-^{d}Ištaran

139: 2

Ur-iti-ma

288: 18

Ur-ki-bi

23: 7 (dumu géme-kíkken)

Ur-ki-gu-la

12: 9; 15: 24 (father of Ur-ša$_{6}$-ga); 19: 2 (šu-ḫa), 27 (ugula); 20: 2 (šu-ḫa), 26 (ugula); 54: 15; 309: 4 (dumu Lugal-ezen)

Ur-kisal

14: 18, 52, 67; 266: 13 (lú-^{ĝeš}tukul gu-la)

Ur-kù-nun-na

192: 9 (sukkal); 284: 10

Ur-^{d}Lama

14: 20, 54 (dumu Ur-ĝar); 15: 18 (šeš Ì-kal-la); 27: 7; 57: 22, 37 (dumu Me-luḫ-ḫa); 62: 6; 67: 9 (dumu Ú-du-ku); 100: 4; 104: 11 (dumu dab$_{5}$-ba); 137: 2 (dumu Un-íl); 147: 3 (saĝa ^{d}Nin-šubur), 6; 206: 15 (sukkal); 222: 17 (Mar-tu); 224: 9, 13 (sukkal); 277: 3; 288: 5 (utul)

Ur-li

67: 16 (father of Ur-ab-ba)

Ur-^{d}Li$_{9}$-si$_{4}$

74: 26 (dumu Ab-ba-mu); 311: 25 (utul *Na-ra-am-ì-lí*)

Ur-lugal

310: 6 (santana)

Ur-^{d}Lugal-bàn-da

76: 21

Ur-ma-ni

198: 16 (lú-kaš$_{4}$)

Ur-mes

12: 15; 13: 9; 19: 40 (father of Ur-^{d}Ba-ú); 20: 37 (father of Ur-^{d}Ba-ú); 60: 14 (gu-zà-la); 61: 14; 65: 9; 68: 10, 18, 21; 82: 15 (father of [ ]); 93: 34; 103: 5 (nu-bànda); 138: 4 (dumu Ba-ad-da); 148: 4

Ur-mes-[ ]-è

249: 4

Ur-mes-bànda

39: 19; 40: 20

Ur-Namma

15: 21 (engar); 18: 4 (engar)

Ur-^{d}Namma

316: 1 (dumu Da-a-mu)

Ur-^{d}Nanna:

185: 15 (sukkal); 210: 19; 261: 20 (aga-ús-gal-gal); 263: 17 (sukkal); 288: 45

Ur-^{d}Nanše

1: 65 (dumu Na-ba-ša$_{6}$), 222 (dumu Lú-du$_{10}$-ga); 14: 48, 61; 19: 33 (nu-bànda); 20: 30 (nu-bànda); 30: 5 (dub-sar, son of Ku-li); 56: 32, 57 (father of Ur-dam); 57: 19, 30, 34 (father of Ur-dam); 59: 17; 66: 6; 67: 76, 107; 86: 7; 91: 2; 118: 12 (ḫé-dab$_{5}$ ^{ĝeš}tukul-e dab$_{5}$-ba), 24 (dumu NUN-[ ]); 129: 4 (dumu Ur-^{d}Ig-alima); 183: 3 (dumu Lú-du$_{10}$-ga); 184: 5 (nu-bànda); 186: 15 (Mar-tu); 197: 17 (dumu Ur-é-an-na); 256: 26 (Mar-tu); 309: 2 (dumu Ur-ḫé-ĝál)

Ur-^{d}NE.ZI

269: 2

Ur-ni$_{9}$-ĝar

64: 48, 114 (dumu Lú-^{d}Nanše); 131: 4 (father of Ur-^{d}Ba-ú); 288: 94; 300: 3; 301: 8

Ur-^{d}Nin-[ ]

36: 13

Ur-^{d}Nin-da

288: 32

Ur-^{d}Nin-gal
22: 5
Ur-^{d}Nin-ĝír-su
56: 18 (dumu Na-ba-ša$_{6}$); 74: 20; 150: 7, 11 (nu-bànda)
Ur-^{d}Nin-ĝeš-zi-da
5: 4; 12: 20; 19: 7 (dumu Géme-ba), 21 (aslag); 20: 7 (dumu Géme-ba), 20 (aslag); 24: 6 (nu-bànda); 60: 11, 26 (dumu Lugal-kù-ga); 82: 18 (dam-a-ni); 85: 18; 86: 10; 125: 3: 135: 3; 146: 4; 256: 13
Ur-^{d}Nin-kára
67: 75, 108
Ur-^{d}Nin-mar-ki
1: 269; 19: 15 (tur); 20: 14 (tur); 56: 22 (dumu Lú-^{d}Utu); 87: 6 (ugula); 174: 5, seal (dub-sar, dumu Lugal-ušumgal)
Ur-^{d}Nin-mug
239: 14 (sukkal)
Ur-^{d}Nin-piriĝ
86: 12
Ur-^{d}Nin-sún
73: 40
Ur-^{d}Nin-šar
19: 16 (šeš Ur-^{d}Ba-ú); 20: 15 (šeš Ur-^{d}Ba-ú)
Ur-^{d}Nin-tu
79: 5 (ugula)
Ur-^{d}Nin-zu
12: 21
Ur-^{i_7}Nina^{ki}-šè-ĝen
12: 7
Ur-ninnu
64: 104
Ur-^{d}Nun-gal
24: 4; 143: 5; 211: 25 (Mar-tu)
Ur-saĝ-ku$_{5}$
35: 4 (dumu Ur-^{ĝeš}gigir)
Ur-saĝ-na-ra
288: 100
Ur-saĝ-pa-è
1: 118, 167
Ur-^{d}Saḫar-^{d}Ba-ú
174: 4; 311: 9
Ur-^{d}SAR-da
36: 8 (father of Ur-^{d}En-ki)
Ur-^{d}Suen
12: 23; 291: 33, 105 (dumu Ù-ša$_{6}$-a)
Ur-^{d}Ša-u$_{x}$-ša
15: 20
Ur-ša$_{6}$
12: 3
Ur-ša$_{6}$-ga
1: 63; 14: 2, 16 (nu-bànda, dumu Lugal-igi), 172 (dumu Ur-gu-la); 15: 24 (dumu Ur-ki-gu-la); 23: 8; 27: 6 (nu-bànda, gu-za-lá); 56: 14 (dumu É-úr-bi); 56: 35, 59 (father of Lú-^{d}Nin-šubur); 94: 10 (father of Ur-^{d}Ba-ú); 130: seal (father of *Er-ra-nu-id*); 155: 6; 243: 3, 7 (sukkal)
dam Ur-ša$_{6}$-ga: 317: 5
Ur-^{d}Šára
118: 11 (ḫé-dab$_{5}$ ^{ĝeš}tukul-e dab$_{5}$-ba)
Ur-^{d}Šu-an-na
129: 6 (dumu Ur-^{ĝeš}gigir)
Ur-šu-ga-[ ]
312: 15
Ur-šu-ga-lam-ma
144: 2
Ur-^{d}Šul-gi
63: 122
Ur-^{d}Šul-pa-è
58: 7 (gu-za-lá); 69: 5; 133: 5; 139: 3, 24; 187: 3 (lú-mu$_{13}$-mu$_{13}$); 202: 3 (lú ^{ĝeš}tukul gu-la); 204: 3 (lú ^{ĝeš}tukul gu-la); 226: 10 (dub-sar Lugal-da-DU); 305: 9
Ur-tur
1: 59; 14: 108 (nu-bànda, dumu [ ]-^{d}Nin-ĝír-su); 89: 2
Ur-ud-da-[ ]
Ur-ud-da-[ ]: 312: 3 (dumu Ni$_{9}$-[ ])
dam Ur-ud-da-[ ]: 312: 7
Ur-^{d}Ùr-bar-tab
79: 6, seal (dub-sar; son of Diĝir-ra)
Ur-^{d}Utu
14: 104 (nu-bànda); 184: 6 (nu-bànda); 222: 11 (sukkal Gáraš^{ki})
Ur-zi-mu
32: 3
Ur-zu-a
307: 2
Ur-^{d}x-ra
295: 4
Úr-ra-ni
69: 10
Ùr-re-ba-du$_{7}$
2: 3; 19: 24; 20: 23; 37: 4; 41: 2 (ĝá-nun-

da-tuš-a); 256: 23 (Mar-tu); 257: 6
^{d}Utu-ba-a-zi
5: 1
^{d}Utu-ba-è
36: 2
^{d}Utu-bar-ra
87: 5 (engar); 101: 8 (šu-ḫa); 111: 4 (gala-maḫ); 113: 7 (gala-maḫ)
^{d}Utu-*be-lí*
225: 3
^{d}Utu-du$_{10}$
15: 23 (engar)
^{d}Utu-kalam-e
19: 13
^{d}Utu-kam
73: 7 (nagar)
^{d}Utu-me-lám
311: 23 (utul lugal)
^{d}Utu-*ši-la-at*
232: 10 (sukkal)

-Z-

Za-an-ti
5: 12
Za-lí-a
66: 15
ZA.SÁ.A
206: 23 (sukkal)
Zabar-dab$_5$
287: 7 (maškim); 291: 27, 57; 303: 10
Zi-zi-ig?
203: 11
Zu-dam-du$_{10}$
123: 4
Zu-zu
92: 13 (engar nu-bànda)

-[ ]-

[ ]-^{d}Ba-ú
119: 7
[ ]-Èr-ra
294: 2
[ ]-gi-na
104: 2 (na-gada)
[ ]-ḫé-ĝál
88: 6
[ ]-ḫi-ĝál
288: 95
[ ]-*ì-lí*
15: 15 (nu-bànda gu$_4$)
[ ]-ì-ša$_6$
15: 10 (nu-bànda gu$_4$)
[ ]-kal-la
15: 7 (engar); 104: 3 (dumu dab$_5$-ba)
[ ]-kù-ge
104: 31 (dumu dab$_5$-ba)
[ ]-ma
82: 11 (dumu *Ku-ku-um*)
[ ]-^{d}Nanše
88: 20
[ ]-^{d}Nin-ĝír-su
14: 108 (father of Ur-tur); 119: 6
[ ]-sila$_4$-ni
89: 10
[ ]-^{d}Šul-pa-è
104: 32 (na-gada)
[ ]-^{d}Utu
288: 59
[ ]-^{d}Utu-*illat*
294: 9

Divine Names

^{d}Amar-^{d}Suen
293: 3
An-nu-ni-tum
289: 12; 290: 5
^{d}Ba-ú
82: 4, 17
^{d}*Be-la-at-dar-ra-ba-an*
289: 11; 290: 4
^{d}*Be-la-at-šuḫ-ni-ir*
^{d}*Be-la-at-šuḫ-ni-ir*: 289: 10
^{d}*Be-la-at-šuḫ-ne-er*: 290: 3
^{d}Dumu-zi
28: 3; 67: 74, 81, 113
^{d}En-ki
283: *passim*
^{d}En-líl-lá
138: 3; 191: 6; 236: 10; 287: 1; 298: 2; 317: 2
^{d}Ĝá-tùm-du$_{10}$
31: 6
^{d}Ĝeš-bar-è
226: 14
^{d}Ḫendur-saĝ
117: 18
^{d}IM
116: 6
^{d}Inanna
257: 11; 292: 5, 29; 316: 5
^{d}Lama
98: 2; 316: 2
^{d}Lú-làl
292: 6
^{d}Lugal-bàn-da
292: 19
^{d}Muš-a-igi-ĝál
292: 16
^{d}Na-na-a
292: 3
^{d}Na-rú-a
75: 6; 112: 3
^{d}Nanna
283: 28
^{d}Nanše
67: 60; 82: 22; 142: 6; 184: 14; 283: *passim*
^{d}Nin-dar-a
67: 73, 79
^{d}Nin-ĝír-su
146: 2
^{d}Nin-ĝeš-zi-da
17: 9
^{d}Nin-ḫur-saĝ
292: 18
^{d}Nin-líl
287: 2
^{d}Nin-mar-ki
136: 3; 137: 6
^{d}Nin-sún
292: 32
^{d}Nin-šubur
147: 3
^{d}Nin-urta
287: 5
^{d}Nusku
287: 4
^{d}Si-ĝar-an-na
292: 17
^{d}Suen
84: 9
^{d}*Šu*-^{d}Suen
293: 2
^{d}Šul-gi
110: 7; 112: 6; 118: 20; 145: 4
^{d}Šul-pa-è
44: 5; 82: 16; 272: 28
^{d}*Ul-ma-ši-tum*
289: 13; 290: 6

Toponyms

A-dam-šáḫ^{ki}
105: 4; 195: 8; 207: 3; 214: 6; 215: 10; 226: 20; 229: 4, 17; 233: 17
A.GÍN^{ki}
185: 16
A-la-a^{ki}
62: 12
A-pi$_4$-sal$_4$^{ki}
272: 37
Á-sún
44: 13
Adab^{ki}
307: seal
An-ša-an^{ki}
189: 19; 192: 21; 193: 19, 21; 206: 26; 208: 13; 214: 19; 217: 4; 220: 16; 230: 13, 15; 231: 21; 236: 22, 23; 241: 17; 243: 11; 248: 18; 251: 20; 252: 19; 260: 23; 261: 23
An-ta-sur-ra
113: 6; 116: 12
Babili^{ki}
291: 75
Bàd-an
uru Bàd-an-na: 311: 3, 17
Du$_8$-du$_8$-lí^{ki}
192: 19; 210: 12; 213: 22
É-saĝ-da-na
303: 32
Ga-eš
210: 3
Gàr-šum^{ki}
94: 3
Gáraš^{ki}
222: 11
Gi-gi-li^{ki}
228: 8
Gi-ša^{ki}
205; 4; 208: 6; 219: 15; 232: 18, 20
Gú-ab-ba^{ki}
Gú-a-ab-ba: 216: 4
Gú-ab-ba: 35: 2, 3; 44: 11; 72: 24; 73: 55; 75: 15; 80: 19; 96: 3; 109: 3; 184: 17; 212: 6; 234: 15; 259: 6
šà Gú-ab-ba gu-la: 75: 7
Ĝír-su^{ki}
19: 5; 20: 5; 64: 39; 70: 25; 75: 1; 93: 25; 96: 19; 184: 12
Ḫa-ar-ši^{ki}
296: 2
Ḫu-bu-la^{ki}
205: 7, 9
Ḫu-ḫu-nu-ri^{ki}
195: 11; 207: 20
Ḫu-rìm^{ki}
44: 15
i$_7$-NE-tum-mal
érin i$_7$-NE-tum-mal: 93: 35
Inim-inim-ma^{ki}
206: 4; 216: 11
Ki-maš^{ki}
195: 15; 199: 3, 5; 205: 1, 3; 206: 21; 213: 12; 218: 16, 18; 227: 20; 232: 4; 253: 7
Ki-nu-nir^{ki}
76: 71; 77: 12; 96: 15; 164: 6
Ki-sur-ra
131: 6
Lagaš^{ki}
2: 12; 100: 7; 108: 2; 194: 13
Má-gan
115: 2, 8
Nag-su^{ki}
80: 9; 158: 7
Nibru^{ki}
147: 7; 189: 19; 192: 21; 206: 26; 208: 13; 210: 12; 214: 19; 216: 22; 220: 17; 231: 21; 236: 22; 241: 17; 243: 6; 248: 18; 252: 19; 253: 14; 287: 6; 295: 1
Nina^{ki}
2: 10; 29: 6; 30: 2; 32: 7; 75: 11; 93: 33; 127: 7; 147: 2; 184: 4; 187: 4
Sa-bu-um^{ki}
193: 10; 203: 19; 210: 22; 211: 19; 215: 3; 218: 13; 223: 12; 227; 9; 228: 16; 230: 19; 232: 12; 233: 9; 243: 6; 244: 5; 250: 25; 257: 15; 259: 10
Sag-da-na^{ki}
19: 58; 20: 47
Saḫar^{ki}
221: 11; 226: 7; 239: 29

Si-ù^{ki}
191: 2, 4
Si-ù-na^{ki}
196: 4, 6
Sippar^{ki}
292: 38
Ši-ma-aš-ki
190: 18; 213: 3, 5; 215: 6; 229: 23, 25; 231: 18; 241: 13
Ši-ma-aš-gi$_4$^{ki}: 204: 8; 210: 12
Šušina^{ki}
187: 14; 193: 8, 23; 195: 4, 200: *passim*; 202: 12; 207: *passim*; 209: 3; 212: 6, 9, 15; 213: 9; 215: 14; 218: 3, 7, 9; 223: 7, 16; 224: 6, 14; 227: 6; 228: 3, 18; 229: 9; 230: 4, 17; 232: 7, 23; 233: 12, 22; 247: 5; 254: 7; 255: 12, 17; 259: 15; 263: *passim*
Ú-lum^{ki}
209: 10, 12
Unug^{ki}
269: 13; 282: 6; 292: 37
ÚR×Ú^{ki}
295: 5
Urí^{ki}
19: 39; 20: 36; 140: 6; 217: 9; 219: 20
URU×A^{ki} (Ú.URU.A^{ki}★/Ú.URU×A^{ki}★★/ Ú.URU×A.A^{ki}★★★)
193: 25★★; 209: 18★★; 213: 14★; 227: 3★★★, 12★★★, 23★★★; 229: 20★★★; 230: 7★★★; 233: 4★★★, 25★★★; 253: 14
URU×gána*tenû*^{ki}
1: 5; 150: 3
Uru-kù^{ki}
111: 3
Za-ul^{ki}
189: 17; 193: 6, 30, 32; 227: 14, 16

Temples, Households, and Institutions

é [ ]: 11: 9; 14: 109, 157
é ^{d}Ba-ú: 82: 4
é ^{d}Dumu-zi: 14: 101, 154
é ^{d}En-ki: 11: 5
é-gal: 93: 13, 18: 5; 18; 56: 50, 66; 102: 2; 126: 2; 140: 6; 143: 4; 145: 3; 147: 4; 149: 5; 155: 2; 297: 2
é-gibil: 64: iii 61; 142: 9
é-gidri: 249:8
é gu-zal-lá: 27: 3
é gu$_4$: 292: 21; 306: 6
é Ig-alima: 1: 342; 24: 3
é ^{d}IM: 116: 6
é-kaš$_4$: 41:13
é-kíkken-a: 19:57; 20:46
é-kìšib-ba: 4: 7; 63: 21; 165: 5; 166: 2; 184: 3; 288: 75; 305: 8; 316: 9
é kurušda: 184: 12
é-lugal: 155: 10
é-muḫaldim: 184: 16; 287: 15
é Nam-ḫa-ni: 1: 215
é ^{d}Nanše: 82: 22; 142: 6; 184: 14
é ^{d}Nin-ĝír-su: 21: 11; 82: 9
é ^{d}Nin-ĝeš-zi-da: 1: 319, 343; 26: 8
é ^{d}Nin-mar-ki: 14: 33, 81; 57: 48
é-nun saĝa: 6: 4
é ^{d}Šul-gi: 1: 110, 341; 118: 20
é temen-na: 276: 11
é udu: 10:9; 37: 5; 155:2
é-udu-ĝá-nun-ĝeš: 171: 6
é Ur-^{d}Ig-alima: 256: 10
é uz-ga: 287: 11

Fields, Storehouses, and Gardens

a-šà [ ]: 1: 187, 189, 192,
a-šà a-gú-na: 15: 26
a-šà a-NÍĜ.ḪU: 149: 4
a-šà ambar-a-šeš: 3: 23
a-šà Ar-ša-ti-a-^{d}Nanše: 1: 163
a-šà Ar-ša-ti-a-^{d}Nin-dar-a: 1: 2
a-ša Ar-ša-ti-a ù é-duru$_5$-Ur-^{ĝeš}gigir: 1: 55
a-šà a-saĝ-dù-du: 1: 137, 181
a-šà ^{d}Ba-ú-tùr-šù-ta: 174: 3
a-šà Bur-su-šè: 6: 2
a-šà da-ad: 11: 13
a-šà ^{kuš}e-sír-dúb-ba: 1: 78
a-šà ^{d}En-líl-lá: 1: 37, 90, 143, 251, 300, 323
a-šà En-nu-lum-ma: 1: 239, 286
a-šà gíd-da-ta: 61: 4
a-šà-gíd gána: 1: 236, 289
a-šà-gíd gána-gu-la: 1: 29, 82, 135
a-šà ĝeš-bi-ĝeš-e-ĝar-ra: 1: 64
a-šà ĝír-ĝír: 1: 140, 178, 249, 298
a-šà ḫi-ĝál-ta: 160: 2
a-šà Igi-zi-mu-pàd: 18: 9
a-šà im-bi-a-ba: 1: 33, 86
a-šà ^{ú}KI.NUMUN: 12: 25
a-šà Lugal-šà-ga: 4: 11
a-šà Mar-tu kur-ba: 256: 20
a-šà nam-niĝin$_5$-a-ni-du$_{10}$: 16: 8
a-šà Nam-šid apin-a: 14: 165
a-šà ^{d}Nanše-ĝar-ra: 17: 5
a-šà NI-zi-na: 1: 132, 184; 16: 4
a-šà Nin-e-gù-ba-dé: 14: 171
a-šà Nin-gána-gi-ambar-sur-ra: 14: 161
a-šà ^{d}Nin-ĝír-su: 1: 35, 88
a-šà ^{d}Nin-mar-ki: 1: 247, 296
a-šà Sirarà^{ki}-ḫé-ĝál-ta: 1: 4, 53, 114
a-šà ^{d}Šul-pa-è: 272: 28
a-šà ^{ĝeš}tir-gaba-gíd-da: 1: 23, 73
a-šà ^{ĝeš}tir-ma-nu: 1: 26, 76
a-šà ú-sar-du$_8$-gíd-da: 162: 1
a-šà Ú-šim-^{d}Ba-ú: 7: 14
a-šà Ù-ma-ni-ka: 10: 7
a-šà úkuš-x-zi: 12: 11
a-šà uru-ni: 1: 243, 292
a-šà [x]-bi-sur-ra: 3: 30
ì-dub A.K[A] muš-bi-ed[in]: 148: 3
ì-dub a-šà a-saĝ-dù-du: 56: 37
ì-dub a-šà ambar-sur-ra: 22: 4; 24: 5
ì-dub a-šà Ar-ša-ti-a: 1: 112, 271
ì-dub a-šà Ar-ša-ti-a-^{d}Nanše: 1: 221
ì-dub a-šà Ar-ša-ti-a-^{d}Nin-dar-a: 1: 162, 219
ì-dub a-šà ḫi-ĝál-ta: 137: 5
ì-dub a-šà Inim-ma-AN: 56: 39
ì-dub a-šà Pú-du: 56: 42
ì-dub a-šà Sirara$_4^{\text{ki}}$-ḫé-ĝál: 1: 165, 217, 273
ì-dub a-šà uru-ul-ta: 173: 3
ì-dub á-gul-ta: 124: 2
ì-dub ambar-sug: 28: 4
ì-dub ELAM-ne-ta: 127: 3
ì-dub Gàr-šum: 94: 3
ì-dub ḫi-ĝál-ta: 168: 2
ì-dub Inim-ma-an-né: 25: 10
ì-dub ki-tuš DA.AN.LA.KI: 56: 44
ì-dub me-si-za: 152: 3
ì-dub ^{d}Nin-ḫur-saĝ: 26: 4
ì-dub U-ša-núm-ma: 94: 11
ì-dub URU×GÁNA*tenû*: 150: 3

^{ĝeš}kiri$_6$ a-ru-a Lú-^{d}Nanše: 74: 13
^{ĝeš}kiri$_6$-Gar-šum-šè: 8: 2
^{ĝeš}kiri$_6$ gu-la šà-uru: 74: 27
^{ĝeš}kiri$_6$ ^{d}Ištaran: 74: 8
^{ĝeš}kiri$_6$ Lú-^{d}Nin-ĝír-su ša$_{13}$-dub-ba: 74: 16
^{ĝeš}kiri$_6$ ^{d}Nin-mar-ki gú-a diri: 74: 5
^{ĝeš}kiri$_6$ Ur-^{d}Nin-ĝír-su gu-la: 74: 20

Seal Inscriptions

Text 10

Ku-li
dub-sar
dumu Lú-kiri$_4$-zal

Text 130

Èr-ra-nu-id
dub-sar
dumu Ur-ša$_6$-ga

Texts 151, 163

Lú-^{d}Nin-ĝír-su
dub-sar
dumu Ba-zi

Text 177

Lú-^{d}Nin-ĝír-su
dub-sar
dumu Ìr-mu

Text 178

[Á]-na-[mu]
dub-[sar]
dumu Ur-$^{[d]}$Ba-[ú]

Text 281

Lú-^{d}Nin-šubur
dub-sar
dumu Lú-^{d}Ba-ú

Text 307

Ḫa-ba-lu$_5$-gé
énsi Adab
Amar-šúba
dub-sar ir$_{11}$-zu

Cornell University Studies in Assyriology and Sumerology
(CUSAS)

David I. Owen, Editor-in-chief

CUSAS 1: *The Cornell University Archaic Tablets*
Salvatore Monaco. 2007. Pp. xiv + 370. ISBN 978-1934309-001

CUSAS 2: *Sumerian Proverbs in the Schøyen Collection*
Bendt Alster. 2007. Pp. xvi + 156. ISBN 978-1934309-018

CUSAS 3: *The Garšana Archives*
David I. Owen and Rudolf H. Mayr with the assistance of Alex Kleinerman. 2007. Pp. xii + 528. ISBN 978-1934309-025

CUSAS 4: *Analytical Concordance to the Garšana Archives*
Alexandra Kleinerman and David I. Owen. 2009. Pp. x + 795. ISBN 978-1934309-032

CUSAS 5: *Workers and Construction Work at Garšana*
Wolfgang Heimpel. 2009. Pp. xx + 394. ISBN 978-1934309-049

CUSAS 8: *A Late Old Babylonian Temple Archive from Dūr-Abiešuḫ*
Karel van Lerberghe and Gabriella Voet. 2009. Pp.xviii + 276. Pl. 22. ISBN 978-1934309-079

CUSAS 9: *Babylonian Tablets from the First Sealand Dynasty in the Schøyen Collection*
Stephanie Dalley. 2009. Pp. xviii + 320. Pl. 182. ISBN 978-1934309-087

CUSAS 10: *Babylonian Literary Texts in the Schøyen Collection*
A. R. George. 2009. Pp. xx + 160. Pl. 62. ISBN 978-1934309-094

CUSAS 11: *Early Dynastic and Early Sargonic Tablets from Adab in the Cornell University Collections*
Giuseppe Visicato and Aage Westenholz. 2010. Pp. xxvi + 124. Pl. 94. ISBN 978-1934309-100

CUSAS 12: *The Lexical Texts in the Schøyen Collection*
Miguel Civil. 2010. Pp. xxii + 308. ISBN 978-1934309-117

CUSAS 13: *Classical Sargonic Tablets Chiefly from Adab in the Cornell University Collections*
Massimo Maiocchi. 2009. Pp. xxii + 334. Pl. 38. ISBN 978-1934309-124

CUSAS 15: *Cuneiform Texts in the Carl A. Kroch Library, Cornell University*
Alhena Gadotti and Marcel Sigrist with the assistance of Nicole M. Brisch and David I. Owen 2010. Pp. xx + 184. Pl. 30. ISBN 978-1934309-254

CUSAS 16: *Ur III Tablets from the Columbia University Libraries*
S. Garfinkle, H. Sauren, and M. Van De Mieroop. 2010. Pp. xxviii + 341. ISBN 978-1934309-285

In Preparation

CUSAS 6: *Garšana Studies*
David I. Owen

CUSAS 7: *Seal Impressions and Sealing Practices in the Garšana Archives*
Rudolf H. Mayr

CUSAS *Middle Sargonic Tablets in the Cornell University Collections*
M. Elena Milone and F. Pomponio

CUSAS *The Late Sargonic "mu-iti" Tablets in the Cornell University Collections*
Amadeo Alberti and P. Notizia